The Shoah in Ukraine

The Shoah in Ukraine

HISTORY, TESTIMONY, MEMORIALIZATION

Edited by
Ray Brandon and Wendy Lower

INDIANA UNIVERSITY PRESS
BLOOMINGTON AND INDIANAPOLIS

Published in association with the
United States Holocaust Memorial Museum

This book is a publication of

Indiana University Press
601 North Morton Street
Bloomington, IN 47404-3797 USA

www.iupress.indiana.edu

Telephone orders	800-842-6796
Fax orders	812-855-7931
Orders by e-mail	iuporder@indiana.edu

First paperback edition 2010
© 2008 by Indiana University Press

Frontispiece: Ivanhorod, Ukraine, 1942. USHMM, courtesy of Jerzy Tomaszewski.

The Library of Congress cataloged the original edition as follows:

The Shoah in Ukraine : history, testimony, memorialization
/ edited by Ray Brandon and Wendy Lower.
        p. cm.
  "This volume originated in a summer research workshop held at the
United States Holocaust Memorial Museum in 1999"—Introd.
  "Published in association with the United States Holocaust Memorial Museum" T.p. verso.
  Includes bibliographical references and index.
  ISBN-13: 978-0-253-35084-8 (cloth)
  1. Holocaust, Jewish (1939–1945)—Ukraine—Congresses. 2. Ukraine—History—German
occupation, 1941–1944—Congresses. 3. Germany—Politics and government—1933–1945—
Congresses. I. Brandon, Ray. II. Lower, Wendy. III. United States Holocaust Memorial Museum.
  DS135.U4S535 2008
  940.53'1809477—dc22
                                2007038871
ISBN 978-0-253-22268-8 (pbk.)

1 2 3 4 5   15 14 13 12 11 10

CONTENTS

Maps

This volume originated in a Summer Research Workshop held at the United States Holocaust Memorial Museum in 1999. Since that initial gathering, the editors sought out additional contributors who were doing groundbreaking research on the Holocaust in Ukraine. During the years in which this book took shape, we received much help from numerous institutions, colleagues, friends, and family members. The editors would like to sincerely thank staff and scholars at the United States Holocaust Memorial Museum, in particular Paul Shapiro, Director of the Center for Advanced Holocaust Studies, and Robert Ehrenreich, Director of University Programs, who supported our proposal for the workshop. In the Center's publications department we received valuable advice and encouragement from Benton Arnovitz and Aleisa Fishman. We appreciate the friendly and valuable assistance of the Museum's librarians and archivists Judith Cohen, Caroline Waddell, Michlean Amir, and Henry Mayer. Across the Atlantic, our search for maps and photos was aided by the generous support of Berit Pistora at the Bundesarchiv-Koblenz, Günter Scheidemann at the Political Archive of the German Foreign Office, and Noa Katz at Yad Vashem. Peter Palm in Berlin created the maps for this volume.

The editors wish to acknowledge Janet Rabinowitch, Director of Indiana University Press, for recognizing the importance of the research in this volume and facilitating its publication. An anonymous reviewer provided very helpful comments on the manuscript, allowing us to improve its presentation. The editorial staff and marketing staff at the Press are also owed a debt of gratitude, in particular Miki Bird, Anne Clemmer, Brian Herrmann, Daniel Pyle, and of course our copyeditor, Candace McNulty.

Lastly the editors wish to thank the contributors to this book who patiently stuck with us in the extended editorial process. Their forbearance was only outdone by the continuous support of the editors' partners and family, Andrea Böltken, Christof Mauch, and Ian and Alexander Mauch. Thank you for your patience and understanding.

The Shoah in Ukraine

Introduction

RAY BRANDON AND
WENDY LOWER

Before the Second World War, the Jews of Ukraine constituted one of the largest Jewish populations in Europe.[1] They were without a doubt the largest Jewish population within the Russian Empire and the Soviet Union.[2] And between July 1940 and June 1941—after Stalin occupied the interwar Polish territories of eastern Galicia and western Volhynia as well as the interwar Romanian territories of northern Bukovina and southern Bessarabia—the number of Jews in the Ukrainian Soviet Socialist Republic (UkrSSR) rose to at least 2.45 million persons, thus making it for a brief period home to the largest Jewish population in Europe.[3] Despite the size of Ukraine's Jewish population, academics and laypersons alike have for over two generations tended to talk about the Holocaust in the Soviet Union, Poland, Romania, or Hungary, but not about the Holocaust in Ukraine, which is the subject of this book.

The reason for this traditional approach is evident. Unlike any of the aforementioned countries, Ukraine from the mid-thirteenth until the mid-twentieth century was but an ensemble of disparate territories partitioned among several neighboring powers. Ukrainian efforts to establish a state in these lands in the aftermath of the First World War were thwarted by internecine factionalism as well as Polish national aspirations and Soviet revolutionary ambitions. Between the Polish-Soviet peace of 1920 and the Nazi-Soviet pact of 1939, the lands of modern Ukraine were split among Poland (eastern Galicia and western Volhynia), Czechoslovakia (Transcarpathia), Romania (northern Bukovina and southern Bessarabia), and the Soviet Union. Inside the Soviet Union, the Crimea remained in Russia, while the rest of Ukraine lay within the UkrSSR. The calamities that swept the Soviet Ukrainian lands between the world wars tore apart Ukrainian and Jewish society alike. The Ukrainian lands of Poland were subjected to similar brutality in the 22 months between Soviet occupation in September 1939 and the German invasion of the Soviet Union in June 1941.

Although so many Jews lived throughout the Ukrainian lands, the Jewish inhabitants of Ukraine did not form a cohesive Jewish community. Nor did the Jews of Ukraine form a culturally Ukrainian Jewry. The Jews of Ukraine were greatly influenced by whichever occupying country they found themselves a part of—this applies in particular to the legacies of Austrian and then Polish rule in western Ukraine in the first four decades of the twentieth century. When the Jews of these lands identified with a culture outside their community or assimilated, they most often chose the dominant culture in the towns where they resided, whereas Ukrainians overwhelmingly lived in the countryside. Those urban cultures therefore tended to be Austro-German, Polish, or Russian. Nonetheless, when Nazi Germany invaded the Soviet Union in June 1941, almost all the Jews of Ukraine found themselves in the recently aggrandized UkrSSR.

Stalin—in a spectacle of revolution played out against a backdrop of *Realpolitik*—had by July 1940 nearly unified Ukraine for the first time in history. Hitler would dismantle Ukraine again. This re-partitioning of Ukraine was not intended by Alfred Rosenberg, the Nazis' chief ideologue and later Germany's minister for the occupied eastern territories. He had hoped to create an enormous unified Ukrainian state under German suzerainty stretching from Lviv to Stalingrad (today Volgograd).[4] Hitler equivocated for several months, but ultimately dispensed with Rosenberg's proposals shortly before a key meeting of Germany's highest leadership on July 16, 1941.[5] Parts of Ukraine fell to the General Government (those parts of the occupied interwar Polish state not incorporated into Germany) and Romania instead of Rosenberg's Reich Commissariat Ukraine (*Reichskommissariat Ukraine*, RKU). (See map 1.2 in chapter 1.)

As a consequence of this impromptu partitioning of Ukraine in July 1941, the term Holocaust in Ukraine has come to refer first and foremost to the Wehrmacht-administered territories and the RKU. The Holocaust in Galicia is technically a part of the Holocaust in Poland, while the Holocaust in Transnistria is a part of the Holocaust in Romania and the Holocaust in Transcarpathia is a part of the Holocaust in Hungary. These distinctions in Holocaust history reflect the role of the various occupying powers and their administrations in shaping and implementing policies of mass murder in their respective parts of Ukraine. However, in all of these various regions, the majority of the population was Ukrainian, and regardless of the nature of the regime in place, large numbers of the co-perpetrators, the rescuers, the bystanders, and of course the fellow victims were Ukrainian. And no matter who held these territories in early 1939, 1940, or late 1941, these lands now make up one country: Ukraine.

A comprehensive history of the Holocaust in Ukraine as a whole has not been written. This may surprise general readers, but they must bear in mind that Holocaust Studies as an academic field began to develop only in the late 1970s. Until the mid-1990s, Holocaust survivor and historian Philip Friedman and historian Shmuel Spector of Yad Vashem, Israel's Holocaust memorial authority, were among the few scholars to focus specifically on Ukraine.

Before the Second World War, Friedman, a native of what is today the Ukrainian city of Lviv, was already an established historian of Polish Jewry and, like Emmanuel Ringelblum in Warsaw, collected materials during the war to ensure that the history of the Holocaust could be written. After the war, Friedman served as the first director of the Central Jewish Historical Commission in Poland, and he is considered by many the "father of Holocaust history" due to his early postwar writings. However, Friedman's scholarly career was cut short when he died in 1960 at age 59. Friedman's work was of course well known to the few specialists studying the Holocaust at the time, but not until 1980 were Friedman's numerous essays and lectures collected and published in English under the title *Roads to Extinction*. One chapter of the Friedman collection was an 80-page essay on the Holocaust in Lviv. This essay, as historian Lucy Dawidowicz wrote in her review in *The New York Times*, was "the definitive work on the subject and an unfulfilled promise of what could have been a book-length history of the major community of Galician Jews."[6]

Aside from Friedman, the only major work to address the Holocaust in Ukraine in detail was Shmuel Spector's *The Holocaust of Volhynian Jews, 1941–1944*, which appeared in Hebrew in Israel in 1986, followed by an English edition in 1990.[7] This book was the first systematic regional history of the Holocaust in Ukraine and in many ways a model in terms of its scope and its range of sources (in all the major languages). Drawing from contemporary German documents and survivor testimony housed in archives in the United States, Poland, and Israel as well as from the memorial books (*yizkor bikher*) compiled by survivors from various prewar Jewish communities, Spector shed new light on the history of the ghettos, Jewish councils, massacres, rescuers, and resistance movements in this rural western region. The works of Friedman and Spector remained exceptions, however. Ukraine was of course mentioned in general Holocaust histories,[8] works dedicated to certain aspects of the Holocaust,[9] studies of key German institutions involved in the Holocaust,[10] examinations of Nazi occupation policy in the Soviet Union,[11] Ukrainian history,[12] and surveys about Soviet Jewry,[13] to name the most obvious fields. But references to the Holocaust in Ukraine usually drew from many of the same sources and focused on many of the same episodes. Not only could these materials become redundant in this respect, but an effort to synthesize them would not on its own yield a comprehensive overview. Save for a few exceptional works such as Raul Hilberg's three-volume study *The Destruction of the European Jews*,[14] many of these studies were limited to the mass shootings of Jews carried out by the mobile SS-police task forces, the Einsatzgruppen, in 1941 and early 1942.

This small body of literature, together with the *Encyclopedia Judaica*[15] and Ilya Ehrenburg and Vasily Grossman's *The Black Book: The Ruthless Murder of Jews by German-Fascist Invaders throughout the Temporarily-Occupied Regions of the Soviet Union*,[16] constituted most of what was available in English. There also existed a few published memoirs by survivors, but these too were scarce before the early 1980s and dedicated primarily to the unrepresentative region of Galicia, with particular attention given the region's principal city, Lviv.[17] Even after the appearance of dozens of memoirs in the mid-1980s and 1990s, the bulk of the material available still addressed primarily eastern Galicia. This focus on Lviv in particular was probably reinforced in part by a set of photographs taken during the pogrom there immediately after the Germans arrived.

The other significant work concerning the fate of Ukraine's Jews that bears mentioning here is Anatolii Kuznetsov's 1967 book *Babi Yar: A Documentary Novel*, which told the story of Dina Pronicheva, one of few survivors of the massacre of Kievan Jewry carried out by Special Commando 4a and several Order Police battalions at the ravine Babi Yar.[18] Due to the size of this massacre—33,771 Jews were shot in two days—it was inevitable that this particular Nazi killing operation came to stand out. Thus, to the extent that the general public in the West gave any thought to the murder of Ukraine's Jews prior to the 1990s, attention was given by and large to Lviv, July 1941, and the Kiev massacre, September 1941.

Lviv and Kiev were no doubt significant episodes, but they provide limited insight into the history of the Holocaust in Ukraine as a whole. With regard to pogroms in general, the available evidence shows that these took place primarily in Galicia and Volhynia, the interwar Polish territories seized by the Soviet Union in September 1939.[19] Where the Lviv pogrom is concerned, the mixture of German incitement and participation, spontaneous Ukrainian action, and advance planning by Ukrainian nationalist extremists—all of which were involved—is still being debated. The Lviv pogrom was partly fueled by the murder of some 2,500 Soviet political prisoners *before* the Red Army's retreat.[20] The subsequent anti-Jewish violence, however, revealed that a large number of local Gentiles believed strongly enough in "Judeo-Bolshevism" to vent their fury on thousands of innocents. In the light of what followed, the Lviv pogrom was also a brief episode in the destruction of that city's Jewish population. Most of Lviv's Jews were shot, gassed at Bełżec, or worked to death over a period of three years.

Outside Galicia, neither "resettlement" to death camps, nor pogroms, nor forced labor was typical for the fate of Ukraine's Jews. Far more frequent in these lands was the kind of slaughter that took place at Babi Yar. However, the Kiev massacre was itself a unique episode in that the major *Aktion* here took place within days of the city's occupation as opposed to weeks in other large cities.[21] The immediate pretext here was a series of massive explosions in Kiev caused by Soviet mines timed to explode after the Germans arrived. Instead of being registered, isolated, forced to clear rubble, tank obstacles, and mines, and perhaps exploited for other kinds of labor—a period of time that usually lasted six to eight weeks—Kiev's Jews were shot almost within two weeks of German occupation. Here the Wehrmacht worked particularly closely with the SS and police forces in Kiev, from making the decision, to printing the posters telling the Jews where to gather, to blasting the walls of the ravine to cover the dead. The decision may even have involved coordination with the authorities in charge of housing seeking to shelter those made homeless by the Soviet mines and the subsequent fires. Rather than being quintessential examples of how the murder of Ukraine's Jews unfolded, Lviv and Kiev were singular episodes, the most extreme examples of the 1941 pogroms on one hand and the first wave of mass shootings on the other.

The relatively slow development of research on the Holocaust in Ukraine stemmed from a combination of at least four major factors. First, as Holocaust Studies established itself as a field, it addressed other key issues first. The records of the German military, the various German ministries and occupation authorities, the catalogued records of the Nuremberg Trials, the Einsatzgruppen reports, survivor testimonies and the yizkor books as well as some records of postwar German criminal investigations were all available to scholars in the West before the 1980s. Instructive, useful preliminary studies at the regional level could have been written. Shmuel Spector did so. In the beginning, however, Holocaust Studies had other problems to tackle, the main ones being the highest decision-making levels of the Third Reich and the debate that erupted early on between "the intentionalists" and "the functionalists," the argument between those who believed that the extreme antisemitism of Hitler and his top leaders drove the policy of the "Final Solution" deliberately toward mass murder versus those who believed that conflicts among competing bureaucracies and ambitious lower-level functionaries had the cumulative effect of pushing anti-Jewish policy toward a program of systematic, mass murder.

Second, and in some ways an extension of the above, was what might be called an "Auschwitz syndrome." For understandable reasons, many historians, philosophers, and political scientists as well as the general public focused on the killing centers and the use of railroads to deport Jews to Auschwitz-Birkenau, as well as to Sobibór, Chełmno, Bełżec, Majdanek, and Treblinka, where altogether as many as 3 million men, women, and children were gassed and cremated in the way a factory receives and processes raw materials and disposes of the remnants. A uniquely horrific and criminal invention on the part of Nazi Germany, Auschwitz became the central symbol of modernity derailed, the nadir of Western civilization. Almost inevitably, academic and public interest in one aspect was bound to lead to neglect elsewhere. Country and regional studies had to wait. Ukraine was hardly alone in this respect.

Third, until 1991, scholars lacked access to the regional archives of the former Soviet Union. It was not until the successor states opened these repositories that the study of the Holocaust (and other previously taboo topics) could incorporate materials that had been located behind the Iron Curtain. Throughout the Cold War, Soviet officialdom—with few exceptions—sought to repress any discussion of the unique fate of Jews under Nazi rule, i.e., the fact that the Germans aimed for "100-percent solutions" where the Jews were concerned. Instead of being acknowledged as Jews, the Jewish victims of the Holocaust in the Soviet Union were often relegated to the category of "peaceful citizens." This manifestation of Soviet antisemitism guaranteed that the archives in Ukraine remained closed until the Soviet Union collapsed.

Fourth, Ukraine's prewar and wartime history of partition at the hands of Poland, Russia, Romania, Hungary, and Germany placed considerable linguistic demands on any scholar trying to gain an overview of how the Holocaust unfolded in Ukraine. In addition to the German, Russian, Ukrainian, and Polish secondary literature and primary sources to be considered, any study would naturally benefit from the use of Yiddish and Hebrew materials and literature. These are but the most obvious languages. Romania contributed two armies to the German invasion of the Soviet Union, while Hungarian and Slovak troops not only marched through central Ukraine in 1941, they also provided security forces for civil and military administered Ukraine in 1942 and 1943.[22] Overall, the study of most aspects of Ukrainian history and Holocaust history is linguistically demanding, the combination of the Holocaust in Ukraine all the more so.

Consequently, more than 30 years after Friedman's death, and 15 years after Dawidowicz's review of *Roads to Extinction*, in which she hinted that the field was wide open, scholars had yet to pick up where Friedman left off and address the Holocaust in Ukraine as a specific topic within the emerging field of Holocaust Studies.[23] It was only in 1996, when two major works on Galicia, by Dieter Pohl and Thomas Sandkühler, appeared in Germany, that the study of the Holocaust in Ukraine was given new impetus.[24]

This volume aims to build on what is generally known about the Holocaust in Ukraine outside the city limits of Kiev and Lviv and to take the study of these events beyond 1941 and 1942. Geographically, these chapters cover almost all of present-day Ukraine. Chronologically, they span the prewar, wartime, and postwar periods. This collection provides a greater context for understanding the causes, forms, and consequences of the Holocaust in Ukraine. It sets familiar issues such as the Einsatzgruppen, ghettos and camps, and local collaborators against the backdrop of Jewish-Ukrainian relations, Ukrainian history, German-Ukrainian ties, Soviet crimes, the German home-front, Polish-Ukrainian inter-communal violence, and the German-Romanian alliance.

For sources, the chapters here draw not only from the records long available in the United States, Germany, Poland, and Israel, but also from archives in the former Soviet Union and the extensive holdings of the United States Holocaust Memorial Museum (USHMM). The archival material also includes postwar criminal investigations of alleged perpetrators in West Germany as well as the court records of cases that went to trial and the verdicts that followed. Several of the scholars in this volume were among the first Holocaust historians to explore the contents of the former Soviet archives—whether in Ukraine or at the United States Holocaust Memorial Museum. The USHMM, through its program of microfilming material from across Europe, has guaranteed that the vast holdings of the many regional and national repositories in Ukraine are now accessible in a central archive in Washington, D.C. The existence of a U.S.-based repository and an institution such as the Center for Advanced Holocaust Studies, where scholars can meet and exchange ideas, was central to the completion of this book, as was the funding provided by the museum through the Summer Research Workshop Program and other fellowships.

The first chapter—by Dieter Pohl, senior researcher at Munich's Institute of Contemporary History—is essentially two chapters in one: an overview of the Holocaust in Ukraine during military administration, and a survey of the Holocaust in the civil administered RKU. He places the first mass killings by the Einsatzgruppen in the context of German military planning and the Wehrmacht's desire for security and stability behind the front, and then outlines the escalation of the shootings to include an ever expanding pool of victims, from select groups of mostly Jewish male victims to shootings organized partly in response to immediate pretexts, such as the murders committed by the Soviet secret police before retreating from Galicia and Volhynia, to the indiscriminate and near total liquidation of entire communities starting in late August 1941. He shows how the ideologically driven food and POW policies facilitated cooperation between military administration commands and the Einsatzgruppen in implementing mass murder, and he gives the higher SS and police leaders (Höhere SS-und Polizeiführer, HSSPF) active in Ukraine—Friedrich Jeckeln, Hans-Adolf Prützmann, and Gerret Korsemann—and the Order Police troops the attention they deserve for their role in the mass killing.

Where the forces of HSSPF Russia South and the Wehrmacht failed to eliminate the Jews before handing over territory to the civilian-run RKU, the civil administration continued this task. Here Pohl analyzes the major turning points in the evolution of Nazi anti-Jewish policy in Ukraine, and when relevant, he shows where mass killing actions in Ukraine paralleled similar activity elsewhere in Nazi-occupied Europe. He describes the scale of destruction, the involvement of Ukrainian police, what Moscow knew about what was happening to the Jews in Ukraine, and the thoroughness of the German perpetrators—first in the actual killing, then in trying to destroy the evidence.

Historian Timothy Snyder of Yale University focuses on a region within the RKU to provide an intricate account of interethnic relations during the Holocaust in the prewar Polish region of Volhynia. Drawing on a wide array of memoirs, testimonies, and contemporary documents, Snyder portrays the economic and social discontent and mutual suspicion among the ethnic groups, which were exacerbated by grievous missteps by the Polish government and then exploited and radicalized by the Soviet and Nazi occupations. Snyder offers portraits of individual Jews, Ukrainians, and Poles whose actions were shaped by differences in generation, ideology, social standing, and many other variables.

Snyder's chapter also looks at the occupation regime in the RKU at the grass roots. However, life for Ukrainians, or almost anybody in the RKU, cannot be compared with life for Ukrainians in District Galicia in the General Government. Key Ukrainian civic leaders in Galicia were, even by Nazi standards, skillfully manipulated in a policy of divide and conquer vis-à-vis Poles and Jews. To make this policy work, Ukrainians were favored over the Poles, and it is clear from postwar memoirs that the Ukrainian intelligentsia in Galicia considered the Nazis preferable to both the Poles and Soviets in areas such as the cooperative movement, religious life, and education policy.

Frank Golczewski of Hamburg University presents Galicia as an important case study for understanding German-Ukrainian relations during the Holocaust. Much of the Galician Ukrainian intelligentsia had been pro-German before 1939, the result of 146 years of attachment to Austria and Austro-German support during the Polish-Ukrainian war over Galicia in 1919. Like so many other European peoples outside the Soviet Union, Galician Ukrainians also had their interwar extremists: the authoritarian and antisemitic Organization of Ukrainian Nationalists. The combination of a pro-German sentiment and an extremist ideology enabled the Third Reich and right-wing Galician Ukrainian civic leaders to cooperate during the war. One result was the voluntary enrollment of many Galician Ukrainian men into the Nazis' machinery of annihilation, primarily as the camp guards and policemen who often figure so prominently in many survivor accounts. Without losing sight of how ordinary Galician Ukrainians suffered under Nazi rule, Golczewski explores the cooperation between Nazi administrators and Galician Ukrainian civic leaders at the cultural, economic, and political level and how this succeeded in creating a tranquil environment against which the destruction of Galician Jewry could unfold.[25]

While Ukrainian cooperation with Nazi Germany took place at the level of German-created institutions of occupation, especially in Galicia, in the case of Romania, cooperation was state to state. Dennis Deletant's chapter reexamines the deportation of the Jews from the Romanian-held borderlands of Bessarabia and Bukovina to Transnistria and the fate of these Jews together with those indigenous to the land between the Dniestr and Southern Bug rivers. Deletant, professor of Romanian studies at University College of London, argues that Romania's deportations were part of a broader policy of "ethnic purification," conceived and implemented by Antonescu. Based on extensive research in archives in Romania and the archives of the USHMM, Deletant argues that Romanian dictator Ion Antonescu originally envisioned Transnistria not as the final destination of the Jews and the Roma (Gypsies) but merely as a "holding-station" for their expulsion across Transnistria's eastern border into Russia. Deletant's work presents the diplomatic exchanges and ideological overlap between Romanian and German officials equally eager to implement deadly social engineering programs in southern Ukraine.

Despite the deaths of tens of thousands in this "Jewish reservation"—the result of both mass shootings and exposure and starvation—Transnistria nonetheless created a reservoir of Jews that the SS sought to exploit for the largest forced labor project in Ukraine, road construction on Thoroughfare IV, one of the German Armed Forces' key supply lines on the eastern front. Andrej Angrick of Berlin provides a history of this relatively unknown project. Using memoirs, German documents, and postwar West German criminal investigations, Angrick reveals the extensive planning that went into the project and portrays the involvement of Hitler, the Ministry of Munitions, the Wehrmacht, the SS, the Order Police, and Organization Todt (the Nazi party's paramilitary construction service) in implementing a project that ultimately cost the lives of 25,000 Jewish forced laborers in central and eastern Ukraine (and tens of thousands of prisoners of war). Angrick's chapter, a detailed journey through the German bureaucracy, demonstrates the forethought that could go into forced labor projects and the ruthless expenditure of human beings as a raw material. In the process, Angrick also brings to light previously unpublished information about the camp system along this thoroughfare.

To coordinate this construction project, the police and engineers on Thoroughfare IV were subordinated to high-ranking SS supervisors, who had often been appointed the post of SS and police leader (SSPF) in a region that had yet to be conquered. Thoroughfare IV was to provide on-the-job training for coordinating forced labor "recruiters," dealing with the Order Police and indigenous police units, liaising with the Security Police and Security Service (Sicherheitsdienst, SD) regional offices and outposts, and cooperating with the top German civil administrators at the county level, the county commissars. The chapter by Wendy Lower provides a case study of these county commissars in General Commissariat Zhytomyr. These were not agents of the SS and police or the military, but a motley assortment of German functionaries—almost all party members—hand picked by senior officials in the Reich Ministry for the Occupied Eastern Territories. Little has been written about these "ordinary" men on the ground who governed anti-Jewish policies in the remote outposts of Ukraine. What was their social and educational background? What motivated them to push through the mass murder? Most were part of the first generation of "old fighters," "brown shirts" who had been too young for military service in the First World War but had been socialized and hardened during the rise of the Nazi movement. Many were the product of Nazi "finishing schools" known as "castles of the order," which were designed to fashion an elite of professional administrators. Prior literature has not stressed enough that many of these county leaders arrived in the Ukrainian "frontier" of the Reich with utopian and colonialist illusions. They saw the Jews collectively as a Bolshevik enemy and racial threat in the fight to secure and settle an all German *Lebensraum*.

Working together with the SS and police at the county and precinct level, the county commissars in General Commissariat Zhytomyr often decided or helped coordinate final ghetto liquidations, selected Jewish laborers, and managed the general welfare of the local population. This caste of adventurers and administrators in General Commissariat Zhytomyr found that they could fulfill their imperialist ambitions and impress their superiors by making their future fiefdoms "free of Jews." While German policies toward ethnic Germans and Ukrainians fueled bureaucratic conflicts and stoked partisan activity, the Nazi anti-Jewish campaign drew upon widespread support inside and outside the German administration.

General Commissariat Zhytomyr was particularly important for the Nazis. It was home to Werwolf, one of Hitler's headquarters, and to Hegewald, an experimental German settlement overseen by Heinrich Himmler, the national leader of the SS and the chief of the German police. The settlers were ultimately to include Germans from the Reich, but in the interim, Hegewald served as a place of resettlement for ethnic Germans in Ukraine. The ethnic Germans played a key role not only in encouraging dreams of empire but, more important, in laying its foundations. Martin Dean, senior researcher at the USHMM Center for Advanced Holocaust Studies and a well-known expert on the history of Ukrainian collaboration, takes a closer look at an important example of collaboration that has been largely overlooked. He shows how ethnic Germans in the police precincts participated in carrying out the Holocaust in their home regions. He demonstrates that Nazi leaders, wherever possible, integrated indigenous Germans into the occupational apparatus, placing them in key positions in the civil administration and the police, whether in stationary local units or the mobile Einsatzgruppen. Dean's work is based on in-depth research in regional archives of the former Soviet Union and war crimes trials held in the late 1990s. The perception of Ukraine's ethnic Germans as "double victims" of history—first as victims of Soviet rule before the war, then as targets of anti-German acts of revenge toward war's end—has generally overshadowed the role they played in implementing Nazi killing policies.

In the process of seeking "100-percent solutions" in the treatment of the "Jewish question"—immediately when possible, after some degree of exploitation as forced laborers when necessary—the perpetrators discussed in these chapters killed at least 1.4 million Jews. Overall, estimates for those Ukrainian citizens who perished as a result of Nazi policies range from 5.5 million to 7 million people (including Transcarpathia and the Crimea), which would mean Jewish deaths accounted for 17–22 percent of those killed in Ukraine in the course of the war. Precise figures, however, are very difficult to determine.[26] Alexander Kruglov of Kharkiv has spent years culling figures from Soviet reports and German documents to provide a region-by-region, month-by-month estimate of Jewish losses in Ukraine during the Holocaust. In addition to documenting losses, he also attempts to quantify evacuation and rescue efforts. Kruglov's chapter offers the latest data on the numbers of Jews killed in Ukraine, from the largest towns to the smallest villages. Those who work in Russian and Ukrainian know how useful his work can be in revealing previously unknown references to camps, ghettos, and killing sites throughout Ukraine. His chapter provides scholars and students with useful data about the scope and chronological development of the Holocaust in Ukraine.

An additional challenge to studying the Holocaust in Ukraine, a challenge that faces researchers in many fields, is the issue of how to deal with personal testimony. Karel Berkhoff of the Center for Holocaust and Genocide Studies in Amsterdam analyzes the dozen known testimonies of Babi Yar survivor Dina Pronicheva. Pronicheva's accounts, which she gave between 1944 and her death in 1977, are the most widely cited sources of the mass shootings at Babi Yar and formed the basis of the famous book by Anatolii Kuznetsov. Berkhoff analyzes both the content of her testimony and its varied political and legal uses after the war. He shows that Pronicheva's story did not change dramatically and also suggests which versions are probably most historically reliable. Berkhoff's chapter offers a summary and overview of the latest research on the history of Babi Yar as well as a look at the perils and possibilities of Holocaust testimony as a source.

Jews were of course not the only ones killed at Babi Yar, but they were the largest group. Other groups included Soviet POWs and political activists, Communist and nationalist alike. For example, the road around the site of Babi Yar is today named for Oleha Teliha, a poet shot at the ravine in February 1942. While Teliha is a martyr for nationalist Ukrainians, her affiliation with the faction of the Organization of Ukrainian Nationalists in Kiev, the faction that most likely provided the auxiliary police for the murder of Kiev's Jews at Babi Yar the previous September, places her in a suspicious light in the eyes of Jews who memorialize their victims at this same ravine.[27] In recent years, Ukrainian attempts to establish a non-Soviet national history have produced similar awkward juxtapositions in marking of Holocaust-related sites and the architectural remnants of Ukrainian Jewish history. In his chapter, Omer Bartov, professor of European history at Brown University, takes readers on a journey through half a dozen towns and cities in modern-day Galicia and explores how the multi-ethnic, multi-denominational past is treated in this region.

From Lviv to Drohobych, Ivano-Frankivsk to Kosiv, Ternopil to Zhovkva, Bartov shows how present-day Galicia is determined not to remember the past as it was, but to magnify the ethnic Ukrainian past and minimize, if not erase, the others. Galicia is today the product of successive campaigns of ethnic cleansing. The Soviets and the Nazis for the most part rid this corner of Ukraine of its Poles and Jews respectively between 1940 and 1946. The Jews who fled to the woods were pursued by the Organization of Ukrainian Nationalists and then by the Ukrainian People's Self-Defense Force (later merged with the Ukrainian Insurgent Army, or UPA). And in 1943–1944, the Ukrainian Insurgent Army also began systematically terrorizing Galicia's Poles in a campaign of murder and expulsion from the countryside (a campaign to which Polish armed groups responded with great brutality). For most Galician Ukrainians, any genuine, thoroughgoing acknowledgement of their murdered or expelled neighbors means confronting a part of the past they wish not to remember. The synagogues are in ruins; cemeteries serve as pasture for goats; and the sites of ghettos are dominated by monuments to leaders of the Organization of Ukrainian Nationalists.

Some of the issues raised in these chapters bear highlighting here. For one, even before the Germans invaded the Soviet Union, military and civilian planners in Berlin, as Dieter Pohl explains in this volume, had already envisioned the death of millions of Soviet citizens in urban areas by sealing off and starving the cities. Because the Soviet Union's Jews were concentrated in the cities, the Germans had in effect already arranged the annihilation of the majority of Jews before decisions were made about the eradication of entire Jewish communities by mass shootings. However, during the invasion, Himmler pressed his immediate representatives in the field to expand the pool of Jews to be shot—from select groups of male Jews targeted on the basis of ideology or function within the Soviet state, to able-bodied men, to women and children—until at some point around mid-August entire Jewish communities were being totally liquidated, primarily in pre-1939 Soviet Ukraine.

The Holocaust in those Ukrainian lands that fell to the RKU was of course very much like the Holocaust in the rest of prewar Soviet territories. It was carried out almost exclusively by shooting, with a small percentage of victims being asphyxiated in gas vans. Just as important as the dozen large-scale massacres usually epitomized by the ravine Babi Yar in Kiev were the hundreds of smaller shootings ranging from 100 to 3,000 victims in towns such as Malyn, Samhorodok, Ustynivka, and Krasnopilka. The Nazi-led destruction of Jewish communities in the RKU still falls within the generally accepted chronology of a first wave and second wave—August to December 1941 and late May 1942 onward—but even in between, the shooting of individuals or small groups of people, whether intended as an instrument of terror or as a means of eliminating exhausted or sick workers, was relentless. In these lands, the killers went to the victims or, eventually, they were recruited from among their neighbors. Men, women and children were murdered in broad daylight in or not far from the towns or villages where they grew up. Despite German efforts to maintain secrecy, the Holocaust in Ukraine was a public event.

It is also worth underscoring here the varying regional responses of the non-Jewish population to the anti-Jewish violence, in particular the pogroms. This subject still requires greater study. However, one important point needs to be stressed: The occurrence of pogroms in Ukraine was uneven. As stated earlier, pogroms in central and southern Ukraine were rare. This is all the more interesting because these are the territories that were hardest hit by the pogroms of 1918–1920 and by Stalin's artificial famine in 1932–1933, a famine that popular antisemitic myth (then and now) ascribes to "Judeo-Bolshevik" perfidy against the Ukrainian peasantry.[28] Yet despite this history of antisemitic violence in these lands and the existence of such myths in the 1940s, the Ukrainian population in central and southern Ukraine—with few exceptions—apparently refrained from anti-Jewish violence even when the Einsatzkommandos tried to incite it. Antisemitism had certainly not been eradicated by Soviet rule, but the readiness to resort to anti-Jewish violence had clearly receded.[29]

In the regions of western Volhynia and eastern Galicia, by contrast, dozens of pogroms occurred during the first six weeks of the German invasion in summer 1941. While western Volhynia had also seen numerous pogroms after the First World War, in neighboring eastern Galicia very few occurred.[30] As parts of Poland between the wars, these regions were spared the enervating devastation of a full generation of Soviet rule, in particular the famine and the purges (1936–1938). However, the interwar Polish state committed numerous blunders that in the end served to exacerbate tensions between the various ethnic groups inhabiting western Volhynia and eastern Galicia. Nonetheless, when Stalin seized these regions in September 1939, they were in turn subjected to a brief and brutal encounter with Soviet Communism, but neither this encounter, nor the German Einsatzgruppen alone explain the local violence against Jews in the opening weeks of the German–Soviet war, as Tim Snyder and Frank Golczewski show in their chapters.

With regard to rescuers, the extent of Ukrainian rescue efforts has only come to light since the demise of the Soviet Union. As of January 1, 2007, Yad Vashem has recognized 2,185 Righteous among the Nations from Ukraine, the vast majority of them in the last 15 years. Overall, the number of rescuers relative to the size of Ukraine's population compares favorably with the ratio for

France, but less favorably to that of Poland. Examples of courage and charity amid enormous hardship can be found throughout Ukraine, and members of almost every ethnic group and religious faith are represented among the rescuers. In western Volhynia and, later, eastern Galicia, rescue efforts were complicated by the partisan war. Snyder describes here how Jews in hiding quickly got caught between the partisan movements fighting one against the other as well as against the Germans. Especially vulnerable were those Jews hiding with Poles, whom the Ukrainian Insurgent Army (UPA) sought to expel from Volhynia. This also took place in Galicia, where the UPA pursued a similar policy of ethnic cleansing.

Finally, none of the German institutions involved in the invasion and occupation of Ukraine operated in complete isolation from the others. Several of the chapters here help us to keep this in mind. At the local and regional level of rule, the Wehrmacht, German civil administrators, the SS, and the Order Police worked together to form an integrated, mutually reinforcing system throughout German-occupied Ukraine, whether the RKU or District Galicia. The purpose of this system was to eliminate those considered "unworthy of life," exploit Ukraine's human and agriculture resources, and make way for a German empire governed by local ethnic Germans and Reich Germans; the colonized territory stretched from District Galicia and the middle of General Commissariat Zhytomyr, down the Dniepr River to the Crimea. The division of labor entailed in this empire building—expressed here in the chapters by Andrej Angrick and Wendy Lower—shows how they worked (and competed) with one another across occupation regimes, especially with regard to Thoroughfare IV, one of the main arteries that was to support this empire.

This integration of institutions extended of course to the realm of foreign policy and Germany's allies as well. For Hitler and the top Nazi leadership, Ukraine was not just for plundering and resettling. It could be carved up in order to pay off allies for their military and economic contributions to the campaign against the Soviet Union, which, as Dennis Deletant shows here, was the German dictator's intent when he presented his Romanian counterpart with the land that became Transnistria. German influence on the Romanians' treatment of the Jews (and the Roma) can be seen, but the Romanian zone of occupation in Ukraine seems to be a case unto itself, mixing mass shootings (e.g., Bohdanivka and Odessa), forced labor, and sheer neglect similar to German policy towards POWs. With regard to Bukovina and Transnistria, local histories of interethnic relations, collaboration, rescuers, and resistance require greater research.[31]

Nonetheless, whether in Bukovina, Galicia, or Dniepr Ukraine, the Holocaust in all of these regions unfolded against a

Ukrainian backdrop, and the local responses—rescuers, bystanders, and collaborators (and the shades of grey in between)—thus constitute both a part of the history of the Holocaust in Ukraine *and* the history of the Second World War in Ukraine. Ukrainians as a whole suffered tremendously under the Nazis, but the behavior of specific Ukrainian political groups and certain individuals within the precinct-level administration and local police (whether in the RKU or District Galicia) has cast a shadow over that greater suffering. The role of the OUN in the 1941 pogroms and that of the UPA in killing Jews in hiding in 1942-1944 (even when these organizations were fighting Erich Koch's civil administration) are two key examples. But even in examining these groups, it is important not to lose sight of overall Ukrainian losses and the leading role of the German occupiers and their allies.

This volume is meant to examine the Shoah within the context of Ukraine and establish the investigation of the events in Ukraine in the field of Holocaust Studies. The chapters offer in-depth treatments of various topics and do so based on newly available sources. Nonetheless, they raise as many questions as they answer. As Pohl points out, little is known about the responses of ordinary German soldiers to the various campaigns of mass murder in Ukraine and the role of the precinct-level administration in implementing anti-Jewish measures across Ukraine. A study of interethnic relations in the borderlands of eastern Ukraine—meaning here the six eastern oblasts that experienced only military occupation—would be most welcome, for example.[32] The premeditated annihilation of Soviet POWs, Roma, the mentally and physically disabled, and parts of the civilian population caught up in anti-partisan operations also require greater study, on their own terms as well as in relation to the destruction of Ukraine's Jews.

Going beyond the fundamental questions of what happened where in Ukraine, on whose authority, and with how much planning, an entire array of other themes awaits investigation. These concern both the aftermath of the Holocaust across Soviet Ukraine and its historical treatment in post-Soviet Ukraine. A separate volume could explore issues such as the systematic suppression of public discourse about the Holocaust in Soviet Ukraine, Ukrainian dissident treatment of the Holocaust in the Khrushchev and Gorbachev eras, and the handling of the Holocaust by émigré Ukrainian historians. How did the Soviet Ukrainian justice system tackle criminal investigations into collaboration involving the Shoah? Does the Holocaust have a place in Ukrainian culture today? In its literature? In its films? How do the politics of commemoration and victimization influence Holocaust education and remembrance in post-Soviet Ukraine? Is the Holocaust covered extensively, or at all, in Ukrainian textbooks today?[33]

The editors of this volume hope that this collection encourages further research on the Holocaust in Ukraine that is rooted in the social, cultural, political, and geographic setting where the genocide occurred. The destruction of Ukraine's Jews, and the murder of millions of others on Ukrainian soil during the war, must be placed in a context that truly reflects this vast territory's ethnic, historical, and regional variations. Similarly, students of Ukrainian history must better come to terms with the Holocaust as an integral part of, not a sidebar to, Ukrainian history. Research on the Holocaust in Ukraine, and elsewhere, has shown us human behavior at its worst in the complicity of tens of thousands, and at its best in the rescue efforts of thousands. The assumption that any ethnic group fell completely and consistently within either of these extremes or was totally isolated from the others obscures the complexities that this volume's contributors seek to bring into sharper relief.

Notes

1. Unless otherwise stated, Ukraine here generally means the lands within the boundaries of the modern Ukrainian state.

2. Drawing from the 1897 Russian census, the *Encyclopaedia Judaica* put the number of Jews in "Ukraine and Bessarabia" at 2,148,059 persons (*Encyclopaedia Judaica*, Vol. 14, "Russia," p. 450 [Jerusalem: Encyclopaedia Judaica, 1971]). Subtracting the Jews of Bessarabia—228,620 persons (*Encyclopaedia Judaica*, Vol. 4, "Bessarabia," p. 705)—leaves 1,919,439 Jews in the Russian Empire's ten Ukrainian provinces (*gubernii*). Russian Poland—meaning the then ten provinces of the Kingdom of Poland—accounted for 1,316,576 Jews, according to the *Encyclopaedia Judaica*. A comparison of the figures of the *Encyclopaedia Judaica* with the 1897 census data published on http://demoscope.ru/weekly/ssp/rus_lan_97.php?reg=0 yields slightly different figures (1,267,194 Jews for the Polish provinces, 49,382 fewer than in *Encyclopaedia Judaica*, and 1,908,465 Jews for the Ukrainian provinces, a difference of 10,974), but the gap between the Polish lands and Ukrainian lands of the Russian Empire is such—roughly 640,000—that the number of Jews within the ethno-linguistic Polish parts of the provinces Grodno and Vilnius could not make up the difference. For prewar figures on the Soviet Union, see Mordechai Altshuler, *Distribution of the Jewish Population of the USSR 1939* (Jerusalem: Centre for Research and Documentation of East-European Jewry, 1993), pp. 9–11.

3. A precise figure is impossible to determine due to imperfect statistics, shifting borders, refugees, deportations, and internal migration. Our figure is based on adding the 1.532 million Jews in the UkrSSR prior to 1939, a minimum of 575,000 from Galicia, 226,000 from Volhynia (including the strip of territory from Polesie Voivodeship added to the Rivne and Volhynia oblasts) as well as at least 120,000 Jews from northern Bukovina and southern Bessarabia, which Stalin seized from Romania in June 1940. This yields 2.453 million Jews in the UkrSSR in June 1941—without refugees from central and western Poland. Nazi-occupied Poland, by contrast, was home to at least 1.906 million Jews, according to the *Statistisches Gemeindeverzeichnis des bisherigen polnischen Staates* (Berlin: Selbstverlag der Publikationsstelle, 1939), table 15, which is based on 1931 Polish census

data. German planners throughout 1940 worked from the assumption that Nazi-occupied Poland had roughly 2.8 million Jews, see "eingegliederte Ostgebiete" and "Generalgouvernement" in the table on p. 303, Götz Aly, *Endlösung: Völkerverschiebung und der Mord an den europäischen Juden* (Frankfurt am Main: S. Fischer Verlag, 1995). This inflated figure is probably based on the 1931 statistics, adjusted for estimated population growth until 1940, assimilated Jews, and refugees from the Polish lands incorporated by the Soviet Union as well as other European countries, etc. Frank Golczewski has produced data showing the figure to be closer to 2.3 million Jews in the second half of 1940—1,945,000 in the General Government and 352,446 in the territories annexed to Germany—see Frank Golczewski, "Polen" in *Dimension des Völkermords: Die Zahl der jüdischen Opfer des Nationalsozialismus,* Wolfgang Benz, ed. (Munich: Oldenbourg, 1991), pp. 448–457. This sounds plausible when compared with the 1931 Polish census. For a contemporary Ukrainian breakdown of the Jewish population in Ukraine, see W. Kubijowytsch, *Lage, Grenzen und Territorium der ukrainischen Gebiete* (Berlin: Selbstverlag der Publikationsstelle, 1942), pp. 28f., which puts the Jewish population for the lands that made up the UkrSSR in 1940 at 2.484 million. In a postwar publication, Kubiiovych's figures for the territories of the UkrSSR in its 1940 boundaries total 2.565 million Jews, see *Encyclopedia of Ukraine, Map and Gazetteer,* Volodymyr Kubijovyč, ed. (Toronto: University of Toronto Press, 1984). In each publication, Kubiiovych based his estimates on the 1926 Soviet census and the 1931 Polish census, which were then adjusted to reflect the situation as of January 1933.

4. Cf. Timothy Mulligan, *The Politics of Illusion and Empire* (New York; Westport, CT; London: Praeger, 1988), pp. 10–13; Ernst Boog et al., *Der Angriff auf die Sowjetunion. Das Deutsche Reich und der Zweite Weltkrieg,* Band 4 (Stuttgart: Deutsche Verlags-Anstalt, 1983), p. 413–421; Roman Ilnytzkyj [Il'nyts'kyi], *Deutschland und die Ukraine, 1934–1945: Tatsachen europäischer Ostpolitik: Ein Vorbericht,* Band 2 (Munich: Osteuropa-Institut München, 1958), pp. 2–76; Alexander Dallin, *German Rule in Russia, 1941–1945: A Study of Occupation Policies* (New York: St. Martin's Press, 1957), pp. 44–58.

5. The protocol of this meeting constituted Nuremberg Document L-221, Besprechung im Führerhauptquartier, July, 16, 1941. Participants at the meeting were Hitler, Rosenberg, Reich Chancellery Chief of Staff Hans Heinrich Lammers, Party Chancellery Chief of Staff Martin Bormann, *Reichmarschall* and Plenipotentiary for the Four-Year Plan Hermann Göring, and Chief of the High Command of the Wehrmacht Wilhelm Keitel. The key reasons for turning over Galicia to the General Government were General Governor Hans Frank's wish to expand his realm and Germany's relations with Romania. Frank was likely lobbying Hitler to this end before Germany invaded the Soviet Union—i.e., before Stepan Bandera's faction of the Organization of Ukrainian Nationalists declared the restoration of Ukrainian statehood in L'viv on June 30, 1941. To what extent Ukrainian nationalist aspirations in Galicia informed this decision appears to be unknown. The issue is not mentioned in the protocol of the aforementioned gathering, which suggests that Hitler, Frank, and others *at the very top* of the Nazi hierarchy saw neither Ukrainian nationalism nor the OUN as a major concern. Both factions of the OUN in mid-1941 were at the time merely two elements of highly factional Ukrainian politics, and neither of them enjoyed a significant following outside Galicia. Still, it may be that the June 30 declaration helped tip Hitler in favor of turning Galicia over to Frank. On this decision, see Sandkühler, pp. 64f. and 473, as well as Ilnytzkyj, Band 2, p. 215.

6. Lucy S. Dawidowicz, "Holocaust Historian," January 11, 1981, *New York Times*. Philip Friedman's essay on L'viv was published first in Polish, *Zagłada Żydów Lwówskich* (The Fate of the Jews of Lvov) (Munich: n.p., 1947). It appears in Philip Friedman, *Roads to Extinction: Essays on the Holocaust* (New York: Conference on Jewish Social Studies, Jewish Publication Society of America, 1980).

7. Shmuel Spector, *Sho'at Yehude Vohlin, 1941–1944* (Jerusalem: Yad va-shem: ha-Federatsyah shel Yehude Vohlin, 1986), and idem, *The Holocaust of Volhynian Jews, 1941–1944* (Jerusalem: Yad Vashem and Federation of Volhynian Jews, 1990). Although important for the scope of its sources and the breadth of topics explored, the English edition of this book was hurriedly translated and rushed to publication. It could stand to be revised, corrected, expanded, and reissued.

8. In addition to Hilberg's study, other general histories included Gerald Reitlinger, *The Final Solution: The Attempt to Exterminate the Jews of Europe, 1939–1945* (London: Vallentine, Mitchell, 1953); Nora Levin, *The Holocaust: The Destruction of European Jewry, 1933–1945* (New York: Crowell, 1968); and Lucy S. Dawidowicz, *The War Against the Jews, 1933–1945* (New York: Holt, Rinehart and Winston, 1975).

9. For example, Isaiah Trunk, *Judenrat: The Jewish Councils in Eastern Europe under Nazi Occupation* (New York: Macmillan, 1972); Reuben Ainsztein, *Jewish Resistance in Nazi-Occupied Eastern Europe* (London: Elek, 1974); and Jean Ancel, *Documents Concerning the Fate of Romanian Jewry during the Holocaust* (New York: Beate Klarsfeld Foundation, 1986).

10. The first major study of the Einsatzgruppen appeared in 1981, Helmut Krausnick and Hans-Heinrich Wilhelm, *Die Truppe des Weltanschauungskrieges: Die Einsatzgruppen der Sicherheitspolizei und des SD 1938–1942* (Stuttgart: Deutsche Verlags-Anstalt, 1981).

11. Examples here are Alexander Dallin, *German Rule in Russia, 1941–1945: A Study of Occupation Policies* (New York: St. Martin's Press, 1957); Gerald Reitlinger, *The House Built on Sand: The Conflicts of German Policy in Russia, 1939–1945* (New York: Viking Press, 1960); Norman Rich, *Hitler's War Aims* (New York: Norton, 1974); and Timothy Patrick Mulligan, *Politics of Illusion and Empire: German Occupation Policy in the Soviet Union, 1942–1943* (New York: Praeger, 1988).

12. John A. Armstrong, *Ukrainian Nationalism, 1939–1945* (New York: Columbia University Press, 1955). While there are about half a dozen references to the Holocaust as such, most of the information on the collaboration of extremist Ukrainian nationalist circles and the German army and police stops short of discussing in detail what that collaboration meant for Ukraine's Jews, particularly those in Galicia.

13. Prominent examples from the Cold War era are Solomon M. Schwarz, *The Jews in the Soviet Union* (Syracuse: Syracuse University Press, 1951); Salo W. Baron, *The Russian Jew under Tsars and Soviets* (New York: Macmillan, 1964); and Nora Levin, *The Jews in the Soviet Union since 1917: Paradox of Survival* (New York: New York University Press, 1988).

14. The most recent printing of this standard work is Raul Hilberg, *The Destruction of the European Jews*, 3rd ed. (New Haven, CT: Yale University Press, 2003).

15. *Encyclopaedia Judaica* (Jerusalem: Encyclopaedia Judaica, 1971).

16. *The Black Book: The Ruthless Murder of Jews by German-Fascist Invaders throughout the Temporarily-Occupied Regions of the Soviet Union and in the Death Camps of Poland during the War of 1941–1945*, Ilya Ehrenburg and Vasily Grossman, eds. (New York: Holocaust Publications, c. 1981). After the fall of Soviet Union, censored passages from the *Black Book*

emerged, which led to a new translation and edition, *The Complete Black Book of Russian Jewry,* Ilya Ehrenburg and Vasily Grossman, eds. (Brunswick, NJ.: Transaction, 2002).

17. Leon Weliczker Wells, *The Janowska Road* (New York: Macmillan, 1963); Paul Trepman, *Why?: Extermination Camp Lwów (Lemberg), 134 Janowska Street, Poland: A Documentary by an Inmate* (New York: Vantage Press, 1975); and Paul Trepman, *Among Men and Beasts* (South Brunswick: A. S. Barnes, 1978) were among the few memoirs existing prior to 1980. The overwhelming majority of published memoirs appeared starting in the mid-1980s. Books by survivors from Galicia outnumber by far those written by survivors from elsewhere in Ukraine, see Karel C. Berkhoff, "Ukraine under Nazi Rule (1941–1944): Sources and Finding Aids, Part II," *Jahrbücher für Geschichte Osteuropas,* 45 (1997), No. 2, pp. 299–304, here 302f.

18. Anatoly Kuznetsov, *Babi Yar: A Documentary Novel* (New York, Dial Press, 1967). The story of Babi Yar survivor Dina Pronicheva and Kuznetsov's book are discussed in detail by Karel C. Berkhoff in this volume.

19. The difference in frequency of documented 1941 pogroms between pre-1939 Polish Ukrainian territories and pre-1939 Soviet Ukrainian territories is circa 70 vis-à-vis 5 (Bilopil'e, Chudniv, Khmil'nyk, Olevs'k, and Hnivan'). There were almost certainly more, but the pattern seems clear, and Einsatzgruppe C, reporting from prewar Soviet Ukrainian territory, complained on two occasions that pogroms were nearly impossible to incite east of the old Polish-Soviet border. A pogrom did occur in Uman', but it was instigated and carried out for the most part by German soldiers. The Zhytomyr pogrom consisted primarily of Sonderkommando 4a trying to animate the local Ukrainians, who were rather reluctant to follow the example. In the zone of operations for Einsatzgruppe D, pogroms were generally Romanian, two exceptions being Chernivtsi and Khotyn. It is hard to assess how many of the Galician and Volhynian pogroms were truly spontaneous, but it is clear that the population was receptive to whatever German incitement was involved. Pogroms also broke out in Galicia where Einsatzgruppe C was not present, for example, in Hungarian occupied areas, and in some cases before the Germans arrived. A crucial role in inciting pogroms in both Galicia and Volhynia was played by the Organization of Ukrainian Nationalists as well.

20. An exact figure has yet to be determined. Contemporary Soviet records found after the Cold War document the killing of 2,464 prisoners. While in custody in Nuremberg Hans Frank, the former head of the General Government, spoke of some 2,400 dead. The source for Frank's statement—Hans Frank, *Im Angesicht des Galgens* (Munich: F. A. Beck, 1953), p. 416—is tendentious and to be consulted with the greatest caution, but this figure so closely reflects the Soviet figure that it cannot be ignored. This and the fact that it lay in Frank's interest to exaggerate the number of dead in L'viv suggests that a number around 2,500 may be more accurate. Cf. Krzysztof Popiński, Aleksandr Kokurin, Aleksandr Gurjanow, eds., *Drogi śmierci. Ewakuacja więzień sowieckich z Kresów Wschodnich II Rzeczypospolitej w czerwcu i lipcu 1941* (Warszawa: Karta, 1995), pp. 31 and 176.

21. For example, in Kirovohrad, occupied on August 14, the greater part of the Jews left behind were murdered on September 30 (4,200 Jews), while in Dnipropetrovsk, captured over the course of several days between August 25 and 28, the main shooting took place on October 13–14 (10,000 Jews). In Kryvyi Rih, which was taken between August 15 and 17, the largest massacre occurred on October 14–15 (over 4,000 Jews); in Kremenchuk, which was occupied incrementally between September 9 and 14, on October

28 (3,000 Jews). In smaller towns, the total or near total liquidation of entire communities usually took place soon after the arrival of a detachment of Einsatzgruppe C.

22. Italy and Croatia also provided troops to Army Group South, which suggests some most likely marginal supplemental information could be secreted away in archives in Rome and Zagreb. Given that Volhynia was also home to Czech settlements, the existence of Czech testimonies is at least theoretically a possibility.

23. A glance at Karel C. Berkhoff's survey, "Ukraine under Nazi Rule (1941–1944): Sources and Finding Aids," shows how little the Holocaust in Ukraine had been examined.

24. Dieter Pohl, *Nationalsozialistische Judenverfolgung in Ostgalizien 1941–1944: Organisation und Durchführung eines staatlichen Massenverbrechens* (Munich: Oldenbourg, 1997) and Thomas Sandkühler, *"Endlösung" in Galizien: Der Judenmord in Ostpolen und die Rettungsinitiativen von Berthold Beitz, 1941–1944* (Bonn: Dietz, 1996).

25. An indication of just how successful the Nazis were in this part of Ukraine can be seen in the way some Ukrainian historians treat Otto Wächter (1901–1949), the governor of District Galicia, and Alfred Bisanz (1890–1949), the head of the Department of Demography and Social Affairs in District Galicia. The two men are commended in various Ukrainian encyclopedias as representatives of a "moderate policy" in Galicia. All of the entries for both omit their role in the deportation of hundreds of thousands of Jews to the death camps of District Lublin (as well as the persecution of Poles). See the entries for Bisanz and Wächter in *Entsyklopediia istoriï Ukraïny* (Kiev: Naukova Dumka, 2003), t. 1, pp. 271 and 498; *Entsyklopediia Suchasnoï Ukraïny* (Kiev: Instytut Entsyklopedychnykh Doslidzhen' NAN Ukraïny, 2003 and 2005), t. 2, pp. 750–751, and t. 4, p. 325; and *Encyclopledia of Ukraine* (Toronto: University of Toronto Press, 1985 and 1993), v. 1, p. 273, and v. 5, p. 677. "Moderate policy" is quoted from the Ukrainian articles for Wächter.

26. See Taras Hunczak, "Ukrainian Losses in World War II," in Michael Berenbaum, ed., *A Mosaic of Victims: Non-Jews Persecuted and Murdered by the Nazis,* (New York: New York University Press, 1990), p. 122. Cf. Alexander Kruglov's chapter for this volume.

27. See Karel Berkhoff's discussion of auxiliaries in his chapter for this volume.

28. A shocking contemporary example of this antisemitic myth's persistence is the appendices to the published papers of the 2002 All-Ukrainian Academic Conference on the Hunger-Plague, *Holodomor 1932–1933 rokiv, iak velychezna trahediia ukrains'koho narodu* (Kiev: Mizhrehional'na akademiia upravlinnia personalom, 2003), pp. 271–277. These include a section entitled "The ruling class of the USSR in 1936–1939" (pp. 272–275), which lists only Bolsheviks of Jewish origin and their government or party posts at the national level. The insinuation is that "the Jews" are to blame for Bolshevism and the 1932–1933 famine. No less disturbing is the fact that this collection is otherwise mainstream in many respects, with contributions by former Ukrainian President Leonid Kravchuk, a half dozen members of the National Academy of Sciences of Ukraine, a dozen university professors, and several editors in chief of periodicals, one of whom is also given as the head of the PEN Club in Ukraine. The appendices are not just a calumny against Jews. They denigrate efforts to call greater attention to the 1932–1933 famine.

29. Whatever the reasons for this restraint in the summer of 1941, after the war, pogroms broke out in several places in Ukraine; see Amir Weiner,

Making Sense of War: The Second World War and the Fate of the Bolshevik Revolution (Princeton University Press, 2000), pp. 192–193.

30. Alexander Victor Prusin, *Nationalizing a Borderland: War, Ethnicity, and Anti-Jewish Violence in East Galicia, 1914–1920* (Tuscaloosa: University of Alabama Press, 2005), pp. 100–101.

31. A foundation has been laid by Jean Ancel, *Transnistria* (Bucharest: Atlas, 1998) and Radu Ioanid, *The Holocaust in Romania: The Destruction of Jews and Gypsies under the Antonescu Regime, 1940–1944* (Chicago: Ivan R. Dee, 2000).

32. With regard to German occupation policy, several studies addressing the Crimea and the Donbas have appeared in recent years; see footnote 8 in Dieter Pohl's chapter. Tanja Penter's recent work on the Donbas goes down to the grassroots and draws on Ukrainian and Russian language sources as well as German ones; see Tanja Penter, "Zwangsarbeit —Arbeit für den Feind: der Donbass unter deutscher Okkupation (1941–1943)," *Geschichte und Gesellschaft*, 31 (2005), 1, pp. 68–100, and idem, "Die lokale Gesellschaft im Donbass unter deutscher Okkupation 1941–1943," *Beiträge zur Geschichte des Nationalsozialismus*, 19, pp. 183–224. By contrast, the oblasts of Kharkiv, Sumy, and Chernihiv have received comparatively scant attention.

33. Initial efforts on some of these topics in English are Elena Ivanova, "Ukrainian High School Students' Understanding of the Holocaust," *Holocaust and Genocide Studies*, 18 (2004), pp. 402–420; Wilfried Jilge, "The Politics of History and the Second World War in Post-Communist Ukraine (1986/1991–2004/2005)," in Stefan Troebst and Wilfried Jilge, eds., *Divided Historical Cultures? World War II and Historical Memory in Soviet and Post-Soviet Ukraine* (Wiesbaden: Franz Steiner Verlag, 2006) (= Themenheft, *Jahrbücher für Geschichte Osteuropas*, 54 [2006], no. 1), pp. 50–81; Alexander Victor Prusin, "'Fascist criminals to the gallows!': The Holocaust and Soviet War Crimes Trials, December 1945–February 1946," *Holocaust and Genocide Studies*, 17 (2003), pp. 1–30; Rebecca L. Golbert, "Holocaust sites in Ukraine: Pechora and the Politics of Memorialization," *Holocaust and Genocide Studies*, 18 (2004), pp. 205–233.

I

The Murder of Ukraine's Jews under German Military Administration and in the Reich Commissariat Ukraine

DIETER POHL

From the moment the German armed forces entered Ukraine on June 22, 1941, the Jews of the Ukrainian Soviet Socialist Republic, the largest Jewish minority in the Soviet Union, faced near certain death. In the 18 months that followed, the Germans, together with their allies and satraps, killed almost every Ukrainian Jew who failed to flee with the retreating Red Army.

Although Soviet Ukraine's Jews represented the second largest Jewish community in Europe prior to the Second World War, scholars have largely neglected the history of this community's destruction (and even more so the destruction of the Russian Federation's Jews). By contrast, the persecution and killing of Jews elsewhere in the Nazi-occupied Soviet territories have been subjected to considerable examination by historians, especially since the collapse of the Soviet Union in 1991. This chapter aims to provide a basic outline of the National Socialists' "Final Solution of the European Jewish question" as it applied to Ukraine's Jews.

This is by no means an exhaustive study. Here, only the Ukrainian territories that were administered by the Wehrmacht and the civilian-run Reich Commissariat Ukraine (RKU) are addressed. For analytical reasons, the regions of eastern Galicia, northern Bukovina, and Transnistria are left out. Eastern Galicia (today in western Ukraine) was annexed to the General Government (the German-occupied Polish territories not incorporated into the Reich); the fate of its Jewish population was interwoven with that of the Jews of Poland during the Nazi era.[1] Similarly, northern Bukovina (today Ukraine's Chernivtsi province) and Transnistria (a swath of territory between the Southern Buh and Dniestr rivers awarded Romania by Germany) concern primarily Romanian anti-Jewish measures, even though German officials greatly influenced Romanian policy.[2] Finally, the area of operations of Einsatzgruppe D, the SS task force behind the lines of the German 11th Army and the Third Reich's Romanian allies, is also omitted, for this Einsatzgruppe was not subordinated directly to Rear Area Army Group South.[3]

Galicia and Transnistria aside, the state of research into the murder of Ukraine's Jews is hardly satisfactory.[4] Even German occupation policy in Ukraine still awaits a more thorough investigation.[5] At this writing, substantial studies on the Holocaust in Ukraine are available only for a few regions outside Galicia and Transnistria, in particular Volhynia[6] and Zhytomyr.[7] Related works have also appeared or are expected to appear soon.[8]

At the start of the Second World War, the Jewish minority in Soviet Ukraine numbered over 1.5 million people. After the Soviet Union annexed eastern Poland in the early weeks of the war, the number of Jews in the expanded Ukrainian Soviet Socialist Republic rose to 2.35 million Jews.[9] With that, the percentage of Jews in Ukraine increased from 5 to 6 percent.

Just over 85 percent of Ukrainian Jews lived in urban areas. East of Kiev, Ukraine's Jews tended to concentrate in large cities; west of Kiev, large communities of Jews could be found in almost every mid-sized town. In the larger population centers of western prewar Soviet Ukraine—Vinnytsia, Zhytomyr, and Kamianets-Podilsky—Jews made up between one third and two thirds of the population.[10] In those places, assimilation—especially vis-à-vis the non-Jewish population—was low. Nevertheless, in Soviet Ukraine as a whole, according to figures for 1938, 17–18 percent of Jews were married to non-Jews.[11]

The Bolshevik Revolution initially brought with it an unambiguous break with the systematic discrimination against Jews of the tsarist era. Many Jews—especially those in large cities such as Kiev, Odessa, and Kharkiv—were quick to take advantage of the new opportunities that came with emancipation. The nationalization of the economy in the 1920s may have placed considerable restrictions on craftsmen and retailers, traditional professions for East European Jews, but jobs in education and administration offered new perspectives for Ukraine's Jews. As time passed, however, these gains were thrown into doubt. In the 1930s, religion and the various official Soviet national cultures were subject to growing repression—including Judaism and the Yiddish proletarian culture originally sponsored by Moscow. In the final phase of the Great Terror of 1938–1939, many Jews lost their state positions, while others lost their lives.[12]

The Jews of the annexed Polish regions of Volhynia and Galicia experienced Sovietization only at the end of 1939, but at an accelerated pace. During the interwar period, the *shtetl*—the impoverished Eastern European Jewish townlet, where traditional religious life shaped most social interaction—had maintained itself in Poland to a much greater extent than in the Soviet Union. Heavily exposed to economic upheaval in world agricultural markets, the inhabitants of Volhynia and Galicia suffered greatly during the global depression of the 1930s. With the outbreak of the war, a part of the Jewish population in eastern Poland warmly greeted the arrival of the Red Army in September 1939, seeing in it protection from the German threat. Hundreds of thousands of Polish Jews fled east to the Soviet zone of occupation seeking refuge from the Nazis. In most of the Ukrainian territories, however, the German threat seemed less immediate—until the Germans actually invaded in mid-1941.

Only a small number of the Jews in western Ukraine managed to escape the Nazi onslaught that began on June 22, 1941. Time was too short, and the Soviets had failed to prepare effective evacuation measures. Estimates suggest that 40,000–50,000 Jews fled western Ukraine in the first weeks of the German invasion—many of whom were nonetheless captured by the Germans at a later date.[13] The situation farther east varied. While over half of the Jews in major cities such as Zhytomyr and Kiev escaped, Jews in central Ukrainian towns fared less well. The largest refugee movements occurred in territories east of the Dniepr, which the Wehrmacht began crossing only in mid-September. There, the Germans found less than a fifth of the prewar Jewish population, mainly elderly people and individuals living on their own.

Exact figures are unavailable, but estimates suggest that at least one third of the Jews living in pre-invasion Soviet Ukraine managed to flee. Thus some 1.4 million to 1.5 million Jews came under the various German and Romanian occupation regimes. Some 650,000 of these Jews were in territories first occupied by Army Group South and then turned over to the RKU. The fate of these Jews is discussed below.[14]

Mass Murder Operations under Wehrmacht Administration

For the campaign against the Soviet Union, the Wehrmacht and the German police developed a graduated "security system," which de facto dealt largely with annihilating certain groups of persons. Frontline officers were ordered to have captured Red Army commissars summarily executed. It was assumed that many of these commissars would be Jews. During the first days of the campaign, this directive—now known as the "commissar order"—was implemented all along the eastern front. Some commanding officers even ordered the shooting of all prisoners of war.[15]

In northern and central Ukraine, the Wehrmacht's armies were followed by the four commandos of Einsatzgruppe C, the Security Police and Security Service task force assigned to the northern half of Ukraine. Special Commando 4a (*Sonderkommando* 4a, Sk 4a) swept through Volhynia, while Special Commando 4b (Sk 4b) moved through Galicia and Podolia. Contrary to prewar planning, which foresaw the restriction of the special commandos to the army rear areas, Sk 4a and Sk 4b were soon called up close to the combat zone. Close ties between Sk 4a and 6th Army High Command (*Armeeoberkommando* 6, AOK 6) developed early in the campaign,[16] with a similar arrangement between Sk 4b and 17th Army High Command (AOK 17) coming later. Cooperation between the special commandos and the 1st Armored Group was limited to visits by commando leaders to the armored group's chief intelligence officer.[17]

Behind the army rear areas was Rear Area Army Group South under Karl von Roques. There, security measures were split up between the Wehrmacht and SS and police forces. Military affairs and technical administrative matters were handled by three army security divisions (the 213rd, 444th, and 454th), which oriented themselves along the main supply lines. Each of these divisions was reinforced by a battalion of German regular police, or Order Police (318, 311, and 82, respectively). Working alongside the military authorities was the Higher SS and Police Leader Russia South (HSSPF Russia South), who oversaw "police work" in Ukraine. Friedrich Jeckeln, the holder of this office, was the direct and personal representative of Heinrich Himmler, the leader of the SS and the chief of the German police. Jeckeln's forces included Einsatzgruppe C commandos 5 and 6, Police Regiment South (Order Police battalions 45, 303, and 314), and, in reserve, three other police battalions (304, 315, and 320).[18] The division of labor between the Sonderkommandos near the front and the Order Police battalions in Rear Area Army Group South initially worked more or less according to plan during the first months, but when the Germans reached central Ukraine, this division began to blur.

The term "police work" encompassed a wide range of activities. Einsatzgruppe C's commandos operated as a secret police, analyzing captured enemy records and gathering information, especially by interrogation. Initially, the commandos' main "executive activity" was the murder of Soviet political functionaries. The tasks of the six Order Police (Orpo) battalions under Jeckeln's command were less clear at first. Since they were not deployed for investigative purposes and were not assigned to set up police offices, their duties depended on Jeckeln's instructions. Often the battalions were given guard duty, for example along the most important supply lines. The three battalions assigned to the security divisions were expected to be involved in missions more military in nature.[19]

The main goal of the Russian campaign, however, was not the immediate, indiscriminate annihilation of large segments of the Soviet population, but—in that day's jargon—"securing the occupied territories," i.e., exploiting those territories to the greatest extent possible. Because the Germans expected to find few industrial goods in the Soviet Union, exploiting those territories primarily entailed seizing produce and raw materials. In early 1941, various German agencies had begun working out plans for the widespread confiscation of harvests and foodstuffs in the occupied territories and the near simultaneous starvation of 30 million people. Included in these plans were provisions for sealing off major urban areas in order to keep provisions from reaching them—which meant the vast majority of Soviet Jews, especially those farther east, had been condemned to death long before any decisions about mass shootings were made.[20]

The orders for mass shootings, by contrast, appear to have resulted from an antisemitic and anti-Communist security policy of terror that required the murder of every person seen by the Germans to pose a potential threat. Carrying out these orders was divided between the Wehrmacht and the SS and police. Frontline units were instructed by the aforementioned "commissar order" not to treat captured Red Army political commissars as regular POWs, but to have them shot under an officer's supervision without delay. (In reality, the sorting out process often took place later on in transit camps.) The HSSPFs and the Einsatzgruppen were to execute certain groups of Soviet functionaries, especially any Jews found among them. Thus, at the outset of the German-Soviet war, only a small part of the Jewish population was to be shot immediately.

Within the first days of the invasion, however, the pool of potential victims was expanded. One reason for this, but not the only one, was the discovery of atrocities committed by the NKVD, the Soviet secret police, in the prisons of western Ukraine before the Red Army retreated. The local non-Jewish population and the Wehrmacht held the Jewish minority responsible for these crimes. As a result, large groups of able-bodied Jewish men were indiscriminately rounded up in many cities and towns and held in provisional camps. No longer were selections and shootings limited to certain groups of functionaries; instead, those who were still needed—skilled laborers, doctors, and specialists—were selected and spared. The rest were shot.

Numerous German soldiers were also involved in the Lviv pogrom, which began on June 30, 1941.[21] The 17th Army High Command, in whose area of operations Lviv lay, even recommended staging pogroms, as Einsatzgruppe C reported to Berlin.[22] A platoon of infantry participated in the mass shooting of 1,160 Jewish men in Lutsk on July 2 and soon thereafter in Dubno.[23] While individual Wehrmacht units mur-

dered Soviet commissars, Roques tried to prevent soldiers from participating in pogroms in Rear Area Army Group South.[24]

In the second half of July, orders for persecuting and murdering
Jews became more radical. On July 21, Himmler traveled to western
Ukraine, where he visited Roques.[25] Meanwhile, Reinhard Heydrich,
the chief of the Security Police (or Sipo, which included the Gestapo)
and Security Service (*Sicherheitsdienst*, the Nazi party intelligence service), began urging his commandos to single out not only Jews who belonged to the Soviet Communist Party or held state office but all Jewish
prisoners—military and civil personnel alike—mostly men between 17
and 45. If army officers could locate a Sipo-SD commando near a POW
camp, selection and killing were to follow.[26] It was also around this
time that Jeckeln ordered his forces to kill anybody suspected of having
"abetted the Bolshevik system."[27]

Finally, toward the end of July 1941, individual SS and police units
began shooting Jewish women and children as well. It has yet to be
clearly determined whether this took place as a result of orders from
above or initiative by SS officers in the field. The evidence so far tends to
suggest that commanding SS officers initially treated women and children differently from case to case. From early July until early August the
number of killings in Ukraine barely increased, even though another
homicidal formation had been sent to Ukraine: the 1st SS Infantry Brigade, a part of the Waffen SS, Himmler's armed forces.[28]

The reasons for this brief leveling off in the number of victims are
to be found above all in the expansion of the area of operations to the
east, but also in absence of any immediate pretext for large-scale reprisals east of the prewar Polish-Soviet border. In the first weeks of
August, Einsatzgruppe C commando leaders were informed that, in
principle, Jewish women and children should be shot as well. Jeckeln
was the decisive force in the expansion of mass shootings in Ukraine.
His Orpo battalions are known to have carried out their first mass killings in the last week of July, somewhat later than the police battalions in
the central sector of the eastern front.[29] Police Battalion 314 conducted
its first massacre in Matsiïv on July 22; two days later, in Shepetivka,
Police Battalion 45 began killing operations as well.[30] Orpo participation in the murder of Ukraine's Jews had long been underway, however. Einsatzgruppe C had been assigned an Orpo company before the
invasion.[31]

The 1st SS Infantry Brigade, meanwhile, was operating in northern Ukraine. In its first four days of activity near Novohrad-Volynsky
(Zviahel), it reported killing "around 800 Jews and Jewesses between the
ages of 16 and 60."[32] Although the brigade's second regiment, SS Infantry Regiment 10, carried out shootings regularly, Himmler complained
about the brigade's lack of "activity" and ordered Jeckeln to report to
him on August 12.[33] Despite this meeting, the death toll from this
formation's activity barely increased in August. The brigade had been

turned over to AOK 6 to fight straggling Red Army units. On September 4, however, the brigade murdered 686 Jews in Lelchitsy.[34]

The Massacre at Kamianets-Podilsky[35]

The Ukrainian town of Kamianets-Podilsky, then a regional administrative center with 40,000 inhabitants located near the prewar Polish-Soviet border, was captured by German and Hungarian troops in early July. Jews made up a third of the town's population. A few thousand had fled, but some 12,000 Jews remained behind. The only Germans in Kamianets-Podilsky were from the Wehrmacht; no detachments of Einsatzgruppe C were stationed there. As was the case throughout the newly occupied territories, the Wehrmacht took over the town's administration. The 183rd Field Administration Command (FK 183) reestablished a local administration, set up an auxiliary police, regulated the distribution of provisions to the population, and monitored public life. According to Wehrmacht directives, the administration commands also had to register Jewish populations, convene Jewish councils, and ensure that Jews wore an armband or Star of David. These activities were part of the military administration commands' routine duties in the east. Rear Area Army Group South, the army rear areas, and the security divisions all maintained a senior councilor for military administration, who was also in charge of "Jewish questions."[36]

At the end of July 1941, thousands of Polish, Czechoslovak, and Hungarian Jews began arriving in Kamianets-Podilsky, expelled on orders from government officials in Budapest. During the dismemberment of Czechoslovakia in 1938 and 1939, Hungary had annexed Carpatho-Ukraine, the easternmost tip of its northern neighbor. This region contained not only large indigenous Jewish communities, but thousands of Jewish refugees from the Greater German Reich and Poland as well. Hungarian bureaucrats saw the invasion of the Soviet Union as a chance to rid themselves of a mostly foreign and "undesirable" minority by expelling it eastward. The first large town east of Carpatho-Ukraine happened to be Kamianets-Podilsky. German army officials from FK 183 reacted to this policy with indignation:

> The numerous Jews were increased by the influx of Jews expelled from Hungary, of which some 3,000 have arrived in the last few days. Feeding them is proving enormously difficult; danger of epidemic also exists. Immediate order for their evacuation is urgently requested.[37]

Ultimately, well over 10,000 Jews from Carpatho-Ukraine entered Kamianets-Podilsky and the surrounding area, where they could be provided only makeshift housing. Diplomatic efforts to convince the Hungarians to take back these Jews failed. On August 25, during talks between the High Command of the Army and the Reich Ministry for the Occupied Eastern Territories on establishing civil administration

Photos taken in Kamianets-Podilsky on August 27, 1941, by Gyula Spitz, a Jewish truck driver in the Hungarian Army in Ukraine, as Jews were led to an execution site by Hungarian soldiers and field police who assisted the Germans in supervising the digging of mass graves by the Jews and also took part in the mass shootings. USHMM, courtesy of Ivan Sved.

in Ukraine, an ominous "solution" began to loom. Participants at the meeting noted that Jeckeln was said to have already announced "the liquidation of these Jews by September 1, 1941,"[38] the very day that this part of Ukraine was to be turned over to German civil administration. The representatives of the civil administration and the Wehrmacht at least took note of Jeckeln's intent, for the suggestion of evacuating the Hungarian Jews had originated with the military to start with.

By this time, Einsatzgruppe C's commandos were farther east. Whether Jeckeln called in a small execution commando for the operation is unclear.[39] Jeckeln had at his disposal only his own staff and its platoon of Orpo men. Bigger units were necessary to carry out such a large killing operation. Jeckeln therefore called in Police Battalion 320, which was reinforced by an Orpo company of ethnic Germans from the Baltic region. Jeckeln almost certainly briefed FK 183 before taking this decisive step; the town lay not only in the latter's area of command, it served as regional headquarters for Wehrmacht administration. In any event, Jeckeln informed the Hungarian military authorities, which then may have taken part in providing cordons.

On August 26, four days before the transfer to civil administration, Jeckeln flew to Kamianets-Podilsky to lead the *Aktion*. On the operation's first day, 4,200 men, women, and children were escorted to the site and shot. The victims were forced to run through a gauntlet of Orpo

men and to hand over any valuables; others were also forced to undress. They then had to climb down into the pits and lie down on the ground, or on top of each new layer of fresh corpses, where they were shot in the back of the head. According to eyewitnesses, Jeckeln stood nearby on a hill and observed events together with several Wehrmacht officers.[40] On the second day, when more than 11,000 Jews were killed, policemen from the 3rd Company of Police Battalion 320 were also deployed in the operation as shooters. Postwar testimony has it that Jeckeln's use of Police Battalion 320 in the actual shooting provoked a fierce exchange between the HSSPF Russia South and the battalion's commander.[41]

The operation entailed the murder not only of the Jews from Carpatho-Ukraine, but also of two-thirds of Kamianets-Podilsky's indigenous Jewish population. When the shooting stopped, Jeckeln radioed Berlin that 23,600 Jews, some 14,000 from Carpatho-Ukraine, had been killed.[42] The High Command of Army Group South, the highest military authority in Ukraine, was also promptly informed of the number of victims.[43] Only after the massacre did the Germans establish a ghetto for the remaining 4,800 Jews. At this time, ghettos were rather unusual in Ukraine, most being set up only in spring 1942.[44] A year later, Hungarian officials tried anew to deport "undesirable" Jews to the east. This time, Himmler immediately intervened to prevent a repetition of these events.[45] The Kamianets-Podilsky massacre was, at the end of August

1941, the largest of its kind and signaled a turning point in the Holocaust, the break with killing targeted groups of mostly Jewish males
to the indiscriminate murder of entire Jewish communities. A month
later, however, events at Kiev's Babi Yar would overshadow this enormous massacre.

The Total Destruction of Jewish Communities

In the two months prior to the massacre at Kamianets-Podilsky, the SS
and police units in Ukraine had shot around 40,000 Jews, mostly men.
This unimaginably high number took on a new dimension as events
unfolded. In the following five weeks, between August 27 and September 30, 100,000 Jews were killed, with women and children making up
the majority of victims.

One key factor for this development was that Einsatzgruppe D, operating along Ukraine's Black Sea coast, had begun organizing indiscriminate mass shootings of Jews.[46] The decisive factor seems to be that
the SS and police forces under the HSSPF Russian South, wherever they
were stationed, began eradicating almost all the Jews they found in their
vicinity. As late as mid-August 1941, the commander of Einsatzgruppe C, Otto Rasch, had still wondered aloud whether "annihilation by
work," forced labor until death, was more suitable for murdering Jews.[47]
After Kamianets-Podilsky, and especially after mid-September, the SS
and police set out to annihilate all Jews. Kamianets-Podilsky had shown
not only that the decision-making levels within the Wehrmacht tolerated and encouraged the shooting of able-bodied Jewish males, which
had been taking place since the first days of the invasion,[48] but that the
military administration commands were ready to cooperate in the mass
murder of all Jews regardless of age or gender.

The question thus arises whether the transition to the total destruction of Jewish communities between August and October 1941
was spurred on not just by instructions from on high but also by negotiations between senior SS and police officers and military administration commandants in the field.[49] Until recently, it was assumed that
this transition was based on a decision by Hitler. For this period, however, no documents referring to such an order have been found. What
is certain is that Himmler ordered another intensification of killings
during a visit to Ukraine in early October 1941.[50] Shortly thereafter,
Einsatzgruppe C drew up a list of criteria for mass shootings; the last
point read "Jews in general."[51] It was simultaneously noted, "The areas
recently occupied by the commandos were rendered free of Jews."[52]

Why were the higher levels of the Wehrmacht, especially the army
high commands and the field administration commands, willing to
help the police organize this genocide? The issue of security remained
largely unchanged; there was hardly any partisan activity to speak of
at the time. In late July, however, it was already becoming clear that the

war against the Soviet Union could not be won as soon as expected. The delay in victory subjected Germany's entire economic planning to changes; autumn was approaching, and the strategy of starvation still could not be implemented. Instead, something unforeseen had set in: In September and October, large numbers of exhausted Soviet POWs, whose rations were curtailed once they could no longer work, began dying. A similar development also began taking shape among Jews, as they had been completely dispossessed and robbed of their primary means of subsistence. Until Kamianets-Podilsky, the first sweep had been aimed primarily at Jewish males of working age, i.e., heads of households, whose families were now at the mercy of German military administration. But the military administration considered feeding these families a burden it could not accept; it was beginning to experience its own difficulties in feeding the troops. The search for a solution to food shortages also helped transform the selection criteria for the mass killing of Jews in September 1941 to include mostly women, children, and elderly people. In addition, the farther east the Wehrmacht pushed, the less industry it found, and subsequently, the fewer workers it needed for the war effort.[53]

These preconditions were what encouraged the military administrators, above all the administration commands, to accept, indeed in some cases even request, mass murder for "the removal of part of the i.[n] p.[art] superfluous mouths in the cities."[54] Wehrmacht commanders could also stop a mass murder when it seemed militarily advantageous to do so. For example, the German 11th Army instructed Einsatzgruppe D where to operate until July 1941.[55] AOK 17, which on occasion requested mass killings, could just as well order the police to refrain temporarily from a massacre, as happened in Artemivsk in December 1941.[56]

Within the officer corps, the policy of mass murder was hardly uncontroversial. There was little criticism of the mass shootings of grown Jewish men; these were considered legitimate within the framework of reprisal measures. But even as early as July, officials from the Wehrmacht departments responsible for the wartime economy began protesting the murder of Jewish workers who in their view were still needed.[57] There is also the infamous case of the internal Wehrmacht debate over the fate of a group of Jewish children in Bila Tserkva in August 1941.

After Sk 4a had shot all of the grown men and many of the women in Bila Tserkva, Wehrmacht chaplains went to their superiors to plead on behalf of the remaining family members. The field administration commandant, Josef Riedl, considered the murder of the Jewish women and children "urgently necessary," because, as he put it, "this lot must be eradicated."[58] Despite numerous protests, Walter von Reichenau, the commander of AOK 6, decided to have the remaining Jews killed, which indeed happened not long after the Kamianets-Podilsky massacre.

Two weeks later, on September 12, the chief of the High Command of the Wehrmacht, Wilhelm Keitel, called for "ruthless and vigorous action" not only in the struggle against Soviet Russia but "above all also against the Jews, the main carriers of Bolshevism." Exceptions were made only for those Jews providing forced labor in work details.[59] The 454th Security Division's administrative section had the following to say about the murder of the children:

> There can hardly be any more talk of a Jewish question. In several places, the provisioning of Jewish children and infants left without parents sometimes created difficulties; also in this regard, however, remedial action has since been taken by the SD.[60]

As more and more Jewish communities were eradicated, Einsatzgruppe C stressed the cooperation it received from the higher levels of Wehrmacht, especially in the area of operations of the 6th Army, which was apparently regularly informed in advance of large-scale killing operations.[61] At the same time, however, Einsatzgruppe C found fault with some lower-level Wehrmacht officers, such as POW camp commandants who refused to release Jewish prisoners for killing:

> Only in the Jewish question was, until most recently, complete understanding not to be found among *subordinate* Wehrmacht authorities [emphasis added, D.P.]. . . . All too often, the Einsatzkommandos were forced to endure more or less veiled rebukes concerning their determined position in the Jewish question.[62]

In the wake of such criticism and discussions within the officer corps, the highest-ranking Wehrmacht commanders in Ukraine in October and November 1941 issued a series of orders justifying the mass killing of Jews.[63] The most famous of these—Reichenau's order of October 10, 1941—is a typical example. The commander of Army Group South, Gerd von Rundstedt, was aware of the mass murder and appeared "completely in agreement" with the justifications provided for the genocide.[64] Similarly, Roques supported the explanations provided for this policy of mass murder as a "binding guiding principle."[65]

At almost every large massacre after Kamianets-Podilsky, the same process can be observed: Upon entering a city, the Sipo and SD would shoot several hundred Jewish men. Then the military administration would register the remaining Jews. After negotiations between HSSPF Russia South or Einsatzgruppe C and the responsible field administration command or army high command, the majority of Jewish inhabitants would be shot, often with the assistance of the Wehrmacht, which regularly provided trucks, ammunition, and soldiers for cordons. This process is seen in the mass shootings in Zhytomyr, Kiev, and Kharkiv.

Zhytomyr, for example, was captured in early July 1941 and, starting on July 18 or 19, had begun serving as headquarters for the command of Einsatzgruppe C. The Ukrainian city administration had already summoned the local Jews for registration on July 11.[66] Sk 4a and the 1st SS Infantry Brigade, upon their arrival in the area, set about murdering Jewish men in and around the city; in several instances, Wehrmacht troops also took part in the killings.[67] Events in Zhytomyr show most clearly the transition from a selective policy of destruction to one of total eradication. It was there in July that Paul Blobel, the commander of Sk 4a, first announced to his men that he was aiming for the total destruction of the city's Jews.[68] During planning, Blobel contacted FK 197:

> Thus, on September 10, 1941, a meeting with the field administration commandant on this issue took place, as a result of which [it] was *decided* [emphasis in the original, D.P.] definitively and radically to liquidate the Jewish community.[69]

FK 197 also provided trucks for the operation.[70] On September 19, Sk 4a shot 3,145 Jews outside Zhytomyr, but Blobel failed to eradicate the entire community. Presumably at the insistence of the military administration, 240 Jews were left alive.[71]

Meanwhile, Jeckeln turned to the second largest community in the area: Berdychiv, just 43 km (27 miles) south of Zhytomyr. On August 26, a ghetto had been set up there to accommodate 20,000 Jews. On September 4, Police Regiment South reported the murder of 4,144 Jews, mostly in Berdychiv.[72] Just over ten days later, in the early hours of September 15, German policemen surrounded the ghetto and escorted the vast majority of Jews there out of town. Upon reaching the airport, circa 12,000 Jews—mostly women, children, and elderly people—were shot by HSSPF Russia South and Police Battalion 45. As in Zhytomyr, a part of the Jewish community was spared, 2,500 workers and their families.[73]

Starting in mid-September, the areas of operations for the Sonderkommandos immediately behind the front and the Order Police units in the rear began to overlap. Prior to the Babi Yar massacre in Kiev, which is not discussed in detail here,[74] a meeting between Jeckeln, Blobel, and the city commandant, Kurt Eberhard of FK 195, was arranged.[75] Four days later, the military administration reported to the Army High Command in Berlin: "Greater measures against undesirable parts of the population will however prove to be necessary."[76] "Greater measures" appears to have meant the shooting of over 33,700 people.[77]

The interaction of Wehrmacht officers and SS and police officials can also be seen in the last large-scale mass murder to take place under military administration. Upon capturing Kharkiv, AOK 6 began to worry about rationing the city's foodstuffs; these after all were to be rerouted to the Wehrmacht. As a former officer confirmed after the war:

> A solution had to be found for what to do with these people. This was determined by the provisions situation. Supplies could no longer keep pace, and we had enormous difficulties with rations. I was present at this meeting.[78]

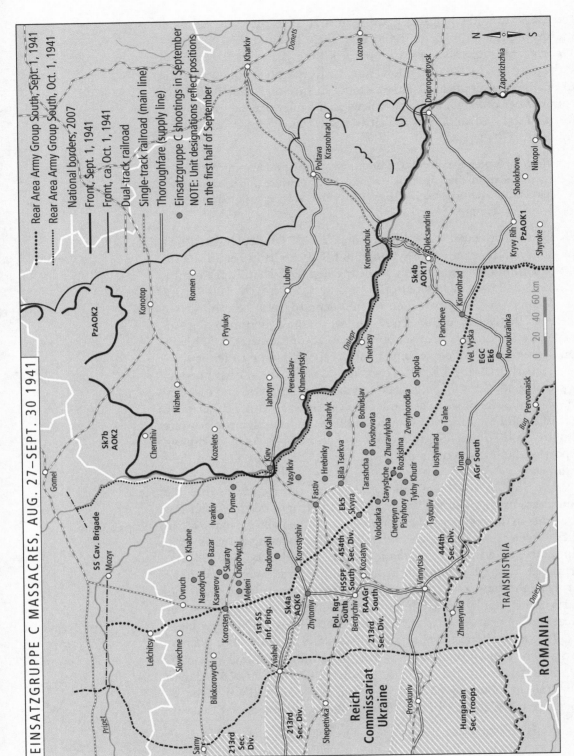

Einsatzgruppe C Massacres, Aug. 27–Sept. 30 1941

In November, the chief intelligence officer of AOK 6 recommended the registration of all Jews and other undesirable elements: "Detention and further treatment of these elements would be the task of the SD, which, however, is itself too weak and therefore requires support from the troops."[79] An initial registration showed 10,271 Jews in Kharkiv.[80] Once again, agreement and close cooperation prevailed between the police and the military, including the field administration command. The city commandant even issued the order telling Jews when and where to gather.[81]

The organization of a mass murder operation on this scale in Ukraine was normally a task for the HSSPF Russia South, which had been taken over by Hans-Adolf Prützmann in November. By this point, a second HSSPF was also operating in Ukraine: the HSSPF for Special Purposes (HSSPF z.b.V.). Gerret Korsemann had been dispatched to Ukraine in late summer 1941 to familiarize himself with the duties of an HSSPF until the Caucasus, his designated posting, had been conquered.[82] Effective January 5, 1942, Korsemann assumed Prützmann's duties in the military occupied territories, while Prützmann looked after affairs in the civil administered parts of Ukraine.[83] It thus fell to Korsemann and his staff to kill the last Jews of Kharkiv, who since December 16 had been interned in a tractor factory. Soon after Korsemann arrived, Sk 4a and Police Battalion 314 went into action, shooting some 12,000 Jews in Drobytsky Yar ravine and murdering several hundred others in a gas van. The killing lasted weeks.[84]

Here, the connection between the Wehrmacht's seizure of food stores, its ideological perception of the food situation, and the decision to murder the Kharkiv Jews is particularly clear. As early as December 1941, starvation was quite frequent, even among the non-Jewish population, and by March 1942, almost half as many people were starving to death in Kharkiv each month as in the Warsaw Ghetto.[85]

The cooperation between the military authorities and the SS and police apparatus in a number of other killing operations has yet to be studied. Between September 19 and 20, 1941, a detachment of Einsatzkommando 6 (Ek 6), working together with Police Battalions 45 and 314, committed one of the largest massacres of the war in Vinnytsia, murdering around 15,000 Jews.[86] German and Soviet postwar investigations arrived at significantly different figures for the number of victims. Ten days later, Police Battalion 304—presumably together with Sk 4b—carried out a mass killing in Kirovohrad; a participant noted in his diary: "Search in Kirovo[hrad] and shooting of 4,200 Jews, among them 600 prisoners of war."[87] Vinnytsia and Kirovohrad and their environs were still under military administration at the time of these killings.

The same can be said for Dnipropetrovsk, the site of the last large massacre to take place in Ukraine under Jeckeln's supervision. This operation occurred on October 13 and 14, 1941, but in this case the killing was organized "without the knowledge of the field administration command" and was carried out solely by Police Battalion 314 and the

Ukrainian auxiliary police.[88] FK 240 clearly had a better picture of the situation five days later, when it reported:

> The Jewish question, at least where the city of Dnipropetrovsk is concerned, can for the most part be viewed as solved. At the start of the occupation, around 35,000 Jews were still present. Around 15,000 Jews were caught up in the SD's measures, another part of around 15,000 Jews fled as a result of these measures, and a remainder of about 5,000 Jews is still present.[89]

By mid-January 1942, there were few large Jewish communities left in Wehrmacht administered Ukraine. A small number of Jews, however, had been left alive in many places, most likely spared to fulfill some specific form of labor. The majority of Jews in eastern Ukraine who had not fled were killed within the first months of 1942, for example in Stalino (today Donetsk) on January 9 and in Kramatorsk on January 26. The murder of the Jews in Artemivsk, temporarily halted by AOK 17 in December 1941, took place in February 1942. Senior officers from Sk 4b and the chief intelligence officer of the 44th Corps chose the killing site together.[90] The last large Jewish community in military occupied eastern Ukraine was in Zaporizhzhia. Its 3,700 members were murdered on March 21 or 24.[91] The killing in this region did not stop there, however. At the end of May 1942, the inhabitants of the Jewish collective farms of Novo-Kovno (Yiddish, Nay-Kovna) and Novy Vitebsk (Yiddish, Nay-Vitebsk) in Stalindorf Precinct fell victim to German commandos.[92]

Meanwhile, another mobile Sipo unit was operating in Rear Area Army Group South: Sonderkommando Plath, named for Karl Julius Plath, commander of the Sipo-SD outpost in Kremenchuk. Formed in late 1941 and subordinated to Korsemann, this commando bore responsibility for killing operations at over 35 sites in the vicinity of Dnipropetrovsk.[93] Even with the campaign of annihilation so nearly complete, Rear Area Army Group South issued an ideologically colored directive for murder in May 1942:

> Whenever it can be determined that Jews are inciting the partisans' struggle, are in contact with them, or even actively operating [as such], they are to be reported straightaway to the SD. In the event the Jews are liquidated by the SD, the greatest care is to be taken that the execution occurs at night or in the early morning hours in a way that the population hears and sees nothing of it.[94]

Elsewhere under Wehrmacht occupation, FK 197 in Nizhyn, in northeastern Ukraine, called on the Security Police for "the soonest possible settling of the local Jewish question." The police responded by massacring 1,200 Jews in Pryluky in June.[95]

In September 1942, the structure of military administration was reorganized once again in the wake of the summer drive on Stalingrad. Rear Area Army Group South was split into Rear Area Army Group A and Rear Area Army Group B. The former covered the rear of the German armies marching toward the Caucasus, while the latter was responsible for eastern Ukraine as well as the rear of the armies heading to Stalingrad. By this point, only a few thousand Jewish workers were still alive in Wehrmacht occupied Ukraine, including about 1,000 Jewish men in Dnipropetrovsk and 1,038 Jews in Voroshilovhrad (today Luhansk).[96]

The commander of Rear Area Army Group B, Erich Friderici, instructed his units, such as the local military administration command in Valuiki (just over the Ukrainian-Russian border) to "discuss the question of bandits and Jews with SD. . . . Jews caught and are to be detained until the SD comes."[97] In the summer of 1942, the 403rd Security Division was deployed to the rear areas in eastern Ukraine and soon joined in hunting down the region's last Jews, ordering local mayors to prevent Jews from fleeing and to continue reporting Jews who had been "overlooked."[98] In August 1942, when the Wehrmacht made a last transfer of territory to the RKU, it was duly noted: "Jewish question cleared up."[99]

Wehrmacht occupation administrators participated mainly in organizing genocide in large cities or large Jewish communities. By contrast, there is little evidence to suggest that the SS and police murdered Jews in the towns and countryside after coordinating with the military in advance. Local commandants stepped in when larger segments of the Jewish population were found under military administration.[100] In some cases, commandants circumvented the SS and police units and directly ordered the Ukrainian auxiliary police to murder Jews, as happened in Troianiv in the Zhytomyr region.[101] The evidence also shows that local commandants in the Crimea, which at the time did not belong to Ukraine, worked particularly closely with Einsatzgruppe D in murdering the peninsula's Jews. Indications of this kind of close cooperation also exist for Sk 4a's area of operations.[102]

Where mass killings were ostensibly reprisal operations, Wehrmacht units in Ukraine murdered Jews on their own initiative. In the event of attacks on the Wehrmacht or local infrastructure, commanders were instructed to take only Jews and Russians hostages; in practice, however, this usually affected only Jews. This racist hostage policy functioned similarly in Serbia, where the Wehrmacht killed all of that country's male Jews under the pretext of excessive reprisals between late summer 1941 and early 1942. What distinguishes the situation in Serbia from that of Ukraine, however, is that Wehrmacht units operating in remote areas of Ukraine shot not only Jewish men but also Jewish women and children.[103]

The 62nd Infantry Division, for example, shot 168 Jews in Myrhorod on November 3, 1941. There is also documentation showing that the 202nd Replacement Brigade and various Home Defense formations (*Landesschützeneinheiten*), which were sent to Ukraine for guard duty, carried out mass murders.[104] Wehrmacht records reveal some references to the activities of the German military police in Ukraine: "The field gendarmes executed a Jewish family that *allegedly* [emphasis added, D.P.] maintained contact to the partisans."[105] There are indications that Hungarian security formations also took part in shootings.[106] Finally, the 12 Secret Field Police groups deployed in Ukraine killed hundreds of civilians, including Jews, every month.[107] Altogether, the number of Ukrainian Jews murdered by the Wehrmacht alone is probably around several thousand. This is significantly less than in Belarus, where regular Wehrmacht troops in Minsk killed around 19,000 Jews with assistance from an Order Police battalion.[108]

Einsatzgruppe C had overall responsibility for carrying out the murder of the Jews in Ukraine within the zone of operations of Rear Area Army Group South, with Sk 4a and Einsatzkommando 5 (Ek 5) standing out in this regard.[109] Operating under Jeckeln's supervision and coordinating with AOK 6 and the military administration commands of the 454th Security Division, Blobel's Sk 4a moved east from one large city to the next organizing the annhilation of one Jewish community after another. Ek 5, under Erwin Schulz and, later, August Meier, began expanding its operations only at the end of August 1941, but ultimately murdered 10,000 Jews in the Kiev region alone.[110] Afterward, Ek 5 provided the core personnel for the stationary Sipo-SD offices within the RKU. Sk 4b and Ek 6 also carried out scores of mass killings, but their operations seldom affected the largest Jewish communities in Ukraine.

The "rank and file of the 'Final Solution'"[111] came from the Order Police. This applied to Police Battalions 82 and 311 as well, although they had been assigned to Wehrmacht security divisions for military purposes and had nothing to do directly with the HSSPF Russia South.[112] The Orpo battalions assigned to the HSSPF Russia South—in addition to Einsatzgruppe C—became the decisive factor in carrying out this enormous campaign of mass murder. There were two key reasons for this. First, the Einsatzgruppen did not enter every town with a large Jewish community, or, until around mid-September, they raced ahead with the Wehrmacht, leaving the majority of Jews encountered alive. Second, the commandos were too small to carry out large massacres such as the one in Kamianets-Podilsky. From the point of view of the HSSPF Russia South in the field and the Order Police Main Office in Berlin, the police battalions solved the manpower problem, since these units were hardly needed to fight partisans at the time.[113]

Altogether, the six police battalions subordinated to the HSSPF Russia South killed considerably more Ukrainian Jews than Einsatzgruppe C and Einsatzgruppe D combined. Under Wehrmacht administration, almost every massacre that claimed more than 2,000 to 3,000 lives was carried out by Sipo-SD commandos and Orpo battalions operating together or by the Orpo acting alone. In joint operations, Einsatzgruppe C usually provided the shooters, but almost inevitably, the Sipo and SD men were eventually relieved by regular policemen.

German or Hungarian police and Ukrainian auxiliaries near Chernihiv force Jewish women to undress before they are shot in 1942. The Chernihiv Region remained under German military administration throughout the occupation; however, security troops for this part of Ukraine were provided by Hungary. USHMM, courtesy of Magyar Nemzeti Múzeum Történeti Fényképtár.

The Murder of the Jews in the Reich Commissariat Ukraine

With the establishment of the Reich Commissariat Ukraine (RKU) on September 1, 1941, a German civil occupation authority came into being in the southern Soviet Union. The Reich commissar for Ukraine, Erich Koch, had his small staff set up headquarters in Rivne, but Koch himself rarely visited Ukraine, preferring instead to reside in Königsberg, East Prussia, where he remained the regional Nazi party leader. To staff the offices of the RKU territorial administration, Koch drafted colleagues from the East Prussian National Socialists. The Main Political Department, under Paul Dargel, and its Section IIa, under Joachim Paltzo, were responsible for Jewish policy; the RKU administration's "expert for Jews" was Hentschell, who had once worked in the Reich Propaganda Office for East Prussia.[114] The small offices at the regional level, known as general regions (*Generalbezirk*) or general commissariats (*Generalkommissariat*), were organized similarly.[115] The commissars in the county commissariats (*Gebietskommissariat* or *Kreiskommissariat*), the next administrative level down, exercised the most influence in shaping and implementing policy on the ground. The counties in turn consisted of precincts (*Rayon*), which were usually headed by Ukrainians or ethnic Germans.

Instructions for the civil administration foresaw the convening of Jewish councils and the establishing of ghettos in towns with more than 200 Jews.[116] Within the RKU, it was the civil administration, not the Wehrmacht's economic and armaments inspectors and their regional offices, that oversaw the rationing of food. Unemployed Jews were generally granted half of the lowest food allowance permissible.[117] In those parts of central and southern Ukraine turned over to the RKU in October and November 1941, the civil administration hardly had to concern itself with Jews. East of Zhytomyr, almost all of the Jewish communities had already been thoroughly eradicated during military rule.

As the RKU took shape, debates over whether to establish a Jewish reservation in southern Belarus and the Pripet Marshes fizzled out. German officials finally decided to assign these territories to the RKU and not to occupied Belarus, where they had been under Soviet rule. Nonetheless, in August 1941, Berlin had entertained the possibility of annexing the marshes to the General Government,[118] and it was only in October that the various schemes for the Pripet Marshes were shelved for good. Reich Minister for the Occupied Eastern Territories Alfred Rosenberg informed General Governor Hans Frank that, for the time being, the deportation of Polish Jews into the occupied Soviet Union would not be considered, while Hitler proposed using the marshes as a Wehrmacht training center.[119]

Plans for the deportation of European Jews to Ukraine were not totally finished, however. On October 10, Heydrich spoke of setting up camps in Einsatzgruppe C's area of operations, to which Jews could be deported. This brief reference has been neglected by scholars, but no such deportations are known to have taken place.[120] In January 1942, the deportation of German Jews to Shepetivka, where they were to be put to work building roads, was raised. This project, however, fell through due to opposition from the local county commissar.[121]

While Berlin debated deportations and the shape of the occupied Soviet territories' new order, the possibility of liquidation loomed large for Jews in the RKU. Einsatzgruppe C's new commander, Max Thomas, insisted on expanding the process of destruction to the civil administered territories:

> Under prevailing circumstances, the only possibility of putting an end to the carryings-on of the Jews in Volhynia and thus depriving Bolshevism of its most fertile breeding ground is the complete eradication of the Jews, who unquestionably bring fewer benefits as workers than [the amount of] harm they cause as the 'bacteriological carriers' of communism.[122]

Fearing a shortage of workers, the civil servants of the RKU, which at first only consisted of General Commissariat Volhynia-Podolia, were apparently at first unwilling to let all the Jews be killed.

Nevertheless, throughout the autumn of 1941, several large-scale mass murders took place in Volhynia-Podolia. On the very day the RKU was officially established, on September 1, 1941, 2,500 Jews were shot in Ostroh. Six weeks later, on October 15, the ghetto there was disbanded, and another 3,000 people were killed.[123] Similar massacres were carried out at almost the same time in other prewar Polish territories of the occupied Soviet Union. In early October 1941 the Germans liquidated several ghettos in western Belarus, and on October 6 and 12 large-scale mass shootings occurred in District Galicia.[124] It is quite possible that these murders were coordinated by a higher authority.[125]

The organization of mass murders on the same scale as those in the military administered territories was slow in starting. The largest of the autumn massacres took place in Rivne. This *Aktion* had been in planning for some time, with the initiative for it probably coming from the civil administration, especially Koch. On November 5, Rivne County Commissar Werner Beer instructed the local Jewish council to register all of the town's Jews without work papers. In October, as planning for the massacre got underway, the only Sipo-SD representation in Rivne was a detachment of Ek 5 under Hermann Ling. The office of the regional Sipo and SD commander had yet to be created. Consequently, Otto von Oelhafen, the territorial commander of the Order Police in Ukraine, was assigned to oversee this massacre. After consultations with Beer, the police—Orpo Battalions 69, 315, and 320 (together with *Ostlandkompanie*) and the detachment from Ek 5—murdered some 17,000 Jews near the village of Sosenki.[126] Rivne's new status as an administrative center probably played a key role in the decision for this massacre. Koch wanted as few Jews as possible near his seat of government. Despite the massacre, however, several thousand Jews remained in Rivne.[127]

Large-scale killings in Volhynia-Podolia also took place during this time in Kostopil, Polonne, and Proskuriv (today Khmelnytsky). In October–November 1941, for example, Police Battalion 320's 1st Company shot several hundred women and children in Kostopil; the Jewish men had been killed during the summer.[128]

In total, during the first six months of the German-Soviet war, around 300,000 Jews were murdered in the territories of the Ukrainian Soviet Socialist Republic that passed from Rear Area Army Group South to the RKU.[129] At the start of 1942, approximately the same number of Jews was still living in the RKU, the overwhelming majority of whom were in General Commissariat Volhynia-Podolia. Under military administration, there remained only a few thousand Jewish forced laborers.[130]

For the civil administrators and the military's economic inspectors, the question of whether to leave Jews alive as forced laborers applied only to the western half of the RKU. A large part of the male workers who were actually needed had been murdered in the opening weeks of the invasion. A report from the Wehrmacht's arms inspectorate for Ukraine, written shortly after the Rivne massacre, contains a summary of the genocide near the end of 1941 that bears quoting at length:

> Immediately after the end of combat operations, the Jewish population was at first left alone.[131] Only weeks, in part months, later were systematic shootings carried out by formations of the Order Police specifically assigned to do so. This action moved on the whole from east to west. It took place completely in the open with the enlisting of the Ukrainian militia, in many cases, unfortunately, also with the voluntary participation of Wehrmacht members. The means of carrying out of this action, which extended to men and elderly people, women and children of all ages, was appalling. The action is in its enormity as large as any other measure taken in the Soviet Union before it. In all, some 150,000 to 200,000 Jews from the part of Ukraine belonging to the RK[U] have probably been executed. Only during the last executions was a "useful" part of the Jewish population (the craftsmen) singled out and not executed, previously no consideration was shown for these economic interests.[132]

The Reich Ministry for the Occupied Eastern Territories made clear immediately thereafter that in the future economic interests were not to be taken into consideration. In practice, however, RKU officials often chose to ignore these instructions.[133] At a meeting of officials from the Reich Ministry for the Occupied Eastern Territories concerning workers in Ukraine on March 10, 1942, it was decided to leave Jewish skilled workers and specialists alive for the time being.[134] This decision did not apply to the areas under military administration. In short, there was no German interest in keeping other Jews alive.

There were few forced labor projects for Jews in Ukraine. The largest was Thoroughfare IV (*Durchgangsstrasse IV*, DG IV). The main supply line for the Army Group South, DG IV had been of special interest to the German war effort since the invasion. At first, Reich officials foresaw using only Soviet prisoners of war for road construction. However, Jews were soon put to work repairing and improving the road, as occurred near Vinnytsia.[135] In eastern Ukraine, roadwork lay mainly in the hands of the military administration in 1941, but in central Ukraine it was the province of the civil administration.[136]

Between October 1941 and February 1942, the administrative structure of the DG IV project underwent a slow and thorough reorganization, as the SS took a growing interest in supplies and reinforcements for the front. In September 1941 Jeckeln had assumed responsibility for guarding a stretch of DG IV between Uman and Dnipropetrovsk.[137] Shortly thereafter, work on the DG IV in the General Government was turned over to SS and Police Leader District Galicia Friedrich Katzmann, who almost exclusively deployed Jews as forced laborers for the project. The road only became a major SS project after Himmler visited the southeastern front during Christmas 1941. Initially, the Reichsführer-SS had envisioned a "Road of the SS" stretching from Romania to the Azov Sea[138] and had transferred several newly appointed SS and

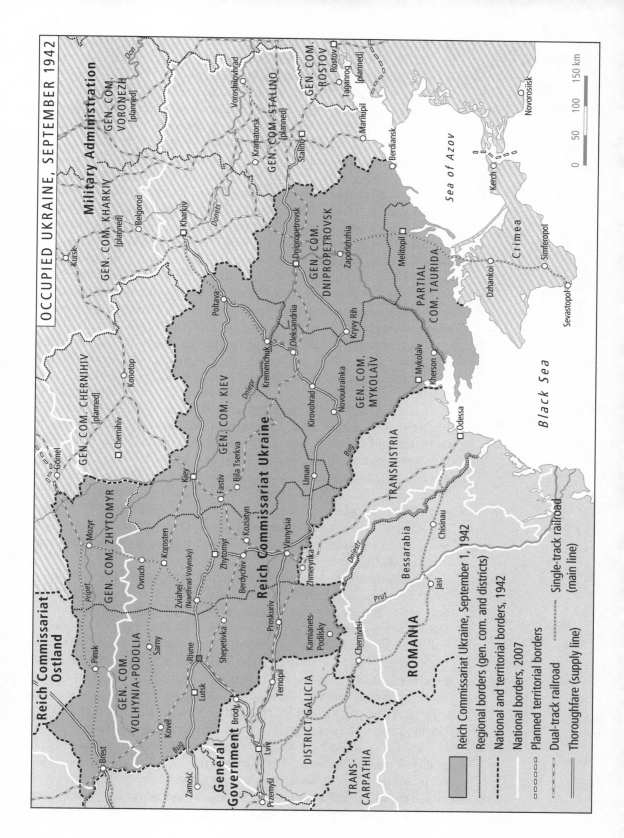

OCCUPIED UKRAINE, SEPTEMBER 1942

Reich Commissariat Ostland

Military Administration

GEN. COM. VORONEZH [planned]

GEN. COM. KHARKIV [planned]

GEN. COM. STALINO [planned]

GEN. COM. ROSTOV [planned]

GEN. COM. CHERNIHIV [planned]

GEN. COM. KIEV

Reich Commissariat Ukraine

GEN. COM. DNIPROPETROVSK

PARTIAL COM. TAURIDA

GEN. COM. ZHYTOMYR

GEN. COM. VOLHYNIA-PODOLIA

GEN. COM. MYKOLAÏV

TRANSNISTRIA

General Government

DISTRICT GALICIA

TRANS-CARPATHIA

ROMANIA

Bessarabia

Sea of Azov

Black Sea

Crimea

Don
Donets
Dniepr
Bug
Bug
Pripet
Pripet
Prut
Dniestr

Gomel
Chernihiv
Konotop
Kursk
Belgorod
Kharkiv
Voroshilovhrad
Kramatorsk
Stalino
Rostov
Taganrog
Mariïupil
Berdiansk
Novorosiisk
Kerch
Simferopol
Sevastopol
Dzhankoi
Melitopol
Zaporizhzhia
Dnipropetrovsk
Kryvy Rih
Kherson
Mykolaïv
Odessa
Kherson
Kirovohrad
Novoukraïnka
Oleksandriïa
Kremenchuk
Poltava
Uman
Vinnytsia
Zhmerynka
Chernivtsi
Jasi
Chisinau
Kamianets-Podilsky
Proskuriv
Berdychiv
Zhytomyr
Zviahel (Novohrad-Volynsky)
Korosten
Ovruch
Mozyr
Pinsk
Brest
Kovel
Lutsk
Rivne
Shepetivka
Ternopil
Lviv
Przemyśl
Zamość
Brody
Samy
Koziatyn
Fastiv
Bila Tserkva
Kiev

Reich Commissariat Ukraine, September 1, 1942
Regional borders (gen. com. and districts)
National and territorial borders, 1942
National borders, 2007
Planned territorial borders
Dual-track railroad
Single-track railroad (main line)
Thoroughfare (supply line)

0   50   100   150 km

police leaders to Rear Area Army Group South. After talks at the highest level of the Reich government in February 1942, German officials settled on a construction project running from the General Government to Dnipropetrovsk via Vinnytsia and Uman, the DG IV.[139] Construction zone chiefs along the road then set up numerous forced labor camps to which what was left of local Jewish communities was assigned.

In addition to the special SS and police apparatus for DG IV, a system of regional and local police offices was also set up in the RKU between September 1941 and May 1942. The core personnel for this came from the command of Einsatzgruppe C and from Ek 5, which had set up headquarters in Kiev in October. The command of Einsatzgruppe C, which became the Territorial Command of the Security Police and Security Service in Ukraine (*Befehlshaber der Sicherheitspolizei und des Sicherheitsdienstes in der Ukraine*, BdS Ukraine), organized the regional commands of the Sipo and SD (*Kommandeur der Sicherheitspolizei und des Sicherheitsdienstes*, KdS) for the general commissariats and their local outposts, using personnel in Kiev and reinforcements from the Reich.

The Territorial Command of the Order Police in Ukraine (*Befehlshaber der Ordnungspolizei in der Ukraine*, BdO Ukraine) organized the deployment of Orpo troops and the regional and local Orpo offices in murder operations. BdO Ukraine Otto von Oelhafen, chief of staff Hans Müller-Brunckhorst, and chief of operations Hermann Engelhaupt were primarily responsible for planning such activities.[140] Oelhafen and his successor, Adolf von Bomhard, smoothly integrated the Orpo into the killing process. Bomhard, who arrived in Kiev in November 1942, wrote Kurt Daluege, the chief of the Order Police, that "partisan warfare is the most fun of all," in other words, operations that sometimes included the clearance of ghettos.[141] Each general commissariat also had a regional commander of the Order Police (KdO), which maintained an extensive system of indigenous police at the precinct and municipal level.

The Wehrmacht Territorial Command in Ukraine (*Wehrmachtbefehlshaber Ukraine*, WBU), under Karl Kitzinger, continued the hostage policy initiated by Rear Area Army Group South. Acts of sabotage against the local infrastructure were met with the seizure of hostages, half of which had to be Jews. If the guilty party were not found within 48 hours, the hostages were shot.[142] The WBU was also regularly informed in advance of large massacres such as the one in Rivne. Military offices subordinated to the WBU continued to take part in the persecution and killing of Jews into mid-1942.[143] Kitzinger's staff also asked the SS for clothing from murdered Jews to hand over to Ukrainian workers.[144]

With few exceptions, RKU county commissars began establishing ghettos between December 1941 and April 1942. Some ghettos had been set up under military rule in August and September, but these were rare occurrences and often served merely as a preparatory step for a killing operation. The county commissars received authorization to establish

"Jewish residential areas" only in December.[145] The ghettoization process in the RKU in March and April 1942 affected primarily the Volhynian Jews. Often these ghettos were not sealed city districts but fenced off streets guarded by local policemen with orders to shoot anyone who strayed beyond the boundaries.

Ultimate responsibility for Jewish policy in Ukraine was sometimes the subject of heated debates among the Germans. While Prützmann acquainted himself with his new duties as HSSPF Ukraine, a limited power struggle between him and Koch evolved—a development that took place elsewhere in German-occupied Europe. Nevertheless, Prützmann and Koch basically understood each other rather well. They had known each other for years in Königsberg. Not least for that reason, Koch officially turned over authority for "Jewish questions" to Prützmann,[146] who in turn delegated this responsibility to the KdS offices under his command.[147]

In January 1942 at the latest—after what is now known as the Wannsee Conference—Himmler and Heydrich laid claim to overall responsibility for the genocide against the Jews in the occupied Soviet territories under civil administration.[148] Not to be sidelined on this key issue, Rosenberg continued to insist that he and his ministry exercised sovereign authority in this matter, with the Sipo serving merely as executor of the decisions made by his administrators.[149] Despite such bureaucratic rivalries, however, the civil authority and the police cooperated relatively smoothly in mass murder, each initiating massacres as deemed necessary.

The Complete Extermination of Ukrainian Jews in 1942

Relatively few massacres of Ukrainian Jews are known to have taken place in the RKU between December 1941 and May 1942. Those that did take place usually came about due to local initiative. The best-documented case concerns the Vinnytsia area, where a new headquarters for Hitler was to be built. In January 1942, units from Organization Todt, the Nazis' paramilitary labor organization, and the Wehrmacht's Secret Field Police turned over to the Sipo 227 Jews living directly along the headquarters' perimeter. These were murdered on January 10. The Sipo murdered another 8,000 Jews in nearby Khmilnyk on January 9 and 16.[150] Shortly thereafter, the Reich Security Service, which was responsible for Hitler's personal security and is not to be confused with the SD, tried to have the remaining 5,000 Jews in Vinnytsia killed. Only three months later could Hitler's bodyguard report: "As already reported, the Jews living in Vinnytsia were knocked off on April 16, up to 4,800 [in all]."[151] The last 1,000 skilled workers in the area were murdered in July 1942 on orders from BdS Ukraine.[152]

Part of the pressure for murdering the Jews in and around Vinnytsia developed around New Year's 1942 with the internment of 60,000 Jews, under the worst imaginable conditions, in the northeastern part of Romanian occupied Ukraine, which bordered on Vinnytsia County. "It is a fact, however, that the Romanian government is leaving the Jews there to starve to death, since [Bucharest] shies away from shooting according to the German example," reported Hitler's bodyguard.[153] In reality, the Romanian police and the German Sonderkommando R, a task force of the Ethnic German Liaison Office (*Volksdeutsche Mittelstelle*), another one of the main offices under Himmler's purview, had begun murdering these Jews on orders from the Romanian government.[154]

Initiatives for other mass killings came from elsewhere in the RKU during the relative lull of early 1942. In February and March, the remaining Jews in General Commissariat Mykolaïv were murdered at the instigation of the civil administration. For example, on February 2, 202 Jews from the Zlatopil ghetto were "eliminated, on orders from the county commissar, by the militia by gassing with Lorpicrin. It was possible to carry out the elimination of the Jews without any disruption and without any commotion."[155] The general commissar in Mykolaïv was soon able to report: "As of April 1, 1942, there are no longer any Jews or half-Jews in General Region Mykolaïv."[156]

It remains to be fully explained why RKU officials decided to launch another large-scale wave of mass killings in May 1942. Just one month earlier, BdS Ukraine announced that undesirable phenomena such as black market activity emanating from the ghettos had been "abolished by means of harsh state-police measures."[157] By May, new instructions were clearly in effect. This development ran parallel to events in other parts of Eastern Europe under German civil administration,[158] which could well point to an order from Berlin.[159] Civil officials in General Commissariat White Ruthenia, the western part of occupied Belarus, had been urging a resumption of mass killings since late March 1942.[160] It can be assumed that the RKU administration's position was hardly any different; Rivne regularly requested the murder of Jews not working on behalf of German interests.[161]

Around May 20, a new wave of mass murder was launched in the general commissariats of Volhynia-Podolia and Zhytomyr, and by late summer, it swelled into the total destruction of almost every Jew in the RKU. The first murders played out mainly in Dubno and Korets in General Commissariat Volhynia-Podolia, as well as in several smaller towns in General Commissariat Zhytomyr. In June, mass shootings followed in Kovel and Lutsk.[162] In line with instructions from Himmler, Jewish workers between 16 and 32 years of age were spared during these operations,[163] thus leaving a small number of Jews alive.

After a short interruption, the mass killings were expanded considerably. Rivne was again the starting point, no longer the capital of the RKU but still the seat of government. On July 13 and 14, KdS Rivne and indigenous police, together with help from the 1st Company of Police Battalion 33, murdered the last 5,000 Jews of Rivne. The second large ghetto liquidation in Volhynia took place on July 27 and 28 in and around Olyka, claiming the lives of 5,673 Jews.[164] Within General Commissariat Zhytomyr, the Sipo-SD outpost in Berdychiv murdered that town's last Jews on July 15 and 16.[165]

The transition from singling out a handful of workers to the total destruction of all the Jews in the RKU also corresponds to events in the General Government. Trainloads of Polish Jews had been rolling to the death camps since March 1942, but only on July 22 did the total eradication of Jewish communities set in. In the two RKU general commissariats where Jews were still living, ghetto clearance "actions" were not yet so systematically organized. The Sipo and Orpo, however, soon implemented a systematic process of clearing the ghettos in the RKU, starting in the vicinity around Kamianets-Podilsky. From there, KdS Rivne's outposts filed almost daily reports on the shooting of thousands of Jews in Kamianets, Kremenets, Kamin-Koshyrsky, and Bar.[166] Not all of the Jews were killed immediately, however; DG IV passed through Podolia, and large numbers of workers were still needed for that project.

What was most likely the largest massacre in Soviet Ukraine in 1942 occurred in Lutsk. Between August 19 and 23, some 14,700 Jews were driven into the Polanka Hills and shot. Only 500 Jewish workers remained in the town.[167] The Lutsk massacre marked the start of another acceleration in the campaign of murder. Koch was pushing for the rapid murder of all the Jews in the RKU under the pretext of drastically reducing the number of consumers of food in his territory. Koch's delivery quota for foodstuffs for the Reich had been raised, and he thought he could meet his new target via mass murder.[168] At a conference of Volhynia-Podolia's county commissars between August 28 and 31, the civil administration agreed with the regional Sipo-SD chief, Karl Pütz, to kill all the Jews in the general commissariat—save for 500 specialists—within five weeks:

> At the county commissars' conference in Lutsk, August 28 to 31, 1942, it was explained in general terms that, in principle, 100-percent solutions were to be carried out. It was announced to the county commissars by the representative of the Reich commissar in attendance—Chairman Dargel—that these 100-percent cleansings are the express wish of the Reich commissar himself. . . . Before such actions are carried out, they are to be discussed in good order with the county commissars, not only with the Gendarmerie [the German rural police], and agreement is to be reached.[169]

The Jews were supposed to be brought from the outlying areas to key towns, so as to murder them in "large-scale actions." In fact, the Jews of a given area were murdered in coordinated groups of shootings that took place simultaneously in or near the towns where they had been living. At the same time, the Germans began replacing the indigenous Jews along DG IV with Jews from Transnistria and Bukovina.[170] What followed was an uninterrupted 67-day campaign of murder against the Jews of Volhynia-Podolia as well as the few remaining Jews in General Commissariat Zhytomyr.[171] The SSPF Volhynia-Podolia explained to the RKU administration:

The actions are being carried out so that the resettlement [of Jews] in county seats and precincts takes place as simultaneously as possible. . . . I feel that given the scope of the large-scale actions a few incidents will be unavoidable, and that the smooth conclusion [of operations] that has nevertheless taken place so far seems all the more remarkable.[172]

At first, the killers drove through Volhynia, moving from south to north and destroying one Jewish community after another throughout September and into October. The massacre in Volodymyr-Volynsky in early September claimed an especially high number of victims, some 13,500 of the 15,000 Jews living there as of July 1942.[173] With the liquidation of the Dubno ghetto on October 5, 3,000 people were killed.[174] The last mass murder of Ukrainian Jews on such a large scale was in Liuboml on October 1 and 2. No fewer than 10,000 Jews were killed there over two days.[175] In November, the killing operations spread north into what had been part of the Belarusian Socialist Soviet Republic before the German invasion. The death squads then headed south again. After the Jewish forced laborers in Lutsk were murdered on December 12, Jewish laborers in Podolia met a similar end: 4,000 victims in Kamianets-Podilsky in November and a similar number in Starokonstiantyniv on December 29, 1942.[176]

The killings were carried out exclusively by the KdS Rivne and its outposts, the Gendarmerie, and the indigenous police. The SSPFs in Lutsk and Zhytomyr, Waldemar Wappenhans and Otto Hellwig respectively, coordinated their various police forces accordingly. They also oversaw the Orpo officers deployed as "SS and police base leaders" (SS- *und Polizei-Standortführer*) in Brest (General Commissariat Volhynia-Podolia) and in Berdychiv and Vinnytsia (General Commissariat Zhytomyr). The RKU administration in Rivne was not the only decisive force behind this campaign of total annihilation on such short notice; the county commissars also contributed significantly to organizing the individual massacres. A number of civil servants, not to be underestimated, also took part in the killing, as in the case of the director of the Labor Office in Kamianets-Podilsky:

> [My] impression was confirmed by a remark from the county commissar, who told me that he was forced to forbid this government councilor from actively taking part in the Jewish actions, that is to say, from doing in Jews by his own hand (!).[177]

Jews who emerged from hiding after the liquidation of a ghetto were handed over by the civil administrators to the police to be murdered.[178] And during the final phase of the killing, Koch even tried to have the former possessions of the murdered Jews turned over to his administration.[179]

In all, some 160,000 Volhynian Jews, 35,000 Podolian Jews, and several thousand Jews from the Zhytomyr region fell victim to the police and civil administration between May and December 1942.[180] By

Jews held in a ravine at Zdolbuniv, General Commissariat Volhynia-Podolia, shortly before their murder on October 14, 1942. USHMM, courtesy of Instytut Pamięci Narodowej, Warsaw.

year's end there were almost no Jews left in the RKU; as one report put it, "Jewry. The cleansing of the territory is in its final stages."[181] Only several thousand specialists considered essential to the war effort were left. In early April 1943, BdS Ukraine surveyed the KdS offices to learn how many Jews remained in the RKU. In the rear areas of the Wehrmacht forces in Ukraine, the surviving Jews numbered only in the hundreds. These Jews were soon murdered as well.[182]

The last large groups of Jewish victims in the RKU were not indigenous to Ukraine but had been deported there from Hungary and Romania. The great majority were Romanian Jews, mostly Jews who had made their way to the RKU from Bukovina or Transnistria and had been put to work on DG IV. These Jews were almost swept up in the ghetto liquidations in the summer of 1942, when police shot the inmates of a DG IV camp in Nemyriv on September 14, 1942. Most of these forced laborers, however, fell victim to the construction project's own contingent of Order Police between February 2 and 5, 1943. A key factor in determining which DG IV Jews to eliminate was the stage of completion of each construction zone.[183] As late as October 1943, some construction zones were still exploiting Jewish forced laborers. A member of Organization Todt near Vinnytsia noted: "Even if poorly clothed, Jews are still very useful as workers."[184] Only a few DG IV camps, among them Bratslav (in Transnistria), were liberated by the Red Army.

An unusual and little known fact is that during the Soviet campaign, the Royal Hungarian Army brought along several battalions of Jewish forced laborers from Hungary.[185] At a point when there were hardly any Jews left alive in eastern Ukraine, Jewish Hungarians continued to enter Ukraine, something German authorities viewed with suspicion.[186] Many of these forced laborers were surrounded in Stalingrad and died either there or in Soviet POW camps. Sometimes, battalions of Hungarian Jews fell into German hands. Sk 4a shot a group of Hungarian Jews near Sumy, while further west a labor battalion's infirmary was set on fire in 1943: "On April 29, the stables at the [collective farm] in Kupyshche (Korosten County) burned down, 300 Hungarian Jews burned with it."[187]

The last known mass killing of Jews in the RKU took place in December 1943. Around 1,000 Jews had been left alive in Volodymyr-Volynsky in 1942. They were quartered in a ghetto of roughly 40 buildings. Although a detachment from a former commando of Einsatzgruppe D had been stationed there for some time, Sk 4b, which had recently deployed there from Stalino, was given the order to kill these Jews. On December 13 or 14, this Sonderkommando shot the Jews in a wooded area after a motorized platoon of Gendarmerie and Ukrainian auxiliaries had cordoned off the area. The rails for a pyre to cremate the bodies had been prepared there in advance.[188]

Resistance and Survival

In general, the Jews of Ukraine put up comparatively little resistance to the Germans, since the preconditions for doing so were quite poor.[189] Going into hiding and taking up armed resistance depended largely on two key factors: the availability of forests and assistance from partisan groups that were not antisemitic. The forests, especially those in western and northwestern Ukraine, offered the only way to escape German "actions." Tens of thousands fled to the woods, but less than 10 percent of them survived. Most were eventually forced to return to the ghettos for lack of food, or they fell victim to raids.

The Soviet partisan movement was relatively poorly developed in Ukraine until mid-1942. Only after the Germans began deporting large numbers of Ukrainians to the Reich for forced labor did the Communist partisan movement begin to find widespread local support, and at first it was only able to do so in northeast Ukraine, between Sumy and Chernihiv.[190] There, however, Jews were relatively few in number, and not all Soviet partisan units in Ukraine were prepared to help Jews.[191]

The greatest numbers of Jews to survive the first wave of killings were located in Volhynia, where the Communists were comparatively weak. Even Soviet research puts the number of Communist underground members and partisans in the Volhynia and Rivne provinces of Soviet Ukraine at just 300 members in October 1942.[192] There, the nationalist Ukrainian Insurgent Army (UPA) gained the upper hand, and in the best of circumstances, the UPA was only interested in the recruitment of Jewish doctors. Many UPA units consisted of deserters from the indigenous police who had persecuted and killed Jews before defecting.[193] By the time the Communist partisans had infiltrated Volhynia in large numbers, the genocide against the Jews was nearly complete.[194]

For this reason, German anti-partisan warfare in Ukraine—in contrast to Belarus—was seldom used as a cover for murdering Jews. There were, however, cases where Jews were caught up in anti-partisan operations. In autumn of 1941, skirmishes with the partisans broke out on the lower reaches of the Dniepr, around Pavlohrad and Novomoskovsk as well as in Nikopol. German forces seized the opportunity to murder Jewish civilians of all ages and both genders.[195] Anti-partisan operations were also used as a pretext for the mass killing of Jews in the northern reaches of General Commissariat Volhynia-Podolia in the autumn of 1942, as the Soviet partisan struggle in General Commissariat White Ruthenia began spilling into the RKU. Thousands of Jews, possibly even tens of thousands, were hidden in the forests there.[196] In the course of 1943, hundreds of Jews were found each month in the towns or woods and subsequently murdered.[197]

A direct correlation between Jewish resistance and the German campaign of destruction existed sporadically and only in the opposite direction from that claimed by the Germans. That is to say, resistance was a response to the mass killings, not the other way around. In some Volhynian ghettos the police encountered organized Jewish resistance in the autumn of 1942; these included Tuchyn, Mizoch, Kremenets, and the forced labor camp in Lutsk. Beyond that, there were numerous examples of individual armed resistance,[198] to which German offices reacted with irritation: "[It is] now being observed that this riff-raff is defending itself, and in recent days, it has come to the severe wounding of guard units entrusted with the task of resettlement."[199]

Only Jews who managed to join the partisans, usually Soviet units, had a greater chance of surviving, and this was possible only for younger people, mostly men. Between 1,700 and 1,900 Volhynian Jews fought in such units or formed their own small Jewish partisan groups.[200] In other areas, these figures were considerably smaller. Even among the partisans, though, only a fraction of Ukraine's Jews survived the war.

Destroying the Evidence

The final act in the murder of the Ukrainian Jews was supposed to be the destruction of the evidence of this enormous crime. The Soviet counteroffensive in December 1941 had shown senior German police officials just how quickly mass graves could be discovered. After some initial preparations in 1942, the setting up of Special Commando 1005 (Sk 1005), a special unit for digging up and burning the bodies of Jews killed in 1941 and 1942, went into high gear in April 1943. By then, the Soviets had reconquered the eastern rim of Ukraine. Destroying the evidence of German crimes became a matter of great political importance for the Nazis, because they had used the discovery of the NKVD's victims in Katyn and Vinnytsia to great propaganda effect. Furthermore, Soviet officials had also begun opening the mass graves of Nazi victims in the northern Caucasus.[201]

The presence of Sk 1005 in western Ukraine is documented for June 1943, when the unit was in Lviv. In the rest of Ukraine, it took some time before the "unearthing" could begin. Blobel returned to Kiev in July or August 1943 to set up other commandos similar to Sk 1005.[202] BdS Ukraine, meanwhile, determined where these commandos were to deploy. On August 3, KdS Rivne distributed a circular to the Gendarmerie in General Commissariat Volhynia-Podolia, asking for lists of mass graves in the precincts. Some 200 sites were apparently reported.[203] By August 1943, two commandos were in operation, Sk 1005-A and Sk 1005-B, each with eight to ten Sipo and SD men, 30 German municipal policemen, and over 300 prisoners, mostly POWs.[204] Both commandos worked on excavations at Babi Yar in the second half of August 1943. Sk 1005-B then went to Dnipropetrovsk, Kryvy Rih, and Mykolaïv before leaving Ukraine in January 1944. On September 29, 1943, prisoners in Sk 1005-A tried to escape while the unit was still in Kiev. Fourteen of the men survived the war. With new prisoners, Sk 1005-A then excavated mass graves at Berdychiv, Bila Tserkva, and Uman. After murdering this team of forced laborers, the commando's German members then turned to Kamianets-Podilsky.[205] Despite their efforts, the Germans never came close to opening but a small fraction of the mass graves in Ukraine, let alone burning the bodies and crushing the bones. After the Red Army's return, Soviet investigators were able to find almost all of the mass graves and to examine them.

Ukrainian Society, Soviet Officialdom, and the West

Another one of the less researched aspects of the Holocaust in Ukraine is the attitude and reaction of the non-Jewish population toward the mass killings.[206] The role of the Ukrainian local police is relatively easy to reconstruct.[207] In western Ukraine and parts of central Ukraine, the two rival factions of the Organization of Ukrainian Nationalists helped set up the local militias that were among those responsible for organizing the pogroms in western Volhynia and eastern Galicia during the German advance in June and July 1941. The military administration generally tolerated these militias, but soon it began disarming them and having their members screened by Einsatzgruppe C. Thus the Ukrainian auxiliary police, known as *Schutzmannschaften* after July 30, 1941, was not identical to the militias from the first days of the German-Soviet war.[208] The auxiliary police were first subordinated to the local military administration commands, then to the Orpo, above all the Gendarmerie in the countryside.[209] Locals generally served as individual patrolmen in posts of 10 to 20 men in the villages; in the cities, they numbered as many as several hundred, in Kiev several thousand. The first mobile battalions of indigenous policemen under German command were set up in October 1941.[210] By the end of November 1942, there were over 19,000 men in 53 indigenous police battalions, 14,163 men in the indigenous municipal police, and 54,794 men in the indigenous rural police in the RKU and military administered Ukrainian territories. In all, over 100,000 men served in the RKU's indigenous police forces.[211]

The participation of local policemen in persecuting and killing Ukraine's Jews took many forms.[212] After the more or less spontaneous excesses during the first days of military occupation, it was the local police that had the most direct contact with Ukraine's Jews. They helped register Jews, conduct raids, and guard ghettos. Starting in August 1941, the local police also played an important role in mass shootings. The Schutzmannschaft of a given town or village drove the Jews together, loaded the convoys to the killing sites, and cordoned off the scene of the shooting. Part of the 300 auxiliary policemen at the disposal of FK 195 in Kiev at the end of September 1941 probably helped organize the massacre at Babi Yar.[213] The auxiliary police were already active during the killing operations in the first weeks and months of the German invasion. During the killing of Kryvy Rih's Jews, "the entire Ukrainian auxiliary police was put to use."[214] At a massacre of Jews in Dnipropetrovsk, cooperation between the Sipo and auxiliary police, the field administration command noted, ran "smoothly in every way."[215] In some cases, local commandants ordered the murder of Jews using the auxiliary police.[216] Many Ukrainians were never disarmed. Einsatzgruppe C also maintained its own auxiliaries starting in August 1941. These, too, carried out shootings sometimes, especially when it came to killing Jewish children.[217]

The massacres in Volhynia-Podlia between May and November 1942 were characterized by the systematic use of the Schutzmannschaft.[218] In almost every town or village where Jews were still living, the Gendarmerie and its auxiliaries took part in the killing. Several Schutzmannschaft battalions have also been documented as participating in shootings. Since these formations were sometimes deployed outside their home territory in other Soviet republics, Ukrainian battalions were not the only ones in the RKU and the military administered parts of eastern Ukraine. Four Lithuanian battalions were employed to guard forced laborers on DG IV during 1942. Of the Ukrainian battalions, at least battalions 102, 103, and 117 were used in mass shootings.[219] The role of the almost thoroughly Ukrainian precinct level administration in organizing the mass killings still awaits investigation. Its responsibilities included registering Jews and establishing ghettos. Mayors also sometimes detained Jews on their own initiative.[220]

The same applies to the reaction of the non-Jewish population in general, above all the Ukrainians but also the Poles in Volhynia and the Russians in the urban areas of eastern Ukraine.[221] The ethnic Germans in Ukraine occupy a special place in the study of the Holocaust in Ukraine, especially those from the Odessa, Zhytomyr, and Zaporizhzhia regions.[222] In Romanian occupied Transnistria, the Ethnic German Self-Defense Force, comprising mostly young, male villagers, made a particularly devastating contribution to the Holocaust in Ukraine, murdering tens of thousands of Jews. Assuming the contemporary situation reports are reliable, the indigenous Germans in other settlements were also as hostile to Jews as the Germans from the Reich, even if they played a smaller role in the killing process.[223]

The situation reports of the Sipo and SD and those of the Wehrmacht regularly noted that the Ukrainian population welcomed the killing "actions" against the Jews.[224] The distribution of foodstuffs appears to have played a key role in shaping this attitude. As famine took hold in central and eastern Ukraine in late 1941, denunciations of hidden Jews began pouring in to the German or Ukrainian police on a daily basis. According to Einsatzgruppe C: "Kharkiv's population is, with few exceptions, absolutely negatively disposed to Jewry."[225] Still, the brutal wave of mass killings in Volhynia in the autumn of 1942 apparently provoked a largely negative reaction among the population. The Polish minority even feared that it would be the next victim of this policy of annihilation.[226] In fact, in 1943, Volhynia's Poles were less threatened by the German occupants than by the UPA. Despite the revulsion felt by much of the Volhynian population toward the slaughter of the Jews, denunciations continued to come in to the German police without interruption.[227]

As for Soviet officials in Moscow, they were often informed in detail about the massacres of the Jews by the Red Army's political departments and the NKVD's underground cells behind the German lines.[228] The first reports on Babi Yar reached Moscow within eight weeks of the massacre, and on December 19, 1942, *Pravda* reported mass killings in Konotop that had taken place two months earlier.[229] Soon thereafter, the Soviet government began covering up the fact that these massacres were a well-orchestrated campaign against the Jews. Later, one spoke only of the massacre of "peaceful Soviet citizens."[230]

Information about the anti-Jewish killings also leaked to the West. The British secret service was able to intercept numerous Orpo radio messages containing body counts until September 13, 1941. After that, such reports were sent only by courier.[231] Exact information about the Holocaust spread through Europe not only via various intelligence services; German officials on business trips and soldiers on leave in Europe discussed with others what they had seen or heard on the Ukrainian front. Rumors about Babi Yar quickly made the rounds in Wehrmacht officer clubs in Paris. The Swiss authorities were also able to get a good idea of the enormous crimes being committed in Ukraine.[232]

Total Losses and Legal Consequences

The number of Jewish deaths in Ukraine during the Second World War, in contrast to most of the other territories under German occupation, can only be determined with great difficulty. The estimated number of unreported deaths in Ukraine is comparatively high, so much so that the chief statistician of the SS and the Reich Security Main Office could no longer maintain an overview.[233] An estimated 1.4 million indigenous Jews in all of Soviet Ukraine (including Transnistria and Galicia) were murdered. The two Einsatzgruppen in Ukraine along with the other forces of the HSSPF Russia South murdered around 300,000 people in the Wehrmacht administered territories and the RKU in 1941 and early 1942; 20,000 Jews fell victim to the pogroms of June and July 1941; 530,000 Jews from District Galicia were killed on site or deported to the Bełżec death camp; 185,000 Jews died as a result of German-Romanian cooperation in Transnistria; and 350,000 Jews were murdered in 1942 and 1943 in the RKU.[234] Hitler himself spoke of half a million Jews being killed in the RKU; within the German occupation apparatus, some of the figures circulating put the number over one million.[235] Not included here are the Hungarian Jews from the work battalions, the Romanian Jews deported from Bessarabia and northern Bukovina, and Jewish POWs from Ukraine.

Only the Ukrainian collaborators were ever prosecuted in large numbers for these crimes, less so the Germans responsible for organizing them.[236] The NKVD conducted several thousand investigations into the activities of former Schutzmannschaft members and local administrators. In many cases, killing Jews lay at the heart of the legal proceedings. Draconian sentences were handed down for collaboration, especially for participating in killing operations; from 1943 to 1947, the death sentence was common; from 1948 on, 25 years in the Soviet labor camps was a typical sentence. Trials of collaborators continued until the early 1990s.[237] Some of the German principals were also captured by the Soviets.[238]

The Western allies and the West German courts prosecuted almost solely Einsatzgruppe members.[239] Few of the former SS officers who had been active at BdS Ukraine or one of the KdS regional offices were ever convicted.[240] A small group of men from Sk 1005 received relatively light sentences.[241] Comparatively few of the perpetrators from the ranks of the Orpo were ever convicted for their role in the Holocaust in Ukraine.[242] The same goes for former military or civil administrators. No former military administrator ever appeared before a German court,[243] and the number of trials against functionaries of the civil administration was minimal. Koch was tried in Poland for crimes committed in the Polish territories annexed to East Prussia, but his crimes in Ukraine were not part of the case against him.[244] Criminal investigations into the activities of county commissars such as Werner Beer (Rivne) or Wilhelm Westerheide (Volodymyr-Volynsky) were either closed or ended in acquittal.[245] The trial against former Zdolbuniv County Commissar Georg Marschall ultimately degenerated into the grotesque. His case was reopened after he received a sentence to life in prison, because the prosecution's chief witness, Fritz Gräbe, had provided inexact information regarding his own Nazi past. In a second trial, Marschall received five years in prison.[246] Only Erich Kassner of the Kovel County Commissariat was found guilty of murder and sentenced to life in prison.[247]

Concluding Observations

The above outline of events in the Ukrainian territories under German military and civil administration reveals a series of differences between the two. From June 1941 to July 1942, the policy of mass murder in Wehrmacht administered Ukraine passed through all of the identified stages of escalation. Annihilating a large part of the Soviet civilian population was not the chief objective of the war against the Soviet Union. The murder of real or alleged enemies was seen as a means of defeating the Soviet Union and breaking potential sources of opposition. This position was shared by the Nazi leadership and the Wehrmacht (most generals and a large part of the officer corps). The main victims of this strategy were the Jews, who were seen as the social basis of Bolshevism. When it became clear that the war against the Soviet Union would not end as quickly as planned, the Nazi leadership and the police, and then parts of the military administration, decided to kill the vast majority of Jews. Economic considerations had little moderating influence on this process. Instead, economic considerations often provided the rationale for mass murder, sometimes having even an accelerating effect. In Wehrmacht administered Ukraine, the Germans for the most part believed they could do without Jewish labor. At the same time, from the Wehrmacht's point of view, the Jews, especially those from the Soviet Union in its pre-1939 borders, represented not only the basis of Bolshevism but an ethnic minority the German military did not want to feed.

Military administration provided, as it were, the cover for the disfranchisement, dispossession, and murder of Jews throughout most of Ukraine until October 1941, thereafter only in the eastern parts of the Soviet republic. Only the German military had sovereignty over this territory, and only its bureaucracy possessed the infrastructure for registering the Jewish population. The army high commands and many of the field administration commands supported the genocide; in several divisional commands and in the officer corps in general, opinions varied. What the rank-and-file soldier thought about the killing is only now being researched.[248]

The civil administration of the RKU established itself at a point when the total annihilation of the Jews was already underway. As at the highest levels of the military, a general consensus existed within the civil administration that the Jews "had to go." However, the civil administration wanted to maintain its sovereignty in every aspect of policy, meaning it also sought to determine the course of events in the "Jewish question" and thus decided for a while not to give up its Jewish workers. For that reason, mass killing in the RKU was suspended during the autumn of 1941, save for Rivne and its environs. At this point ghettos were set up. By late May 1942, parallel to the acceleration of the "Final Solution" elsewhere in Europe, RKU officials began urging that all Jews without work be shot. In July or August, the RKU leadership agreed with the Sipo and SD to annihilate all of the territory's remaining Jews, which was all but completed by December 1942.

Seen in this light, the SS and police appear not as a separate center of power, but much more as an executor of RKU policy. Division of labor was most decisive, not conflict of interests. Responsibility for the mass killings in the early months of the German-Soviet war lay with the HSSPF Russia South. Einsatzgruppe C, the police battalions, and the 1st SS Infantry Brigade were his troops, each with different tasks. With the establishment of the stationary BdS and KdS structure at the end of 1941, the Sipo and SD took over coordinating massacres, especially in the summer of 1942. The Orpo, which was strongest in numbers, operated via its own system of municipal and rural police and mobile formations. Together with the auxiliary police, the Orpo provided the backbone of manpower for "Jewish actions."[249] In the killing process, it often acted autonomously. The majority of the Orpo's officer corps saw the annihilation of hundreds of thousands of people as its task. Within this group, however, there were noteworthy exceptions.[250] Nevertheless, the overwhelming majority of those Orpo men involved in the mass killings helped to ensure that the Jews in the RKU and in the eastern parts of Ukraine under military administration were almost completely annihilated.

Notes

An earlier version of this article was published under the title "Schauplatz Ukraine: Der Massenmord an den Juden im Militärverwaltungsgebiet and im Reichskommissariat 1941–1943," in Norbert Frei, Sybille Steinbacher, Bernd C. Wagner, eds., *Ausbeutung, Vernichtung, Öffentlichkeit. Neue Studien zur nationalsozialistischen Lagerpolitik* (Munich: Saur, 2000), pp. 135–173.

1. Ya. S. Khonigsman, *Katastrofa evreistva Zapadnoi Ukrainy* (L'vov, 1998); Dieter Pohl, *Nationalsozialistische Judenverfolgung in Ostgalizien 1941–1944. Organisation und Durchführung eines staatlichen Massenverbrechens* (Munich: Oldenbourg, 1996); and Thomas Sandkühler, *"Endlösung" in Galizien. Der Judenmord in Ostpolen und die Rettungsaktionen von Berthold Beitz* (Bonn: Dietz, 1996).

2. Radu Ioanid, *The Holocaust in Romania. The Destruction of Jews and Gypsies Under the Antonescu Regime, 1940–1944* (Chicago: Ivan R. Dee, 2000); Jean Ancel, *Transnistria* (Bucharest: Atlas, 1998) (in Romanian); idem, "The Romanian Campaigns of Mass Murder in Transnistria, 1941–1942," in Randolph L. Braham, ed., *The Destruction of Romanian and Ukrainian Jews during the Antonescu Era* (Boulder, CO: Social Science Monographs, 1997), pp. 87–134; Shemuel Ben-Siyon, *Yeladim yehudim be-Transnistriya bi-tequfat has-sho'a* (Haifa: Yad Vashem, 1989); Avigdor Shachan, *Burning Ice. The Ghettos of Transnistria* (New York: Columbia University Press, 1996).

3. Andrej Angrick, *Besatzungspolitik und Massenmord. Die Einsatzgruppe D in der südlichen Sowjetunion 1941–1943* (Hamburg: Hamburger Edition, 2003); idem, "Die Einsatzgruppe D," in Peter Klein, ed., *Die Einsatzgruppen in der besetzten Sowjetunion 1941/42. Die Tätigkeits- und Lageberichte des Chefs der Sicherheitspolizei und des SD 1941/42* (Berlin: Edition Hentrich, 1997), pp. 88–110.

4. Initial efforts to present a comprehensive overview have been made by Alexander I. Kruglov, *Kholokost na Ukraine 1941–1944 gg.: Monografiia*, manuscript from ca. 1993; idem, *Unichtozhenie evreiskogo naseleniia Ukrainy v 1941–1944 gg. Khronika sobytii* (Mohyliv-Podil's'kyi, 1997); idem, *Katastrofa ukrainskogo evreistva 1941–1944 gg. Entsiklopedicheskii slovar'* (Kharkiv: Karavella, 2001). Also see S. Ia. Ielisavets'kyi, ed., *Katastrofa ta opir ukraïns'koho ievreistva (1941–1944)* (Kiev, 1999).

5. See the exhaustive study of sources by Karel Berkhoff, "Ukraine Under Nazi Rule (1941–1944): Sources and Finding Aids," in *Jahrbücher für Geschichte Osteuropas*, Vol. 45, no. 1–2 (1997), pp. 84–103 and pp. 273–309.

6. Shmuel Spector, *The Holocaust of Volhynian Jews 1941–1944* (Jerusalem: Yad Vashem, 1990); and *Encyclopedia of Jewish Communities. Poland*, Band 5: Polesie-Volhynia (Jerusalem: Yad Vashem, 1990) (in Hebrew). Christian Gerlach, *Kalkulierte Morde. Die deutsche Wirtschafts- und Vernichtungspolitik in Weissrussland* (Hamburg: Hamburger Edition, 1999), also discusses events in the general commissariats of Volhynia-Podolia and Zhytomyr in the RKU, as they included parts of Soviet Belarus.

7. Martin Dean, "The German *Gendarmerie*, the Ukrainian Schutzmannschaften and the 'Second Wave' of Jewish Killings in Occupied Ukraine: German Policing at the Local Level in the Zhitomir Region, 1941–1944," in *German History*, Vol. 14, no. 2 (1996), pp. 168–192; Wendy Lower, "Nazi Colonial Dreams: German Policies and Ukrainian Society in Zhytomyr, Ukraine 1941–1944," PhD diss., American University, Washington, 1999.

8. For example, on the Crimea: Manfred Oldenburg, *Ideologie und militärisches Kalkül. Die Besatzungspolitik der Wehrmacht in der Sowjetunion 1942* (Cologne, Vienna: Böhlau, 2004); Norbert Kunz, *Die Krim unter deutscher Herrschaft 1941–1944* (Darmstadt: Wissenschaftliche Buchgesellschaft, 2005).

9. Mordechai Altshuler, *Distribution of the Jewish Population of the USSR 1939* (Jerusalem: Centre for Research and Documentation of East-European Jewry, 1993), pp. 9ff., V. S. Kozhurin, "O chislennosti naseleniia SSSR nakanune Velikoi Otechestvennoi voiny," *Voenno-istoricheskii zhurnal*, no. 2 (1991), pp. 21–26.

10. For example, in Liubar and Dunaïvtsi, Jews made up 70 percent and 68 percent of the population respectively; Altshuler, *Distribution*, pp. 22f.

11. Mordechai Altshuler, "Unique Features of the Holocaust in the Soviet Union," in Yaacov Ro'i, ed., *Jews and Jewish Life in Russia and the Soviet Union* (Newbury Park Ilford: Frank Cass and Company, 1995), pp. 171–188, here p. 180.

12. Reuben Ainsztein, *Jewish Resistance in Nazi-Occupied Eastern Europe* (London: Elek, 1974), pp. 208ff.; Matthias Vetter, *Antisemiten und Bolschewiki. Zum Verhältnis von Sowjetsystem und Judenfeindschaft 1917–1939* (Berlin: Metropol, 1995), pp. 324ff.; Vadim Dubson, "On the Problem of Evacuation of the Soviet Jews in 1941 (New Archival Sources)," *Jews in Eastern Europe*, Vol. 40, no. 3 (1999), pp. 37–55.

13. Dov Levin, "The Fateful Decision. The Flight of the Jews into the Soviet Interior in the Summer of 1941," *Yad Vashem Studies*, Vol. 20 (1990), pp. 115–142 (which address western Ukraine); Mordechai Altshuler, "Escape and Evacuation of Soviet Jews at the Time of the Nazi Invasion," in Lucjan Dobroszycki and Jeffrey S. Gurock, eds., *The Holocaust in the Soviet Union* (Armonk, New York: M. E. Sharpe, 1993), pp. 77–104, here p. 99.

14. In Galicia there remained about 530,000 Jews, in Transnistria around 200,000 Jews. Shmuel Spector, "The Holocaust of Ukrainian Jews," in Zvi Gitelman, ed., *Bitter Legacy. Confronting the Holocaust in the USSR* (Bloomington: Indiana University Press, 1997), pp. 43–50, here p. 49, assumes 1.5 million Jews in German occupied Ukraine as a whole; see his data in the Hebrew-language *Shvut*, Vol. 12, no. 1 (1987), pp. 55–66.

15. Christian Streit, *Keine Kameraden. Die Wehrmacht und die sowjetischen Kriegsgefangenen 1941–1945* (Stuttgart: Deutsche Verlags-Anstalt, 1978), p. 89, contains one of the first analyses of the sources related to this matter. See also Bernd Boll and Hans Safrian, "Auf dem Weg nach Stalingrad. Die 6. Armee 1941/42," in Hannes Heer and Klaus Naumann, eds., *Vernichtungskrieg* (Hamburg: Hamburger Edition, 1995), pp. 260–296, here pp. 266f.; Pohl, *Judenverfolgung*, p. 73, for June 1941.

16. Boll and Safrian, *Auf dem Weg nach Stalingrad*, pp. 269ff.

17. Fritz Braune, a later commander of Sk 4b, claimed after the war that his predecessor, Günther Herrmann, was warmly seen off by Colonel-General Hermann Hoth upon departing the Ukrainian theater, Bundesarchiv-Ludwigsburg (BA-L), 208 AR-Z 6/60, questioning of March 20, 1964. On PzAOK 1 and Sk 4b, see Bundesarchiv-Militärarchiv Freiburg (BA-MA), RH 21-1/470, Tätigkeitsbericht PzAOK 1/Ic, December 19, 1941.

18. On the individual battalions, see Stefan Klemp, *"Nicht ermittelt": Polizeibataillone und Nachkriegsjustiz—ein Handbuch* (Essen: Klartext, 2005).

19. BA-MA, RH 22/12, Berück 103 an Sich.Div., June 11, 1941.

20. Christian Gerlach, "Die Ausweitung der deutschen Massenmorde in den

besetzten sowjetischen Gebieten im Herbst 1941," in Gerlach, *Krieg, Ernährung, Völkermord. Forschungen zur deutschen Vernichtungspolitik im Zweiten Weltkrieg* (Hamburg: Hamburger Edition, 1998), pp. 10–84.

21. Hannes Heer, "Einübung in den Holocaust: Lemberg Juni/Juli 1941," *Zeitschrift für Geschichtswissenschaft*, Vol. 49, no. 5 (2001), pp. 409–427.

22. Bundesarchiv Berlin (BA-B), R 58/214, p. 52, Ereignismeldung (EM) 10, July 2, 1941.

23. *Verbrechen der Wehrmacht: Dimensionen des Vernichtungskrieges 1941–1944. Katalog zur Ausstellung*, Hamburger Institut für Sozialforschung ed. (Hamburg: Hamburger Edition, 2002), pp. 123–127.

24. BA-MA, RH 22/170, Befehl des Berück Süd Abt. Ic, July 29, 1941. Rear Area Army Group South came into existence on July 9, 1941. Roques was represented by Erich Friderici for two months starting October 27, 1941.

25. Pohl, *Judenverfolgung*, p. 65.

26. Richtlinien für die in die Stalags abzustellenden Kommandos, appendix to Heydrich's Einsatzbefehl no. 8, July 17, 1941, printed in Klein, *Einsatzgruppen*, pp. 331–340. These guidelines applied not only to the POW main camps (Stalags), which did not exist at this point in the occupied Soviet Union, but also to the POW transit camps in the rear area of the army (Dulags), see ibid., p. 333. These guidelines were drawn up by June 28, 1941, see Nuremberg Document PS-78.

27. Einsatzbefehl Jeckeln an 1. SS-Brigade, July 25, 1941, quoted in Prosecutor's Office Munich, Einstellungsverfügung, I 118 Js 12/71 ./. Tzschoppe u.a., July 5, 1972. Cf. BA-B, NS 19/2551, Kommando-Stab RFSS Kommandosonderbefehl, Betreff: Sumpfgebiete, July 28, 1941.

28. Bernd Boll, "'Aktionen nach Kriegsbrauch.' Wehrmacht und 1. SS-Infanteriebrigade 1941," *Zeitschrift für Geschichtswissenschaft*, Vol. 48, no. 6 (2000), pp. 775–788. See also Martin Cüppers, *Wegbereiter der Shoah: Die Waffen-SS, der Kommandostab Reichsführer-SS und die Judenvernichtung 1939–1945* (Darmstadt: Wissenschaftliche Buchgesellschaft, 2005).

29. See, for Army Group Center, Andrej Angrick et al., "'Da hätte man schon ein Tagebuch führen müssen.' Das Polizeibataillon 322 und die Judenmorde im Bereich der Heeresgruppe Mitte während des Sommers und Herbstes 1941," in Helge Grabitz, Klaus Bästlein, and Johannes Tuchel, eds., *Die Normalität des Verbrechens* (Berlin: Edition Hentrich, 1994), pp. 325–385, here pp. 331ff.

30. Klemp, *"Nicht ermittelt,"* pp. 124f., 276ff.; Peter Longerich, *Politik der Vernichtung* (Munich: Piper, 1998), p. 385; for a micro study of Police Battalion 45, see *Täter: Wie aus normalen Menschen Massenmörder werden* (Frankfurt: Fischer, 2005). It has not been fully determined whether Police Regiment South also ordered the shooting of women and children in Shepetivka.

31. For the first "test shootings" carried out in Rivne by the Order Police platoon assigned Sk 4a, see the unpublished master's thesis by Martin Wiedemann, "Führerwille und Eigeninitiative: 'Der Vernichtungskrieg in der Sowjetunion am Beispiel der Tätigkeit des Sonderkommandos 4a,'" Munich, 1990, p. 69.

32. Cüppers, *Wegbereiter des Shoah*; Tätigkeitsbericht 1. SS-Brigade für 27.-30.7.1941, *"Unsere Ehre heisst Treue." Kriegstagebuch des Kommandostabes RFSS. Tätigkeitsberichte der 1. und 2.SS-Infantrie-Brigade, der 1. SS-Kavallerie-Brigade und von Sonderkommandos der SS*, Fritz Baade et al. ed. (Vienna and Frankfurt am Main: Europa Verlag, 1965), pp. 105f. In all, 1,658 Jews were shot during these "cleansing actions." See also Prosecutor's Office Munich, Einstellungsverfügung, I 118 Js 12/71 ./. Tzschoppe u.a., July 5, 1972; Cüppers, *Wegbereiter der Shoah*.

33. Christian Gerlach, *"Deutsche Wirtschaftsinteressen, Besatzungspolitik und der Mord an den Juden in Weissrussland,"* in Ulrich Herbert, ed., *Nationalsozialistische Vernichtungspolitik 1939 bis 1945* (Frankfurt am Main: Fischer, 1998), pp. 263–291, here p. 278.

34. *"Unsere Ehre heisst Treue,"* pp. 35 and 149. By September 16, the brigade was in the Dniepr Bend, where it continued operations until mid-October. Afterward, it was deployed to the Sumy region.

35. Klaus-Michael Mallmann, "Der qualitative Sprung im Vernichtungsprozess: das Massaker von Kamenez-Podolsk Ende August 1941," *Jahrbuch für Antisemitismusforschung,* Vol. 10 (2001), pp. 239–264.

36. BA-MA, RH 22/5, orders of the Rear Army Group Area South, Abt. VII, no. 3/41 and no. 17/41, July 12 and 21, 1941, respectively; BA-MA, RH 22/203, Bericht über die verwaltungsmässigen Verhältnisse im Befehlsbereich des Berück Süd, July 28, 1941; regarding Section VII as the "Jews desk," see R 94/26, pp. 1ff., Richtlinien des Berück Süd zu Abt.VII, Sich.Div. 444, 454; Geschäftsverteilungsplan 454. Sich.Div./Abt. VII.

37. USHMM, RG-11.001 (Former Special [Osobyi] Archive Moscow, now part of the Rossiiskii Gosudarstvennyi Voennyi Arkhiv), Reel 92, 1275/3/667, p. 49, FK 183/Ia an 444. Sich.Div., July 31, 1941.

38. Nuremberg Document PS-197, Vermerk Reichsministerium für die besetzten Ostgebiete, August 27, 1941. Two days earlier, Economics Staff East had decided to substitute Jewish labor with prisoners of war, see Gerlach, *Kalkulierte Mord,* p. 579.

39. Mallmann, "Sprung," does not see any participation by Einsatzgruppe C; witnesses do mention the presence of an "SS Major Meyer" in Kam'ianets', *Verbrechen der Wehrmacht,* p. 135. SS Major August Meier was at the time Einsatzgruppe C's liaison to HSSPF Russia South, Pohl, "Einsatzgruppe C," in Klein, *Einsatzgruppen,* p. 71.

40. Andrej Angrick, "The Escalation of German-Rumanian Anti-Jewish Policy after the Attack on the Soviet Union," *Yad Vashem Studies,* Vol. 26 (1998), pp. 203–238, here pp. 228f.

41. Prosecutor's Office Frankfurt am Main, 4 Js 901/62, 4 Ks 1/71, Vol. 41, pp. 7,754–7,769, testimony of Ottmar L., April 20, 1961; Klemp, *"Nicht ermittelt,"* p. 285.

42. *Verbrechen der Wehrmacht,* p. 134; BA-B, R 58/217, EM 80, September 11, 1941.

43. Nuremberg Document NOKW-1554, Notiz über eine Besprechung bei der Heeresgruppe Süd am 2.9.1941. Kam'ianets'-Podil's'kyi is also discussed in Richard Breitman, *Official Secrets: What the Nazis Planned, What the British and Americans Knew* (New York: Hill and Wang, 1998), pp. 63ff. The British secret service, which intercepted a considerable amount of Order Police radio traffic concerning massacres between June 22 and September 13, 1941, was almost certainly aware of this operation as well.

44. A general regime for setting up ghettos was issued by the High Command of the Army on August 19, 1941. Rear Area Army Group South did the same on August 28, 1941, Gerlach, *Kalkulierte Morde,* p. 525.

45. Politisches Archiv, Auswärtiges Amt, Berlin, Inland II g. 208, pp. 89–93, Luther an Gesandtschaft Budapest, December 24, 1942. Even after the August 1941 massacre, individual Hungarian Jews made their way to Kam'ianets'-Podil's'kyi; Yigal Zafoni, "Bibliography on the Holocaust for those Regions of the Soviet Union Occupied by German Forces from June 1941," *Journal of the Academic Proceedings of Soviet Jewry,* Vol. 1, no. 1 (1986), pp. 82–103, here p. 88.

46. Andrej Angrick, *Besatzungspolitik und Massenmord: Die Einsatzgruppe D in der südlichen Sowjetunion 1941–1943* (Hamburg: Hamburger Edition, 2003), pp. 225ff.; Ralf Ogorreck, *Die Einsatzgruppen und die Genesis der "Endlösung,"* (Berlin: Metropol, 1996), pp. 204ff.

47. BA-B, R 58/216, EM 52, August 14, 1941; EM 81, September 12, 1941.

48. BA-B, R 58/216, EM 58, August 20, 1941.

49. This was also the thesis of a presentation given by Hans Safrian on April 11, 1998, at a conference held by the University of Florida at Gainesville.

50. *Der Dienstkalender Heinrich Himmlers 1941/42*, Peter Witte et al., eds. (Hamburg: Christians, 1999), p. 224f., entries covering October 2–4, 1941.

51. BA-B, R 58/218, EM 111, October 12, 1941.

52. Klein, *Einsatzgruppen*, p. 232.

53. Gerlach, *Kalkulierte Morde*, pp. 574ff. The heavily industrialized Donets' Basin and Kharkiv were the only exceptions.

54. Nuremberg Document PS-2174, Bericht der Rüstungsinspektion Ukraine, November 29, 1941.

55. Angrick, *Besatzungspolitik und Massenmord*, pp. 172ff.

56. AOK 17 Ic/AO, September 22, 1941, "SD commando IVb is requested [to conduct] reprisal actions against Kremenchuk Jews." See also Manfred Oldenburg, *Ideologie und militärisches Kalkül: Die Besatzungspolitik der Wehrmacht in der Sowjetunion 1942* (Cologne, Vienna: Böhlau, 2004), p. 255; Breitman, *Official Secrets*, pp. 98f.; BA-MA, RH 26–97/100, Tätigkeitsbericht 97. ID/Ic, November 13, 1941.

57. For example, BA-MA, RW 31/138, p. 211, Wirtschaftsstab Ost, July 15, 1941.

58. Helmuth Groscurth, *Tagebücher eines Abwehroffiziers*, Helmut Krausnick et al., eds. (Stuttgart: Deutsche Verlags-Anstalt, 1970), pp. 534–542.

59. Erlass, Oberkommando der Wehrmacht, September 12, 1941, printed in Norbert Müller, ed., *Deutsche Besatzungspolitik in der UdSSR* (Cologne: Pahl-Rugenstein, 1980), p. 72.

60. BA-B, R 94/26, pp. 28–38, Abschrift Lagebericht 454. Sich.Div./VII, September 23, 1941.

61. Tätigkeitsbericht Gruppe Ic/AO AOK 6, September 2, 1941, in Helmut Krausnick and Hans-Heinrich Wilhelm, *Die Truppe des Weltanschauungskrieges: Die Einsatzgruppen der Sicherheitspolizei und des SD 1938–1942* (Stuttgart: Deutsche Verlags-Anstalt, 1981), p. 243.

62. Krausnick and Wilhelm, *Truppe des Weltanschauungskrieges*, p. 258.

63. Order of the commander in chief of the 17th Army, Hermann Hoth, Verhalten der Truppe im Ostraum, November 17, 1941, printed in Gerd R. Ueberschär and Wolfram Wette, eds., *"Unternehmen Barbarossa." Der deutsche Überfall auf die Sowjetunion 1941* (Paderborn: Schöningh, 1984), pp. 341ff.

64. For example, BA-B, R 58/215, EM 47, August 9, 1941, contains a message from HSSPF Russia South to Army Group South on mass shootings in the Shepetivka area. Additional antisemitic statements by Rundstedt can be found in Detlef Vogel, "Generalfeldmarschall von Rundstedt," in Gerd R. Ueberschär, ed., *Hitlers militärische Elite. Von den Anfängen des Regimes bis Kriegsbeginn* (Darmstadt: Primus, 1998), pp. 223–233, here p. 229. See also Charles Messenger, *The Last Prussian. A Biography of Field Marshal Gerd von Rundstedt, 1875–1953* (London: Brassey, 1991), p. 145ff.

65. Jürgen Förster, "Die Sicherung des 'Lebensraumes,'" in *Das Deutsche Reich und der Zweite Weltkrieg*, Band 4, pp. 1,030–1,078, here p. 1,051.

66. Tsentral'nyi Derzhavnyi Arkhiv Vyshchykh Orhaniv Ukraïny (TsDAVO) in Kiev, R-3833/2/104, p. 6, Ukraïns'ka presova sluzhba, July 30, 1941.

67. Wendy Lower, *Nazi Empire-Building and the Holocaust in Ukraine* (Chapel Hill: University of North Carolina Press, 2005), pp. 69ff.

68. Ogorreck, *Einsatzgruppen*, pp. 202f.

69. BA-B, R 58/218, EM 106, October 7, 1941, printed in Jörg Friedrich, *Das Gesetz des Krieges. Das deutsche Heer in Russland 1941 bis 1945* (Munich: Piper, 1993), p. 793.

70. BA-MA, RH 22/204, Lagebericht FK 197/VII, September 20, 1941.

71. Wila Orbach, "The Destruction of the Jews in the Nazi-Occupied Terri-

tories of the USSR," *Soviet Jewish Affairs*, Vol. 6, no. 2 (1976), pp. 14–51, here p. 51. Spector, "The Holocaust of Ukrainian Jews," p. 47, and Leni Yahil, *The Holocaust* (New York: Oxford University Press, 1990), p. 272, speak of much higher figures and later shootings.

72. Browning, *Ganz normale Männer*, p. 38

73. Lower, *Nazi Empire-Building*, pp. 76f.; this massacre is not fully described in the Einsatzgruppen Reports on Events in the USSR. Likewise, the Prosecutor's Office Regensburg, in an indictment in the case I 4 Js 1495/65 ./. Rosenbauer u.a., dated February 2, 1970, assumes 1,000–3,000 Jews were murdered on September 12, 1941, p. 39. Different figures are to be found in Orbach, "Destruction of the Jews," pp. 32–36; Ilya Ehrenburg and Vasily Grossman, *The Complete Black Book of Russian Jewry*, David Patterson, ed., (New Brunswick, NJ, and London: Transaction, 2002), pp. 15–18. Additional accounts of events in Berdychiv are contained in Breitman, *Official Secrets*, p. 65, and S. Ia. Elisavetskii, *Berdichevskaia tragediia. Dokumental'noe povestvovanie* (Kiev: UkrNIINTI, 1991); more problematic, Carol and John Garrard, *The Bones of Berdichev* (New York: Free Press, 1996). Yehoshua Büchler, "Kommandostab Reichsführer-SS Himmler's Personal Murder Brigades in 1941," *Holocaust and Genocide Studies*, Vol. 1, no. 1 (1986), pp. 11–25, here p. 21, notes the presence of units from the 1st SS Brigade in the immediate vicinity of Berdychiv on September 14, 1941, as well.

74. See Karel Berkhoff's contribution to this volume.

75. Gerlach, in *Kalkulierte Morde*, p. 595, argued that an approximate number of victims based on the city's catastrophic food and housing situation might even have been predetermined for Kiev.

76. BA-MA, RH 22/7, Berück Süd/Ia an OKH/Kriegsverwaltung, September 30, 1941.

77. The Germans continued to kill Jews at Babi Yar after the first massacre. In all, the total number of Jews killed at the site could be as high as 50,000; see Orbach, "Destruction of the Jews," pp. 39f. A census showed only 20 Jews in the city as of April 1, 1942; A. L. Perkovskii, "Istochniki po natsional'nomu sostavu naseleniia Ukrainy v 1939–1944 gg.," in *Liudskie poteri SSSR v period vtoroi mirovoi voiny* (St. Peterburg: Rossiiskaia Akademiia Nauk, Otdelenie Istorii, 1995), pp. 49–61, here p. 56.

78. Wiedemann, *Führerwille und Eigeninitiative*, pp. 109f.

79. BA-MA, RH 20–6/494, Ic/AO, AOK 6, November 6, 1941; on provisioning, see USHMM, RG-11.001 (Osobyi), Reel 92, 1275–3–670, p. 9, Berück Süd an 444. Sich.Div., December 25, 1941.

80. Complete census material is to be found at USHMM, RG-31.010M (Derzhavnyi Arkhiv Kharkivs'koï Oblasti), Reels 1–21, 2982–4–52–129 and 2982–6–1–95; cf. Raul Hilberg, *Täter, Opfer, Zuschauer. Die Vernichtung der Juden 1933–1945* (Frankfurt am Main: Fischer, 1992), pp. 107 and 308; Iu. M. Liakhovitskii, ed., *Poprannaia mezuza. Kniga Drobitskogo Iara* (Kharkiv: Osnova, 1991), pp. 36ff.; idem, ed., *Kholokost na Ukraine i antisemitizm v perspective* (Kharkiv: Bensiakh, 1992), pp. 91–148; idem, *Perezhivshie katastrofu. Spasshiesia, spasiteli, kollaboranty, martirolog: svidetel'stva, fakty, dokumenty* (Kharkiv, Jerusalem: Biblioteka gazety Bensiakh, 1996).

81. BA-B, R 58/219, EM 156, January 16, 1942, and EM 164, February 4, 1942.

82. Korsemann was presumably also involved in preparing the murder of Kiev's Jews, Ogorreck, *Einsatzgruppen*, p. 321.

83. USHMM, RG-11.001 (Osobyi), Reel 80, 1323–1–53, pp. 65f., Rundschreiben HSSPF beim RKU, January 5, 1942.

84. A. I. Kruglov, "Istreblenie evreiskogo naseleniia na levoberezhnoi Ukraine," in Ielisavets'kyi, ed., *Katastrofa ta opir*, pp. 172–201; Ehrenburg and Grossman, *Black Book*, pp. 37f.; *Neizvestnaia chernaia kniga* (Jerusalem, Moscow:

Yad Vashem, 1993), pp. 86ff. The "unknown black book" contains material not found in *The Black Book*.

85. Hilberg, *Täter*, p. 222; *Verbrechen der Wehrmacht*, pp. 328–346. On Kiev, Nicholas G. Bohatiuk, "The Economy of Kiev Under Foreign Conquerors, 1941–1944," *Ukrainian Quarterly*, Vol. 42, no. ½ (1986), pp. 35–58.

86. This killing operation is not mentioned in the Reports on Events in the USSR; see Dean, "German *Gendarmerie*," p. 174; *Nazi Crimes in the Ukraine 1941–1944. Documents and Materials* (Kiev: Naukova Dumka, 1987), p. 149; and BA-B, NS 33/293, p. 58, HSSPF Russland-Süd an Kdo.-Stab RFSS, September 19, 1941. It has not been determined which Orpo unit carried out this massacre: Police Battalion 69, as noted in Ernst Klee, Willi Dressen, and Volker Riess, eds. *"Schöne Zeiten." Judenmord aus der Sicht der Täter und Gaffer* (Frankfurt am Main: Fischer, 1988), pp. 79, 116, and 120; or Police Battalions 45 and 314, as recorded in Browning, *Ganz normale Männer*, p. 38.

87. USHMM, RG-31.012, Verfahren Bezirksgericht Halle, diary entry in testimony of R.M., February 9, 1978.

88. USHMM, RG-11.001 (Osobyi), Reel 92, 1275-3-666, Bericht FK 240/VII, October 19, 1941; see a report compiled by Germany's coordinating office for the investigation of Nazi era crimes, Central Office of the Judicial Authorities of the Federal States for Investigation of National Socialist Crimes, Ludwigsburg (now a branch of the Bundesarchiv, hereafter BA-L), 114 AR-Z 67/67, "NS-Verbrechen im ehemaligen Generalkommissariat Dnjepropetrowsk," Vol. 1, pp. 33ff.

89. Krausnick and Wilhelm, *Truppe des Weltanschauungskrieges*, pp. 243f.; USHMM, RG-11.001 (Osobyi), Reel 92, 1275-2-661, p. 59, Lagebericht Dnepropetrovsk, November 15, 1941; see also Ehrenburg and Grossman, *Black Book*, pp. 42f. The exact number of victims was close to 13,000. Hungarian troops were also informed; Gerald Reitlinger, *Die Endlösung*, 5th edition (Berlin: Colloquium, 1979), p. 265.

90. Judgment, LG Düsseldorf I 21/73 S ./. Günther Herrmann u.a., January 12, 1973, p. 260; see also Tätigkeits- und Lagebericht der Einsatzgruppen für März 1942 in Klein, ed., *Einsatzgruppen*, p. 309.

91. *Nazi Crimes in the Ukraine*, p. 143; Zafoni, "Bibliography on the Holocaust," p. 102, says the killing took place on March 24; USHMM, RG-22.002M, Reel 1, Report of the Investigation Committee for Zaporizhzhia says March 21.

92. Orbach, "Destruction of the Jews," p. 44.

93. Anweisung des Berück Süd, March 20, 1942, printed in Müller, *Deutsche Besatzungspolitik*, p. 91; here the enlistment of the Wehrmacht to cordon off the killing site is foreseen. See also BA-L, Abschlussbericht Exekutionen des Sonderkommandos 4a der Einsatzgruppe C, December 30, 1964, pp. 104–107, 284–304. Sk Plath also had to file reports to Rear Area Army Group South, BA-B, R 70 SU/18, pp. 104f., Soko an Berück B, August 15, 1942.

94. BA-MA, RH 22/204, Berück Süd an FK 197, May 10, 1942.

95. Quote from BA-MA, RH 22/204, Lagebericht FK 197/VII, April 20, 1942; Lagebericht FK 197/VII, June 19, 1942; see also Orbach, "Destruction of the Jews," p. 45.

96. TsDAVO, R-3206/2/26, pp. 27–42, Reisebericht Prof. Grünberg (RKU IIIg) vom 13.8.-3.9.1942, September 10, 1942; BA-MA, RH 22/206, Lagebericht Oberfeldkommandantur Donez, September 24, 1942.

97. BA-MA, RH 22/98, pp. 271–276, Besichtigungsreise des Berück im Einsatzraum der 403. Sich.Div., September, 15, 1942; ibid., pp. 282–298, Besichtigungsreise des Berück, 6.-16.9.1942.

98. BA-MA, RH 22/204, Lagebericht Sich.Div. 403/VII, October 23, 1942.

99. BA-B, R 6/302, p. 45, Übergabeverhandlung Berück/VII an RKU, August 27, 1942.

100. USHMM, RG-11.001 (Osobyi), Reel 92, 1275-3-664, Bericht Ortskommandantur 829 (Novoukraïnka), September 14, 1941, where a "clearing up" is announced; also, RH 22/201, Monatsbericht FK 239/VII, February 16, 1942: "A definitive solution of the question by the police battalion in Myrhorod is in view."

101. Dean, "German *Gendarmerie*," p. 175.

102. BA-B, R 58/217, EM 80, September 11, 1941; BA-B, R 58/219, EM 135, November 19, 1941.

103. Truman Oliver Anderson III, *The Conduct of Reprisals by the German Army of Occupation in Southern USSR, 1941–1943*. PhD diss., University of Chicago 1995, pp. 227ff.; Truman Oliver Anderson III, "Die 62. Infantrie-Division. Repressalien im Heeresgebiet Süd, Oktober bis Dezember 1941," in Heer and Naumann, *Vernichtungskrieg*, pp. 297–314. Additional evidence has emerged from the practice of military administration commands turning over valuables after killings; Martin C. Dean, "Jewish Property Seized in the Occupied Soviet Union in 1941 and 1942. The Records of the Reichshauptkasse Beutestelle," *Holocaust and Genocide Studies*, Vol. 14, no. 1 (2000), pp. 83–101.

104. BA-MA, RH 22/203, Lagebericht FK 194 (Novhorod-Sivers'kyi), February 11, 1942.

105. BA-MA, RH 22/204, Bericht FK 198 über Rajon Krasnokutsk, February 24, 1942.

106. Krisztián Ungváry, "Ungarische Besatzungskräfte in der Ukraine 1941–1942," *Ungarn-Jahrbuch*, 26 (2002/2003), pp. 125–163, and BA-MA, RH 22/3, KTB, Berück Süd, December 22, 1941.

107. Klaus Gessner, *Geheime Feldpolizei* (Berlin: Militärverlag der DDR, 1986), pp. 83 and 142ff.; a report by the Zentrale Stelle, "Neue Erkenntnisse über die Geheime Feldpolizei, Einsatz Südrussland," February 13, 1968, looks into GFP groups 1, 626, 647, 706, 708, 719, 720, 721, 725, 730, and 739; see in particular Anderson, "Conduct of Reprisals," p. 221; Boll and Safrian, "Auf dem Weg nach Stalingrad," p. 275; BA-MA, RH 22/204, Lagebericht FK 197/VII, December 15, 1941.

108. Peter Lieb, "Täter aus Überzeugung? Oberst Carl von Adrian und die Judenmorde der 707. Infanteriedivision 1941/42," *Vierteljahrshefte für Zeitgeschichte*, 50 (2002), pp. 523–557.

109. Yaakov Lozowick, "Rollbahn Mord. The Early Activities of Einsatzgruppe C," *Holocaust and Genocide Studies*, Vol. 2, no. 2 (1987), pp. 221–242; Dieter Pohl, "Die Einsatzgruppe C." Sk 7b of Einsatzgruppe B murdered Jews in the Chernihiv area in September 1941, Klein, *Einsatzgruppen*, p. 230.

110. Judgment, LG Düsseldorf in 8 I Ks 1/66 ./. Jung u.a., August 5, 1966, printed in *Justiz und NS-Verbrechen*, Vol. XXIV (Amsterdam: Amsterdam University Press, 1979), no. 636.

111. This phrase borrows from the title of Klaus-Michael Mallmann, "Vom Fussvolk der 'Endlösung'. Ordnungspolizei, Ostkrieg und Judenmord," *Tel Aviver Jahrbuch für deutsche Geschichte*, Vol. 26 (1997), pp. 355–391.

112. On shootings by Pol. Batl. 82 in Chervone, see BA-MA, Film 59103, KTB 454. Sich.Div., 31.8.1941 and Judgment, Bezirksgericht Neubrandenburg ./. Johannes P., 1981, printed in *DDR-Justiz und NS-Verbrechen*, Vol. I (Amsterdam: Amsterdam University Press, 2002), no. 1013. Concerning shootings by Pol. Batl. 311 near Pavlohrad, see BA-MA, RH 26–444/6 and Prosecutor's Office Stuttgart 84 Js 79/73.

113. USHMM, RG-22.002M (Gosudarstvennyi Archiv Rossiiskoi Federatsii), 7021-148-101, p. 75, Runderlass des Chefs der Ordnungspolizei, January 13, 1942.

114. TsDAVO, R-3206/1/110, pp. 1ff., Geschäftsverteilungsplan RKU zum 1.1.1942; TsDAVO, R-3206/2/36, p. 18, Personalverzeichnis RKU, undated.

115. TsDAVO, R-3206/1/72, p. 7, Besetzung der GK zum 15.2.1942.

116. TsDAVO, R-3206/1/69, RKU/IIc an GK Wolhynien-Podolien, September 5, 1941; see also Sh. Spector, "Getaot v Yudenratim b Shtahei HaKibush HaNazi b Brit HaMoazot (b Gvulot September 1939)," in *Shevut* 1991, pp. 263–276.

117. TsDAVO, R-3206/1/65, Rundschreiben RKU/III, February 20, 1942.

118. Sandkühler, *"Endlösung" in Galizien*, pp. 63ff.

119. Rosenberg's statement of October 14, 1941 is printed in Werner Präg and Wolfgang Jacobmeyer, eds., *Das Diensttagebuch des deutschen Generalgouverneurs in Polen 1939–1945* (Stuttgart: Deutsche Verlags-Anstalt, 1975), p. 413; Hitler's suggestion, made on October 29, 1941, is recorded in Werner Jochmann, ed., *Adolf Hitler. Monologe im Führerhauptquartier* (Hamburg: Knaus, 1980), p. 113.

120. Peter Longerich, ed., *Die Ermordung der europäischen Juden* (Munich: Piper, 1989), p. 173. The background for a trip to Lublin by Prützmann on January 18, 1942, to visit Odilo Globocnik, who was then building death camps, remains unknown. I thank Christian Gerlach for this reference. A concentration camp for Kiev was in planning: Pohl an Himmler, April 30, 1942, Document R-129, printed in *Der Prozess gegen die Hauptkriegsverbrecher vor dem Internationalen Militärgerichsthof*, Blue Series, Vol. 38 (Nuremberg, 1947–1949), pp. 363 ff. The camp in the Syrets'k district of Kiev was mainly for POWs but some Jews were kept there. A death camp was indeed planned for Mogilev in Belarus; see Christian Gerlach, "Failure of Plans for an SS Extermination Camp in Mogilev, Belorussia," *Holocaust and Genocide Studies*, Vol. 11, no. 1 (1997), pp. 60–78.

121. USHMM, Derzhavnyi Archiv Zhytomyrs'koï Oblasti, 1151-1-137, p. 8, Runderlass RKU, January 12, 1942; BA-L, II 204 AR-Z 21/58, Vol. 9, p. 219, questioning of Kurt Syplie, November 27, 1959. I thank Wendy Lower and Christian Gerlach for this reference. Similar rumors circulated in L'viv in late 1941, Sandkühler, *"Endlösung" in Galizien*, p. 156.

122. BA-B, R 58/219, EM 132, November 14, 1941. The original report from Einsatzgruppe C must have been filed several days earlier.

123. Spector, *Holocaust*, pp. 111f.; *Encyclopaedia Judaica* (Jerusalem: Encyclopaedia Judaica, 1971), Vol. 12, Col. 1,513f.

124. Gerlach, *Kalkulierte Morde*, pp. 585ff.; Pohl, *Judenverfolgung*, pp. 139ff.

125. Gerlach, "Wirtschaftsinteressen," p. 283.

126. Spector, *Holocaust*, pp. 113–115; BA-B, R 58/219, EM 143, December 8, 1941; see also the Rivne case at BA-L, 204 AR-Z 48/58 (Zentralstelle Dortmund, 45 Js 7/61) ./. Wiemer u.a.). The number of victims was general knowledge to German soldiers serving in the region at the time; see interrogation of German POW Wilhelm Sudbrack printed in Ehrenburg and Grossman, *Black Book*, pp. 578f. After excavating the site in 1944, Soviet officials estimated the number of corpses to be around 17,500; *Nazi Crimes in the Ukraine*, p. 131.

127. IfZ, MA 1569/15, questioning of Otto Oelhafen, May 7 and 28, 1947; Oelhafen's final message to the HSSPF on November 9, 1941, was intercepted by British intelligence, Public Records Office, HW 16/32 (I thank Steve Tyas for this reference); BA-L, 204 AR-Z 48/58, Vol. I, pp. 60–78, questioning of Hans P., March 16, 1959; as well as questioning of Kristina Novakovska, who escaped from Sosenki, November 30, 1944, contained in Yitzhak Arad, ed., *Unichtozhenie evreev v SSSR v gody nemetskoi okkupatsii (1941–1944). Sbornik dokumentov i materialov* (Jerusalem: Yad Vashem, 1992), pp. 151f.; see also Barbara Baratz, *Flucht vor dem Schicksal. Holocaust-Erinnerungen aus der Ukraine 1941–1944* (Darmstadt: Darmstädter Blätter, 1984), pp. 64ff.

128. Spector, *Holocaust*, p. 112.

129. Einsatzgruppe C, which operated almost solely in Ukraine, reported some 108,000 victims in Ukraine, Einsatzgruppe D 75,000–80,000 victims. In addition, there were the massacres carried out by the Orpo but not mentioned in the Reports on Events in the USSR, at least 6,000 victims of the 1st SS Brigade, and the murders committed by the Secret Field Police and other army units.

130. At the Wannsee Conference in January 1942, the number of Jewish inhabitants given for Ukraine was 2,994,684 Jews. The figure is probably based on numbers provided by Ukrainian émigrés and the RKU envisioned by Rosenberg in May 1941. The number can only be considered fictitious, consisting of census data from 1939 (1,553,000) plus overestimated figures for Volhynia (ca. 300,000), eastern Galicia (ca. 670,000), and the territories annexed by the Soviet Union from Romania. In any event, the figure is too high.

131. The report omits the killing of men during the invasion's first weeks.

132. Nuremberg Document PS-2174, Bericht Prof. Seraphim mit Anschreiben der Rüstungsinspektion Ukraine, November 29 and December 2, 1941, merged in Nuremberg Document PS-3257 and printed in *Prozess gegen die Hauptkriegsverbrecher*, Vol. 32, pp. 73f. By the time the report was written, the Wehrmacht had made two more transfers of territory to the RKU so that the territory in question extended to the Dniepr.

133. Nuremberg Document PS-3666, Bräutigam an Lohse, December 18, 1941, printed in *Prozess gegen die Hauptkriegsverbrecher*, Band 32, p. 437.

134. BA-B, R 6/69, pp. 157–169.

135. BA-MA, Film 59104, Befehl Berück Süd/Qu, around September 19, 1941; USHMM, RG-11.001 (Osobyi), Reel 92, 1275-3-662, FK 675/VII an 444. Sich.Div., August 11, 1941. For a more thorough discussion of DG IV, see Andrej Angrick's contribution to this volume.

136. The civil administration in September 1941 sent a senior construction official to Uman' to take over an additional stretch of the road, TsDAVO R-3206/2/164, p. 49, Bericht GK Brest/IV, September 12, 1941.

137. BA-MA, RH 22/3, KTB Berück Süd, September 18, 1941.

138. *Dienstkalender Himmlers*, p. 298, entries for December 24–26, 1941.

139. *Dienstkalender Himmlers*, pp. 339ff. and 355f. entries for February 7 and 19, 1942; Hermann Kaienburg, "Jüdische Arbeitslager an der 'Strasse der SS,'" *Zeitschrift für Sozialgeschichte des 20. und 21. Jahrhunderts*, Vol. 11, no. 1 (1996), pp. 13–39; BA-B, R 6/18, pp. 67–68, Vermerk RMfbO (gez. Labs), March 9, 1942.

140. TsDAVO, R-3206/1/110, p. 5, Geschäftsverteilungsplan RKU zum 1.1.1942.

141. Bomhard an Daluege December 15, 1942. See also Bernd Gottberg, *Die höheren SS- und Polizeiführer im Okkupationsregime des faschistischen deutschen Imperialismus in den zeitweilig besetzten Gebieten der Sowjetunion 1941 bis 1944*, unpubl. diss., Berlin 1984, p. 72; Martin Hölzl, "Grüner Rock und weisse Weste: Adolf von Bomhard und die Legende von der sauberen Ordnungspolizei," *Zeitschrift für Geschichtswissenschaft*, Vol. 50, no. 1 (2002), pp. 22–43.

142. TsDAVO, R-3206/1/2, pp. 7f., Befehl WBU/Ia, October 10, 1941. On October 17, 1941, the WBU endorsed Reichenau's order; Förster, "Sicherung," p. 1,051.

143. BA-B, NS 19/1798, Fernschreiben Krüger an Himmler, October 9, 1942.

144. The Ukrainian translation of a decree dated June 1, 1941, from the city commandant of Kiev requesting the addresses of Jews is provided in *Nimets'ko-fashysts'kyi okupatsiinyi rezhym na Ukraïni (1941–1944): Zbyrnik dokumentiv i materialiv* (Kiev: Naukova Dumka, 1963), p. 104.

145. Verordnung über Meldepflichten und Aufenthaltsbeschränkungen in den besetzten Ostgebieten, December 19, 1941.

146. TsDAVO, R-3206/2/14, pp. 5ff., Runderlass des RKU über Polizeikompetenzen, March 1, 1942, printed in Ukrainian in *Nimets'ko-fashysts'kyi okupatsiinyi rezhym*, pp. 92ff.

147. BA-Zwischenarchiv Dahlwitz-Hoppegarten (BA-DH), FW 490, A. 27, p. 2, BdS Ukraine an SSPF Shitomir, February 2, 1942 (Zur Kenntnisnahme an alle Gebietskommissare, February 10, 1942). I thank Christian Gerlach for this reference.

148. BA-Koblenz, ZSg. 144/2, Rundschreiben Heydrichs an alle BdS, January 25, 1942. On the debate surrounding the "Brown Folder for Ukraine," Nuremberg Document NO-4882, Heydrich an Rosenberg, January 10, 1942; Himmler an Rosenberg, ca. February 3, 1942, quoted in Yitzhak Arad, "Alfred Rosenberg and the 'Final Solution' in the Occupied Soviet Territories," *Yad Vashem Studies*, Vol. 13 (1973), pp. 263–286, here, pp. 281f.

149. BA-B, R 43 II/684a, pp. 139ff., Denkschrift Rosenbergs (ca. Mai 1942); Heydrich an Rosenberg, May 17, 1942, printed in Hans Buchheim, Martin Broszat, Hans-Adolf Jacobsen, and Helmut Krausnick, eds., *Anatomie des SS-Staates*, Vol. 1 (Munich: Deutscher Taschenbuch Verlag, 1979), pp. 87f.

150. Ehrenburg and Grossman, *Black Book*, pp. 24f.

151. TsDAVO, R-3637/4/116, pp. 28ff. Reichssicherheitsdienst, Sicherungsgruppe Eichenhain an Rattenhuber, January 12, 1942, quote from May 16, 1942. Cf. BA-L, II 204a AR-Z 4/69; Prosecutor's Office Munich, I 111 Js 2/69.

152. TsDAVO, R-3637/4/116, p. 56, KdS Shitomir an KdS-ASt. Winniza, July 11, 1942.

153. TsDAVO, R-3637/4/116, Reichssicherheitsdienst, Sicherungsgruppe Eichenhain an Rattenhuber, undated (after January 12, 1942).

154. Ancel, *Romanian Campaigns*, pp. 116ff. addresses this operation, but discusses only Romanian participation. Himmler had the *Volksdeutsche Mittelstelle*, one of the many main offices under his purview, set up Sonderkommander R for the invasion of the Soviet Union, see Robert Koehl, *RKFDV: German Resettlement and Population Policy, 1939–1945* (Cambridge: Harvard University Press, 1957), p. 64.

155. TsDAVO, R-3676/4/317, p. 71, fragment of a situation report from BdO Ukraine (gez. Müller-Brunkhorst), ca. March 1942 (title page missing); cf. the witness I. Butovetskii, in Arad, *Unichtozhenie*, pp. 246–249. On the killing of Jews by the Kamenka County Commissar in March 1942, see Yitzhak Arad, "Der Holocaust an den sowjetischen Juden in den besetzten Gebieten der Sowjetunion," in Ilja Ehrenburg and Wassilij Grossman, *Das Schwarzbuch. Der Genozid an den sowjetischen Juden*, Yitzhak Arad and Arno Lustiger, eds. (Reinbek: Rowohlt, 1994), pp. 1,044f. Zlatopil' was located in Mala Vys'ka County.

156. Centre de Documentation Juive Contemporaine in Paris, CXLIV-474, Lagebericht GK Nikolajew für Februar 1942, February 24, 1942; quote from Lagebericht GK Nikolajew für April 1942, undated.

157. BA-B, R 58/221, EM 191, April 12, 1942.

158. Pohl, *Judenverfolgung*, pp. 206ff.

159. On Heydrich's trip through the eastern territories in April 1942, see Klein, *Einsatzgruppen*, pp. 406ff. The Gestapo chief at KdS Kiev after November 1941, Hans Schumacher, told investigators on November 7, 1973, that Max Thomas, BdS Ukraine, received instructions from Heydrich to murder Jews, see BA-L, 213 AR-Z 370/59.

160. Gerlach, *Kalkulierte Morde*, p. 689.

161. BA-B, R 6/243, pp. 9–12, Niederschrift Tagung HA III GK Wolhynien 27.-29.3.1942, April 13, 1942, when General Commissar Heinrich Schoene spoke on the "Jewish question."

162. Spector, *Holocaust*, pp. 180 and 184; *Encyclopaedia Judaica*, Vol. 6, Col. 249ff. and Vol. 10, Col. 202f.; Orbach, "Destruction of the Jews," p. 47; Dean, "German Gendarmerie," p. 182; BA-B, R 6/310, p. 17, Lagebericht GK Shitomir, June 3, 1942. *Encyclopaedia Judaica*, Vol. 10, Col. 1,228f., dates the liquidation of the Kovel' ghetto to July 22, 1942, but BA-B, R 94/6, Lagebericht Stadtkommissar Brest, says July 12, 1942.

163. Müller an KdS Litauen, May 18, 1942, printed in Klein, *Einsatzgruppen*, pp. 410ff.

164. Spector, *Holocaust*, pp. 184f.

165. Judgment, LG Berlin 3 PKs 1/57 ./. Knop u.a., March 9, 1960, printed in *Justiz und NS-Verbrechen*, Vol. XVI, no. 490; cf. Michel Mazor, "La fin de Ber-ditschew," *Monde Juif*, Vol. 25, no. 55 (1969), pp. 21–25. Ehrenburg and Grossman, *Black Book*, p. 19, cite as the date June 15, 1942.

166. Instytut Pamięci Narodowej (IPN), Zbiór zespołów szczątkowych jednos-tek SS i policji, no. 77, pp. 1–10, Meldungen KdS-ASt. Kamenez-Podolsk, August 6, 1942, KdS Rowno, August 15 and 17, 1942, ASt. Kamenez Podolsk, August 13, 1942, Meldung KdS Rowno, August 20, 1942; Gendarmerie Bar an KdS Rowno, August 27, 1942; letter from Technical Sergeant of the Gendarmerie Jacob printed in Klee, Dressen, and Riess, eds., *"Schöne Zeiten,"* pp. 149–151.

167. *Encyclopaedia Judaica*, Vol. 11, Col. 589; Spector, *Holocaust*, p. 177. Jews were also brought from various locations via trains to a central killing site near Sarny and shot, Spector, *Holocaust*, p. 179.

168. Christian Gerlach, "Die Bedeutung der deutschen Ernährungspolitik für die Beschleunigung des Mordes an den Juden 1942," in Gerlach, *Krieg, Ernährung, Völkermord*, pp. 167–257, here pp. 240ff.

169. BA-B, R 6/243, pp. 20ff., Niederschrift Tagung HA III GK Wolhynien 28.-31.8.42, September 4, 1942; quote from IPN, Zbiór zespołów szczątkowych, no. 77, KdS Wolhynien-Podolien an KdS-ASt., August 31, 1942.

170. IPN, Zbiór zespołów szczątkowych, no. 77, p. 7, GK Wolhynien an RKU, August 25, 1942.

171. Dean, "German *Gendarmerie*," p. 184.

172. IPN, Zbiór zespołów szczątkowych, no. 77, p. 7, SSPF Wolhynien-Podolien an RKU, August 31, 1942.

173. BA-B, R 58/222, Meldungen aus den besetzten Ostgebieten, no. 12, July 17, 1942, and *Enzyklopädie des Holocaust* (Berlin: Argon, 1992), p. 1,611. Events in the ghetto of Lokache (southeast of Volodymyr-Volyns'kyi) around September 9, 1942 are described in detail in Michael Diment, *The Lone Survivor. A Diary of Lukacze Ghetto and Svyniukhy, Ukraine* (New York: Holocaust Library, 1992), pp. 106–147.

174. *Enzyklopädie des Holocaust*, p. 373. See also Hermann Gräbe's witness statement printed in Reitlinger, *Endlösung*, pp. 231–233, and Bericht des Rüstungs-kommandos in Luts'k printed in Raul Hilberg, *Die Vernichtung der europäischen Juden* (Frankfurt: S. Fischer 1990), p. 400.

175. *Encyclopaedia Judaica*, Vol. 11, Col. 629f.; *The Memorial Book of a Vanished Shtetl* (Hoboken: KTAV Publishing House, 1997).

176. *Nazi Crimes in the Ukraine*, pp. 135 and 160.

177. BA-B, R 6/70, p. 49, Beobachtungen bei den Gebietskommissaren in der westlichen Ukraine, September 1, 1942 (presumably by Otto Bräutigam).

178. BA-B, 11.01/17, pp. 6f., 175, Lagebericht GK Nikolajew, October 30, 1942.

179. BA-B, R 6/243, Niederschrift Tagung HA III GK Wolhynien 30.10.1942, November 11, 1942.

180. Spector, *Holocaust*, p. 186; Kruglov, *Unichtozhenie*, p. 79; BA-B, NS 19/2566, Meldung über "Bandenbekämpfungserfolge" HSSPF Russland-Süd, Ukraine und Nordost, December 26, 1942, which for the period from August until the end of November reports the murder of 363,000 Jews. This figure includes victims from Białystok Region in East Prussia and from the Belarusian parts of the RKU. De-ducting for these regions leaves 180,000 to 190,000 victims on the Soviet Ukrai-nian territory of GK Volhynia-Podolia; Gerlach, *Kalkulierte Morde*, p. 723.

181. Centre de Documentation Juive Contemporaine, CXLVIIa-29, Lagebericht GK Wolhynien-Podolien, December 31, 1942.

182. Zentralstelle Dortmund, 45 Js 31/61 ./. Körting u.a., p. 118, Verfügung December 20, 1968.

183. Concerning crimes on DG IV, see BA-L, 213 AR-Z 20/63, Prosecutor's Of-fice Lübeck, Abschlussvermerk, May 26, 1970; Kaienburg, "Jüdische Arbeitslager."

Additional camp liquidations took place in March, May, and December 1943. On Khmil'nyk, see Ehrenburg and Grossman, *Black Book*, pp. 25f. (March 3, 1943). The *Polizeisicherungsabteilung* was a special four-company unit set up by the Order Police Main Office for the DG IV project.

184. BA-MA, RH 2/2559, p. 151, Informationsbericht Organisation Todt Russland-Süd, here October 18, 1943.

185. Martin Broszat, "Die jüdischen Arbeitskompanien in Ungarn," in *Gutachten des Instituts für Zeitgeschichte*, Vol. 1 (Munich: Institut für Zeitgeschichte, 1959), pp. 200–214; Randolph L. Braham, *The Hungarian Labor Service System, 1939–1945* (New York: East European Publications, 1977), pp. 25ff.; Braham, ed., *The Wartime System of Labor Service in Hungary* (Boulder, CO: East European Publications, 1995).

186. BA-MA, RH 22/90, p. 23, FK 197 an Berück Süd, July 30, 1942, on such units in Konotop; Orientierung über ungar. Abeits-Bataillone, AOK 2, May 11, 1942, printed in Ernst Klee and Willi Dressen, eds., *"Gott mit uns." Der deutsche Vernichtungskrieg im Osten* (Frankfurt am Main: Fischer, 1989), p. 114.

187. TsDAVO, R-3637/4/480, p. 195, FS RKU an RMfbO, May 25, 1943; cf. O. I. Kruhlov, "Znyshchennia fashystamy inozemnykh hromadian na okupovanii terytoriï Ukraïny (1941–1944 rr.)," *Ukraïns'kyi istorychnyi zhurnal*, no. 5 (1989), pp. 82–87, here p. 84. It is possible that two different fires are being described here. A list of all 34,000 missing Hungarian Jews is given in Gavriel Bar Shaked, ed., *Nevek Munkaszázadok Veszteségei a keleti Magyar hadmüveteli területeken, Names of Victims of Hungarian Labour Battalions*, 2 Volumes (New York, Jerusalem: Yad Vashem, [1992]).

188. Prosecutor's Office Dortmund 45 Js 24/62, Vermerk, July 20, 1965.

189. Shmuel Spector, "Jews in the Resistance and Partisan Movement in the Soviet Ukraine," *Yad Vashem Studies*, Vol. 23 (1993), pp. 127–144; Ielisavets'kyi, ed., *Katastrofa ta opir*, pp. 226–417; and idem, "Ievreï v antyfashysts'komu oporu i radians'komu pidpil'no-partyzans'komu rusi v Ukraïni," *Ukraïns'kyi istorychnyi zhurnal*, no. 3 (1995), pp. 59–72.

190. BA-B, NS 19/2566, Prützmann zur Bandenlage, December 27, 1942.

191. The murder of Jews by a Soviet partisan unit is mentioned in Ainsztein, *Jewish Resistance*, p. 357.

192. Nikolai V. Starozhilov, *Partizanskie soedineniia Ukrainy v Velikoi Otechestvennoi voine* (Kiev: Vyshcha Shkola, 1983), p. 23.

193. Spector, *Holocaust*, pp. 269ff., and Frank Golczewski, "Die Revision eines Klischees. Die Rettung von verfolgten Juden im Zweiten Weltkrieg durch Ukrainer," in Wolfgang Benz and Juliane Wetzel, eds., *Solidarität und Hilfe für Juden während der NS-Zeit*, Band 2 (Berlin: Metropol, 1998), pp. 9–82, here pp. 40ff.

194. This was the case around October 26, 1942; Ainsztein, *Jewish Resistance*, p. 348.

195. John A. Armstrong, ed., *Soviet Partisans in World War II* (Madison: University of Wisconsin Press, 1964), pp. 633ff.; Orbach, "Destruction of the Jews," pp. 44f.; and BA-MA, RH 26-444/6, p. 2, KTB 444. Sich.Div., January 3, 1942.

196. Spector, *Holocaust*, pp. 198ff. Spector's high figure of 47,500 refugees has been revised downward with time.

197. For example, Lagebericht GK Wolhynien-Podolien, April 30, 1943, printed in *History Teaches a Lesson* (Kiev: Politvydav Ukraïni, 1986), pp. 111f.

198. Ainsztein, *Jewish Resistance*, pp. 259ff.; Spector, *Holocaust*, pp. 206ff.; Spector, "Jews in the Resistance," p. 136.

199. BA-B, 11.01/17, p. 15, Lagebericht GK Wolhynien, November 1, 1942.

200. Spector, *Holocaust*, pp. 273ff., and "Jews in the Resistance," pp. 140f. Spector has since finished a book on Jewish partisan groups in Ukraine. For more on the Gildenman group, see Yuri Suhl, *Uncle Misha's Partisans* (New York: Four Winds Press, 1973).

201. On April 13, 1943, the discovery of a mass grave in Katyn' was made public; two days laters, a Soviet commission exhumed mass graves in Yeisk (in the Kuban') and near Voroshilovhrad (today Luhans'k), *Dokumenty obviniaiut: Sbornik dokumentov o chudovishchnykh zverstvakh germanskikh vlastei na vremen-no zakhvachennykh imi sovetskikh territoriiakh*, Vol. 2 (Moscow: Ogiz, Gosudarst-vennoe izdatel'stovo politicheskoi literatury, 1945), pp. 115f., and *Nazi Crimes in the Ukraine*, pp. 54f. By August 1943 at the latest, Soviet radio broadcast news of the exhumations. BA-B, 11.01/14, pp. 149–157, Seehaus-Dienst, August 5, 1943.

202. Reitlinger, *Endlösung*, p. 262. Blobel claimed he visted BdS Ukraine Max Thomas in late autumn 1942 for negotiations on Sk 1005's mission. Thomas, Blobel said, dismissed the "unearthing" project as a "fool's errand."

203. Drawing from captured German records, Radio Moscow reported this on March 11, 1944. BA-B, 11.01/14, p. 9, Seehaus-Dienst.

204. Prosecutor's Office Stuttgart 17 Js 270/64; IfZ Gs 05.33, Judgment, LG Stuttgart Ks 22/67 ./. Sohns u.a., March 13, 1969, printed in *Justiz und NS-Verbre-chen*, Vol. XXXI, no. 701; TsDAVO R-3679/1/57, p. 134, Finanzbericht SSPF Dnje-propetrowsk, June 20, 1943; IPN, UWZ Litzmannstadt, 204, p. 139, Inspekteur der Sipo Posen an RSHA IA1, September 20, 1943.

205. Shmuel Spector, "Aktion 1005—Effacing the Murder of Millions," *Holo-caust and Genocide Studies*, Vol. 5, no. 2 (1990), pp. 157–173, here pp. 162ff.

206. See Karel C. Berkhoff, *Harvest of Despair: Life and Death in Ukraine un-der Nazi Rule* (Cambridge, Mass.: Belknap Press of Harvard University Press, 2004); Spector, *Holocaust*, pp. 238ff.; John-Paul Himka, "Ukrainian Collabora-tion in the Extermination of the Jews During the Second World War. Sorting Out the Long-term and Conjunctural Factors," in Jonathan Frankel, ed., *The Fate of the European Jews 1939–1945: Continuity or Contingency?* (New York: Oxford University Press, 1997), pp. 170–189; Golczewski, "Revision eines Klischees," pp. 37ff.; M.I. Koval', "The Nazi Genocide of the Jews and the Ukrainian Population, 1941–1944," in Gitelman, *Bitter Legacy*, pp. 51–60; Iakiv Suslens'kyi, *Spravzhni heroï. Pro uchast' hromadian Ukraïny u riatuvanni ievreïv vid fashysts'koho he-notsydu* (Kiev: Ukraïna, 1993).

207. Dieter Pohl, "Ukrainische Hilfskräfte beim Mord an den Juden," in Ger-hard Paul, ed., *Die Täter der Shoah* (Göttingen: Wallstein, 2002), pp. 205–234.

208. Förster, "Sicherung," p. 1,058. BA-B, R 19/326, Runderlass RFSS, July 25, 1941; BA-B, R 19/281, Runderlass RFSS, November 6, 1941.

209. Dean, "German Gendarmerie," pp. 178ff. Distinguishing among the vari-ous local police forces is complicated by the parallel existence of "Hilfspolizei" and "Ordnungsdienst" under military administration and "Schutzmannschaft" or "Gemeindepolizei" under civil administration. In addition, the Wehrmacht maintained "Hilfswachmannschaften," mostly for local guard duty.

210. Richard Breitman, "Himmler's Police Auxiliaries in the Occupied Soviet Territories," *Simon Wiesenthal Center Annual*, 7 (1990), pp. 23–39, here p. 25. See also Frank Golczewski, "Organe der deutschen Besatzungsmacht: die ukrai-nischen Schutzmannschaften," in Wolfgang Benz, Johannes Houwink ten Cate, and Gerhard Otto, eds., *Die Bürokratie der Okkupation. Strukturen der Herrschaft und Verwaltung im besetzten Europa* (Berlin: Metropol, 1998), pp. 173–196; and Martin Dean, *Collaboration in the Holocaust: Crimes of the Local Police in Belorus-sia and Ukraine, 1941–44* (London: Macmillan, 1999).

211. Hans-Joachim Neufeldt, Jürgen Huck, and Georg Tessin, *Zur Geschichte der Ordnungspolizei 1936–1945*, Teil II, (Koblenz: Bundesarchiv, 1957), pp. 64–67 and 104–106.

212. Hilberg, *Täter*, pp. 111f.

213. The unit in question was set up on September 19, 1941, and entered Kiev on September 27 and 29, 1941, BA-MA, Film 59104, Befehl Berück Süd/Qu., ca. September 19, 1941; BA-MA, Film 59103, KTB 454. Sich.Div., September 27 and

29, 1941; BA-MA, RH 22/7, 454. Sich.Div./Ia an Berück Süd/Ia, September 29, 1941; see also Berkhoff's chapter in this collection.

214. USHMM, RG-11.001 (Osobyi), Reel 92, 1275-3-665, OK I/253 Krivoj Rog an FK 240, October 15, 1941.

215. USHMM, RG-11.001 (Osobyi), Reel 92, 1275-3-666, Bericht FK 240/VII, October 19, 1941.

216. BA-B, R 58/217, EM 88, September 19, 1941.

217. Dean, "German *Gendarmerie*," p. 183.

218. See, for example, footnote 101.

219. For Schutzmannschaft-Batl. 103, see BA-L, Dok.-Sammlung UdSSR, Band 245e, pp. 419–422; for Schutzmannschaft-Batl. 117, see Band 245Ag, pp. 180–205; and for Schutzmannschaft-Batl. 102, see Dean, *Collaboration*, p. 63.

220. For Kremenchuk, see BA-MA, RH 22/201, Monatsbericht FK 239/VII, October 10, 1941; for Romny, see *Nazi Crimes in the Ukraine*, p. 103.

221. Cf. Berkhoff, *Harvest of Despair*; Amir Weiner, *Making Sense of War. The Second World War and the Bolshevik Revolution* (Princeton: Princeton University Press, 2001), pp. 241ff.; Hiroaki Kuromiya, *Freedom and Terror in the Donbas: A Ukrainian-Russian Borderland, 1870s-1990s* (Cambridge and New York: Cambridge University Press, 1998), p. 285.

222. See Martin Dean's contribution to this collection.

223. Meir Buchsweiler, *Volksdeutsche in der Ukraine am Vorabend und Beginn des Zweiten Weltkrieges—ein Fall doppelter Loyalität?* (Gerlingen: Bleicher, 1984), pp. 375ff.; Ingeborg Fleischhauer, *Das Dritte Reich und die Deutschen in der Sowjetunion* (Stuttgart: Deutsche Verlags-Anstalt, 1983), pp. 139ff. The Germans registered 163,000 ethnic Germans in the RKU as of March 1943; Włodzimierz Bonusiak, *Polityka ludnościowa III Rzeszy na okupowanych obszarach ZSRR (1941–1944)* (Rzeszów: Wydawnictwo Wyższej Szkoły Pedagogicznej, 1992), p. 128.

224. BA-MA, Film 59105, p. 178, Tätigkeitsbericht Ic 454. Sich.Div., November 2, 1941, reported after the Babi Yar massacre: "The action against the Jews has been welcomed in general."

225. BA-B, R 58/221, EM 191, April 12, 1942.

226. BA-B, 11.01/17, pp. 6f., Lagebericht GK Wolhynien, November 11, 1942.

227. TsDAVO, R-3676/4/161, p. 48, Bericht über ukrainische Propagandisten für Ostarbeiter, November 30, 1943.

228. Tsentral'nyi Derzhavnyi Arkhiv Hromads'kykh Orhanizatsiï Ukraïny (TsDAHO), Kiev, P-1/23/688, pp. 2–27, NKVD Situation Report, Poltava, July 2, 1942.

229. Report of the Poltical Department of the Southwestern Front to the Political Main Administration of the Red Army, November 21, 1941, printed in F. D. Sverdlov, ed., *Dokumenty obviniaiut. Kholokost: Svidetel'stva Krasnoi Armii* (Moscow, 1996), p. 46. Cf. TsDAHO, P-62/9/4, pp. 149–155, Report from the southern front, January 15, 1941; BA-MA, RH 2/2538, pp. 72–76, translation Abt. Fremde Heere Ost from *Pravda*, December 12, 1942.

230. A. Blium, "Otnoshenie sovetskoi tsenzury (1940–1946) k probleme kholokosta," *Vestnik Evreiskogo Universiteta v Moskve*, Vol. 2, no. 9 (1995), pp. 156–167.

231. Francis H. Hinsley, *British Intelligence in the Second World War*, Vol. 2 (London: HMSO, 1981), p. 671; decoded radio message from the chief of the Order Police, September 13, 1941, printed in Klein, *Einsatzgruppen*, p. 397; Breitman, *Official Secrets*, pp. 67f. The British secret service received additional reports via an agent at BdO Prague, Detlef Brandes, *Grossbritannien und seine osteuropäischen Alliierten 1939–1943* (Munich and Vienna: Oldenbourg, 1989), pp. 201f.

232. Ulrich Herbert, *Best. Biographische Studien über Radikalismus, Weltanschauung und Vernunft 1903–1989* (Bonn: Dietz, 1996), pp. 313 and 607; David Bankier, *Die öffentliche Meinung im Hitler-Staat. Die "Endlösung" und die Deutschen* (Berlin: Berlin Verlag, 1995), p. 148; Gaston Haas, *"Wenn man gewusst*

hätte, was sich drüben im Reich abspielte . . . " 1941–1943. Was man in der Schweiz von der Judenvernichtung wusste (Basel, Frankfurt: Helbing & Lichtenhahn, 1994), pp. 107f. and 140ff. touches on Kiev, Vinnytsia, and Rivne.

233. The Korherr Report, which describes the situation as of December 31, 1942, shows only half of the victims or fewer. The Reich Security Main Office ordered monthly reports for killings starting only on July 4, 1942, Klein, *Einsatzgruppen*, pp. 361f.

234. Bonusiak, *Polityka ludnościowa*, p. 76; Pohl, *Judenverfolgung*, p. 67 and 385; Spector, "The Holocaust of Ukrainian Jews," p. 49; and Jean Ancel, "Transnistrien," in *Enzyklopädie des Holocaust*, p. 1,422. Kruglov, *Unichtozhenie*, p. 96, reaches similar figures based on a very detailed method of counting. His total is ca. 1.5 million victims including northern Bukovina, Carpatho-Ukraine, and the Crimea. See Kruglov's contribution to this volume.

235. Hitler to Keitel and Zeitzler during a meeting on June 8, 1943, Helmut Heiber, ed., *Hitlers Lagebesprechungen. Die Protokollfragmente seiner militärischen Besprechungen 1942–1945* (Stuttgart: Deutsche Verlags-Anstalt, 1962), p. 259. Hitler was quoting Koch here; see also reference to a report by Propaganda Ministry official Hans-Joachim Klausch on his travels in Ukraine and the Crimea, June 26, 1943, in Max Weinreich, *Hitler's Professors* (New York: YIVO, 1946), pp. 165f.

236. A paradoxical category of legal proceedings are the wartime judgments of the SS and field courts concerning the "unauthorized" murder of Jews. Such killings were accompanied by such brutality that even the German authorities felt compelled to intervene. See excerpts from SS proceedings against Max Täubner (1st SS Brigade) in Klee, Dressen, and Riess, eds., *"Schöne Zeiten,"* pp. 184–192, and the judgment against Johann Meisslein in Proskuriv, mentioned in Christopher Browning, *Ordinary Men*, enlarged ed. (New York: Penguin, 1998), p. 257.

237. On the first trials, see TsDAHO, P-1/23/684, pp. 6–15, report of the NKVD-military tribunals for the Ukrainian region from July to September 1943 (October 22, 1943). Concerning later trials, see *Nazi Crimes in the Ukraine*, pp. 353–357, Judgment, October 28, 1982. David Rich of Washington pointed out to me a trial in Zhytomyr in 1991. Of the 54,000 investigations of alleged collaborators in Ukraine, several thousand cases probably concerned the murder of Jews; see also A. S. Chaikovskii, *Plen. Za chuzhie i svoi grekhi (Voennoplennye i internirovannye v Ukraine 1939–1953 gg.)* (Kiev: Parlamentskoe izdatel'stvo, 2005), p. 539.

238. HSSPF Russia South Friedrich Jeckeln; KdO Kiev Paul Albert Scheer; 17th Army commander Erwin Jaenecke; AOK 6 rear area commander Karl Burckhardt; 213th Security Division commander Eckart von Tschammer und Osten; Melitopol County Commissar Georg Heinisch, etc. A show trial was held in Kharkiv in December 1943 to prosecute mostly low-level German functionaries. See also Manfred Zeidler, *Stalinjustiz contra NS-Verbrechen. Die Kriegsverbrecherprozesse gegen deutsche Kriegsgefangene in der UdSSR in den Jahren 1943–1952* (Dresden: HAIT, 1996), p. 28; *Kyïvs'kyi protses. Dokumenty ta materialy* (Kiev: Lybid, 1995); Alexander Victor Prusin, "'Fascist Criminals to the Gallows!': The Holocaust and Soviet War Crimes Trials, December 1945–February 1946," *Holocaust and Genocide Studies*, Vol. 17, no. 1, pp. 1–30.

239. Klein, *Einsatzgruppen*, pp. 82f., 104. Criminal investigations of later commando leaders, Friedrich Schmidt(-Schütte) and Theodor Christensen, both of Sk 4a, as well as Waldemar Krause of Sk 4b were either closed or ended in acquittal, see Judgment, LG Darmstadt Ks 1/68 ./. Christensen, April 18, 1969, *Justiz und NS-Verbrechen*, Vol. XXXII, no. 703, and Judgment, LG Kiel ./. Schmidt, May 20, 1968, printed in *Justiz und NS-Verbrechen*, Vol. XXIX, no. 677. Schmidt was sentenced to two years in prison for crimes committed in Schleswig-Holstein.

240. These included officers from Sipo-SD outposts in Uman' (KdS Kiev) and Berdychiv (KdS Zhytomyr) and from KdS Kiev.

241. Judgment, LG Stuttgart Ks 22/67 ./. Sohns u.a., March 13, 1969.

242. Klemp, *"Nicht ermittelt"*; Judgment, LG Kaiserslautern ./. Heinemann, June 25, 1982; Judgment, LG Nuremberg 1070 Ks 7/62 ./. Paur u.a., May 27, 1963, printed in *Justiz und NS-Verbrechen*, Vol. XIX, no. 553; Judgment LG Regensburg Ks 6/70 ./. Kreuzer, August 5, 1971; Judgment LG Traunstein ./. Bauer u.a., June 25, 1982; see also Heiner Lichtenstein, *Himmlers grüne Helfer. Die Schutz- und Ordnungspolizei im "Dritten Reich,"* (Cologne: Bund, 1990), pp. 124–143. Additional verdicts against former Orpo members were handed down in East Germany: Judgment, Bezirksgericht Neubrandenburg, June 26, 1981, and Judgment Bezirksgericht Frankfurt an der Oder BS 3/85, July 4, 1985, printed in *DDR-Justiz und NS-Verbrechen*, Vol. 1, no. 1006.

243. Karl von Roques was sentenced to 20 years in prison by a U.S. military court on October 28, 1948, see *Fall 12. Das Urteil gegen das Oberkommando der Wehrmacht* (Berlin: Rütten und Loening, 1961), pp. 217ff. Friderici died in 1964 without ever standing trial.

244. Korsemann, who led the massacre at Kharkiv, was sentenced by a Polish court for his activity in Lublin, but after his return to West Germany in 1949, it appears that he was never questioned. He died in Munich in 1958.

245. Judgment, LG Dortmund ./. Westerheide, December 20, 1982. Criminal investigations into the activities of German civil administrators elsewhere in occupied Europe met a similar end, see Uwe Danker, "Der gescheiterte Versuch, die Legende der 'sauberen' Zivilverwaltung zu entzaubern. Staatsanwaltschaftliche Komplexermittlungen zum Holocaust im 'Reichskommissariat Ostland' bis 1971," in Robert Bohn, ed., *Die deutsche Herrschaft in den "germanischen" Ländern 1940–1945* (Stuttgart: Steiner, 1997), pp. 159–186.

246. Judgment, LG Nürnberg 225 Ks 1/64, June 9, 1965, printed in *Justiz und NS-Verbrechen*, Vol. XXI, no. 592; Judgment LG Stade 9 Ks 1/63, May 9, 1967, printed in *Justiz und NS-Verbrechen*, Vol. XXI, no. 642. For his blunt testimony, Graebe was subjected to considerable hostility in West Germany and ultimately emigrated to the United States, see Douglas K. Huneke, *The Moses of Rovno. The Stirring Story of Fritz Graebe* (New York: Dodd, Mead, 1985), pp. 165ff., and the attacks on him in *Der Spiegel*, December 29, 1965.

247. Judgment, LG Oldenburg 2 Ks 1/64 ./. Kassner, September 26, 1966, *Justiz und NS-Verbrechen*, Vol. XXIV, no. 638.

248. Examples of antisemitic mail are printed in Walter Manoschek, ed., *"Es gibt nur eines für das Judentum: Vernichtung." Das Judenbild in deutschen Soldatenbriefen 1939–1944* (Hamburg: Hamburger Edition, 1995). It is not clear how representative these are.

249. A list of most Orpo crimes in Ukraine can be found in Wolfgang Curilla, *Die deutsche Ordnungspolizei und der Holocaust im Baltikum und in Weissrussland 1941–1944* (Paderborn: Schoeningh, 2005), pp. 791–817.

250. David H. Kitterman, "Those Who Said 'No!' Germans Who Refused to Execute Civilians during World War II," *German Studies Review*, Vol. 11, no. 2 (1988), pp. 241–254, here pp. 244ff.; Alfred Streim, "Zum Beispiel: Die Verbrechen der Einsatzgruppen in der Sowjetunion," in Adalbert Rückerl, ed., *NS-Prozesse* (Karlsruhe: C. F. Müller, 1971), pp. 65–106, here, p. 98. The examples named require further examination.

Translated by Ray Brandon

II

The Life and Death of Western Volhynian Jewry, 1921–1945

TIMOTHY SNYDER

Henryk Józewski, governor of Poland's eastern province of Volhynia in the interwar years, remembered Volhynia's Jews as he saw them in the village of Kolky (Polish, Kółki), during the good times. The village, as Józewski recalled, was "cut off from people and the world." Home to about 2,000 souls—Jews, Poles, and Ukrainians—Kolky was 45 miles of bad road from the nearest bus station. Józewski visited on horseback, on his way north to his favorite hunting grounds, in a part of Volhynia where the Styr River flows wide and strong. Returning home to Lutsk (Polish, Łuck), passing the little Jewish houses on each side of Kolky's main street, he would contemplate the lamp suspended before each door. He found the glow of candles through the dusk unforgettable. Outside the village, he passed a gentle figure in priest's garb, fishing in the Styr. Once, Józewski took part, in his official capacity of governor of the Polish province of Volhynia, in the celebration of the completion of a new Roman Catholic church in Kolky. The Roman Catholic priest had invited the Orthodox priest and the rabbi. As the Roman Catholic priest told Józewski of the construction, the Orthodox priest interrupted to note his contribution: the beams and the rafters. Then the rabbi burst in: "And the glass, that's my work."[1]

Józewski saw Volhynian Jewry as a community out of time, separated from Christian neighbors, living by its own lights. As Józewski knew, the history of Polish power in Volhynia was old, but the history of Jewish settlement was older. Rabbi Benjamin the Generous, known for his Halakic rulings, was active in 1171.[2] Jews had settled 13 localities in Volhynia by the fourteenth century. Volhynian Jews witnessed the Lublin Union of 1569, which established the Polish-Lithuanian Commonwealth and brought Volhynia under the Polish crown. For the next 200 years, Volhynian Jewish communities founded schools and produced rabbis known throughout Europe. The school, or yeshiva, in Ostroh (Polish, Ostróg) in the first half of the seventeenth century shared the town with an Orthodox academy, a Unitarian church, and a mosque. Jews helped Polish lords colonize Volhynia and the rest of Ukraine in the sixteenth and seventeenth centuries and were killed along with Poles during the Khmelnytsky Uprising of 1648. Jewish communities recovered from this onslaught, and their communal autonomy in Volhynia continued so long as the Commonwealth survived.

The Polish-Lithuanian Commonwealth was a republic of nobles. Jews could not be citizens of the Commonwealth, unless they converted to Christianity. Their legal and social status was defined communally, by the *kehilla,* the organized community. (*Kahal* and *gmina* are other names of the same institution.) The community was legitimated internally by Halakic law and externally by the recognition of Polish princes. The community collected taxes from its members and regulated Jewish relations with the outside world. In return, the community received military protection and a certain advisory role in the government. Communities elected regional councils, which in turn elected the Council of the Four Lands, the highest body of Jewry within the Commonwealth. In the seventeenth and eighteenth centuries, Volhynian Jews led the Council of the Four Lands. Efraim Fishel was honored by the title Servis Regis by Polish King Jan Sobieski. The efforts of Meir of Dubno led to the papal bull that defended the Jews from the accusation of ritual murder.[3]

The Polish-Lithuanian Commonwealth's tolerant practices made it a haven to Jews, even as they were expelled from western and central Europe. In demographic, economic, and cultural terms, Poland-Lithuania became the center of Jewish civilization in Europe. Its destruction in the late eighteenth century by three neighboring empires, Prussian, Austrian, and Russian, ended this conjuncture. The final partition of the Polish-Lithuanian Commonwealth, in 1795, left the Russian Empire with most of Europe's Jews.[4] In the Russian Empire, the Jewish community operated within an imperial legal system lacking extensive experience with Jews and possessing a marked tendency toward centralization. Tsar Nicholas I extended compulsory military service to the Jews in 1827. This underscored the weakening of the community, whose historical function was to negotiate the terms by which non-Jewish men at arms would protect the stability of Jewish life. The community was also required to choose which young men would serve, which presumably worsened divisions between rich and poor. Russia formally abolished Jewish communal autonomy in 1844. Though communities continued to function informally, they lost their coercive power as the Russian state increased its capacity, in the 1860s and 1870s, to tax and draft its Jewish subjects as individuals. Volhynian Jewry inclined to Hasidism; the first Yiddish edition of *In Praise of the Baal Shem Tov,* the first collection of stories about the founder of Hasidism, was published in Volhynia in 1815. Some Jews continued to prosper as the agents of the great Polish lords, who continued to dominate Volhynian economic life despite Russian rule. By the middle of the nineteenth century, some three-quarters of merchants in Volhynia were Jews.[5] Most Jews scratched out a living from petty trade or artisanry. After five generations of Russian rule, almost all Jews had lost contact with Polish traditions and the Polish language. The communities remained, impotent and quiet, representing a Jewish-Russian rather than a Jewish-Polish tradition.[6]

Interwar Poland

The western and central portions of the former Russian imperial province of Volhynia, largely Ukrainian by population, were attached to Poland by the terms of the Riga Treaty, which was signed by the Polish and Bolshevik governments in 1921. Volhynian Jews were indifferent, or sometimes hostile, to the Polish state established in 1918. Their Slavic language was Russian rather than Polish. They suffered pogroms during the Great War (1914–1918), the Russian Civil War (1917–1918), and the Polish-Bolshevik War (1919–1920). The worst perpetrators were soldiers and irregulars of the short-lived Ukrainian People's Republic, although the Red Army and the Polish Army carried out pogroms as well. The dominant current in Polish political life in the 1920s, as Jews soon understood, was the integral nationalism of the National Democrats. Their leader, Roman Dmowski, was the pioneer of modern anti-semitism in Poland.

Yet during the ascendancy of the National Democrats during the early 1920s, Volhynian Jews managed a rare feat of local governance. Although the National Democrats and their allies had skewed electoral laws such that the eastern districts (and thus the national minorities) were under-represented in the central parliament in Warsaw, local elections were democratic. Jews, a plurality or a majority in all the main towns, controlled Volhynia's town councils. National Democrats believed that Jews could not be integrated into the Polish political community and had few policy ideas applicable to areas where Jews outnumbered Poles. Jews were about 10 percent of the population of the Volhynia province as a whole, but because 90 percent of Jews lived in the towns, they predominated in urban life. This was the state of affairs when Józef Piłsudski took power in Poland by military coup in May 1926. He dispatched two of his associates, first Władysław Mech and then Henryk Józewski, to govern Volhynia.

The National Democrats were antisemitic in orientation, but lacked a program for Volhynia in the 1920s. Piłsudski was a former socialist and an etatist and endorsed loyalty to the state rather than propagating ethnic ideas of nationalism. He and his lieutenants, however, had several clear programs with direct implications for Poland's larger minorities: the five million Ukrainians, the three million Jews, the one million Belarussians. In Poland's sensitive eastern districts, state power was to be secured, and Russian influence was to be minimized. Upon becoming governor of Volhynia in 1928, Józewski put an end to Jewish majorities in town councils. He fixed local elections until he got a Polish majority. He explained to Jewish leaders that ostentatious domination was not in their interest, the implication being that it would provoke antisemitism. Józewski also removed Poles he found unyielding from Polish town councils, yet Jews were removed simply for being Jews. His true concern was probably to remove Russian speakers from any visible position of power.[7]

In other respects, Józewski meant to endorse continuity of Jewish tradition and to protect Jewish institutions with Polish laws. The end of local democracy in town councils was compensated, in some measure, by the revival of the Jewish organized community and the redefinition of its legal relationship to a modern Polish state. To be sure, even when the legal status of the community was undefined, the rabbis in Volhynia mediated between Jews and the state. Rabbis were entrusted with the life rituals of their followers and expected to record all Jewish births, deaths, marriages, and divorces, which they (or their scribes) did in beautiful flowing Polish cursive.[8] Just after the establishment of Polish independence, a decree was issued formalizing the relationship between the Jewish community and the state in central Poland. After Piłsudski's return to power in 1926, the legal foundations for the reestablishment of the community in eastern Poland as well were laid in 1927, and communal elections were held in 1928.[9] By 1928, Jewish communal autonomy was established on a unitary legal basis throughout Poland. The Polish state registered Jewish voters, who had to be male and 25 years of age or older, using bilingual forms. The illiterate signed with a thumbprint.[10]

The communities funded themselves. They made some net income from cemetery services and ritual slaughter, which they arranged for a fee. Annual contributions from individual Jews, though mandatory, were moderate and indexed to personal wealth. The very poorest did not have to pay. The community's contribution was often supplemented by donations from Jewish emigrants. For example, in 1932, the Korets (Polish, Korzec) community expected to receive more than four times as much funding from American Jews as it did from the mandatory contributions of its own members.[11] Services provided by the communities supplemented those administered by the state. Jewish children could and did attend Polish schools in Volhynia, and Jewish patients (and Jewish doctors) could be found in state clinics and hospitals. But all institutions for Jews were to be funded by the Jewish communities. With communal contributions, the secular Zionist Tarbut network founded Hebrew schools throughout Volhynia. The religious Zionist Yavneh movement also founded dozens of academies, as well as *yeshivas* and *cheders* (supplementary programs for Jewish children attending Polish public schools). The internationalist socialists of the Bund had established 20 Yiddish schools by 1925. The Bund's commitments were to socialist revolution and to remaining in the lands of historic Jewish habitation, and its preferred language was thus Yiddish rather than Hebrew. In the 1938–1939 school year, there were seven functioning private Jewish high schools in Volhynia. By comparison, there was only one Ukrainian high school, and it was public. Every town in Volhynia had a Jewish library, and the larger towns had Yiddish weeklies. Jewish children attended Jewish summer camps of various religious and political orientations, and two Jewish soccer teams played in the regional first division.[12] Nonetheless, Józewski's officials did not fully respect the autonomy of the communities, intervening in problematic cities such as Kovel (Polish, Kowel) to force the appointment of sympathetic rabbis.[13]

Józewski was one of the organizers of Piłsudski's non-party electoral bloc, designed to allow Piłsudski to dominate the parliament. The bloc appealed to those who believed that any great change in Poland would be for the worse. Throughout Poland, the bloc was most popular among Jews, who saw in Piłsudski a guarantor of stability, a friend of the Jewish people, or at least preferable to the antisemitic National Democrats.[14] In Volhynia, membership in Piłsudski's electoral bloc was mostly Jewish, and two Jews were elected from its ranks in 1928.[15] The bloc was meant to be a safe form of political expression for the apolitical, to provide a ritualized opportunity to support the existing state of affairs without taking a defined political stand. It provided national and religious minorities with a center position, between Polish nationalism and leftwing radicalism. There was a brief moment of overlap between political and religious orthodoxy. Just as Christian Orthodox priests marched their congregations to the polling stations to vote for the bloc, so did the traditionalist rabbis of the main Volhynian congregations urge their followers to vote for Piłsudski.[16] The bloc thereby allowed Jews some representation in national politics, although it was an instrument to support a non-democratic form of government. Its Volhynian Jewish members probably cared less about democracy and more about stability. It was a non-democratically elected parliament dominated by the bloc that categorically removed, in 1931, all restrictions flowing from language, nationality, or religion on the individual rights of Polish citizens.[17]

In Volhynia, as elsewhere in Poland, the effort to create a political center around the idea of loyalty to the state was a very partial and tentative success. The state's alliance with traditional Jewry naturally excluded the secular right and the secular left. The Bund was popular in some

Volhynian towns, such as Kovel. It competed for influence over labor unions with the Labor Zionists of Poalej Zion Left and the Communist Party of Western Ukraine[18] and organized at least one strike of Jewish workers in Lutsk, in March 1936, to protest boycotts of Jewish shops and rising antisemitism.[19] The Bund maintained that only a complete transformation of the existing order could solve such problems. Although in principle the Bund stood for international revolution, it was no ally of the Soviet Union, where it had been dissolved by the Bolsheviks. In the here and now, Bundists mainly represented the interests of the Jewish working class, an agenda that allowed them to declare their loyalty, at least for the time being, to the Polish state.

More popular still, especially in the late 1930s, were the Revisionist Zionists, who cooperated with the Polish state in their efforts to settle Palestine with Polish Jews as quickly as possible. Their leader, Vladimir Jabotinsky, cultivated relationships within the Polish state and with Ukrainian elites. Zionists were also revolutionaries, but their national and social revolution was to take place in Palestine rather than Poland. Their quarrel was not with the Polish authorities, who increasingly agreed with Zionists that Jews should voluntarily leave Poland, but with the Jews, few of whom wished to go. Because Zionists wished to leave Poland rather than harm it, they too could introduce all public gatherings with declarations of loyalty to Poland.[20] Zionists could even treat eastern Poland as kind of staging area for future emigration and thereby achieve a provisional modus vivendi with the state. HeHalutz founded a kibbutz in Volhynia to teach Zionist emigrants stonework before they left for Palestine. With the assistance of the Polish Army, Bejtar, a Revisionist Zionist youth organization, trained young Jews in the use of firearms.[21]

Communism, in its various guises, was the most popular form of opposition politics in Volhynia. The Communist Party of Western Ukraine was an illegal, conspiratorial organization whose influence through front organizations and protest movements far exceeded what one might expect from its small formal membership. According to party records, most members in the countryside were Ukrainians; most members in the towns were Jews.[22] In the provincial capital of Lutsk in 1933, for example, party records indicate that all members of the party and its youth organization were Jews.[23] There were a few Polish Communists as well, but Poles in Volhynia were a privileged caste and had little reason to support the far left, especially since the far left was explicitly anti-Polish. The Communist Party of Western Ukraine, a cooperative project of Ukrainians and Jews, used the national and land questions to attract the Ukrainian peasant to revolution. This meant that Jewish Communist propagandists were some of the early articulators of Ukrainian nationalism in Volhynia. In the 1930s, Volhynia was in a state of persistent social and national conflict, as the Polish police raided Communist Party cells and the Communists tried to organize violent resistance to Polish rule in the countryside.[24] Jews were prominent in the leadership of the Communist Party of Western Ukraine, but Józewski did not treat Communism as Jewish.[25]

West Ukrainian Communists characterized Polish government in Volhynia as a "Petliurite occupation."[26] The Petliurites, the followers of Symon Petliura, were former officers and officials of the Ukrainian People's Republic. Several Petliurites were indeed employed by Józewski in Volhynia, as part of a larger project to use the Ukrainian question against the Soviet Union.[27] For Jews, a "Petliurite occupation" would have meant pogroms. Although none of the Petliurites employed by Józewski was known to be personally involved in the pogroms of 1919–1921, most of the pogroms had in fact been carried out by his army. Many soldiers of the Ukrainian People's Republic had treated Communism as a Jewish movement, and some of their officers used this to justify pogroms.[28] Even as violence against Jews increased in central Poland in the late 1930s, there were few recorded antisemitic outbursts in Volhynia.[29] Although the politically motivated association of Jews and Communists had both a past and a future in Volhynia, it appears to be absent during the period of Józewski's rule. Józewski was an anti-Communist, but not an antisemite. The Petliurites advocated democracy, the separation of church and state, and equal rights for all citizens of a future independent Ukraine. Even their secret plans for a Ukrainian constitution after the recapture of Soviet Ukraine included provisions for minority rights, religious freedom, and the separation of church and state.[30] The propaganda sent from Warsaw to Soviet Ukraine by way of Volhynia was supposed to be anti-antisemitic.[31] Jews were presented as the state nation in the Soviet Union, so went the argument depicted in posters printed in Warsaw, but in fact Communist rule was not in the interests of Ukrainian Jews.[32] Yet another poster designed in Warsaw, one commemorating the anniversary of Petliura's death, mentioned that his assassin was a Jew.[33] It also appears that Ukrainian agents working covertly in Soviet Ukraine designed their own pamphlets, explicitly linking Jews and Communism. However, in Poland appearances were at least maintained.

In Volhynia, Józewski was able, for a time, to persuade moderate elements from the Ukrainian and Jewish communities to support the Polish state. Ukrainians and Jews figured on the same party lists in elections, and Ukrainians and Jews, when they voted for Piłsudski's non-party bloc, chose the same candidates. This is not to say that all of the Petliurite activists in Volhynia would have endorsed this situation, if left to their own devices. Other Ukrainian political groups, mainly the Organization of Ukrainian Nationalists, carried out antisemitic violence in Volhynia. The OUN was far weaker in Volhynia than in its native Galicia, but it did attack Jews. In 1937, the OUN undertook 830 violent actions against Polish citizens or their property, of which 540 were classified as anti-Polish, 242 as anti-Jewish, 67 as anti-Ukrainian, and 17 as anti-Communist. Yet only a few of these outbreaks took place in Volhynia, the vast majority in Galicia.[34] Ukrainian nationalist attacks on Jews in Volhynia were sufficiently rare that Józewski could believe, or at least claim, that Polish nationalists were the true culprits. In one incident in 1936, Ukrainian nationalists apparently burned down several Jewish houses in Kostopil County (Polish, Kostopol). Józewski claimed that the assailants were in fact Polish nationalists, but either way the victims were Jews.[35] Still, the OUN was relatively weak in Volhynia before the Second World War and at times compromised with the local Communists. Because the latter party was a Ukrainian-Jewish venture, such cooperation probably dampened expressions of antisemitism.

Piłsudski died in 1935, and his successors moved Poland to the right. A new Camp of National Unity, explicitly ethnic in composition, replaced the non-party bloc as the basis of rule. Policies directed against the national minorities sharpened, and advocates of toleration lost their positions. In April 1938, Józewski was replaced by Aleksander Hauke-Nowak as governor of Volhynia. In the 16 months of his tenure, Hauke-Nowak presided over a policy of modernization, designed to secure Poland's eastern flank against future Soviet attack by polonizing the local population. Just as Ukrainians had been the key to the previous policy of toleration, so they occupied the central position in the modernization policy. The cities were less urgent, and more complex. After more than a decade of Polish settlement, Jews were no longer a clear majority in most Volhynian towns by the late 1930s, but they were still a plurality in most towns and managed to hold on to a majority in some others. By 1936, Jews constituted 49.5 percent of Volhynia's urban population, Poles only 26.3 percent.[36]

In trade and commerce, Jews continued to dominate in Volhynia. Jews were about a tenth of the population in 1937, while two of three traders in the province were Jewish, and Jews owned as many industrial enterprises as the rest of the population combined. Jews controlled the profitable oak lumber and brewery industries, although in the late 1930s the Polish state began to seize control of the former. In the late 1930s, the logic of the policy of polonization indirectly protected Jews: Polish authorities believed that any weakening of the Jews' position would only help Ukrainians, which was viewed as undesirable, since Ukrainians were seen as less reliable than Jews in the Volhynian context. This was a reservation only of practice, not of principle.

Had Polish rule continued, the policy of state-led modernization would likely have turned against the Jews; in the event, it was mainly turned against the Ukrainians. The state began to campaign for popular support to "polonize" the towns as well, which seemed to imply the removal of the Jews. This was the minority program of Poland in the late 1930s: Slavs were to be assimilated, and Jews were to emigrate. No truly effective measures were found, and little was achieved. But such was the emerging design.[37]

Soviet Occupation

On September 1, 1939, Nazi Germany invaded Poland from the west; on September 17, the Soviet Union entered Poland from the east. Poland's Jews were divided, it appeared, into two communities of fate. The Jews of Łódź, Warsaw, and Cracow fell under German occupation; the Jews of Volhynia along with those of Galicia and Belarus under Soviet occupation. About 200,000 Jews fled east from the Germans, joining a native Jewish population of about 1.2 million Jews in the Soviet zone of occupied Poland.[38] In the first half of September, before the Red Army arrived, many of them were sheltered and provided for by the local Jewish communities where they found refuge.

In Volhynia, in late September 1939, the Red Army was welcomed everywhere, which is not to say that it was welcome to everyone. Soldiers were greeted warmly by local Communists and by some Jewish refugees from the west. Israel Weiner's description of the Volhynian town Shumsk (Polish, Szumsk) is typical: "Satisfaction was displayed by the few sympathizers of the Communist ideology among the local population, as well as by refugees from the western regions of Poland."[39] Local Communists in Volhynia were mainly Ukrainians and Jews, but they greeted the Red Army as Communists. Moshe Kleinbaum's account of the Soviet arrival in Lutsk is much the same:

> Ukrainian peasants, who came en masse from neighboring villages, as well as Jewish youth, especially Jewish Communist girls, greeted the soldiers with toasts and loud salutes to friendship. The number of such Jewish admirers was not especially high. Nevertheless, their behavior that day, their noisiness, aroused suspicion. In these conditions one could draw the false impression that Jews were the happiest guests at the party.[40]

Where the Communist party was stronger, as in Kovel, observers emphasize the Communist element: "The Soviet invasion was greeted with full enthusiasm by communized Jews and Ukrainians, the former recent arrivals from central Poland as a result of the war."[41] Kovel was the site of an enthusiastic welcome, as Jews threw flowers at Russian soldiers, who for their part just wanted into Jewish shops.[42] Everywhere the Red Army was greeted with bread and salt, mainly by Communists, sometimes by refugees or Jewish and Ukrainian youth.[43] All Volhynians knew that Communists were numerous in their province, and locals were far from surprised by Communists' reaction to Soviet occupation. As one Pole had told a Polish military investigator in 1938: "When the Bolshevik comes to Lutsk, we [Poles] will be the ones who have to escape."[44]

Once Poland was destroyed, many Jews and Ukrainians saw no reason for it to be restored. This distinguished both groups from local Poles, who had been the privileged group and now found themselves at the bottom of the political and social ladder. Beyond their shared newfound superiority over Poles, the position of Jews and Ukrainians was quite different. Many Ukrainians imagined that the occupying authorities would grant them greater sovereignty than Poland had and even dreamed of independent statehood. Between 1939 and 1941, Ukrainians were indeed preferred to Poles by both the Nazi and the Soviet occupation regimes. Jews, however, had obvious reasons to prefer one occupation to the other. German policies to Jews were well known: 17,000 Polish Jews had been expelled from Germany in October 1938, 11 months before the war began.[45] The Wehrmacht, in September 1939, had crossed briefly into borderlands of Volhynia before the Soviets arrived and abused Jews and burned synagogues (in Liuboml [Polish, Luboml], for example) before withdrawing.[46] Jews thus had a strong case for preferring the Red Army to the Wehrmacht, and these two occupying armies appeared as clear alternatives. In Volhynia, the Jews experienced the Communist diversions and peasant rebellions of the first half of September. Yet by autumn 1939, with the Polish Army dispersed and the Soviets and Germans effectively allied with each other, Jews envisioned that the new order would be durable.

The mass transfer of Germans from Volhynia to the Reich must have confirmed that impression. The Nazi-Soviet agreements of August and September 1939 had left some 100,000 to 120,000 Polish citizens who considered themselves Germans in the Soviet zone. The German occupation of western and central Poland had created a new German question in the enlarged Soviet Union. The two allies moved quickly to resolve the issue, agreeing on November 16, 1939, that Germans from eastern Poland would be exchanged for Ukrainians and Russians who remained in western Poland. As these territories were officially attached to the Soviet Union, SS officers screened the population to allow Germans to escape to the Reich. These Germans, until recently citizens of Poland, had an obvious preference for Germany over the Soviet Union. Many non-Germans also asked to be included in the repatriation. Beginning on December 22, 1939, Germans from Volhynia and elsewhere in eastern Poland began their journey to the Reich. Their trains or horse-drawn wagons were met in Łódź, which the Nazis renamed Litzmannstadt and had incorporated into the Reich. Here, Germans from Volhynia, who as Polish citizens had no official nationality in passports or even censuses, escaped Soviet rule for the Nazi racial paradise. In Łódź, where the Germans governed in the offices occupied by Józewski after he was transferred west in 1938, the ethnic Germans of Volhynia were racially screened for a second time. Those with positive racial classifications ("O" for *Ost* [east], as opposed to "A" for *Altreich* [old Reich]) were assigned to Germanize the Polish territories absorbed by the Reich. Some 365,000 Poles were "ethnically cleansed" from the enlarged German Reich to the General Government to create space for the new arrivals.[47]

In the Soviet zone, only the Communists had much cause for real satisfaction. The Polish state, their great foe, had been destroyed. Rival political and social organizations, including the Polish political parties, Ukrainian cooperatives, and the Jewish community, were liquidated.[48] Communists, joined by sympathetic or opportunistic Ukrainian and Jewish youth, formed the militias that supplied the local police power throughout the Soviet occupation. Due to Volhynia's demographics, Jews were prominent in the towns (although Ukrainians also served in cities such as Lutsk and Rivne [Polish, Równe]), whereas the militiamen were usually Ukrainians in the countryside.[49] Jews replaced Poles in the local administration in the towns, which Jewish refugees noted as a particular cause of Polish dissatisfaction.[50] None of this meant that Volhynian Jews controlled their own fate. Jews, like Ukrainians, were certainly favored over Poles, whom the Soviets identified as the class and national enemy. In 1937 and 1938, the Soviet secret police, the NKVD, had killed 111,091 Soviet citizens, mostly Poles, for supposed contacts with Polish intelligence. Poles has been executed in numbers hugely disproportionate to their representation in the Soviet population as a whole, while Soviet Jews and Soviet Ukrainians had been repressed in about the same proportions as the Soviet population as a whole during this period.[51] In 1939–1941, no one doubted that Soviet repressive organs targeted Poles first and foremost in Volhynia. Yet under Soviet rule, Jews had no independent organizations (such as the kehilla) by which to create a civil society and no ability to affect the composition of supposedly representative bodies. As before the war, Jews were under-represented in city councils.[52] Ukrainians were over-represented, and Poles and Jews all but absent. Only one local Jew (from Kovel) was elected to the Ukrainian Supreme Soviet in March 1940.[53]

Real power in Volhynia, now part of Soviet Ukraine, was exercised by the Ukrainian section of the Bolshevik party, which expanded westward in the months following September 1939, and by the NKVD, which followed on the heels of the Red Army. For reasons having to do with events that took place later, during the German occupation, much attention has been paid to the "ethnic" character of these organizations. The Germans portrayed Soviet organs as Jewish, and sometimes people who profited from or collaborated in the Nazi genocide of the Jews made (or make) similar claims. Irrespective of the national composition of these Soviet organizations, they did not represent any national group, since no national group chose to be ruled by them. Even if one insists (in my view, quite erroneously) on equating self-declared ethnicity of officers and officials with the representation of a nation, the identification of Soviet organs with Jews fails in 1939.

By the time the Soviet Union invaded Poland, the Ukrainian section of the Bolshevik party was numerically dominated by Ukrainians. Even as show trials and purges crushed the nascent Ukrainian cultural intelligentsia, and famine silenced the Ukrainian peasantry, ethnic Ukrainians deemed trustworthy were promoted through the ranks of the party. Between 1922 and 1940, the proportion of Russians in the Ukrainian section of the party fell from 54 percent to 19 percent, while that of Jews remained steady at about 13 percent. Among the higher ranks, Ukrainians made noteworthy gains at the expense of Russians and Jews. By 1938, for example, there were only two Jews among the 304 members of the Soviet Ukrainian parliament.[54] A similar trend is evident in the most important state organization, the secret police. As late as 1936, 60 of 90 ranking officers (captain and above) of the NKVD in Soviet Ukraine had declared themselves to be of Jewish nationality.[55] As late as March 1937, Jews outnumbered Russians (38 percent and 32 percent respectively) in the highest positions of the Soviet NKVD as a whole. The Great Terror of 1937–1938 reached into the highest levels of the internal security apparatus, and the promotions that followed radically changed its ethnic composition. Again, according to declared nationality, Russians were predominant in the Soviet NKVD by the outbreak of the Second World War (67 percent, versus 4 percent Jews and 12 percent Ukrainians in July 1939).[56]

In the new western territories of Soviet Ukraine, local Jews were trusted more than local Poles, but this was only a relative distinction, and Jews had no authority as such nor any institutional representation in Soviet organs. Insofar as local Volhynian Communists, Jewish or otherwise, had any discretion in local affairs, it was in autumn 1939, before Soviet power had been fully established. Sovietization of the economy and society began in earnest in January 1940. In February 1940, local militias aided the NKVD in the organization of the first major deportation of 17,851 Polish elites, largely Polish colonists and state officials. Perhaps 500 Polish Jews were among them.[57]

By 1940, it seems likely that few Volhynian Jews had any illusions about the Soviet Union. Jews were legal equals in a system in which all were subject to deportation and terror. Jews had access to Jewish culture, but only in officially sanctioned versions. A society that was still generally Orthodox and observant was exposed to Soviet religious policy. The destruction of the community meant that the rites of life and death, if they were to be organized by Jews rather than officials, had to be arranged secretly. Jews could participate without prejudice in the economy, but the open market itself was disappearing. Jews dominated the black market, which further worsened relations with gentiles. Communists of Jewish origin had played an important role in local militias in late 1939, but by 1940, they had been replaced by men from the east. The year 1940 saw the liquidation of legal private trade, and the dissolution of remaining Hebrew schools. In 1940, cadres from the east took full control of state administration and banned private trade.[58] Just as many Ukrainians were disillusioned by collectivization, so many Jews were disappointed by the end of private enterprise. While Polish landlords saw their state destroyed and their estates expropriated, prosperous urban Jews lost their stone houses, factories, banks, and hotels to the new authorities. Savings accounts were liquidated, wiping out the Jewish middle class.[59]

Communists and refugees, the groups most welcoming of Soviet forces in 1939, had second thoughts in 1940. Many Jewish refugees from western Poland refused Soviet passports, on the logic that Poland would be reestablished, and that Polish citizenship was preferable to Soviet. They were likely a majority of the 12,752 people removed from Volhynia in the June 1940 wave of Soviet deportations.[60] By 1941, the Soviet administration was supported by almost no one, but had implicated Ukrainians, Poles, and Jews in a kind of fearful general collaboration.[61] All inhabitants came to understand that the Soviet state required no ideological enthusiasm to entrench itself, but functioned very well in the elimination of rival ideas and organizations.[62] It could not be turned to serve the purposes of other groups, and attempts by members of one group to exploit others only served its purposes. Distrust and denunciation were its ideal conditions. This made Ukrainians, Jews, and Poles mistrustful of each other, but also eroded internal cohesion within each group. As one Jew recalled,

> Already under the [Soviet] regime, before the Nazi tragedy, fathers of families had become like loosely hanging limbs. The framework of their lives was torn away, their families became unsteady, their desire for society disappeared, and the authority of Jewish conscience crumbled.[63]

As another Volhynian Jew summarized the state of affairs, "we thought it would get better, but it got worse."[64]

German Occupation

For Volhynian Jews, the worst began in summer 1941. Hitler's racial policies, already unthinkably ambitious, would find vast new horizons as his armies raced eastward in the Soviet Union. The Soviet Union was unprepared for the German attack, and the Wehrmacht swept across Volhynia and the other formerly Polish territories in a matter of days in late June 1941. By early July 1941, all of Volhynia was in German hands. The Soviet occupation, seemingly so durable, lasted a scarce 22 months. Most Jews in Volhynia remained where they were. There was little possibility of moving eastward faster than German troops, little certainty where Jews would go. In September 1939, Jews from western Poland fled east, believing that they would find shelter among organized Jewish communities in eastern Poland. The next flight east, for most Jews, would be a leap into the unknown, into territories that had been Soviet before 1939, where there was no organized Jewish life. Volhynian Jews knew a good deal about Soviet rule by 1941 and had every reason to believe that flight east could only lead to Siberian exile. Volhynia was largely woods and marshland, and while nature provided some shelter, it offered little sustenance. Many Jews who left Volhynian towns as the Wehrmacht invaded were induced to return. The Soviets sometimes halted refugees at the 1939 Soviet-Polish border. In the end,

"Peasants, seize the grain! It will be yours!" reads this flyer from the records of the German Foreign Office representative attached to the 6th Army, which passed through Volhynia. The flyer, which began circulating in mid-July 1941, mixes social discontent, animosity toward the Soviet police, and antisemitic tropes. Various German authorities, including the Foreign Office and the Wehrmacht, collaborated in creating such flyers. Political Archive/ Federal Foreign Office, Berlin, R 105173.

only about 1.5 percent of Jews from Lutsk and Kovel escaped to the east. Jews from Rivne and Ostroh, further east in Volhynia, escaped in somewhat higher numbers. After the deportees of 1940, these refugees were probably the second-largest group of Jewish survivors of the German occupation.

Yet in summer 1941, Jews also did not know what they were fleeing. They might suspect that German occupation would be worse than Soviet occupation, but this was still far from certain. Even when they knew something about Nazi occupation practices, they had no reason to expect total annihilation. To be sure, the Nazi invasion of Poland had involved mass executions of prisoners of war and mass retributions against civilians for individual acts of resistance.[65] Nazi policies in occupied Poland between 1939 and 1941 involved mass expulsions of Polish citizens from territories annexed to the Reich, and ghettoization in cities with Jewish populations. Yet the vast majority of those expelled from their homes by the Germans had been non-Jewish Poles, and the major killing actions had been directed at the Polish intelligentsia, not against the Jews. Hitler's first priority in Poland was to destroy any potential national leadership: a policy that resulted in the murder of many Jews, to be sure, but certainly had not revealed an intention to murder all Jews in general.[66] As of June 1941, it was still possible to believe that the Germans killed to prevent resistance, rather than to destroy a racially defined group. The mass murder of Jews as such began with the second eastward march of the German Army, on the new eastern front. At first, in summer 1941, the main perpetrators were the mobile SS and police killing units, the Einsatzgruppen. Similar task forces had engaged in mass murder in occupied Poland against the Polish population, and in the east, they initially engaged in the murder of Jews: first Jews in party and state positions, then able-bodied men, then all "suspicious" elements, and by September 1941 entire communities.

Einsatzgruppe C (commanded by Dr. Dr. Otto Rasch, doctorates in law and political economy) followed the Wehrmacht's Army Group South into Ukraine in June 1941. As elsewhere on the eastern front in June 1941, in Volhynia Einsatzgruppe C tried to induce the local population to kill Jews and Bolsheviks in "self-cleansing actions." This policy led to pogroms in a broad arc of territory from the Baltic to Bukovina.[67] Sometimes, the Germans failed to incite pogroms; in certain places, pogroms were probably instigated with little or no German involvement. The Germans ably exploited the Soviet legacy. The NKVD had murdered its prisoners before fleeing to the east, and that many of these prisoners had been Ukrainians. In Volhynia, the most deadly pogrom was apparently in Kremenets (Polish, Krzemieniec), where the NKVD had murdered some 100–150 prisoners before hastily departing, and where the disinterred bodies revealed signs of torture. Here, the local population killed about 130 Jews. In Lutsk, the NKVD machine-gunned its prisoners after a revolt, leaving behind 2,800 corpses.

Special Commando 4a reported that it organized the murder of 2,000 Jews as retribution.[68]

These actions ranged across a spectrum in which, at one extreme, the local population killed Jews with (and sometimes without) the support of the Germans and, at the other, the Germans killed Volhynian Jews hoping to gain the support of the local population. As the summer of 1941 progressed, however, the vast majority of mass murders came to be committed by the Germans. In June and July 1941, the German police and the SS killed about 12,000 Volhynian Jews, mostly but by no means entirely young men.[69] In Melnytsia (Polish, Mielnice), an Einsatzkommando detachment appeared with a list of political activists.[70] In Klevan (Polish, Klewań), Ukrainians told the SS which homes were Jewish, and that all of the Jews were Communists. About 700 of the 2,500 Jews of that shtetl were killed during the first days of the occupation, their bodies left on the street to be eaten by dogs and swine for three days. Then the Germans made Jews take the bodies to the local synagogue and burned it.[71] In late June, the Germany Army ordered all Jewish men to report for work at the Lubart Castle by the Styr River. When it transpired that ten German soldiers had been killed, the army murdered 1,160 Jews within the walls of the castle.[72] In Rivne, the town that became the administrative center of the civil administered zone of occupation known as the Reich Commissariat Ukraine (RKU), the German Order Police, assisted by a detachment from Einsatzkommando 5, killed 15,000 Jews on November 6–7, 1941.[73] Overall, the Germans killed perhaps 20,000 Volhynian Jews in autumn 1941.

These death tolls, high as they were, remained lower in Volhynia than in Ukrainian lands further east. The front had passed through Volhynia very quickly, before the killing of Jews had become a policy of total annihilation. In central Ukraine, starting in early September 1941 at the latest, entire Jewish communities were simply eliminated: Berdychiv on September 12, Vinnytsia on September 19, Kiev on September 29–30, Dnipropetrovsk on October 13. In Volhynia, some semblance of Jewish life remained, and some shadow of Jewish social order could return. Even in Rivne, nearly 10,000 Jews were still alive as 1942 began. In Volhynia, these mass murders could still perhaps be understood as a wartime pogrom, something to be weathered until the war had finished.

There were some signs that the Germans regarded Jewish communities as durable. In July 1941, German authorities required Volhynian Jews to reconstitute the Jewish community in the form of the Jewish council, or *Judenrat*.[74] Since the Soviets had dissolved Jewish institutions, the German revival of the trappings of communal institutions was greeted by some Jews as step toward normality. Refugees from western Poland sometimes joined the community; the chairman of the Jewish Council in Vyshnivets (Polish, Wiśniowec) was from Łódź.[75] But most of the Jewish communities in Volhynia were led by the same men who led them in 1939, under Polish rule.[76] In smaller villages bypassed

WESTERN VOLHYNIA

GEN. COM. VOLHYNIA-PODOLIA

Reich Commissariat Ukraine

General Government

--------- National and territorial borders, 1942
========= National borders, 2007
-·-·-·- Polish regional borders, 1939
··············· Regional borders, 1942
========= Soviet regional borders (oblast), 1940

========= Dual-track railroad
·········· Single-track railroad (main line)
————— Thoroughfare (supply line)
● Documented pogrom, 1941
▲ NKVD prison, 1941

by the wave of killing in summer 1941, the Germans' call for the creation of Jewish councils recalled the relatively peaceful German occupation during the First World War.[77]

In late 1941, however, the traditional institution of communal autonomy was perverted to support the Germans' "new order." Jewish leaders did exercise some responsibilities that recalled their traditional role. The communities appealed to the Germans to allow Jews to return to the jobs they had held before the Soviet occupation, and issued certificates to qualified workers. In larger towns the community ran health clinics and moderated in Jewish disputes.[78] Yet the basic responsibilities had been fundamentally warped. Perceptibly or imperceptibly, a page had been turned. The communities used the backs of interwar Polish kehilla forms, printed in Polish and Yiddish, to handwrite petitions in the languages of power of 1941, German and Ukrainian. The community was traditionally responsible for raising taxes; under the Germans it was required to pay unsustainable contributions in gold, jewelry, and goods. It became an instrument by which the German authorities extracted Jewish wealth before murdering Jewish populations.[79] The community had never traditionally disposed of a police force; the Germans created such forces in order to direct their supreme power within the ghetto. The Jewish Order Service was charged with keeping order in the ghetto, collecting the contributions, and organizing forced labor. During German-led killing actions, Jewish policemen found Jews in their hiding places and turned them over to the Germans.

Even at the most local level, the existence of Jewish policemen did not signify Jewish power.[80] The Ukrainian police established by the Germans in July 1941 was granted far more discretion and responsibility. Under the Soviet occupation, Ukrainians and Jews had often worked together in the local militias; now the local organs of coercion that mattered were usually staffed by Ukrainians, occasionally also by local Germans (Volksdeutschen). Importantly, policemen were generally Ukrainians chosen by the Germans or by the advance groups of Ukrainians nationalists that swept east behind the Wehrmacht. Jews who fought with Ukrainians that summer inevitably got the worst of it, as Jews had no coercive power, and Ukrainians, at the local level, had some. A Jewish high school student in Lutsk, for example, fought his schoolmates, who now treated him as an enemy. He was brutally murdered, crushed in a waterwheel.[81] In the countryside, the Ukrainian police was often the only authority, and policemen robbed Jews.[82] Since young Ukrainian policemen were expected to do the heavy work for their middle-aged German superiors, and because the ratio of the former to the latter was five to one and climbing, the face of German power in the Volhynian countryside was Ukrainian. Before 1939, the police in Volhynia had been Polish; under both Soviet and Nazi occupation, the police were predominantly Ukrainian.[83] The Ukrainian policemen were trained to associate local Jews with Soviet Communism. One Jewish fugitive was called "Kaganovich" by his Ukrainian pursuers: The Nazis presented Lazar M. Kaganovich, a leading member of the Soviet Politburo, as a central figure in the 1939–1941 Soviet occupation, and he was known as one of the Soviet officials responsible for the artificial famine of 1932–1933 (although the famine had not directly affected Volhynia, which had been in Poland at the time). The Germans worked hard to make Ukrainians see a connection between local Jewry and the famine.[84] There were, however, a few Ukrainian policemen who, despite the direction of German policy, helped Jews to escape.[85]

Soviet police power had also been heavily based in the Ukrainian population between 1939 and 1941; now Nazi police power was as well. Ukrainians were the majority population of Volhynia and less objectionable to the two occupiers than the great local enemy: Poles for the Soviets, Jews for the Germans. Under Nazi rule, some Ukrainian policemen were ideologically motivated, although some of the Ukrainian militiamen under Soviet rule had also been ideologically motivated. Ukrainians in the smaller towns probably served in both Soviet and Nazi militias. In many cases, the Germans simply kept the Soviet militias as a matter of convenience. In some localities, the Germans left the organization of the militia to Galician Ukrainians from the Organization of Ukrainian Nationalists.

This organization had been weak in Volhynia before 1941 and had cooperated with and tried to penetrate the Communist Party of Western Ukraine. The Organization of Ukrainian Nationalists had treated the Communist Party of Western Ukraine, and quite correctly, as the organization spreading Ukrainian nationalism in Volhynia. It therefore seems very unlikely that even militias recruited by the Organization of Ukrainian Nationalists would have been free of some previous association with Communism, during the Soviet period, during the interwar years, or both.[86] In 1941, under the Germans, as in 1939, under the Soviets, some Ukrainians had simply responded to the official summons to join the police. For most, the motives were probably economic or social: to get a salary, and to gain status. For some, the motives were political: to gain military training, arms, or information. Under both occupations, Ukrainian young men hoped to avoid deportation. The NKVD sent suspect elements to Kazakhstan, and the German police sent fit young men as forced labor to the Reich. Service in the police was protection from deportation.[87]

When taking orders from local commissars (sometimes Jews) under the Soviets or taking orders from the Germans, Ukrainian policemen were not pursuing an independent policy. They were not even legally permitted to plunder the Jews (although of course some did); instead, they were supposed to turn over all property of deceased Jews to the office of Reich Commissar for Ukraine Erich Koch.[88] In all likelihood, the Germans overlooked the plundering of Jews by Ukrainians, in order informally to compensate collaboration. From the local Jewish point of view, the Ukrainian police were powerful: They were often armed and decided upon life or death.

Ukrainian policemen identified Jews to the Germans, so that even Jews who had "a good appearance" and had escaped the September 1941 regulations about wearing armbands were soon placed on lists.[89] In Povorsk (Polish, Powórsk), Ukrainian policemen could force a Jewish man to dance at night naked while being whipped.[90] Ukrainian policemen answered to the German police, who numbered about 1,400. German methods left no ambiguity about the place of Jews in the new order. In Volodymyr (Polish, Włodzimierz), for example, they chose a strong young Jewish man, buried him up to his neck, poured gasoline over his head, and burned him to death.[91] In the provinces Jews, not Ukrainians, were ordered to simply give any material goods they had accumulated under Polish and Soviet rule to the new Ukrainian authorities.[92] It was the Jews who had to clean the cities and repair the buildings in September 1941 to prepare for the arrival of the German civil administration.[93]

In autumn 1941, the German civil administration, Erich Koch's RKU, replaced the German Army as the source of executive power in Volhynia and became the local organizer of the "Final Solution." In general, German organs of power cooperated smoothly with one another, despite occasionally competing institutional interests.[94] Real power remained with the Germans, even as some local administration passed to local ethnic Germans and Ukrainians. In some cases, Ukrainians who had just claimed to be loyal Communists now presented themselves as loyal German collaborators.[95] Although the Germans sought to eliminate any possible Soviet insurgency, they could not remove every schoolteacher or police officer who had exercised authority under the Soviets. Indeed, this was one difference between the German occupation and the Soviet: The Soviets essentially deported everyone with an education who had played any role in the previous Polish regime in any capacity. Because the Soviets had only occupied half of Poland, they also had the spare personnel to send to Volhynia. As Germany's occupation spread rapidly east, administrative capacity wore thin. Had the Germans deported or killed everyone who knew how to use a piece of chalk or a hold a club, they would have been left with no one to run the schools and the police forces. Indoctrination and extermination were two branches of public administration that the Germans could not, given their colonial priorities, do without.

German policemen and their ever more numerous Ukrainian counterparts began to establish ghettos in Volhynia and, insofar as Jewish populations remained alive, across the RKU.[96] In towns, this meant expulsions from homes and the erection of barriers; in villages Jews were simply banned from leaving their current place of residence. In the smallest settlements no formal ghetto was established.[97] In Lutsk, Poles and Ukrainians left work to watch as Jews were forced into the ghetto.[98] During the first half of 1942, epidemics raged through the overcrowded Volhynian ghettos. Jews began to starve to death; people who tried to bring food from the outside were killed by the Germans.[99] Within the ghettos, the same hierarchy of power remained. The community still raised contributions from Jews to pay Germans: Whereas the previous hope had been to avoid the ghetto, now the hope was to preserve life.[100] The Jewish police collected the money, organized the forced labor, and prevented escape. The Ukrainian and German police guarded the ghetto. Surviving Jews were intentionally worked to death. All Jews between the ages of 14 and 60 were subject to slave labor. Any Jew found beyond the ghetto not engaged in slave labor was to be shot. Even in these circumstances, communities continued to care for their members, trying to move clinics into the ghettos before they were fenced off, and appealing to the Germans to restrain their demands for labor. As late as May 1942, after two-thirds of Rivne's Jews had already been killed, its communal authorities still tried to negotiate with local authorities so that survivors could preserve some means of subsistence.[101]

By that time, a second sweep of mass murder had begun. Its purpose, at first, was to murder all Jews deemed unfit for labor. It quickly became a policy of total annihilation of all Volhynian Jews. Between April and July 1942, another 30,000 or so Volhynian Jews had been killed by the German police, with the help of Ukrainian policemen. In late August 1942, local leaders of the RKU administration learned that all remaining Jews were to be killed in the next few weeks.[102] The police in the RKU administrative center, Rivne, had been seeking to eliminate the Jews entirely since November 1941. Local authorities understood perfectly well that they were engaged in "the liquidation of the Jews."[103] By summer 1942, the Jews of General Commissariat Volhynia-Podolia, horribly reduced as they were, constituted the only sizable community left in the RKU.[104] In Volhynia, as throughout the RKU, the German and Ukrainian policemen murdered Jews in death pits near their homes.[105] From Lutsk, for example, the Jews were driven about seven kilometers into a forest, where pits had already been dug. Jews were forced to strip and lie face down in the pits. There they were shot to death, or buried alive if they survived the first salvo. So perished about 17,000 Jews.[106] The last Jews of Rivne, Volhynia's second important Jewish community, were murdered in the same way in woods near Kostopil.[107] Because these actions took place in public and over months, Volhynian Jews had few doubts about their fate. The very openness of the "Final Solution" in Volhynia encouraged some Jews to flee for their lives. After the deportees of 1940 and the refugees of 1941, these escapees of 1942 were the third largest group of survivors. Survival after escape was an endeavor of almost unimaginable difficulty. Leaving the ghetto was the easiest part.

Partisan War

The overwhelming majority of Volhynian Jews perished during the German occupation. All escapes, then, were exceptions, each requiring an explanation.[108] Yet there were a few patterns. Jews in the Tuchyn ghetto (Polish Tuczyń) and the workshop in the Lutsk ghetto rebelled, allowing a few people to escape in the general confusion. A few hundred more Jews were protected from ghetto liquidations by German engineer Hermann Friedrich Gräbe. Given this second chance, some of them escaped to the forests. Gräbe also furnished his last 25 employ-

Jews wearing circular badges (in contrast to the Star of David common in Western and Central Europe) walk through Kremenets, Volhynia. The coats and scarves suggest that the picture may have been taken during the ghettoization of the town's Jews, which took place on March 1, 1942. The ghetto was liquidated on August 18, 1942, in a shooting operation typical for this region of Ukraine. USHMM, courtesy of Instytut Pamięci Narodowej, Warsaw.

ees with false Aryan papers (German identity documents, like Soviet but unlike Polish, specified nationality) and sent them to a fictitious branch of his company in Poltava, where they survived.[109] A few Jews succeeded in impersonating Poles or Ukrainians from the beginning of the war and thereby avoided the ghetto. A few individuals were outside the open ghettos of the countryside during the liquidations and escaped after their families had been killed. Many Jews slipped away from the ghettos before liquidation, only to be betrayed by those they had paid to protect them.[110] The sense of vulnerability outside the ghetto meant that few Jews tried to escape before the liquidations began. Those who did escape the larger closed ghettoes such as Lutsk or Rivne were often children who hid themselves in attics during the liquidations, slipped out of the ghetto thereafter, and found shelter with Polish, Ukrainian, or Czech peasant families. Children could do useful work around the farm, aroused pity as orphans, were easier to hide, and were less unwilling than adults to convert to Christianity.[111]

A Jew who survived a ghetto's liquidation had to find shelter, food, and water, a task impossible without help. The law of the land was German and prescribed death not only to Jews but to those who hid them. Even without this draconian threat, most gentiles were cowed by German force and saw the presence of a Jew outside a ghetto as something alarming and threatening. As elsewhere in German-occupied Europe, much of the local gentile population was corrupted by the acquisition of Jewish property, and many gentiles came to see the murder of Jews as corresponding to their personal economic interests. A Dubno survivor remembered only one Pole in Dubno who refused his share of plundered Jewish property.[112] Many Volhynian Ukrainians and Poles, no doubt, were indifferent to the Jews' fate. Some, certainly, approved of German policy. Others, Poles and Ukrainians alike, warned friends inside the ghetto to escape, although warning is easier than rescue.

To support and hide a human being is an enormous effort, even when one's own life and the life of one's family are not at stake. Since a single informant could destroy a rescue attempt, the undertaking was often the work of families working in conspiracy right in front of their neighbors as well as the Ukrainian and German police. In these conditions, very few people offered disinterested assistance, and many of these soon became frightened. Prewar friends sometimes proved unreliable during this war of annihilation. Prewar employees sometimes turned in their Jewish employers to the Germans. Prewar political comrades, fellow Communists especially, were perhaps more trustworthy. As elsewhere in Europe, gentile spouses and suitors were sometimes able to protect Jewish loved ones, although in Volhynia Jewish-Christian marriages were very rare.[113]

Some gentiles risked their own lives to save the lives of Volhynian Jews without financial, personal, or ideological motivation. Fanye Pasht hid with her Ukrainian peasant rescuer, one Lavrov, behind his stove. Mikołaj Kuriata took in Estera Guz, who was deaf, blind, tubercular, and no longer young. Zygmunt Kuriata rescued Szyja Flajsz, a young boy. Franciszek Broczek and his son and daughter gave shelter to no fewer than 25 Jews, 21 of whom survived the war. Bogdan Bazyli and his family saved at least 22 Jews. He built a dugout for them, and every evening brought food and water and collected urine and feces. His children brought mushrooms and fruit at dawn. Bazyli lived in the Polish colony of Pańska Dolina, which became a base for the Polish Home Army, and which gave shelter to other Jewish families. Here, as in the Polish colony of Trzesłaniec, neighbors did know about the presence of Jews and helped keep them alive.[114] Many others gave shelter to Jews for a time and then led them to nearby Soviet partisans. There was nothing ideological about this: Everyone in Volhynia, from the Ukrainian Baptists to Polish patriots, knew that the Soviet partisans had the capacity and sometimes the willingness to save Jews. Most stories of Jewish survival in Volhynia involve the Soviet partisans.

Soviet partisans appeared in northern Volhynia in June 1942, just as the ghetto liquidations began. Armed forces opposed to Hitler were in proximity to the killing fields, and every Jew knew that the partisans were the best hope for survival.[115] The Soviet partisan soldiers were no less antisemitic than other Ukrainians or Russians, but most of their officers enforced internationalism, and some understood the Jewish plight.[116] Anton Brynsky, the commander of an important group of Soviet partisans in Volhynia, was believed by some of the Jews he saved to be a Jew. He was an ethnic Ukrainian. One of his officers, "Maks," is most often mentioned as a friend of the Jews of Volhynia. Maks (who was a Pole named Józef Sobesiak) and other partisan officers separated Jews into those ready for combat (perhaps 1,000) and those who would be protected as civilians (perhaps another few thousand). His partisans protected "civilian camps" of Jewish survivors in the Volhynian forests.[117] Maks was perhaps the only partisan leader to make contact with ghettos before their liquidation and was perhaps the most devoted to the protection of the civilian camps. He recalled that three of the camps were named "Birobidzhan" (after the Soviet Jewish national homeland), "Nalewki" (after the principal street in Jewish Warsaw), and "Palestine."[118] Polish and Ukrainian rescuers sent Jews into the local woods to seek the civilian camps by listening for conversations in Yiddish.[119]

Jews with Communist pasts were assigned important work. Jakub Mendziuk, for example, seems to have been in contact with Soviet partisans from the ghetto and to have brought a number of Jewish refugees into the partisan ranks. He was then assigned to recruit Volhynian Poles for a special Polish unit of the Soviet Ukrainian partisans (which was commanded by a Jewish husband and wife, the Satanowskis.).[120] Izrael Pinczuk was also an agitator, or in his words a "politruk." His job was to gain the support of the local population for the Soviet cause, which meant working with and among Ukrainians. He seems to have enjoyed some success: He had "a whole staff of people I recruited, among them local peasants, Ukrainians who had once served the Germans and now came over to our side."[121] Pinczuk's account of his accomplishments is confirmed by Ukrainian nationalists, who looked on with great concern as the Ukrainian police, recruited by Jewish Communists, left the Germans to fight for the Soviets in late 1942.[122] Local Jews who were less well known to the Soviet officers still performed important functions. Some gathered intelligence; others served as guides.[123] Jews were also sent on diversionary missions designed to weaken the German war effort, destroying supplies and mining bridges.[124] Jews with a "German physiognomy" were taught literary German and sent to assassinate German officials. One Jewish woman worked as a waitress and assassinated some Germans by leaving a bomb under a restaurant table.[125]

Jews seem to have played a more important role in the Soviet partisan effort in Volhynia than anywhere else.[126] Partisan warfare gave many Volhynian Jews a wartime occupation that they could experience and remember as meaningful. This is not to say that the Soviets were virtuous practitioners of guerilla warfare. On the contrary, they set a standard for brutality in partisan warfare that Ukrainian nationalists later worked hard to match. Soviet partisans cleansed territories they regarded as theirs of anyone they found there. They retaliated against whole villages thought to collaborate with the Germans. They assassinated individuals seen as agents of Germans. In some cases, they intentionally provoked reprisals against villages that they regarded as too passive.[127]

Jews took part in such actions and engaged in direct combat with German police forces.[128] Combat, more than anything, was remembered as redeeming life. As one partisan put it, "I was glad that I could avenge myself somewhat. I felt a bit lighter with every German I killed." Another recalled that "with the partisans, life had for me its full value." A third remembered "the splendid feeling of the deed, of the struggle for victory." A young woman accepted for reconnaissance work wrote that "from that moment I began to live."[129] On a limited scale, the partisans fought to make Volhynia safer for Jews still in hiding. Revenge expeditions (usually led by Ukrainians) were sent to kill Ukrainians who turned in Jews to the Germans. The goal was to force a change in the moral balance of the countryside, to make Ukrainian peasants inclined to shelter wandering Jews rather than summon the police.[130] For this to work, the peasants had to fear the Soviets more than they feared the Nazis. None of this fell within the initial mission of the partisans, which was to weaken the Wehrmacht from behind the lines. Yet the simple fact that Soviet arms were used to rescue Jewish life and dignity was impossible for survivors to forget.[131]

By 1943, the Soviet partisans were one of two guerilla armies battling for control of the region in anticipation of the defeat of the Germans. To general surprise, Ukrainian nationalists established the Ukrainian Insurgent Army (UPA) in Volhynia in early 1943, and it began its major operations in Volhynia by attacking the Polish population.[132] The Polish colonies that sheltered many Jewish survivors were a main target of its attacks.[133] As the UPA brought much of the countryside under its control, Jews who were staying with Poles were killed along with their rescuers, presumably sometimes as Poles and sometimes as Jews.[134] Polish rescuers fled their villages, as the Jews they sheltered had done the previous summer. Fleeing Poles sometimes met Jewish refugees in the forest and fought with them against Ukrainian nationalists. These smaller groups were absorbed by the Soviet partisans.[135] Jews sometimes joined Poles in their flight to the towns, which were still under German control. There Jews fought with Poles in Polish self-defense units, supported sometimes by the German authorities, sometimes by the Soviet partisans, and sometimes by the Polish Home Army.[136] Some Jews adjudged the risks differently, and remained in the countryside to work the fields of their Polish friends. Some of these were also discovered by the UPA and killed as Jews. In at least one case, Jews who had shelter in 1943 rescued Poles from Ukrainians.[137] In another case, Jews who had taken shelter with Poles watched as they were murdered by Ukrainians on western-rite Christmas Day.[138] The very fact that Poles were in flight created an opportunity for Jewish refugees, who could now present themselves to Germans as Poles fleeing from the UPA. At the same time, Jews who were posing as Ukrainians with Ukrainian families were verified anew, by Ukrainian nationalists who suspected that the Jews might be Poles.[139]

Throughout 1943, Volhynia was the battlefield of a multi-sided civil war, with Soviet Ukrainian partisans, Ukrainian nationalist partisans, Polish self-defense outposts, and the German police all engaged. The Soviet Ukrainian partisans fought the Ukrainian nationalist partisans and the German police. The Ukrainian nationalists fought the German police and the Soviet Ukrainian partisans. The Polish bases tried to protect civilians, aided variously by the Soviet partisans and the German police. The German police fought the Soviet Ukrainian partisans and the Ukrainian nationalist partisans, and recruited from and sometimes aided Polish self-defense units. Jewish survivors understood this matrix rather well and knew where they were most and least endangered: They were most at risk where Ukrainian nationalists controlled the terrain, very much still at risk in towns under German control (although they could pass for Poles), often protected by Polish self-defense units (although these could be defeated by the UPA), and most reliably defended by the Soviet partisans (although the partisans did not always want them and were sometimes forced to withdraw).

This was not quite a war of all against all, but it was a war of most against most, within which surviving Jews had to make sudden and difficult choices. The Volhynia they had known had been destroyed for good: burned were the ancient synagogues, gone were the habits of social life established under Polish rule, murdered were traditional authorities, families, and friends. By the end of 1943, almost all of the Jews had been killed. Perhaps a fifth of the Poles had been killed; during the Soviet occupation another seventh had been killed or deported. The civil war of 1943 quieted only when the Red Army returned to Volhynia in early 1944. The UPA then consolidated its forces, so as to prepare for their major struggle against Soviet power. Meanwhile, Soviet authorities then completed the process of ethnic homogenization that others had begun. The Soviet "population exchanges" of 1944–1946 ostensibly concerned citizens of prewar Poland, but in fact Poles and Jews were sent west, whereas Ukrainians had to stay in Soviet Ukraine. The real criterion was one of ethnicity, not citizenship. The ethnic criterion was applied to everyone in Volhynia, Ukrainians forced to stay despite their prewar Polish citizenship, Poles and Jews forced to leave despite their ancient traditions in the region. Jewish survivors of the Holocaust and Polish survivors of the ethnic cleansing were generally willing to depart. The history of Volhynia, as an ancient multi-confessional society, had come to an end.

Kolky and Kovel

The end of this history was experienced as such. The collective anticipation of murder was sometimes understood, by some traditional Jews, in traditional eschatological terms. Whole communities of Jews dreamed of the Messiah, and respected rabbis proclaimed the signs of his coming.[140] Since great suffering of Jews is supposed to attend the "birth-pangs" of the Messiah (*hevlei Mashiah*), this interpretation of 1942 is unsurprising. Those who escaped to the forest brought messianism with them or found it among allies and friends. Everyone who hoped to survive knew that "the Russians were the messiah."[141] Some Jews still believed in communism and understood the return of Soviet power as revolution, a fundamental change to take place on this earth.[142] Other Jews, fighting in the Soviet ranks, found their Zionist beliefs confirmed, or became Zionists in the forest.[143] In rough terms, Zionism was a secularization of religious faith, a desire to return to Palestine before the Messiah or without Him. It meant an end to the world of the diaspora. Like religious messianism or communism, it allowed people to describe the end of the world and impart significance to their experience.

Ukrainian and Polish Baptists who saved Jews took part in this system of belief, calling the Jews of Volhynia "the People of Israel," treating war as an occasion to demonstrate a side of their faith about which the Jews had heretofore known nothing. Because Protestants trusted one another, they could also move Jews from one family to another at need.[144] On one occasion, Jews promised to take their Baptist rescuer to Palestine.[145] Jewish refugees, forced to calculate and choose by day, had fearful dreams by night. In the traditions of practical cabbala (and gentile pagan survivals), they told these dreams to their rescuers, who interpreted them. The Baptists, adherents to a Protestant faith of distant origin, excelled in the native Ukrainian art of dream interpretation. A dream of a cracked wooden shoe, for example, signified the loss of a family member.[146] Yet faith, ancient or modern, native or novel, was not the only motivation of rescue. Some rescuers acted as they did not because of history, but rather despite it, not from belief in the significance of the end of the world, but from the wish to behave humanely in this one so long as it lasts. The words "help" and "humanity" are often found together in the accounts of survivors and witnesses. A Jewish survivor wrote from Israel that "he who wanted to help others in that terrible time, helped."[147] A Pole from the Kolky region recalled that "the Holocaust brought out the humanity in Poles, or the lack thereof."[148]

Kolky was the village that Henryk Józewski regarded as an emblem and instance of Jewish timelessness. Even under the Polish rule of the 1920s and 1930s, the Volhynian town changed, and Volhynian Jews endorsed modern political trends.[149] Józewski's Volhynia, with its creaky and ambiguous policies of toleration, its references to the multi-national past, and its tactics to rescue Polish power, was undone and swept away by the Second World War. Neither Moscow nor Berlin offered the Ukrainian majority of Volhynia political independence, and both thereby contributed to the emergence of Ukrainian nationalist partisans. The Soviets banned traditional Jewish institutions and gave some Jews a taste of political responsibility. The Nazis revived and perverted communal autonomy. In 1943, the UPA controlled much of the Volhynian countryside, having fought both German and the Soviet invaders and killed both Polish and Jewish natives. Traditional Jewish belief continued, inflecting these trends and opposing them, under Polish rule as under the two occupations.

The general sense of the coming end was also recorded individually, in ways that reveal fundamental, perhaps timeless, human concerns. At this point, at the edge of the abyss, humanity, or the lack thereof, was simply asserted. Packed into the synagogue of Kovel in September 1942, awaiting certain death, some of the town's remaining 12,000 Jews set down a few parting words on the wall, in Polish, Yiddish, and Hebrew.[150] Some left their names, with the date and fact of death. Two young girls, signing only first names, wrote that "one so wants to live, and they won't allow it. Revenge, revenge." An unsigned note was less personal: "For our innocent blood, for the tears of mothers and children. A tragedy such as the world as never seen, and dear God we will not be silent! We ask for revenge." A nearby line, with a simple surname and date, asserts that "God will avenge." Another young person tried to describe the experience of awaiting the end: "I write the last time before my death. If anyone should survive, may he remember the fate of our brethren. I am strangely calm, although it is hard to die at 20." A woman wrote her husband, so that "should he come to the *shul*" he would learn of the death of his wife and daughter. A mother and father asked for *kaddish* to be said for them, and for the holidays to be kept. A parent recorded that: "I die, innocent, with my little son." A girl wrote to her mother: "My beloved mama! There was no escape. They brought us here from outside the ghetto, and now we must die a terrible death. We are so sorry that you are not with us. I cannot forgive myself this. We thank you, mama, for all of your devotion. We kiss you over and over."

Notes

1. Henryk Józewski, "Zamiast pamiętnika (2)," *Zeszyty historyczne,* no. 60 (1982), p. 81. On the mutual influence of Christian and Jewish sacral architecture in Volhynia, see Eleonora Bergman, "Gates of Heaven," *Polin,* Vol. 14, 2001, pp. 358–374. On modernization and the countryside, Włodzimierz Mędrzecki, "Przemiany cywilizacyjne i socjotopograficzne miast województwa wołyńskiego 1921–1939," *Kwartalnik Historii Kultury Materialnej,* no. 1 (1995), p. 113.

2. Israel M. Ta-Shma, "On the History of Jews in Twelfth- and Thirteenth-Century Poland," *Polin,* Vol. 10, 1997, p. 307.

3. Szmuel Spektor, "Żydzi wołyńscy w Polsce międzywojennej i w okresie II wojny światowej (1920–1944)," in Krzysztof Jasiewicz, ed., *Europa Nieprowincjonalna* (Warsaw: Instytut Studiów Politycznych PAN, 1999), pp. 566f.; M. J. Rosman, *The Lord's Jews* (Cambridge: Ukrainian Research Institute, 1990), pp. 1–22. See also Jacob Goldberg, "Polish Attitudes to Jews," in Antony Polonsky, ed., *From Shtetl to Socialism* (London: Littman Library of Jewish Civilization, 2000), p. 55, and Gershon David Hundert, "Some Basic Characteristics of the Jewish Experience in Poland," in ibid., pp. 19–25. Classic studies are Salo Wittmayer Baron, *A Social and Religious History of the Jews* (New York: Columbia University Press, 1976), Vol. 16, although important conclusions have since been revised. On the

kehillot, Anna Michałowska, ed., *Gminy żydowskie w dawnej Rzeczypospolitej* (Warsaw: Dialog, 2003).

4. Austria took Galicia in the first partition of 1772, thereby creating the political framework for the emergence of Galician Jews. Theirs is a rich history quite different from that of their northern neighbors, the Volhynian Jews. Although Poles and Jews alike continued to imagine themselves within enduring communities after the partitions, imperial borders mattered.

5. Benjamin Nathans, *Beyond the Pale: The Jewish Encounter with Late Imperial Russia* (Berkeley: University of California Press, 2002), pp. 27f. on communities; p. 40 on merchants.

6. Robert Moses Shapiro, "Jewish Self-Government in Poland: Lodz, 1914–1939," PhD diss., Columbia University, 1987, pp. 2f., 50; Moshe Rosman, "In Praise of the Ba'al Shem Tov: A User's Guide to the Editions of Shivhei haBesht," *Polin*, Vol. 10, 1997, pp. 189–192.

7. Polish military intelligence had no illusions about the Ukrainian and Jewish populations of Volhynia in the 1920s. See Więckowski, Dowództwo Okręgu Korpusu II w Lublinie, do Oddziału II Sztabu Generalnego w Warszawie, "Raport Narodowościowy," April 16, 1925, Centralne Archiwum Wojskowe, Rembertów (CAW), I.371.2/A.80. On mayors: Spektor, "Żydzi wołyńscy," 570f. On manipulation of elections, Józewski's own account: "Zamiast Pamiętnika (2)," p. 151; cf. Mędrzecki, "Przemiany cywilizacyjne i socjotopograficzne miast województwa wołyńskiego," p. 111. There were about 165,000 Jews in Volhynia in 1921, and about 208,000 in 1931.

8. Record books (Księgi metrykalne) of Volhynian towns and villages in Derzhavnyi Arkhiv Rivnens'koi Oblasti (DAR) 259/1/16 = United States Memorial Holocaust Museum (USHMM) RG-31.017M-8; DAR, 261/1/28 = USHMM, RG-31.017M-8; DAR, 261/1/21 = USHMM, RG-31.017M-6; DAR, 261/1/20 = USHMM, RG-31.017M-6; DAR, 261/1/18 = USHMM, RG-31.017M-6; DAR, 259/1/19 = USHMM, RG-31.017M-5; 259/1/17[8]. In Volhynia, Jews rarely married Christians.

9. Shapiro, "Jewish Self-Government," pp. 88ff.; Jolanta Żyndul, *Państwo w państwie? Autonomia narodowo-kulturalna w Europie środkowowschodniej w XX wieku* (Warsaw: DiG 2000) pp. 110, 122.

10. For example, "Deklaracja/Deklaratse," Numbers 156 and 208 for the Klevan' kehilla, DAR, 217/1/1 = USHMM, RG-31.017M-6.

11. "Budżet na rok kalendarzowy 1932 gminy wyznaniowej w Korcu," DAR, 216/1/2 = USHMM, RG-31.017M-6; "Lista platników składki Gminy Wyznaniowej Żyd. w Korcu an rok 1932," DAR, 216/1/1.

12. Spektor, "Żydzi wołyńscy," pp. 571ff.; Stanisław Mauersberg, *Szkolnictwo powszechne dla mniejszości narodowych w Polsce w latach 1918–1939* (Wrocław: Ossolineum, 1968) p. 184. See also Shaul Stampfer, "Hasidic Yeshivot in Interwar Poland," *Polin*, Vol. 11, 1998, pp. 3–24.

13. This particular maneuver, of January 1931, was overruled by the minister of religion after a parliamentary interpolation; Jerzy Tomaszewski, "Walka polityczna wewnątrz gmin żydowskich w latach trzydziestych w świetle interpolacji poselskich," *Biuletyn Żydowskiego Instytut Historycznego*, no. 85, 1973, pp. 100–103.

14. The clearest finding of Jeffrey S. Kopstein and Jason Wittenberg, "Who Voted Communist? Reconsidering the Social Bases of Radicalism in Interwar Poland," *Slavic Review*, Vol. 67 (2003), no. 1, pp. 87–109.

15. See Alfred Wiślicki, "Wacław Wiślicki—Działacz polityczny," *Biuletyn Żydowskiego Instytutu Historycznego*, no. 158, 1991, pp. 73–85.

16. This was true throughout the country; Andrzej Ajnenkial, *Polska po przewrocie majowym* (Warsaw: Wiedza Powszechna, 1980), pp. 87, 94. See generally

Gershon C. Bacon, *The Politics of Tradition: Agudat Yisrael in Poland, 1916–1939* (Jerusalem: Magnes Press, 1996).

17. On Jews in the Non-Partisan Bloc for Cooperation with the Government, Dowództwo Okręgu Korpusu II, "Referat o sytuacji polityczno-narodowościowej DOK II za czas od 1 V do 1 VIII 1929," August 1, 1929, p. 17; CAW, I.371.2/A.88. On rabbis, Dowództwo Okręgu Korpusu II, "Referat o sytuacji polityczno-narodowościowej DOK II za trzeci kwartał 1930 r.," CAW, I.371.2/A.88. Cf. Spektor, "Żydzi wołyńscy," p. 570. On citizenship, Jerzy Tomaszewski, "The Civil Rights of Jews in Poland, 1918–1939, *Polin*, Vol. 8, 1995, p. 125.

18. For KPZU interest in the Jewish masses, Centralny Komitet KPZU, "Okolnik Nr. 3 w sprawie akcji antysjonistycznej," June 1931, Archiwum Akt Nowych, Warsaw (AAN), Komunistyczna Partia Zachodniej Ukrainy (KPZU) 165/V-7.

19. Jan Kościołek, Starosta Powiatowy Łuck, "Strajk pracowników Żydów," March 17, 1936, and strike announcements in Yiddish, AAN Urząd Województwa Wołyńskiego (UWW) 979/85/9.

20. On the popularity and activities of the Bund, Poalej Zion Lewica, and the Zionists, see Dowództwo Okręgu Korpusu II, "Referat o sytuacji polityczno-narodowościowej DOK II za czas od 1 V do 1 VIII 1929," August 1, 1929, p. 41, CAW, I.371.2/A.88; Dowództwo Okręgu Korpusu II, "Referat o sytuacji polityczno-narodowościowej DOK II za czas od 1 VIII do 1 X 1929," pp. 10, 26; CAW, I.371.2/A.88; Dowództwo Okręgu Korpusu II, "Referat o sytuacji polityczno-narodowościowej DOK II za czas od 1 X do 31 XI 1929," p. 30, February 1, 1930, CAW, I.371.2/A.88; Dowództwo Okręgu Korpusu II, "Referat o sytuacji polityczno-narodowościowej DOK II za pierwszy kwartał 1930 r.," p. 22, May 1, 1930, CAW, I.371.2/A.88.

21. On Zionist organizations: Spektor, "Żydzi wołyńscy," p. 573. On Zionist success in elections, see Shapiro, "Jewish Self-Government in Poland," pp. 177, 227.

22. See for example "Orhanizatsiinyi zvit OK Lutsk," AAN, KPZU 165/VII-1 t. 10 43.

23. "Zvit z zhovtnevoi konferentsii OK KPZU," AAN, KPZU 165/VII-1 t. 10 24.

24. On popular support for communism among Jews, see Więckowski, Dowództwo Okręgu Korpusu II w Lublinie, do Oddziału II Sztabu Generalnego w Warszawie, "Raport Narodowościowy," April 16, 1925; CAW, I.371.2/A.80; Generał brygady Drapella, Dowódca 27. Dywizji Piechoty, "Sytuacja bezpieczeństwa na terenie dywizji," Kovel', April 24, 1937, CAW, I.371.1.2/A.103. The best evidence is perhaps the uncorrected election results of 1928, which reveal that some of the Jewish towns of Volhynia voted for communist parties. Of the votes cast in Kovel', for example, 50 percent were invalidated. Ministerstwo Spraw Wewnętrznych, Wydział Bezpieczeństwa, "Udział ugrupowań wywrotowych w wyborach do ciał ustawodawczych w Polsce w roku 1928," Warsaw 1928, AAN, MSW 1/1186/15.

25. Later in life, when Józewski was arrested and interrogated by officers of Communist Poland's Public Security, he also did not connect Jews and Communism. At the time of his interrogation, about 35 percent of the 450 most important officers of the Communist security apparatus were prewar communists of Jewish origin; Andrzej Paczkowski, *Od sfałszowanego zwycięstwa do prawdziwej klęski: Szkice do portretu PRL* (Cracow: Wydawnictwo Literackie, 1999), pp. 40.

26. "Rezolucje VI rozszerzonego siedzenia CK.KPZU," Lwów 1932 (summary by the KOP), CAW, I/303/4/7016.

27. For details see Timothy Snyder, *Sketches from a Secret War: A Polish Artist's Mission to Liberate Soviet Union* (New Haven: Yale University Press, 2005).

28. Henry Abramson, *A Prayer for the Government: Ukrainians and Jews in Revolutionary Times, 1917–1920* (Cambridge: Harvard University Press, 1999), pp. 112f.

29. Jolanta Żyndul records none in her *Zajścia antyżydowskie w Polsce w latach 1935–1937* (Warsaw: Fundacja Kelles-Krauza, 1994), p. 53 and passim. There were

surely some, for example those committed by the Organization of Ukrainian Nationalists (see below).

30. "Osnovni zasady pidhotovnoi pratsi do povorotu ta vidnovlennia ukraïns'koi derzhavnosty," [1937], CAW, I.380.2.27.

31. [Third Section, URL Army], "Treść polityczna propagandy," 1927, Józef Piłsudski Institute, New York, UMW 7/4/1/34.

32. Ukraïns'kyi Revolutsiinyi Komitet [UNR Army, Second Section, Third Referat], "Do ukraïns'kykh żydiv," CAW, I.380.2.342.

33. Ukraïns'kyi Revolutsiinyi Komitet [UNR Army, Second Section, Third Referat], "V tretiu richnitsiu smerti Velikoho Vozhda Ukraïns'koho Narodu Symona Petlury," May 25, 1929, CAW, I.380.2.342.

34. Ministerstwo Spraw Wewnętrznych, Wydział Bezpieczeństwa, Referat Ukraiński, "Sprawozdanie z przejawów ruchu nielegalnego /UWO-OUN/ w Małopolsce Wschodniej i na Wołyniu za rok 1937," June 9, 1938, CAW, VIII.72.1.

35. Dowództwo Okręgu Korpusu II w Lublinie to I Wiceminister Spraw Wojskowych w Warszawie, "Likwidacja UNO w pow. kostopolskim—informacje," September 19, 1936, CAW, I.371.2/A.87

36. "Województwo Wołynskie: Referat specjalny," AAN, UWW 277 I-1.

37. On trade and industry generally, "Omówienie wydawnictwa Wołyńskiego Urzędu Wojewódzkiego p. t. 'Wołyń'," June 1937, CAW, I.371.2/A.100. On lumber and beer, Spektor, "Żydzi wołyńscy," p. 569. On the indirect protection, "Podstawowe Wytyczne do Polonizacji Chełmszczyzny," CAW, I.371.2/A.105. First signs of polonization of towns, Janina Stobniak-Smogarzewska, *Kresowa osadnictwo wojskowe, 1920–1945*, (Warsaw: Instytut Studi<o,ACU>w PAN, 2003), p. 212. On the general design, Marek Wierzbicki, *Polacy i żydzi w zaborze sowieckim* (Warsaw: Fronda, 2001), p. 21, as well as Robert Potocki, *Polityka państwa polskiego wobec zagadnienia ukraińskiego w latach 1930*, (Lublin: IES-W, 2003).

38. Regarding the number of Jewish refugees, Andrzej Żbikowski, "Konflikty narodowościowe na polskich Kresach Wschodnich (1939–1941) w relacjach żydowskich bieżeńców," in Krzysztof Jasiewicz, ed., *Tygiel narodów: Stosunki społeczne i etniczne na dawnych ziemiach wschodnich Rzeczypospolitej 1939–1953* (Warsaw: Rytm, 2002), p. 413.

39. Hoover Institution, Stanford (HI), 209/10/9721.

40. Cited after Żbikowski, "Konflikty narodowościowe na polskich Kresach Wschodnich (1939–1941) w relacjach żydowskich bieżeńców," p. 583. Kleinbaum's description matches that of a non-Jewish Polish observer: HI 210/4372.

41. HI, 209/8/10405.

42. HI, 209/7/4775. On Kovel', see Dov Levin, *The Lesser of Two Evils: Eastern European Jewry Under Soviet Rule, 1939–1941*, Philadelphia: Jewish Publication Society, 1995, p. 33.

43. For example in Dubno, HI, 209/1/3917/1 and 209/1/10888; Antonivka, HI, 209/8/10405; Kremenets', HI, 209/9/6105; and Luboml', HI, 209/13/8034. The question of the "Jewish welcome" of the Red Army is raised in the secondary literature. It is not the case that Polish observers claim that all Jews welcomed the Soviets. There are some witnesses who overemphasize the Jewish element, but the majority of literate observers writing close to the events in question mention Jewish and Ukrainian Communists, or simply Communists, rather than Jews or Ukrainians. Polish observers also mention Polish Communists (for example, HI, 209/3/3535; 209/3/3492; 210/4372; and 209/3/9240). Nor do available Jewish memoirs especially minimize the participation of Jews. One is tempted to say that many observers of these painful days were more fair-minded than their later chroniclers.

44. Dr. Jan Wojnowski, "Reportaż z powiatów Kowelskiego, Łuckiego, Horochowskiego, Włodzimierskiego z Chełmskiego," July-August 1938, CAW, DOK I.371.2/A.97 27.

45. Jerzy Tomaszewski, *Preludium zagłady: Wygnanie Żydów polskich z Niemiec w 1938 r.* (Warsaw: PWN, 1998), p. 5 and passim.

46. Levin, *Lesser of Two Evils,* 32.

47. Valdis O. Lumans, "A Reassessment of Volksdeutsche and Jews in the Volhynia-Galicia-Narew Resettlement," in Alan E. Steinweis and Daniel E. Rogers, eds., *The Impact of Nazism: New Perspectives on the Third Reich and its Legacy* (Lincoln: University of Nebraska Press, 2003), pp. 85–100.

48. Some Zionists went underground, but had little influence on the course of events. *Sefer Lutsk* (Tel Aviv: Irgun Yots'e Lutsk be-Yisrael, 1961), "Calendar of Pain, Resistance and Destruction"; Grzegorz Motyka and Rafał Wnuk, "Żydzi w Galicji Wschodniej i na Wołyniu w latach 1939–1941," in Jasiewicz, ed., *Europa nieprowincjonalna,* p. 588; Levin, *Lesser of Two Evils,* pp. 235–256. Since the *kehilla* was responsible not only for religious and communal affairs but for basic rites such as bar mitzvahs, weddings, and funerals, its liquidation was a change in Jewish life. Such rituals continbued in private homes, although the private life of Jews in eastern Poland under Soviet occupation has not been studied.

49. HI, 209/11/4217 (Kremenets' County); HI, 209/13/2935 (Luboml' County); HI, 209/1/7956 (Dubno County); HI, 209/3/2570 (Horokhiv County); HI, 209/3/4817 (Horokhiv County); HI, 209/5/6034 (Horodenko County); HI, 209/7/85685 (Kovel' County); HI, 209/8/10630; HI, 209/11/4217 (Kremenets' County); HI, 209/10/688 (Kremenets' County); HI, 209/11/3238 (Kremenets' County); HI, 209/13/2935 (Luboml' County); HI, 210/1/746 (Luts'k city); HI, 210/1/8531 (Luts'k city). Cf. Krzysztof Jasiewicz, *Pierwszi po diable: Elity sowieckie w okupowanej Polsce 1939–1941* (Warsaw: Rytm: 2001), p. 162; Motyka and Wnuk, "Żydzi w Galicji Wschodniej i na Wołyniu w latach 1939–1941," p. 586.

50. Andrzej Żbikowski, "Lokalne pogromy Żydów w czerwcu i lipcu 1941 r. na wschodnich rubieżach II Rzeczypospolitej," *Biuletyn Żydowskiego Instytutu Historycznego,* no. 162–163, 1992, pp. 10f.

51. G. V. Kostyrchenko, *Tainaia politika Stalina: Vlast' i antisemitizm* (Moscow: Mezhdunarodnye otnosheniia, 2001), p. 132; cf. Terry Martin, *Affirmative Action Empire: Nations and nationalism in the Soviet Union, 1923–1939* (Ithaca: Cornell University Press, 2001), pp. 426f.

52. Ben-Cion Pinchuk, *Shtetl Jews Under Soviet Rule* (Oxford: Blackwell, 1990), p. 49.

53. Levin, *Lesser of Two Evils,* p. 52.

54. Jasiewicz, *Pierwszi po diable,* pp. 125–134. Party membership taken from Basil Dmytryshyn, *Moscow and the Ukraine 1918–1953* (New York: Bookman Associates, 1956), pp. 240, 246. Ukrainian Supreme Soviet figure is from Solomon Schwartz, *Jews in the Soviet Union* (Syracuse: Syracuse University Press, 1972), p. 302.

55. Vadim Zolotar'ov, "Nachal'nyts'kyi sklad NKVS USRR u seredyni 30-x rr.," *Z arkhiviv VUChK-HPU-NKVD-KGB,* no. 2 (2001), pp. 326–331.

56. NKVD figures from N. V. Petrov and K. V. Skorkin, *Kto rukovodil NKVD 1934–1941* (Moscow: Zven'ia, 1999), p. 475; see also Kostyrchenko, *Tainaia politika Stalina,* p. 200.

57. A. E. Gurianov, "Pol'skie spetspereselentsy v SSSR v 1940–1941 g.," in *Repressii protiv poliakov i pol'skikh grazhdan* (Moscow: Zven'ia, 1997), p. 119; Jan T. Gross, *Revolution from Abroad: The Soviet Conquest of Poland's Western Ukraine and Western Belorussia* (Princeton: Princeton University Press, 2002), pp. 201f.

58. Motyka and Wnuk, "Żydzi w Galicji Wschodniej i na Wołyniu w latach 1939–1941," p. 586; Żbikowski, "Konflikty narodowościowe na polskich Kresach Wschodnich (1939–1941) w relacjach żydowskich bieżeńców," p. 420; Jasiewicz, *Pierwszi po diable,* p. 120; Marek Wierzbicki, *Polacy i żydzi w zaborze sowieckim* (Warsaw: Fronda, 2001), pp. 176f.

59. Marek Wierzbicki notes that 78 percent of the owners of expropriated

buildings in Pinsk were Jews. The figures were probably comparable in larger Volhynian towns; "Ofiary i kolobaranci," *Rzeczpospolita,* September 27, 2003, internet version, p. 3.

60. On the motives, Fortunoff Video Archive, Yale University (FVA), T-1627; Motyka and Wnuk, "Żydzi w Galicji Wschodniej i na Wołyniu w latach 1939–1941," p. 587. Regarding numbers, Gurianov, "Pol'skie spetspereselentsy v SSSR v 1940–1941 g.," 119.

61. Jasiewicz, *Pierwsi po diable,* p. 95; Wierzbicki, *Polacy i żydzi w zaborze sowieckim,* p. 111.

62. This is a major argument of Gross, *Revolution from Abroad,* the fundamental study of the Soviet occupation of eastern Poland.

63. "A Survivor," "The Nazi Horrors in Wiśniowec," in Haim Rabin, ed., *Vishnivits: sefer zikaron li-kedoshe Vishnivits she-nispu be-sho'ath ha-natzim* (Tel Aviv: Irgun 'ole Vishnivits, 1979), p. 315.

64. FVA, T-1344. Cf. FVA, T-640. The point about trust among Jews was made by Pinchuk, *Shtetl Jews Under Soviet Rule,* p. 5.

65. Alexander Rossino, *Hitler Strikes Poland: Blitzkrieg, Ideology, and Atrocity* (Lawrence: University Press of Kansas, 2003), pp. 58–190.

66. Christopher Browning, *The Origins of the Final Solution: The Evolution of Nazi Jewish Policy, September 1939–March 1942* (Lincoln and Jerusalem, University of Nebraska Press and Yad Vashem, 2004), pp. 93–112.

67. Jedwabne is the best known incident. See Jan Gross, *Neighbors: The Destruction of the Jewish Community in Jedwabne, Poland* (Princeton: Princeton University Press, 2001); Paweł Machcewicz and Krzysztof Persak, eds., *Wokół Jedwabnego,* 2 vols. (Warsaw: Instytut Pamięci Narodowej, 2002).

68. Karel C. Berkhoff, *Harvest of Despair: Life and Death in Ukraine Under Nazi Rule* (Cambridge: Harvard University Press, 2004), pp. 14ff.; Yitzhak Arad, Shmuel Krakowski, and Shmuel Spector, eds., *The Einsatzgruppen Reports* (New York: Holocaust Library, 1989), pp. 11, 31, 39; Rudnyts'ka, *Zakhidna Ukraïna za bolshevikami,* p. 491.

69. Estimate based upon A. I. Kruglov, *Entsiklopediia Kholokosta* (Kiev: Evreiskii sovet Ukrainy, 2000), pp. 30, 146. Spektor, "Żydzi wołyńscy," p. 575, gives a similar estimate.

70. Żydowski Instytut Historyczny, Warsaw (ŻIH), 301/299.

71. ŻIH, 301/1190.

72. Arad et al., *Einsatzgruppen Reports,* p. 32. Whereas German reports speak of two mass executions of 1,160 and 2,000 Jews, Jewish survivor accounts say 3,000 Jews were killed and do not mention the dead German soldiers or the NKVD victims; see also *Sefer Lutsk,* "Calendar of Pain, Resistance and Destruction"; ŻIH, 301/5657 and 301/1982.

73. Raul Hilberg, *The Destruction of the European Jews* (New York: Octagon Books, 1978), p. 196; Christian Gerlach, *Krieg, Ernährung, Völkermord: Forschungen zur deutschen Vernichtungspolitik im Zweiten Weltkrieg* (Hamburg: Hamburger Edition, 1998), p. 238; Kruglov, *Entsiklopediia Kholokosta,* p. 147.

74. The *kehilla* is usually called the *Judenrat* in this wartime context. The role of the *kehillot* has been an especially sensitive issue in the historiography of the Holocaust. See Raul Hilberg, *The Politics of Memory: The Journey of a Holocaust Historian* (Chicago: Ivan R. Dee, 1996), pp. 150f.

75. "A Survivor," "The Nazi Horrors in Wiśniowec," in Rabin, ed., *Vishnivits,* pp. 320f. On westerners in the Luts'k *kehilla,* ŻIH, 301/5657.

76. Spector, *Holocaust of Volhynian Jews,* pp. 169–172. Isaiah Trunk found that, in Poland in general, 43 percent of *Judenrat* members had been active in prewar *kehillot. Judenrat: The Jewish Councils in Eastern Europe Under Nazi Occupation* (New York: Macmillan, 1972), p. 574.

77. Dodl Abramovitsch, "Khurbm un Vidershtand," in D. Abramovitsch

and Morskhay V. Bernshtayn, eds., *Pinkes Biten: Der Oyfkum un Untergang fun a Yidisher Kehile* (Buenos Aires: Bitener Landslayt in Argentine, 1954), pp. 323f. The source is from lands further north.

78. On permission to work, Zhydivs'ka Rada m. Rivne, "V vidpovidi. . . ." [1941], DAR, 33/3/2 = USHMM, RG-31.017M-2; Zhydivs'ka Rada m. Rivne, Do Pana Burmistra, [1941], DAR, 33/1/8 = USHMM, RG-31.017M-1. On qualifications, Zhydivs'ka Rada, Viddil Remisnytstva ta Promyslovosti, "Na pidstavi . . ." August 1941, DAR, 33/3/2 = USHMM, RG-31.017M-1. Regarding clinics: "Poliklinyka Zhydivs'a T7073," DAR, 33/3/2 = USHMM, RG-31.017M-1. On dispute resolution, Judenrat in Rowno, "Die Schlichtungsordnung . . ." January 9 [1942], DAR, 22/1/19–USHMM, RG-31.017M-2.

79. This was part of a systematic policy throughout much of German-occupied Europe; Götz Aly, *Hitler's Volksstaat: Raub, Rassenkrieg und nationaler Sozialismus* (Frankfurt am Main: Fischer, 2005).

80. Spector, *Holocaust of the Volhynian Jews,* pp. 155ff.; ŻIH, 301/5737; *Sefer Lutsk*, "Testimony of Fanye Pasht."

81. ŻIH, 301/5657.

82. ŻIH, 301/1623.

83. Whereas the Nazis associated Jews with Communism, Ukrainians escaped this taint. Even though far more Ukrainians than Jews in Volhynia had in fact been Communists before 1939, no Nazi stereotype associating Ukrainians with communism ever emerged. This is perhaps unsurprising, as Nazi stereotypes of Jews were based upon abstractions on a global scale, not upon knowledge of local political life. Nazi knowledge of Ukrainians was provided by revolutionary Ukrainian nationalists from Galicia, who had no interest in dispelling Nazi illusions about the pliability of the local population.

84. ŻIH, 301/1393. On the scale and content of German propaganda, Shmuel Spector, "The Jews of Volhynia and their Reaction to Extermination," in Michael R. Marrus, ed., *Jewish Resistance to the Holocaust* (Westport: Meckler, 1989), p. 192.

85. *Sefer Lutsk*, "Testimony of Fanye Pasht"; ŻIH, 301/2879.

86. This analysis seeks to render plausible the facts conveyed by John Armstrong, *Ukrainian Nationalism* (New York: Columbia University Press, 1963), p. 218; John-Paul Himka, "Ukrainian Collaboration in the Extermination of the Jews During the Second World War: Sorting Out the Long-Term and Conjunctural Factors," in Jonathan Frankel, ed., *The Fate of the European Jews, 1939–1945: Continuity or Contingency?* (Oxford: Oxford University Press, 1997), p. 179; Dieter Pohl, "Russians, Ukrainians, and German Occupation Policy," in Andreas Kappeler, Zenon Kohut, Frank Sysyn, and Mark von Hagen, eds., *Culture, Nation, and Identity: The Ukrainian-Russian Encounter, 1600–1945* (Edmonton: Canadian Institute of Ukrainian Studies, 2003), p. 285.

87. Martin Dean treats these matters sensitively in his *Collaboration in the Holocaust: Crimes of the Local Police in Belorussia and Ukraine* (London: Macmillan, 2000), pp. 67, 71.

88. Wendy Lower, "The 'Reibungslose' Holocaust? The German Military and Civilian Implementation of the 'Final Solution' in Ukraine, 1941–1944," in Gerald Feldman and Wolfgang Seibel, eds., *Networks of Persecution: The Holocaust as Division of Labor-Based Crime* (New York: Berghahn Books, 2004), p. 248.

89. ŻIH, 301/2519. On the armband regulations, Dr. [Werner] Beer, "Bekanntmachung," September 17, 1941, Amtsblatt des Gebietskommissar in Rowno, April 1, 1942, DAR, 33/1/3 = USHMM, RG-31.017M-2.

90. ŻIH, 301/5737.

91. ŻIH, 301/5737. See also Zev Sobol, "The Ghetto in Wiśnowiec," in Rabin, ed., *Vishnivits*, pp. 298–310.

92. Nimets'ka Komendatura m. Mizocha, "Nakaz no. 1," July 22, 1941, DAR, 22/1/15 = USHMM, RG-31.017M-2.

93. See the lists of Jewish workers under the title "Vidomist'": DAR, 33/4/11 = USHMM, RG-31.017M-2, 33/4/15 = RG-31.017M-2.

94. Lower, "The 'Reibungslose' Holocaust?" pp. 238–258.

95. The local administration of Dubno, for example, was made up of Ukrainians who had previously taught in Soviet schools and presented themselves as Communists. Moshe Vaysberg, "Life and Destruction of the Jews in Dubno," in Ya'acov Adini, *Dubno: sefer zikaron* (Tel Aviv: Irgun yots'e Dubno be-Yisra'el, 1966) pp. 698–701.

96. For a review of the debate on the timing of this decision, see Christopher Browning, *Nazi Policy, Jewish Workers, German Killers* (Cambridge: Cambridge University Press, 2000), pp. 1–57; also Browning, *The Origins of the Final Solution,* pp. 309–351.

97. Spektor, "Żydzi wołyńscy," p. 576; *Sefer Lutsk,* "Calendar of Pain, Resistance and Destruction."

98. *Sefer Lutsk,* "Occupation, Ghetto, Destruction."

99. ŻIH, 301/1623.

100. ŻIH, 301/1477; *Sefer Lutsk,* "Calendar of Pain, Resistance and Destruction."

101. Deutsche Bürgermeister der Stadt Rowno, An den Judenobmann Dr. Bergmann, May 8, 1942; Judenrat in Rowno, An Herrn deutschen Bürgermeister der Stadt Rowno, May 10, 1942, DAR, 22/1/19 = USHMM, RG-31.017M-2.

102. Dean, *Collaboration in the Holocaust,* p. 93.

103. The phrase from a letter from the Kostopil' County commissar, An den Herrn Generalkommissar fuer Wolhynien und Podolien, September 29, 1942, DAR, 21/1/3 = USHMM, RG-31.017M-3.

104. Stephen Pallavacini, "The Liquidation of the Jews of Polesie: 1941–1942," PhD diss., Macquarie University, 1999, chapter 6, pp. 1ff.

105. A good discussion by a survivor is FVA, T-3237.

106. ŻIH, 301/1982 and 301/5657; *Sefer Lutsk,* "Calendar of Pain, Resistance and Destruction."

107. Spektor, "Żydzi wołyńscy," p. 577.

108. On the difficulties: Spector, "Jews of Volhynia," pp. 193–197.

109. Regarding rebellions by Luts'k workers: ŻIH, 301/1982, *Sefer Lutsk,* "German Workshops in Łuck." On Lakhva, ŻIH, 301/652; on Tuczyn, ŻIH, 301/652 and Spektor, "Żydzi wołyńscy," p. 578. Concerning Gräbe, Spector, *The Holocaust of Volhynian Jews,* pp. 253ff.; ŻIH, 301/1795. On Koch, ŻIH, 301/1190. Cf. Raul Hilberg, *Perpetrators Victims Bystanders,* (New York: Harper Collins, 1992), p. 174.

110. *Sefer Lutsk,* "Occupation, Ghetto, Destruction."

111. On Betrayals, *Sefer Lutsk,* "Occupation, Ghetto, Destruction." On individuals: ŻIH, 301/260, FVA, T-1627. On children, ŻIH, 301/1982; 301/2992; 301/2739; and 2794.

112. Moshe Vaysberg, "Life and Destruction of the Jews in Dubno," in Adini, *Dubno: sefer zikaron,* pp. 705f.

113. Regarding betrayal by friends, ŻIH, 301/1477 (by both Poles and Ukrainians). On employees, Berkhoff, *Harvest of Despair,* p. 81. On Faithful (Communist) comrades: ŻIH, 301/305 and 301/717; cf. Spector, "Jews of Volhynia," p. 215.

114. On Pasht, *Sefer Lutsk,* "Testimony of Fanye Pasht." On Mikołaj Kuriata, ŻIH, 301/3470. On Zygmunt Kuriata, ŻIH, 301/2739. On Broczek, ŻIH, 301/1470. On Bazyli, ŻIH, 301/6335. On Trzesłaniec (family Nazarek or Olczarek), ŻIH, 301/451. On Pańska Dolina, Stanisław Wroński and Maria Zwolakowa, *Polacy Żydzi 1939–1945,* (Warsaw: Książka i Wiedza, 1971), p. 265.

115. FVA, T-097.

116. ŻIH, 301/299; 301/53; and 301/1499.

117. ŻIH, 301/299 and 301/53. Regarding estimates, Spektor, "Żydzi wołyńscy," p. 578; Spector, *The Holocaust of the Volhynian Jews*, p. 323. Bryns'kyi's memoirs, A. P. Bryns'kyi, *Po toi bik frontu*, 2 vols. (Kiev: Politvydav Ukraïny, 1976–1978).

118. Michał Grynberg, *Księga sprawiedliwych* (Warsaw: PWN, 1993), p. 501; Wroński and Zwolakowa, *Polacy Żydzi 1939–1945*, pp. 262f.

119. Conversations: ŻIH, 301/5737. Compare Yitzhak Arad, "Jewish Family Camps in the Forests: An Original Means of Rescue," in Marrus, ed., *Jewish Resistance*, pp. 234–245. Arad says Jewish fighters better protected the camps before the arrival of the Soviets, who drew away the armed men.

120. On Mendziuk, ŻIH, 301/1795. On the Satanowskis, Spector, *The Holocaust of the Volhynian Jews*, p. 324; Ster Elisavetskii, *Polveka zabveniia* (Kiev: Mezhdunarodnyi Solomonov Universitet, 1998), pp. 86, 392. Mojżesz Edelstein was another Jew who recruited among Poles for the Soviets, ŻIH, 301/810.

121. ŻIH, 301/717.

122. "Postanovy III. Konferentsii Orhanizatsii Ukraïns'kykh Natsionalistiv Samostiinikiv Derzhavnikiv, 17–21 liutoho 1943 r.," in *OUN v svitli postanov Velykykh Zboriv* (n.p.: Vydavnytstvo Zakordonykh Chastyn Orhanizatsiï Ukraïns'kykh Nacionalistiv, 1955), p. 82; cf. Oleksander Panchenko, *Mykola Lebed': Zhyttia, Diial'nist', Derzhavno-pravovi pohliady* (Lokhvytsia: Kobeliaky, 2001), p. 75.

123. FVA, T-0927; ŻIH, 301/5657.

124. ŻIH, 301/719; 301/1811; and 301/1488.

125. ŻIH, 301/718.

126. Spector, *Holocaust of Volhynian Jews*, p. 323.

127. Amir Weiner, *Making Sense of War: The Second World War and the Fate of the Bolshevik Revolution* (Princeton: Princeton University Press, 2001), p. 161.

128. FVA, T-1845 and T-2484.

129. Respectively, ŻIH, 301/1487; 301/1499; 301/955; and 301/2519. Misha Gildenman, a Jewish officer in the Soviet Ukrainian partisans, has published memoirs in Yuri Suhl, ed., *They Fought Back: The Story of Jewish Resistance in Nazi Europe* (New York: Crown Publishers, 1967), pp. 261–274.

130. ŻIH, 301/5737 and 301/53.

131. Mordechai Altshuler, "Jewish Warfare and the Participation of Jews in Combat in the Soviet Union as Reflected in Soviet and Western Historiography," in Zvi Gitelman, ed., *Bitter Legacy: Confronting the Holocaust in the USSR* (Bloomington: Indiana University Press, 1997), pp. 151–166, proposes methods for rediscovering evidence of Jewish combat in Soviet sources. In regions such as Volhynia, the files from the eastern provinces housed at the Jewish Historical Institute in Warsaw may be easier to handle. On the aftermath, see also Weiner, *Making Sense of War*, pp. 209–235.

132. The ethnic cleansing operation and its consequences are treated here only in their direct connection with the fate of Jews. On these events, see Timothy Snyder, *The Reconstruction of Nations: Poland, Ukraine, Lithuania, Belarus, 1569–1999* (New Haven: Yale University Press, 2003), pp. 154–216; also Berkhoff, *Harvest of Despair*, pp. 285–300.

133. ŻIH, 301/1011.

134. FVA, T-1740 and T-1645; ŻIH, 301/1222.

135. ŻIH, 301/5980/B.

136. ŻIH, 301/1982 and 301/1222; Archiwum Wschodnie, Ośrodek Karta, Warsaw (AW), II/1362/2kw and II/1350; "Położenie na Wołyniu i w Małopolsce Wschodniej," 8 January 1944, Studium Polskiej Podziemnej, London, 3.1.1.13.2.

137. On farming, FVA, T-1740, ŻIH, 301/1982 and 301/297. On sheltering, FVA, T-1645.

138. Yitshakh Fisher, "In Hiding and in the Woods," in Adini, *Dubno: sefer zikaron*, pp. 717f.

139. ŻIH, 301/2519.

140. ŻIH, 301/717 and 301/397. This sentiment did not preclude the continuation of traditional Talmudic study, as among people swollen from hunger in the Luts'k ghetto. *Sefer Lutsk*, "People Studied the Talmud." See also Gershon Greenberg, "Orthodox Jewish Thought in the Wake of the Holocaust: Tamim Pa'alo of 1947," in Omer Bartov and Phyllis Mack, eds., *In God's Name: Genocide and Religion in the Twentieth Century* (New York: Berghahn Books, 2001), pp. 316–342.

141. FVA, T-640, for example, although this phrase is quite common.

142. ŻIH, 301/1795 and 301/1499.

143. FVA, T-1845.

144. Berkhoff, *Harvest of Despair*, p. 87.

145. ŻIH, 301/397. See also Dean, *Collaboration in the Holocaust*, 128. It appears that the shock of Warsaw's 1938 "revindication" (forced conversion) campaign and the experience of the German occupation favored conversions to Baptism and other Protestant denominations.

146. ŻIH, 301/397; FVA, T-640.

147. ŻIH, 301/6335.

148. AW, II/1328/2k.

149. Kolky, as Józewski perhaps preferred to forget, was also the site of violent clashes between his police and the Communist Party of Western Ukraine in 1935, *Borot'ba za vozz'iednannia Zakhidnoi Ukraïny z Ukraïns'koiu RSR 1917–1939: Zbirnik dokumentiv ta materialiv* (Kiev: Naukova Dumka, 1979), pp. 392ff.

150. ŻIH, 301/1644. As noted by Hanoch Hammer. At the time of his visit, the synagogue was being used by the Soviets to store grain.

III
Shades of Grey: Reflections on Jewish-Ukrainian and German-Ukrainian Relations in Galicia

FRANK GOLCZEWSKI

"The Ukrainians were the worst!" This sentiment or something similar is often mentioned by Holocaust survivors when they reflect on their tormentors in concentration camps and ghettos during the Second World War. Latvian and Lithuanian police and guards sometimes rank equally in terms of brutality, but as a rule, Ukrainians in such positions are singled out as uncommonly cruel. In many cases, the atrocities committed by the Nazis' eastern European accomplices even overshadow those carried out by the Germans. As one survivor put it, "The Ukrainians were indeed much worse than the Germans. When they met a Jew on the street, they killed him."[1]

The stereotype indeed has some basis in fact, but it remains as distorted as it is widely held. This display of selective memory to some extent answers one part of the question of how something like the Holocaust could have happened. After all, whatever else one can say about "the Ukrainians" in general, the behavior of Ukrainian guards in the camps and policeman outside the ghettos cannot be generalized to all Ukrainians. Likewise, one cannot deduce anything about "the Jews" based on the crimes committed by Bolsheviks of Jewish origin in the Soviet Union.

Nevertheless, perceptions of reality can seem to matter more to perpetrators, victims, and bystanders than historical reality. Stereotypes and prejudices often shape the actions of individuals and historical events as much as facts. And a steady stream of narratives concerning harrowing experiences at the hands of Ukrainians during the Holocaust—no matter how important and necessary the repeated testimonies are for posterity—can easily end up perpetuating distortions and resuscitating stereotypes, lending them a dimension and vibrancy that is larger than life. That the sample of Ukrainians in question is quite limited is quickly forgotten.

No matter how widespread some popular generalizations, no matter how morally repulsive the behavior of Ukrainian guards in the German camps, historians have to address something as complicated as Ukrainian-Jewish relations from a different point of view than survivors and their audiences. Historians have to consider the preconditions that helped create such impressions, and how representative such impressions were in fact. They must consider, as John-Paul Himka has suggested, whether the preconditions for Ukrainian collaboration were rooted in "long-term factors," i.e., historical experience over the centuries, or "conjunctural factors," i.e., contemporary events within the recent memory of the actors.[2] Historians have to sift through the evidence as provided by all sides and explain the cultural, material, and political frames of reference in which these activities occurred.

There are plenty of examples of false impressions in Ukrainian-Jewish relations: Practically every faction involved in the Russian Civil War, which broke out after the Bolsheviks took power, carried out pogroms between 1917 and 1921. Yet popular history in the east and the west has seized on the violence committed by forces of the Ukrainian People's Republic (UNR) during the rule of Symon Petliura. These forces were indeed guilty of most pogroms, but the Bolsheviks carried out scores of pogroms as well. The collaboration of militant Ukrainian nationalist groups with certain German political circles and intelligence services has left such an impression that it is largely forgotten that a good part of Ukrainian nationalist leaders in the 1920s embraced the Soviet Union's policy of Ukrainization and returned to Ukraine after a short exile. And while thousands of Ukrainians from Galicia and occupied Poland rallied to German-sponsored paramilitary and military formations, millions of Ukrainians from prewar Soviet Ukraine—the very Ukrainians who experienced the worst of Soviet rule during the 1930s—fought for the Soviets.

Postwar surveys of Ukraine during the Second World War have tended to generalize the experience of Ukrainians under Nazi rule as one all-Ukrainian disaster that inflicted an equal amount of damage throughout the Ukrainian lands. Reality, however, was much different. German rule varied in style of administration from region to region: military administration, civil administration, Reich Commissariat Ukraine, and General Government. Seen in their entirety, all these occupation regimes were without a doubt destructive, but Nazi designs on certain lands meant rule in some parts of Ukraine was less severe than in others as far as Ukrainians were concerned. This was the case in the General Government, that part of interwar Poland that was not directly incorporated into the Greater German Reich.

The Ukrainian reception accorded the Germans also varied. Ukrainians and the territories they inhabited have been shaped through the centuries by numerous partitions, annexations, occupations, and brief interludes of semi-independence. In addition to Russia, the powers that held vast stretches of Ukrainian territory at one time or another included Lithuania, the Ottoman Empire, and Poland, as well as Germany, Hungary, and Romania. And there was Austrian rule in Galicia (Eastern Galicia to Austrians, Little Poland to the Poles between the world wars, and western Ukraine to Ukrainians).

From 1772 and the first partition of Poland until 1939 and the Soviet occupation of what was then eastern Poland—167 years—Galicia was divorced from the remaining 90 percent of Ukraine. For a variety of reasons, this region during the Second World War was assigned to the General Government. As a result of a German policy of divide and rule and the pursuit of political goals via Ukrainian welfare organizations, Ukrainians in the General Government experienced a very different form of German occupation than their compatriots in the Reich Commissariat Ukraine (RKU). In discussing Ukrainians during the Second World War, it is necessary to treat these two occupation regimes separately. While overlap certainly does exist, the experiences cannot be conflated.

Most recently, Karel Berkhoff has made a major contribution to both the study of Nazi occupation policies and Ukrainian studies in his history of everyday life in the RKU. His volume addresses Galicia only on the periphery.[3] The Holocaust in Galicia has received considerable attention in recent years, in particular in the works of Thomas Sandkühler and Dieter Pohl.[4] The topic of interethnic relations in eastern Poland in the first half of the twentieth century—particularly in northwestern Poland and Volhynia—has also been receiving growing attention since the collapse of Communism in Poland and the demise of Soviet Union.[5] And at least two works on Lviv during the war are known to be in the making.[6]

So far, however, the Ukrainian-German symbiosis in the General Government and Galicia has been largely neglected in favor of the German occupation of the RKU. When this topic has been discussed, particularly in the Soviet bloc during the Cold War, it has frequently been distorted beyond the point of recognition. This chapter examines two sides of the Ukrainian-German-Jewish triangle in Galicia—Ukrainian-Jewish relations and German-Ukrainian relations—and how these intertwined to facilitate the Holocaust during the three years of Nazi Germany's occupation of Galicia. The subject is important because *Ukrainian* anti-Jewish violence was rare *in Galicia* throughout the nineteenth century and immediately after the First World War. By the start of the Second World War, however, this had changed—for the worse.

Ukrainians and Jews in Galicia from Khmelnytsky to the First World War

Jews, Germans, and Ukrainians began interacting with one another and developing their mutual stereotypes centuries ago. Sometimes perceptions were based on acceptance of particular traits, sometimes on rejection. With a few major exceptions—primarily the Khmelnytsky Uprising of 1648–1649—Ukrainians and Jews tended to coexist in relative peace until the last quarter of the nineteenth century, particularly in Galicia. Their relations steadily developed according to each group's understanding (and misunderstanding) of one other's place in society, their distinct cultural traditions, and their religious practices. These relations were the product of a permanent discourse that continually adapted to the contemporary situation. Yet in the process of this evolution, certain historical episodes came to acquire greater significance than others.

With the Union of Lublin in 1569, the Kingdom of Poland, which had come into possession of Galicia in 1349, and the Grand Duchy of Lithuania, which had come to rule most of the remaining Ukrainian lands at about the same time, merged to form the Polish-Lithuanian Commonwealth. With that, almost all of Ukraine was briefly united under the Polish crown. In the wake of this event, Polish nobles began colonizing their new domains. This practice involved the dispossession and enserfment of the local Slavic inhabitants and the recruitment of local Jews to oversee and manage the Polish lords' holdings. One result was the dramatic impoverishment of Ukrainians. With time, other sources of discontent such as Cossack privileges, tensions between the Orthodox and Roman Catholic faiths, and personal vendettas combined to create a volatile atmosphere in central Ukraine. In the mid-1640s, the Ukrainian territories erupted in rebellion. The rebels' fury was directed at the Polish nobility and, by proxy, their Jewish intermediaries. By the time Khmelnytsky's men reached Galicia, they were slaughtering Poles and Jews alike.

What began as a social conflict also took on religious significance, when in 1649 the local Orthodox clergy convinced Khmelnytsky that part of his task was to defend Orthodoxy, seen to be under siege from the Muslim Ottomans as well as from the Roman Catholic Poles and their allies the Greek Catholic Church (often called the Uniate Church), which had emerged 50 years earlier in the 1596 Act of Union at Brest. The existence of the Greek Catholic Church, which uses Orthodox liturgy but recognizes papal authority, especially infuriated Orthodox leaders farther east. Indeed, Khmelnytsky's men frequently treated Greek Catholics no less ruthlessly than Jews or Poles.[7] The injection of this religious element into the conflict exacerbated Ukrainian-Jewish relations. Ukraine's Jews, already regarded as the Poles' colonial partners, came to be seen as agents of Roman Catholic infidelity as well. The twin association further fueled the massacres of Jews.

Although news of the pogroms quickly spread throughout Europe and gained a foothold in popular imagination, it would be wrong to see in these events the start of an uninterrupted modern tradition of Ukrainian antisemitism.[8] The "Ukrainian" quality of the seventeenth-century population was not a national one, as some nationalist authors would have it. (Indeed, Khmelnytsky was not initially interested in statehood for the Dniepr Cossacks, but in privileges within the Polish Commonwealth.) National consciousness in these parts of Europe developed at best in the nineteenth, if not in the twentieth century. Cossack-Jewish antagonisms cannot be seen without the broader social context—the conflict between the Poles and the Eastern Slavs native to Ukraine.

The Cossacks established a quasi-state astride the Dniepr River under Russian protection, but in less than a generation, the Right Bank (save for Kiev) was back under Polish control. Decades passed when real or relative peace was the rule in Ukraine. Among foreign observers, the image of a vibrant, multicultural society in Galicia and Ukraine took root. There, on the edge of Europe, the peoples of different cultures seemed to deal with each other amicably, attended each other's festive events, and generally refrained from violence, the key exceptions being the Northern War and the Battle of Poltava, an event of international significance, and the Haidamak Uprisings (1734, 1750, and 1768), which were regional in character. The lands affected by the Haidamak Uprisings were still a part of Poland at the time, but only the first uprising involved Galicia. Toward the last quarter of the eighteenth century, Prussia, Austria, and Russia helped themselves to Polish territory in a series of three partitions. In the first partition, in 1772, Austria gained Galicia, while in the subsequent partitions of Poland, Russia seized most of Right Bank of Dniepr Ukraine (1793) and the bulk of Volhynia (1795).

In eastern Galicia and post-Ottoman Bukovina, Austrian Ukraine as it were, Jewish-Ukrainian relations were much more peaceful than east of the Zbruch and north of the Dniestr rivers. Anti-Jewish violence lay largely outside the narrative of Ukrainian-Jewish relations in Galicia during this period. The waves of pogroms that became synonymous with tsarist Ukraine (and Russian Poland) after 1881 did not affect Galicia. In fact, Jews and Ukrainians in Galicia actually collaborated with one another politically around the turn of the century. Despite anti-Jewish agitation on the part of Polish parties in Galicia—such as the Polish Peasant Parties and the National Democrats—these efforts resonated only in western Galicia, where few Ukrainians lived. When the Austrian Empire fell apart in November 1918 and war broke out between the Galician Ukrainians and the Poles over the future of eastern Galicia, the Jews of the region declared neutrality, a decision the Ukrainian side respected. Consequently, Ukrainian-led pogroms were quite rare in Galicia. The Polish side, however, viewed neutrality as pro-Ukrainian, which resulted in a greater frequency of Polish-led pogroms in the region, the most infamous being the one that ensued after Polish troops recaptured Lviv.[9]

It was during this period that life for Jews in what had been tsarist Ukraine deteriorated precipitously. During the Civil War, pogroms became a regular feature of life in Dniepr Ukraine, Volhynia, and Podolia. All the parties to the conflict indulged in anti-Jewish violence at some point: the Whites (forces loyal to the tsar and the idea of a united Russia), the Anarchists of Nestor Makhno, the Red Guards, and the undisciplined formations led by various local strongmen or warlords (*atamans*).[10] Antisemitism was not a hallmark of UNR policy, though. The fledgling Ukrainian republic had proclaimed far-reaching political and cultural autonomy for the Jews and other non-Ukrainians, and Jews served as ministers in the new government. However, the UNR was quite powerless and was forced to rely on irregular troops such as those supplied by the atamans, who easily changed sides. Often based in railroad cars, the UNR government under Symon Petliura frequently turned a blind eye to the atrocities committed by its soldiers. And although Petliura's government issued statements condemning atrocities, it at the same time promoted officers implicated in pogroms. Despite Petliura's prewar record on Jewish-Ukrainian relations and the constructive measures that he initially promoted, the failings of his state quickly came to outweigh its accomplishments, and these were propagated among his enemies and picked up by the European press. In the eyes of Jews around the world, Petliura soon came to personify the anti-Jewish violence of the day, while conventional wisdom even claimed that Petliura's government had ordered pogroms.[11] This perception had grim consequences in Galicia in later years.

Germany and Ukraine Prior to Versailles

Before the First World War, the most significant encounters between Germans and Ukrainians occurred during the eighteenth century, when German colonizers settled in areas such as Volhynia and the Dniepr and Dniestr basins, and Austria annexed the Ukrainian-populated territories of eastern Galicia and Bukovina. There was no opportunity for German-Ukrainian relations on a political level. Germany was, until 1871, a collection of kingdoms, principalities, and free cities, and Ukraine was throughout this period but a territory divided between the Russian Empire and Austria.

The impact of Austrian rule on Galician Ukrainians cannot be underestimated. The presence of this province in Austria-Hungary for 146 years led to a peculiar affinity between the German Habsburgs and the Galician Ukrainians. With the annexation of Galicia to Austria, a pocket of Ukrainians, former Polish subjects, remained in Central Europe, thus positioning the region to absorb the main currents of nationalist politics that circulated within the Austrian Empire in the nineteenth century. Overall, Austrian policy sought to treat its Ruthenians—as Ukrainians were called under the Habsburgs—the same as its Polish ones. While tsarist officials fought every manifestation of Ukrainian national consciousness it encountered, the Ukrainian intelligentsia in Galicia evolved along the lines of similar movements in the rest of Central Europe. In turn, during the period of Ukrainian national awakening in Galicia, Ukrainians regularly competed with the Poles for Vienna's favors—a competition Habsburg officials took care to nurture.

With the outbreak of the First World War, both the Entente Powers (England, France, and Russia) and the Central Powers (Germany and Austria-Hungary) tried to exploit nationalism to their own ends. The French set up Polish units drawing on Austrian POWs and volunteers of Polish origin from the United States, while the Russian Empire used a similar approach to organize a Czech legion, which was to disseminate unrest within the Habsburg Empire. The Germans and Austrians also went so far as to establish a Polish kingdom (a puppet state), while the Austrians and the Russians raised Polish legions for their armies.

The Russian occupation of Galicia in 1914, which included efforts to undermine the Ukrainian movement and promote russification, served to convince Galician Ukrainians to stand by the Habsburg crown. Austria responded by organizing able-bodied, national-minded Ukrainians into a legion known as the Ukrainian Sich Sharpshooters. Socialist Ukrainian emigrants from the Union for the Liberation of Ukraine, which was founded in August 1914 to promote the Ukrainian cause among the Central Powers, prompted Austria and Germany to raise the national consciousness of Russian POWs from Ukrainian for later military service.[12]

Despite its skill at manipulating the Ukrainian movement in the past, Austria was inconsistent in its treatment of its Ukrainian population. The more numerous Poles frequently had gained the upper hand over the Ukrainians, while the latter were often suspected of being pro-Russian. The fear was not altogether unfounded. A strong Russophile current did exist in Galicia prior to the war. More important, however, by March 1917, the tsar had abdicated and Dniepr Ukraine was edging toward independence. With the former Russian Empire in a state of disarray, Galicia's more strongly nationalist-minded Ukrainians were feeling drawn to the east.

Not long after the Bolsheviks seized power in Russia in November 1917, negotiations between the Central Powers and Communist Russia were held in the town of Brest with the aim of ending hostilities on the eastern front. To facilitate this agreement and maintain its hold on Galicia, Austria made some concessions to Galicia's Ukrainian separatists—such as promises to establish a separate Ruthenian province and to turn over the Chełm region (today in Poland) to Ukraine. This accord, the first Treaty of Brest-Litovsk (February 9, 1918), which also recognized the newly independent UNR (January 25, 1918), was a portentous moment in German-Ukrainian relations.

The Austro-Hungarian Empire never honored these promises. By November of that year, it too was coming apart in the wake of the armistice agreements that ended the First World War as the various national movements began to stake out their claims for future states. The Ukrainians and Poles plunged into a bloody competition for the future of eastern Galicia. In the rush to arms, the hastily formed Ukrainian Galician Army, which included some of the Sich Sharpshooters, lacked officers and began to draw on demobilized German Austrians. As a consequence, Germans held many key commands in the Ukrainian Galician Army. This development, alongside the Treaty of Brest, led key Polish officials in Poland and at the Paris Peace Conference to promote the view that the Austrians and the Germans had invented Ukrainian nationalism to serve their own aims. This belief spread to the Allies, who came to suspect that Ukrainian claims to nationhood and Polish lands were in fact part of a German conspiracy. Laboring under this misperception, the Allies ultimately conferred eastern Galicia to Poland in 1923.

This was the more short-term result of Brest. The longer-term implication was that Ukrainian nationalist circles, particularly in Galicia, became convinced that Ukrainians and Germans were natural allies against Poland, the Entente, and the Versailles Treaty. Particularly, where Poland was concerned, there was some truth to this. This hostility toward the new Polish state and the amity toward Germany would have fateful consequences once the Nazis came to power. German-Ukrainian relations between the wars, however, were not based on relations between two states but between a state, on the one hand, and various competing exile groups and underground organizations on the other.

Ukrainians and Jews in Galicia between the Wars

By 1923, Poland had, under international law, acquired the Ukrainian-populated lands of western Volhynia and eastern Galicia. Then, drawing all the wrong lessons of its past, the Polish state launched a policy of colonizing its newly acquired lands. Despite its treaty obligations to the western powers, Poland began to pursue polonization. Minority rights were disregarded and Ukrainians deprived of state subsidies. Protests became terrorist acts on the part of Ukrainian extremists, to which the Poles responded with bloody raids.[13] In anticipation of the Entente's decision to award eastern Galicia to Warsaw, the more radical Ukrainian nationalists in Galicia chose to go underground, forming the Ukrainian Military Organization (UVO) in 1920. This group, headed up by Colonel Ievhen Konovalets, resorted to terrorist tactics and forged ties with the German military and rightwing organizations in order to destabilize Poland.

The watershed event in Ukrainian-Jewish relations, for Galician Ukrainians, took place on May 25, 1926, when Petliura was killed by Samuel Schwarzbart on the streets of Paris. In the trial that followed, the gunman, who had lost more than a dozen relatives in the Ukrainian pogroms of 1918–1920, declared that he had exacted revenge for the anti-Jewish violence that had taken place under Petliura. Jewish organizations throughout Europe rallied to the assassin's cause.[14]

Most Ukrainians in western Europe and Poland emphasized Schwarzbart's connection to the Soviet Union, seeing in him a Soviet agent. Schwarzbart was acquitted, and Petliura became a martyr, particularly among émigré and student groups in Berlin, Königsberg, Prague, Paris, and Vienna.[15] Even in Galicia, where Ukrainians resented Petliura's abandoning them to the new Polish state in exchange for an anti-Soviet alliance with Warsaw in 1920, Schwarzbart's acquittal provoked outrage, with one widely circulating newspaper warning of a "disproportionate bloody response."[16] Dmytro Dontsov, the most influential thinker for militant Ukrainian nationalists, wrote:

> The Jews are guilty, horribly guilty, because they were the ones who helped secure Russian rule in Ukraine, but the Jews are not guilty of everything. Russian imperialism is guilty of everything. Only when Russia falls in Ukraine will we be able to order the Jewish question in our country in a way that lies in the interest of the Ukrainian people.[17]

The damage done by Schwarzbart's acquittal went further than Jewish-Ukrainian relations. Not only did the murderer's Jewish roots and his Soviet ties seem to confirm the stereotype "Jewish Bolshevism," his defense by a French lawyer and his acquittal by a French court reinforced perceptions of an anti-Ukrainian conspiracy among Communists, western democrats, and Jews. Ukrainians outside the Soviet Union, whose more pragmatic leaders had been willing to win over Jews for their cause, continued to move right in their political thinking. Any chance that Galician Ukrainian nationalism would embrace liberal democracy receded into the background.

Events in the Soviet Union also gave antisemitic and anti-Western thinking among Ukrainians in Galicia and the émigré communities of Europe yet another push. Much of the first decade of Soviet rule corresponded with a campaign of indigenation (korenizatsiia) or nationalization, a policy designed to encourage the development of the Soviet Union's nationalities. The policy was convincing enough that even prominent nationalist Ukrainians scholars, writers, and artists returned to Ukraine from exile or moved east from western Ukraine. Jews in Ukraine also benefited from indigenation. Perhaps the official promotion of Jewish agricultural settlements, Jewish art, and Yiddish letters helped create the impression that Jews mostly benefited from Communist rule. Far more important than that, however, were personnel matters within the Soviet ruling party. Since the Russian Revolution, anti-Soviet writers had identified Jews with communism; Karl Marx,

Lev Trotsky, Lev Kamenev, Grigorii Zinoviev, and Lazar Kaganovich ranked among the most frequently cited examples. "Jewish Bolshevism" became a familiar trope throughout Europe, especially among Germany's Nazis.

The moderate policies of indigenation and the New Economic Policy were not destined to last long. On the cultural front, a wave of arrests swept Ukraine in 1929 in advance of a signal 1930 show trial that would mark the end of the experiment of national communism in the Soviet Union.[18] All faiths—even the Soviet-sponsored Autocephalous Ukrainian Orthodox Church—were labeled reactionary and subjected to repression. Zionism, which had enjoyed a semi-legal position in the Soviet Union, was outlawed in 1928. Hebrew culture, both religious and secular, was eradicated, a fate that was to befall the secular Yiddish culture later in the 1930s.

The era of limited market-driven economics in the Soviet Union had already ended in 1928 with the introduction of the First Five-Year Plan. The outlawing of what was left of private commerce was a disaster for Jewish traders and Ukrainian peasants alike. The most traumatic event for the peasant Ukrainian nation was collectivization: Millions of peasants perished in Soviet Ukraine and other parts of the Soviet Union in the famine that ensued as a result of collectivization. This event went largely unnoticed in the west, but in Galicia, which bordered on fertile Soviet regions such as Podolia, the suffering of Ukrainians across the Zbruch River, however estranged, spurred anti-Communist sentiment and, via established prejudices and antagonisms, antisemitism. Among the Ukrainian intelligentsia in Poland and Ukrainian exile groups abroad, the various streams of hostility toward the democratic west, the Soviet Union, Poland, and Jews began to flow into one torrential river of resentment.

When considering Galician Ukrainian-Jewish relations between the wars, at least three other issues must be kept in mind, in addition to the preexisting prejudices based in folklore, the Petliura affair, and the perception of "Jewish Bolshevism." The first of these was the world economic depression. The decline in economic prosperity and collapse in prices for agricultural products exacerbated relations between Ukrainian peasants and Jewish wholesalers who bought Ukrainian produce, on the one hand, and between Ukrainian consumers and Jewish retailers on the other. Second, Polish discrimination policies toward the Jews, such as restricting the number of Jews who could attend university or excluding Jews from certain civic and social organizations, served to stigmatize and isolate the Jews from the rest of society. Finally, the rise of fascism and authoritarianism throughout Europe showed a clear alternative to liberal democracy.

Ukrainian nationalist circles closely observed events in Germany. The Ukrainian population in Poland was kept abreast of Nazi Jewish policies by the Ukrainian press, which passed on to its readers everything from the boycotts of Jewish shops to the Nuremberg Laws. After the death of Józef Piłsudski, Poland's predominant statesman in the interwar era, in March 1935, Warsaw also began implementing anti-Jewish policies. At the same time, Ukrainian émigré groups in the German and Czech lands were witnessing first hand the Nazi persecution of the Jews. Antisemitism was not yet a major point of convergence for Galician Ukrainians in militant nationalist circles and German National Socialists.

Germany, the Ukrainian émigrés, and Eastern Galicia

As much as Dmytro Dontsov's views can be labeled antisemitic, his dislike of Jews was secondary to his hatred of Russia. The aversion to Russia was central to his concept of Ukrainian nationalism. Since the First World War, Dontsov, who came from eastern Ukraine, had been calling for alliances with any power that was anti-Russian. Save for the brief period of German–Soviet rapprochement during the Weimar era, Germany appeared the natural ally. By the same formula, Poland was not so bad so long as it was anti-Russian. The Germanophile leanings of the former Austrian subjects, reinforced by German military assistance during the Polish-Ukrainian war and the Treaty of Brest-Litovsk, merged with anti-Russian and anti-Communist sentiments and their perception of the west's indifference to the Ukrainian cause.

Throughout the 1930s, the Germans liaised with the various émigré groups in Europe. The main groups were the UNR exile government in Warsaw, the Hetmanites in Berlin, and the Organization of Ukrainian Nationalists in the underground. Located near the center were the last of the liberal democrats, then under Petliura's successor, Andrii Levytsky. This group managed to keep its distance from Berlin longest. In 1935, however, when France entered into an alliance with the Soviet Union, the exile UNR government also established its own secret ties with the German government. Farther right were the Hetmanites, a conservative movement centered on Hetman Pavlo Skoropadsky, a former puppet leader installed by German military leaders to rule Ukraine during the German-Austrian occupation of the country in 1918. On the radical right was the Organization of Ukrainian Nationalists, which Konovalets formed out of the UVO and student organizations in 1928.

The OUN was a rightwing-oriented, authoritarian, and revolutionary organization. Anti-Polish, anti-Russian, antisemitic, anti-democratic, and anti-Communist, the OUN continued to rely on terrorist tactics of the UVO to press its case for Ukrainian independence. The movement was the Galician Ukrainian expression of the extremist rightwing political thought that dominated much of Europe between the wars. Ties to the Nazis went back to the early 1920s, but these were ambivalent until around 1938. Nazi ideologue Alfred Rosenberg and the Nazi party's Foreign Policy Office took a rather cautious view of the OUN and wished to avoid leaning too heavily on a single group, particularly one rooted in a remote corner of Ukraine caught outside the development of 90 percent of the Ukrainian lands. Instead, Rosenberg and his colleagues preferred the Hetmanites. Much more important for the UVO, and later the OUN, were the contacts forged with Abwehr, German military intelligence, which were also established in the 1920s. Save for the years from 1928 to 1932, Abwehr provided support and training for militant Ukrainian nationalists in exchange for intelligence work in Poland.[19]

However, neither the Germanophile orientation of the Ukrainian émigrés and Galician Ukrainians nor the partial ideological overlap between the OUN and the Nazis kept Berlin from pursuing its own foreign policy at the expense of its would-be allies. When the Germans occupied the Czech lands and created an independent Slovakia in March 1939, Ukrainians in Carpatho-Ukraine, encouraged by supporters of the OUN, tried to seize the moment to create a Ukrainian statelet. The German government, however, backed the Hungarian annexation of Carpatho-Ukraine one day after it declared independence.[20] Nevertheless, the Ukrainian nationalist movement in Poland and in the west continued to side with the Germans.

The exposure to Nazism could not but influence the OUN's attitude toward the Jews for the worse. The topic of OUN policy toward the Jews, much debated but little studied, is only now being adequately examined. It is true that some OUN leaders tried to distinguish their party from the German Nazis, but hostility toward Jews can also be traced back to the organization's founding and the work of Dontsov. The antisemitic currents within the OUN received another boost when Konovalets was assassinated by a Soviet agent in May 1938. On the first anniversary of this event, the paper of the OUN-affiliate organization legally operating in Berlin published a poem:

> And know, you Muscovite-Jewish reptile,
> Which has sucked our blood for centuries,
> That the soul nurtures a hellish wrath,
> That we will have to meet with you.[21]

When the Germans invaded Poland in September 1939, a small Ukrainian legion headed by Colonel Roman Sushko took part in the attack. This legion had barely crossed the San River before being withdrawn to allow for the Soviet occupation of Galicia in accordance with the secret protocols of the German-Soviet agreements. Once again, the Germans sold out the Ukrainian cause in pursuit of their own interests.

Ukrainians and Jews in German Occupied
Poland until June 1941

Ukrainian nationalists were, of course, disappointed when the German-Polish war led not to the establishment of a Ukrainian state but to Soviet rule in Galicia. The Germans, however, skillfully compensated for this disappointment by granting numerous privileges and advantages to the Ukrainian minority under its rule. The Ukrainian Central Committee (UTsK) was established by the Germans in occupied Poland initially as a welfare and relief agency. Although Ukrainians did not participate officially in any decision-making body of the General Government, the UTsK, which was headed by the ostensibly politically independent geographer Volodymyr Kubiiovych but maintained close ties to the OUN (and later the OUN faction loyal to Andrii Melnyk), became "the only officially sanctioned Ukrainian political and community organization in the Generalgouvernement."[22] As such, the UTsK functioned for the Germans as the conduit for bestowing favors and, for the Ukrainians in the General Government, as the channel for pursuing nationalist goals.

The German policy of divide and rule did not aim to play the various nationalities in the General Government against one another to an equal extent. Instead, it aimed to exploit sympathetic Ukrainian circles at the expense of both Poles and Jews. Ukrainians were made mayors and local administrators in both Ukrainian and Polish-Ukrainian villages and regions, and the Orthodox Church in Poland was partly ukrainized. The Ukrainian cooperative movement, an essential element of nineteenth-century nation-building in eastern Europe, was freed from the restrictions imposed upon it during Polish rule. For Kubiiovych and Sushko, this policy was crucial so as to liberate the prewar system of trade, which "had been mainly directed at the exploitation of the Ukrainian peasant," from "Jewish hands."[23] The Ukrainian cooperative movement in the General Government subsequently grew from 212 cooperatives in 1939 to 995 by early 1941.[24] Sushko was able to use the men from his legion to form a Ukrainian police force under German command and supervision.[25] Despite the police force's limitations, the UTsK and OUN saw this as a step in the direction of self-administration. Thus the General Government's limited Ukrainian community largely supported the Germans, who seemed to empower it, raise its standard of living, and improve its cultural life.

But not all of the OUN was so easily placated. A split within the organization's ranks took place in early 1940. The reasons for this split lay mainly in tactics rather than ideology, but included OUN German policy. Both factions counted on German support; however, the younger, more radical men, led by Stepan Bandera, were unwilling to wait too long for future developments. This faction, the OUN-B, wanted to force Ukrainian independence on the Germans immediately. The older nationalists, most of whom had come of age under Austrian rule and sided with Andrii Melnyk—a former Austrian officer and the successor to Konovalets—thought Ukrainian independence would come through prolonged cooperation with the Germans during the war. Although no less dedicated to the goal of Ukrainian independence, the OUN-M was ready to accept years of German dominance, and even humiliation, in the hope of achieving statehood after the war.

The first twenty-two months of Nazi rule in Poland set the tone for Ukrainian-Jewish relations in the General Government. The UTsK, both factions of the OUN, and probably a large part of the Ukrainian population at large in the General Government had a very clear picture of what was happening to the Jews. The German invasion of Poland had been accompanied by the looting of Jewish property, the shooting of Jews in large numbers, and the desecration or destruction of synagogues, including those in towns with notable Ukrainian populations such as Łańcut, Leżajsk, Gorlice, and Przemyśl. Thousands of Jews in these Ukrainian settled parts of Poland had either fled from the Germans or been forced at gunpoint across the Bug River, the later demarcation line between the Soviet and the Nazi zones of occupation.

German civil administration brought with it the confiscation of Jewish-owned property and the introduction of forced labor. The Ukrainian daily *Krakivski Visti* was full of ads for former Jewish businesses under new Ukrainian proprietorship. In District Lublin, at least 28 labor camps existed by the end of 1939. The identification of Jews by a white armband bearing the Star of David was introduced throughout the General Government in November 1939. Mass deportations of Jews from cities such as Cracow and Lublin as well as from those parts of Poland incorporated into the Reich had led to overcrowding in the Ukrainian populated southeast of the General Government and put an enormous strain on resources in towns such as Zamość, Chełm, and Nowy Sącz. By June 1941, ghettos existed in Biłgoraj, Gorlice, and Sanok as well as in Chełm, Nowy Sącz, and Zamość. And in early 1941 in Cracow, where the UTsK had its headquarters, the Jews were expelled from the main city to a walled ghetto in the district of Podgórze on the other side of the Vistula River. It was against this backdrop that Kubiiovych, on April 18, 1941, petitioned General Governor Hans Frank to purge the ethnic Ukrainian territories in the General Government of "Polish and Jewish elements."[26]

Ukrainians and Jews in Soviet Occupied Poland until June 1941

The Soviet occupation of eastern Poland, also known as "the liberation of western Ukraine and western Belarus"—a term coined by the Soviets and still in use in eastern Ukraine today—was based on the secret protocols of the Ribbentrop-Molotov accord of August 23, 1939. The 22-month occupation, which began with the Soviet invasion of September 17, 1939, had an enormous impact on interethnic relations in Galicia.

With the end of military operations in October, Moscow began sovietizing the newly seized areas. Soviet rule, however, had two sides to it. While the sovietization of Galicia entailed the enormous and violent transformations that had already occurred in central and eastern Ukraine, it also brought with it the pro forma recognition of many aspects of Ukrainian nationhood. On the other hand, almost all of the

Ukrainian lands were now unified into one republic; the Ukrainian language was promoted more than in prewar Poland; and the same process of elevating Ukrainians into the administrative positions as had occurred in the Soviet Union in the 1920s and 1930s was introduced.[27] For almost a year, the Soviets tread a careful path, particularly in Galicia. Private business was of course abolished. The Greek Catholic Church in Galicia was harassed, but was not closed—although the Soviets did close the church's school system. And the politically inactive intelligentsia was largely left alone.[28] Ukrainian cooperatives corresponded remotely with Soviets aims and were thus exploited to facilitate collectivization.[29] Around mid-1940, however, this began to change. The border was sealed, economic transformation was intensified, the Soviet secret police succeeded in rolling up a good part of the OUN, and large numbers of party and state administrators from outside Galicia were settled into the region.[30] Worst of all for Galician Ukrainians, the Soviet policy of deporting unwanted segments of the population began affecting large numbers of Ukrainians.

In addition to many members of the Ukrainian intelligentsia and lower class, some Jews also benefited from Soviet rule. One cannot stress enough the word "some." Some historians, for example, Bogdan Musial, have succumbed to broad generalizations when speaking of the Jews during the first period of sovietization in Galicia and Volhynia. Ignoring Polish anti-Jewish measures between the wars and German violence against the Jews during the September 1939 invasion and dwelling on a supposed choice that Jews faced between Nazi or Soviet occupation, Musial stresses the Soviet treatment of Jews at the same level as Gentiles and emphasizes the installation of Jews into positions of power and influence in Soviet-occupied Poland. He concludes: "[T]he [emphasis added, F.G.] Jews were happy that the Soviets occupied eastern Poland."[31]

This was certainly the impression of many non-Jews in eastern Galicia. In fact, Jews did sometimes benefit nominally from the official policy of nondiscrimination among nationalities. As a result, some Jews did become more visible as they assumed posts in the new Soviet institutions and municipal administrations. This, however, is a problem of perception: What is conspicuous and registered as such in many cases reflects a contrast but not necessarily reality. Under Polish rule, Jews and Ukrainians were all but barred from holding administrative posts; suddenly under Soviet rule, Jews were visible in positions of power. For many Galician Ukrainians, who saw the new government as at least officially "Ukrainian," it seemed normal—and therefore less problematic—for Ukrainian peasants and workers to accept positions under the Soviets. For the Jewish minority to hold positions of political power, however, was something novel. Moreover, since the inclusion of Jews took place mostly at the communal level, Ukrainians in Galicia tended to encounter these Jews on an everyday basis.[32] Thus, the general public and the nationalist intelligentsia were inclined to see their stereotype of "Jewish Bolshevism" once again reinforced.

This contrast with pre-1939 reality and the contradiction to the officially propagated Ukrainian quality of the Soviet rule, combined with prewar antisemitic prejudices—religious beliefs, economic envy, and differences in education levels—put additional strain on the already tense relations between Jews and non-Jews in eastern Poland. Soviet rule, which persecuted both Polish and Ukrainian nationalists as well as Zionists, was generalized as "Jewish rule" both by anti-Soviet Poles and Ukrainians.[33]

Of course, the idea that "the Jews" gained from Soviet occupation is far from correct. Jan T. Gross introduced two important concepts into the study of this era in his 1988 book on the Soviet occupation of eastern Poland: first, that of the Soviet Union as a "spoiler state"—a state whose aim was to destroy existing social, political, and economic structures via divide and rule—and second, the "privatization of politics"—whereby private or personal rivalries, and not necessarily Marxist-Leninist doctrine, were used to destroy previously stable social structures. In this context, Ukrainian and Polish nationalist perceptions of Jews moving up the social and political ladder was very much how the Soviet leaders wanted them to see it.[34]

If one removes the nationalist blinders, however, one sees that the situation was hard for Jews as well. The economic transformation had a devastating effect on Jews. Since the greater part of small business was in Jewish hands, Jewish traders bore the brunt of Soviet economic policy once private enterprise was outlawed. Soviet religious persecution knew no distinction between Christian and Jew. As the Soviets rounded up "enemies of the state" for deportation to Siberia and Central Asia, they chose Poles, Ukrainians, and Jews alike. Paradoxically, the forced transfer of these Jews to the mines of eastern Ukraine and the logging camps of Siberia ended up saving them from certain death at the hands of the Germans.

In short, the Jewish experience in Galicia during the 22 months of Soviet occupation was just as negative as that of the Ukrainians or Poles (if not more so). As an informant for the German military put it in August 1940, "Only the lowest of the Jewish proletariat is satisfied with the current Bolshevik regime."[35] By the eve of the German invasion, however, the general non-Jewish public tended to see things differently.

German Military Administration in Galicia

On June 22, 1941, the German Armed Forces, supported by troops from Finland, Hungary, Italy, Romania, and Slovakia, attacked the Soviet Union.[36] The invading armies initially made rapid advances, encircling and destroying large concentrations of Red Army forces and capturing hundreds of thousands of Soviet troops. Following in the wake of the German armies were the Einsatzgruppen, special task forces of the Security Police (the Sipo, which included the Gestapo) and Security Service (SD).[37]

At the time of the invasion, eastern Galicia's prisons were full of Jews, Poles, and Ukrainians alike, peasants who had resisted collectivization, townspeople accused of bourgeois nationalist activists, and victims of denunciations. In light of the rapid advance of the invading armies, there was neither the time nor the will to evacuate all the prisoners. Rather than let these "enemies of the people" fall into German hands, the Soviet secret police, the NKVD, acting on direct orders from Moscow, massacred the prison inmates in an unusually brutal fashion. Some prisoners were bludgeoned by hammers, others mangled by hand grenades tossed into their cells. The victims were then hastily buried in courtyards of buildings such as the Brygidki Prison in Lviv or old fortresses, like the one in Zolochiv, that had been turned into prisons.[38] Others were left to rot where they died. When the Germans arrived, they quickly found the mass graves and exhumed the bodies to show to the locals. The body count ran into the thousands. The number of victims in Lviv may have been as high as 3,000.[39] Across Galicia, the number may have been as high as 10,000.[40]

At this point, the process of myth-making takes over and the interplay of imaginations described earlier began to take hold. Antisemitism

According to testimonies collected during and after the war, the Germans and their Ukrainian accomplices rounded up Jews to remove the bodies of those murdered by the Soviet secret police throughout eastern Galicia as the Wehrmacht advanced. This photograph, a still from the German Wochenschau newsreel of July 10, 1941, depicts such a scene at a Lviv prison in the first days of the German occupation. The military policeman on the right is at the head of a column of cowed civilian men. As one group comes out, he ushers another group in. Bundesarchiv, Filmarchiv Berlin/Transit Film, Munich.

had been rampant in prewar Poland. Not only had it rubbed off on the militant Ukrainian nationalists, the OUN stood firm in the conviction that Jews were "Moscow's agents." The popular belief that all Bolsheviks were Jews was turned on its head to suggest all Jews were Bolsheviks. Supported by a wave of German (and OUN) propaganda against the "Judeo-Bolshevik" Soviet regime, many Ukrainians accused "the Jews" for the NKVD murders. By contrast, they saw in the Germans the people that had remedied so many Polish injustices and put "the Jews" in their place in the General Government. The Germans had come to liberate Ukraine, so it was widely thought; they had created Ukrainian legions, and they were going finally to take care of "the Jews," allegedly Moscow's primary source of support in Ukraine. In many Galician towns where NKVD massacres took place, pogroms followed.

The NKVD massacres are not the end of the story, however. Dozens of pogroms took place where the NKVD had not carried out massacres. Throughout western Ukraine, pogroms broke out in the wake of the Soviet retreat. The number of documented pogroms in Galicia runs into the dozens, with the number of victims believed to be around 12,000.[41]

This development was not unique to the Ukrainian lands. A similar course of events unfolded in Lithuania and Latvia, where locals also looted and killed their Jewish neighbors. The scenario played itself out in Polish towns and villages as well, the most famous case being Jedwabne.[42] Despite historical evidence to the contrary, many nationalist-minded historians—whether Polish, Ukrainian, Latvian, or Lithuanian—find it hard to accept that anti-Jewish feelings were ever so strong in their country as to lead their compatriots to find common cause with the Nazis in the "Jewish question."

The Germans certainly aimed to encourage pogroms, but the search for the extent of German involvement in sparking pogroms has led to some obfuscation. Ukrainian historians, for example, tend to play up the German role and call into question or ignore local participation,[43] as illustrated in this passage from Paul Robert Magocsi's general history of Ukraine:

> The Germans helped to circulate rumors that "Jewish Bolsheviks" had been involved in the murders of thousands of Ukrainian political prisoners killed by the Soviet authorities before their hasty retreat. In consequence, in Lviv, for instance, after the prisons were opened, about 4,000 Jews were massacred between 30 June and 7 July by German extermination task forces with the assistance of what some sources describe as "Ukrainian auxiliary police" (*Ukrainische Hilfspolizei*).[44]

Without denying Ukrainian participation in the pogroms during the summer of 1941, Magocsi blames the Germans first and foremost for *motivating* the Ukrainians to act. He fails to mention that pogroms sometimes often broke out before the Germans arrived or in places occupied not by the Germans but by the Hungarians. Where his narrative turns to mass executions, he equates the use of "local Ukrainians, Russians, Poles, Germans, and even Jews (through the so-called Jewish Councils: *Judenräte*) in the organization and implementation of their murderous missions." Without making further distinction, he adds: "Some of the local population participated, either willingly or under various forms of coercion."[45]

Responsibility for the setting in which the pogroms took place lies squarely with the Germans. A June order from Reinhard Heydrich, the chief of the Security Police and the SD, to the Einsatzgruppen shows that the Sipo-SD anticipated the outbreaks of violence and planned to capitalize on them:

> No obstacles are to be put in the way of self-cleansing efforts on the part of anti-Communist and anti-Jewish circles in the territories to be occupied. To the contrary, they are to be triggered leaving no traces whatsoever, to be intensified when necessary, and to be guided in the right direction, without these local "self-defense circles" being able to refer later to orders or political promises made.[46]

There can be no doubt that the Germans touched off some pogroms, and that their approval of such activity encouraged such riots with or without direct prodding. Likewise, the mass killings carried out by the Einsatzgruppen were committed for the most part by Germans. But German rumors alone would have failed if they had not fallen on receptive ears. Report on Events in the USSR No. 19 of July 11, 1941, noted that the Germans "inspired" the murder of 600 Jews in Ternopil, while making clear that many of the local inhabitants harbored a good deal of hostility toward the Jews. This must have been the case. Otherwise, the inspiration could not have worked.[47]

Even non-Ukrainian scholars have sometimes gone too far in downplaying the depth of anti-Jewish, anti-Communist, and anti-Russian sentiment in these regions. Raul Hilberg, for example, argues that "truly spontaneous pogroms, free from Einsatzgruppen influence, did not take place," and that "all pogroms were implemented within a short time after the arrival of the killing units."[48] This, however, does not explain the pogroms that broke out in places such as Stanyslaviv (today, Ivano-Frankivsk), Kolomyia, Horodenka, and Obertyn, towns that were in the Hungarian zone of operations and occupation in Galicia.[49]

Dieter Pohl also hesitates to rush to judgment with regard to spontaneous anti-Jewish riots in Galicia. He instead has collected evidence of an OUN network that cooperated with and cleared the way for the Germans, spreading anti-Jewish propaganda and advocating "German methods" in "the struggle against Jewry in Ukraine."[50] The existence of such a network could explain how some pogroms broke out in advance of the occupying forces in both the German and Hungarian zones of occupation.[51]

The origins of the Ukrainian *militsiia* responsible for so many pogroms in western Ukraine have yet to face in-depth scholarly scrutiny and remain murky. One witness suggests that Soviet Ukrainian police-men—*militsiia* being the Soviet term for "police"—left behind by the Soviets formed the first nationalist Ukrainian militsiia in Lviv at the end of June 1941. It is logical that they would have tried to divert attention from their Soviet-era collaboration and prove their conversion by joining in the murder of those deemed to be the new enemies. In such cases, former Soviet policemen would have been interested in equating Jews and Communists, so as to cover up their own prior activities.[52] In preparing for the invasion, however, both factions of the OUN trained Ukrainians for police duty and schooled instructors for a future police force in Ukraine.[53] They also prepared to organize Ukrainian administrative structures for the territories "liberated" by the Germans.

Germans and Ukrainians in Galicia

No sooner had the Germans captured Lviv on June 30, 1941, than Iaroslav Stetsko, the OUN-B's top representative in the field, issued a declaration of Ukrainian statehood and formed a cabinet that was to act as a government. The Germans quickly thwarted this embryonic administration and, over the course of July and August, rounded up leading OUN-B figures in Galicia, replacing them with representatives of the OUN-M or with Ukrainian figures not officially affiliated with any party. Despite this setback, as late as August 14, 1941, the OUN-B was still urging "cooperation with Germany not for opportunistic considerations, but due to the necessity of such cooperation for the good of Ukraine."[54]

In the meantime, on July 16, Hitler decided to remove Galicia from what was to become the Reich Commissariat Ukraine and allocated it, effective August 1, to the General Government. This decision, as well as Hitler's decision to return all of Bukovina to Romania *and* award the Ukrainian territory west of the Southern Buh River to his Romanian ally, unleashed a flood of petitions from Ukrainians throughout the Reich and Galicia. Nevertheless, the Ukrainian population in the General Government and the Reich continued to lend their support to the German war effort. General Governor Hans Frank expanded his policy of divide and rule into the new holdings of his aggrandized realm, and the Ukrainian agencies under his purview continued to exploit their privileged position vis-à-vis the Poles and Jews.

Barely one month later, Kubiiovych presented Frank with a memorandum calling for the official "recognition of the Ukrainian ethnic group's special status" within the General Government and "its right to autonomously shape the Ukrainian ethnic community." Kubiiovych requested "military formations under joint German-Ukrainian leadership," a solely Ukrainian police force, exclusion of Poles from key positions in the administration, expansion of Ukrainian schools, the restoration of land appropriated by the Soviets, and a revitalization of the cooperative movement in Galicia. Kubiiovych also asked to see "a very significant part of confiscated Jewish wealth turned over to the Ukrainian people"; after all, in his view, it mostly belonged to the Ukrainians in the first place and ended up in Jewish hands "only through ruthless breach of law on the part of the Jews and their exploitation of members of the Ukrainian people."[55]

Kubiiovych did not get everything on his list, but advances for the Ukrainians in Galicia were significant. The Greek Catholic Church was granted considerable leeway and provided subsidies, while the Roman Catholic Church suffered extensive persecution.[56] Whereas the Polish intelligentsia was oppressed, Galician Ukrainian intellectuals thrived (so long as they did not openly belong to the OUN-B or to the Communist Party).[57] Despite the hardships and shortages of life during wartime, art and literature flourished such that nationalist-minded Ukrainian writers would later look back on this period as the most liberal and influential in recent history.[58] Over 70 Ukrainian periodicals existed in the General Government for the four million Ukrainians there. Polish university preparatory schools were closed, Ukrainian ones opened. While Ukrainian children in the RKU were forced to make do with just four years of grammar school, a government-sponsored Ukrainian school system became reality in the General Government, and Ukrainians from the General Government were sent to study at German universities. The former head of the Main Department for Academic Affairs and Teaching within the administration of the General Government, Ludwig Eichholz, remarked:

> The Ukrainians also hardly ever raised any serious complaints about school policy in [Galicia], they greeted the building up of their national school system after the inclusion of their territory in the General Government as the beginning of a general national renaissance.[59]

The Ukrainian version of Germany's compulsory manual labor service, the Construction Service (*Baudienst*), was given a Ukrainian patriotic varnish and christened Ukrainian Service for the Fatherland (*Ukraïnska Sluzhba Batkivshchyni*). Despite some initial disappointment, the organization even came to enjoy the support of UTsK functionaries who had long called for Ukrainian genuine military units. The Germans threw their weight behind the Ukrainian cooperative movement, although they used these agencies of rural self-organization to collect agricultural goods for feeding Germany. And the new rulers seemed prepared to reverse Soviet collectivization policy and to accept Ukrainian self-organization in economic matters. Thus, Ukrainians in Galicia saw the increasing number of cooperatives, and their growing importance in filling the void left by the isolated and murdered Jews and the disenfranchised Poles, as a positive step.[60]

The General Government, however, was hardly a "Ukrainian paradise." The top Nazi leadership had no desire to realize Ukrainian statehood, and those Ukrainians who openly and forcefully advocated the idea, especially the leading cadres of the OUN-B, were tracked down and sent to concentration camps such as Sachsenhausen or Auschwitz. The same applied to Communists in Galicia. It is also unclear whether the particular advantages enjoyed by the Ukrainian intelligentsia and the UTsK in larger towns filtered out to the countryside. The Germans, for their part, were just as capable of preferring the stick to the carrot in Galicia as elsewhere in occupied Europe when pursuing their interests. Thus average Ukrainians in Galicia saw themselves very much under a harsh German occupation regime.

In early 1943, a special operation against "asocial elements" resulted in the arrest of 5,000 people in District Galicia. However, members of the Ukrainian business community and of the various local aid committees, as well as artists, were also caught up in the sweep. Mass shootings were sometimes carried out in reprisal for the death of a German or an act of sabotage, even in cases where the damage done was probably an accident. This was the case in Lubycza (today in Poland) on October 4, 1942, when a barn burned down killing three horses.[61] The fear of Bolshevism, however, remained so great that even in September 1943, the Sipo and SD could report to Berlin that the Ukrainian resistance, i.e., the OUN-B, was hesitant to launch a full scale campaign against the Germans because the peasants and the intelligentsia would refuse to go along with such a struggle.[62]

The greatest source of discontent among average Ukrainians in Galicia (and elsewhere in occupied Ukraine) was the German drive for manpower for farms and factories in Germany. During the last three months of 1942, "wild ruthless manhunts" for workers for the Reich became so frequent in District Galicia that some Ukrainians were afraid to go out on the street by year's end. The situation was such that some Ukrainians there circulated the following quip: "During Austrian and Polish times, Lviv lay in Europe, from 1939 to 1941 . . . in Asia, and now it is in Africa."[63] During the first year of German rule, most appear to have gone to Germany voluntarily. By late 1942, however, this readiness was dissipating.

Nonetheless, the UTsK worked to convince Ukrainians under its purview to go to Germany so as to support the German war effort. Kubiiovych spoke regularly of the "completely voluntary" deployment of Galician Ukrainians in the Reich or "hundreds of thousands of volunteers for labor in the Reich"[64] and advised the German authorities on how best to arrange for local contingents of workers via local communities or aid committees.[65] The governor of District Galicia, SS Brigadier General Dr. Otto Wächter, saw worker conscription under his rule similarly. In a speech to SS officer cadets after the Germans had evacuated Galicia, Wächter revealed that "out of a population of 4.5 million inhabitants, 350,000—for the most part voluntarily—went to Germany as workers."[66] Furthermore, the Ukrainian workers from the General Government were granted a number of privileges. Unlike their compatriots from the RKU, they were accorded the status of Ukrainian nationals, allowed to dispense with the badge OST (used to designate workers from the occupied territories of the Soviet Union), and granted their own newspaper.[67]

Despite the Ukrainians' relative advances in the General Government compared with Polish and Soviet rule, one thing weighed heavily on the minds of the Galician Ukrainian civic leaders: Ukrainian armed forces. Since the start of the German-Soviet war, Kubiiovych and Melnyk had tried to convince the Germans to create a Ukrainian army drawing on Ukrainians in the General Government and the "liberated Ukrainian territories."[68] In early 1943, Himmler decided to allow Galician Ukrainians to join his pan-European crusade against Bolshevism. Hitler signed off on the idea, justifying the matter for himself with the assertion that Galician Ukrainians were "interwoven" with Austrians, because they had "lived for a very long time under Austrian rule."[69]

There was a hitch for the Galician Ukrainians, however. Although the word "Ukrainian" was used for practically every other institution or agency the Germans permitted—the Ukrainian Central Committee, the Ukrainian National Union, the Ukrainian Service for the Fatherland, the Ukrainian Police, the Ukrainian Publishing House—Himmler forbade the use of "Ukrainian" with regard to the division. Instead, only "Galicia" or "Galician" was allowed, as in SS Rifles Division Galicia, the unit's original designation, or Galician SS volunteers. This affront to Ukrainian nationalist sensibilities and aspirations did not stop the UTsK and the Greek Catholic Church from running an extensive and elaborate recruitment drive for the new formation. During the first month of recruitment more than 80,000 Ukrainians volunteered, of which ultimately 13,000 became soldiers.[70] Recruitment, wrote historian Taras Hunczak, "proved easier and more successful than anyone could have possibly anticipated."[71]

The nationalist school of Ukrainian historiography has tried to link the division to Austria's Ukrainian legion from the First World War and the Ukrainian struggle for independence. For Galician Ukrainians, it is even argued, the initials SS recalled the Austrian legion Sich Sharpshooters. Since 1945, nationalist historians have tried to pluck the division from the SS establishment and to present it as a regular military formation. However, it is indisputable that Himmler's SS trained and indoctrinated the division's Ukrainians, and that many of the division's German commanding officers came from SS and police units that had participated in the Nazis' murderous policies; the division also took part in the German war effort against the Soviets, in particular the suppression of the Slovak uprising in late 1944. Furthermore, before being transferred to the division, thousands of its rank-and-file members had served with SS and police formations involved in anti-partisan activity against Polish and Soviet partisans, or the persecution of Jews. In the late summer of 1944, around 1,300 members of the division were attached to 5th SS Armored Division Wiking.

Overall, Ukrainian civic and community leaders in the General Government considered German rule an improvement on Polish and

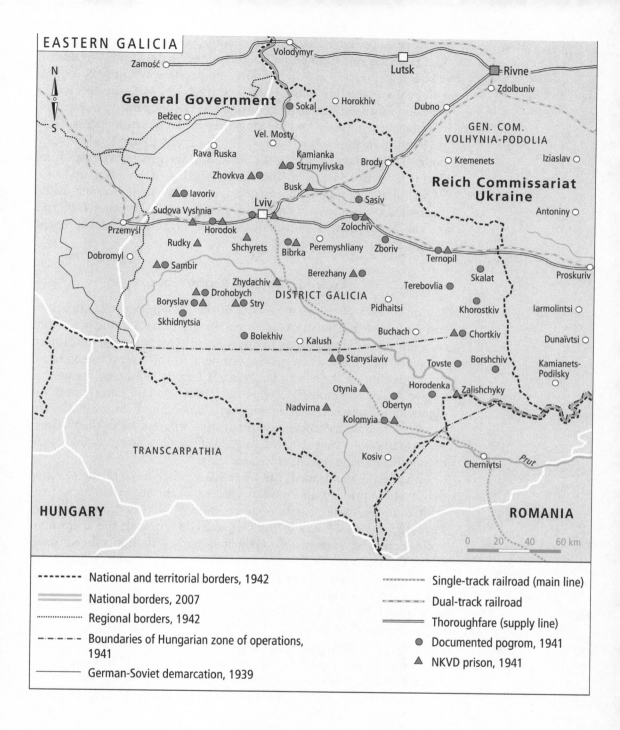

EASTERN GALICIA

General Government

GEN. COM.
VOLHYNIA-PODOLIA

Reich Commissariat
Ukraine

DISTRICT GALICIA

TRANSCARPATHIA

HUNGARY

ROMANIA

Zamość
Volodymyr
Lutsk
Rivne
Zdolbuniv
Sokal
Horokhiv
Dubno
Bełżec
Vel. Mosty
Rava Ruska
Kamianka
Strumylivska
Brody
Kremenets
Iziaslav
Zhovkva
Busk
Iavoriv
Lviv
Sasiv
Antoniny
Sudova Vyshnia
Zolochiv
Przemyśl
Horodok
Rudky
Shchyrets
Bibrka
Peremyshliany
Zboriv
Ternopil
Dobromyl
Sambir
Berezhany
Skalat
Proskuriv
Zhydachiv
Terebovlia
Boryslav
Drohobych
Stry
Pidhaitsi
Khorostkiv
Iarmolintsi
Skhidnytsia
Bolekhiv
Kalush
Buchach
Chortkiv
Dunaïvtsi
Stanyslaviv
Tovste
Borshchiv
Kamianets-
Podilsky
Otynia
Horodenka
Zalishchyky
Nadvirna
Obertyn
Kolomyia
Kosiv
Chernivtsi
Prut

0   20   40   60 km

------- National and territorial borders, 1942

National borders, 2007

.... Regional borders, 1942

—·—·— Boundaries of Hungarian zone of operations,
1941

——— German-Soviet demarcation, 1939

Single-track railroad (main line)

Dual-track railroad

——— Thoroughfare (supply line)

● Documented pogrom, 1941

▲ NKVD prison, 1941

Soviet rule. In light of the options considered—the maintenance of Nazi rule or a return to either Poland or the Soviet Union—Nazi rule was seen as preferable. Furthermore, cooperation with the Nazis was seen by the leadership of the UTsK and the OUN-M as the best way of pursuing short-term goals in education and the cooperative movement, to name but two fields, and the longer term goal of a homogenous ethnic Ukrainian state after the war. The Germans understood this and made sure that Ukrainians in the General Government benefited from Nazi rule in the short term. This in turn facilitated rounding up workers for the Reich, requisitioning grain, and selecting policemen. Later, this policy made it easy to recruit support personnel for the Waffen-SS and the Wehrmacht and ultimately to raise a frontline division for the Waffen-SS.

Police Forces and Camp Guards

The discussion of the whereabouts of the SS Division Galicia's rank and file before the division was formed brings us back to the police and concentration camp guards in the General Government. Ukrainian collaboration in the General Government in this respect centers on three institutions: the Ukrainian Police (*Ukrainische Polizei*), the guards known as Trawniki men (*Wachmannschaften*), and the battalions of indigenous policemen (*Schutzmannschafts-Bataillone,* Schuma-Batl.). On paper, there were technical, administrative differences. To the victims, such distinctions meant nothing. And in fact, in practice, there was regular overlap among these various forces.

As already mentioned, the Ukrainian police force in the General Government prior to the German invasion of the Soviet Union was recruited under Roman Sushko's supervision. With the addition of these formerly Austrian lands to the General Government, the Ukrainian Police expanded into eastern Galicia as well. Although subordinated to the Germans and prevented from establishing a central command at the regional level, the mere existence of the Ukrainian Police stood out in a stark contrast to the pre-1939 situation when Polish policemen lorded over the Ukrainian population.

An in-depth history of the Ukrainian Police in the General Government has yet to be written.[72] Of the rank and file as a whole, it is safe to say that they were voluntary. The establishment of a Ukrainian police force in Galicia was seen as a step toward self-administration, and both factions of the OUN struggled to infiltrate it. Of the Ukrainian police commanders, it is believed that most of the officers sympathized with the OUN-M or the Front of National Unity, a pro-German, fascist-oriented prewar movement that rejected the OUN's revolutionary methods.[73] These were no mere "scoundrels" or "criminal elements."[74] Liudomyr Ohonovsky, a captain of the Ukrainian police in Lviv city, and Ivan Kozak, the commandant of the Ukrainian police academy in Lviv, were respected veterans of the Ukrainian Galician Army. Ohonovsky, the son of a prominent educator and the nephew of a famous linguist, was even a hero of the November 1918 Ukrainian Lviv uprising.[75] The Ukrainian police in Galicia were also comparatively well paid. Rank-and-file policemen earned more than secretaries and unskilled workers, and the officers received higher wages than skilled workers. More important, a successful applicant could also expect a range of social benefits ranging from supplemental rations to social and health care. The benefits culminated in evacuation with the Germans in 1944.[76]

The activities of this police force are rather well known. In addition to regular law enforcement duties in rural or urban precincts, the Ukrainian police enforced the ghettoization process, provided cordons during ghetto clearance operations and mass shootings, escorted Jews to local killing sites or to the trains headed for the death camp Bełżec, carried out house-to-house searches, and combed forests for hidden Jews. Jews found in hiding or caught trying to flee were usually shot or handed over to the Germans. The police were also deployed in mass shootings and often committed individual acts of murder on their own initiative, especially in villages or ghettos.[77] Guard duty in the forced labor camps along Thoroughfare IV, one of the Wehrmacht's main supply lines, was carried out in Galicia by both the Ukrainian police and guards from the SS training camp in Trawniki.[78]

The "Trawniki men," as the guards trained by the SS in the Polish town of Trawniki, near Lublin, came to be known, rank among the most notorious perpetrators of the Second World War. Based on both German and Jewish wartime documents and postwar testimonies, these men appear to have been mostly Ukrainian, but they included Lithuanians, Latvians, ethnic Germans, Poles, and Russians. Recruiting began in the autumn of 1941, with drives conducted primarily in POW camps.

At the time of recruitment, conditions in the POW camps were appalling. Soviet POWs had begun dying off in droves by the autumn of 1941. Practically any German agency offering release and a job was bound to generate a flurry of applicants. Selection was based on German roots, non-Russian nationality, hatred of the Bolsheviks, and state of health.[79]

Just how much duress played a role for non-Russian POWs must be carefully considered. For example, the Germans had been officially releasing Ukrainian POWs (and other non-Russians) since early September, a policy that continued well into December although formally it ended in November.[80] Also, the UTsK and Ukrainian Red Cross had managed to intervene on behalf of ethnic Ukrainian POWs imprisoned in the General Government. Furthermore, the POWs were over time joined by Ukrainian volunteers from District Lublin and District Galicia.[81] Just as important as the factor of duress is the question why the German recruiters and trainers felt they could rely mostly on Ukrainians for the tasks they had in store for recruits.

Some 3,000 to 5,000 men were ultimately trained at Trawniki. They were initially deployed as guards at economic installations and forced labor camps in District Lublin. Above all, they helped in the operation of the death camps of Bełżec, Treblinka, and Sobibór. But they were also transferred to camps in the other four districts of the General Government and to camps in "Greater Germany." Thus Ukrainian guards were soon found in Auschwitz and Płaszów as well as Mauthausen (Austria), Sachsenhausen (near Berlin), and Stutthof (near Danzig [Gdańsk]). Trawniki men also participated in suppressing the Warsaw Ghetto Uprising and in operations against Polish partisans. The latter task, however, was more frequently set aside for the mobile police battalions.

The use of mobile police battalions recruited from the General Government began in September 1941 with Schuma-Batl. 201, which was raised from two Abwehr-trained Ukrainian units and deployed in Belarus before being disbanded in late 1942.[82] A second Ukrainian battalion, Schuma-Batl. 203, was created in 1942 from Trawniki men and frequently used in anti-partisan operations.[83] It was followed by another battalion at the SS training center Heidelager (Dębica), District Cracow. This formation, Schuma-Batl. 204, was eventually absorbed by the SS Division Galicia. The unit provided the guards not only for the training center's perimeter but for the concentration camp Pustków, which was located within the center.[84] Also worth mentioning is Schuma-Batl. 205; this unit was formed in April 1943 and drew from Ukrainians who had been serving in a Wehrmacht commandant's guard battalion in Lviv. That this battalion was deployed in a scattered fashion throughout District Galicia just as the Germans began accelerating the final liquidation of the region's remaining ghettos raises questions about this unit's possible participation in the mass murder of Jews as well.[85]

The role of the UTsK and the OUN in these various police forces is unclear. Kubiiovych and the UTsK constantly pressed for the enlargement of Ukrainian police forces at the expense of Polish ones.[86] The disbanding of police formations, as was the case of Schuma-Batl. 201, produced "indignation" and "extensive disquiet" among Galician Ukrainians, including the intelligentsia.[87] With the support and encouragement of local Ukrainian aid committees and Ukrainian village elders and mayors, ethnic Ukrainians from the districts Cracow, Lublin, and Galicia were recruited into the police. Furthermore, local aid committees and churches facilitated recruitment by providing certification of "Aryan ancestry" for Ukrainian policemen.[88]

The UTsK and the OUN had nothing to do with the recruitment from Soviet POWs, but as eager as they were to have the Ukrainian police expand, to see their able-bodied men receive at least some paramilitary training, to defend Ukrainian gains, and to demonstrate loyalty to the German war effort, the UTsK and its subordinate local aid committees contributed to later drives for Trawniki recruits. There is also absolutely no known concrete evidence that the UTsK or the OUN had a direct say in the deployment of any of these police forces—even if they did happen to promote such nationalist goals as an ethnically homogenous Ukrainian territories.

Ukrainian Nationalist Partisans in Galicia

By July 1943, the Reich Commissariat Ukraine was in the middle of a complicated partisan war between the Ukrainian Insurgency Army (UPA), the German police and SS, Polish underground and self-defense forces, and Soviet partisans. Originally comprising various groups of different ideologies, the UPA had gradually fallen under the influence of the OUN-B. Throughout the last months of 1942, Soviet partisans had been infiltrating into the northern woods of Volhynia, where Ukrainian nationalist forces had been forming but remained too weak to go head to head with the Germans. The ensuing competition for "hearts and minds" of Volhynian Ukrainians degenerated into a treacherous and bloody campaign to prove who was the true defender of the people against the German occupiers. When it appeared that the Red Army might push the Germans back to the Dniepr River in February 1943 (advance units briefly reached the outskirts of Dnipropetrovsk), the UPA also began fighting the Poles of Volhynia to keep any future Polish government from having a pretext for annexing the region again. Calls for Poles to leave Volhynia "voluntarily" soon turned into a campaign of murder—to which Polish partisans responded in kind.[89]

In the General Government, however, the Germans had been able to keep things under control. The SD chief in District Galicia, Walter Schenk, was able to report in July 1943, "District Galicia's security situation . . . is still to be considered sound and not dangerous."[90] Kubiiovych noted in one of his postwar works, *Ukraine: A Concise Encyclopedia*, that Galicia in mid-1943 was "the only relatively peaceful island in the great expanse of eastern Europe conquered by the Germans, and the only place where conditions were close to normal."[91] The primary reasons for this were the pragmatic German policy toward the Ukrainians in Galicia and Galicia's distance from any serious zone of operations for Soviet partisans. This changed, however, when Soviet partisans under Sidor Kovpak raided Galicia in July 1943.

Kovpak's raid had three consequences. First, it shook the Galician Ukrainian population's confidence in the Germans' ability to protect them. Second, it gave new life to the region's Communist partisans. Third, it led the Germans to introduce their brand of anti-partisan operations into Galicia. In the meantime, the underground OUN-B formed a Galician version of the UPA under the name Ukrainian People's Self-Defense Force (UNSO). By the end of the year, although Kovpak had long since withdrawn to eastern Ukraine, Communist cells, UNSO, various Polish units, and German forces were fighting one another as well. Around 15,000 non-Jewish Galicians were killed, starting in late 1943.[92] In early 1944, the UPA, which absorbed UNSO in late 1943, be-

This poster, an issue of the bulletin board newspaper *Novi Visti* from late 1943, bears the headline "to arms." It demonstrates how ideas shared by the Nazis and Galician Ukrainians converged during recruitment for the SS Volunteer Rifles Division Galicia. The poster combines written and graphic appeals to "annihilate the Judeo-Bolshevik monster," references to the 1932–1933 artificial famine in Soviet Ukraine and the Gulag system, and patriotic appeals drawn from the poets Taras Shevchenko and Ivan Franko. A prose translation of the lines in capital letters reads: "... and with the enemy's evil blood consecrate your freedom..." and "... to attain for you, our native land, glory and freedom and honor!" *Bundesarchiv.*

gan trying to rid Galicia of its Poles as well, killing at least 10,000 in the process.[93]

Jews trying to flee German persecution in Galicia were very much on their own during the first two years of the German occupation. After the Kovpak raid, they could hope to find shelter with Kovpak's raiders or with the revitalized local Polish or Ukrainian Communists. They did so not because they were Communists, but because a chance existed that the Communist partisans would accept them. Joining the nationalist Ukrainian partisans was not entirely out of the question, but very difficult. Many of UPA members and leaders, for example, were still convinced that "the Jews" supported the Bolsheviks. After all, Jews appeared to be joining only the Soviet partisans groups. Furthermore, nationalist Ukrainian partisans (like their Polish counterparts) were fighting for a nation-state, and one basic tenant common to both groups was the belief that it was optimal to have as few members of different nationalities as possible. Thus, very few Jews were able to join nationalist partisans—primarily those who could offer some needed form of skilled labor, i.e., doctors, tailors, shoemakers and the like. This issue also requires more research.

The OUN-B officially moderated its position toward Jews at its August 1943 conference and dispensed with other trappings of far-right militant groups such as the fascist salute. In the field, however, the new resolutions changed little in UPA's actions toward Jews in hiding, particularly in Galicia. Dieter Pohl concludes, "the consistency of antisemitism [is] astounding."[94]

The conflict between the Germans and UPA in Galicia peaked around April 1944. Afterward, with the Red Army pressing on the Bug River and into eastern Galicia, mutual interests made it easier to overcome differences and enabled the UPA and Germans to return a level of tactical cooperation similar to that of 1941. The Germans provided training and supplies for the UPA, while the UPA assisted the Germans with reconnaissance.[95] The overlapping interests also included the "Jewish question." As the 1st Armored Army High Command noted in May 1944:

> In the event of an agreement [with the UPA] the following would be expected: an end to the threat to rear-area lines of communications; active help against Soviet paratroopers, Red Army stragglers, Bolshevik, Polish and Jewish gangs; combat operations behind enemy lines; the transfer of enemy information.[96]

There is also evidence of a certain level of cooperation with at least a part of UPA with regard to what was left of the Jewish question in Galicia, as is seen in the following excerpt from another Wehrmacht intelligence report:

> By our own reconnaissance, a gang of Jews was observed east of Bibrka, the planned destruction of which could not ensue due to use of the intended troops in another operation. The UPA has successfully taken up pursuit of the Jewish gangsters and up to now shot almost 100.[97]

Relations between OUN-B and the Germans continued to improve until Bandera and his imprisoned comrades were released from the concentration camps where they were held in the autumn of 1944. Earlier that summer, after the Red Army had expelled the Germans from Ukraine, the various Ukrainian organizations had finally managed to reestablish a sufficient degree of cooperation among themselves in order to form the Ukrainian Supreme Liberation Council (*Ukraïnska Holovna Vyzvolna Rada*). Within Soviet territory, the council served to coordinate the Ukrainian struggle against Soviet rule; farther afield, the council's foreign representation was used to establish contact with the Western Allies.

Rescuers

So far, the focus has been on those Ukrainians or Ukrainian groups within the General Government who sided with the Germans and tried to profit from it. This picture, however, is incomplete. There were Ukrainian rescuers in the General Government, and theirs is a sad story, for historical discourse has lost sight of these courageous individuals and institutions.[98]

One reason for the neglect is that efforts by Ukrainian emigrants to present a different picture often read like apologetic attempts to white-wash Ukrainian collaboration and to play down the long tradition of Ukrainian anti-Jewish violence.[99] While on the Jewish side, shrill titles such as S. F. Sabrin's *Alliance for Murder* have served more to fire tempers than to cool them. Taras Hunczak speaks of an "invisible wall" that divides Jewish and Ukrainian historians.[100]

Another reason for this neglect was that in the Soviet Union, discussion of the Shoah was all but impossible.[101] So long as the mass killing of Jews in Ukraine was left untouched by Soviet historians, one could hardly discuss Ukrainian rescuers. Thus, until 1991, Yad Vashem, Israel's Holocaust remembrance authority, had very little information on Ukrainian Righteous among Gentiles. Most of the information that was on record came by way of Poland despite that country's place in the Soviet bloc. There was a drawback, though. Such cases usually concerned only western Ukraine, and frequently the rescuers were of Polish nationality.

The taboos against discussing the Shoah in Ukraine disappeared with the collapse of the Soviet Union. Since then, it has become possible to gain a more comprehensive overview of Ukrainian rescue efforts. The first publication on Ukrainian rescuers was published in Ukraine in 1993.[102] Over the past decade, reports of rescuers from all across Ukraine and from all levels of Ukrainian society now complement this picture. As of January 1, 2005, Yad Vashem had recognized 2,079 Righteous among the Nations from Ukraine.

The Greek Catholic Church, despite its German subsidies and ties to both OUN factions, also contains several examples of clergy who tried to save Jews, first and foremost Metropolitan Andrei Count Sheptytsky, the head of the church, who rescued at least 150 Jews.[103] With Sheptytsky's help, Rabbi David Kahane spent the war disguised as a Greek Catholic librarian and taught Greek Catholic monks Hebrew. Kliment Sheptytsky, the metropolitan's brother and the head of the Greek Catholic Church's Studite convents, together with convent abbess Ihumena Iosefa, helped hide Kahane's wife and daughter.[104] Natalia Dresdner of Lviv hid for eight months in Mosty under the protection of a priest by the name of Korduba.[105]

The Greek Catholic Church, it should also be noted, also used baptism to save some Jews, but this was not widespread. The Sipo-SD in District Galicia counted 40 cases of Jews being officially baptized in the first half of 1942. The practice was officially ended after consultation between the Sipo-SD command in Lviv and Sheptytsky.[106] Although the metropolitan issued a decree forbidding the baptism of Jews, it appears that this practice continued. In Peremyshliany, the Greek Catholic priest Omelian Kovch was deported to Majdanek and murdered there for baptizing large numbers of Jews.[107]

Kahane also later related how the director of the Ukrainian city library in Lviv, Omelian Masliak, constructed specials shelves for the purpose of hiding Jews and sold rare books to earn the money necessary to feed them.[108] A watchman at the Lviv Botanic Gardens hid the musician and jurist Julius Sperber as a gesture of gratitude for free violin lessons given to his son before the war.[109] Beyond Lviv, reports from Peremyshliany speak of 1,700 Jews who were able to survive the occupation in the woods protected and supplied by Ukrainian and Polish foresters.[110] Mass rescues also took place in towns such as Sambir, where Oleksandr Kryvoiaza rescued 58 Jews, and Pidhaitsi, where Levko and Roman Biletsky saved 23 Jews.[111] Another notable example is that of the Przemyśl gymnasium teacher Zahaikevych who saved a family.[112] This was dangerous work, as illustrated by the case of a Ukrainian woman by the name of Anna Masiaga, who was sentenced to death for aiding and abetting Jews in Stry in early 1944.[113]

The behavior of the largely uneducated, highly religious Galician Ukrainian peasantry does not allow itself to pigeonholed either. David Kahane noted that peasants in Galicia were just as likely to help Jews jumping from the trains heading toward the death camp Bełżec as to turn them in.[114] The stereotype would probably have peasants turning over the vast majority of fleeing Jews. In late 1943, the SS and police in Galicia noted that peasants stood out among Christians being prosecuted for aiding and abetting Jews.[115]

Sometimes, rescue came from the most unexpected quarters. Ukrainian policemen discovered Mundek Margulies, who hid in the sewers of Lviv, during one of his nightly excursions in search of food. One of the policemen pointed a flashlight in Margulies's face and said, "Let him go. I know him well." In the flashlight's glare, Margulies was unable to recognize the policeman who saved him.[116] The Ukrainian policeman Vavryniuk of Lviv hid Clara Zimmels-Trope in his apartment, thus enabling her to survive the war.[117] After an anti-Jewish *Aktion* in Ternopil on April 7, 1943, a Ukrainian policeman let a Jew emerging from a tunnel escape: "He told me I should disappear fast, and so I was again saved in a miraculous way."[118]

Even the Ukrainian Regional Committee under Kost Pankivsky—the UTsK's branch office in District Galicia—saved a handful of Jews by providing them Ukrainian papers. Pankivsky specifically mentions in his memoirs a friend, Martin Liebesmann, and the Jewish wives of Ukrainians. Jews were also employed by some of the aid committees until the Germans put an end to the practice. However, Pankivsky himself concedes that "these were especially exceptional cases, and that there were not many of them."[119]

Marginal groups for Galicia also took part in saving Jews. The ethnically mixed family Iatskiv in Terebovlia—the husband a Ukrainian, the wife a Pole—hid around ten Jews without asking for anything in return.[120] The Baptist Vasyl Dzyvulsky of Chortkiv County saved a 17-year-old boy as well as another 12 people from Buchach.[121] Seventh-Day Adventists and Jehovah's Witnesses also ranked among rescuers in Galicia. Elsa Silver from the Pidhaitsi region and Simon Schechter of

Korolivka survived the occupation with the help of the former, while a member of the latter rescued Yehoshua Shiloni.[122]

Some Ukrainians, including Metropolitan Sheptytsky, remain unrecognized by Yad Vashem. Such cases usually involve very complicated circumstances. It is undisputed, for example, that Metropolitan Shepytsky saved many Jewish lives, and that he condemned antisemitism among his followers. On the other hand, Sheptytsky welcomed the Germans in a pastoral letter dated July 1, 1941—the very moment when pogroms were sweeping Lviv. Later, he congratulated Hitler on the occupation of Kiev and declared himself a "friend of Germany" in the fight against Bolshevism.[123] In a January 1942 letter to Hitler, Sheptytsky—along with Andrii Melnyk, Mykola Velychkivsky, chairman of the short-lived OUN-M sponsored Ukrainian National Council in Kiev, and Andrii Levytsky, the president of the UNR's Warsaw-based exile government—criticized the German government's actions regarding Ukrainian nationalist aspirations, but nevertheless continued to offer close cooperation.[124] Sheptytsky's initial endorsement of the German invasion stemmed from the repression experienced under the Soviets. With time, he was disabused of whatever misconceptions he had about the Germans, and in August 1942, he made it very clear to the Pope what the Germans were doing to the Jews and declared the Nazis to be worse than the Soviets.[125] Yet half a year later, he bestowed his blessing on the creation of the SS Division Galicia.

Indulging in a discussion on the number of rescuers or ratio of rescuers to population, as conducted for many years among Polish and Israeli historians, rarely leads to any clear conclusions.[126] Whether there were thousands or hundreds or merely scores of "righteous" in a population of millions is a question of ethics. For the historian, it suffices to realize that there were too many acts to make them irrelevant, yet too few to change the overall picture.

Conclusion

Ukrainian nationalism in the twentieth century (like most nationalisms) espoused a view of the contemporary world based to a large extent on partly understood lessons of history. Many of the lessons drawn from the Ukrainian past had nothing at all to do with reality but rather an idealized form of what reality should be. As a result, the expectations and values of key Ukrainian nationalist groups ultimately led to a scenario where the Ukrainian people were but puppets in a larger power play. And no matter what happened, against all odds and contrary to their experiences with Berlin, these groups continued to side with the Germans right up until May 8, 1945.

The Germans used Ukrainian nationalism for their own ends—and not unsuccessfully. The Germans repeatedly duped and disappointed the Ukrainian nationalists, from 1918, when they toppled the UNR government, to 1939, when they turned over Carpatho-Ukraine to Hungary and Galicia and Volhynia to the Soviets, to 1941, when they arrested the militant nationalists of OUN-B. Nonetheless, the Ukrainian nationalists continued to cooperate with the Germans, especially in the last seven months of the war.

The build-up of Ukrainian auxiliary police formations in 1942 and 1943 in District Lublin and District Cracow, the SS Division Galicia in 1943, the UPA-Wehrmacht cooperation in Galicia in the late spring of 1944, the release of the Ukrainian nationalists from prisons and concentration camps in the autumn of 1944, and the cooperation with the Germans in creating a Ukrainian National Committee in March 1945: All of these events stand for examples of certain political priorities pursued by Ukrainian nationalist political elites in the General Government. For politically minded Ukrainian nationalists, autonomy, independence, statehood at the expense of Russia and Poland—these were the key reasons to collaborate. For others, there were materialist incentives. The extermination of the Jews was not the main reason Ukrainians collaborated and, with few exceptions, it was not a reason for nationalist organizations to resist either.

Returning to our starting point, we can say that historical predispositions worked against a more humane stand against the Holocaust. The Germans used this setting for their own objectives. There were many more reported cases in which Gentiles participated in the murder, but there were cases that were very different. If history teaches anything, it warns us of the dangers of generalizing and labeling a people as a whole as an enemy. It tells us that one should not believe in historical "laws" that motivate fanatics to take violent action. And it tells us that people will continue to do so when they believe that their "historical rights" or political dreams allow them to violate the sanctity of life.

Notes

1. Interview with Isaac W., p. 236, in Donald L. Niewyk, *Fresh Wounds* (Chapel Hill, London: University of North Carolina, 1998). The same volume, which is a collection of testimonies gathered shortly after the war, contains a similar comment in the interview with Jacob M., p. 310: "[The Ukrainians] were frightful, they were the worst evil." In his book *The Righteous: The Unsung Heroes of the Holocaust* (London: Black Swan, 2003), p. 14, Martin Gilbert quotes a letter from a survivor whose father, who passed through four concentration camps, used to say that the "Ukrainian and Baltic States' concentration camp guards often far surpassed the cold, calculated cruelty of the Germans."

2. John-Paul Himka, "Ukrainian Collaboration in the Extermination of the Jews During the Second World War. Sorting Out the Long-term and Conjunctural Factors," in Jonathan Frankel, ed., *The Fate of the European Jews 1939–1945: Continuity or Contingency?* (New York: Oxford University Press, 1997), pp. 170–189.

3. Karel Berkhoff, *Harvest of Despair* (Cambridge: Belknap Press of Harvard University Press, 2004).

4. See Thomas Sandkühler, *"Endlösung" in Galizien: Der Judenmord in Ostpolen und die Rettungsaktionen von Berthold Beitz* (Bonn: Dietz, 1996); and Dieter

Pohl, *Nationalsozialistische Judenverfolgung in Ostgalizien 1941–1944: Organisation und Durchführung eines staatlichen Massenverbrechens* (München: Oldenburg, 1996).

5. See, for example, Werner Benecke, *Die Ostgebiete der Zweiten Polnischen Republik: Staatsmacht und öffentliche Ordnung in einer Minderheitenregion 1918–1939*, Beiträge zur Geschichte Osteuropas, Bd. 29 (Köln, Weimar, Wien: Böhlau, 1999); Cornelia Schenke, *Nationalstaat und nationale Frage: Polen und die Ukrainer 1921–1939*, Hamburger Veröffentlichungen zur Geschichte Mittel- und Osteuropas, Vol. 12 (Hamburg: Dölling und Galitz, 2005). Polish authors working on these and similar topics include Andrzej Żbikowski, Grzegorz Hryciuk, and Marek Wierzbicki.

6. Christoph Mick of Warwick University is readying for publication a study of interethnic violence in Lviv in 1918 and 1939–1945. Christine Kulke of the University of California at Berkeley is working on a dissertation of everyday life in Lviv during the Second World War.

7. Henry Abramson, *A Prayer for the Government* (Cambridge: Harvard University Press, 1999), p. 3.

8. Some contemporary reports, many of which strongly exaggerated the numbers of victims, are published in English in Nathan Hanover, *Abyss of Despair* (New Brunswick, London: Transaction Books, 1983). For a broader discussion of the Khmel'nyts'kyi era, see Bernard D. Weinryb, "The Hebrew Chronicles on Bohdan Khmel'nyts'kyi and the Cossack-Polish War," *Harvard Ukrainian Studies*, 2 (1977), pp. 153–177; and Frank Sysyn, "The Cossack Insurrections in Jewish-Ukrainian Relations," in Peter Potichnyj and Howard Aster, eds., *Ukrainian-Jewish Relations in Historical Perspective* (Edmonton: Canadian Institute of Ukrainian Studies, 1988), pp. 43–56.

9. Frank Golczewski, *Polnisch-jüdische Beziehungen 1881–1922* (Wiesbaden: Steiner, 1981), pp. 185–205 and pp. 213–217. See also Alexander Victor Prusin, *Nationalizing a Borderland: War, Ethnicity, and Anti-Jewish Violence in East Galicia, 1914–1920* (Tuscaloosa: University of Alabama Press, 2005).

10. Matthias Vetter, *Antisemiten und Bolschewiki* (Berlin: Metropol, 1995); Peter Kenez, "Pogroms and White Ideology in the Russian Civil War," in Shlomo Lambroza and John D. Klier, eds., *Pogroms: Anti-Jewish Violence in Russian History* (Cambridge: Cambridge University Press, 1992), pp. 293–313.

11. There is a sizeable literature on the Petliura era. For the central arguments, see Saul S. Friedman, *Pogromchik* (New York: Hart Publishing, 1976). A short debate is to be found in two articles: Taras Hunczak, "A Reappraisal of Symon Petliura and Ukrainian-Jewish Relations, 1917–1921," *Jewish Social Studies*, 31 (1969), pp. 163–183, and Zosa Szajkowski, "A Reappraisal of Simon Petliura and Ukrainian-Jewish Relations, 1917–1920: A Rebuttal," ibid., pp. 184–213.

12. Cf. Omelian Terlets'kyi, *Istoriia ukraïns'koï hromady v Rastati 1915–1918* (Kiev, Leipzig: Ukrainska nakladnia, 1919) and Ihor Sribniak, *Poloneni Ukraïntsi v Avstro-Uhorshchyni ta Nimechchyni (1914–1920 rr.)* (Kiev: Derzhavnyi Lingvistychnyi Universytet, Kafedra Istoriï Ukraïny, 1999).

13. The worst of these was the "pacification" operation of early autumn 1930. The death toll in this largest of Polish operations against Ukrainians ranges from 7 to 35 people. The former figure is from Stephan Horak, *Poland and Her National Minorities, 1919–39* (New York: Vantage Press, 1961), p. 162. The latter comes from Petro Mirchuk and is cited in Hans-Jürgen Boemelburg, "Die polnisch-ukrainischen Beziehungen 1922–1939: Ein Literatur- und Forschungsbericht," *Jahrbücher für Geschichte Osteuropas*, 39 (1991), p. 90. The financial damage in the middle of the depression was considerable, topped only by the damage done to any possibility of Polish-Ukrainian reconciliation within the Polish state.

14. On the Schwarzbart trial, see Henry Torrès, *Le procès des pogroms* (Par-

is: Les Éditions de France, 1928); Andrii Iakovliv, *Paryzhs'ka trahediia* (Praha: Vydavnyts'tvo Komitetu oborony pam'iaty S. Petliury ta Komitetu budovy UAPTS khramu sv. Symona v Paryzhi, 1930).

15. Ivan Kedryn, "Kul't Symona Petliury," in *Symon Petliura* (Munich, Paris: Ukraïnskyi Vil'nyi Universytet, 1980), pp. 209–217.

16. *Novy Chas* quoted in "Mniejszowci narodowe w Polsce," *Sprawy Narodowosciowe*, no. 3/4 (1928), p. 412f.

17. Dmytro Dontsov, "Symon Petliura," *Literaturno-Naukovyi Vistnyk*, 5 (1926), p. 327. For more reactions, see Alexander J. Motyl, *The Turn to the Right: The Ideological Origins and Development of Ukrainian Nationalism, 1919–1929* (Boulder, CO: East European Monographs, 1980), pp. 50f.

18. For more information on the trial of the Union for the Liberation of Ukraine, see Terry Martin, *Affirmative Action Empire: Nations and Nationalism in the Soviet Union, 1923–1939* (Ithaca: Cornell University Press, 2001), pp. 249–254.

19. Volodymyr Martynets', *Ukraïns'ke Pidpillia* (Winnipeg, 1949), pp. 59–61.

20. Vincent Shandor, *Carpatho-Ukraine in the Twentieth Century: A Political and Legal History* (Cambridge: Harvard University Press, 1997).

21. V. K., "Do pomsty, do zbroï, do mesty!" *Ukraïns'kyi Vistnyk*, 4 no. 5–6 (24–25) (1939), p. 1.

22. *Encyclopedia of Ukraine*, Volume 5, entry "Ukrainian Central Committee," p. 367.

23. NS43/42, Denkschrift der Ukrainer an Herrn Generalgouverneur Reichsminister Dr. Frank in Krakau, November 17, 1939, pp. 136–146. The memo is signed by Kubiiovych, Sushko, and nine other civic leaders.

24. Mirosław Sycz, *Spółdzielczość ukraińska w Galicji w okresie II wojny światowej* (Warsaw: Pracowia Wydawnicza, 1997), pp. 68, 80, and 162f.

25. John A. Armstrong, *Ukrainian Nationalism 1939–45* (New York: Columbia University, 1953), p. 50.

26. Volodymyr Kubiiovych, *Ukraïntsi v Heneral'nii Hubernii 1939–1941: Istoriia Ukraïns'koho Tsentral'noho Komitetu* (Chicago: Denysiuk, 1975), p. 569. For more details about this meeting between Frank and Kubiiovych and the proposals put forward, see also Werner Präg and Wolfgang Jacobmeyer, eds., *Das Diensttagebuch des deutschen Generalgouverneurs in Polen 1939–45* (Stuttgart: DVA, 1975), pp. 358f.

27. Armstrong, *Ukrainian Nationalism*, p. 67.

28. Armstrong, *Ukrainian Nationalism*, p. 67, 190.

29. Sycz, *Spółdzielczość ukraińska*, pp. 106–119.

30. Armstrong, *Ukrainian Nationalism*, p. 68f.

31. "Die Juden waren daher froh, dass die Sowjets Ostpolen besetzten." Bogdan Musial, *"Konterrevolutionäre Elemente sind zu erschießen"* (Berlin, München: Propyläen, 2000), p. 57.

32. Pohl, *Judenverfolgung*, p. 38.

33. See Jan T. Gross, *Revolution from Abroad: The Soviet Conquest of Poland's Western Ukraine and Western Belorussia* (Princeton: Princeton University Press, 1988), and idem, "The Jewish Community in the Soviet-Annexed Territories on the Eve of the Holocaust. A Social Scientist's View," in Lucjan Dobroszycki and Jeffrey S. Gurock, eds., *The Holocaust in the Soviet Union. Studies and Sources on the Destruction of the Jews in the Nazi-Occupied Territories of the USSR, 1941–1945* (Armonk, NY: M. E. Sharpe, 1993), pp. 155–171.

34. Gross, *Revolution from Abroad*.

35. Cited in Pohl, *Judenverfolgung*, p. 38.

36. Two Ukrainian-German units trained by German military intelligence also accompanied the Wehrmacht: Special Formation Nachtigall, which served

under the 17th Army from June 22 until July 22, and Organization Roland, which was assigned to the 11th Army from July 26 to August 17. OUN members provided the Ukrainian contingent for both units.

37. For Einsatzgruppen activities, see Helmut Krausnick and Hans-Heinrich Wilhelm, *Die Truppe des Weltanschauungskrieges* (Stuttgart: DVA, 1981); and Peter Klein, ed., *Die Einsatzgruppen in der besetzten Sowjetunion 1941/42: Die Tätigkeits- und Lageberichte des Chefs der Sicherheitspolizei und des SD* (Berlin: Edition Hentrich, 1997).

38. Regarding Zolochiv, see the memoirs of one of the few survivors, Shlomo Wolkowicz, *Das Grab bei Zloczow* (Berlin: Wichern-Verlag, 1996).

39. Using contemporary NKVD documents, the editors of one Polish work show 2,464 prisoners being shot prior to the Soviet evacuation; Krzysztof Popinski et al., eds., *Drogi Smierci* (Warsaw: Karta, 1995), esp. p. 31 and p. 176. To this it necessary to add as many as 200 killed in Lviv during an abortive uprising before the Germans took the city.

40. Pohl, *Judenverfolgung,* p. 55.

41. See the regional entries for Drohobych, Lviv, Ivano-Frankivs'k, and Ternopil' regions in Alexander Kruglov, *The Losses Suffered by Ukrainian Jews in 1941–1944* (Kharkiv: Tarbut Laam, 2005). See also Pohl, p. 54–67; and Andrzej Żbikowski, "Lokalne pogromy Żydów w czerwcu i lipcu 1941 roku na wschodnich rubieżach II Rzeczypospolitej," *Biuletyn Żydowskiego Instytutu Historycznego,* no. 2–3 (1992), pp. 3–18, published in English as "Local Anti-Jewish Pogroms in the Occupied Territories of Eastern Poland, June–July 1941," in Dobroszycki and Gurock, eds., *The Holocaust in the Soviet Union*; and Ahron Weiss, "The Holocaust and the Ukrainian Victims," in Michael Berenbaum, ed., *Mosaic of Victims: Non-Jews Persecuted and Murdered by the Nazis* (New York: New York University Press, 1990). This figure is based on Kruglov, *The Losses Suffered by Ukrainian Jews.* Cf. Pohl, who also arrives at an estimate around 12,000, while Weiss, "Holocaust and Ukrainian Victims," p. 110, puts the figure as high as 24,000. The small part of Volhynia included in Ternopil' region has been taken into account here.

42. Jan Tomasz Gross, *Sąsiedzi* (Sejny: Pogranicze, 2000).

43. Wolodymyr Kosyk, *The Third Reich and Ukraine* (New York: Peter Lang, 1993). Kosyk states that "Hitler" and the "German police" identified the Jews "as the main agents of bolshevism" (p. 92), and that this was how the Einsatzgruppen rationalized their tasks. He omits, however, that the OUN-B included the same statement in its program.

44. Paul Magocsi, *A History of Ukraine* (Toronto: University of Toronto Press, 1996), p. 631.

45. Ibid.

46. Bundesarchiv-Berlin (BA-B), R70-SU/32, pp. 11f., Heydrich to Chiefs of the Einsatzgruppen, Schnellbrief, June 29, 1941.

47. BA-B, R58/214.

48. Raul Hilberg, *The Destruction of the European Jews: Revised and Definitive Version,* Vol. 1 (New York: Holmes and Meier, 1985), p. 312.

49. See Żbikowski; Juliusz Feuerman, "Pamiętnik ze Stanisławowa (1941–1943)," *Biuletyn Żydowskiego Instytutu Historycznego,* 59 (1966), pp. 63–91; Markus Willbach, "Skupisko Żydowskie w Obertynie podczas II wojny światowej," *Biuletyn Żydowskiego Instytutu Historycznego,* 35 (1960), pp. 106–128. Numerous reports are also printed in S. F. Sabrin's *Alliance for Murder* (New York: Sarpedon, 1991). Aside from the testimonies and documents reproduced here, this book makes for a less than constructive contribution to the literature. Żbikowski, p. 177. The Hungarian army not only refused to tolerate pogroms, it also disarmed Ukrainian militias found committing them. It should be noted that Budapest did deport from its annexed territories to German-occupied Ukraine Jewish refugees who had fled the Soviet Union and Poland earlier in the war, and that this policy

ultimately led to the murder of those Jews at Kam'ianets'-Podil's'kyi in August 1941. Klaus-Michael Mallmann, "Der qualitative Sprung im Vernichtungsprozess. Das Massaker von Kamenez-Podolsk Ende August 1941," in *Jahrbuch für Antisemitismusforschung 10* (Frankfurt am Main: Campus-Verl., 2001), pp. 239–264.

50. Pohl, *Judenverfolgung,* pp. 54–59. The quote, from Bandera's deputy, Iaroslav Stets'ko, is cited on p. 49.

51. Armstrong, *Ukrainian Nationalism,* p. 69f.

52. I. T. Lipschütz-Lipinski, *Hans Duda und die Askaris* (Tel Aviv: Hamenora, 1971), pp. 61–63; Hans Raschhofer, *Der Fall Oberländer* (Tübingen: Schlichtenmayer, 1962), pp. 57ff.; Leo Heiman, "They Saved Jews," *The Ukrainian Quarterly,* 17 (1961), pp. 320–332, here p. 322.

53. On OUN-M, see Armstrong, *Ukrainian Nationalism,* p. 73. For OUN-B, Pohl, *Judenverfolgung,* pp. 57f.

54. See Stepan Bandera an Reichsminister Alfred Rosenberg, August 14, 1941, in *Akten zur deutschen auswärtigen Politik 1918–1945,* Serie D, Bd. XIII, 1 (Göttingen: Vandenhoeck und Ruprecht, 1970), pp. 261f.

55. Kubiiovych to Frank, August 29, 1941, NAC, MG 31, D203, Vol. 26, File 31. Reprinted in *The Correspondence of the Ukrainian Central Committee in Cracow and Lviv with the German Authorities, 1939–1945,* Part 1, compiled with an introduction by Wasyl Veryha (Edmonton: Canadian Institute of Ukrainian Studies Press, 2000), pp. 336–343, here p. 342.

56. Christoph Klessmann, "Nationalsozialistische Kirchenpolitik und Nationalitätenfrage im Generalgouvernement (1939–1945)," *Jahrbücher für Geschichte Osteuropas,* Vol. 18, no. 4 (1970), p. 596. The Greek Catholic Church received 535,383 zloty per month in 1942. Using official fixed exchange rates (RM 2.5/U.S. $1, 1941), this worked out to about $107,000 at the time, which today would be worth around $1.48 million (2006 U.S. dollars). The sum was bound to be somewhat less, as this figure fails to take into account purchasing power and the more realistic exchange rates that most likely existed on the black market.

57. In the first days of the German occupation of Lviv, the Gestapo killed a group of Polish university professors who had survived the Soviet ordeal.

58. Ostap D. Tarnavs'kyi, *Literaturnyi Lviv 1939–1944: Spomyny* (Lviv: Prosvita, 1995), pp.128f.

59. Georg Hansen, *Schulpolitik als Volkstumspolitik: Quellen zur Schulpolitik der Besatzer in Polen 1939–1945* (Münster-New York: Waxmann, 1994), p. 548.

60. Sycz, *Spółdzielczość ukraińska,* p. 245.

61. All of the above excesses are drawn from Nuremberg Document PS-1526, Kubiiovych to Frank, February 25, 1943. This document is reproduced along with its 16 annexes in *Correspondence of the Ukrainian Central Committee,* Part 1, pp. 493–529.

62. Meldungen aus dem Generalgouvernement, September 1943, reproduced in Boberach, ed., *Regimekritik, Widerstand und Verfolgung,* Microfiche 7.

63. Meldungen aus dem Generalgouvernement, December 1942, reproduced in the microfiche collection: Heinz Boberach, ed., *Regimekritik, Widerstand und Verfolgung in Deutschland und den besetzten Gebieten: Meldungen und Berichte aus dem Geheimen Staatspolizeiamt, dem SD-Hauptamt der SS und dem Reichssicherheitshauptamt, 1933–1945,* Pt. 2 (München: Saur, 1999), Microfiche 5.

64. See, for example, *Correspondence of the Ukrainian Central Committee,* Part 1, Behandlung der Ukrainer aus dem Generalgouvernement im Deutschen Reich, June 1942, p. 394, and Grundlagen der deutsch-ukrainischen Beziehungen, December 1942, p. 470.

65. In November 1942, Kubiiovych suggested the Germans assign local communities contingents for delivery, see National Archives Canada, Kubiiovych Files, MG 31, D 203, Vol. 18, File 10, conference Siebert, Föhl, and Kubiiovych, November 19, 1942, and on December 17, 1942, Kubiiovych suggested

that the Ukrainian Auxiliary Committees be employed to this end, and that workers be selected by lists, ibid., conference Kubiiovych and Bühler, December 17, 1942.

66. BA, R6/597, Über die politische Führung fremdvölkischer Gebiete, p. 4.

67. Regarding national status, see entry in *Encyclopedia of Ukraine*, Vol. 3, entry "Ostarbeiter," on p. 729. On the OST badge, see Bohdan Krawchenko, "Soviet Ukraine under Nazi Occupation, 1941–4," p. 28, in Yury Boshyk, ed., *Ukraine during World War II: History and its Aftermath* (Alberta: Canadian Institute of Ukrainian Studies, 1986). The newspaper, *Visti, Wochenzeitung für ukrainische Arbeiter aus dem Generalgouvernement,* can be found in German libraries.

68. Kubiiovych to Frank, July 7, 1941, *Correspondence of the Ukrainian Central Committee,* Part 1, pp. 317–318. For more examples when Kubiiovych pressed Hans Frank for Ukrainian military units, see Kubiiovych to Frank, August 29, 1941, *Correspondence,* Part 1, p. 342, and Präg and Jacobmeyer, eds., *Diensttagebuch Frank,* p. 463.

69. BA-B, R58/1005, p. 12, Bormann protocol of meeting on May 19, 1943, between Hitler, Reich Minister for the Occupied Eastern Territories Alfred Rosenberg, Reich Commissar Ukraine Erich Koch.

70. Myroslav Yurkevich, "Galician Ukrainians in German Military Formations and in the German Administration," in Boshyk, ed., *Ukraine during World War II,* p. 77. Wächter's own tally of Galician Ukrainians who eventually served under arms was 35,000; see BA, R6/597, Über die politische Führung fremdvölkischer Gebiete, p. 5. A German division at the time would have consisted of around 13,500 soldiers.

71. Taras Hunczak, *On the Horns of a Dilemma: The Story of the Ukrainian Division Halychyna,* (Lanham, MD: University Press of America, 2000), p. 31.

72. The activities of the Ukrainian Police are mentioned in passim in Thomas Sandkühler, *"Endlösung"* and Pohl, *Judenverfolgung.* The first long article to address this topic separately is Gabriel N. Finder and Alexander Prusin, "Collaboration in Eastern Galicia: The Ukrainian Police and the Holocaust," *East European Jewish Affairs,* 34, no. 2 (Winter 2004), pp. 95–118.

73. Ryszard Torzecki, *Kwestia ukraińska w polityce III Rzeszy, 1933–1945* (Warsaw: Książka i Wiedza, 1972), p. 242.

74. Taras Hunczak, "Ukrainian-Jewish Relations during the Soviet and Nazi Occupation," in Michael R. Marrus, ed., *The Nazi Holocaust,* Vol. 5, Pt. 1, Public Opinion and the Relations to the Jews in Nazi Europe (Westport and London: Meckler, 1989), p. 403.

75. Entries for Ivan Kozak and Liudomyr Ohonovs'kyi in *Entsklopediia Ukraïnoznavstva,* Vol. 3, p. 1,066, and Vol. 5, p. 1,813, respectively. Neither man appears in the English-language *Encyclopedia of Ukraine.*

76. Finder and Prusin, "Collaboration in Eastern Galicia," p. 109, 117, ft. 62. Lev Shankovs'kyi's entry on the Ukrainian Auxiliary Police in the *Encyclopedia of Ukraine,* Vol. 5, p. 354, maintains that the police were poorly paid and enjoyed few benefits.

77. Pohl, *Judenverfolgung,* pp. 277f. and 311f.

78. Pohl, *Judenverfolgung,* p. 339.

79. Peter Black, "Die Trawniki-Männer und die "Aktion Reinhard," in Bogdan Musial, ed., *"Aktion Reinhardt": Der Völkermord an den Juden im Generalgouvernement 1941–1944,* Einzelveröffentlichungen des Deutschen Historischen Instituts Warschau, no. 10 (Osnabrück: Fibre, 2004), pp. 315f.

80. On the start of recruitment see Peter R. Black, "Rehersal for 'Reinhard': Odilo Globocnik and the Lublin *Selbstschutz,*" *Central European History,* 25, no. 2 (1992), p. 225. On the release of Ukrainian POWs, see Berkhoff, *Harvest of Despair,* p. 106. The asynchrony regarding the ending of the policy arises from the

time required—around two weeks—for orders to move from Berlin to the battalion and company level in the field.

81. Wolfgang Scheffler, "Probleme der Holocaustforschung," in Stefi Jersch-Wenzel, ed., *Deutsche—Polen—Juden, Ihre Beziehungen von den Anfängen bis ins 20. Jahrhundert* (Berlin: Colloquium Verlag, 1987), p. 278.

82. The Schutzmann-Battallions in the General Government are briefly discussed in Hans-Joachim Neufeldt, Jürgen Huck, and Georg Tessin, eds., *Zur Geschichte der Ordnungspolizei 1936–1945*, Teil II, (Koblenz: Bundesarchiv, 1957), pp. 53 and 106. Schuma.-Batl. 202 was recruited from Poles and deployed in anti-partisan operations in Belarus and Volhynia.

83. Maria Wardzyńska, *Formacja Wachmannschaften des SS- und Polizeiführers im Distrikt Lublin* (Warsaw: Główna Komisja Badania Zbrodni przeciwko Narodowi Polskiemu, 1992), pp. 46f.

84. Stanislaw Zabierowski, *Pustków Hitlerowskie obozy wyniszczenia w Służbie Poligonu* (Rzeszów: RSW "Prasa—Książka—Ruch," 1981), p. 34.

85. Pohl, *Judenverfolgung*, p. 93.

86. Early in 1943 Kubiiovych petitioned the Germans to disband the Polish police in the Chełm region of District Lublin, to dimiss Polish members of the Criminal Police in District Galicia, and to expand the Ukrainian auxiliary police in general; see Vorsprache des Leiters des Ukrainsichen Hauptasschusses im Generalgouvernement . . . bei SS-Gruppenführer Müller, Berlin, February 19, 1943, in *Correspondence*, Pt. 1, pp. 488f. The Müller in question here is Gestapo chief Heinrich Müller.

87. Meldungen aus dem Generalgouvernement, January 1943, reproduced in Boberach, *Regimekritik,* Microfiche 6.

88. See, for example, various records of individual Ukrainian policemen for Przemyśl at Institut Pamięci Narodowy, MSW 893. The use of the word "Aryan" stems from the Ukrainian side in these records.

89. The first balanced treatment of these issues is Timothy Snyder, "The Causes of Ukrainian–Polish Ethnic Cleansing 1943," *Past and Present,* May 2003, pp. 197–234.

90. Pohl, *Judenverfolgung*, p. 257.

91. *Ukraine: A Concise Encyclopedia,* Vol. I (Toronto: University of Toronto Press, 1963), p. 889, cited in Pohl, *Judenverfolgung,* p. 12.

92. "Mobilizacja Lwowa," *Karta,* no. 35 (2002), p. 64. This figure appears in the introduction to a photo essay on the SS Division Galicia, where it is used to contrast the propagandistic nature of the photos with the grim reality of Nazi occupation. However, the great majority of these 15,000 non-Jewish civilians, a good number of whom were certainly Polish, fell victim to German anti-partisan operations months after the photos were taken. The enthusiasm in the photos, which were indeed used for propaganda, was real, as ultimately shown in the recruiting figures.

93. Pohl, *Judenverfolgung*, p. 376.

94. Pohl, *Judenverfolgung*, p. 382f.

95. The ups and downs of these negotiations are documented in Taras Hunczak, ed., *The UPA in Light of German Documents,* Book one and two (*Litopys UPA,* Vol. 6 and 7).

96. BA-MA, RH 21-1/184, Pz. AOK 1, Abt. Ic, Unterhandlungen mit Banden, May 22, 1944. The goal of the negotiations here was practical, not political.

97. Staatsanwaltschaft Dortmund, 45 Js 24/62, Bd. "Reste von Gutachten und Dokumenten aus dem Bestand des Pz. AOK 4." These are photocopies from BA-MA, RH-21-4, Pz. AOK 4, Abt. Ic/AO, Tätigkeitsbericht, April 1944.

98. For a treatment of this issue that addresses eastern and western Ukraine alike see Frank Golczewski, "Die Revision eines Klischees. Die Rettung von verfolg-

ten Juden im Zweiten Weltkrieg durch Ukrainer," in Wolfgang Benz and Juliane Wetzel, eds., *Solidarität und Hilfe für Juden während der NS-Zeit*, Band 2 (Berlin: Metropol, 1998), pp. 9–82. Many of the individual cases cited in "Revision eines Klischees" are repeated below.

99. Worthy exceptions are H. Aster and P. Potichnyj, *Jewish-Ukrainian Relations: Two Solitudes* (Oakland, Ontario: Mosaic Press, 1983), and idem, *Ukrainian-Jewish Relations*.

100. Hunczak, "Ukrainian-Jewish Relations," in Marrus, ed., *Nazi Holocaust*, Vol. 5, Pt. 1, p. 396.

101. See the articles by Zvi Gitelman and Lukasz Hirszowicz, in Dobroszycki and Gurock, eds., *The Holocaust in the Soviet Union*.

102. See Iakiv Suslens'kyi, *Spravzhni heroï* (Kiev: Tovarystvo "Ukraïna," 1993).

103. Philip Friedman, "Ukrainian-Jewish Relations during the Nazi Occupation," in Marrus, ed., *Nazi Holocaust*, Vol. 5, Pt. 1, p. 392. The most important works concerning Sheptyts'kyi are: Shimon Redlich, "Sheptyts'kyi and the Jews during World War II," in Paul R. Magocsi, ed., *Morality and Reality The Life and Times of Andrei Sheptyts'kyi* (Edmonton: Canadian Institute of Ukrainian Studies, 1989), pp.145–162; Shimon Redlich, "Metropolitan Andrei Sheptyts'kyi, Ukrainians and Jews during and after the Holocaust," *Holocaust and Genocide Studies,* 5 (1990), no. 1, pp. 39–51; Kurt I. Lewin, "Andreas Count Sheptytsky [...] and the Jewish Community in Galicia During the Second World War," *Annals of the Ukrainian Academy of Arts and Sciences in the United States,* 7 (1959), pp. 1,656–1,667.

104. Kahane was later a rabbi in the Polish People's Army. For his full story, see David Kahane, *The Lvov Ghetto* (Amherst: University of Massachusetts Press, 1990); regarding his wife and daughter, see pp. 60f., 77, 125, 148ff.

105. Friedman, "Ukrainian-Jewish Relations," in Marrus, ed., *Nazi Holocaust*, Vol. 5, Pt. 1, p. 393.

106. Meldungen aus dem Generalgouvernement, January 1943, reproduced in Boberach, *Regimekritik,* Microfiche 6.

107. In September 1999 Kovch was named a Righteous Ukrainian by the Jewish Council of Ukraine. See the biography written by his daughter, Anna Maria Kowc-Baran, *For God's Truth and Human Rights* (in Ukrainian, 1994), English excerpts and the Ukrainian edition available at: http://www.baran.ca/HumanRights. htm. His rescue activities are also mentioned in Philip Friedman's "Ukrainian-Jewish Relations during the Nazi Occupation," in *Roads to Extinction: Essays on the Holocaust* (New York, 1980): 176–208, and in Hunczak, "Ukrainian-Jewish Relations," in Marrus, ed., *Nazi Holocaust*, Vol. 5, Pt. 1, p. 405. Hunczak received this information from Ida Pizem-Karezag, who was hidden by the Sokoluk family in Borshchiv.

108. Heiman, "They Saved Jews," p. 331.

109. Yad Vashem Archive 216, cited in Mordecai Paldiel, *The Path of the Righteous* (Hoboken: KTAV Publishing House, 1993), p. 280.

110. Friedman, "Ukrainian-Jewish Relations," in Marrus, ed., *Nazi Holocaust*, Vol. 5, Pt. 1, p. 388.

111. On Sambir, see Friedman, "Ukrainian-Jewish Relations," in Marrus, ed., *Nazi Holocaust*, Vol. 5, Pt. 1, p. 388. On Pidhaitsi, see Hunczak, "Ukrainian-Jewish Relations," in Marrus, ed., *Nazi Holocaust*, Vol. 5, Pt. 1, p. 404.

112. Gay Block and Malka Drucker, *Rescuers* (New York, London: Holmes & Meier, 1992), pp. 241–245.

113. See facsimile of poster announcing death sentences in Yurkevich, "Galician Ukrainians," in Boshyk, ed., *Ukraine during World War II*, p. 79. Of the 20 people sentenced to death here, Masiaga was the only one accused of aiding Jews. The rest were accused of membership in the OUN or aiding and abetting gangsters, i.e., partisans. The same fate befell Stefan Kulak, Nikolaus Kulak, and Ma-

ria Nazar also of the Stryi region, see excerpt from a similar poster in Friedman, "Ukrainian-Jewish Relations," in Marrus, ed., *Nazi Holocaust,* Vol. 5, Pt. 1, p. 388.

114. Kahane, *Lvov Ghetto,* p. 76.

115. See Friedman, "Ukrainian-Jewish Relations," in Marrus, ed., *Nazi Holocaust,* Vol. 5, Pt. 1, p. 206.

116. Robert Marshall, *In the Sewers of Lvov* (London: Collins, 1990), p. 108.

117. Hunczak, "Ukrainian-Jewish Relations," in Marrus, ed., *Nazi Holocaust,* Vol. 5, Pt. 1, p. 403.

118. Israel Goldfliess, "Fragments of My Holocaust Experiences," in Sabrin, *Alliance for Murder,* p. 106.

119. Kost' Pankivs'kyi, *Roky nimets'koï okupatsiï* (New York and Toronto: Shevchenko Scientific Society, 1965), p. 73.

120. Israel Goldfliess, "A Shelter in the Forest," pp. 110, 120, in Sabrin, *Alliance,* p. 106. Other Jews hidden in the woods were looked after by the Iats'kiv's as well.

121. YVA, 265, cited in Paldiel, *Path of the Righteous,* p. 271.

122. Friedman, "Ukrainian-Jewish Relations," in Marrus, ed., *Nazi Holocaust,* Vol. 5, Pt. 1, ft. 82, p. 393.

123. V. Zarechnyi, "Al'ians OUN-SS," *Voenno-istoricheskii Zhurnal,* 4 (1991), pp. 53–62.

124. BA-Lichterfelde, R6/69, pp. 139ff., Mel'nyk, Sheptyts'kyi, and others to Hitler, January 14, 1942. Kosyk cites this letter, but omits the quintet's offer of "closest possible cooperation"; see also Wolodymyr Kosyk, *The Third Reich and Ukraine* (New York: 1993), p. 208.

125. Sheptyts'kyi to Pius XII, August 29–31, 1942, *Actes et documents du Saint Siège relatifs à la seconde guerre mondiale,* Vol. 3, Deuxième partie, *Le Saint Siège et la situation religieuse en Pologne et dans les Pays Baltes 1939–1945* (Vatican City: Libreria Editrice Vaticana, 1967), Document no. 406, p. 625.

126. Yisrael Gutman and Władysław Bartoszewski, "Polish-Jewish Relations during the Second World War: A Discussion," *Polin,* Vol. 2, 1987, pp. 337–358.

IV
Transnistria and the Romanian Solution to the "Jewish Problem"

DENNIS DELETANT

In recent years, a number of studies of Transnistria have appeared in Romania, among the most notable being Jean Ancel's three-volume work *Transnistria*, published in Romanian in 1998, which painstakingly reconstructs the fate of the Jews deported from Bessarabia and Bukovina and that of the indigenous Jews of Transnistria.[1] For the English-reading public, Marshal Ion Antonescu's treatment of the Jews and Roma (Gypsies) has been elucidated in works such as Matatias Carp's *Holocaust in Rumania: Facts and Documents on the Annihilation of Rumania's Jews, 1940–1944*,[2] translated from the Romanian in 1994. One of the more important titles is Alexander Dallin's *Odessa, 1941–1944: A Case Study of Soviet Territory Under Foreign Rule*, originally written as a RAND report in 1957 and reissued in 1998. As pioneering as Dallin's work was at the time, he did not enjoy the cooperation of the Soviet or Romanian authorities, nor was he able to consult the thousands of pages of Romanian and Soviet documentation now available to researchers.

The collection of Romanian records housed at the United States Holocaust Memorial Museum formed the basis of Radu Ioanid's recent history, *The Holocaust in Romania. The Destruction of Jews and Gypsies under the Antonescu Regime, 1940–1944*. This work provides a groundbreaking synthesis, cataloging and describing Antonescu's systematic measures to expel and eliminate Romania's Jews and Roma (Gypsies). In addition to Ioanid, other eminent scholars such as Randolph Braham have taken a regional approach to Romania's Holocaust history, examining the fate of Jews from Bukovina and Bessarabia.[3] And since most of the Jews from these regions were deported to Transnistria, these local studies also shed light on the history of Transnistria itself.

This chapter reviews the deportation of the Jews from Bessarabia and Bukovina to Transnistria and argues that deportation was part of a broader policy of "ethnic purification," conceived and carried out by Marshal Ion Antonescu, Romania's pro-German military dictator. It seeks to show that Transnistria was originally intended by Antonescu to be not the final destination of the Jews but merely a "holding station" for their expulsion across Transnistria's eastern border, the Southern Buh River, into Russia.

Transnistria was the name given by the Antonescu regime to the region of Ukraine between the Dniestr and the Southern Buh, which Romania occupied following the joint German-Romanian attack on the Soviet Union on June 22, 1941. The region became the graveyard of some 250,000 Jews and more than 12,000 Roma. Many of these were victims of the deportations of Jews ordered by Antonescu in August 1941 from Romanian-controlled Bukovina and Bessarabia, and of Roma from Romania proper in May 1942. Of the 147,000 Jews who were deported from these two areas between 1941 and 1943 to Transnistria, at least 90,000 died in makeshift camps and ghettos, the majority from typhus and starvation.[4] During the same period, between 130,000 and 170,000 local Ukrainian Jews are also estimated to have been murdered or left to die of disease in the same province.[5] A large number of these were shot by the Romanians. Romanian forces killed 15,000–20,000 Jews in Odessa in October 1941 in reprisal for the blowing up of Romanian Army headquarters in the city; according to records from a Romanian war-crimes trial, between 43,000 and 48,000 Jews were massacred on orders from local Romanian officials in the district of Bohdanivka at the end of December 1941, while several thousand other Jews were handed over the following spring to ethnic Germans in Transnistria, who in turn murdered them (especially in Berezivka County).

The Creation of Transnistria

No doubt aware of his Romanian ally's wishes regarding northern Transylvania, Hitler on July 27, 1941, for the first time dangled the prospect of Ukrainian territory southwest of the Southern Buh before Antonescu. As Romanian troops marched on Odessa, on August 14 Hitler again wrote to Antonescu proposing that the Romanian leader take over the entire area between the Dniestr and the Dniepr. Three days later, Antonescu explained that, since he lacked "the means and trained staff," he could only assume responsibility for the administration of the territory between the Dniestr and the Buh; for the remaining area—that between the Buh and the Dniepr—he would be willing to supply security troops only. At the same time, Antonescu asked Hitler to specify the rights and duties of a Romanian administration in what would become Transnistria.[6]

As a result of this correspondence, Romanian and German military officials signed an agreement at Tiraspol on August 19 that allowed Antonescu to decree officially the creation of Transnistria in the area between the Dniestr and the Buh and the establishment of Romanian occupational government there, although the decree was not publicized until October 17, the day after Odessa fell. The agreement was consolidated by a convention signed at Tighina, Bessarabia, on August 30, which gave the Germans control of the main railway lines and the port facilities of Odessa. Save for these exceptions, which were vital to supplying the Wehrmacht on the eastern front, the convention otherwise left practically everything else to the Romanians.[7]

The new territorial entity created in these agreements encompassed a swath of territory beginning on the eastern shore of the Dniestr and extending to the Southern Buh, which empties into the Black Sea just south of Mykolaïv. Bounded in the south by the Black Sea and in the north by the Liadova River, it covered some 40,000 square kilometers (15,445 square miles), about half the size of South Carolina. According to the Soviet census of 1926, the land turned over to Transnistria supported a population of 2.5 million people. The great majority were Ukrainian and Russian, but among the Slavic majority there also lived 290,000 Romanians, 125,000 Germans, and 300,000 Jews.[8] Unlike Bukovina or Bessarabia, Transnistria had no historical pedigree as a separate administrative or regional entity. It had never been ruled by Romanians, and as indicated by the numbers above, Romanians amounted to about 10 percent of the population.

Antonescu's Policy of "Ethnic Purification" and Deportation

The Jews were the principal victims of Ion Antonescu's minority policies. Romania's largest ethnic minority, their deportation constituted the principal means for satisfying Antonescu's desire to "purify" and "homogenize" Romania's population. It was not by chance that the word "purification" came most frequently from the lips of Ion Antonescu and his Deputy Prime Minister Mihai Antonescu when referring to the need to deport the Jews; this connotation underlines the racial character of their policy toward the Jews. When examining the regime's minority policies, it should be borne in mind that the legislation regarding the Jews in the period 1941–1944, like that in the years immediately preceding, was directed against the Jews as a race, and the Jews in Romania were the only minority population to suffer such racial discrimination. The deportation of the Jews represented the fundamental objective of Antonescu's minority policy and was accompanied by a project to bring into Transnistria the 10,000 Romanians estimated to be living east of the Southern Buh.

The expulsion of the Jews from Romania was a primary tool of Ion Antonescu's policy of "ethnic and political purification." Mihai Antonescu made this clear at a cabinet meeting over which he presided on June 17, 1941, only a few days before the German-Romanian attack on the Soviet Union:

> We must use this hour to carry out the purification of the population. For this reason, Bessarabia and Bukovina will experience Titus's[9] policy with regard to certain ethnic groups—and I assure you, not only in respect of the Jews, but of all nationalities; we will implement a policy of total and violent expulsion of foreign elements.

Mihai already had in mind territorial expansion as far as the Buh River as an instrument for removing unwanted peoples:

> Gentlemen, I think that we must use this moment—although when we were discussing this problem a few months ago. . . . General Antonescu called me a megalomaniac—to extend our frontier to the Buh and to reaffirm our old historical settlements; let us use this moment to pursue the great fight against the Slavs.[10]

Eight days later, at another ministers meeting, Mihai revealed that Ion Antonescu had already taken the decision to round up the Jews in preparation for deportation:

> General Antonescu has taken the decision—while he is in Moldavia—to remove the Jews from this very moment from all the villages in Moldavia, Bessarabia and Bukovina. This measure is already being applied in Moldavia.[11]

The deportations—the preferred term in Romanian official parlance was "evacuation"—were carried out by the Romanian Army and Gendarmerie in retaliation for the hostility that Antonescu alleged was shown by Jews toward the Romanian Army during its withdrawal from these provinces during the Soviet occupation in June 1940, and the subsequent behavior of Jews toward the Romanian population in these territories under Soviet rule from June 1940 until July 1941. Antonescu also invoked security grounds, namely that he did not want Jews, whom he considered unreliable, behind the Romanian lines.[12] Angered by the heavy losses suffered by the Romanian Army in its advance eastward, losses he attributed entirely to "the Jewish commissars" in the Red Army, Antonescu erupted into a paroxysm of rage against the Jews in a directive sent to Mihai Antonescu from the front on September 5, 1941. Returning to his refrain of "purification," he predicted that victory would allow the Axis to "cleanse" the world of Jews:

> The soldiers at the front run the great risk of being wounded or killed because of the Jewish commissars, who with a diabolical perseverance drive the Russians from behind with revolvers and keep them in their

positions until they die to the last man. I have found out about this and am disgusted.

Referring again to the commissars, Antonescu ranted:

> He, and only he, leads the slaves like a herd of cattle and causes their death by firing the last bullet. Hence our great losses. Had the Jewish commissars not been around, we would have reached Odessa long ago.[13]

The clearest insight into Ion Antonescu's motives for deporting the Jews is provided by his response to two petitions sent to him in October 1941 by Wilhelm Filderman, the head of the Federation of Jewish Communities in Romania, in protest of the deportations.[14] Antonescu's reply, dated October 19 and published in the national and local press (Filderman's petitions were not) at the end of the month, reignited a vigorous antisemitic campaign:

> Mr. Filderman, no one can be more sensitive than I am to the suffering of the humble and defenseless. I understand your pain, but all of you should, and especially should have, understood mine at the time, which was the pain of an entire nation. Do you think, did you think, of what we were going through last year during the evacuation of Bessarabia and what is happening today, when day by day and hour by hour, we are paying generously and in blood, in a great deal of blood, for the hatred with which your co-religionists in Bessarabia treated us during the withdrawal from Bessarabia, how they received us upon our return, and how they treated us from the Dniestr up to Odessa and in the area around the Sea of Azov?[15]

Reliable accounts of the behavior of the minority population toward the departing Romanians are lacking. Although there was allegedly some photographic evidence of such behavior by Jews during the withdrawal of June 1940, and there were several reports of such incidents from the Romanian troops withdrawn from the two provinces, the latter suggest that it was not only Jews who welcomed arrival of Soviet troops and ridiculed the departing Romanians.[16] Russians and Ukrainians living in Bessarabia were glad to see the back of the Romanian administration and made no secret of their feelings. That Jews should express relief at the prospect of release from crude antisemitic policies, and do so in a demonstrable manner, is hardly surprising. Yet other Jews, the more wealthy among them, fearing for their fortunes at the hands of a Communist regime, were apprehensive at the prospect of Soviet rule and showed that concern by withdrawing with the Romanian forces. Finally, if retaliation against the Jews for their treatment of the withdrawing Romanian forces from the provinces in June 1940 was one of the motives invoked by Antonescu for deportation, then it made no sense to include the Jews from southern Bukovina and Dorohoi County in northern Moldavia, which were not annexed by the Soviet Union in June 1940.[17]

Concentration of the Jews in towns was a prelude to their deportation. This can be inferred from Mihai Antonescu's speech at the Ministry of Internal Affairs on July 3:

> Ethnic and Political Purification. We find ourselves at the broadest and most favorable moment for a complete ethnic unshackling, for a national revival and for the cleansing of our people of all those elements alien to its spirit, which have grown like mistletoe to darken its future. To avoid losing this unique opportunity, we must be implacable. . . . The action of purification would be carried out by concentrating or isolating all the Jews—as well as the other foreigners whose attitude is doubtful—in places where they could not exercise their baneful influence.[18]

Five days later, he was most explicit. At another meeting of the cabinet, over which he presided in the absence of Ion Antonescu, he declared:

> At the risk of not being understood by some traditionalists who may still be among you, I am for the forced migration of the whole Jewish population in Bessarabia and Bukovina, which must be expelled *over the frontier* [emphasis added]. Similarly, I am for the forced migration of the Ukrainian population, which has no place here at this time. . . . I do not care. The Roman Empire carried out a series of barbarous deeds against others yet it was still the grandest and most extensive political entity.
>
> I do not know how many centuries will elapse before the Romanian people will have a greater freedom of action to carry out the ethnic purification and national revision. . . . There is no moment in our history more favorable. . . . for a complete ethnic unshackling, for a national revision and purification of our people. . . .
>
> So let us use this historic moment to cleanse the Romanian land and our nation of all the misfortunes that have befallen it down the centuries, in which we could not be our own masters. . . . If we have to, we should use the machine gun.[19]

It is also worth noting that Mihai Antonescu spoke here of *all the Jews in Bessarabia and Bukovina.*

Originally, Antonescu saw the expulsion as a one-step operation, a corollary to the German-Romanian advance through Bessarabia and Bukovina, which would sweep all the Jews before it and cast them into Russia. The Romanian leader admitted as much in a cabinet meeting of September 6, 1941:

> Our aim must be that the state of Galicia be founded to provide a link between us and the Germans, while this Galicia should be cleansed of Yids and Slavs, just as I am fighting now to cleanse Bessarabia and Bukovina of Yids and Slavs. . . . We have tens of thousands of Jews whom I intend to cast into Russia.[20]

But the German refusal to accept the influx of Jews on territory under their control forced Antonescu to modify his timetable and conduct a holding operation, leaving the Jews on the Bessarabian bank of the Dniestr in makeshift camps. His enthusiasm to rid Romania of its Jews

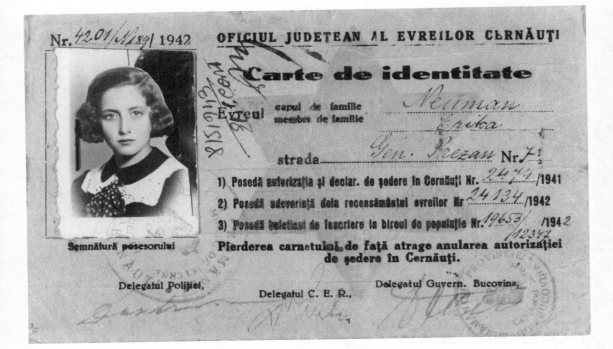

Nr. 42.01/189/1942   OFICIUL JUDEȚEAN AL EVREILOR CLRNĂUȚI

Carte de identitate

Evreul   capul de familie   *Neuman*
         membru de familie   *Erika*

         strada   *Gen. Prezan* Nr. 7!

1) Posedă autorizația și declar. de ședere în Cernăuți Nr. 2477 /1941
2) Posedă adeverință dela recensământul evreilor Nr 24134 /1942
3) Posedă buletinul de înscriere la biroul de populație Nr. 19653 /1942
                                                          /12347

Pierderea carnetului, de față atrage anularea autorizației de ședere în Cernăuți.

Semnătură posesorului

Delegatul Poliției,   Delegatul C. E. R.,   Delegatul Guvern. Bucovina,

Official identification card issued to Erika Neuman of Chernivtsi (Romanian, Cernăuți; German, Czernowitz), authorizing her to remain in Chernivtsi rather than be deported to Transnistria. The item is an example of how the Romanian occupation authorities applied discriminatory measures of isolation and registration. USHMM courtesy of Erika Neuman Kauder Eckstut.

got the better of his military judgment, as the German High Command was quick to demonstrate. Pushing tens of thousands of Jews into combat zones created problems of logistics and security that the German Army had no time or inclination to address.

Yet several thousand Jews did not survive the German-Romanian invasion of the Soviet Union to be expelled across the Dniestr.[21] From the earliest days of the attack, the mass killing of Jews was a feature of the combined Axis advance through northern Bukovina and Bessarabia.[22] The ground for such action had been prepared by General Constantin Vasiliu, head of the Gendarmerie in the Ministry of Internal Affairs, who on June 17 relayed to Gendarmerie units to be deployed in Bessarabia Antonescu's idea for "cleansing the terrain" of Jews.[23] This policy was described as

> the extermination on the spot of all Jews in rural areas, enclosing them in ghettos in urban areas, and the arrest of all those suspected of being Communist Party members or of having held important functions under Soviet rule.[24]

Vasiliu's orders to the Gendarmerie were categorical:

> The Jewish minority is to be pursued with the utmost vigor, since it is known that the Jews, almost in their entirety, collaborated with Communism and perpetrated acts of the greatest hostility against the Roma-

nian Army, authorities, and population. As regards this population, one should exercise the greatest vigilance, so that not a single guilty individual escapes the retribution he deserves.[25]

In Chernivtsi, more than 2,000 Jews were killed within 24 hours of the entry of Romanian troops on July 6, according to one source.[26] On July 7, 400 others, including Chief Rabbi Dr. Mark, were murdered by German SS and police troops.[27] During the reconquest of northern Bukovina at least 4,000 Jews are believed to have been murdered by Romanian and German troops and by Romanian and Ukrainian villagers.[28] In Bessarabia, it is estimated that more than 12,000 Jews were shot by German and Romanian forces by the end of the summer; about half of these deaths are ascribed by some scholars to the mobile German death squads of SS Colonel Otto Ohlendorf's Einsatzgruppe D, which was operating with the support of the German and Romanian armies in Bessarabia and northern Bukovina.[29]

Pride in the efficiency with which Einsatzgruppe D meted out death prompted it to record its dissatisfaction with the arbitrary fashion in which Romanian troops murdered Jews. In a report dated July 31, 1941, Einsatzgruppe D complained:

> The Romanians act against the Jews without any idea of a plan. No one would object to the numerous executions of Jews if the technical aspect of their preparation as well as the manner in which they are carried out were not wanting. The Romanians leave the executed where they fall, without burial. The Einsatzkommando [present] urged the Romanian police to proceed with more order from this point of view.[30]

A similar complaint was relayed to his superiors by SS Major Josef Gmeiner on July 16:

> The Ic [staff officer for intelligence] has tried to see whether anything appropriate could be done about the unrealistic and sadistic executions carried out by the Romanians and whether they can be prevented. He would be particularly pleased if objects and belongings could be secured against pillage.[31]

In continuing this policy of "cleansing the terrain" Romanian Gendarmerie drove columns of Jews on foot from Bukovina and Bessarabia toward the north of the latter province and over the Dniestr into what was at the time German-controlled territory. The mass character of the deportation—children, women, the aged and infirm included— shows clearly that Antonescu's intention was to ethnically cleanse the two provinces of Jews. Those that had the opportunity took with them clothes, food, money, and jewelry. The Germans were unwilling to accept large numbers of them and sent them back.[32] The Romanian Gendarmerie in Soroca—in northern Bessarabia—reported that on 5 August the Germans had sent 3,000 Jews back across the Dniestr to Atachi "from the 12,000 that had been sent across the Dniestr" by the Romanians at Mohyliv-Podilsky.[33] On the same day, the Romanian Army telegraphed General Ioan Topor that there were about 20,000 Jews from the county seats of Khotyn and Storozhynets on the road to Atachi whom the Germans had refused to accept. Three days later, the Gendarmerie inspectorate in Chernivtsi telegraphed that 20,000 from Khotyn County had been driven across the Dniestr, but that the Germans on 7 August had begun to send back from Ukraine everyone from Bessarabia and northern Bukovina, irrespective of their ethnic background.[34] In the words of a German report, the Jews were "chased back and forth until they dropped . . . Old men and women lay along the road at short distances from each other."[35]

With nowhere to send the Jews, the Gendarmerie set up transit camps for Bukovina Jews at Sokyriany and Edineț, and in Bessarabia at Vertujeni and Mărculești, into which more than 50,000 Jews were herded.[36] In a report of the Romanian Security Police drawn up in reply to a "request by telephone made on September 10, 1941"—from whom is not said—the sites for concentrating Jews in Bessarabia were listed. The ghettos ranged in size from 11,328 Jews at Chișinău ghetto to 65 at Tighina.[37] The living conditions were appalling. Poor sanitation, a shortage of water, and a lack of food quickly led to the outbreak of disease. The mortality rate soared. In a review of the situation in Sokyriany and Edineț submitted on September 11 to the provincial administration, Colonel Ion Mănecuță, head of the Gendarmerie in Bukovina, pointed out that the majority of the Jews

> have no clothing and nothing to cover themselves with. Since most were sent to Ukraine and then forced back by the Germans, they have either lost or had taken from them in Ukraine everything they had. They have nothing available to prepare food, each person cooks in the house where they are staying. There is a shortage of medicines.[38]

Antonescu and his senior officials had never regarded the camps as anything more than a way station.[39] The initial thrust to deport the Jews had been frustrated by objections from the Germans in command of the area between the Dniestr and the Buh, but once Antonescu had been given control of this territory under the Tighina Agreement of August 30—creating in the process Transnistria—the second stage of the deportations began. Romanian rule of Transnistria gave Antonescu a "dumping ground" for the Bessarabian and Bukovinan Jews, but this was envisaged by Antonescu as a temporary location for the Jews; deportation across the Buh was to be eventual destination of the Jews as the agreement specified:

> The evacuation of the Jews beyond the Buh cannot be accomplished at this time. Therefore, they should be concentrated in work camps and used for labor until the moment when, after the conclusion of operations, their evacuation to the east will be possible.[40]

Antonescu's longer-term aim was to colonize Transnistria with Romanians living not only beyond the Buh, but also west of the Dniestr, as he made clear in December 1941:

We will give some compensation to those who have lost land in Transnistria, but we will seek to drive them beyond Transnistria, because Transnistria is destined to be colonized with Romanians of ours, Romanians whom we shall bring from beyond the Buh and even from this side [i.e., the Romanian side] of the Dniestr.[41]

It was at Tighina that Antonescu convened the governors[42] of Bessarabia, Bukovina, and Transnistria late in August 1941 and gave them the order for the deportation of Jews across the Dniestr to resume. General Cornel Calotescu, General Gheorghe Voiculescu, and Gheorghe Alexianu, the governor-designates of Bukovina, Bessarabia, and Transnistria, respectively, were given details as to how the Jews were to be sent across the Southern Buh.[43] In an undated memorandum to Antonescu, written at the end of the year, Voiculescu wrote that the governors had received "precise instructions" on the way in which the deportation of the Jews to the Southern Buh was to be carried out.[44] Antonescu himself referred to his plans in this respect at a cabinet meeting of December 4, 1941:

> I warned you—you, General Voiculescu, and you too, Alexianu—that it was my intention to take the Jews to the Buh. Instead of eating the bread of the land of Romania, let them eat the bread there. I told you to take steps so that the execution of the plan should be flawless. The operation began in November. From August to November, we had three months, and we organized it as we did. The same thing is valid for Bukovina.[45]

General Ioan Topor, who held the senior legal position in the Romanian Army known as *marele pretor,* was charged orally by Antonescu and in writing by Colonel Petrescu, head of counterintelligence of the Romanian Army, with coordinating the deportation.[46] He issued orders on September 7 to the inspector of Gendarmes in Bessarabia, Colonel Teodor Meculescu, to proceed with the deportations on September 12, starting with the camp at Vertujeni, and laid down guidelines for their implementation.[47] These guidelines were applied at other camps and in the Chişinău ghetto.[48] The commandant of the Vertujeni camp, which held 22,969 Jews according to a Gendarmerie statistic of early September,[49] was instructed by Topor through Meculescu to form the Jews into convoys of 1,600 persons and to send them across the Dniestr at a rate of 800 per day; between 40 and 50 wagons were to be provided for each convoy of 1,600 Jews to carry the old, the sick, and children; the convoys were to leave Vertujeni every other day; and gendarmes along the designated routes were to assist local inhabitants in burying the dead.[50] The punishment for those Jews who did not conform to these procedures was disguised as the code-word "Alexianu," the name of the governor of Transnistria; it meant "execution on the spot."[51]

The use of the codeword is confirmed in testimony to a Gendarmerie commission of Lieutenant Augustin Roşca, who accompanied one such convoy on October 8. His orders, received from a general staff officer, included the use of a codeword, as the commission report reveals:

This special codeword was relayed to him [Roşca] by the commander of the Khotyn legion [of gendarmes], Major Drăgulescu, who told him that on the orders of the Army General HQ, Jews who could not keep up with the convoys, either through incapacity or through illness, should be executed. To this end, he ordered him [Roşca] to send a man ahead, two days before the departure of each convoy, to dig pits with the help of the local gendarmes every ten kilometers that could take around 100 bodies—those who had fallen behind and had been shot. . . . Lieutenant Roşca carried out these orders to the letter, which resulted in the shooting of about 500 Jews among those deported along the route Sokyriany-Cosăuţi. The same procedure was applied to the convoys between Edi-neţ and Cosăuţi, where the deportations were carried out by Lieutenant Popovici from the same unit, under the orders of Lieutenant Augustin Roşca.

Because of the steps taken to dig the pits in preparation for the burials, the peasants in the villages along the routes learned of what was to occur. They therefore waited at the edge of the route, hiding in corn-fields or other places, for the executions to take place in order to throw themselves onto the bodies to rob them. From the verbal declaration of Lieutenant Augustin Roşca, it emerges that the preparations for, and es-pecially the carrying out of, the executions produced such moments of drama that the participants would bear for a long time the impression of those events.[52]

It took several day of consultation involving Topor and the gover-nor of Bessarabia, Gheorghe Voiculescu, before Meculescu issued the deportation order for Vertujeni. In the event, its execution added to the misery of the Jews. Witnesses at the trial of the camp commandant as a war criminal, which opened in Bucharest on May 14, 1945, testified that never at any time were more than six to eight wagons supplied for the convoys of 1,600 persons. A Gendarmerie officer escorting the con-voys stated that the deportees were not given food on departure and that there were insufficient wagons for the elderly, infirm, and children. Only a light guard accompanied the Jews, which made them easy prey for civilians who attacked and robbed them en route. "The road between Vertujeni and Cosăuţi [on the Dniestr across from Iampil]," the officer went on, "was dotted with those who did not have the energy even to get to the crossing-point."[53]

At the Mărculeşti camp, officials from the Romanian National Bank were sent to buy up the valuables of the Jews in exchange for the cur-rency introduced by the German authorities in occupied Ukraine and in circulation in Transnistria. According to witnesses at the Bucharest war crimes trials of 1945, one official, Ioan Mihăescu, after initially pur-chasing jewels and gold objects from some Jews at bargain prices, took to simply confiscating these valuables from others. Mihăescu himself painted a harrowing picture of the camp:

Mice swarmed in the thousands down the dirt-alleys and through the houses, the flies, in a totally inordinate number, were extremely tire-some. Because of this, sleep was impossible. Many of the officials' belongings were gnawed on by rats . . . We were all dirty, and there were no washing facilities . . . The Jews gave a watch or two in exchange for a loaf of bread.[54]

A colleague of Mihăescu described the scene on his arrival at the camp: "I found there thousands of deportees who were living in a state of indescribable misery. The corpses of the deportees were lying everywhere, in cellars, in ditches, in courtyards."[55] Antonescu himself recognized the scale of Jewish dead. Reacting to a claim in November from one of his ministers that all the Jews had left the city of Iași, the Marshal retorted: "The Yids have not yet left Iași. I have enough problems with those I drove to the Southern Buh. Only I know how many died en route."[56]

Antonescu's responsibility for the deportations and their consequences is evident from his remarks at a meeting of the Council for Supply on October 6, 1941:

> As regards the Jews, I have taken measures to remove them entirely and once and for all from these regions [Bessarabia and Bukovina]. The measure is being applied. I still have in Bessarabia approximately 40,000 Jews, who in a few days will be driven across the Dniestr, and, if circumstances permit, *they will be driven beyond the Urals* [emphasis added].[57]

Deportation, he emphasized yet again, was the instrument of ethnic purification:

> As regards commerce, it is beyond dispute that we must start from the beginning, because I have excluded the Yids and slowly, slowly I am driving out the other foreigners as well, apart from those who have long had business there. But my tendency is to carry out a policy of purification of the Romanian race, and I will not give way before any obstacle in achieving this historical goal of our nation.
>
> If we do not take advantage of the situation that presents itself today on the international and European level in order to purify the Romanian nation, we shall miss the last chance that history offers us. And I do not wish to miss it, because if I do so future generations will blame me. I can get back Bessarabia and Transylvania, but if I do not purify the Romanian nation then I have achieved nothing, for it is not frontiers that consolidate a nation, but the homogeneity and purity of its race. And that is my principal goal.[58]

Deportation from Bukovina to Transnistria

In Bukovina, the governor, General Cornel Calotescu, acted on orders received through Topor's delegate, Lieutenant Colonel Petrescu. In a subsequent report on the deportations for Antonescu, Calotescu pointed out that he did not see a copy of the deportation order, even though he requested one, but that he had merely been informed by Topor's delegate that "on the Marshal's orders all Jews in Bukovina would be evacuated to Transnistria in ten days." The deportations began in the south of the province (in Suceava, Câmpulung, and Rădăuți) between October 10 and 15. Calotescu drew up a program for the Jews in Chernivtsi to be gathered into a ghetto on October 11, prior to deportation.[59] This operation involved herding about 50,000 Jews into a small area of the town that, according to Mayor Traian Popovici, could house a maximum of 15,000 persons. Popovici recorded in a memorandum the details of the deportations, which commenced on October 13. Between this date and November 15, when the deportations were suspended because of the bad weather and, it appears, a shortage of freight cars, 28,391 Jews were deported to Transnistria in fourteen trains supervised by the Gendarmerie. In addition, a further 395 Jews identified as Communists or considered undesirable were deported.[60]

According to Popovici, Calotescu ordered that before deportation the Jews should go through a screening process; between 15,000 and 20,000 were to be selected "for their usefulness to the Romanian state." Mihai Antonescu had been advised of the damage that the deportation of the Jews was causing to the economy and thus laid down guidelines for the exemption of those vital to the national interest. Calotescu charged the army and the mayor's office with setting up a selection committee to issue permits to those chosen to remain in Chernivtsi. Initially, they were given four days in which to carry out this complicated procedure. Popovici wrote:

> . . . for fear that the trains provided for the evacuation of the Jews to Transnistria might be given another purpose and therefore we would be placed in the situation of not being able to proceed with the evacuation of the Jews.

An ad hoc committee of Jews was set up on Popovici's orders to provide a list of all the Jews remaining in the ghetto according to their skills; this list was submitted to Calotescu who, in discussion with Popovici and the military commander in Chernivtsi, General C. Ionescu, decided on the percentage of each professional category of Jews who should remain. In fact, many Jews entered their names under more than one category, as a hedge against deportation, and consequently received multiple permits, which then found their way into the hands of those with similar names. Faced with this situation, the committee set about verifying whether the recipients of permits were entitled to them, an exercise that took 18 days. As a result, 16,569 Jews received authorization to remain in Chernivtsi.[61]

Details of the manner in which the deportation was carried out in Dorohoi were provided by a lawyer, Constantin Muşat, who was commissioned by the Federation of Jewish Communities in Romania under Filderman to carry out an enquiry.[62] By placing Muşat's report alongside the official account given by the county prefect, Colonel Ion Bărcan, a comprehensive picture of events can be drawn.[63] On November 5, the prefect had been handed a deportation order from Calotescu, issued on October 28, by Lieutenant Colonel Petrescu. The order set out the conditions under which the deportations were to take place, with guidelines as to who was to be exempted. These guidelines, drawn up by Mihai An-

tonescu, ordered that "property owners, industrialists, traders, craftsmen and intellectuals vital to the national economy as well as public
officials and public service pensioners should not be deported."[64] The
pensioners included war veterans and their families. A selection committee was set up to determine who would be deported, according to
these guidelines, but the guidelines were not respected.[65]

As the prefect admitted:

> In spite of the rigor of the selection, exceptions to the norm which we
> followed crept in. . . . we could not exempt all those who had fought in
> the war of 1916–1918 (there were none from 1877), since these together
> with their families represented more than two-thirds of the total num-
> ber of Jews and thus the deportation would have been rendered almost
> pointless.[66]

Muşat presented a different story; the selection was far from rigorous,
on the contrary it was done

> in a completely arbitrary fashion, with no objective criterion. . . . because
> certain people had a decisive influence with the committee and paid
> sums ranging from 200,000 [lei] to 1 million lei, or gave valuables such
> as astrakhan coats and jewels in order to obtain a provisional authoriza-
> tion [for exemption], which was cancelled within 24 hours.[67]

The sick, the old, invalids, young children, war veterans, and war widows were swept up in the operation, which began on November 7.

The first Jews deported were those who had gathered in the town of
Dorohoi from Darabani and Rădăuţi. They hired carts to take them and
their belongings to the station, where they were searched by gendarmes
and had fabrics and leather goods they were carrying confiscated. The
prefect confirmed the search but denied claims that clothing was confiscated: "The only food confiscated was that considered to be surplus
and considered to be hoarded."[68] Carpets, cushions and mattresses
were also confiscated on the grounds that on arrival at Atachi on the
Dniestr River, the deportees would be taken from the train and driven
in columns on foot to Transnistria. On previous occasions when other
deportees reached the Dniestr, they had had heavy baggage that had to
be left in the station at Atachi and Mărculeşti.[69]

The Jews were herded into freight cars. "No more than 50 were put
in each car," the prefect wrote,

> since there was no space for any more, while the doors to the cars were
> locked on only one side of the train, the doors on the other side being
> left unlocked so that the guard escort could inspect the cars more easily
> when the trains stopped in stations.[70]

In the second train, which left on November 8, were Jews from Săveni
and Mihăileni. Four days later, the deportation of the local Jews from
Dorohoi town itself began. Their houses were sealed by officials from
the town hall with a notice: "State property—whoever disturbs it will
be shot on sight."[71] On November 14, the last third of the Jews in Do-

rohoi town were ordered to the station, but they were sent back to their homes after being told that an order suspending their deportation had been given "due to a lack of freight cars."[72] Some 6,000 Jews were deported from Darabani, Rădăuti, Săveni and Mihăileni, and about 3,000 from Dorohoi town. At the time of his enquiry—the end of November— Muşat stated that 2,500 Jews were left in Dorohoi.[73]

A commission set up by Antonescu to investigate the conduct of deportations from Bukovina found that at the end of January 1942 there were 21,626 Jews left in Chernivtsi, of whom 16,391 had permits, 235 were Communist suspects waiting deportation, and around 5,000 had remained illegally.[74] At the end of March 1942, Antonescu approved a request from Governor Voiculescu of Bessarabia that 425 Jews who were left in ghettos in the province or had been left free "according to orders from above" be sent to Transnistria by train."[75] Shortly afterward, Antonescu ordered the resumption of deportation from Bukovina.

A balance sheet of the progress of deportation, provided at Antonescu's request by Governor Voiculescu on August 21, 1942, reported that 55,867 Jews from Bessarabia had been deported to Transnistria, and 45,867 Jews from Bukovina via Bessarabia. Following the resumption of deportation in May 1942, a total of 231 Jews had been deported from Bessarabia.[76] On the same day, Governor Calotescu informed Antonescu's office that during July 4,094 Jews had been deported from Bukovina and that a further 19,475 remained to be deported. He proposed to deport all of the latter, except those assigned to compulsory labor and those exempt under orders given previously. The subtraction of those in the two latter categories left a figure of 6,234 Jews to be deported from Chernivtsi, and 592 from the town of Dorohoi; their deportation was planned for October.[77]

Jews were not the only victims of deportation. Driven by a mixture of social and racial prejudices, Antonescu adopted a similar policy toward the Roma.[78] More than 25,000 of a total of 208,700 Roma (the estimated size of the Roma population in 1942) were deported, roughly 12 percent.[79] Antonescu took his decision to deport the Roma in May 1942, but not all Roma were targeted. On May 22, the Marshal ordered the Ministry of Internal Affairs to deport certain categories of Roma who were considered "a problem." A census was made by the police and Gendarmerie three days later to determine which Roma fell into this category.[80] Those included were nomadic Roma and their families and, among sedentary Roma, those who had a criminal record, repeat offenders, and the unemployed. A total of 40,909 Roma were recorded, 9,471 nomadic and 31,438 sedentary Roma.[81]

Once in Transnistria, the Roma were settled in villages in the southeast of the territory. Most of the nomadic Roma were placed in Golta, and almost all of the sedentary ones in Ochakiv. For some, their dwellings were hovels dug out of the earth with a cover of reeds or corn stalks. The more fortunate were given houses. To make room for them, Ukrainians had to double up with neighbors. Several villages on the

Jews on the banks of the Dniestr River near Vascauti, Moldova, on June 10, 1942, await their expulsion into Transnistria. Yad Vashem.

Buh were completely evacuated to this end and the Ukrainian population moved inland. These villages were termed colonies by the Transnistrian authorities. They were neither camps nor ghettos, as in the Jewish experience, even though Romanian documents also use these terms, but areas reserved for Roma in the center or on the periphery of a village. Although guarded by Gendarmes, the Roma were allowed to move within the community so as to earn a living.[82]

Many of the deported Roma died in Transnistria from hunger and illness. There were no organized executions of Roma by the Romanian authorities, as in the case of the Jews. There were, however, instances of Roma being shot by the Gendarmerie, as happened at Trykhaty in Ochakiv County, where a report from May 1943 states that Gendarmes killed a number of Roma who had arrived in search of work.[83]

The total number of Roma who died in Transnistria is unknown. A May 1944 Gendarmerie assessment of the numbers who made their way back to Romania after the occupation found only 6,000 persons, but this census was made at a time of upheaval. Those parts of Romania already taken by Soviet troops were not accessible to the census takers. Some Roma who lived in tolerable conditions may have remained in Transnistria. It is almost certain that more than half of the 25,000 Roma deported to Transnistria died.

Reversal of the Deportation Policy

In the summer of 1942, Antonescu made a fundamental change to his policy toward the Jews. This shift underlined a basic difference in approach to what both Hitler and Antonescu termed "the Jewish problem." The change involved two momentous decisions by Antonescu. The first was his refusal to participate in the "Final Solution," the second his reversal of the policy of deportation to Transnistria. He refused to accede to German requests that the remaining Jewish population of Romania—from the Banat, southern Transylvania, Wallachia, and Moldavia—be sent to the death camps in Poland, and he suspended the deportations to Transnistria.

On July 10, 1942, Colonel R. Davidescu, the head of Antonescu's office, instructed the Ministry of Internal Affairs to compile figures for the number of Jews in Transylvania and to study the feasibility of

> [sending] to the Buh all the Jews in Transylvania except the intellectuals essential for our needs (doctors, engineers, etc.) and the industrialists necessary for the management of different enterprises, in order to make room for the shelter of the Romanian refugees from the ceded part of Transylvania.[84]

Rumors of a plan to deport Jews from southern Transylvania and Banat startled Jewish leaders, particularly those in the regions targeted. The Romanian Intelligence Service reported that Baron Alfred Neuman, the owner of textile and chemical factories in Arad, traveled to Bucharest "around August 20" in an effort to get the deportations postponed until the following spring, "when the conditions for transport would be better."[85] His efforts included his promise of a 100-million-lei contribution by the Jewish communities of Banat and southern Transylvania—scheduled to be the first to be deported—for the construction of the "Palace of the Handicapped," whose project director, Dr. Stoenescu, was Antonescu's personal doctor.[86] The leaders of the democratic parties raised their voices in protest, much to the Marshal's annoyance. On August 10, he wrote on a report giving statistics of the urban Jewish population:

I shall ignore everyone and every difficulty in cleansing this nation totally of this blight. I shall castigate in due course all those who have
come—the most recent being Mr. Maniu [National Peasants' Party][87]—
and will come to stop me from responding to the wishes of the vast majority of this nation.[88]

A particular impact on the Marshal was made, according to a declaration of the chief rabbi of Romania, Alexander Safran, by Metropolitan
of Transylvania Nicolae Bălan; Safran recalled in 1961 that

> the interventions which we attempted to make with the government and
> with Romanian persons of influence had been unsuccessful. There was
> a last chance: an approach to the metropolitan of Transylvania, Monsi-
> gnor Bălan. The latter, in reply to my personal request, came from Sibiu,
> the bishop's residence, to Bucharest, to talk to me. My meeting with the
> prelate took place in the house of General Vaitoianu. It was dramatic.
> After only a few hours, Metropolitan Bălan informed me that he had
> persuaded the Marshal to cancel the decision to deport the Jewish popu-
> lation of Transylvania.[89]

On September 12 Iuliu Maniu, the National Peasants' Party leader,
stated that the Jewish question was becoming of matter of great international importance in the wake of Roosevelt's message and Churchill's
declaration that those who deported Jews would be subject to punish-
ments without precedent in history. Two days later, Ion Mihalache,
Maniu's deputy, voiced his disapproval of the deportation, adding that
according to his information these measures had been taken at the suggestion of foreign circles "alien to the humanitarian traditions of our
people." On September 16, Maniu declared:

> I have said it once and will go on saying it: we will pay dearly for the
> mistreatment of the Jews. I have been told, for example, that impor-
> tant wealthy Jewish families have also been removed from Arad and
> Timişoara. Why wealthy families? I do not understand.

Constantin Brătianu, the liberal leader, was even more forthright.
Speaking on September 25, he expressed his outrage:

> The deportation of the Jews is continuing under different pretexts that
> discover new guilty persons who are dispatched. These horrors, which
> represent a slap on the country's face, are all the more revolting because
> in their innocence, the old, women, and children are being sent to their
> death.

At a meeting of the board of the Romanian Bank on October 7, 1942,
Brătianu said that Maniu had the impression that he had furnished the
Marshal with arguments that had made him reflect more closely on the
consequences of deportation.[90]

At an international level, the interventions of the papal nuncio, Andrea Cassulo, had a considerable impact on Antonescu's thinking. In
July, there was discussion in Jewish circles of the news that the nuncio
had instructed Catholic parishes to hold a special service on Wednes-

days for Jews deported to Transnistria.[91] In September, President Roosevelt sent a special representative, Myron Taylor, to tell the Pope at first hand of his concern at the physical destruction of the Jews by the Nazis. Some back-pedaling on the proposed deportation of the Jews from Banat and southern Transylvania is hinted at in the response received from Antonescu's office to the guidelines put forward on September 18 by Radu Lecca, plenipotentiary for Jewish affairs in Romania, for the deportation of the Jews in these areas:

> The evacuation [deportation] of the Jews from Transylvania is only the subject of study. It will only begin at the opportune moment. Until then, preparations are being made, down to the smallest detail, on the basis of instructions given by Marshal Antonescu.[92]

The decision to suspend the deportation of the Jews to Transnistria was conveyed by Mihai Antonescu to a meeting of the Council of Ministers on October 13 from which the Marshal was absent. Since the beginning of July rumors had been circulating in Bucharest about Ion Antonescu's health. Throughout the summer he had been laid low by a mysterious ailment that had severely limited his public appearances.[93] Mihai prefaced his announcement by referring, albeit obliquely, to the international concern expressed at his regime's treatment of its Jews:

> Recently, a great deal of dissatisfaction and in particular an unfavorable attitude has been created in connection with the treatment of the Jews. There is no point in my telling you that I, who signed the law on expropriation of Jewish property, am not a philosemite, and I take no honor in considering—however much I might be driven by the universal laws for the protection of man—that it is a duty for us to look after these elements, as we would look after Romanians. I consider, however, that because of the international situation, and because of the fact that in other countries the treatment of the Jews is different from that in Romania, we must avoid creating—given that the Romanian soldier, through his genuine heroism, is raising our history to new levels and is building around the Romanian people an atmosphere of civilization and national consciousness—we must avoid creating a situation in which it appears that, through administrative measures or our own omissions, we do not care if, at the level of degrees of civilization, the Romanian government is not contributing to this prestige created by the army, or, on the contrary, is working against it.

The prestige of the government was at stake over its handling of the Jewish "problem":

> The main reason I have convened you here is this problem of the Jews that also threatens the government. If you want to know the truth, I can tell you that recently I have received a whole series of details on this subject even from German circles from whom I was informed last year about such matters. It was pointed out to me that people attribute these measures [against the Jews] to German initiative and influence when the Germans have nothing to do with them.

Mihai Antonescu underlined his point when turning to the "romani-anization" of commerce that involved the "removal of Jews from the important positions in the national economy":

> I am not carrying out antisemitic reform for the Germans and under the doctrine of Dr. Rosenberg,[94] however powerful and healthy it is, and however great the danger that Jewish Communism or simply the Judaic ideology might represent. What interests me is to make Romanian nationalism and to take from Dr. Rosenberg's reform and the German experience the wise decisions and not any measure that does not suit our country.... We must make our antisemitic reform a creative reform, not a demagogic one, to prevent damage to ourselves and remaining fixed in the positions we create. This is our situation.

These words brought Antonescu to the heart of the business of the meeting. As was customary in the parlance of the Antonescu regime, the word "deportation" was avoided:

> For the time being, all transports of Jews across the Dniestr are suspended. The transports will henceforth be organized by a joint body, which will be set up by the General Staff, the Ministry of Internal Affairs, the Ministry of Finance and the Presidency of the Council of Ministers.... The General Staff gives the orders, the Ministry of Internal Affairs must carry them out, the prefecture of police begins the manhunt in Bucharest in order to catch those [Jews] on the list.... We hold to the principle that all Jews who are dangerous because of their subversive or Communist activity will be subjected to all rigors and the harshest measures will be applied to them, including the death penalty, to avoid agitation over this measure.[95]

This suspension of deportation also affected those Jews currently in custody for shirking compulsory labor. While Mihai Antonescu's words made it clear that the deportation of Jews was to be *suspended,* it was equally plain that resumption was envisaged once the new body he had referred to was set up.

When advised by the Bucharest police chief that some Jews paid large sums of money to his men to avoid being picked up, Antonescu recognized the practice:

> Not only do policemen take money to save those who are subject to being sent across the Dniestr, but they go and threaten others who do not enter this category, thus getting more money and making the name of Romanian administration mud by their behavior. For this reason, a temporary halt is to be put to the sending of Jews [to Transnistria].[96]

The broad details of the application of the systematic liquidation of the Jews as a goal of state policy—Hitler's "Final Solution"—had been elaborated at the Wannsee Conference on January 20, 1942. Pressure was exerted by SS Captain Gustav Richter, the counselor for Jewish problems at the German legation in Bucharest, for Romania to apply the policy against its own Jews, and on July 22, 1942, he reported to Berlin that Mihai Antonescu had given his government's agreement to the deportation of Romanian Jews to the death camps in the General Government (those parts of occupied Poland not annexed to the Reich).[97] On July 26, Heinrich Himmler, the head of the SS and chief of the German police, was informed that preparations for the deportations were under way, and that the first of a number of trains would leave "around September 10" for the General Government's District Lublin, "where those fit for labor would be put to work, while the rest would be subjected to special treatment [liquidation]."[98] On September 23 the director general of the Romanian railway, General T. C. Orezeanu, wrote to Radu Lecca informing him that the head of the German railroad's office for east Berlin had convened a conference for September 26–28 to draw up a timetable for special trains to carry Jews from Romania to the General Government, and requesting details so that the Romanian delegates to the conference could come to a decision in the matter.[99] In his reply of the following day, Lecca confirmed that Marshal Antonescu had "given orders that the evacuation[100] of the Jews from Romania be prepared in the smallest detail by the Ministry of Internal Affairs, on the basis of instructions given by Mr. Mihai Antonescu."[101] At the same time, however, Franz Rademacher, the head of the Jewish Section of the German Department—the German Foreign Office body responsible for the "Jewish question"—relayed to Berlin the information

> [from] two sources in Romania, Dr. Emil Hoffman [the press attaché at the German legation in Bucharest and an adviser to the Romanian government], and a member of the Iron Guard, that [Marshal] Antonescu in fact had no intention of deporting the Romanian Jews.[102]

Antonescu's real intentions on this subject are a puzzle. Certainly Lecca's reply to the director general of the Romanian railway bears out Richter's report of Mihai Antonescu's assent to deportation. If Lecca is to be believed (he was writing to a Romanian official and not a German one), Mihai was telling Richter the truth when he said that his government had agreed to deportation. The Marshal then changed his mind.[103] Whatever the explanation, steps to implement the deportation of Romanian Jews to Poland were never taken. Romanian railway representatives failed to attend the meeting in Berlin organized by Adolf Eichmann on September 26, when they were expected to discuss the transport of Jews from Romania "by special trains" every other day, each carrying 2,000 Jews to Bełżec. A German railway expert was sent to Bucharest to make arrangements, but no deportations took place.[104] Antonescu may well have considered capitulation to German pressure as an affront to Romanian sovereignty, since the German plan not only targeted Jews from Wallachia and Moldavia, the Banat, and southern Transylvania, but proposed their deportation to a foreign territory.[105]

When rumors spread of the plan for deportation of the Jews to Poland, Mihai Antonescu recognized that he and the Marshal had considered the matter. At a Council of Ministers meeting of September 29, 1942, he declared:

Rumor factories are being organized which have an ingenious and diabolical machine for launching rumors designed to paralyze the moral effects of an action of ours and to replace them with other elements of unease, or even to create elements of unease. My conviction is that the principal organizer of this machine is the Yid. And if this system continues, be certain that we will adopt the most severe measures. I have checked this against one fact. At a certain point, the issue of sending some Jews from our country elsewhere was discussed. Nobody except the Marshal, me, and a person liaising with the government of the Reich knew about this. Only three lines were written, very vague, and the only one to know about this problem was somebody in the German SS. Well then, exactly five days after this conversation, the whole of Transylvania was invaded by the news that the Romanian government was expelling the entire Yid population from Transylvania in order to create room for 20,000 or 100,000 German families from towns bombed by the British.[106]

In October 1942, the Marshal called a halt to deportation to Transnistria. Mihai Antonescu explained the change in policy at a Council of Ministers meeting on October 13 that the Marshal did not attend:

> Lately, a whole lot of discontent arose and, especially, a very unfavorable atmosphere was created in connection with the treatment of the Jews.... I am not a philosemite ... but because of the international situation and the fact that the Jews elsewhere are treated differently than in Romania ... we must not create a situation to look as if it is all the same to us, on the level of civilizing measures, the Romanian government contributes to the prestige of the army or, on the contrary, works against it.... We must examine Romanian economic positions and realities ... From our antisemitic reform we must also produce a creative reform.... For the time being, all transfers of Jews across the Dniestr are suspended.[107]

The Marshal never explained his decision; it was probably influenced by a conjunction of factors rather than by one specific consideration. He was aware that the deportations had exacerbated Romania's already negative image in Washington—this was underlined by a call to the Romanian government by the US Secretary of State Cordell Hull in September 1942 for a halt to the deportations to Transnistria on pain of measures being taken against Romanians living in the United States. On top of this, vigorous protests against the plan for the deportations of Romanian Jews had been made by the Swiss *chargé d'affaires* René de Veck, Apostolic Nuncio Andrea Cassulo, and Metropolitan Nicolae Bălan of Transylvania, who pointed out that deportation, the institution of ghettos, and the wearing of the Star of David had been measures taken only in satellite and occupied countries such as Croatia and Poland, and not in other sovereign Axis members such as Italy and Hungary.[108]

A crucial influence on Antonescu's decision was Helen, the Queen Mother. She was identified in Nazi circles as the leading opponent of the measures taken against the Jews in Romania.[109] A report from Richter dated October 30, 1942, is eloquent in this respect:

A Swiss journalist reports the following: "On the occasion of the last[110] transport of Jews to Transnistria, the philologist Barbu Lăzăreanu (Lazarovici) was also due to be arrested and deported. The police commissioner, however, gave him a breathing-space of "two days" to arrange his situation. Lăzăreanu, therefore, contacted a friend, the well-known doctor Victor Gomoiu, who is well-regarded by Helen, the Queen Mother. Gomoiu, a man so nice that he could not imagine that the Jews are so persecuted, went in person to Strada Sfântul Ion Nou [a building where the Jews were assembled for deportation] to see for himself the pitiful state of these unfortunate persons."

As a result Dr. Gomoiu immediately got in touch with the Queen Mother and the latter with King Michael. The Queen Mother told the King that what was happening to people in this country was a disgrace, and that she could not bear it any longer, all the more so because the King (her son) and her name would be permanently associated in Romanian history with the crimes committed against the Jews, while she would be known as the mother of "Michael the Wicked." She is said to have warned the King that, if the deportations were not immediately halted, she would leave the country. As a result the King immediately telephoned Deputy Prime Minister Mihai Antonescu and, as a consequence, a meeting of the Council of Ministers took place following which not only were those arrested released, but a communiqué of the Presidency [Marshal Antonescu] was issued. Among the Jews deported recently, several hundred were shot, some by the Germans, others "by the Romanians."[111]

One can only speculate whether the drawn-out battle for Stalingrad (August 1942–February 1943) was also a factor in Antonescu's decision, but Antonescu was astute enough to realize that a short war against the Soviet Union offered the best chance of a victory, and he may well have had an eye on the eventual peace settlement when considering the consequences of his reversal of policy on deportation.[112] Antonescu, therefore, turned to emigration to Palestine as a solution to the "Jewish problem."

Emigration was not an option for the Jews surviving in Transnistria. Return to Romania was expressly forbidden unless a case for wrongful deportation could be made. A Decree-Law of September 22, 1942, instituted the death penalty for Jews of both sexes above the age of 15 who had been deported to Transnistria and who returned "in a fraudulent manner to Romania." Those who abetted this "crime" through instigation, complicity, or failure to report it were liable to a term of forced labor of between five and 25 years.[113] Jews largely resigned themselves to life in the ghettos and the camps.

By summer 1943, pressure from two fronts was beginning to have an effect on Romanian policy toward the deported Jews. The first was the eastern front, where Soviet advances reminded the Romanian dictator and his closest associates of the precariousness of their position and a probable reckoning with the Allies. The second was Wilhelm Filderman, chairman of the disbanded Federation of Jewish Communities in Romania, who bombarded Antonescu and General Constantin Vasiliu, the head of the Gendarmerie, with memoranda demanding the repatriation of *all* Jews from Transnistria. Some progress was made in this respect when on September 30 the Romanian Council of Order, a new state body for repatriation, ordered the Gendarmerie in Transnistria to repatriate all Jews sentenced for contraventions of the forced labor requirements who had completed their terms of punishment.

On October 12, 1943, Filderman pressed for the repatriation of the Jews deported to Transnistria in a memorandum to the Romanian government proposing that the deported Jews be brought back to their places of residence in Romania proper.[114] After consultations between Mihai Antonescu, Vasiliu, and the Marshal, the order was given on December 8 for the repatriation of the Jews from Dorohoi who had been deported to Transnistria and of the 16 survivors of the group of 568 Jews deported for having requested repatriation to the Soviet Union after the loss of Bessarabia and northern Bukovina.[115] The first group of Jews from Dorohoi, numbering around 1,500, returned to Romania on December 20. At the same time, another 70 deportees were repatriated, among them the 16 survivors mentioned above. Between December 20 and 25, a group of 6,107 Jews, mostly from Dorohoi, were moved from Transnistria to Moldavia. On March 6, 1944, 1,846 orphans under 15 were repatriated, and later in the month 2,518 deportees returned with the help of Jewish aid committees in Bucharest. Most of the latter were allowed to return to their homes, with the exception of 563 Communists interned at Vapniarka who were sent under escort to Târgu-Jiu.[116]

Time was of the essence for the survival of the Jews in Transnistria. As the Soviet forces pushed back the Germans, Antonescu prepared to withdraw from the area, and on February 15 it was announced that the "government of Transnistria" had been abolished and replaced by "The Military Administration of the Territory between the Dniestr and the Buh." This was merely one step away from the cession of the whole area to the retreating Germans. Within a month, the Romanian authorities had handed over control; on March 13, Antonescu resolved that the Romanian administration be withdrawn from Transnistria, and that all Jews there should be brought for their own safety to Bessarabia and Bukovina.[117] Over 10,700 Romanian Jews were repatriated at this time, including 1,846 orphaned children.[118] As Romanian officials left Odessa they plundered the Jewish cemetery, removing marble tombstones and sending them by rail to various masons in Bucharest for sale as building material. News of this vandalism reached Antonescu, who condemned this profanation as "an odious and thoughtless act that could have consequences for the whole nation." He ordered the return of the stones at the expense of those responsible on pain of internment and commensurate confiscation of their wealth.[119]

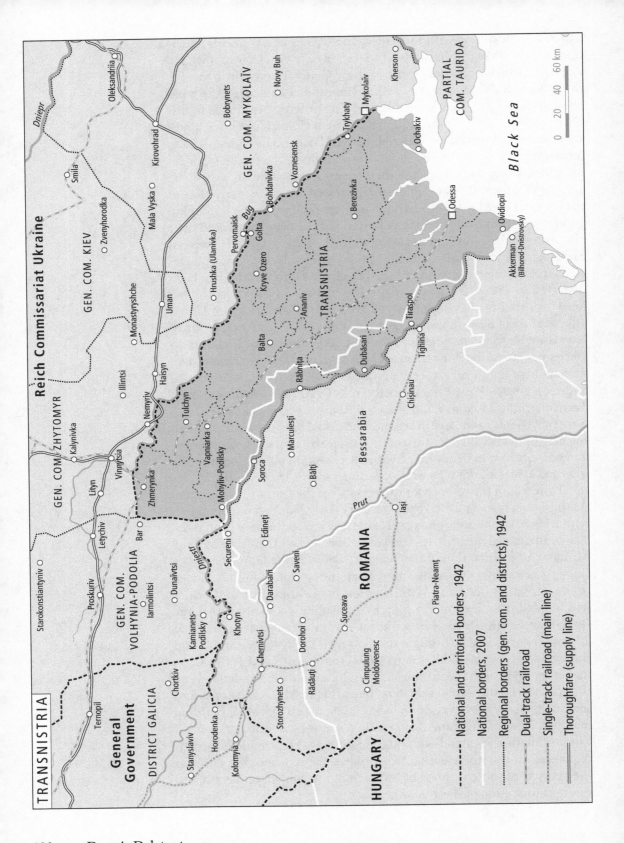

TRANSNISTRIA

PARTIAL COM. TAURIDA

Black Sea

Reich Commissariat Ukraine

GEN. COM. MYKOLAÏV

GEN. COM. KIEV

GEN. COM. ZHYTOMYR

GEN. COM. VOLHYNIA-PODOLIA

TRANSNISTRIA

Bessarabia

ROMANIA

HUNGARY

General Government

DISTRICT GALICIA

Dnipr

Oleksandriia

Smila

Kirovohrad

Mala Vyska

Zvenyhorodka

Monastyryshche

Uman

Illintsi

Haisyn

Nemyriv

Tulchyn

Vinnytsia

Litynbar

Letychiv

Proskuriv

Kalynivka

Zhmerynka

Starokonstiantyniv

Iarmolintsi

Kamianets-Podilsky

Dunaïvtsi

Khotyn

Chortkiv

Stanyslaviv

Horodenka

Kolomyia

Ternopil

Bobrynets

Novy Buh

Kherson

Mykolaïv

Trykhaty

Ochakiv

Odessa

Ovidiopil

Akkerman (Bilhorod-Dnistrovsky)

Voznesensk

Berezivka

Tiraspol

Tighina

Chişinău

Dubăsari

Râbniţa

Ananiv

Balta

Kryve Ozero

Golta

Pervomaisk

Bohdanivka

Bug

Hrushka (Ulanivka)

Vapniarka

Mohyliv-Podilsky

Soroca

Marculeşti

Bălţi

Secureni

Edineţi

Prut

Iaşi

Saveni

Darabani

Dorohoi

Rădăuţi

Storozhynets

Chernivtsi

Suceava

Cîmpulung Moldovenesc

Piatra-Neamţ

Dnister

0   20   40   60 km

- - - - National and territorial borders, 1942

——— National borders, 2007

· · · · Regional borders (gen. com. and districts), 1942

═══ Dual-track railroad

──── Single-track railroad (main line)

——— Thoroughfare (supply line)

180 • Dennis Deletant

Summing Up

Altogether, Transnistria was the graveyard of between 220,000 and 260,000 Jews and between 10,000 and 20,000 Roma, most of whom died as a result of malnutrition and disease in internment camps. Although several thousand Jews were shot between 1941 and 1943 by Romanian and SS units (the latter often aided by ethnic Germans), administrative incompetence and corruption caused the death of most Jews trapped in or deported to Transnistria between 1941 and 1944. As a result, as Ioanid has pointed out, tens of thousands who might otherwise have survived ultimately died.

Antonescu's treatment of the Jews was an ambivalent one. For the Jews of Bukovina, Bessarabia, and Transnistria, Antonescu was a murderous antisemite; for the Jews of Moldavia, Wallachia, and southern Transylvania, he was a providential antisemite. At the ideological level, he shared the Nazis' identification of Jews with Bolshevism, frequently referring in his speeches to the "Judeo-Bolshevik menace," but his method of dealing with this "menace" differed from that of Hitler. While German and Romanian forces joined in mass executions of Jews in Bessarabia and northern Bukovina in the summer of 1941, after that date Romanian treatment of the Jews broadly speaking followed a separate course. If, in the German case, discrimination was followed by deportation to the gas chambers, deportation in the Romanian case did not lead to the gas chambers but to degradation, callous neglect, and starvation.

Jews residing in Ukraine beyond Transnistria were likely to suffer a quick death by shooting at the hands of the Germans, but in Transnistria, Jews, after the massacres at Bohdanivka in December 1941, faced slow death by typhus or starvation as a result of Romanian neglect. The contrast between German and Romanian actions is illustrated by the fact that the largest proportion of Jews to survive Axis rule during the Second World War in Ukraine was in Transnistria. This is of no consolation to the dead, but it is of immense importance to those who made their way back to their homes in the spring and summer of 1944.

Notes

1. Jean Ancel, *Transnistria* (Bucharest: Atlas, 1998).

2. Matatias Carp, *Cartea Neagră. Suferinţele Evreilor din România, 1940–1944* (Bucharest: Editura Diogene, 1996). This three-volume study first appeared in 1946–1948.

3. Randolph L. Braham, ed., *The Destruction of Romanian and Ukrainian Jews During the Antonescu Era* (New York: Columbia University Press, 1997).

4. These figures are based on the reports sent to Antonescu by the governors of Bessarabia, Bukovina, and Transnistria. They reveal the numbers of Jews deported and surviving in Transnistria as of November 15, 1943. United States Holocaust Memorial Museum (USHMM), RG 25.006M (Archive of the Romanian Ministry of Foreign Affairs), reel 10, file 21, 133–135; reel 11, file 21, p. 589. Radu Ioanid estimates a similar death toll in *The Holocaust in Romania. The Destruction*

of Jews and Gypsies under the Antonescu Regime, 1940–1944 (Chicago: Ivan R. Dee, 2000), p. 174. Bancoş gives a figure of 149,000 for the number of Jews deported to Transnistria by Antonescu and puts the total number of victims among the Jewish community in Romania at the hands of the Antonescu regime at 119,000; D. Bancoş, *Social şi national în politica guvernului Ion Antonescu* (Bucharest: Editura Eminescu, 2000), p. 173. If we add the estimated 130,000–170,000 local Ukrainian Jews who perished in Transnistria under Romanian administration, we have a total figure of 250,000–290,000 Jewish dead.

5. A reflection of the callousness of the Romanian authorities in Transnistria toward the local Ukrainian Jews was the often cavalier attitude with which names and numbers were recorded. This makes an accurate calculation of the numbers of Ukrainian Jews who perished difficult. Furthermore, there is no reliable figure of the numbers of Ukrainian Jews who left Transnistria with the Soviet forces in summer and autumn 1941. Consequently, the researcher is reduced to making estimates. Of the 300,000 Jews recorded there in the 1939 Soviet census, 100,000–150,000 Jews are thought to have stayed behind when the Soviet forces withdrew; Ioanid, *The Holocaust in Romania*, p. 177. Estimates of Ukrainian Jewish victims in the period from September 1941 to November 1943 range from 130,000 (Ioanid, *The Holocaust in Romania*, p. 289) to "at least 170,000" (Ancel, *Transnistria*, Vol. III, pp. 300f). As regards the provinces of Bessarabia and Bukovina, Ioanid concludes that a total of 124,000 Jews—81,000 from Bessarabia and 43,000 from Bukovina—fled these provinces with the retreating Soviets in July 1941, leaving approximately 190,000 to face the Romanian and German advance, Ioanid, *The Holocaust in Romania*, p. 172.

6. *Antonescu-Hitler. Corespondenţă şi întîlniri inedite (1940–1944),* Vol. 1 (Bucharest: Coresi, 1991), pp. 116, 119–122.

7. The agreement was followed by a German order of September 4 establishing a border separating Transnistria from the German Rear Area Army Group South and stipulating which persons and goods were to be permitted across in either direction; Alexander Dallin, *Odessa, 1941–1944: A Case Study of Soviet Territory under Foreign Rule* (Iaşi, Oxford, Portland: The Centre for Romanian Studies, 1998), p. 59. The area beyond the Southern Buh was later to be known as the Reich Commissariat of Ukraine.

8. Dallin, *Odessa,* pp. 198–206. The figure of 300,000 Jews was confirmed by the census of 1939, which recorded the Jewish population by oblast (a Soviet regional-level administrative unit) as follows:

Odessa	233,155
Autonomous Moldavian Soviet Socialist Republic	37,035
Mohyliv	8,703
Tul'chyn	5,607
Iampil'	1,753
Vapniarka	711
Bershad'	4,271
Zhmerinka	4,630
Bar	3,869

See Mordechai Altshuler, ed., *Distribution of the Jewish Population of the USSR, 1939* (Jerusalem: The Hebrew University of Jerusalem, 1993), Tables 1–5.

9. Titus Flavius Vespasianus, Roman Emperor (79–81 BC). During the reign of his father, Vespasian, Titus was commander of the Roman armies in Judea, where he put down the rebellion of the Jews in 70 B.C. and destroyed Jerusalem.

10. Marcel-Dumitru Ciucă, Maria Ignat, and Aurelian Teodorescu, eds., *Stenogramele şedinţelor Consiliului de Miniştri. Guvernarea Ion Antonescu, Vol. III (aprilie-iunie 1941)* (Bucharest: Arhivele Naţionale ale României, 1999), p. 570.

11. Ciucă et al., *Stenogramele,* Vol. III, p. 618.

12. In a memorandum of August 22, 1942, against the proposed deportation of Romanian Jews to Poland, Filderman wrote: "Marshal Antonescu justified the deportation of Jews from Bessarabia and Bukovina as punishment for the acts of hostility that the latter allegedly carried out against the army, and from the need to remove an important number of uncertain elements in the war zone." Jean Ancel, ed., *Documents Concerning the Fate of Romanian Jewry During the Holocaust* (New York: Beate Klarsfeld Foundation, 1986), Vol. III, pp. 259–262, and Vol. IV, p. 126.

13. Arhivele Naționale Istorice Centrale, fond Preşidenția Consiliului de Miniştri–Cabinet, file 167/1941, pp. 64f. I thank Viorel Achim for this source. The text is in Ancel, *Transnistria,* Vol. 1, pp. 317f.

14. In his letter to Antonescu of October 11, 1941, Filderman wrote: "Today I received a desperate appeal from the leadership of the ghetto in Chişinău. On the morning of October 8, 1,500 people set out on the road, most of them on foot, taking with them only what they could carry. Almost all, therefore, are likely to perish, since it is cold outside and they are naked, without food and without the slightest possibility of getting supplies on a journey of at least eight days in the cold and snow. Only the sick, old, and children have left in carts. Thus not even the sick were spared; thus the women too left on foot. It means death, death, death of the innocents, without any other guilt than that of being Jews. I beg of you, Marshal, not to let such a tremendous tragedy take place. Please accept, Marshal, the assurance of my profound respect." Carp, *Cartea Neagră,* Vol. 3, p. 101, 189f.

15. Ancel, *Documents Concerning the Fate of Romanian Jewry,* Vol. III, pp. 259–262. In a postscript added by hand to the original text and not appearing in the published text, Antonescu added: "A wounded soldier from Piatra Neamț was buried alive on the orders and under the eyes of the Yid Soviet commissars despite the poor man's pleas that he had four children," Carp, *Cartea Neagră,* Vol. 3, p. 192. Antonescu gave an explicit explanation of his reasons for deporting the Jews—he preferred the term "evacuation"—in a letter dated February 4, 1944, to the Jewish architect Harnet Clejan: "As I have declared to you verbally, I was forced to evacuate the Jews from Bessarabia and Bukovina because, due to their horrible behavior during the occupation of those territories by the Russians, the population was so strongly incensed against them that without this security measure even more terrible pogroms would have taken place. Given all of this, I decided to evacuate all of the Jews of Bessarabia and Bukovina, but through various interventions, I was impeded from doing so. Today, I regret that I did not do this, because it has been established that, among the Jews that remained there, dishonorable elements were recruited by the adversary of the country. There has not been a single Communist or terrorist organization discovered by our police in which Jews have not been members, and frequently they are constituted only of Jews." See also Larry Watts, *Romanian Cassandra. Ion Antonescu and the Struggle for Reform, 1916–1941* (Boulder, CO: East European Monographs, 1993), p. 372.

16. USHMM, RG 25.003, reel 116, file 941.

17. Dorohoi became part of Bukovina for administrative purposes under Article 15 of Decree-Law 2506, which was published on October 15, 1941, in the official bulletin *Monitorul Oficial.* This decree stipulated that Bukovina comprised the counties of Câmpulung, Chernivtsi, Khotyn, Rădăuți, Storozhynets', Suceava, and Dorohoi.

18. Carp, *Cartea Neagră,* Vol. 3, p. 95.

19. Ciucă et al., *Stenogramele,* Vol. IV, p. 57.

20. Minutes of Meeting of the Council of Ministers, September 6, 1941, in Lya Benjamin, ed., *Evreii din România între anii 1940–1944. Problema Evreiască în stenogramele Consiliului de Miniştri,* Vol. II (Bucharest: Hasefer, 1996), pp. 302f.

21. For most Romanians, crossing into Bessarabia and northern Bukovina did

not constitute an "invasion" of the Soviet Union, since both territories had been wrested from Romania under threat of war by the Soviet Union in June 1940.

22. It has been estimated that up to 100,000 of the approximately 285,000 Jews in the two provinces had left, having either been sent into internal exile by the Soviets following the annexation of the provinces in June 1940 or having fled with the Red Army after the Romanian reannexation in July 1941. In December 1940, thousands of families of various nationalities were deported from Akkerman (Bilhorod-Dnistrovs'kyi) by the Soviet authorities to western Siberia and to Kazakhstan—the numbers have yet to be ascertained from the relevant Soviet documents. The Soviet regime also targeted its class enemies in the two provinces—the bourgeois, capitalists, and landowners—and its political opponents—nationalists, Zionists, priests, and pastors.

23. The phrase in Romanian *was curățirea terenului*. Paul A. Shapiro, "The Jews of Chișinău (Kishinev): Romanian Reoccupation, Ghettoization, Deportation," in Braham, *The Destruction of Romanian and Ukrainian Jews*, p. 140.

24. Ibid.

25. USHMM, RG 25.004M (Serviciul Român de Informații), reel 24, file 20725, Vol. 5, Order of Vasiliu, no. 37.519/1941, annex 00022.

26. Carp, *Cartea Neagră*, Vol. 3, p. 37.

27. Ibid.

28. Details in Ioanid, *The Holocaust in Romania*, pp. 134–139, and Carp, *Cartea Neagră*, Vol. 3, pp. 31–35.

29. Andrej Angrick, "Die Einsatzgruppe D," in Peter Klein, ed., *Die Einsatzgruppen in der besetzten Sowjetunion 1941/42* (Berlin: Hentrich, 1997), pp. 88–110.

30. Henri Monneray, ed., *La Persécution des Juifs dans les Pays de l'Est* (Paris: Editions du Centre, 1949), p. 291, cited in Ioanid, *The Holocaust in Romania*, p. 151.

31. Bundesarchiv Militärarchiv, RH 20–11/488, Niederschrift über die Besprechung mit dem Ic 11 Armee, July 16, 1941, p. 18. I am grateful to Ottmar Trașca of the Institute of History in Cluj-Napoca for showing me this report.

32. For the German reaction to the expulsions of Jews by the Romanian authorities, see Andrej Angrick, "The Escalation of German-Rumanian Anti-Jewish Policy after the Attack on the Soviet Union," *Yad Vashem Studies*, Vol. 26 (1998), pp. 203–238.

33. Carp, *Cartea Neagră*, Vol. 3, p. 101.

34. Ibid.

35. Dallin, *Odessa*, pp. 198–206.

36. Between August 9 and 23, 1941, the average number of Jews in Edineț was 10,000, in Sokyriany 21,000, and in Vertujeni 22,000; Radu Ioanid, "The Antonescu Era," in Randolph L. Braham, ed., *The Tragedy of Romanian Jewry* (New York: The Rosenthal Institute for Holocaust Studies, 1994), p. 148.

37. Anatol Petrencu, *Basarabia în al doilea război mondial 1940–1944* (Chișinău: Lyceum, 1997), p. 325.

38. Carp, *Cartea Neagră*, Vol. 3, p. 124.

39. Shapiro, "The Jews of Chișinău (Kishinev)," p. 160.

40. Ibid.

41. Council of Ministers Meeting, December 16, 1941, in Ciucă et al., *Stenogramele*, Vol. V, p. 492.

42. At the time these officials were termed "plenipotentiaries," being appointed governors, in the case of Bukovina and Bessarabia, by Antonescu on September 5, 1941.

43. According to Mihai Antonescu, a distant relative of the Marshal, the decision to deport the Jews from Bessarabia and northern Bukovina was not taken at any cabinet meeting but "was taken by the Marshal when he was in Moldavia, near

the front." Under questioning on April 17, 1946, before his trial, Mihai Antonescu declared that Ion Antonescu had taken the decision "to begin the deportation of Jews from Chernivtsi and from Chişinău" while he was in Iaşi [in early July 1941]. This was done because "it seemed to him that there were too many Jews in Bessarabia and Bukovina, and because in 1940 they showed an inappropriate attitude, and because of the atmosphere that the Marshal claimed existed in Bessarabia and Bukovina, that he made the hasty decision to evacuate the Jews." See Interrogation of Mihai Antonescu, April 17, 1946, USHMM, RG 25.004M (Serviciul Român de Informaţii), reel 31, file no. 40010, Vol. 43, pp. 14, 16, 19; see also Jean Ancel, "Antonescu and the Jews," *Yad Vashem Studies*, Vol. 23 (1993), p. 243; Jean Ancel, "The Romanian Campaigns of Mass Murder in Transnistria, 1941–1942," in Braham, *The Destruction of Romanian and Ukrainian Jews*, p. 129, note 49.

44. Memorandum of General Gheorghe Voiculescu, governor of Bessarabia, regarding the situation in the Chişinău ghetto, addressed to Ion Antonescu. From references within the text, the document can be dated to late December 1941, see Ion Şerbănescu, ed., *Evreii din România*, Vol. III, Part 1, doc. 373, p. 48, and Ancel, "Antonescu and the Jews," p. 241.

45. Ciucă et al., *Stenogramele*, Vol. V, p. 323. The deportations began on September 16, 1941, not in November.

46. Shapiro, "The Jews of Chişinău (Kishinev)," p. 161; Ancel, "Antonescu and the Jews," p. 243; Ancel, "The Romanian Campaigns," p. 129, note 49.

47. Carp, *Cartea Neagră*, Vol. 3, p. 128. Figures compiled for Antonescu put the number of Jews in Bessarabia, "as of September 25, 1941," at 53,800, including those in the ghetto of Chişinău; Ancel, "Antonescu and the Jews," p. 243.

48. Shapiro, "The Jews of Chişinău (Kishinev)," p. 161.

49. Carp, *Cartea Neagră*, Vol. 3, p. 123. In the instructions issued by Colonel Meculescu, head of the Gendarmerie in Bessarabia, to the commandant of Vertujeni, Colonel Vasile Agapie, the number of Jews in the camp was 22,150, ibid.

50. Ibid., p. 130.

51. Shapiro, "The Jews of Chişinău (Kishinev)," p. 188, note 85.

52. Alex Mihai Stoenescu, *Armata, Mareşalul şi Evreii* (Bucharest: RAO, 1998), pp. 332f.

53. Carp, *Cartea Neagră*, Vol. 3, p. 130.

54. Ibid., p. 131.

55. Ibid.

56. Council of Ministers Meeting, November 13, 1941, Ciucă et al., *Stenogramele*, Vol. V, p. 126.

57. Ibid., pp. 4f.

58. Ibid., p. 8.

59. Ion Şerbănescu, ed., *Evreii din România*, Vol. III: *Perioada unei Mari Restrişti*, Part 2 (Bucharest: Hasefer, 1997), pp. 21f.

60. Ibid., doc. 367, p. 39.

61. Ibid.

62. Ibid., doc. 399 (dated November 22, 1941), pp. 88–92.

63. Ibid., doc. 406 (dated December 30, 1941), pp. 98ff.

64. Memorandum of October 12, 1943, sent by Mihai Antonescu to General C. Z. Vasiliu, state secretary at the Ministry of Internal Affairs, on the abuses committed during the deportations of 1941 and 1942, USHMM, RG.25.004M (Serviciul Român de Informaţii), reel 13, file 2757/82, p. 38.

65. This was recognized in the memorandum of October 12, 1943: "War widows and war orphans, descendants of veterans of the War of Independence [1877–1878], women and children whose husbands were and still are doing compulsory labor in Romania, had all been victims. There were also Jews who, on the outbreak of war, had been sent to Wallachia from the area of the front in Bukovina and Dorohoi but who, on the intervention of the Ministry of Finance, had been

sent back to their homes in the autumn of 1941, in order to subscribe to the war loan to which Jews were required to do by law. After subscribing, the order for deportation came, and they were deported. Had they remained in Wallachia, they would have been safe."

66. Şerbănescu, *Evreii din România*, Vol. III, Part 2, doc. 406, p. 99.

67. Ibid., doc. 399, p. 90.

68. Ibid., doc. 406, p. 99.

69. Ibid.

70. Ibid.

71. Ibid., doc. 399, p. 90.

72. Ibid., doc. 399, p. 91.

73. Ibid.

74. Bancoş, *Social şi national*, p. 162.

75. Şerbănescu, *Evreii din România*, Vol. III, Part 2, doc. 513, p. 228. Confusingly, the Inspectorate of Gendarmes reported that on January 1, 1942, there were only 401 Jews left in Bessarabia; ibid., doc. 476, p. 182.

76. Ibid., doc. 534, p. 248.

77. Ibid., doc. 538, p. 252.

78. I am grateful to Viorel Achim for providing me with the results of his research on the deportation of the Roma.

79. The estimate came from the Central Institute of Statistics, which was subordinated to the Presidency of the Council of Ministers, i.e., to Ion Antonescu. The Institute's director was Sabin Manuilă.

80. Viorel Achim, "Deportarea ţiganilor în Transnistria," *Anuarul IRIR 2002*, (Bucharest, 2003), pp. 130f.

81. Ibid.

82. Ibid., p. 134.

83. Ibid., p. 139.

84. "Transylvania" meant southern Transylvania, since the northern part had been ceded to Hungary in August 1940.

85. Şerbănescu, *Evreii din România*, Vol. II, doc. 179, p. 537.

86. Radu Ioanid, "The Antonescu Era" in: Braham, *The Tragedy of Romanian Jewry*, p. 162.

87. Iuliu Maniu, the leader of the National Peasant Party.

88. Ancel, *Documents Concerning Romanian Jewry*, Vol. X, p. 215.

89. Declaration of Alexander Safran, Geneva, January 10, 1961; in Ancel, *Documents Concerning Romanian Jewry*, Vol. VIII, p. 599.

90. Şerbănescu, *Evreii din România*, Vol. II, doc. 179, pp. 538f.

91. Ibid., p. 539.

92. Ibid., p. 453, note 1.

93. Some claimed that he had suffered a nervous breakdown, others that he had contracted syphilis as a young officer and that its effects had resurfaced. Mihai Antonescu gave a blander explanation: The problem was food poisoning. See the diary of the Swiss Minister René de Weck, *Jurnal* (Bucharest: Humanitas, 2000), p. 135.

94. Alfred Rosenberg, the Nazis' principal ideologist.

95. Şerbănescu, *Evreii din România*, Vol. II, doc. 147, pp. 455–459.

96. Ibid.

97. Watts, *Romanian Cassandra*, p. 362.

98. Ancel, *Documents Concerning Romanian Jewry*, Vol. IV, p. 120.

99. Ibid, p. 250, and *Martiriul Evreilor din România, 1940–1944. Documente şi Mărturii* (Bucharest: Editura Hasefer, 1991), p. 218.

100. "Evacuation" was the term in official usage for deportation.

101. Ancel, *Documents Concerning Romanian Jewry*, Vol. IV, p. 252, and *Martiriul Evreilor*, p. 219.

102. Watts, *Romanian Cassandra*, p. 363.

103. Ibid.

104. Christopher R. Browning, *The Final Solution and the German Foreign Office. A Study of Referat DIII of Abteilung Deutschland 1940–1943* (New York: Holmes and Meier, 1978), p. 115, quoted in Watts, *Romanian Cassandra*, p. 363. Light is shed on the absence of Romanian railway officials at Eichmann's meeting by a report of the director general of Romanian railway, General T. C. Orezeanu, to Antonescu of October 27, 1942: the German railway directorate for east Berlin had convened a conference on September 26, 1942, to arrange special trains for Jews from Romania to be sent to the General Government. He, Orezeanu, had no prior knowledge of this matter and approached the Ministry of Internal Affairs and Radu Lecca, the plenipotentiary for Jewish affairs in Romania. Both, he wrote, were also unaware of the issue. Orezeanu sent a request to German Railways to postpone the conference, but it was ignored, and the conference went ahead without Romanian representation. According to information received by Orezeanu, it was resolved at the conference to provide special trains for the deportation of 280,000 Jews made up of 50 freight cars and one passenger car (for the guards) that would carry 2,000 Jews every other day. The trains would depart from Adjud in southern Transylvania for Bełżec via Orășeni and Sniatyn, the frontier station for the General Government. In view of this situation, Orezeanu ended his report by asking Antonescu for instructions. Antonescu simply responded in a hand-written note in the margin of the report that, at the meeting of the Council of Ministers on October 13, 1942, he had stopped the deportations of the Jews. See Ancel, *Documents Concerning Romanian Jewry*, Vol. X, minutes of conference held in Berlin, September 26–28, 1942, regarding the evacuation of the Jews from the General Government and the dispatch of Jews from Romania to the General Government, pp. 237f.

105. Such was Richter's enthusiasm for the deportation of Romanian Jews to the death camps in Poland that he drew up his own detailed plan.

106. Șerbănescu, *Evreii din Romania*, Vol. II, doc. 145, p. 442.

107. Ibid., p. 458. The word "deportation" was avoided. The Romanian Intelligence Service noted on October 9, 1942, that deportations were still taking place: "We are informed that at Botosani 30 more families have been arrested in order to be deported to Transnistria," USHMM, RG.25.004M (Serviciul Român de Informații), reel 14, file 2869/208, p. 334. On September 8, 1942, the deportation began of almost all the Jews—407—among the Communists interned in Târgu-Jiu to Vapniarka camp in Jugastru (Iampil') County, Transnistria. They arrived there on September 16. In addition, 523 Jews who had requested repatriation to the Soviet Union after the loss of Bessarabia and northern Bukovina in June 1940 and whose names had been found in the Soviet legation in Bucharest after the withdrawal of Soviet representation in June 1941 were deported on the same date. The latter were sent to Slivina camp in Ochakiv County; Carp, *Cartea Neagră*, Vol. 3, p. 449. The number of Communists in the camp at Vapniarka totaled 619 in November 1943, out of a total of 1,312 inmates who included Christian common-law criminals. An exception to those Jewish Communists deported was Iosif Chișinevski who remained in Caransebeș. Born in 1905 in Bessarabia, Chișinevski is believed to have studied at the Communist Party school in Moscow during the late 1920s. He was arrested in 1941 as the head of a Bucharest Communist cell and sent to Caransebeș jail. He was spared deportation to Transnistria because only Jewish Communists with sentences under 10 years were sent to the province. Those with heavier sentences, like Chișinevski, Simion Zeiger, and Radu Mănescu, stayed in Caransebeș until their release on August 23, 1944; Pavel Câmpeanu, "Pe marginea unei recenzii. Mistere și pseudo-mistere din istoria PCR," Vol. 22, no. 34 (1995), p. 12.

108. Jean Ancel, "Plans for the Deportation of the Rumanian Jews and their

Discontinuation in Light of Documentary Evidence (July-October 1942)," *Yad Vashem Studies*, Vol. 16 (1984), pp. 388f. Filderman also prepared a memorandum on August 22, 1942, against the proposed deportation of Romanian Jews to Poland, but it is unclear for whose eyes it was intended. It casts light on Flderman's thoughts on how to attenuate the consequences of such a plan for the Jews of Romania: "Marshal Antonescu justified the deportation of Jews from Bessarabia and Bukovina as punishment for the acts of hostility that the latter allegedly carried out against the army, and from the need to remove an important number of uncertain elements in the war zone, while the German armies have justified the deportation of some of the Jews in the occupied countries on the grounds of the repeated attacks on the German army, etc. Not only has no such allegation similar to the one leveled against the Jews of Bessarabia and Bukovina been made to date against the Jews in Transylvania and the Banat, nor against those remaining in Bukovina, not to mention those in the Old Kingdom, but everyone recognized that both on the occasion of the cession of part of Transylvania and afterward that both the Jews in the territories that remained and—what is even more important— those in the ceded territories behaved irreproachably. . . . If, against all possibility, Romania finds herself faced by problems which forced the government to take decisions contrary to the program announced by Marshal Antonescu, then, in the light of what precedes and what follows, it would be politic on the one hand that as far as possible the execution of the plan be postponed, and on the other that the deportations apply only to those who have settled clandestinely in Romania, to those sentenced to crimes against the security of the state, and to those born in regions other than those claimed by Romania as being Romanian. Under no circumstances should children, women, and old people—that is those under one year of age and those over 55—be deported. Deportation could be postponed by making emigration legal and organizing the emigration of Jews earmarked for deportation through reliable agencies and giving the Jews several months notice." Ancel, *Documents Concerning Romanian Jewry*, Vol. IV, p. 126.

109. A half-century later, Queen Helen was to be recognized by the Israeli authorities as one of the Righteous Among Nations. The memorandum of her activities during the war which the Israeli government based its decision stated: "Queen Helen identified herself openly with the plight of the Jews. She even threatened to leave the country if their deportation continued. The contact she made through her Jewish doctors with the underground Jewish leadership enabled her to provide 'vital and irreplaceable support,' which made it possible to save tens of thousands. By doing so (as had her son when advocating a break with the Axis in his New Year broadcast in 1942 [*sic*]), she put her life at risk. She knew that her royalty would not save her; her sister Irene had been arrested by the Germans in Italy, her cousin Princess Mafaldi had died in Buchenwald. Hitler pressed Marshal Antonescu to 'eliminate Queen Helen physically.' Her opposition to the barbaric treatment of Jews in Romania constituted a daily risk to her life," Yad Vashem, undated memorandum, On Assistance to Romanian Jews Rendered by Queen Elena During World War II, quoted in manuscript of Ivor Porter, *King Michael of Romania: The King and the Country* (Stroud: Sutton, 2005), p. 107.

110. In the original German, *letzen* "last" could either be interpreted as "final" or "most recent."

111. Ancel, *Documents Concerning Romanian Jewry*, Vol. IV, pp. 314f.

112. Watts dismisses the argument that Stalingrad and a wish to "save his own skin" were instrumental in Antonescu's decision; Watts, *Romanian Cassandra*, pp. 364f.

113. *Martiriul Evreilor*, p. 218.

114. Carp, *Cartea Neagrǎ*, Vol. 3, pp. 444–447.

115. Ibid., p. 410. At a Council of Ministers meeting on October 13, 1942, General Vasiliu, the undersecretary at the Ministry of Internal Affairs, reported

that Jewish Communists and Jews who had requested repatriation to the Soviet Union following the Soviet annexation of Bessarabia and northern Bukovina numbered 2,161. Of these, 1,538 had been sent to Transnistria; Şerbănescu, *Evreii din România*, Vol. II, doc. 147, p. 455.

116. Carp, *Cartea Neagră*, Vol. 3, p. 412.

117. Ion Şerbănescu, ed., *Evreii din Romania intre anii 1943–1944: Bilanţul Tragediei-Renaşterea Sperantei*, Vol. IV (Bucharest: Hasefer, 1997), doc. 346, p. 382.

118. Ioanid, *The Holocaust in Romania*, p. 257.

119. Şerbănescu, *Evreii din România*, Vol. IV, p. 298.

V
Annihilation and Labor: Jews and Thoroughfare IV in Central Ukraine

ANDREJ ANGRICK

When Reinhard Heydrich announced on January 20, 1942, at what we now call the Wannsee Conference, that the further emigration of Jews from German-occupied Europe would be suspended due to the war, and that the Jews would instead be "evacuated" to the east, a large part of Soviet Jewry had already been killed. Most of the largest mass shootings of Jews in the Second World War had already taken place. Upon finishing the outline of his plan for the "Final Solution of the European Jewish question," the chief of the Reich Security Main Office (RSHA) nonetheless turned to the occupied Soviet Union, where it was planned to put the Jews to work "in the east in an expedient manner in the course of the Final Solution" with those who were able to work "moved into those territories constructing roads."[1]

It must have been clear to those at the conference that the word "evacuation" was a euphemism for state-sponsored mass murder. The representatives of the Foreign Office, the Plenipotentiary for the Four-Year Plan, and the Ministry of Justice may have lacked detailed knowledge of what this entailed, but all those present were at least informed of the mass shootings in the Soviet Union. All of them had already played a part in the process, each according to his ministry's responsibilities, interests, and powers. But even within this circle of insiders, was the formulation that the Jews would be sent east for road construction—where "a large part will drop off by a natural process of attrition," while those who remained "will have to be treated accordingly"[2]—simply a generalization with no basis in reality, since all Jews were to be murdered anyway? Or was there something else, a specific project, that Heydrich had in mind?

Historians Wolfgang Scheffler, Helge Grabitz, and Hermann Kaienburg were the first to suggest that Heydrich's digression on road construction was in no way a euphemism for mass murder, but instead a reference to the Jewish forced labor camps along the supply line Thoroughfare IV (*Durchgangsstrasse IV,* or DG IV) in Ukraine. Those camps, in particular those in Galicia, were already putting into practice what Heydrich disclosed as his intent at Wannsee.[3] Yet the chief of the RSHA, home office to the state Security Police (which included the Gestapo) and Nazi party's Security Service, was uncharacteristically imprecise, which might have had something to do with his desire to remind his audience in his opening remarks that, on July 31, 1941, Hermann Göring, then Hitler's closest colleague and designated successor, had appointed him "plenipotentiary for the *preparation* of the Final Solution of the European Jewish question." The reason for this reminder lay in Heydrich's realization that, in the first weeks of the war against the Soviet Union, he faced competition within the SS and police where the mass murder of the Jews was concerned.

In the summer of 1941, Heinrich Himmler, both the national leader of the SS and the chief of the German Police, deployed three higher SS- and police leaders (HSSPF) to the Soviet Union as his direct representatives. These three men were the driving force behind what appeared to British intelligence as a "competition with each other as to their scores" in shooting Soviet Jews.[4] In addition to employing their own battalions of regular police and SS combat brigades, the HSSPFs used the four Einsatzgruppen, Heydrich's infamous death squads, which were made up largely of Security Police (Sipo) and Security Service (SD) personnel. But it was the HSSPFs who forced the transition from the murder of select Jewish men to the mass murder of all Jews regardless of age or gender.[5] For example, Friedrich Jeckeln, HSSPF Russia South until October 31, 1941, seized the initiative within the SS at Kamianets-Podilsky at the end of August 1941, overseeing the murder of 23,600 Jews over three days, by far the largest massacre in the war to that date.[6] And it was Himmler who traveled the eastern front, personally ordering the HSSPF to accelerate the campaign of mass murder and to expand the scope of operations to include women and children.[7] By contrast, Heydrich appears to have been unusually inactive during this period. The question therefore arises whether Heydrich was aware of his limited powers of authority—at least in internal SS power struggles over policy in the Soviet Union—and for this reason made the aforementioned inaccurate and passing reference to DG IV—especially since DG IV was by January 1942 the responsibility of another Himmler confidant, Hans-Adolf Prützmann.[8]

Sections of Thoroughfare IV have already been the subject of academic interest, but these have examined primarily the western parts of the project. Sybille Steinbacher has analyzed segments of this thoroughfare in Upper Silesia; Thomas Sandkühler and Dieter Pohl have studied the role of DG IV in Galicia, Wendy Lower its role in Zhytomyr.[9] This study will focus on DG IV in the Reich Commissariat Ukraine between Pidvolochysk, due east of Ternopil, and Uman, due south of Kiev. Because the labor camp commandants on this stretch drew on the Jewish population in Galicia and the Romanian occupied region of Transnistria, they were able to exploit and persecute Jewish workers throughout the German occupation. The inclusion of Jews from Galicia and Transnistria in this murderous undertaking as well as the enormous scope of the DG IV made the project the subject of postwar criminal investigation by West German prosecutors and so produced valuable collections of testimonies to complement surviving Wehrmacht and SS records. Given the distance of camps east of Uman from Transnistria and Galicia, far fewer Jews appear to have been used on the Uman-Taganrog stretch, which must remain the subject for later study.

What emerges here, based on the analysis of the available records, is a project that entailed extensive planning and a highly managed division of labor and coordination of offices, involving multiple institutions and individuals ranging from Hitler and Himmler in Berlin to local mayors and indigenous policemen in Ukraine itself. In this particular chapter of Holocaust history, Heydrich's Reich Security Main Office and his secret police and security commanders in the field tended to play marginal roles.

DG IV's Origins and Progress until December 1941

Stretching some 2,175 kilometers (ca. 1,360 miles) from Lviv to Taganrog, DG IV was the southernmost of the Wehrmacht's main supply lines in the east. It had not existed before the war, but was a series of country roads and highways joined by SS and Wehrmacht planners, beginning in the largest city in eastern Galicia (occupied by the Soviets in September 1939) and running through the southern half of Ukraine via Proskuriv (today Khmelnytsky), Vinnytsia, Uman, Kryvy Rih, Dnipropetrovsk, and Stalino (today Donetsk) to Taganrog.

DG IV projects included two main connecting roads: DG IVb (Lviv-Brody-Dubno-Rivne) and DG IVc (Kirovohrad-Oleksandriia-Kremenchuk-Poltava). These linked DG IV with DG V, which led through the northern half of Ukraine (Volodymyr Volynsky-Rivne-Zhytomyr-Kiev-Chutovo). Under the auspices of the DG IV operation, two other major projects were also carried out: the bringing on line of a dam at Zaporizhzhia and the construction of bridges across the straits at Kerch (in the Crimea) and across the Southern Buh River at Mykolaïv.[10] DG IV was planned as the continuation of the autobahn construction projects under Organization Schmelt in Silesia, which in turn involved the extension of the Breslau-Gleiwitz autobahn in the Reich.[11] Planning envisioned the extension of DG IV to Rostov on the Don and into the Caucasus along the German military's foreseen line of advance.

Plans for expanding the system of Soviet roads that comprised DG IV originated at the urging of the High Command of the Wehrmacht (OKW) soon after the attack on the Soviet Union. As the Soviet Union lacked railways running west to east (especially lines with two sets of tracks), the OKW chose to link and improve certain roads to facilitate the convoys of heavy vehicles needed to keep the troops supplied. As a supply line, DG IV was more than simply a road. It served as the base for a network of support units such as tow platoons, motor pools, tire depots, veterinarian facilities, corrals for horses, infirmaries, field hospitals, and accommodations for soldiers in transfer, much of which was often in the same location as forced labor camps.[12] Given DG IV's southeasterly course, the supply line appears to have provided a greater strategic service in that it helped the Wehrmacht maintain forces as far away as the outskirts of Kirovohrad until March 1944, by which point the Red Army had expelled the Germans from almost all of northern Ukraine.

Responsibility for maintaining and improving DG IV in Ukraine was given to Organization Todt, the Nazi party's paramilitary labor service named for founder Dr. Fritz Todt, after negotiations between it and the OKW. Todt, who had overseen autobahn construction in the Reich and was now the German minister for arms and munitions, in turn delegated the realization of this project to the Office of the General Construction Inspector under Albert Speer (best known as Hitler's favorite architect and Todt's successor). Work on DG IV in Galicia got under way in September 1941, when the O.T. supply-line superintendents set up their offices in Lviv.[13]

The German military's willingness to use Jews for forced labor projects in the occupied Soviet territories also goes back to the early weeks of the Soviet campaign. Having received inquiries from various offices, the Armed Forces Economics and Armaments Office announced its basic support for the idea that the Jews be "billeted and deployed in cohesive work details," as the inspector for Economic Staff East, Hans Nagel, put it—after consulting Göring—at a meeting of the economic inspectorate chiefs of the German army groups on the eastern front.[14] The use of Jews as workers for projects such as road construction was of course nothing new. Since 1940, Organization Schmelt had been using Jewish labor extensively for building roads. Although the Armed Forces Economics and Armaments Office could exert but limited influence on the High Command of the Army in Berlin or the armies in the field, the OKW after some delay issued an order in September 1941 stating that, with regard to the "treatment" of Jews—"the main carriers of Bolshevism"—their use as laborers could take place only "in specially assembled work details" and "under German supervision." The Wehrmacht was explicitly instructed not to issue papers to individual Jews assuring them of work. Given that this order was issued at the very moment when the annihilation of entire Jewish communities under military administration was shifting into high gear, one is left to conclude that one purpose of limiting work permits to details was to help prevent Jews from escaping.[15]

At almost the same time, Einsatzgruppe C, which was operating in the northern half of Ukraine, recommended a strategy combining roadwork on the eastern front's southern sector with the annihilation of the Jews, so as to fulfill both objectives:

> In western and central Ukraine, Jewry is almost identical with the urban stratum of workers, craftsmen, and traders. *Should Jewish labor be dispensed with completely, the economic reconstruction of Ukrainian industry as well as the strengthening of the urban administrative centers will be almost impossible.*
>
> There is only one possibility, which the German administration in the General Government has underestimated for a long time:
> *Solving the Jewish question through the extensive use of Jews for labor.*
> That would lead to the gradual liquidation of Jewry—a development that would be in line with the economic conditions of the country.[16]

It is not clear whether the Einsatzgruppe, based at the time of its report on DG IV in Novoukraïnka, had discussed this idea with any part of Army Group South, but it is known that Jews, in accordance with the army leadership's wishes, were conscripted into forced labor immediately upon the capture of a Soviet cities—usually to clear debris or search for mines.

What Einsatzgruppe C was calling for does not appear to have been adopted immediately in central Ukraine. However, Fritz Katzmann, the SS and police leader in District Galicia, had been charged with applying the idea on the stretch of DG IV under his purview, starting in October 1941. The Wehrmacht, which had originally proposed using Jewish forced labor back in the summer, naturally took an interest in this development. Few POWs had been captured in western Ukraine, and the civilian administration in Galicia could not count on POWs from further east.[17] Katzmann, who all too well understood that Galicia's craftsmen were "90 percent Jewish workers," adopted the policy of using Jews for hard labor, thus complying in part with the strategy called for by Einsatzgruppe C. It was also clear to him that all of the Jewish workers could not be murdered in one sweep, at least not without harming the war effort. Instead, his men initially focused on annihilating what they saw as "the work-shy and asocial Jew[ish] riff-raff" before turning to the rest.[18]

This calculated system of extermination—which did not really involve "annihilation through work," but annihilation after a period of forced labor—was at this point restricted to the Galician part of DG IV. Katzmann quickly went about filling his DG IV camps with Jewish forced laborers. For him, however, killing his Jewish workers was more important than their work—as he demonstrated by filling key posts along DG IV with outspoken antisemites, who then set about realizing the goal of "using up" human beings by working them to death. Accordingly, Katzmann also gave orders to shoot Jews who were unfit for work and to liquidate entire work details as punishment should a prisoner make a successful escape. He apparently believed that he enjoyed access to an inexhaustible reservoir of Jews fit for work to make up for such losses.[19] According to Katzmann's report on the annihilation of eastern Galicia's Jews, 254,989 Jews were "evacuated or resettled" by November 10, 1942. How many of these victims had passed through his DG IV camps by then is unclear, although Katzmann himself suggested that the number amounted to "only" 20,000. He also claimed that Jewish prisoners had completed work on 160 kilometers (100 miles) of road. Forced labor on DG IV in central Ukraine, however, has to be considered in a different light than events on DG IV inside Galicia.

Further east, the use of Jewish labor remained sporadic at first—especially in the rear area behind the lines immediately west of the Dniepr River. There, the annihilation of the Jews had taken top priority. So long as the front kept moving east, labor- and time-intensive projects such as DG IV were of lesser importance. The HSSPF Russia South, the Einsatzgruppen, and the Wehrmacht went about eradicating entire communities of Jews with little regard for economic interests. Unsurprisingly, by the end of 1941, maintenance on DG IV was relatively modest in scope. This changed at the end of December, however, when the German campaign on the southern sector of the eastern front came to a halt.

New Priorities

Germany's failure to take Moscow and Leningrad in 1941 and unexpectedly high losses of men and materiel made it impossible for the Wehrmacht to consider offensive operations on all three sectors of the front simultaneously. Although Army Group South had yet to achieve all of its objectives for 1941—the Crimea had yet to be conquered and the Red Army had repulsed the Wehrmacht advance on Rostov—German hopes for forcing an end to the war in 1942 concentrated on this front and dual lines of advance east to Stalingrad and south to the Caucasus. The supply lines in this sector of the eastern front, especially DG IV, would be of crucial importance to German planning for the next phase of the war, but DG IV still lacked a powerful sponsor to ensure its expansion and repair.

By coincidence, two divisions of the Waffen-SS, the SS armed forces, bogged down in the mud near the Black Sea town of Taganrog in December 1941 just as Himmler embarked on an inspection tour to the front. The experience was to teach him a lesson in the importance

In mid-1943, SS and Police Leader Galicia Fritz Katzmann filed a report to Reichsführer-SS and Chief of the German Police Heinrich Himmler on the solution of the Jewish question in District Galicia. Contained in the report was a photo album, which includes this photo of Jewish men at work on Thoroughfare IV during the summer of 1942. Instytut Pamięci Narodowej, Warsaw.

of good supply lines. Whenever underway by car, Himmler regularly encountered difficulties. A meeting at IIIrd Armored Corps command was cancelled due to miserable road conditions, while various reviews of the troops could only take place with the help of a plane.[20] Legend has it that on the way to review SS Division Wiking, a visit made possible only by an all-terrain vehicle, the all powerful Reichsführer-SS and chief of the German police had to help push his car through enormous patches of mud.

Upon arriving at the headquarters of SS Division Wiking, Himmler ordered division command to look after the roads leading to its positions. He was informed that the dilapidated roads—as well as the completely over-burdened and insufficient railroads—were preventing the division from receiving the supplies it needed to fight, let alone to undertake road repairs. Upon hearing this, Himmler resolved to make sure the supply lines were put in order.[21] While the effects of this decision would take time to produce tangible results, Himmler had at least grasped that the country roads in the Soviet Union did not correspond to German autobahns. From that point on, the Reichsführer-SS began to take an active interest in the movement of supplies on DG IV.

Upon leaving the Wiking division, Himmler traveled to Army

Group South headquarters, where he took part in a situation conference with Field Marshal Walter von Reichenau on December 28, 1941.[22] Here and in subsequent telephone conversations, Himmler and Reichenau discussed the future of the "road of the SS."[23] In the meantime, Himmler informed Jürgen Stroop, later an inspector on DG IV, of the new project. Stroop noted after the war that part of the importance of DG IV lay not only in sending supplies to the front but also in conveying plundered raw materials and foodstuffs to the Reich.[24]

Initially, Himmler merely instructed Prützmann to establish contact with the Army Group South and its combat engineers. Himmler himself wanted to talk about the matter with Reich Commissar for Ukraine Erich Koch.[25] A few days later, however, Reichenau died, leaving Himmler without his principal collaborator within Army Group South. Nevertheless, Himmler urged Prützmann, in addition to forcing road construction, to build up the railways as much as was in his powers and to order the SS and police leaders (SSPF) under his command to assist him as needed.[26] Field Marshal Fedor von Bock, Reichenau's successor, also complained about supplies failing to reach the front, but he was content to leave the matter to Speer, who subsequently became Himmler's main ally in the DG IV project.[27] This was the state of affairs concerning DG IV at the time of the Wannsee Conference and Heydrich's reference to roadwork in the east.

While negotiations with Speer were still underway, Himmler informed the main office chiefs within his SS and police empire that Prützmann had orders to repair DG IV (identified here as "the Black Sea Road"), "practically speaking, to build [it] anew" by spring, and that the main offices were to lend him their full support. Within the office of the HSSPF Russia South, Paul Otto Geibel was entrusted with running the project, but was soon succeeded by Walter Gieseke, in summer 1942. The Operations Staff on DG IV, a special command unit of mechanics, architects, policemen, construction engineers, cartographers, and communications experts as well as numerous support personnel, was also set up.[28]

On February 17, 1942, the first meeting on DG IV took place between Speer, Prützmann, and Hans Kammler, who ran the building and construction office within the SS Economics and Administration Main Office. Two days later, Himmler met with Prützmann, Geibel, and Kammler as well as Arnold Adam (supply line superintendent for DG IV) and Dr. Gerhard Fränk (head of the O.T. Construction Staff Speer). It was agreed here that Himmler's organization would take tasks that lay within the prerogatives of the SS—the mustering of workers and providing guards—while the O.T. was to provide the construction supervisors and technicians and to be responsible for the technical aspects of the project. That same evening at Hitler's headquarters, DG IV was on the agenda for Himmler during a presentation by Hans-Joachim Riecke of the Wehrmacht's Economics Staff East. There, it was agreed that DG IV's route was to be brought into line with Nazi policy for German settlements in the east. Speer meanwhile informed Hitler of his agreement with Himmler. The dictator gave his approval but insisted that the road be "expanded only in the most primitive way," and that the road's surface have "a durability of only 2 to 3 years."[29]

Hitler's limits on the project reflected the lessons learned from the events of winter 1941–1942. Not only had almost all the Jews under Wehrmacht administration been murdered, the greater part of the 3 million Soviet POWs that Hitler once imagined exploiting for forced labor had since starved to death, been shot, or succumbed to sickness or deprivation. As a result, DG IV had been reduced to what seemed possible—but at the same time, independent of supplies and reinforcements for the front, Hitler's ethnic-based utopia still remained in play. In the next 10 years, Hitler planned to have 4 million Germans, and then, in 20 years, some 10 million Germans living along DG IV, from Lviv to Rostov, in model settlements with administrative centers for the National Socialist German Workers Party, the SS, the Wehrmacht, and the civilian state apparatus.[30] Such were the dreams of the overconfident dictator.

Organizing and Supervising DG IV

In early 1942, the main challenge was getting the regional organization of this enormous project going. The O.T. had road superintendent Adam set up his office in Vinnytsia, while the HSSPF Russia South chose Dnipropetrovsk for the headquarters of the Operational Staff on DG IV.[31] For administrative and practical purposes, the roads that were to comprise DG IV were divided into regional construction zones (*Oberbauabschnitt*) and construction zones (*Bauabschnitt*). Headquarters for regional construction zones were established in Vinnytsia, Kirovohrad, Kryvy Rih, and Stalino, with administrative centers for construction zones in Letychiv, Haisyn, Uman,[32] Novoukraïnka, Oleksandriia, Hurivka, Sofiïvka, Dnipropetrovsk, Pavlohrad, Hryshyne, and Makiïvka.

The regional construction zones and construction zones were run by SS officers from the General SS (*Allgemeine-SS*), a part of the SS Command Main Office (*SS-Führungshauptamt*). They were deployed along DG IV as "specialist-officers" (*Fachführer*) with a patch (F) behind their insignia. Notably, several SS officers waiting to deploy as SSPF further east ended up on DG IV overseeing various construction zones. Work on DG IV was evidently considered a good way for SSPF-designates to familiarize themselves with their future duties: One had to cooperate with different, sometimes competing, agencies and SS offices and coordinate with them.[33] By mid-1942, the DG IV project employed some 5,000 German officers, engineers, managers, security personnel, and other specialists.

Responsibility for securing DG IV and guarding the forced laborers fell to the Police Security Section on DG IV, a special four-company formation set up by the Order Police Main Office. The security section was stationed along the construction zones, but clearly a formation of 546 men, including a good number of older policemen, was hardly enough to guarantee security on DG IV. Consequently, local police battalions (*Schutzmannschaft* battalions) made up of Lithuanians, Latvians, Cossacks, and Ukrainians were also assigned to the security force. These formations (as large as 500 men, but frequently smaller) had to guard even the smallest bases—some of which were often only 10–15 kilometers (6–9 miles) from one another.[34] The battalions set up in areas of military administration were established in cooperation with the Wehrmacht, as is seen in instructions issued to the legal and administrative department of Rear Area Army Group South:

> DG IV from Dnipropetrovsk via Pavlohrad to the Donbas region is being upgraded by the SS. By request, the raising of a special Ukrainian police formation of 400 men for overseeing the prisoners of war deployed along the construction zone of Dnipropetrovsk-Bohuslav has been officially approved. This protective force is a special formation with tasks limited to time and place. It is subordinated to the SS; [however] in situations of pressing military interest, the bearer of executive authority has immediate right of disposal. A condition was posed that this police force, upon completion of the construction zone, be subordinated to the commander [of Rear Area Army Group South].[35]

For transport between construction zones, the 17th company of Transport Regiment Speer, Speer's motor pool, was sent to Ukraine.

Overall technical planning for the project, repair work, and maintenance lay with the O.T.—as did responsibility for housing and feeding prisoners and remunerating those workers formally employed by O.T. The O.T. coordinated the work of the various construction and civil engineering companies from the Reich and established how many civilian workers would be necessary at each stage of the project. The task of the Police Security Section and the indigenous police battalions was to guard against partisan attacks and oversee the forced laborers during transfer to and from the camps and throughout the workday. The police formations could receive basic instructions from the chief engineers and specialists in the construction zones, but the latter lacked the authority to enforce orders or discipline the police, not even the indigenous police. Watching over the construction zone inspectors were in turn the regional construction zone inspectors, who had the task of coordinating and mediating between the SS and the O.T. (which was not subordinated to the SS), and who were authorized to take independent action and keep an eye on the project as a whole. They reported to their own supervisors in the Operations Staff on DG IV, where everything came together. When necessary, regional construction zone inspectors intervened to guarantee control farther down the chain of command. They also liaised with local Sipo-SD offices.[36]

For construction expertise, the Nazis turned to the private sector, taking bids (or bribes) and awarding contracts to private companies on

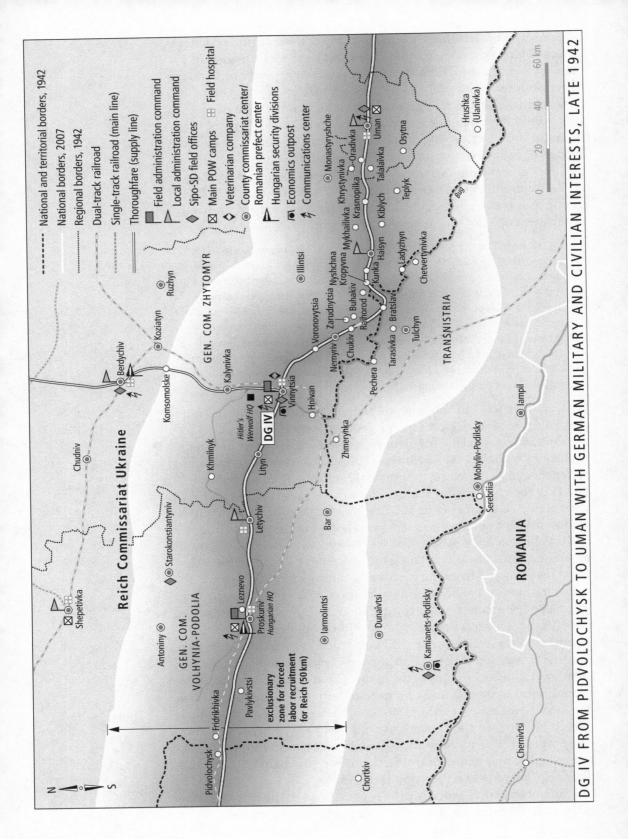

Legend:

- — — — — National and territorial borders, 1942
- ———— National borders, 2007
- ·········· Regional borders, 1942
- ═══════ Dual-track railroad
- ———— Single-track railroad (main line)
- ········· Thoroughfare (supply line)
- ▮ Field administration command
- ▲ Local administration command
- ◆ Sipo-SD field offices
- ⊠ Main POW camps
- ◈ Veterinarian company
- ◉ County commissariat center/ Romanian prefect center
- ▲ Hungarian security divisions
- ■ Economics outpost
- ⚡ Communications center
- ⊞ Field hospital

Reich Commissariat Ukraine

GEN. COM. ZHYTOMYR

GEN. COM. VOLHYNIA-PODOLIA

TRANSNISTRIA

ROMANIA

exclusionary zone for forced labor recruitment for Reich (50 km)

Hitler's Werwolf HQ

DG IV

Hungarian HQ

Pidvolochysk · Fridrikhivka · Pavlykivtsi · Proskuriv · Leznevo · Letychiv · Lityn · Khmilnyk · Komsomolske · Kalynivka · Berdychiv · Koziatyn · Ruzhyn · Chudniv · Starokonstiantyniv · Antoniny · Shepetivka

Chortkiv · Iarmolintsi · Bar · Zhmerynka · Hnivan · Vinnytsia · Voronovytsia · Nemyriv · Chukiv · Zarudnytsia · Buhakiv · Rajhorod · Nyshchna · Kropyvna · Mykhailivka · Khrystynivka · Krasnopilka · Oradivka · Monastyryshche

Kamianets-Podilsky · Dunaivtsi · Tarasivka · Pechera · Bratslav · Tulchyn · Chetvertynivka · Ladyzhyn · Kunka · Haisyn · Kiblych · Talalaivka · Teplyk · Osytna · Uman · Hrushka (Ulanivka)

Mohyliv-Podilsky · Serebriia · Iampil · Chernivtsi

Illintsi · Bug

0 20 40 60 km

N ← S

DG IV FROM PIDVOLOCHYSK TO UMAN WITH GERMAN MILITARY AND CIVILIAN INTERESTS, LATE 1942

200 · Andrej Angrick

the basis of evaluations and cost estimates. Company employees were officially enrolled in the O.T. so they could work in areas under military occupation and were then deployed to construction zones or regional construction zones. More than one company could be based in a construction zone. These companies either worked separate stretches of DG IV or collaborated on the same segment based on the principle of division of labor. For example, the company Kaiser (Hanau) and Ufer (Koblenz) worked together at Teplyk and Kiblych.[37]

The structure of the DG IV project presented thus far should make clear that it was a highly important undertaking for the Germans, thoroughly planned in almost every detail. Its success, however, depended solely on the efficient use of forced labor. Given the large number of Ukrainian forced laborers deported to the Reich and the need for agricultural workers within the RKU, DG IV's builders never had a sufficient numbers of workers at their disposal. This shortage of workers was in turn exacerbated by a tendency to allow groups of workers to be "reduced" by exhaustion and shooting. As a result, forced labor and annihilation were always in conflict with one another.

The Manpower Issue

The actual road work on DG IV—which took place under the filthiest and most hazardous conditions—was carried out by prisoners of war, local civilians, and Jews. By spring 1942, there were 50,000 POWs, 50,000 civilians, and 10,000 Jews working on DG IV. Despite the importance of the thoroughfare, each construction zone inspector had to concern himself with the "procurement" of everything from civilian workers to wooden carts for transporting construction materials. Since the construction zone inspectors did not have access to their "own" pools of local workers, they turned to various offices based near their construction zone: agricultural specialists (Germans in charge of collective farms), mayors (usually Ukrainians, but sometimes ethnic Germans), and commandants of POW camps. Only in this way could the construction zone inspectors pull together the necessary contingents of workers, find the carts, and secure whatever other materials the SS needed for DG IV. The manpower needs were so great that a 50 kilometer (31 mile) exclusion zone was established on either side of DG IV, from which Fritz Sauckel, the general plenipotentiary for the deployment of labor, could not "recruit" workers for the Reich.[38]

As for Jews, they were not used in large numbers on DG IV before spring 1942. The SS and police, in coordination with the Rear Area Army Group South and its military administration commandants, had eradicated almost all of the Jewish communities within the borders of prewar Soviet Ukraine by early 1942. Few Jewish craftsmen were still alive, which meant that in German-occupied central and eastern Ukraine, there could be no resort to Jewish forced labor as had been done in District Galicia in the General Government.[39] Other sources had to be found, starting with Red Army prisoners of war.

Prisoners of War and Non-Jewish Civilians

The first group the SS, O.T., and Wehrmacht counted on was the Soviet prisoners of war; it was believed that they existed in unlimited numbers. Army Group South, on September 19, 1941, issued an order stating that prisoners of war were to be organized in large numbers for road and bridge work—wherever possible in "construction units" consisting of no more than 1,000 men (organized in four companies of 250 men each)—for work solely on "Russian land."[40] The POWs, according to a supplemental order to Adam from December 20, 1941, were to be escorted from their camps to their work sites, or camps were to be set up for them along the road. The number of prisoners of war working on DG IV and DG V were to be listed separately from POWs working on other projects and passed on in monthly reports to the general of the pioneers in Army Group South.[41]

The use of Soviet POWs was considered most desirable for the construction of DG IV. There seemed to be plenty of them; they were rarely locals and so elicited limited sympathy among the local peasants; and there were no Jews among them, as these had been singled out and shot. However, the productivity of prisoners compared to that of German pioneers, who were bound by orders and filled with a sense of duty, was not held in high esteem. As one report from a construction battalion to the commander of 45th Construction Troop put it, the prisoner of war only worked when he "knows supervision is behind him and [he] is spurred on." Furthermore, the Germans considered the POWs to be less intelligent and full of "ill will" toward their captors. So as to boost productivity, it was recommended to use threats of punishment or a return to the POW main camps, which the battalion's scribe knew would conjure up vivid images of death by starvation or sickness. But even this writer could not help but point out a crucial reason for maintaining the policy of exploiting Red Army POWs: Living and work conditions on DG IV were so bad for prisoners put to work outside main camps that, of the 1,052 POWs taken on by this construction battalion, 183 were already dead and 174 were sick.[42] In other words, the threat to return POWs to main camps would probably provide no incentive to work harder.

It was clear that the use of prisoners of war for work on DG IV could meet the high expectations set by the Germans only to a certain extent. It is even possible that the death rate for prisoners of war on DG IV was higher than in POW camps at that time in the war. By spring 1942, just as SS involvement in the DG IV project was getting underway, the DG IV's managers had already "used up" such large numbers of prisoners of war that they had begun to resort to civilians. Using the local field hands posed another problem.

As spring approached, the Germans noted that workers from the surrounding villages would be needed in the fields as well as on DG IV. Due to the long thaw, the streets dried out only rather late in the spring, which in turn led to work delays. Erosion on DG IVc (between Kirovohrad and Kremenchuk) and on DG V had left both supply lines "not yet usable for through traffic" as late as May 1942. It was impossible, however, to hold onto workers for construction and then send them to the fields, since the timeframes for both tasks overlapped. The problem was compounded by the continued presence of Sauckel's forced labor recruiters. In their deliberations over what to do, the German authorities ultimately gave the recruitment of local civilians for DG IV higher priority than that of forced labor for the Reich.[43] Would-be workers outside DG IV's 50-kilometer exclusion zone could decide whether to go with Sauckel's recruiters or stay in Ukraine. Thus competition and chaos ran rampant, as the Nazis competed among themselves for manpower.[44] The decision-making process was more clear-cut for the civilian workers. According to Gieseke, they were skeptical of Sauckel's recruiters and "preferred to work in their own country than go to Germany."[45]

Meanwhile, shortages in construction materials also bedeviled the Germans in spring 1942. These shortages stemmed in part from the poor road conditions and the shortage in manpower to heave the wooden carts still widely used in transporting raw materials. But part of the problem also lay in the greater strategic situation: German troop movements to and from the front in preparation for the summer offensive clogged the roads and kept shipments of raw materials from reaching DG IV camps on time. The field administration command in Zaporizhzhia lamented that, although necessary material was located in the Crimea, it could not be transported where it was wanted.[46] The German civilian administration and the Wehrmacht tried to alleviate the situation by building log roads (thus eliminating the need for gravel) and by restricting civilian use of the main roads (thus forcing the peasants and others to use only sandy roadside trails or to avoid the main roads altogether).[47]

At this point, things began to change to a small extent for that group of workers whose rights counted for nothing in the eyes of the Nazis, a group whose help was desperately needed due to the growth of the DG IV project: Ukraine's surviving Jews. In light of the aforementioned considerations, however, it should not be so surprising that the Germans fell back on using Jews to advance road construction and work in the quarries that provided the sand and gravel needed to give the road a solid foundation.

Jews as Forced Laborers on DG IV

The Germans had begun using Jewish labor in Ukraine in isolated cases as early as September 1941, when Jews, instead of captured Red Army soldiers, were put to work on a stretch of DG IV in Vinnytsia.[48] Something similar had also taken place in Kremenchuk, where the mayor had 1,100 Jews brought to a camp with barracks and employed "several hundred in road work everyday."[49] Such occurrences, however, had their basis in orders from on high.[50] Now, what had evolved on its own in 1941 was to become officially sanctioned practice in 1942. The notes of the field administration command based in Konotop provide an example of what was starting to happen in general throughout the areas under Wehrmacht administration:

> The Jewish question in this area was taken care of in the months of October and November 1941 by the 1st SS Infantry Brigade, which was deployed here. In May 1942, a further 24 Jews were discovered in the town of Bilopillia, whose housing in mass accommodations and later sending away to forced labor was authorized.[51]

This formulation "sending away" was in no way a euphemism for murder. Those 24 Jews who had survived the 1941 massacres were indeed transferred for forced labor. The Germans needed them. The problem was where to find them. Since the "Final Solution" in these parts of Ukraine had been carried out so thoroughly between August 1941 and May 1942, there had been no need for ghettos in central and eastern Ukraine. The few ghettos that were created in these parts of Ukraine were not very large. Where DG IV was concerned, the situation in central Ukraine stood in stark contrast to the situation in eastern Galicia, where hundreds of thousands of Jews were still alive at this time. While Katzmann could still draw on this pool of potential forced laborers for his stretch of DG IV, Prützmann found himself with a limited number of Jews in the areas surrounding the supply line.

Of the towns along DG IV, Uman provided Prützmann with the largest contingent of local Jews. The selection process here took place in conjunction with the liquidation of town's Jewish quarter in May 1942. The ghetto was sealed and the inhabitants told to gather at a given assembly point. There the men, women, and children were divided up according to lists prepared in advance. Most were taken away by truck; some left town on foot. After the trucks departed, the ghetto was combed for hidden Jews. Anybody caught trying to flee was to be shot. A few kilometers outside of Uman, the Germans unloaded the Jews in the woods, where those who were young and fit for work were separated from the rest. It is unclear whether this was a new selection or a roll call to make sure none had fled. Those deemed fit for work were transported to DG IV camps within Construction Zone Haisyn, while the rest were then shot by Ukrainian and Lithuanian policemen. Members of the 2nd Company of the Police Security Section are also said to have taken part in the massacre. This shooting was organized by Xaver Schnöller, the inspector for Construction Zone Uman. Schnöller, known to his victims as the "King of Uman," admitted his role in the massacre years later, but claimed that he was following Stroop's orders, which, given the size of the operation, is plausible.[52] The liquidation of the ghettos in Vinnytsia, Letychiv, Nemyriv, and Teplyk and the selection and transfer of Jews deemed fit for work to DG IV camps followed a similar pattern. Jews from more far-flung locations were also added to the camps.[53]

These small groups of selected Jewish forced laborers could in no way meet the Germans' manpower needs on DG IV. The SS officers overseeing the project thus began looking for regions where the "Final Solution" had yet to murder all the local Jews. They hoped to have surviving Jews transferred from such regions to DG IV. An example of this process was the dispatch of 500 Jews from Lviv to Odessa, where they were used as mechanics from January to June 1942. The authorities in Galicia insisted on the return of these specialists, and at the end of June 1942, these Jews began their long journey back to Lviv. Upon reaching Zhytomyr, however, they were held up for several days, while German officials tried unsuccessfully to seize them for DG IV.[54] Obtaining Galician Jews for work on DG IV outside of the General Government also failed to solve the problem. Although DG IV was the most important German construction project in Ukraine, it was not the only one needing Jewish labor. There was still the railroad bridge at the mouth of the Southern Buh River, where some 1,000 Jews from the forced labor camp in Trykhaty worked,[55] and General Government officials had their own projects requiring Jewish labor.

The SS officials on DG IV even went so far as to inquire formally at Sipo and SD outposts and police stations throughout Ukraine in their search for Jewish forced laborers. The inspector for Regional Construction Zone Vinnytsia, Theobald Thier, made a successful attempt in this regard, as can be seen from a telex of August 17, 1942, when Hermann Ling reported a successful recruitment from the area around Kamianets-Podilsky:

> Through personal consultation with the SD outpost in Kamianets-Podilsky and the responsible county commissars, [I] have secured 500 Jews from Kamianets-Podilsky, 600 Jews from Dunaïvtsi, 800 Jews from Bar, 400 Jews from Iarmolyntsi for DG IV's purposes. The inspector for DG IV in Vinnytsia, SS Senior Colonel[56] Thier, assumes transport and employment. I was forced to realize, however, that without my intervention these Jews would have been executed; for example, executions in Dunaïvtsi County and Bar had already been prepared. I ask that [you] work toward seeing to it that in the future in the counties bordering DG IV all Jews still fit for work are turned over to DG IV and no longer executed.[57]

The Sipo-SD headquarters for General Commissariat Volhynia-Podolia (where Kamianets-Podilsky was located) disapproved of these instructions, for they contravened standing orders. Ling's recommendation prompted the following comment, which also amounted to a rebuke of his colleagues in Kamianets-Podilsky:

I note here that the ordered resettlements of the Jews are to be carried out further according to plan and without disruption. The timely separation of Jews fit for work for DG IV is a matter [at least one word is missing here] SS Major Ling. Furthermore, all of the county commissars were informed from here some time ago about the need for Jews for labor for DG IV.[58]

Sipo-SD headquarters in Volhynia-Podolia went along with Ling's arrangements, but Ling had to make his selections quickly. The Sipo and SD commandos were not going to delay shootings on his behalf.

Indeed, just two weeks later, Paul Dargel, the head of the RKU administration's political department, declared at a gathering of county commissars in Lutsk that, with regard to Jewish actions, "100-percent solutions are to be carried out in principle." Exceptions were to be made only for specialists, who, after a two-month transition period following each large-scale action, also had to "disappear."[59] Despite the need for manpower on DG IV and despite the special powers of the SSPF-designates overseeing the project, not enough Jews could be provided for DG IV—not least because other Nazi agencies (including the Sipo and SD)—refused to cooperate.

To assume that the Jews Ling secured for DG IV automatically had a better chance of surviving is but wishful thinking. They too—at least those 300 whose fates can be somewhat reconstructed—faced near certain death, ending up as forced laborers at Leznevo, where the Germans had set up a camp for Jews in spring 1942. There the O.T. maintained an office on the grounds of a large collective farm, while a consortium of companies, Meister-Jehle-Grimminger-Stork, put the Jews to work in road construction. Several indigenous police units and parts of the 1st company of the Police Security Section watched over them.

Although relatively healthy Jews fit for work were deported to Leznevo, several of them quickly contracted typhus. Initially, they were sent to a still functioning Jewish hospital in Proskuriv. A little while later, a truck arrived outside the hospital. Clad only in shirts, these ailing Jews were loaded into the back of the truck, driven to a sand pit, dumped there, and shot by Lithuanian policemen.[60] That autumn, Lithuanian auxiliaries, acting in the presence of German policemen, murdered another 80–100 Jewish prisoners, men and women alike. Siegfried Scherer of the Police Security Section is believed to have phoned in the order for the shooting. Other Jews were shot while "trying to escape" or carrying out their tasks. For example, an older Jew was murdered as he struggled with a road roller.[61] How many prisoners died from hunger, exhaustion, or sickness is unknown, as is the date the Leznevo camp was disbanded. The circumstances surrounding the fate of the Jews from the area around Kamianets-Podilsky were repeated in many other camps.

Even before Dargel's meeting with the county commissars, the SS inspectors on DG IV were starting to realize that they were not going to find an adequate number of Jewish workers from within the German-run territories. The unrelenting destruction of Jewish life in District

Galicia and General Commissariat Volhynia-Podolia had priority over all economic considerations, even those of the SS.[62] In their search for a way out of the dilemma of needing manpower but being unable to find it in the required numbers, SS officers on DG IV settled on a new plan. Franz Christoffel, a former SS officer and inspector of Construction Zone Haisyn, claimed after the war that he came up with an idea in August 1942, which was approved by Gieseke and the inspector for Regional Construction Zone Vinnytsia: the "recruitment" of Jewish forced laborers from Transnistria, that part of Ukraine under Romanian rule.[63] It may have seemed the obvious thing to do for the perpetrators, but in hindsight, it is a curious and grotesque chapter in the Shoah's history.

Despite a policy of malign neglect toward the Jews located in Transnistria—whether Jews native to the region or deportees from Bukovina and Bessarabia—the Romanians in this part of Ukraine still had by the summer of 1942 a much larger reservoir of Jewish forced laborers than their German allies along DG IV—even if one considers only the relatively small part of the Jewish population that was living and working in camps along the Transnistria-RKU border.[64] The Jews in these camps were the ones that Christoffel and his "recruiters" wanted to convince to volunteer for transfer to the German side of the Southern Buh.

Around mid-August, Christoffel and his men visited the camps at Ladyzhyn and Chetvertynivka as well as a camp known to its inmates as "the quarry." According to Matatias Carp, a survivor, the O.T. discussed the recruitment plan with the Rumanian prefect for Tulchyn County in advance. A few days later, on August 19, 1942, around 3,000 prisoners followed Christoffel and his team out of Transnistria.[65] There are several reasons these Jews fell for Christoffel's promises. Many of them had arrived in the Ladyzhyn area only in July. They had been deported from Serebriia (near Mohyliv-Podilsky) and Chernivtsi and sent to the quarries without any provisions.[66] Measured against their experience with Romanians to that point, these Jews found the Germans rather friendly and obliging. They seemed to care about the Jews' well-being. The Germans promised the Jews provisions, accommodations, and even homes for the young and the infirm. That the SS and police, as well as the Wehrmacht, had committed heinous crimes receded into the background.[67]

These Jews quickly learned that they had been duped. Upon leaving the Romanian camps, they were mistreated and beaten along the road to Ladyzhyn. Not all of the "recruits" were allowed to cross the Southern Buh on the ferry; some of the men were forced to swim to the RKU. After they arrived in German-administered territory, they were then searched for anything of value. Finally, the disillusioned souls were distributed to camps at Nemyriv, Mykhailivka, Bratslav, Teplyk, Chukiv, and Krasnopilka.[68] Jews from Transnistria were also transferred to the camps at Osytna and Kunka.[69]

In mid-September 1942, 550 Jews—250 locals and 300 deportees—

were "picked up" in Ladyzhyn and brought to DG IV camps near Krasnopilka. In November, an additional 500 Jews from Pechera crossed the Southern Buh. Another 600 Jews from the same town followed in May 1943.[70] According to Arnold Daghani, who was transferred to the RKU from Transnistria for the DG IV project and who managed to keep a diary, the SS also earned money by renting out "their" Jews as workers; after all, the SS enjoyed a kind of monopoly over this group of victims as opposed to the POWs and non-Jewish civilians. The road construction companies paid the SS 16 pfennig per prisoner per day.[71]

Other transfers followed with the approval of the Tulchyn County prefect, but some of these had nothing to do with forced labor on DG IV. Rather, they solely provided victims for murder.[72] In September 1942, for example, around 150 Jewish girls aged 14–20 were turned over to camp commandant Hans Rucker by his Romanian counterpart in Pechera. The Germans claimed the girls were needed as nurses in Vinnytsia, but they never arrived. They were abused in a small forest between Bar and Vinnytsia, probably raped, and finally shot. Only one, a girl by the name of Frida Koffler, survived, saved by a man in uniform.[73]

Life and Death in DG IV Camps

Assuming Jewish workers could be found, and assuming they survived the abuse inflicted on them during transfer, they then had to face life in the camps. Upon their arrival in DG IV camps, Jews were assigned the most rudimentary accommodations. The Germans seldom bothered to find proper structures. Sometimes it would be a school, as in Teplyk, or a warehouse, as in Krasnopilka. In Nyshcha Kropyvna, Tarasivka and Naraïvka, Jews were kept in barns. Stalls were used in Kunka and Oradivka.[74] Some of the camps existed for a few months, others for more than a year. In the eyes of the SS, the importance of DG IV and with it the justification for keeping Jewish forced laborers alive were often related to the military situation and the location of the eastern front. Thus, some camps lasted until December 1943.

Survivor Daghani described how shocked he and his colleagues were upon arriving at Mykhailivka camp—two stalls of a former collective farm—and their first encounter with the emaciated, ragged, and dehumanized Jews they found there. At the behest of the Jewish camp leader, separate space was created for the new arrivals who were afraid of contracting diseases or catching lice from the others. Despite their best efforts, the new arrivals were unable to prevent their demise. Daily rations at Mykhailivka consisted of unsalted pea soup mixed with a musty gruel. After the first eight or nine days, the newcomers were given three-quarters of a loaf of bread per person. Another witness spoke of 215 grams (7.5 oz.) of bread, 70 grams (2.4 oz.) unpeeled peas, 260 grams (9 oz.) potatoes, and 20 grams (0.7 oz.) meat, none of which was truly edible. The prisoners were forced—although it was expressly forbidden—to trade with the local peasants, the watchmen, or the Germans themselves for food, assuming one had anything that was worth trading after being searched on the Transnistria-RKU border. Soon the new arrivals were also emaciated. Once well-mannered, disciplined people succumbed to hunger and stole bread from their neighbors, even from good friends.[75] Mykhailivka stands as an example of the other DG IV camps, but it should be remembered that food and shelter were usually the responsibility of the private civil engineering and construction companies—not the SS.[76]

Most of the work was done on the road itself or in the quarries or sand pits, where construction material for DG IV was mined. For the actual widening of the road, which was to be 8 meters (ca. 26 feet) wide, some of the workers had to carry the gravel, while others had to transport the construction material and tools to the place of work by pulling them in wooden carts. The road also had to be protected from the elements, which meant digging drainage ditches, removing snow, and in some cases, building walls to keep out snowdrifts. Those in the quarries were worst off. They had to produce gravel by breaking up larger stones. This was the hardest form of physical labor, involving the swinging of picks and sledgehammers the entire day. Others had to dig pebbles and sand. Those Jews put to work in and around the camps as mechanics, cleaning personnel, workshop assistants, and field hands (DG IV grew some of its own produce) could consider themselves lucky. Not only could they procure additional food, they gleaned bits of information such as the news of the German defeat at Stalingrad, the Warsaw Ghetto Uprising, or the approach of the Red Army.[77]

For most prisoners, above all those on DG IV itself or in the quarries, hard labor combined with exposure, malnutrition, and physical and mental torture, brought about a quick demise. Those who kept their wits (loss of which could mean shooting on the spot) watched their bodies waste away and, with that, their sense of individuality. Many died of exhaustion or sickness, while the rest simply endured, eking out a miserable existence as best they could. A significant number were murdered by Germans indulging in sadistic hazing or were shot for some infringement of camp rules. Those who tried to flee were also killed.[78] The frequency of such cases makes it impossible to mention all of them here. Postwar criminal investigations into DG IV are filled with examples, such as the killing of three infants in Krasnopilka and the murder of a Jewish couple and, on a separate occasion, of ten female prisoners in Naraïvka, which was ordered to enforce camp discipline. Sometimes a camp's Jewish workers were shot after a construction zone was finished. They were so "used up" that the Germans felt it pointless to transfer them to another zone.

The top SS officers on DG IV took this "using up" of prisoners into consideration in their planning, ordering the routine killing of the exhausted and sick. According to Christoffel, whose postwar testimonies are to be read with great care,[79] Prützmann, in consultation with Gieseke, ordered the regular liquidation of those no longer fit for work.

Table 5.1. Documented Selections and Shootings in DG IV Camps in Central Ukraine

Camp	Date	Victims	Pretext	Perpetrators
Fridrikhivka[80]	Late summer 1942	300–400 Jews	Closing of camp	Unknown
Pavlykivtsi[81]	Late summer 1942	Circa 400 Jews	Possibly closing of camp	Unknown
Letychiv[82]	Autumn 1942	Unknown	Selection of least able to work, possibly typhus outbreak	Construction zone chief, Lithuanian auxiliaries, and Sipo-SD post in Starokonstiantyniv
Lityn[83]	Summer 1942	7–10 Jews	Exhaustion	Lithuanian auxiliaries, SS, and possibly SD; Police Security Section DG IV
Hnivan[84]	Summer 1942	At least 50 Jews	Unknown	Police Security Section DG IV, local rural police, and Lithuanian auxiliaries
Vinnytsia[85]	mid-summer 1942	Undetermined number of Jews	Illness; possibly typhus-related	Police Security Section DG IV, Ukrainian auxiliaries, unknown SS officer
Nemyriv	June 1942	Undetermined number of Jews, primarily women, children, and unhealthy individuals	Exhaustion	Camp commandant, mobile squad, and Lithuanian auxiliaries
Nemyriv	September 14, 1942	Undetermined number of Jewish women, elderly people, and children as well as those who were sick	Victims were determined to be "dispensible"	Unknown
Nemyriv[86]	May 1943	180 prisoners	Closing of camp	Unknown
Chukiv[87]	February 1943	Jews from camps at Berezivka, Bratslav, Buhakiv, and Zarudnytsi	Probable consolidation of workers after closure of camp or arrival of Jews from Transnistria	SS auxiliaries, auxiliaries, and camp commandants
Raihorod	Summer 1942	Undetermined number of Jews under 16 and over 40	Unknown	Most likely ordered by construction zone chief
Raihorod[88]	December 28, 1942	Unknown number of Jews	Typhus	Unknown
Nyshcha Kropyvna[89]	Autumn 1942	200–300 Jewish women, children, and sick people	Victims deemed too weak or sick for hard labor	Unknown
Haisyn	October 14, 1942	250 Jewish women, children, and sick people	Victims deemed too weak or sick for hard labor	Unknown
Haisyn[90]	November 6, 1942	1,000 Jews	Probably part of liquidations taking place in RKU at the time	Unknown
Tarasivka[91]	December 10, 1943	400–450 Jews, mostly from Transnistria	Closing of camp	Unknown

Camp	Date	Victims	Pretext	Perpetrators
Mykhailivka	August 19, 1942	16 people	Routine selection after arrival of fresh workers	Unknown
Mykhailivka	Winter 1942–43	107 people	Lack of shelter	Unknown
Mykhailivka[92]	April 26, 1943	55 people	Reduction of workers considered superfluous	Unknown
Krasnopilka[93]	August 1943	Unknown	Probably routine liquidation of sick workers	SS commando and Lithuanian auxiliaries
Naraïvka[94]	September 21, 1941, Yom Kippur	23 sick and elderly people and children	Victims deemed too weak or sick for hard labor	Unknown
Kiblych[95]	December 1942	Unknown number of Jews	Unknown	Camp commandant
Teplyk[96]	September 1941	10–12 children and ill workers	Victims deemed too weak or sick for hard labor	Mobile commando
Talalaïvka[97]	December 1943	Undetermined number of Jews	Closing of camp	German police
Oradivka[98]	December 17, 1943	92 prisoners	Closing of camp	Unknown
Osytna	September 1942, possibly Yom Kippur	Undetermined number of newly arrived Romanian Jews	Victims deemed too weak or sick for hard labor	Unknown
Osytna[99]	December 1942	27 people	Typhus outbreak	Ukrainian guards and unknown commando

Christoffel said he received such orders in writing from Ludolf von Alvensleben, then inspector for Regional Construction Zone Vinnytsia, but he could not say for sure whether this was in summer or autumn 1942.[100] The frequency of these shootings suggests that they must have been ordered from on high.[101]

German prosecutors in Lübeck, in an extensive postwar investigation, documented several shootings that took place in the camps along DG IV in central Ukraine. Their findings, however, are incomplete. By no means could they uncover every crime that occurred along this road, and in many cases, they were unable to determine the set of circumstances surrounding each incident, the number of victims, or the exact perpetrators.[102] Table 5.1 provides the basic data concerning the best-documented selections and killings that took place along the 400 kilometers (roughly 245 miles) between Pidvolochysk and Uman.[103]

Prützmann's Construction Empire Meets Its End

By early 1943, according to the Lübeck prosecutors, there were "only" 70,000 people involved in the construction of DG IV, which would effectively mean a decline of 40,000 workers since the summer of 1942.[104] As losses were generally replaced, this implies an even higher number of

Shooting of Jews in Khrystynivka, just off Thoroughfare IV. This kind of operation was carried out repeatedly near the various camps and ghettos. The shooter is most likely from the Order Police. This photo was intercepted by a Polish Home Army cell controlling German military mail. USHMM, courtesy of Archiwum Akt Nowych, Warsaw.

victims. The results of this investigation, however, contradict a message Prützmann sent Himmler on June 15, 1943, in which he emphasized that he had 140,000 people working on DG IV "in addition to very few German workers" and 12,000 local policemen. Even assuming Prützmann was trying to exaggerate his "achievements," the contemporary document still seems more credible.[105] This suggests that DG IV and the question of supplies and reinforcements had grown more important. This document also indicates that as late as June 1943 Prützmann continued to set very ambitious goals for himself. He still associated the construction of "railways, bridges, arms factories, mineshaft railways, [military] positions, etc." with "the planned deployment" on DG IV. But this was before the Germans lost the battle of Kursk and before the Soviets launched their subsequent summer offensive.

During the spring of 1943, Prützmann's most immediate threat came from other powerful figures in the SS. Exploiting the opportunity posed by partisan attacks on the supply lines, Erich von dem Bach-Zelewski, in his capacity as chief of German anti-partisan forces, began intriguing against Prützmann in an attempt to take over DG IV. Bach, who had the Himmler's permission to negotiate on his own where armaments were concerned, wanted to forge an alliance with Speer and Professor Walter Brugmann, the chief of O.T. operations in the southern Soviet Union. This was rather typical of Bach, who in the summer of 1942—after the establishment of SS and police offices in the occupied eastern territories—involved himself in negotiations with Wehrmacht authorities about the seizure of factories. With regard to DG IV, Prützmann prevented Bach from intervening and took the matter to Himmler. Prützmann reminded the Reichsführer-SS that, during the Easter holidays that year, they had discussed having some unspecified interests within Speer's arms programs put at the disposal of the Waffen-SS as a means of returning a favor for SS cooperation in O.T. projects. Prützmann, worried about the fruits of his labor and determined to put an end to Bach's high-handedness, felt DG IV should be one of those programs.[106]

This internal SS conflict was to be of little consequence for DG IV. With the Red Army's successes in July and, to a lesser extent, the reluctance of Romanian leaders to replace troops lost at Stalingrad, the Third Reich had been forced onto the defensive. Of course supplies would have to keep rolling, if only for defensive purposes.[107] However, in the wake of the summer battles, DG IV construction zones east of the Dniepr soon came under fire, which meant that detours had to be built, and this necessity in turn diverted human resources and materiel. In one case, 800 workers were deployed for five weeks behind the lines of the 15th Air Force Field Division to build a replacement road.[108] Workers were not the only resource in dispute.

In early July 1943, Rear Area Army Group South informed Prützmann that, according to another directive from Bach, the protection of all thoroughfares was to become the Wehrmacht's responsibility, and that the SS was to secure only those structures that were still under construction, meaning primarily bridges. Upon completion, these structures were to be handed over to the Wehrmacht as well. Adolf von Bomhard, commander of the Order Police in the RKU, confirmed Bach's directive on Prützmann's behalf and promised the transfer of those structures—an indication of Prützmann's waning influence.[109]

By August, the military situation was such that the Germans began to evacuate entire regions. In September, as preparations for giving up the area between Kremenchuk and Dnipropetrovsk were under way, Himmler issued a special order stating that the SS and police were to be "particularly active" in supporting "the evacuation work of the Wehrmacht" and its "movement toward the west."[110] The Operations Staff on DG IV was disbanded, and Gieseke together with the Police Security Section and a number of Cossack and Ukrainian police battalions were merged into a regiment and sent to Volhynia in January and February 1944.[111] As the Red Army closed in on Kirovohrad and Kryvy Rih that December, the last camps—such as Talalaïvka, Oradivka, and Tarasivka—were liquidated.

Altogether, according to Kaienburg, at least 25,000 Jewish forced laborers died in the Ukrainian DG IV camps outside Galicia.[112] A few fortunate Jewish prisoners survived DG IV and were transferred west. Their suffering continued until war's end, but they were no longer captives of the DG IV project.

Conclusion

If one looks back at the DG IV camps as more than a special case in the evolution of the "Final Solution" and examines the Wannsee Protocol more closely, Heydrich does not necessarily appear an all-powerful executioner acting on the basis of Göring's authority. It is worth noting that Heydrich himself sent copies of Göring's letter commissioning him with the "Final Solution" to his top Sipo-SD commanders in the field only on January 25, 1942. He emphasized in an accompanying message that he had been entrusted with "the necessary *preparations* for a complete solution to the Jewish question within the German area of influence in Europe with regard to organizational, practical, and materiel matters" and added that the *preparatory* work had begun.[113] What most researchers have interpreted as a demonstration of his omnipotence in matters of mass murder may well be the actions of an official charged with informing others, somebody abetting other senior officials in the German state. Primary responsibility for the crimes on DG IV lies with Prützmann and the other high-ranking SS officers who worked on the thoroughfare, many of whom rose to become HSSPF or SSPF (quite possibly because they proved themselves on DG IV). The role of Heydrich's RSHA and its personnel in this project seems remarkably limited. It may even be that the postwar testimonies of Gestapo chiefs contained a bit more than a grain of truth when they suggested, independent of one another, that until late October 1941 they thought the deportation of the German Jews to the east was—at least initially—indeed for forced labor.[114]

Heydrich may have wanted to appear to the ministerial representatives gathered at Wannsee as the man in charge of such an enormously important administrative task as the "Jewish problem," but it should also be clear that Himmler saw certain ministries and agencies as secondary in importance. Institutional jurisdictions had long since been settled through official channels and a well-ordered division of ministerial authority. Instead, Himmler relied on the principle of personality and like-minded men of action to carry out his orders. While Heydrich called conferences with high-ranking officials to assert his intentions, Himmler held numerous face-to-face meetings with his handpicked representatives, such as the HSSPF. It is hoped that future researchers examining the decision-making process in the murder of the Soviet Jews and the German Jews deported to the east will look more closely at the history of forced labor on major Nazi imperial projects such as road building, and the role of regional SSPF leaders and private industry situated at key Nazi outposts in Ukraine.[115]

Notes

1. Undated protocol of the Wannsee Conference, printed in *Akten zur deutschen Auswärtigen Politik, Serie E, Band I* (Göttingen: Vandenhoeck and Ruprecht, 1969), pp. 267–275. Quote, p. 271.

2. Ibid.

3. See Wolfgang Scheffler and Helge Grabitz, "Die Wannsee-Konferenz. Ihre Bedeutung in der Geschichte des nationalsozialistischen Völkermordes" in *Acta Universitatis Wratislaviensis*, no. 1715. *Studia nad Faszyzmen i Zbrodniami Hitlerowskimi*, XVIII (1995), pp. 197–219, here p. 213; Hermann Kaienburg, "Jüdische Arbeitslager an der 'Strasse der SS,'" in *Zeitschrift für Sozialgeschichte des 20. und 21. Jahrhunderts*, Vol. 11, no. 1 (1996), pp. 13–39, here pp. 13f. Jan Erik Schulte has also made the connection between Jewish forced labor and the Wannsee Conference, but puts it in the context of a meeting of SS main office chiefs on January 14, 1942; Jan Erik Schulte, *Zwangsarbeit und Vernichtung: Das Wirtschaftsimperium der SS. Oswald Pohl und das SS-Wirtschafts-Verwaltungshauptamt 1933–1945* (Paderborn: Schöningh, 2001), pp. 356–360.

4. Richard Breitman, *Official Secrets: What the Nazis Planned, What the British and Americans Knew* (New York: Hill and Wang, 1998), p. 92.

5. Christian Gerlach, "Die Wannsee-Konferenz, das Schicksal der deutschen Juden und Hitlers politische Grundsatzentscheidung alle Juden Europas zu ermorden," in Christian Gerlach, *Krieg, Ernährung Völkermord: Forschungen zur deutschen Vernichtungspolitik im Zweiten Weltkrieg* (Hamburg: Hamburger Edition, 1998), pp. 85–166, here pp. 94f.

6. On the Kam'ianets'–Podil's'kyi massacre, see Klaus-Michael Mallmann, "Der qualitative Sprung im Vernichtungsprozess. Das Massaker von Kamenez-Podolsk Ende August 1941," in *Jahrbuch für Antisemitismusforschung*, 10 (2001), pp. 239–264.

7. Andrej Angrick, Martina Voigt, Silke Ammerschubert, and Peter Klein, "Da hätte man schon ein Tagebuch führen müssen," in *Die Normalität des Verbrechens*, Helge Grabitz, Klaus Bästlein, and Johannes Tuchel, eds. (Berlin: Edition Hentrich, 1994), pp. 325–385. Pages 331–340 describe Himmler's efforts to accelerate the shooting of Jews in Rear Area Army Group Center. In addition to Himmler, the three HSSPFs for the Soviet campaign and Order Police Chief Kurt Daluege—not Heydrich—helped prepare the mobile units for their "operation against Jews." Representative for other units is the "swearing-in ceremony" of Police Battalion 307 in Brest by Daluege and HSSPF Center Erich von dem Bach-Zelewski. See also Zentrale Stelle der Landesjustizverwaltungen (Central Agency for State Justice Administration, ZStL), Ludwigsburg, 204 AR-Z 82/61, Bd. 1, Aussage Friedrich Stüve, p. 131, and Bd. 3, Aussage Max Kayser, p. 471, and Aussage Kuno Kempcke, pp. 522 and 524.

8. This may have also led historians to focus for decades on Hitler, Himmler, and Heydrich and neglect this aspect of the murder of Soviet Jewry. Prützmann took over as HSSPF Russia South on November 1, 1941.

9. On Upper Silesia, see Gruner and Sybille Steinbacher, *Musterstadt Auschwitz, Germanisierungspolitik und Judenmord in Ostoberschliesien* (Munich: Saur, 2000), pp. 138–153 and 275–278. For Galicia, see Dieter Pohl, *Nationalsozialistische Judenverfolgung in Ostgalizien 1941–1944: Organisation und Durchführung eines staatlichen Massenverbrechens* (Munich: Oldenburg, 1996), and Thomas Sandkühler, *"Endlösung" in Galizien: Der Judenmord in Ostpolen und die Rettungsinitiativen von Berthold Beitz 1941–1944* (Bonn: Dietz, 1996). For Zhytomyr see Wendy Lower, *Nazi Empire-Building and the Holocaust in Ukraine,* (Chapel Hill: Univ. of North Carolina Press, 2005), pp. 143–150.

10. ZStL, 204 AR-Z 20/63, Bd. 1, Aussage Walter Gieseke, p. 18.

11. Pohl, *Nationalsozialistische Judenverfolgung in Ostgalizien*, p. 171. By early

1943, Organization Schmelt controlled over 50,000 Jews and was in terms of the number of Jewish forced laborers similar to DG IV in Ukraine; Wolf Gruner, "Juden bauen die 'Strassen des Führers': Zwangsarbeit und Zwangsarbeitslager für nichtdeutsche Juden im Altreich 1940–1943/44," *Zeitschrift für Geschichtswissenschaft,* 44 (1996), no. 9, pp. 789–808.

12. Bundesarchiv-Militärarchiv (BA-MA), Freiburg, RW41/1, Anlage zu Wehrmachtbefehlshaber der Ukraine, Monatsbericht für Januar 1942, Wegweiser für den Bereich des Wehrmachtbefehlshabers Ukraine (mit Übersichtsskizze), February 4, 1942.

13. ZStL, 213 AR-Z 20/63, Bd. 17, Verfügung der StA Lübeck (*Verfügung*), May 26, 1970, pp. 80f.; Franz W. Seidler, *Die Organisation Todt: Bauen für Staat und Wehrmacht 1938–1945* (Koblenz: Bernard & Graefe, 1987), pp. 91f.; Horst Rohde, *Das deutsche Wehrmachttransportwesen im Zweiten Weltkrieg. Entstehung—Organisation—Aufgaben* (Stuttgart: DVA, 1971), pp. 102f. and 220. In addition to DG IV and DG V, the less important DG VII also traversed the RKU, running from the General Government–RKU border at Brest via Kobryn to Bereza Kartuska, near the border with Reich Commissariat Ostland. Regarding Jewish forced labor in the O.T. camps—omitted in Seidler—and the supply lines in the northern part of the occupied Soviet Union, see Bella Guttermann, "Jews in the Service of Organisation Todt in the Occupied Soviet Territories October 1941–March 1942," in *Yad Vashem Studies,* XXIX (2001), pp. 65–107, especially pp. 89–98.

14. BA-MA, Film WF-01/15885, Frames 5882–5887, KTB Wi Rü Amt/Stab, Besprechung Amtschef [Gen. Georg Thomas] mit Gen. Lt. [Wilhelm] Schubert [Chef Wirtschaftsstab Ost], Gen. Weygand [Wirtschaftsinspekteur Mitte Gen. Lt. Wolfgang Weigand], Gen. Lt. [Hans] Leykauf [Rüstungsinspekteur Ukraine], Gen. Lt. Stieler v. Heidekamp [Wirtschaftsinspekteur Süd Gen. Lt. Hans Stieler von Heydekampf], V.-Adm. [Heinrich] Ancker [Wirtschaftsinspekteur Nord], Gen. Maj. [Hans] Nagel [Inspekteur des Wirtschaftsstabes Ost], Oberst Jansen [Stab Wirtschafts- und Rüstungsamt], July 31, 1941.

15. BA-MA, RH 24–14/59, Panzergruppe 1, Ia, Einzelanordnung Nr.16, September 26, 1941. This order was originally issued on September 12, 1941, but apparently required two weeks to reach troops in the field.

16. Bundesarchiv-Berlin (BA-B), R 58/217, Ereignismeldung UdSSR Nr. 86, September 17, 1941, emphasis in the original. Cf. Sandkühler, *"Endlösung" in Galizien,* p. 134. In contrast to Sandkühler, I do not see Einsatzgruppe C's recommendation as limited to the General Government with an eye to further eastward expansion but as a reference to all of Ukraine and other parts of the southern Soviet Union.

17. Sandkühler, *"Endlösung" in Galizien,* p. 142.

18. Nuremberg Document L-18, [Bericht des] Der SS-u. Polizeiführer im Distrikt Galizien, Betr.: Lösung der Judenfrage in Galizien, June 30, 1943, excerpted in *Der Prozess gegen die Hauptkriegsverbrecher vor dem internationalen Militärgerichtshof,* Blue Series, Bd. 37 (Nuremberg, 1947–1949), pp. 391–431.

19. Ibid. According to Katzmann, 15 camps were set up for the DG IV project. Pohl, supported by the Stuttgart Prosecutor's Office, has found 30 camps and sub-camps in all, but only 15 camps in spring 1942 (with two unrelated to DG IV). This would mean that Katzmann's report was based on old information or referred only to spring 1942. See also Pohl, *Nationalsozialistische Judenverfolgung in Ostgalizien,* pp. 169f. and 338–342, and ZStL, 202 AR-Z 294/59, Bd. 19, Verzeichnis der Zwangsarbeiter des SSPF im Distrikt Galizien 1941–1943 Raum Lemberg und Tarnopol mit sämtlichen Lagern der Durchgangsstrasse 4 (DG 4), Sonderheft 4, pp. 4,124–4,200.

20. *Der Dienstkalender Heinrich Himmlers 1941/42,* Peter Witte et al., eds. (Hamburg: Christians, 1999), p. 298; Rudolf Lehmann, *Die Leibstandarte,* Vol. II (Coburg: Nation Europa Verlag, 1995), pp. 276f.

21. Peter Strassner, *Europäische Freiwillige. Die Geschichte der 5. SS-Panzer-division Wiking* (Osnabrück: Munin, 1968), p. 104.

22. *Dienstkalender Heinrich Himmlers*, p. 299.

23. Ibid., p. 314. Reichenau was entrusted with the command of Army Group South on December 1, 1941, after Gerd von Rundstedt failed both to achieve his objectives and to prevent the setback at Rostov. That the supply problem, as well as Hitler's unreasonable demands, contributed to the debacle was not lost on Reichenau. As a result, the rapid expansion of DG IV became a high priority for him, even if it meant enlisting Himmler's support.

24. Kazimierz Moczarski, *Gespräche mit dem Henker: Das Leben des SS-Gruppenführers und Generalleutnants der Polizei Jürgen Stroop aufgezeichnet im Mokotów-Gefängnis zu Warschau* (Düsseldorf: Droste, 1978), p. 162. Stroop said that he was summoned to Himmler to discuss the recruitment of ethnic Germans; ibid., pp. 160f. The meeting Stroop had in mind took place at the end of December 1941. Himmler met with Reichenau and Prützmann on December 27, and two days later, back in Berlin, phoned SS Lt. Gen. Hans Jüttner, chief of staff in the SS Command Main Office, to discuss the conscription of ethnic Germans, *Dienstkalender Heinrich Himmlers*, pp. 299f.

25. Public Record Office (PRO), London, HW 16/6, German Police Summaries, December 16, 1941–January 15, 1942, p. 11, Himmler to Prützmann, January 11 and January 12, 1942. I thank Steven Tyas for this information. See also *Dienstkalender Heinrich Himmlers*, p. 314.

26. PRO, HW 16/6, German Police Summaries, January 15, 1942–February 15, 1942, p. 10, Himmler to Prützmann, January 18, 1942. See also *Dienstkalender Heinrich Himmlers*, p. 314.

27. Field Marshal Fedor von Bock, *Zwischen Pflicht und Verweigerung. Das Kriegstagebuch*, Klaus Gerbert, ed. (Munich and Berlin: Herbig, 1995), pp. 362–365.

28. BA-Berlin, Berlin Document Center, SS Officer File Hans-Adolf Prützmann. Quote from *Dienstkalender Heinrich Himmlers*, p. 339. Cf. *Verfügung*, pp. 120–122.

29. *Dienstkalender Heinrich Himmlers*, p. 355; BA-B, NS 19/3961, p. 10, Dienstkalender Brandt, February 17, 1942; BA-B, R 3/1503, p. 4, Speer's talking points for his appointment at Führer Headquarters on February 19, 1942. A protocol of the meeting between Hitler and Speer on February 19, 1942 is printed in *Deutschlands Rüstung im Zweiten Weltkrieg: Hitlers Konferenzen mit Albert Speer*, Willi A. Boelcke, ed. (Frankfurt am Main: Athenaion, 1969), pp. 64–68, here p. 64. See also observations by Professor Dr. Konrad Meyer about his presentation to Himmler on February 19, 1942, at Hitler's headquarters printed in *Vom Generalplan Ost zum Generalsiedlungsplan*, Czeslaw Madajczyk, ed. (Munich: Saur, 1994), pp. 41f. In addition to Riecke, Himmler, and Meyer, Major Ernst Seifert of the Wehrmacht's Economics Staff East also attended the meeting. Meyer belonged to the staff of the Reich Commissar for the Strengthening of Germandom, also run by Himmler, which played a key role in German settlement plans. Riecke worked at the Reich Ministry for the Occupied Territories in the food and agriculture department.

30. On Hitler's remarks of October 17, 1941, and his projected deployment of Red Army POWs as forced laborers, see Christian Streit, *Keine Kameraden: Die Wehrmacht und die sowjetischen Kriegsgefangenen 1941–1945* (Bonn: Dietz, 1991), pp. 196f. and footnote 38 on pp. 386f. It is unclear whether Hitler himself intended for the POWs to die in the process.

31. The reason for this may be that the O.T.'s main office for the southern Soviet Union, led by Professor Walter Brugmann, was in Dnipropetrovs'k.

32. Uman' was later headquarters for a regional construction zone, *Verfügung*, p. 84.

33. For example, Himmler's former adjutant Ludolf von Alvensleben (SSPF Taurida), Theobald Thier (SSPF Kuban' and SSPF Galicia), and Jürgen Stroop (SSPF Georgia, SSPF Galicia, and SSPF Warsaw) worked on DG IV before taking up their SSPF duties. Stroop and Alvensleben eventually became HSSPF Rhine and HSSPF Elbe respectively. Heinz Roch (briefly acting SSPF Taurida), Johannes Döring (SSPF Stalino), and Karl Schäfer (SSPF Dnipropetrovs'k) worked on the project as inspectors. Wilhelm Günther also spent several weeks on DG IV in May-June 1942 before becoming SSPF Volhynia-Podolia.

34. *Verfügung*, pp. 81–87. The length of DG IV here refers to the stretch from the General Government-RKU border to Makiïvka. The distance varies according to the ever-changing course of the supply line; Kaienburg, "Jüdische Arbeitslager," p. 21. The presence on DG IV of Schutzmannschaft Battalions 4 (based in Stalino), 7 (Vinnytsia), 8 (Uman' and Pishchanyi Brid), 17 (Dnipropetrovs'k), 23 (Dnipropetrovs'k), 268 (Dnipropetrovs'k), 27 (Kryvyi Rih) and 28 (Kryvyi Rih)—which were recruited from the Baltics—as well as Cossack battalion 111 (Kryvyi Rih) and the Ukrainian battalion 124 (Uman') has been documented for the summer of 1942. By early 1943 at the latest, almost all of these units had been rotated out and replaced by Schutzmannschaft Battalions 125 (Kompaniïvka), 126 (Kirovohrad), 134 (Kryvyi Rih), 135 (Kryvyi Rih), 159 (Kryvyi Rih), 160 (Kryvyi Rih), and 161 (Stalino). These later units were Ukrainian or Cossack, Georg Tessin "Die Stäbe und Truppeneinheiten der Ordnungspolizei" in H.-J. Neufeldt, J. Huck, and G. Tessin, *Zur Geschichte der Ordnungspolizei 1936–1945*, Schriften des Bundesarchivs 3 (Koblenz: Bundesarchiv, 1957), p. 101–106; BA-MA, R22/165, Die im H. Geb. Süd einges. Kräfte d. Höh. SS u. Pol. Fhr. Russland Süd, undated (probably early 1943).

35. BA-MA, RH 22/203, Befh. H. Geb. Süd, Abt. VII, Aufgaben für das Übergabegebiet, July 16, 1942.

36. *Verfügung*, pp. 94–150, lists the institutions responsible for DG IV, their organizational structure, and the names of the individuals in charge of each office or department.

37. Hermann Kaienburg, "Zwangsarbeit von Juden in Arbeit- and Konzentrationslagern," in *"Arisierung" im Nationalsozialismus, Volksgemeinschaft, Raub und Gedächtnis*, Irmtrud Wojak and Peter Hayes, ed. (Frankfurt am Main: Campus, 2000), pp. 219–240 and p. 228. Many of the companies involved in work on DG IV are listed under in *Verfügung*.

38. ZStL, 4 AR-Z 20/63, Bd. 1, Aussage Gieseke, pp. 17–20. See also Seidler, *Die Organisation Todt*, p. 93. Contemporary documents confirm that workers living within the 50-km wide strip on either side of DG IV were drafted. Seidler also points to another problem: The RKU was worried about agricultural production along DG IV, since humans and animals were being diverted from producing food. Speer claims that he issued instructions stating that the needs of agriculture had to be considered, which in turn meant that a good number of civilian workers were no longer available to the O.T.

39. BA-B, Film 13677, Frames 1513–1527, Bfh. Rückw. H. Geb. Süd, Abt.VII, Lagebericht, March 16, 1942. This situation report includes a statistical appendix of cities with over 10,000 inhabitants under Rear Area Army Group South. By this point, the only significant number of Jews living in this territory was in Stalino, where some 3,000 were counted. The next largest number of Jews given in the statistics was to be found in Sumy, with 215 Jews. However, the second page of this appendix is imprecise and, for towns such as Zaporizhzhia, Dnipropetrovs'k, and Poltava, does not distinguish between children and Jews, who received the same rations. It is to be assumed that some Jews were still alive in these cities, since several mass murders took place in those places in spring 1942. Nevertheless, it still stands that the "Final Solution" had already taken place in Ukraine. Given the lack of Jews, as well as the shortage of POWs, it is not surprising to find this

report describing the use of civilian Ukrainians for construction work on DG IV at this time. Alone in the area of operations for the 444th Security Division, some 25,000 civilians were at work on the thoroughfare.

40. BA-MA, RH 21–1/241, Oberkommando Heeresgruppe Süd, Ia, General der Pioniere, Betr. Verwendung von Kriegsgefangenen im Grosseinsatz für Strassen-, Brückenbau usw. bei den Baueinheiten, September 19, 1941. The recipients of these instructions included the O.T. liaison for Army Group South and supply-line superintendents 4 and 5, meaning DG IV and DG V.

41. BA-MA, RH 21–1/241, Heeresgruppe Süd, Ib, Betr.: Meldungen über Kgf., December 20, 1941. These instructions did not apply—as the writer stressed—to POWs in camps falling under the Wehrmacht Territorial Commander in Ukraine, the German military's command within the RKU. These POWs were to be counted separately when deployed in Rear Area Army Group South. Officials on the DG V were also informed accordingly.

42. BA-MA, RH 21–1/241, Bau-Batl.109 (K), An den Kommandeur der Bautruppen 45, March 9, 1942. The timeframe for these figures is unclear, but judging from the context, I assume it to be around three months.

43. BA-MA, RH 21–1/241, Kommandeur der Bautruppen 45, Abt. Ib, An Pz. AOK 1/A. Pi. Fü., Betr.: Kgf-Einsatz im Strassen- and Brückendienst, April 3, 1942. Ibid., Oberkommando des Heeres, Gen. StdH/Org. Abt. (II), An die Heeresgruppen, AOK u PzAOK, Befehlshaber der Heeresgebiete, Betr. Bau-Btlne. (K), May 16, 1942.

44. BA-MA, RH 22/204, Sicherungs-Division 213, Abt. VII, Lagebericht für die Zeit vom 16.4.-15.5.1942. See also ibid., FK 197, Militärverwatungstruppe, Lagebericht für die Zeit vom 15.1.42 bis 15.2.1942: "It will be very difficult to determine the repair work on the overwhelming part of the indescribably poor roads in the spring. The [numbers of] civilian workers are not sufficient. It will be even more difficult in spring, because the rural population will be desperately needed for tilling the fields."

45. ZStL, 4 AR-Z 20/63, Bd. 1, Aussage Gieseke, p. 18 (reverse). For DG V, an example of locals choosing work in Germany has survived in the records of the Rear Area Army Group South. In the area under Field Administration Command FK (V) 239, based in Khorol, 500 workers were recruited for work in Germany from mid-April to mid-May 1942. Simultaneously, civilians from the surrounding area along the DG V (60 for every kilometer) had to be handed over for road work. The transfer of the latter to DG V followed in consultation with the Labor Office, county agricultural officials, and the local Wehrmacht economics commando. However, civilians who had been recruited for work in the Reich were also employed on DG V in the construction zone around Borispil', which led to protests both by the recruits and by the Labor Office and had as its consequence the removal of the recruits from DG V and their transportation to Germany; BA-MA, RH 22/201, Feldkommandantur (V) 239, Abtlg. VII, Monatsbericht der Abt. VII für die Zeit vom 16.4. bis 15.5.1942.

46. BA-MA, RH 22/202, FK 774, Abt.VII, Lagebericht für Februar und März 1942.

47. BA-MA, RH 22/205, Zusammenstellung der von der Abt. VII des Bef. H. Geb. B. in der Zeit vom 10.7.41 bis 30.9.42 herausgegebenen Anordnungen and Befehle von allgemeiner Bedeutung zur Durchführung der Aufgaben der Militärverwaltung, Anordnung of July 21, 1942; ZStL, UdSSR Ordner 406, p. 762, Verordnung über den Verkehr auf den Durchgangsstrassen, December 30, 1942. This decree, issued by Reich Commissar Ukraine Erich Koch, echoed a decree from Reich Minister for the Occupied Eastern Territories Alfred Rosenberg of February 16, 1942, and represented only a slight modification based on experiences during 1942.

48. Dieter Pohl, "Schauplatz Ukraine: Der Massenmord an den Juden im Mi-

litärverwaltungsgebiet und im Reichskommissariat 1941–1943," in *Ausbeutung, Vernichtung, Öffentlichkeit: Neue Studien zur nationalsozialistischen Lagerpolitik,* Norbert Frei, Sybille Steinbacher, and Bernd C. Wagner, eds. (Munich: Saur, 2000), pp. 136–173, here p. 156.

49. BA-MA, RH 22/201, FK (V) 239, Abt.VII, Monatsbericht der Abteilung VII für die Zeit vom 15.9.-15.10.41.

50. BA-MA, RH 22/205, Zusammenstellung, Anordnung, July 21, 1941. This collection contains not only the orders of Rear Area Army Group B but also those of its predecessor, Rear Area Army Group South.

51. BA-MA, RH 22/201, FK (V) 200, Abt.VII, Dem Kommandierenden General der Sicherungstruppen and Befehlshaber im Heeres-Gebiet Süd, Abt. VII, Betr.: Tätigkeitsbericht zum 20.6. 1942.

52. *Verfügung,* pp. 530–551. For background information about Schnöller, see *Verfügung,* pp. 647ff.

53. *Verfügung,* pp. 15–18, 218, 225, 259, 463, and 498. After the war, ghetto liquidations that preceded the deportation of survivors to forced labor camps were usually the subject of investigations separate from those into events surrounding DG IV. Cf. ZStL, 204 AR-Z 140/67 for more on the mass killings in Haisyn and Teplyk in spring 1942 and 204 AR-Z 136/67 for Vinnytsia and Lityn.

54. U.S. Holocaust Memorial Museum, Zhytomyr 1465–1–1, Gendarmerie-Gebiet Zwiahel, Gendarmerie-Posten Marchlewsk, An den SS- und Pol.Gebietsführer in Zwiahel, Betr.: Festnahme von drei Juden, die aus einem Transportzug in Shitomir ausgerückt sind, July 10, 1942. Wendy Lower kindly shared this document with me.

55. Andrej Angrick, "Rumänien, die SS and die Vernichtung der Juden," in *Rumänien und der Holocaust: Zu den Massenverbrechen in Transnistrien 1941–1944,* Mariana Hausleitner, Brigitte Mihok, and Juliane Wetzel, eds. (Berlin: Metropol, 2001), pp. 113–138. Here p. 138.

56. The rank of "SS senior colonel" fell between that of a brigadier general (*SS-Brigadeführer*) and colonel (*SS-Standartenführer*). There is no equivalent in the German Army nor in the U.S. or UK armed forces.

57. Instytut Pamięci Narodowej (IPN), Zbiór zespołów szczątkowych jednostek SS i policji, no. 77, Der Kommandeur der Sicherheitspolizei und des SD im Generalbezirk Wolhynien u. Podolien, An die Aussenstelle der Sicherheitspolizei und des SD z. Hd. SS-Hauptscharführer Fermer o.V.i.A. Kamenez-Podolsk. I thank Dieter Pohl for providing me with this document.

58. Ibid.

59. IPN, Zbiór zespołów szczątkowych jednostek SS i policji, no. 77, Der Generalkommissar für Wolynien and Podolien, An die Aussenstellen der Sicherheitspolizei und des SD Brest, Pinsk, Starokonstantinow, Kamenez-Podolsk, Betr.: Judenaktionen, August 31, 1942. I am indebted to Dieter Pohl for this document as well.

60. *Verfügung,* pp. 187–194.

61. Ibid., pp. 195–217.

62. It should be noted that, at this time, decisions regarding which Jews were killed and when were the responsibility of local SS officials. Under different circumstances, Friedrich Wilhelm Rohde, the SS and police base leader (*SS- und Polizei-Standortführer*) in Brest, tried to save his ghetto of Jewish craftsmen (for economic, not humanitarian, considerations) but could only delay, not prevent, the liquidation, BA-B, R 94/6, Der SS- and Polizeiführer für Wolhynien and Podolien, Lagebericht für die Zeit vom 15. August bis 15. September 1942; BA-Berlin, R 94/7, Der Gebietskommissar Brest-Litowsk, Abt. IIa, An den Herrn Generalkommissar für Wolhynien and Podolien, Lagebericht für September 1942; Ibid., Der Gendarmerie-Gebietsführer Brest-Litowsk, An den Herrn Kommandeur der Gen-

darmerie, Lagebericht für Monat Oktober 1942; ZStL, AR-Z 334/59, Bd. 1, Aussage Wilhelm Rompel, pp. 52f., Bd. 3, Aussage Ernst Westermacher, pp. 564f.

63. ZStL, 213 AR-Z 20/63, Bd. 5, Aussage Franz Christoffel, pp. 115f. Christoffel could not remember whether he had discussed the realization of this idea with Alvensleben or with Thier. Given the timeframe—Thier replaced Alvensleben in the summer of 1942—it was probably Thier, since he too was recalled from DG IV in early September, *Verfügung*, pp. 75 and 78.

64. On the performance of Jewish forced laborers in northern Transnistria and the conditions under which they lived, see ZStL, Dokumentation, Verschiedenes 301j 52, Matatias Carp, *Schwarzbuch: Tatsachen und Urkunden. Die Leiden der Juden in Rumänien*, pp. 210–271. This book originally appeared in three volumes in Bucharest in 1946. Volume 3 concerns Transnistria.

65. Carp, *Schwarzbuch*, p. 270, entries for August 19, 1942. The forced laborers at the Quarry who did not volunteer were in turn temporarily sent to Ladyzhyn, while the mentally handicapped workers, most likely Jews, were murdered. The Jews in Ladyzhyn were then returned to the Quarry and resumed work. Carp, *Schwarzbuch*, p. 272, entries for August 26 and 28, 1942. On the dates and recruitment campaign, see Isak Weissglas, *Steinbruch am Bug: Bericht einer Deportation nach Transnistrien* (Berlin: Literaturhaus Berlin, 1995), pp. 52f. and 59.

66. Carp, *Schwarzbuch*, pp. 268f., entries for July 3 and 6, 1942.

67. Testimonies of Zwi Rauchwerger and Bertha Loebel quoted in *Verfügung*, pp. 75f. Loebel's assertion that one was "happy" to be with "German-speaking people" is explained by the history of Chernivtsi (German, Czernowitz), which had belonged to the Austrian Empire. A unique German-Jewish culture shaped the city's life and generated a sense of belonging to German-Austrian culture. Czernowitz fell to Romania after the First World War, but few Jews considered Romanian citizenship desirable. Cf. Weissglas, *Steinbruch am Bug*, p. 53.

68. *Verfügung*, pp. 76f.

69. Events at Kunka and Osytna are described in *Verfügung*, pp. 522–529.

70. Carp, *Schwarzbuch*, p. 273, entry for September 15. On Pechera, p. 277 and 283, entries for November 20, 1942, and May 10, 1943. On Krasnopilka, see *Verfügung*, p. 463.

71. Arnold Daghani, *Lasst mich Leben* (Tel-Aviv: Verlag Weg and Ziel, 1960), p. 8. Using the official contemporary exchange rate for reichsmarks to US dollars, RM2.5 = $1, which was fixed between 1939 and 1941, this wage works out to about 6.5 cents per day at the time. Adjusted for inflation ($1 [1941] = $13.89 [2006]), this would be about 90 cents per day today. This figure, however, does not take into account purchasing power parity or black market exchange rates.

72. Carp, *Schwarzbuch*, p. 287, entry for August 2, 1943, refers to such episodes.

73. Ibid., p. 274, entry for October 16, 1942.

74. See the various entries corresponding to the camps in *Verfügung*.

75. Daghani, *Lasst mich Leben*, p. 13; *Verfügung*, p. 410; notes by Nathan Segall from October 21, 1943, printed in *Verfügung*, pp. 40–48, here pp. 41 and 48. Segall was the leader of the Jewish camp and was murdered on December 10, 1943; Kaienburg, "Jüdische Arbeitslager," pp. 28ff.

76. Segall quoted in *Verfügung*, p. 41. In his capacity as leader of the Jewish camp, Segall could leave the camp for short periods, which assured him "that the picture elsewhere, if not worse, was in no way better than in my camp." See also *Verfügung*, pp. 244, 283, 300, 364, and 498.

77. Kaienburg, "Jüdische Arbeitslager," p. 31; Daghani, *Lasst mich Leben*, pp. 15–18, 37, 44, 52, 55, 69, 72.

78. Daghani reported cases of death from typhus and exhaustion. He also described infestations of worms and lice, and gangrene due to frostbite; Daghani,

Lasst mich Leben, pp. 33, 46, 48, 57f., 91. The evidence here concerns cases of illness and deprivation.

79. Christoffel's inexact dating suggests that he might have confused Gieseke with Geibel at times.

80. *Verfügung,* pp. 154–170.

81. Ibid., pp. 170–185. SS Captain Otto Fach was in charge of the relevant construction zone at the time.

82. Ibid., pp. 218–225. The Germans closed the Letychiv camp in late 1942.

83. Ibid., pp. 225–234. Two large-scale *Aktionen* followed not long after this shooting. ZStL, 204 AR-Z 136/67.

84. Ibid., pp. 238–242.

85. Ibid., pp. 242–250. Otto Ettengruber, a member of the Police Security Section on DG IV, delivered the "mercy shots."

86. Ibid., pp. 251–277. Additional shootings took place during Christmas 1942 and on February 1 and 4, 1943. The Nemyriv camp was run by Technical Sergeant Alfred Jähnig of the Order Police. Daghani, *Lasst mich Leben,* p. 76. It may be that the Nemyriv camp was not supposed to be liquidated in May 1943. Instructions for maintaining the camp were issued, wrote Daghani, but they did not arrive in time.

87. On Berezivka and Buhakiv, see *Verfügung,* pp. 279–285; on the Bratslav camp, which was run by SS Sergeant Paul Stolzmann, and the Zarudnytsi camp, see *Verfügung,* pp. 287–337.

88. Ibid., pp. 338–348. See *Dovidnyk pro tabory,* p. 45, which says 2,758 people were killed at the Raihorod camp. The camp was liquidated in January 1943.

89. Ibid., pp. 348–361. The camp at Nyshcha Kropyvna was liquidated on May 24, 1943.

90. Ibid., pp. 361–365. German investigators did not document a forced labor camp for Jews in Haisyn, but determined that Jews had worked at the train station there. Carp, on the other hand, mentioned a camp at Haisyn and large-scale actions there; Carp, *Schwarzbuch,* pp. 274 and 276, entries for October 14 and November 6, 1942.

91. Ibid., pp. 365–408. The company Dohrmann was offered 50 POWs to replace the Jewish workers.

92. Ibid., pp. 408–456.

93. Ibid., pp. 463–488. Additional selections took place at Krasnopilka around October 1942 and in April 1943.

94. Ibid., pp. 488–491. The Naraïvka camp was closed in late autumn 1942, and its workers distributed among other DG IV camps.

95. Ibid., pp. 492–497. The camp at Kiblych was closed in June 1943 and its labor force turned over to DG IV camps between Haisyn and Osytna.

96. Ibid., pp. 497–517. Although this is the only verifiable incident for Teplyk in the *Verfügung,* additional deliveries of new Jewish workers to the camp have been documented, suggesting in turn more selections and shootings.

97. Ibid., pp. 517–520. An escape attempt was made during the liquidation of the Talalaïvka camp. Of 156 prisoners who fled, 30 were captured and shot.

98. Ibid., pp. 520 ff.

99. Ibid., pp. 522–529.

100. ZStL, 213 AR-Z 20/63, Bd. 5, Aussage Christoffel, p. 113. It should be recalled here that Dargel's orders from August 31, 1942, allowed Jewish specialists to be spared killing for a maximum of two months.

101. *Verfügung,* pp. 602–613.

102. Ukrainian historians have found that additional crimes were also committed on DG IV. See *Dovidnyk pro tabory, tiurmy ta getto na okupovanii terytorii Ukraïny: 1941–1944* (Kiev: Derzhavnyi Komitet Archiviv Ukraïny, 2000). Pages 31, 45, 49, 51, 65, 69, and 93 give evidence of imprisonment and shootings in the precincts (*Rayons*) of Sofiïvka and Shyroke (Dnipropetrovs'k Oblast) as well as in a

DG IV forced labor camp for Jews in Novyi Vitebsk. Additional Jewish forced labor camps along DG IV are listed in Chukiv, Komsomol's'ke, Khmil'nyk, and Pechera (Vinnytsia Oblast), Mala Vyska (Kirovohrad Oblast) and Verkhn'odniprovs'k (Dnipropetrovs'k Oblast).

103. Additional crimes are mentioned only when there is a connection with DG IV.

104. *Verfügung*, p. 81.

105. Prützmann may have simply inserted under the rubric of DG IV workers from other projects in his domain, BA-B, BDC, SS-HO 1249, Fernschreiben, An Feldkommandostelle Reichsführer-SS, June 15, 1943. Prützmann's telex was in response to an inquiry of June 11, no copy of which is known to me.

106. BA-B, R 20/45b, Tagebuch Bach, entries from May 22 and June 19, 1943. For background on these events, see Schulte, *Zwangsarbeit und Vernichtung*, pp. 283 and 320–331.

107. On the German military situation on the eastern front in 1943, Ernst Klink, *Das Gesetz des Handelns: Die Operation "Zitadelle" 1943* (Stuttgart: DVA, 1966). For a Soviet view, *Die Geschichte des Zweiten Weltkrieges 1939–1945*, Bd. 7, H. Hoffmann et al., eds., (Berlin [Ost]: Militärverlag der Deutschen Demokratische Republik, 1979), pp. 146–154.

108. BA-MA, RH 24–29/169, K.V. Insp. Dumtzlaff, V.O. XXIX. AK, Lenkung des Arbeitseinsatzes im Korpsbereich, July 19, 1943.

109. BA-MA, RH 22/116, Bfh. H. Geb. Süd, Ia, An Höh.SS-u.Pol.Führer Russland-Süd, Betr. Sicherung der Brücken an der Dg IV, July 9, 1943; ibid., Der Höhere SS- und Polizeiführer Russland Süd und für die Ukraine, Ia, Betr. Sicherung der Brücken an der Dg IV, July 19, 1943.

110. BA-MA, RH 22/116, Bfh. H. Geb. Süd, Abt. Ic, Besprechung über Erntesicherung, August 2, 1943. At this meeting, the Germans worked out the evacuation efforts north of Kiev and responsibilities for securing key sites. The HSSPF was to assume such responsibilities only "in the event of a disaster"; ibid., Bfh. H. Geb. Süd, Ia, An Okdo. d. H. Gr. Süd, September 19, 1943. This includes a copy of Himmler's basic instructions.

111. Tessin, "Die Stäbe and Truppeneinheiten der Ordnungspolizei," p. 66f. and 95. As a result of high losses, a good number of which were desertions, Police Rifles Regiment 37 was disbanded in late March 1944, BA-B, R19/330, BdO Ukraine an den Chef der Ordnungspolizei, undated.

112. *Verfügung*, p. 519; Kaienburg, "Jüdische Arbeitslager," p. 38.

113. Latvijas Valsts Vestures Arhiva, Riga, 1026–1–3, pp. 161f. Der Chef der Sicherheitspolizei und des SD, IV B 4a, An die Befehlshaber der Sicherheitspolizei and des SD, Betr.: Endlösung der Judenfrage.

114. Staatsanwaltschaft beim Kammergericht Berlin, 1 Js 1/61, Bd. 12, Aussage Christian Woesch, pp. 246ff., Aussage Johann Pfeuffer, pp. 252ff., Bd. 15, Aussage Helmut Lessmann, pp. 58ff., Aussage Otto Schmalz, pp. 65f. According to these testimonies, 50–60 senior members from Gestapo offices across Germany and Luxemburg met with officials from the RSHA's Jewish affairs desk in Berlin on October 23, 1941, to discuss the deportation of German Jews to the east. At the time, according to the testimonies, there was no talk of murdering the Jews to be deported. The witnesses, who were not suspects when questioned, maintained that Adolf Eichmann, the head of Jewish affairs at the RSHA, said the deported Jews would be put to work behind the front. This interpretation contradicts that of other authorities such as Richard Breitman, *Der Architekt der "Endlösung." Himmler und die Vernichtung der europäischen Juden* (Paderborn: Schöningh, 1996) pp. 284f.

115. For example, Ruth Bettina Birn, *Die Höheren SS- und Polizeiführer. Himmlers Vertreter im Reich und den besetzten Gebieten* (Düsseldorf: Droste, 1986).

Translated by Ray Brandon

VI

"On Him Rests the Weight of the Administration": Nazi Civilian Rulers and the Holocaust in Zhytomyr

WENDY LOWER

The Nazis developed sinister, utopian plans for exploiting Ukraine's natural and human resources, and in their view, these plans were absolutely essential to secure the Reich's future. The continued sustenance of the German Army and people was seen to depend on grain, livestock, and other agricultural products from Ukraine, and the survival of the "Aryan race" was considered to hinge on the total defeat of the Nazis' archenemy: the Jew, above all the "bolshevized" Jew. Since the largest population of Soviet Jews resided in this "breadbasket of Europe," there was much to be done, in Nazi thinking, and no time to waste in conquering and exploiting Ukraine.

Flush with the euphoria of victory and fantasies of empire building, Hitler in mid-July 1941 spoke to a small meeting of top government, party, and military leaders about his plans for a "Garden of Eden" in the newly conquered eastern territories and the incorporation of the Crimea into Germany proper.[1] A month later, with the German-Soviet front outside Kiev, Hitler ordered that the westernmost lands of Ukraine (save for Galicia, which had already been turned over to the General Government) be transferred from military administration to a newly created civil administration as early as September 1, 1941.[2] A flurry of Hitler decrees for establishing civilian rule in western Ukraine quickly followed. First, the position of Wehrmacht Territorial Commander Ukraine (*Wehrmachtbefehlshaber Ukraine,* WBU) was created as the supreme military authority within the civilian zone of occupation. Hermann Göring, Hitler's designated successor, saw his role as plenipotentiary for the Four-Year Plan extended to economic matters in the occupied east. Then, Hitler formally established a central authority for the civil administration of Soviet territories and appointed the Nazis' ideologue, Alfred Rosenberg, minister of the occupied eastern territories. Police and security-related issues in these same areas were entrusted to Reichsführer-SS and Chief of the German Police Heinrich Himmler.[3]

Yet the decrees establishing Nazi rule in Ukraine were no more specific in identifying who was ultimately in charge. In the summer of 1941, only the most senior personnel had been appointed, causing Hitler's deputies to rush to find suitable personnel for their outposts in the east. Hitler's minions also had to determine how their respective agencies functioned, and how they would carry out what would in the end turn out to be the most radical colonization campaign in the history of European conquest and empire building. Nazi rule in Ukraine developed in stages and in an ad hoc manner often shaped by personal preferences, tested loyalties, and bureaucratic rivalries rather than by individual competence and professional experience. Within this organized chaos, the one administrative priority that transcended such incongruities in administration and diversity in personnel was the Nazi mass murder of the Jews.

On the eve of the Nazi invasion of the Soviet Union, Rosenberg, Himmler, and Göring had begun to devise the structural framework for German rule in Ukraine. Rosenberg tapped many German and Ukrainian émigrés who offered maps, demographic reports, and other valuable information about the Sovietized eastern territories.[4] Rosenberg planned for a sprawling bureaucracy of administrative commissars, statisticians, and Slavic specialists. Drawing on their experiences in Poland, Himmler and Reinhard Heydrich, the head of the Reich Security Main Office (home to the Gestapo), started with a smaller hierarchical staff of higher SS and police leaders and mobile task forces that later multiplied into a large network of German SS, mobile Order Police battalions, and stationary rural police posts, supported by thousands of Ukrainian, Cossack, Lithuanian, and Latvian auxiliaries. Meanwhile, Göring's plan for controlling the eastern economy with technical inspectors, businessmen, and agricultural overseers represented only one of several highly competitive organizations that ravaged Ukraine's economic resources. Göring's rivals included various Wehrmacht offices for supplies, provisions, and munitions, and SS industrial and construction enterprises.

All of these agencies coexisted independently, and their representatives in the field operated under steadily evolving administrative organs and amid a frustratingly backward infrastructure. Inasmuch as

Nazi leaders and their subordinates believed in a permanent German presence in the east, if not a 1,000-year Reich governing the territory, the day-to-day reality of ruling the conquered land and its peoples was not, as Hitler asserted, simply a matter of organization. The pressures of a war-footing economy combined with incompetent personnel and irrational, destructive policies combined to create an extremely unstable ruling apparatus that was in many ways inherently self-destructive.

Even the most senior Nazi officials could never feel secure in their power due to the unpredictable nature of Hitler's rule, the encroachments of Himmler's SS-police empire, the ever shifting policy priorities, and the unrelenting diversion of manpower to the military. While constantly complaining about labor and material shortages, Nazi officials continued to implement a murderous policy of terror that antagonized the majority of Ukrainian peasants and destroyed the Jewish intelligentsia and craftsmen. These wasteful, criminal policies, although largely dictated from above, were exacerbated by the county commissars, Hitler's colonizers on the ground, a motley ensemble of middle-ranking bureaucrats, party hacks, and marginalized officers from the Storm Troops (SA) who were granted often unchecked power over millions of inhabitants and vast territories. Although their motives differed, most abused the power of their position in the worst ways imaginable.

This chapter focuses on the county level leaders, specifically how they operated on their own initiative, and how they interacted with their superiors at the regional level of administration. In all, there were at least 114 county commissars in the Reich Commissariat Ukraine (RKU). These men answered to one of six general commissars at the regional level. And in turn, the general commissars answered directly to the Reich commissar for Ukraine, who for his part was subordinated, in theory, to Rosenberg's ministry. The commissars were responsible for the welfare of the Jewish population, and thus the course of anti-Jewish policies in the more remote areas of the Nazi empire. According to Hitler's plans for the eastern administration, "the settlement of day-to-day issues [was] left in the hands of the respective county commissars." Rosenberg echoed Hitler's wish when he wrote in his guidelines for ruling the east that the county commissar would direct the local administration and, therefore, "on him rests the weight of the administration."[5]

The county administrators could not issue laws, but they could post decrees and orders, which in effect became local law because of the commissars' power of office. According to Hitler and Rosenberg's design, instructions from Berlin would be so broad that the lower levels could devise their own methods for meeting their superiors' expectations and demands. To this end, county commissars could choose to cooperate or to compete with the other German agencies active in their counties. There was also ample room for the lower-level administrators to pursue their private interests and desires, especially if they coincided with the broader wishes expressed by the central Nazi leadership.

Among the six RKU regional governments that were established was General Commissariat Zhytomyr, which serves as the focal point for this chapter.[6] General Commissariat Zhytomyr was situated in Right Bank Ukraine, roughly 100 miles west of Kiev. It was not the largest territory; however, its administration was, relative to the other commissariats, amply staffed. It also existed longer than the commissariats to the east and south, and most importantly, much of its administrative documentation survived the war.

By the summer of 1942, there were about 870 Reich Germans running the region's 25 counties (later 26), two municipalities, and general commissariat's headquarters centered in the city of Zhytomyr. The commissariat's population numbered some 2.5 million persons, who resided in an area of 64,800 square kilometers (about the size of New Hampshire, Vermont, and Massachusetts together).[7]

Across the RKU, each county commissar governed about 3,000 square kilometers, with populations ranging from 50,000 to 300,000 persons. In Zhytomyr, the county commissar and his staff managed on average a geographic area of 2,300 square kilometers with about 108,000 inhabitants. The county commissars reported to General Commissar Kurt Klemm and, as of October 1942, to his successor Ernst Leyser (an SS brigadier general and member of the Reichstag). In addition to Zhytomyr, which had a population of 42,000, the second and third largest towns in General Commissariat Zhytomyr were Vinnytsia and Berdychiv.[8] A special advisor for the "Jewish question" existed in the general commissar's office, but not in the county commissariat outposts.

The county commissars set up their rural offices with no more than ten German subordinates and dozens of indigenous helpers who worked in six administrative areas: 1) Politics and Propaganda; 2) Administration; 3) Finance; 4) Welfare; 5) Agriculture; and 6) Labor. The Politics and Propaganda Office was the most important of these offices, and its chief usually served as the deputy commissar. The welfare and agricultural chiefs managed the agrarian industries and collective farms through a network of field offices. The head of the Labor Office also operated through a handful of rural stations where a local German commissioner of labor was often posted. The Labor Office chief was notorious among the indigenous population for his brutal methods of seizing and deporting Ukrainians to work in factories and on farms in the Reich. In addition to a few agricultural specialists and foresters, the county commissar had at least one female typist-stenographer and some ethnic German translators.[9]

Like most European colonial administrations, Nazi rule in Ukraine relied heavily on local leaders and collaborators. Rarely did the county commissar venture beyond his headquarters to the more remote villages. During the first year of occupation it was unnecessary, and then, as partisan activity against German rule increased, it was too dangerous. The county commissar supervised scattered rural populations through indigenous collaborators known as precinct (*Rayon*) leaders and village elders (*Starosta*). The commissars used Ukrainian administrators as much as possible and heavily promoted ethnic Germans (many of whom lacked the necessary job skills). A starosta was appointed to each village. He then reported to a Ukrainian or ethnic German representative in the local precinct administration office, and the precinct leader reported directly to the commissar's office. In addition, the commissars formed indigenous advisory boards to deal with matters of administration, culture, and the economy.

The recruiting of commissars for General Commissariat Zhytomyr began in early September 1941 when Rosenberg's deputy, Alfred Meyer, a former chief Nazi party official in the province of Westphalia, contacted one of his fellow Westphalians, Kurt Klemm, a county executive administrator from Münster. Meyer asked him to take the position of general commissar for Zhytomyr. The 47-year-old Klemm, the only professional civil servant found among the six general commissars, moved to a temporary office in Berlin, where he began to contact potential department chiefs for his staff and commissars for Zhytomyr's counties.

Faced with a requirement that 60 percent of his personnel be Nazi party members, Klemm began compiling lists of future commissars to manage Zhytomyr. His candidates shared certain characteristics worth highlighting. On average 36 years old, most grew up during the First World War and had been too young to see combat, but old enough to experience the hardships on the home front and the humiliation that came with Germany's defeat in 1918. These men came of age during the Weimar years, when the radical left and right took their battles from the Reichstag to the streets. A little over one-third of the county commissar candidates joined the National Socialist German Workers' Party (National-Sozialistische Deutsche Arbeitepartei, NSDAP) before January 1933, when the Nazis came to power in Germany. During the 1930s, they oversaw county-level Nazi party operations (serving as *Kreisleiter*), led university student Nazi party organizations (as *Kameradschaftsführer*), or ran offices within regional party organizations (as *Gaustellenleiter*). They were mid-level party officials and managers. The non-party members put forward by Klemm as candidates were younger, on average 30 years old. These men knew no other bureaucratic culture than that of 1930s Nazi Germany. Most were middle-ranking bureaucrats at the level of an assessor. Only one man belonged to one of Himmler's organizations. Dr. Hans Schmidt, who became the county commissar for Novohrad-Volynsky, was an SS first sergeant in the Security Service, the Nazi party's intelligence service.

The educational backgrounds of Klemm's candidates manifested the growing influence of the Nazis' "castles of the order," which were located in Vogelsang in the Eifel, Sonthofen in Allgau, and Krössinsee in Pomerania. Few of the candidates had formal university degrees. Instead, many were indoctrinated at Vogelsang, the first castle of the order, in response to Hitler's call for the continued development of Nazi party elites. According to the Nazi party's plan for a "thorough recon-

Rechitsa
Gomel
Zhitovichi
Vasilevichi
Kalinkovichi
Petrikov
Mozyr
Turov
Khoiniki
Loev
Yelsk
Narovlya
Bragin
Lelchitsy
Chernihiv
Pripet
Komarin

Reich Commissariat Ukraine

Sarny
Slovechne
Ovruch
Olevsk
Narodychi
Luhyny
Bazar
Ivankiv
Korosten
Iemilchyne
Chopovychi
Horodnytsia
Malyn
Barashi
Potiïvka
Volodarsk-Volynsky
Iarun
Zviahel
(Novohrad-
Volynsky)
Chervonoarmiisk
Radomyshl
Kiev
Dovbysh
Zhytomyr
Korostyshiv
GEN. COM. KIEV
Baranivka
Cherniakhiv
Vasylkiv
Dzerzhinsk
Troianiv
Kornyn
Fastiv
Shepetivka
Brusyliv
Dniepr
Chudniv
Andrushivka
Liubar
Berdychiv
Popilnia
Bila Tserkva
Ianushpil
(Ivanopil)
Vchoraishe
Koziatyn
GEN. COM.
VOLHYNIA-PODOLIA
Ulaniv
Ruzhyn
Tarashcha
Komsomolske
Khmilnyk
Samhorodok
Proskuriv
Pohrebyshche
Letychiv
Kalynivka
Lityn
Turbiv
Plyskiv
Orativ
Zvenyhorodka
Brailiv
Lypovets
Vinnytsia
Bar
Voronovytsia
Illintsi
Dashiv
Monostyryshche
Zhmerynka
Nemyriv
Sytkivtsi
Uman
Haisyn
Teplyk
TRANSNISTRIA

Bug
Dzhulynka
ROMANIA

0 20 40 60 km

- - - - - National and territorial borders, 1942
═══════ National borders, 2007
·············· General commissariat borders
═══════ County commissariat borders
═══════ Precinct borders

■ General commissariat administrative center
◉ County commissariat center
○ Precinct center

- · - · - Dual-track railroad
·············· Single-track railroad (main line)
═══════ Thoroughfare

"On Him Rests the Weight of the Administration" · 229

struction of [Germany's] national system of education . . . [the party men were] brought into line with the requirements of practical life [and] comprehension of the state idea," Robert Ley, who was in charge of the German Labor Front as well as internal party educational programs (as Reich Organization Leader) managed the construction of Vogelsang and hand picked the party members to be trained there. The educational curriculum and structure combined historical models of the Teutonic order with a new Nazi emphasis on racial hygiene, sport, and ideological themes found in Hitler's *Mein Kampf* and Alfred Rosenberg's theories of race and anti-Semitism. Elaborate festivals, nature walks, rituals, receptions, and speeches from special guests, including Hitler and Göring, were considered program highlights. The castle was adorned with typical Arno Breker–style sculptures of the "idealized Germanic hero," including an enormous sculpture of a muscular nude man and a carved plaque stating: "You are the torch bearers of the nation. You carry forward the spiritual light in the fight for Adolf Hitler." The castles of the order physically trained and ideologically groomed an emerging caste of Nazi civil servants.[10]

Close to half (12 of the 25) of the county commissars in General Commissariat Zhytomyr graduated from a castle of the order. For example, Wolfgang Steudel, later the commissar for Koziatyn County, got his career boost at Vogelsang. After earning the German graduation certificate that qualified him for university study (*Abitur*), he joined the party in 1930 and pursued a career as an athletics instructor. He worked briefly on the staff of an SA leadership school and then as a sports teacher at a state school. In 1936, he arrived at Vogelsang and became the adjutant of the castle's commandant, remaining there until his transfer to Ukraine in late 1941. Another example was County Commissar Hermann Drechsler, who ran Radomyshl County. He was trained as a master baker, but after joining the SA and graduating from Vogelsang, he became a certified teacher of biology and racial hygiene.

Heinrich Becher, a county-level party leader back in the Reich who became county commissar in Haisyn, was a blacksmith whose imprisonment for "political crimes" during the Weimar era cut short his education. He joined the SA in 1931 and quickly climbed the ranks of the party and state after completing his training at one of the castles. County Commissar Herbert Sittig in Nemyriv, who controlled Jewish camps and ghettos that provided labor for road construction in Ukraine, was a barber and veteran of the First World War. After his business closed in 1934, he enrolled at Vogelsang and stayed on as a trainer.

Among these true believers were other candidates for commissar positions in Ukraine, including a druggist, a factory foreman from a cannery, a convicted member of a paramilitary organization who had fled a sentence of 15 years hard labor, and an agronomist. To his list, Klemm added a colleague from Münster, a mayor who had also been in Zhytomyr when the Germans occupied Ukraine during the First World War.[11] It is clear from the lists of candidates that the future rulers in the east who had enormous power represented both the leftovers in the Nazi system as well as a rising class of revolutionaries who bore the stamp of the party's elitist educational system, the castles of the order. County commissars such as Drechsler, Steudel, and Becher not only graduated from Vogelsang, but were hired to train the next generation of elites in racial science and sport. Previous scholarship by Alexander Dallin and Gerald Reitlinger mentioned that some of the commissars passed through the castles on their way to the east as part of a quick orientation program. But relatively little has been written about the extensive training and curriculum of these castles, and how this Nazi "higher education" undercut the traditional training of civil servants who before 1933 studied law and political science at the university.

Klemm submitted the lists to Koch's deputy, Helmuth von Wedelstädt, for approval.[12] Those chosen as county commissars were not told exactly where they would be posted, but were instructed to identify a secretary, driver, and translator to accompany them. The commissars were then ordered to meet Klemm and Koch on October 13 at Falkenburg Castle on Krössinsee lake in Pomerania for briefings about their duties. From there, a special train was to take them to Zhytomyr.[13]

Little evidence survived the war about what the commissars were told before they were let loose on Ukraine. We know only from one testimony that they received their uniforms, listened to many speeches, and celebrated the anniversary of Hitler's attempted putsch on November 8, 1923. In 1944, one participant in the Krössinsee orientation (W. Dietz) published an essay about his recruitment and preparation for Ukraine. He recalled being summoned to Berlin "by order of the Führer" for a "Special Commission R." At the time, he was not sure if the "R" stood for "Rosenberg" or "Russland." He was among the more enthusiastic who wanted to "make a difference" and quickly responded; according to Dietz, others dragged their heels, trying to avoid a possible transfer to the dangerous east. Eventually "almost all the *Ordensburger*" appeared, and from there, they were sent to Krössinsee.[14]

The Krössinsee meetings and reception with Erich Koch's policy chief, Paul Dargel, were immediately followed by a period of false starts and administrative bungles as the commissars' rail transport to Ukraine was repeatedly delayed by the Reich Railway Office. This prolonged stay, Dietz explained, was all the more frustrating because at Krössinsee the commissars were not given "any information about the concept and form of their mission." What was clear at the outset, however, was that their deployment was key in preparing for the long-term political work in the east.[15]

The "special transport" of 39 railway cars with 150 staff members finally arrived in Zhytomyr in November, when the ground was already covered with snow and the bitterly cold temperature had fallen to below 0° Fahrenheit.[16] The arrival date of the commissars is significant, because in postwar criminal investigations in West Germany, many former commissars tried to obscure this date. The ghettoization of the

Zhytomyr region's surviving Jews, which resulted in the deaths of weak, ill, or elderly Jews, was initiated shortly after the commissars arrived. Some, however, stated in postwar testimonies that they arrived in early 1942, after ghettoization.[17]

Klemm and his departmental chiefs took over the former state museum building for their temporary administrative headquarters. The county commissars were allotted three vehicles, a typewriter, two Nazi flags, a radio set, and several thousand sheets of paper and were sent into the countryside. Before departing, they were also given a few words of encouragement from Klemm, who declared that the administration "will fulfill the tasks that have been conferred upon us by the Führer with a cheerful devotion . . . and without bureaucratic formalism."[18] Although vague references to theories of *Raum und Volk* had been made at Krössinsee, and although the commissars had experienced at least eight years of Nazi antisemitism and its escalating offenses, it was not until they arrived in Ukraine that they grasped the reality of mass murder and their role in carrying it out.

The commissars' tasks concerning the "Jewish question" were spelled out in Alfred Rosenberg's administrative guidelines. There, it was stated that county commissars were responsible for:

1) registering and marking all Jews;
2) establishing and administering ghettos;
3) installing a Jewish Council and Jewish order service;
4) selecting useful Jewish laborers, providing work papers for the laborers, and placing Jewish laborers in special buildings or camps; and
5) coauthorizing and implementing the liquidation of camps and ghettos with regional Sipo-SD offices, which supplied the shooting squads only.

In addition to these measures, the commissars had the authority to determine who was or was not a Jew. In effect, they could decide who lived or died. Beside formal authority, the commissars also possessed ample room for maneuver. Intentionally or not, they were given significant latitude. According to Dietz this freedom was both exhilarating for these self-identified "eastern pioneers" and daunting, because they were ill equipped to respond to extreme demands from superiors and feared that poor performance might result in a transfer to the front.[19]

Despite their relatively small number, the commissars at the regional and county level were notoriously visible, known for strutting about like "golden pheasants" in their insignia-laden brown party uniforms. To the Ukrainian population, they were the "Lord Commissars," the authors of threatening orders and malicious policies of forced labor and grain requisition. Wartime critics and postwar scholarship have branded the entire Rosenberg organization an "administrative monstrosity," led by a group of "egotistical hyenas," "carpetbaggers," and "eastern losers" (*Ostnieten*).[20]

Vogelsang, a "castle of the order," provided training for up-and-coming members of the Nazi elite. The building and the school grounds display the monumentalism and Germanic features of Nazi architecture, intended to instill a nationalist, imperialist megalomania. Sammlung F. A. Heinen.

"On Him Rests the Weight of the Administration" · 233

The Commissars and the Holocaust in Zhytomyr, 1941–1944

The Jews of the Zhytomyr region who had survived the 1941 period of SS and Wehrmacht killing operations were those in hiding, those whose locales had not yet been "cleansed," and those who were assigned to labor details. A few ghettos remained in the region, especially in the areas close to Romanian-occupied Ukraine, for example at Khmilnyk. Individuals who had been able to escape the SS and police roamed the countryside, hiding in barns and hovels.[21] Some were concealed by courageous Ukrainians who risked their lives and the lives of family members.

During the second phase of the Nazi occupation, when the civil administration was in place, mass executions of Jews continued; but with very few exceptions, killing actions did not reach the scale of several thousands as had been the case in 1941. The first killing sweeps in 1941, which were carried out by German military administration and SS and police forces, had killed as many as 70,000 Jews in the Zhytomyr region, mostly in the urban areas in and around Vinnytsia, Berdychiv, and Zhytomyr. At least 50,000 Jews native to the region remained alive when the commissars arrived. Since it had become quite clear that Himmler and his police forces had the upper hand in determining the final fate of the Jews, regional advisers and administrators in Himmler's police and Rosenberg's civil administration simply sought a modus operandi in the field.

In early 1942, one of the insiders among Rosenberg's advisers on Jewish policy, Erhard Wetzel, discussed in his correspondence with SS officials the practical coordination of county commissars and security police. Himmler's security and order police would continue to maintain overall control of Jewish policy; but its implementation, now that nearly all the mobile killing forces under Higher SS- and Police Leader Ukraine Hans-Adolf Prützmann and Einsatzgruppe C Commander Max Thomas, as well as the army security divisions, had moved farther east, required the combined effort of several stationary police and non-police forces, particularly the *Gendarmerie* (the Reich's rural police), the county commissars, the agricultural leaders, the economic specialists, and the foresters.[22] Moreover, the county commissars, who relied on police forces to secure their power, employed a growing number of Ukrainian auxiliaries and other non-German allies, such as Hungarian and Slovakian military forces assigned to General Commissariat Zhytomyr.

Even with the extensive recruiting of Ukrainian police, the German regional and county commissars needed other German agencies to help carry out the "Final Solution." In Ruzhyn County, for example, which was 1,800 square kilometers with 129,000 inhabitants, the Gendarmerie post was equipped with two motorcycles and a moped, but no truck. Therefore, individuals employed in non-police functions were expected to provide assistance and to serve in policing roles. Engineers working on construction projects for Organization Todt, for example, were to contribute the trucks needed for transporting Jews to execution sites, while foresters might come across Jews in hiding, who were supposed to be apprehended but were often shot on the spot.[23]

The involvement of Germans outside of the police hierarchy can be best understood as occurring at two levels: among the bureaucrats of the civil commissariat who were implementing policy and among individuals who simply agreed to join in the killing actions. Sometimes, these two functions overlapped when county commissars themselves not only pushed through the bureaucratic process of organizing mass murder, but also became involved in the killing action itself. The commissar kept abreast of the status of the "Jewish question" in his county by consulting with his Gendarmerie county leader (or in the case of six counties in General Commissariat Zhytomyr, SS- and police county leaders) and other department heads, such as the Labor Office chief. He in turn reported his findings to Rosenberg's ministry in Berlin. Of specific interest to the higher-ups in Berlin were two matters: whether the area was "free of Jews," and the total number of Jews killed. While the county commissars were granted a great deal of leeway to run their fiefdoms as they saw fit, they were subject to restraints from their superiors at the regional level. These included nutrition and health issues, but were applied particularly where the plunder of the murdered Jews was concerned.

Within the regional commissariat apparatus, Jewish matters fell under the Political Policy Office, Main Department II. Although the military administrations had by and large begun to direct certain anti-Jewish measures, such as the obligatory registration and marking of the Jews with stars, the county commissars and their staff in the political department took over these tasks in November 1941. Once the Jews had been forcibly relocated into ghettos, camps, and other locales, the commissars, together with the help of Ukrainian police in their county, were responsible for their food rations, the selection of those who were fit or unfit for work, and labor assignments.

According to Koch's ration instructions, all Jews received the smallest ration (that allotted to children up to 14 years old) if the rations were available; in other words, whatever was left over and in the smallest portions.[24] Jews assigned to hard labor received more. They got two meals per day, one at about 5:30 AM and the other at about 6:30 PM. A typical meal consisted of a watery soup and ersatz bread.[25] Under the supervision of the commissars' nutritional, medical, and labor experts, non-laboring Jews in the camps were, as a matter of policy, left to die of thirst and starvation-related diseases.

Another subsection of the administrative policy department, which was led by Dr. Müssig, controlled the accounting of confiscated Jewish property. In police reports about killing actions, the Gendarmerie post leader or SS-police leader would write that the county commissar and his finance office would be informed of the action.[26] To some degree, it is possible to connect Müssig's finance reports to the timing of anti-Jewish massacres and local Germanization activities. For example, at the end of July 1942, Dr. Müssig ordered that all county and city commissars generate lists of Jewish gold, silver, cash, and other valuables, and that the lists and items be brought to the commissariat's finance department. Müssig reissued this order during the last killing sweeps in the Reich commissariat and added that other items such as clothing should be included for the "urgent" needs of local organizations (e.g., the Ethnic German Liaison Office) when Hegewald, a nearby ethnic German colony, was being created.[27]

Since few Jews in Ukraine possessed any gold, silver, or cash, the greater part of the plundering operation against the Jews centered on the confiscation of apartments, furniture, bedding, and other household items. On December 12, 1941, General Commissar Klemm ordered that all Jewish property be handed over to the commissariat office. During summer and fall 1941, local Ukrainian militiamen grabbed Jewish belongings, which was not only a violation of Nazi decrees but also stirred up local unrest.[28] The regional commissar's housing office and inventory commission took possession of Jewish property and redistributed it among the local officials and privileged groups, to the county commissars, military commanders, and ethnic Germans.[29] In Rivne, in neighboring General Commissariat Volhynia-Podolia, County Commissar Werner Beer held a sale from his office, announcing to other German officials in the area that he had Jewish watches, jewelry, cigarette holders, and other personal effects.[30]

Assisted by local Ukrainian and ethnic German clerks, the county commissar's office carefully listed the addresses of Jews who had been "resettled" and the contents of their dwellings. Letters from local O.T. representatives, ethnic Germans, army officials and other Reich Germans in the area streamed into the inventory commission's office with requests for beds, tables, chairs, and cupboards. In July 1942, Klemm's deputy in the inventory commission, Plisko, issued detailed instructions regarding the confiscation of Jewish property, thus putting a temporary halt to the distribution of Jewish valuables by local officials who were taking items without the proper paperwork. He advised the county commissars not to dispose of the original lists of property registered by the Jews (who were now mostly dead) because these lists (although potentially incriminating) were the most complete records available.[31]

Meanwhile, in the commissar's office of public health, its chief, Dr. Kuhlberg, reported on the outbreak of epidemics, which he attributed to the arrival of Jewish work details in the northern counties of Zhytomyr; no effort was made to provide medical aid to the ill Jewish laborers. In a health policy measure of June 1942, the commander of the Gendarmerie in Zhytomyr ordered all German police who came in contact with the Jews to bathe and check for lice.[32] Again, the timing of this measure coincided with the killings of Jews in the summer of 1942.

The remnant community of Jews in Berdychiv, which (officially) numbered 1,162 in January 1942, was subjected to a salvo of decrees issued by County Commissar Erwin Göllner. First, he ordered all Jews to pay special taxes as of November 1941.[33] In January he called for another registration of all Jews and enforced the wearing of an eight-centimeter white circle. Then he raised taxes by 100 rubles per head. Koch had pressed his county commissars to find more sources of revenue, and like most German commissars, such as County Commissar Dr. Paul Blümel in neighboring Chudniv, Göllner assumed that the Jews could be exploited to this end. The Ukrainian police collected the money. The rubles went directly into his account.[34] Though Nazi leaders prosecuted and even issued the death sentence to the rank and file officials who enriched themselves, corruption was rampant in the system, and top Nazi leaders (for example, Göring and Koch) set the worst examples of state-led plunder for personal gain. Göllner bragged about the "Persian rugs, satin bedding, and Viennese tortes" that he, as a commissar, enjoyed and later requested to be transported with him during the German evacuation of Berdychiv in early 1944.[35]

For some county commissars, merely overseeing the implementation of anti-Jewish measures—whether on their own initiative or carrying out the few guidelines they did receive from above—was not enough. Some felt compelled to join in the actual killing. While Klemm's administrators and technocrats headquartered in the city of Zhytomyr routinely pursued the implementation of anti-Jewish measures in bureaucratic ways, by calculating lists of Jewish property, distributing starvation level rations to the camps, and monitoring epidemics near Jewish camps, many of the German county officials in the rural administrations actually participated in shooting actions.[36] According to Rosenberg's guidelines, the county commissar had unlimited power to enforce police actions against Jews.[37] It was not uncommon that the county commissar himself, after supervising a roundup of Jews, also arrived with the SD commando at the pits and observed the shootings.

In Lityn County, Traugott Vollkammer, an SA colonel, oversaw the action and stood by the pits during the ghetto clearing on December 19, 1941. Subordinate chiefs in the policy department, including one named Sundermeier, took part in shooting one or more Jews in October 1942. Vollkammer's office ordered the final liquidation of the Lityn ghetto on September 18, 1943. Less than 100 Jews remained of the thousands who had resided in the town in summer 1941. Some were able to escape the final destruction of the ghetto, but 14 men, 40 women, and 32 children were not; they died as the Red Army made its advance back into Right Bank Ukraine. In Lityn, the county commissar's office also organized systematic massacres of Roma and collective reprisal measures against Ukrainians in 1943.[38]

The southern counties of the region (Lityn, Vinnytsia, Nemyriv, and Haisyn) were the site of a major road construction project—Thoroughfare IV (*Durchgangsstrasse IV*, DG IV; see chapter 5 of this volume), a main supply line for the Wehrmacht. The use of Jewish labor on this building project meant that the county commissars in these areas continued to be involved in the persecution and killing of Jews throughout 1942 and 1943, more routinely and extensively than in the northern counties where most Jews were killed in the "first sweep" of summer and autumn 1941 and during the final massacres in summer 1942.[39]

In Khmilnyk, hundreds of Jews were killed in the ghetto about every six months or so as part of ongoing selections of laborers and their families (who were assigned to the construction of DG IV). Lityn County Commissar Witzemann led the planning of the massacres and took an active role in the killing, especially in 1942. In fact, Witzemann believed that his mission in the east was to fulfill Nazi political aims, in particular to fully carry out actions against Jews. After the war, a survivor provided testimony about Witzemann:

> On January 2, 1942 the Lityn County Commissar Witzermann [sic] came speeding into town in his car. He was notorious as an inhuman murderer. He summoned the Jewish elder and demanded a large contribution. Immediately after that, he gave the order that elderly Jews were to move from the new section of the city to the old area where a ghetto was being set up. . . . The ghetto had existed for several days when the inevitable German *Aktion* took place. Commanded by County Commissar Wiztermann [sic], the Gestapo men, their assistant, and the police from Lityn and the village surrounded the streets. When the square was filled with people, the county commissar read the list of skilled workers who were permitted to live. The rest were herded to a pine forest about 3 kilometers from the city. Pits had already been prepared there.[40]

The pits had been dug by POWs, who were told that they were preparing an in-ground storage space for potatoes. The ghetto was surrounded by a platoon of army home defense units who had been ordered to shoot any Jews, including women and children, who tried to flee. The ghetto was sealed off at 5:00 AM on January 9, 1942. The half-clothed Jews who had been driven from their homes were forced to stand in the town square in snow and freezing temperatures. Those who could not walk or refused to go were shot on the spot. After some time, an estimated 6,800 Jews were marched to the killing site, where an SD execution squad from Vinnytsia awaited them. Corpses that lay strewn about the ghetto were collected, placed on sleds, and brought to the mass grave in a nearby pine forest. About a week later, local German gendarmes and their Ukrainian auxiliaries searched the ghetto again, discovered 1,240 Jews hiding there, and shot them as well.[41]

Not far from Lityn, in Samhorodok, Wolfgang Steudel, who ran Koziatyn County, implemented the "Final Solution" in his territory. The German Gendarmerie and the Ukrainian police first began to concentrate the Jews there as late as May 16, 1942. During this ghetto operation the German and Ukrainian policemen shot the sick and the elderly and those who resisted. A few weeks later, on June 4, 1942, the remaining population of about 500 Jewish men, women, and children were killed.

Steudel had ordered the Ukrainian mayor of Hermanivka to assign 25 Ukrainians from the nearby collective farm to dig the mass graves. Steudel personally inspected the pits shortly before the Jews arrived. He supervised the entire action, often directing the local Gendarmerie post leader Josef Richter. Two or more SD men from the Sipo-SD outpost in Vinnytsia did the shooting at the pits.[42]

In addition to the local SS-policemen, the county commissar turned to local military personnel in the region for assistance. For example, on May 26, 1942, in Haisyn, a meeting was held in the office of the Wehrmacht's local administration command to plan for the execution of the local Jewish population scheduled for the next day. Haisyn County Commissar Heinrich Becher, who had probably received some prior direction from the SD in Vinnytsia, called the meeting and invited two local Wehrmacht commanders, a certain Major Heinrich and the commander of the Hungarian battalion, along with the station chief of the gendarme post, a certain Dreckmeier.[43] Because they intended to round up the Jews from three villages, Becher split the action into two transports; one of these was led by Heinrich and supported by Ukrainian police and Hungarian infantry. At 3:00 AM they forced the Jews onto trucks and drove them to the execution site at Teplyk, where a shooting commando of SD men stood ready. About 400 Jews were killed in these massacres.[44]

After such mass killings and ghetto liquidations, county commissars continued to be involved in the "Final Solution," because many secretly exploited private Jewish tailors, dentists, and craftsmen in their homes or offices. This was a tacit violation of policy that occurred among the higher ranking civil and police officials in the region, including Otto Hellwig, the SS and police leader for General Commissariat Zhytomyr, and Leyser, the general commissar. In the summer of 1943, about the time that the gendarmes were asked again to turn over any remaining Jews employed in the administration, Leyser identified his Jewish tailor, who was turned over to Hellwig and hanged.[45]

Himmler's agencies maintained supreme control over the mass murder apparatus, but the sheer scope and great importance that Nazi leaders assigned to the "Final Solution" meant that the commissariat and other offices had to contribute to the Holocaust. The commissariat's participation, in contrast to other non-police agencies in the region, was imperative. The county commissars led roundups and incarcerations of the remaining Jewish inhabitants who had survived Wehrmacht administration. They oversaw the ghettoization of the Jews and the management of the ghettos. They also coordinated with various agencies in planning massacres.[46] While there are a few examples of county commissars (among other German officials) who complained about the loss of skilled labor that resulted from the massacres of Jews, these commissars during and after the war did not leave behind or present evidence of any outstanding individual or collective effort to hinder or slow the radical course of the "Final Solution."

Residence of Dr. Hans Schmidt, who served as commissar for Zviahel (Novohrad-Volynsky) County and was an SS first sergeant in the Security Service, the Nazi party's intelligence branch. Schmidt's choice of quarters suggests an attempt to set himself up in Ukraine on a grand scale. Bundesarchiv.

Conclusion

The county commissars' conduct in Zhytomyr reveals that they did what they believed was possible and permissible in their capacity as rulers. They turned the ideological goals set forth by their superiors into everyday practices and some system of rule. At the same time, the county commissars enjoyed a certain independence within their respective areas and could conduct themselves in ways that were not limited by official policies or the expectations of their superiors. Many fancied themselves colonial-style governors in their eastern outposts. Like their forefathers in German Southwest Africa, Nazi commissars at the county level ruled with the whip, conspicuously placing it on their desks during their office hours. They pictured themselves in the "wild east" of Nazi Germany's frontier, where traditional codes of decency seemed irrelevant and violence unrestrained.[47] Commissar Dietz described the "instinctive" ability of his fellow commissars to grasp their historic role:

> The east is a proving ground for pioneers in every respect. The space and never-ending vastness were allowed to play their magical powers and secretly exact a toll from those who were not securely rooted in German thought and its national socialistic duty. The task in the east, in particular as county commissar, allows a free expression of all one's facilities and characteristics. Some developed here talents and capabilities that they could have not developed in the Reich itself. But here were missing the borders that are established in a grown societal order, as in the Reich. Only the clean core and the healthy instinct of the eastern pioneer serves as a pathfinder in the Slavic space . . . our former covenant as members of the Castle of the Order was strong enough to bind together our comrades scattered across the wide space of Ukraine.[48]

Not all the county commissars drank excessively, fraternized, plundered, and ordered executions at whim. From the perspective of senior SS officers in the region, some of the county commissars were too lenient. After a member of Prützmann's office wrote to General Commissar Klemm that a deputy commissar in Novohrad-Volynskyi, a certain Müller, should be reprimanded for not exploiting more labor and facilities in his region, the SS and police, together with the local county agricultural leader, simply disregarded Müller's authority by marching into his county's villages, seizing workers and grain, and murdering village elders who resisted German demands.[49] Usually when a county commissar appeared to be too soft, he was sidelined by others who were willing to do the dirtiest work of Nazi empire building.

In the end, the county commissars, who had minimal resources and worked under extreme pressure from superiors to meet quotas of all kinds, found that their greatest power lay in the central coordinating role that they played in implementing Nazi policy at the lowest levels.[50] The county commissar's office was not strong enough politically, nor was it well enough staffed, to enjoy exclusive control over its county. The prestige that these administrators sought depended on the kind of cross-agency cooperation that occurred in Zhytomyr. Though the entire Nazi ruling apparatus, with its heinous policies, multiple levels of command, and ad hoc structure, constituted a "monstrosity," a necessary system of cooperation emerged at the lower levels in the RKU.

The county commissars embodied an unusual mix of modern colonizers, Nazi revolutionaries, and social outcasts who found their self-worth in the movement and their newfound power in the east. They were amateurs, adventurers, and careerists with worldly ambitions but a narrow outlook and warped education. In many respects, they epito-mized the up-and-coming generation of Nazi bureaucrats in the mak-ing. Having been socialized in the Nazi system, bearing the stamp of the Vogelsang education, and holding the pluralist politics of the Weimar era in contempt, they did not embody the rational, "caged" bureaucrats of the Weberian model, nor were they the banal "desk-murderers" of Hannah Arendt's or Zygmunt Baumann's typologies.[51]

These self-perceived vanguards of the movement were deliberate-ly situated on the Reich's frontier. They carried out the regime's most revolutionary aims with a clear sense of purpose and conviction, not moral numbness and apathy. As Michael Mann has aptly stressed in his study of Nazi perpetrators, "modernity's evil has been more ideologi-cal and blood-spattered than bureaucratic and dispassionate."[52] Raul Hilberg has written that the county commissars, compared with other middle ranking bureaucrats in the Nazi system, possessed "a striking path-finding ability in the absence of directives, a congruity of activities without jurisdictional guidelines, a fundamental comprehension of the task even when there were no explicit communications."[53] One should stress that, in the occupied Soviet territories (as well as Poland), these administrators fancied themselves pioneers in the European imperial tradition, with their own distorted sense of a "manifest destiny" for Germany.[54] While the county commissars did not command the leading role in the "Final Solution," they controlled the main administrative ap-paratus governing Ukraine, which prioritized anti-Jewish policies from the marking of Jews, ghettoization, property confiscation, and labor as-signments to the liquidation of camps and ghettos.

Wartime critiques of the county commissars derided them as cor-rupt, inefficient, and weak rulers, which later contributed to the misper-ception that Rosenberg's staff was not to be pursued seriously as central agents of Nazi criminal activities. Largely overshadowed by Himmler's SS-policemen, many county commissars escaped investigation and prosecution in the postwar era by hiding under this misperception as well as the guise of an ordinary bureaucrat exiled to a remote outpost of the Reich. They were located at the periphery of the empire, but their activities were central to the Nazi's genocidal reordering of Ukraine.[55]

Notes

1. Material in this chapter appeared in my book, *Nazi Empire-Building and the Holocaust in Ukraine* (Chapel Hill: University of North Carolina Press, 2005), pp. 98–161. Nuremberg Document L-221, Besprechung im Führerhauptquartier, July 16, 1941. Participants at the meeting were Hitler, future Reich Minister for the Occupied Eastern Territories Alfred Rosenberg, Chief of the Reich Chancel-lery Hans Heinrich Lammers, Chief of the Party Chancellery Martin Bormann, *Reichmarschall* and Plenipotentiary for the Four-Year Plan Hermann Göring, and Chief of the High Command of the Wehrmacht Wilhelm Keitel.

2. War diary, 454th Security Division, August 20, 1941, U.S. National Ar-chives and Record Administration (NARA), RG 242 T-315/R 2215/000438, and

Commander of Rear Area Army Group South to OKH General Staff, Übergabe an die Zivilverwaltung d. Reichskommissare, September 7, 1941, NARA, RG 242 T-501/R 5/000848. The transfer of the Zhytomyr region to civil administration occurred on October 20, 1941, when the RKU was expanded to the Dniepr and the Cherkasy-Pervomaisk line; this was in accordance with a Hitler decree of October 11, 1941, NARA, RG 242 T-454/R 92/000861-62 and T-315/R 2216/000330. Military affairs in the Reich Commissariat Ukraine were turned over to Wehrmacht Territorial Commander for Ukraine Karl Kitzinger, who was stationed in the RKU capital, Rivne. The territorial commanders in civil administrated territories looked after the passage of troops, POWs, and supplies across the region to and from the front, but they were also drawn into civilian occupation policies. Field Administration Command 811 arrived in Zhytomyr on October 27, 1941; NARA, RG 242 T-315/R 2216/000437.

3. Rosenberg had been forming a staff of eastern experts since early April. On April 20, 1941, Hitler appointed Rosenberg the central authority on the east; Trial of the Major War Criminals before the International Military Tribunal (IMT), NARA, RG 238, PS-865. Himmler (and Heydrich) had also planned since early 1941 to lead the police and security operations of the occupied east, placing Einsatzgruppen, Higher SS and Police Leaders, and Order Police battalions within the military and civilian zones. On Himmler's planning for the war in the east, see Richard Breitman's *The Architect of Genocide: Himmler and the Final Solution* (New York: Knopf, 1991).

4. Alexander Dallin, *German Rule in Russia, 1941–1945: A Study of Occupation Policies* (New York: Macmillan, 1957), pp. 107–118. Gerald Reitlinger, *The House Built on Sand: The Conflicts of German Policy in Russia, 1939–1945* (London: Macmillan, 1960), pp. 129–142.

5. "Die Zivilverwaltung in den besetzten Ostgebieten, Teil II: Reichskommissariat Ukraine," (Brown File), Osobyi Moscow GARF 7021-148-183, p. 10. I am grateful to Jürgen Matthäus for providing me with a copy of this document.

6. The other general commissars were for Volhynia-Podolia, SA Lieutenant General Heinrich Schoene (based in Brest, then Luts'k); for Zhytomyr, Government Executive Administrator (*Regierungspräsident*) Kurt Klemm (and from October 29, 1942, SS Brigadier General Ernst Leyser); for Kiev, Province Office Leader (*Gauamtsleiter*) Waldemar Magunia; for Mykolaïv, NS Aviators Corps Lieutenant General Ewald Oppermann; for Dnipropetrovsk, NSDAP Senior Command Leader (*Oberbefehlsleiter*) Claus Selzner; and for Crimea, former Province Party Leader Alfred Frauenfeld (based in Melitopol). See Karel Berkhoff, *Harvest of Despair: Life and Death in Ukraine Under Nazi Rule* (Cambridge: Belknap Press of Harvard University Press, 2004), p. 39. Frauenfeld, an Austrian, was a fanatical Nazi; after the war he was arrested in 1953 for his involvement in a neo-Nazi plot to overthrow the Bonn government. See Frauenfeld's *Ursache und Sinn unseres Kampfes* (Vienna: Waldheim-Eberle, 1944), "Sowjetunion und Termitenstaat," *Wille und Macht* 22 (Berlin, 1941), pp. 1–4, and *Und trage keine Reu': Vom Wiener Gauleiter zum Generalkommissar der Krim. Erinnerungen und Aufzeichnungen* (Leoni am Starnberger See, 1978), and Alexander Dallin, *German Rule in Russia, 1941–1944*, pp. 264f.

7. General Commissariat Zhytomyr as a geographic construct was a German creation; see *Der Generalbezirk Shytomyr*, Zhytomyr State Archive (ZhSA), P1151-1-51. The general commissariat expanded to 26 counties in 1942.

8. In February 1942, however, three of the 25 counties were still lacking a commissar: Lel'chitsy, Komarin, and Monastyryshche, Kiev Archive of the October Revolution (AOR), United States Holocaust Memorial Museum Archives (USHMM), RG31.003M, reel 3, frames 14ff.

9. See report by the general commissar on the structure of the administration, ZhSA, P1151-1-42. More description of the county commissars' offices is in

Abschlussbericht, Investigation of Zhytomyr county commissars, Bundesarchiv Ludwigsburg, ZSL II 204a AR-Z 135/67, and Case Against Friedrich Becker, Schupo Berdychiv, Bundesarchiv Ludwigsburg, II 204a AR-Z 129/67, Bd. IV.

10. See National Socialists German Worker's Party, *25 Points Regarding a New National Education* in Anton Kaes, Martin Jay, and Edward Dimendberg, eds., *The Weimar Republic Sourcebook* (Berkeley: University of California Press, 1994), pp. 124–126; George Mosse, *Nazi Culture: Intellectual, Cultural and Social Life in the Third Reich* (New York: Grosset and Dunlap, 1966), plate VI; and F. A. Heinen, *Vogelsang: Von der NS-Ordensburg zum Truppenübungsplatz in der Eifel* (Aachen: Helias, 2002). An overview of Vogelsang Castle's history is available on www.lernort-vogelsang.de., accessed on 1 October 2006. A list of county commissars who were active in Zhytomyr and the rest of Nazi-occupied Ukraine is available in *Burggemeinschaft*, no. 7/9 (1944), p. 12. A collection of this alumni newsletter for castle of the order graduates is held at the Deutsche Nationalbibliothek in Leipzig. I am grateful to Mr. Heinen for this reference.

11. On *Ordensjunker*, see Robert Michael and Karin Doerr, *Nazi Deutsch: An English Lexicon of the Language of the Third Reich* (Westport: Greenwood Press, 2002), p. 304. On the Klemm-Meyer correspondence, ZhSA, P1151-1-19; regarding the credentials of staff and party quotas, ZhSA, P1151-1-26 and P1151-1-46; meeting in Berlin on September 23–24, 1941, and naming of Zhytomyr staff, ZhSA, P1151-1-24.

12. Von Wedelstädt (1902–?), head of RKU Main Office I (Policy); after 1945 a lawyer, active in local level politics for the Free Democratic Party. According to British intelligence, Wedelstädt had ties to the postwar underground Nazi organization led by Werner Naumann, a former state secretary in the Propaganda Ministry; see Ernst Klee, *Das Personenlexikon zum Dritten Reich: Wer war was vor und nach 1945* (Frankfurt am Main: Fischer, 2003), p. 658 (Wedelstädt entry) and p. 429 (Naumann entry).

13. Memos regarding special train for commissars traveling to Zhytomyr, November 1941, ZhSA, P1151-1-26; and notes from Klemm meeting of September 23–24, 1941, P1151-1-18.

14. W. Dietz, "Die Ordensburgen im Osteinsatz (Reichskommissariat Ukraine)," *Burggemeinschaft*, no. 7/9 (1944), p. 9.

15. Ibid.

16. Klemm file, ZhSA, P1151-1-26; the commissars' arrival is also described by Fritz Margenfeld, the former city commissar for Vinnytsia. See statement of Margenfeld on the Krössinsee orientation, March 17, 1971, Staatsanwaltschaft (StA) Stuttgart, 84 Js 3/71, p. 2.

17. See, for example, Sittig testimony in Ludwigsburg, Abschlussbericht, II 204a AR-Z 141/67, Bd. II, p. 362f. See also investigation and statement of Fritz Margenfeld (city commissar Vinnytsia), March 17, 1971, StA Stuttgart, 84 Js 3/71, pp. 3–9.

18. Klemm, introductory memo to commissars, December 5, 1941, ZhSA, P1151-1-33.

19. Dietz, "Die Ordensburgen im Osteinsatz," p. 9f.

20. See IMT, NARA, RG 238, NO-1897; tendentious postwar account of Rosenberg deputy, Otto Bräutigam, *Überblick über die besetzten Ostgebiete während des 2. Weltkrieges*, p. 25; and the portrait by historian Jonathan Steinberg, "The Third Reich Reflected: German Civil Administration in the Occupied Soviet Union, 1941–44," *English Historical Review* (June 1995), p. 621.

21. One of the two survivors of Dzerzhyns'k, where the Germans murdered a population of 4,000 Jews, described his ordeal of hiding in old barns and roaming villages in search of food and shelter; see Mikhail Alexeevich Rozenberg, interview (April 25, 1996). Nina Borisovna Glozman also told of her hiding in old barns,

abandoned houses, and factories, interview (February 2, 1995). Eva Abramovna Frankel walked hundreds of kilometers and had to beg for food and shelter in villages around Berdychiv; interviewed by Kira Burova (February 2, 1995), Office of Jewish Affairs and Emigration, Zhytomyr Ukraine. Vladimir Goykher wrote in his memoirs of similar experiences, *The Tragedy in the Letichev Ghetto* (New York: V. Goykher, 1993).

22. In Wetzel's terms, Himmler's forces were in charge. See Otto Bräutigam file, Guidelines for the Treatment of the Jewish Question, NARA, RG 242 T-454/R 154/ MR 334 EAP 99/447.

23. Kommandeur der Gendarmerie, Kommandobefehl, June 6, 1942, ZhSA, P1151-1-9.

24. Jews were allotted rations only if food was left over; if they were given food, it was the ration amount given to a child (up to 14 years old). Report of the RKU, Department for Food and Agriculture, February 20, 1942, Kiev AOR 2206-1-65, in USHMM, RG31.002M, reel 2.

25. On Koziatyn camp and mealtimes, see ZhSA, P1182-1-6. Most of the Jews who were held here were killed before October 1942, though a few remained when the camp was liquidated in May 1943; correspondence between Berdychiv SD Outpost Chief Knop and County Commissar Steudel, May 5, 1943, ZhSA P1536-1-2.

26. SS and Police County Leader Koziatyn to SD Berdychiv, February 11, 1943, pp. 167–168, ZhSA P1182-1-6, and Gendarmerie leader Pohrebyshche to SS and police leader Koziatyn, March 1, 1943, ZhSA, P1182-1-6.

27. Müssig to commissars, July 1942, and October 27, 1942, ZhSA, P1151-1-139.

28. Klemm to commissariat offices, December 12, 1941, ZhSA, P1182-1-6, p.170.

29. See the several cases regarding the disposition of former Jewish housing on Lubarska Street in Zhytomyr city. One mentions that one apartment with Jewish furnishings had been occupied by a German sergeant from the Field Administration Command; memo of May 12, 1942, ZhSA, P1152-1-13. Requests for furniture to the Inventory Commission are in ZhSA, reel 9, P1152-1-16 and P1152-1-13. In 1943, items belonging to Ukrainian men and women who had been arrested and killed as suspected partisans were also among those confiscated and redistributed.

30. Beer announcement, Jewish valuables for sale, November 29, 1941; in USHMM, RG 31.002 (Central State Archive, Kiev, Ukraine), reel 4.

31. On housing and furniture requests, see Plisko's revised procedures for handling of Jewish property, July 29, 1942, ZhSA, P1152-1-16.

32. Kommandobefehl, June 5, 1942, ZhSA, P1182-1-4. The deliberate medical neglect and killing of the insane and handicapped occurred in Vinnytsia under City Commissar Margenfeld. See investigation and statement of Fritz Margenfeld (City Commissar Vinnytsia), March 17, 1971, StA Stuttgart, 84 Js 3/71, 3–9.

33. Göllner order November 1941 and accounting ledgers for Chudniv showing *Judenabgabe* (November 1941–February 1942), ZhSA, P1537-1-282.

34. ZhSA, P1188-2-421. Göllner orders to Berdychiv mayor and precinct chiefs of Berdychiv, Ianushpil and Andrushivka, regarding a Jewish "contribution," November 27, 1941, and January 20, 1942.

35. Göllner inventory, February 8, 1944, ZhSA, 2375-1-1.

36. In the general commissar's office, Klemm and Leyser's personal advisor was Dr. Moyisch; the department chief of justice was Dr. Gunkel; the department chief of public prosecutions was Dr. Derks; the chief of staff of the department of economy was Dr. Amend, whose subordinate chief of industry and manufacturing was Dr. Hollnagel; the chief of labor was Dr. Feierabend. The chief of administration of policy, who oversaw anti-Jewish measures, was Dr. Rauch. See staff charts

and telephone listings in ZhSA, P1151-1-42. These senior officials from the general commissar's office ranged in age from 36 to 45 years, which means that the doctorates were probably granted in late 1920s–mid-1930s.

37. Verordnung über polizeiliche Strafgewalt der Gebietskommissar, August 23, 1941, Brown File, p. 56.

38. Abschlussbericht, Litin Case, Ludwigsburg II 204a AR-Z 135/6, pp. 561ff. Vollkammer was last seen in 1945 in Kurland and was still declared missing in 1973 during a war crimes investigation.

39. Dietz bragged about the commissars' success in exploiting and developing Ukraine's economy and infrastructure, mentioning their support of labor teams assigned to the construction of DG IV, but not specifying their abuse of Jewish laborers there; Dietz, "Die Ordensburgen im Osteinsatz," p. 9

40. Ilya Ehrenburg and Vasily Grossman, eds., *The Black Book* (New York: Holocaust Library, 1980), p. 31f.

41. Home Defense Battalion 466, 1st Lieutenant Hermann Marohn (1891–1948), Abschlussbericht, investigation of commissar in Lityn, Bundesarchiv Ludwigsburg, II 204 AR-Z 135–167, pp. 24ff.

42. Abschlussbericht, Koziatyn Case, Ludwigsburg 204 ARZ 137/67, Band II, pp. 20ff.

43. Ibid., p. 225.

44. Ibid., p. 12. On the SD killing sweep in Teplyk and Sobolivka, see Alexander Kruglov, *Entsiklopediia Kholokosta* (Kiev: Evreiskii sovet Ukrainy, 2000), pp. 9f. The cruel treatment of Hungarian Jewish laborers in Ukraine attached to the 2nd Hungarian Army is detailed in Randolph Braham, *The Hungarian Labor Service System 1939–1945* (New York: Columbia University Press, 1997), pp. 35–38.

45. Bundesarchiv, Ludwigsburg, II 204 AR-Z 8/80 (Franz Razesberger investigation), Bd. I, pp. 41 and 62.

46. The civil administration in Belarus played a similar role, according to the work of Bernd Chiari, *Alltag Hinter der Front: Besatzung, Kollaboration und Widerstand in Weissrussland, 1941–1944* (Düsseldorf: Droste, 1998), p. 59 and chapter 7. See Christian Gerlach's *Kalkulierte Morde: Die deutsche Wirtschafts- und Vernichtungspolitik in Weissrussland, 1941–1944* (Hamburg, 1999), which covers the northern part of General Commissariat Zhytomyr (today in Belarus), pp. 165, 224ff., and 447.

47. On the reference to whips on commissars' desks, see Berkhoff, *Harvest of Despair*, p. 47. On Nazi colonialism and the "wild east," see David Furber, "Going East: Colonialism and German Life in Nazi-Occupied Poland," PhD diss., State University of New York–Buffalo, June 2003.

48. Dietz, "Die Ordensburgen im Osteinsatz," p. 10.

49. On Müller, ZhSA, P1151-1-383. In Vinnytsia, army officers from the agricultural economy section got into a drunken brawl one night and forced Ukrainian militiamen to find them women; they then tried to rape the Ukrainian cleaning woman in their office. Vinnytsia State Archive, P1311-1-2, available in USHMM RG31.011M, reel 1.

50. As Timothy Mulligan has pointed out, "In January 1943, roughly 25,000 Reich Germans governed 16,910,008 inhabitants scattered throughout the Reichskommissariat's five cities and 443 *raions* . . . these dimensions alone ensured that the most basic levels of administration depended entirely on Ukrainians." Timothy Mulligan, *Politics of Illusion and Empire: German Occupation Policy in the Soviet Union, 1942–1943* (New York: Praeger, 1988), p. 64.

51. Donald Bloxham, "Bureaucracy and Genocide," paper presented at conference, Genocide: Causes-Forms-Consequences, The Namibian War (1904–1908), Haus der Kulturen der Welt, Berlin, January 9, 2005.

52. Michael Mann, *The Dark Side of Democracy: Explaining Ethnic Cleansing* (Cambridge: Cambridge University Press, 2005), p. 242.

53. Raul Hilberg, *The Destruction of the European Jews* (New York: Holmes and Meier, 1985), p. 993.

54. On Poland's regional administrators and their colonial mindset, see Furber, "Going East." Reich German women also experienced an "intoxication" with the east and undertook the colonial mission, although their participation in the Holocaust was mainly indirectly oriented toward the rehabilitation of the ethnic Germans; see Elisabeth Harvey's *Women and the Nazi East: Agents and Witnesses to Genocide* (New Haven: Yale University Press, 2004).

55. Of course Rosenberg stressed the primary importance of his commissars to his rival, Himmler. Initially Hitler sided with Rosenberg in this struggle, when Hitler reasserted the governing power of the county commissars in August–September 1942; see Rosenberg-Himmler joint memorandum on commissars, September 1942, NARA, RG 242, T-175/R 17/2521105. In 1944, Dietz described the single-handed contribution and "pioneering work" of the commissars in Ukraine, especially in exploiting agriculture and forced labor; see "Die Ordensburgen im Osteinsatz."

VII

Soviet Ethnic Germans and the Holocaust in the Reich Commissariat Ukraine, 1941–1944

MARTIN DEAN

In late spring 1942, after only a few months of service with the police in Ustynivka Precinct (*Rayon*) in Nazi-occupied southern Ukraine, Ernst Hering, a 19-year-old ethnic German native of the area, was asked to participate in the shooting of Jews from his home region.[1] The Bobrynets County commissar had ordered the police to gather the roughly 25 surviving Jews from the nearby villages at the police station in Ustynivka. Another 35 to 40 Jews were brought in from the nearby town of Bobrynets, where they had been collected from elsewhere in the county.[2]

Around 60 Jews were still living in Hering's home village of Izraïlivka. On the eve of the action, the precinct police chief, Alexander Hübner, also an ethnic German, issued orders for the Jews to be gathered in the village center. After arriving in Izraïlivka, at around 2 AM, the policemen forced the Jews into the school building.[3] Meanwhile, a mass grave was prepared near Kovalivka, a few kilometers outside Izraïlivka on the road to Ustynivka.[4]

The next morning, the *Gendarmerie*, as the rural police from the Reich were known, and the local police (*Schutzmannschaft*) escorted the Jews to the freshly dug pit. The Jews—men, women, and children—were made to undress. Then members of the Security Police (which included the Gestapo), the Gendarmerie, and the local police murdered them by shooting. Other members of these police forces stood guard around the perimeter of the execution site. The commissar for Bobrynets County, a National Socialist official from Germany named Holzmann, and Ustynivka Precinct's top civil administrator, a local ethnic German by the name of Friedrich Strohmeier, stood by and observed the massacre.[5] Having taken away the "racially pure" Jews that morning, some of the local policemen, including Ernst Hering, were sent back to Izraïlivka to collect about 20 half-Jewish children from mixed marriages. The children were then killed as well.

In June 1991, a team of forensic experts employed by the Australian Special Investigations Unit carried out an exhumation of the mass grave near Izraïlivka. The skeletal remains of 19 children aged under 11 years were uncovered lying at the top of the grave. Seven of the children had bullet wounds to the head, while the remainder had fractured skulls caused by a blunt instrument, such as a rifle butt. Under these bodies was a layer of soil and beneath that the remains of adult humans. The Australians estimated that about 100 more bodies were buried there.[6]

Six years later, 55 years after the shooting, Ernst Hering, by then 75, was convicted of abetting the murder of the children at Izraïlivka and given a suspended sentence of 20 months by a German juvenile court in Cologne.[7] According to the court, Hering had joined the German administration's local auxiliary police force in March or April 1942, roughly seven months after the Germans arrived in Kirovohrad Oblast, his home region. The court also found that Hering decided to join the police of his own free will.[8] What would make a 19-year-old man decide to join what was at the time known to be a murderous agency of foreign occupation?

From the available evidence, it does not appear that Hering joined the police out of antisemitism. Between the world wars, ethnic relations in Izraïlivka (also known as Steinthal or Berezovatka) had not been openly hostile. Approximately half of the small town's inhabitants were Jews; the remainder, apart from seven ethnic German families, were Ukrainians. Ernst Hering had even attended the town's Jewish school for a short period prior to its closure by the Soviet authorities.[9]

Hering's parents, devout Christians, disapproved of their son's decision to join the police, but this did not change his mind. He relocated a few kilometers from Izraïlivka to the precinct center of Ustynivka, returning only occasionally to visit his family. Not long after joining the police, Hering learned from his new comrades that their Ukrainian boss, deputy police chief Mefody Marchyk, frequently tortured and shot Jews when he was drunk. This information, however, also failed to move Hering to reconsider. He stayed on, as did his cousin Gustav.[10] It appears that in Ernst Hering's case, more practical matters led to his joining the police. First, unlike service in the German Army, joining the police permitted him to remain behind the front and close to home. In addition, police service was less arduous and better paid than his former job as an agricultural laborer on the collective farms.

This individual's story throws light on a significant yet little known aspect of the Holocaust in Ukraine, that of the ethnic Germans as a link between the occupying force of Reich Germans and the local non-German population. By fulfilling certain key tasks, the local German inhabitants of Ukraine played an important role in the Nazi administration of occupied Ukraine. They made a particularly conspicuous and potent contribution to the effectiveness of the regional and county-level SS and police forces, which, in addition to their many other tasks, were charged with the murder of Ukraine's Jews.

The ethnic Germans of central and eastern Europe cannot be stereotyped as fanatical Nazis or condemned collectively as war criminals. Many ethnic Germans held firm religious beliefs, and some were critical of brutal Nazi policies toward other locals. Nevertheless, a considerable number of the available ethnic German men were recruited into the German administrative structure, including the local police, during the occupation. The exile historian Adam Giesinger noted:

> Because the occupation authorities found them more trustworthy than the rest of the population and because they knew both Russian and German languages, many of them were employed in local government posts and became part of the occupation regime.[11]

Ethnic Germans in Ukraine during the Second World War: Background

Historical analysis of the ethnic Germans to date has concentrated on Nazi policy toward them as a group. In particular, their status as victims of Soviet oppression has diverted attention from the active participation of ethnic Germans in Nazi atrocities. Nevertheless, as translators, local policemen, and officials within the civilian administration, ethnic Germans played important roles in implementing occupation policy in certain parts of Ukraine. In fact, their status as an oppressed minority within the Soviet Union gives added poignancy to the ethnic Germans' response to the Nazis' persecution of the Jews.

Ingeborg Fleischhauer's history of the ethnic Germans of the Soviet Union during the Second World War contains a well-documented overview of the participation of the Ethnic German Self-Defense Force in the murder of Jews in the Romanian occupied territory of Ukraine known as Transnistria.[12] However, with regard to the civil administered Reich Commissariat Ukraine (RKU), her interpretation stresses the condescending attitude of Reich German officials toward the local ethnic Germans. She states that there were only a few ethnic Germans at the lower levels of the administration, and that none held senior positions within the RKU.[13] While this statement is accurate with regard to representation at the higher levels, Fleischhauer does not, for example, examine the service of ethnic Germans within the Gendarmerie and the local police, which were responsible for policing at the precinct level.[14]

The work of Meir Buchsweiler provides a fair assessment of the situation of the ethnic Germans caught up in the struggle between two dictatorships based on terror. He concludes:

> Nearly all ethnic Germans in Ukraine knew what was done to the Jews, even soon after the invasion. Many received some of the property stolen from the Jews and at least several hundred (perhaps even thousands) participated actively in the killing actions.[15]

He also provides examples and evidence from the RKU's general commissariats. In Stalindorf Precinct, which lay in General Commissariat Dnipropetrovsk, a number of Jewish collective farms existed alongside German settlements. Not all of the Jews there were liquidated immediately. Instead, they were depleted by successive police "actions" from September 1941 until the end of 1942. Buchsweiler notes that in this area ethnic Germans were local administrators, while some took over the former homes of the Jews.[16] Nonetheless, the bulk of the evidence he presents concerns the participation of ethnic Germans in atrocities committed in Transnistria.

This chapter will examine the participation of ethnic Germans in crimes against humanity, in the context of the history of their local communities. The aim is to illuminate the various ethnic German responses to Nazi rule in the east and the roles played by ethnic Germans in the Holocaust. Despite the need for a more detailed analysis of the ethnic German Self-Defense Force's role in the murder of local and Romanian Jews in Transnistria,[17] this chapter will concentrate mainly on the hitherto neglected role of ethnic Germans within the German police structure of the RKU.[18] An additional brief case study of an ethnic German serving with Einsatzgruppe D has been included to illustrate the career paths of ethnic Germans who served with the Security Police and the Security Service (SD).

Historical Roots of Ethnic Germans in Ukraine

The history of ethnic Germans in Ukraine extends back to the eighteenth century. The first organized German colonists were encouraged to settle in the Russian Empire by Catherine the Great in the period 1764–1767. Although they initially settled along the Volga River, further large-scale migrations in the late eighteenth and the first quarter of the nineteenth century included the establishment of more than 300 settlements in Ukraine.[19] Many of these Germans migrated for religious as well as economic reasons. By 1914, the ethnic German population in Ukraine had increased to more than 500,000.[20] Soviet census data, however, indicates a decline thereafter to about 400,000 in 1926.[21]

As these figures imply, the fate of the ethnic Germans was deeply affected by mass deportation, famine, and emigration that took place during the First World War, the Russian Civil War, and the initial years of Soviet rule. German investigations conducted during the Nazi occupation reveal that many ethnic German communities in south-central and eastern Ukraine suffered heavy losses at the hands of the anarchist partisans of Nestor Makhno in 1919.[22] In 1921–1922 and again in 1933, large numbers of ethnic Germans fell victim to the famines that followed the collectivization of agriculture. Collectivization also destroyed the prosperity of ethnic German farmers.[23] Many thousands were deported to Siberia prior to 1941—especially in the years 1937–1938—and only a few ever returned.[24] In the summer of 1941, the retreating Soviets rounded up and deported as many ethnic German men aged between 16 and 60 as they could, but only became relatively efficient in doing so in early autumn, when the front reached the Dniepr River. For example, 31,320 ethnic Germans from the Zaporizhzhia Oblast were deported to the Soviet interior at the end of September 1941. Only a small number of ethnic German men from Left Bank Ukraine were able to escape deportation.[25]

Recruitment of Ethnic Germans to Serve the Third Reich

The ethnic German settlements in southern Ukraine were of considerable interest to Heinrich Himmler, the head of the both the SS and the German police, and to various other agencies under his purview, including the office of the Reich Commissar for the Strengthening of Germandom. Several different German organizations prepared detailed reports on these communities. Among the reporting agents were members of Special Commando R (*Sonderkommando R[ussland]*) and Kommando Dr. Karl Stumpp as well as the propagandist Karl Götz.[26] Registration of the ethnic Germans was entrusted to the Ethnic German Liaison Office, an office for ethnic German affairs established on Himmler's orders in 1937.[27] A number of detailed accounts on ethnic Germans can also be found in the monthly situation and activity reports of the Einsatzgruppen.[28]

Many Reich Germans were initially skeptical of the local ethnic Germans' loyalty to the fatherland; they suspected that Bolshevik rule and intermarriage would have had debilitating effects on their capacity to serve the new order.[29] In some areas, measures taken against suspected Communist activists included the arrest and murder of a few ethnic Germans who had "collaborated" with the Soviets.[30] However, indisputable evidence of the survival of German culture and active support for the German administration soon convinced the Nazi invaders that most of the ethnic Germans were "loyal."[31] Even some Mennonites, pacifists by ideology, "expressed ardent support for the occupiers."[32]

In their search for local personnel to staff the new administration, the Reich Germans saw the ethnic Germans as the best candidates for many key posts due to their language abilities and supposed loyalty.

An ethnic German teacher, Ramm, installed by the occupying authorities as the mayor of Pryshyb, south of Zaporizhzhia, poses for a photo taken by a member of a special task force from the Stuttgart-based Institute for the German Abroad (Deutsches Ausland-Institut) in 1942. The portrait in the background reads, in Ukrainian, "Hitler the Liberator." Bundesarchiv.

For instance, ethnic Germans were appointed as mayors in both Zaporizhzhia and Novo-Zaporizhzhia in General Commissariat Dnipropetrovsk. Heinrich Jakob Wiebe of Zaporizhzhia was an experienced communal official from tsarist times and had worked as an accountant under the Soviets. A report filed by the 676th Field Administration Command (FK 676) describes him as "intelligent, hard-working and concerned," and his measures were described as "effective." The mayor of Novo-Zaporizhzhia was a Mennonite named Isaak Johann Reimer, also described as active and energetic but lacking something of the necessary administrative experience. Nonetheless, his practicality enabled him to demonstrate partly good results.[33]

The recruitment of ethnic Germans to serve the Third Reich frequently occurred on a semi-voluntary basis. Owing to the dire need of the Germans for translators to enable them to administer such large swaths of occupied territory, the German authorities from the military, police, and civilian administration energetically sought to recruit those ethnic Germans possessing the necessary language skills.[34]

Ethnic Germans were preferred as administrative and police chiefs at the precinct level, both in the RKU and in the military occupied areas. They were clearly over-represented in these positions and were given responsibility for areas with few or no ethnic German settlements. For instance, of the 11 precincts surrounding the town of Ivanivka, which all ended up in the Partial Commissariat Taurida, there existed only three ethnic German communities. However, two of the 11 precinct administrative heads and three of the precinct police chiefs were ethnic Germans.[35] Some ethnic Germans were even able to benefit from the competition among German agencies for their skills and to choose which organization they worked for.

Service of Ethnic Germans in the Local Police

From the beginning of the occupation, ethnic Germans were also recruited to the local police, also known as the *Miliz* (or *militsiia*, Russian for police) during the period of military occupation. For example, FK 676 noted in early September 1941 that "in the town of Pervomaisk, the militsiia consists of ethnic Germans who are being trained by a staff corporal of the Field Gendarmerie [ed. the Wehrmacht's equivalent of the military police]."[36]

By early 1942, the German Order Police, the regular police, had begun transforming the Miliz into a more organized local police force (*Schutzmannschaft*).[37] They attempted to weed out undesirable elements and took measures to provide the men with proper uniforms and police training. In the RKU, the vast majority of local policemen were Ukrainian, but a number of ethnic Germans were scattered throughout the police, often serving in key positions. In addition to being highly sought after as translators, they were preferred as non-commissioned officers to administer the local police.

Many of the Reich German gendarmes in the RKU came from the reserve of the Order Police. They were too old to serve on the front, but could be counted on to help police the civil administered territories. About two thirds of the Gendarmerie officials assigned to General Commissariat Mykolaïv in 1941 were members of the police reserve.[38] However, the Reich Germans were usually tied up with administrative tasks.[39] As a result, they had to rely considerably on the initiative of the local NCOs within the indigenous police to lead patrols, carry out arrests, and interrogate suspects.

A platoon consisting of roughly 20 to 25 gendarmes from the Reich was based in each county under the command of a "Gendarmerie county leader" (*Gendarmerie-Gebietsführer*).[40] The members of the platoon were in turn deployed in groups of three to five men over several posts, which were generally situated in the various precinct centers of a Gendarmerie county leader's area of responsibility.[41] Each Gendarmerie post usually had 30 or more local policemen, usually recruits from the area. At many posts, at least one or two ethnic Germans were to be found working primarily as translators and senior NCOs within the local police. Records from 1942 for Ruzhyn County, located in the southern part of General Commissariat Zhytomyr, indicate that only three ethnic Germans were working among some 100 indigenous policemen at the county's three main Gendarmerie posts (Ruzhyn, Popilnia, and Vchoraishe). And these records of the local policemen covered only two of the three posts. Two of the ethnic Germans were NCOs, and the other served with the Gendarmerie as a translator.[42]

A rough indication of the number of ethnic Germans in the police in General Commissariat Zhytomyr can be gleaned from details of training courses conducted by the Berdychiv Gendarmerie Captaincy, which consisted of several surrounding counties. Of 120 men called up for a training course in 1943, 30 were ethnic German auxiliaries. The 11th Motorized Gendarmerie Platoon, made up entirely of ethnic Germans, sent 17 men to take part in the course. A further 13 ethnic Germans were made available from three other Gendarmerie platoons in the captaincy.[43] Caution is advised in extrapolating from these figures, as German instructions gave a clear preference to ethnic Germans over Ukrainians for training courses. The percentage of ethnic Germans in the local police units overall is unlikely to have exceeded 10 percent, even including the few purely ethnic German units. For example, the Gendarmerie county leader in Melitopol, an area of ethnic German settlement, had 16 ethnic Germans serving among 143 local policemen in August 1942 in the Novovasylivka Precinct.[44]

More significant is the representation of ethnic Germans among the senior NCOs. In the northern half of General Commissariat Zhytomyr, ethnic Germans appear to have been heavily represented among the senior NCOs of the local police. In a list of decorations issued on April 26, 1943, seven out of nine senior NCOs have German-sounding names.[45] In an area with a relatively strong ethnic German population, as was the case north of Zhytomyr, ethnic Germans provided a strong cadre of NCOs within the local police, in addition to fulfilling their more typical function as translators.

According to a German census of June 1943, there were 169,074 ethnic Germans in the RKU, 130,866 in Transnistria, and 13,365 in the military occupied areas.[46] The number of able-bodied men aged 18 to 35 was only a fraction of these totals due to deportation and conscription into the Red Army. The strength of the Ukrainian local police in the RKU exceeded 36,000 in July 1942 and was more than 50,000 by November 1942.[47] The number of ethnic Germans serving within this force probably did not exceed 5,000, although their strong overrepresentation in leadership positions gave them considerable influence. Older ethnic German males and those not already in the police served in local forces established to help protect ethnic German communities from partisan attack.[48] Surviving German documentation regarding the precise position of ethnic Germans within the Nazi police structure is ambiguous. Evidence from several areas demonstrates that ethnic Germans served alongside Ukrainians in the local police but usually in positions of seniority.

In 1942, ethnic German policemen in General Commissariat Zhytomyr were given the special status of Ethnic German Auxiliary Police (*Volksdeutsche Hilfspolizei*). They ranked above their Ukrainian counterparts in the local police, but they still did not enjoy the full civil service status of the gendarmes from the Reich.[49] The members of the Ethnic German Auxiliary Police wore green uniforms similar to those of the Order Police, which distinguished them from members of the Ukrainian local police.[50] Orders were also issued for all ethnic German policemen to attend training courses.[51] According to postwar witness testimonies from what had been the general commissariats of Mykolaïv and Volhynia-Podolia, ethnic German policemen were sent to train at local police schools during the occupation. Upon their return, they were seen wearing the green uniforms of the Order Police. Subsequently, they worked directly with the Gendarmerie.[52]

The Ethnic German Auxiliary Police was envisioned as an entirely German organization designed to replace the non-German police in areas designated as strictly ethnic German settlements. However, many of the ethnic Germans remained in the Ukrainian police throughout 1942, because it took some time to create the settlements and to train the eligible men. In the Korosten Captaincy, preparations were made in 1942 for all ethnic German policemen to be transferred to a single company. The comments of a Gendarmerie captain in this regard are revealing:

> I remind you again to conduct energetic recruitment of ethnic Germans for an ethnic German company to be established in the future. These men should be enrolled in the local police and held in readiness for the company. The company is to be integrated later into the Gendarmerie. I expect the Gendarmerie county leaders to demonstrate understanding for my plan, to support it freely, and not to complain if I take away some of their ethnic German policemen. We all must have before our eyes the great aim of integrating the ethnic Germans into our community and strengthening the position of Germans in this country. I consider my plan suited to achieve this. Insofar as ethnic Germans are required as translators, they can be replaced by ethnic German women and girls.[53]

How important was the contribution of ethnic Germans to the Nazi criminal policies perpetrated by the SS and police forces? If many ethnic

Germans served as translators, what kind of power could they wield in this capacity? An outstanding example of a translator who sabotaged Nazi policies is to be found at the local police station at Mir (today in Belarus). There, Oswald Rufeisen, who concealed his Jewish identity by claiming to be a Pole, served as a translator in the local police. Through careful mistranslation of police interrogations, Rufeisen succeeded in freeing a man suspected of planning to join the partisans. On another occasion, he used similar tactics to mislead the police about local partisan movements.[54] The translation of interrogations of suspected partisans was a matter of life or death for prisoners, as a great many were shot afterward.[55]

Did ethnic Germans play a key role as perpetrators of Nazi crimes against Jews and other victims of the Nazi terror? The extent of ethnic German participation was influenced by the chronological and structural development of the Holocaust in the different parts of Ukraine. In some areas in central and southern Ukraine, the Einsatzgruppen and police battalions conducted mass killings of the Jews in the summer and fall 1941 before the arrival of the Gendarmerie. In several locations, such as Kryvy Rih and Radomyshl, the participation of the Miliz in mass killings in the summer of 1941 is documented, although no information is available on the participation of ethnic German personnel in these incidents.[56] In Talne, some 40 kilometers northeast of Uman, an ethnic German is reported to have taken over the leadership of the population and carried out a "large action" against the Jews in August 1941.[57]

With regard to what scholars call the "second wave" of killings, which took place in 1942, especially in General Commissariat Volhynia-Podolia and the southern half of General Commissariat Zhytomyr,[58] the specific role of the Gendarmerie and local police is better documented. In these areas, as with the case of Ustynivka noted above, it is possible to identify individual ethnic Germans who took an active part in anti-Jewish measures on the basis of evidence collected for postwar criminal investigations.

In the village of Vchoraishe in Ruzhyn County, the chief of the local police was an ethnic German named Arthur Reglin. According to Soviet evidence, he was present when men under his command rounded up some 200 Jews on May 1, 1942. The local police escorted the Jews to the execution site, where members of the Gestapo carried out the shooting. Reglin was also accused, in 1951, of personally shooting a Jew with his revolver in May 1942 after the Jew was found in hiding.[59] This last accusation is characteristic of the active role played by NCOs in the local police, which combed emptied ghettos and surrounding forests in order to finish off remaining Jews.[60] Further evidence of ethnic Germans acting as police chiefs and participating in the murder of Jews can be found for the towns of Iemelchyne and Kovel in general regions of Zhytomyr and Volhynia-Podolia respectively.[61]

An ethnic German self-defense unit in Halbstadt (Ukrainian: Molochansk) stands at attention for visitors from the Institute for the German Abroad (Deutsches Ausland-Institut) in 1942. Bundesarchiv.

Case Study: Domachevo Precinct

A more detailed case study of the role played by ethnic Germans in the local administration is provided by the events in the Domachevo Precinct of General Commissariat Volhynia-Podolia. Here, the fate of the entire ethnic German community became inextricably linked with that of the Reich Germans as they became drawn into the growing partisan conflict. In the vicinity of the town of Domachevo (now in Belarus), there were a number of ethnic German settlements or colonies. In the winter of 1939–1940, many ethnic Germans left the Soviet Union for the Reich in accordance with a 1939 German-Soviet agreement for the resettlement of the Volhynian Germans.[62] However, the male members of some ethnic German families decided to remain behind in order to look after their property. This was the case with the family of Gustav Ryll, born 1921, who together with his father remained in Domachevo, where they owned the steam mill.[63] When the Wehrmacht arrived, the Rylls were registered as ethnic Germans. The younger Gustav Ryll was among the first to volunteer for service with the local police in 1941.[64]

According to Soviet postwar statements, Gustav Gustavovich Ryll participated in the arrest and shooting of local inhabitants during the occupation.[65] The participation of the local police in the mass shooting of Jews in Domachevo is recorded in a monthly report of the Gendarmerie county leader in Brest:

> On September 19–20, 1942, an anti-Jewish *Aktion* was carried out in Domachevo and Tomashovka by a special commando of the SD together with the cavalry squadron of the Gendarmerie and the local police stationed in Domachevo, and in total, some 2,900 Jews were shot. The action took place without any disturbance.[66]

The story of the ethnic German community in Domachevo is of interest for several reasons. According to the results of a local census of the region reported by the civil administration in February 1942, 284 ethnic Germans were living in the Domachevo Precinct, as well as 3,316 Jews and more than 7,000 Ukrainians.[67] Despite the comparatively small ethnic German community, persons registered as ethnic Germans held a number of key posts in the administration, including the Domachevo village elder, the assistant to the local German agricultural leader, and the Gendarmerie's translator.[68] Ethnic Germans were also requested to use their local knowledge to provide the names of former Communist Party activists.[69]

At the time of the liquidation of the Domachevo ghetto in September 1942, which saw the elimination of all but a handful of the town's Jewish inhabitants, there was also a brutal operation to clear the nearby orphanage. The SD office in Brest conducted this operation, although it is alleged in Soviet documentation that an ethnic German named Vogel informed the orphanage staff that the children would be moved to Brest. The children were instead taken away by truck and murdered nearby.[70]

The probable motive for the murder of the orphans was the desire to establish a German kindergarten in the building, to serve the growing ethnic German community.[71] Ethnic Germans from the region (as well as subsequently some refugees displaced from the east by the German retreat) were being concentrated in Domachevo for their security and to provide schooling for their children. Ethnic German children attending the kindergarten in Domachevo received clothing that had been collected from the Jews just before they were shot.[72]

As partisan warfare intensified in the autumn of 1943, the ethnic German community increasingly became the target of Soviet partisan attacks.[73] In response, available ethnic German men were organized into a self-defense force to help defend the town. Soviet partisans launched a major attack against Domachevo on November 23, 1943. In this attack, two ethnic Germans were killed and one was wounded.[74] A partisan report noted that of the local peasants only the ethnic Germans had not been alienated by the high agricultural levies imposed by the Nazi authorities, as they received preferential treatment.[75] A further partisan raid in early 1944 resulted in the burning of a number of ethnic

German houses. As the security of the 600 ethnic Germans (including women and children) could no longer be guaranteed, they were evacuated to Białystok.[76]

The case of the chief of the police in Khoiniki, a precinct center in the northern part of General Commissariat Zhytomyr, provides further evidence of the direct participation of ethnic German NCOs in the Holocaust. Alexander Ermolshik was born in the Khoiniki area (now in Belarus) in 1915 to an ethnic German father and a Ukrainian mother. He trained with his father as a mechanic and was serving as a corporal with the Red Army in Baranovichi at the time of the German invasion. At the first contact with the enemy, he deserted without firing a shot and returned to his home precinct in the wake of the advancing German troops.[77]

After serving for a brief period as a translator with the German civil administration at the end of October 1941, he took up a position as a criminal investigator with the German Gendarmerie. According to his own testimony, he was mainly involved in interrogations and investigations arising from reports made by the local population.[78] From April 1942 until September 1943, Ermolshik was the leader of Khoiniki's local police, which consisted of about 80 Ukrainian volunteers. At the end of 1943, he retreated with the German forces to Germany, where he worked in a dairy and later in an armaments factory before being drafted into the Wehrmacht. Just prior to his capture by the Americans, he changed his name to Albert Krüger, as he feared that otherwise he might be handed over to the Soviets.[79]

Ermolshik/Krüger was the subject of Soviet allegations after the war, based mainly on the extensive Soviet investigations conducted against lower ranking members of the Khoiniki local police. A number of specific allegations were made against Ermolshik in relation to the murder of members of the local population. One specific incident described by several Soviet witnesses concerned the shooting of a family of seven Roma by a patrol of Ukrainian policemen under Ermolshik's command in November 1942. On their arrival in the village of Strelichev, the local village elder, who was punished by the Soviets after the war for collaboration, showed the policemen the house occupied by the Roma. In 1963 Soviet authorities exhumed the victims' bodies. The remains revealed traces of bullet wounds to the head. Local inhabitants who had been instructed to bury the bodies recalled the policemen departing from the scene singing a well-known folk song.[80]

Evidence of Ermolshik's police service can also be found in the surviving records of the Gendarmerie post in Khoiniki. He is listed as a corporal in the local police in Rechitsa in April 1943, when he received a decoration for "members of the eastern peoples."[81] Just prior to this, on February 18, 1943, he was arrested and his house searched, apparently in connection with the shooting of an "innocent person" without specific orders from the Gendarmerie.[82] In spite of this, Ermolshik still received his decoration. A further report in September 1943 names him as leader of the Khoiniki indigenous police during a battle against partisans. A female partisan captured during the operation was shot four days later after her interrogation and a telephone conversation with the SD.[83]

These contemporary records and postwar investigations indicate the active role played by Ermolschik as a local police chief. His position involved him in the arrest and interrogation of suspects and in the execution of prisoners once authorization had been granted by the SD. It appears that Ermolschik may also have abused his position to settle personal scores. His indispensability, however, protected him from serious consequences.

Service of Ethnic Germans with the Security Police

Some ethnic Germans were recruited directly into the Security Police and served with a mobile Einsatzgruppe unit or a Regional Commander of the Security Police and SD in the occupied territories. All SD prisoners were closely interrogated with the assistance of translators. Witness statements indicate that following the interrogations, there were initially only two options, either release or execution, partly due to the need for more space in the prisons. If the interrogation revealed that a prisoner was Jewish, then the prisoner's execution would automatically follow. Thus, considerable responsibility rested on the ethnic German translators attached to the Security Police and SD.[84]

A 1999 trial in Stuttgart brought to light the participation in mass killings by an ethnic German from Ukraine who had served in the Gestapo.[85] At the time of the German invasion in the summer of 1941, Alfons Josefovich Götzfrid was 21 years old. He lived in the village of Marynivka near Odessa. In the late summer of 1941, he was requested by the German authorities to escort a number of horses to Mykolaïv. There, he was given a job as groom and translator with the command of Einsatzgruppe D. He then received instructions from the Einsatzgruppe to take the horses to Simferopol, where he arrived at the end of November 1941.[86]

In the winter of 1941–1942, members of Einsaztgruppe D command and Sonderkommando 11b shot about 10,000 Jews in Simferopol. The victims were murdered outside the city in anti-tank ditches.[87] According to interrogations conducted by the Soviet authorities, Götzfrid personally took part on the first day of the two-day massacre. Among the victims were women, children, and elderly people.[88] There were several other ethnic Germans from the Soviet Union acting as translators with Einsatzgruppe D in Simferopol at this time.[89]

Later, Götzfrid served with the Caucasian Company, which was formed by Walter Kehrer in Simferopol during the first half of 1942. The company acted primarily as a guard unit for Einsatzgruppe D command. The Caucasian Company was recruited from Soviet prisoners of war, comprising Armenians, Georgians, Azerbaijanis, members of other Caucasian peoples, and Russians.[90] According to Götzfrid's testimony, the Einsatzgruppe conducted regular shootings of prisoners taken from the prison in Simferopol. These took place roughly twice a week until May or June 1942. At this time, a gas van arrived, which was subsequently used to murder prisoners.[91]

In a 1973 statement, Götzfrid admitted that, as a member of the Caucasian Company, he directly participated in the gas van operations in Simferopol: "I helped in forming the corridor and also had to go into the cell in order to hurry the people up. I also had to escort those people who had to bury the dead bodies."[92] According to his Soviet statements, Götzfrid participated several times in gas van "actions" under Kehrer's command in the city of Stavropol in Russia after the Einsatzgruppe advanced toward the Caucasus in the summer of 1942.[93] His unit then retreated in 1943 via Darmstadt (near Melitopol) and Ovruch to Lviv. Götzfrid subsequently worked in the second half of 1943 as a translator and supply clerk for the Caucasian Company.[94] In July 1943, the Caucasian Company participated in the liquidation of the Jewish forced labor camps Kamianky (Kamionki I) and Velyki Birky (Borki Wielki) near Ternopil.[95]

In 1999, a German court convicted Alfons Götzfrid for his participation in Operation Harvest Festival, the liquidation of the Jewish camps in Majdanek, Trawniki, and Poniatowa in the General Government on November 3–4, 1943. Götzfrid, together with other members of the Security Police from Lviv, is believed to have taken part in the shootings at Majdanek, where the number of victims is estimated between 17,000 and 18,000.[96] The numerous self-incriminating statements of Götzfrid recorded by the Soviet authorities are unusual in that he did not subsequently deny them when later questioned by investigators from the West. In fact, he made considerable admissions that ultimately led to his prosecution in Germany. When he was questioned as a witness in 1996, he clearly recalled specific details of the liquidation of the camp at Velyki Birky and freely confirmed other elements of his Soviet statements.[97]

Götzfrid was 21 years old when he left home to serve with Einsatzgruppe D. He started out initially as a groom, but with time, he took on greater responsibility as a translator with the Caucasian Company and served as an active member of the Security Police in Lviv. These successive promotions reflected his loyal service with the Einsatzgruppe. He was punished for his crimes, serving more than ten years in Soviet prisons. These crimes have come back to haunt him in the form of recurring interrogations throughout his life.[98] His story also reflects the experience of many young ethnic Germans who became drawn into mass crimes by their misplaced enthusiasm for the Nazis on their arrival in Ukraine.[99]

Conclusion

What conclusions can be drawn following this survey of the role of ethnic Germans in the various German forces within the RKU? While their numbers remained small and the positions they held were relatively minor, ethnic Germans still acted as an important link between German police officers from the Reich and the local population. In particular, as translators and senior NCOs, they were crucial in enabling the local police to function under German orders. As translators during interrogations, they sometimes held the power of life and death over prisoners in German custody.

The few detailed case studies above demonstrate that many of the ethnic German men were quite young (aged 18–21) at the time of their recruitment and had missed being deported or purged on account of their youth. The direct impact of Soviet repression on their lives, often devastating, made many of them strongly anti-Soviet; thus they willingly served the German occupation authorities, encouraged by the privileges they were offered in relation to the local non-Germans.[100] In turn, the effect of removing young men from their families and integrating them into the police exposed these young men to a great deal of peer pressure. The absence of many fathers, or other figures of moral authority, due to Soviet deportations, may also have played a role.

There were, therefore, a number of reasons why the Nazis were able to exploit young ethnic Germans and convert them into instruments of their criminal policies. The ethnic German communities themselves were not necessarily ideal breeding grounds for Nazi ideology. Despite strong resentment arising from the human and material losses suffered under Soviet rule, there remained a clear demand for the revival of religion among many ethnic Germans, some of whom had also achieved a degree of assimilation within the surrounding population on a personal and professional level.

With time, Nazi policies and the communal experience of complicity in the occupation served to bind the fate of ethnic Germans ever more closely to that of the Third Reich. In addition to widespread service in the police, the Wehrmacht, and the local administration from the start of the occupation, remaining males of military age were conscripted into the Waffen-SS, the armed forces of the SS, during the retreat from the RKU during summer and autumn of 1943.[101]

While ethnic Germans did benefit from privileges granted to them by the Third Reich, they also became a particular target for partisan attacks on account of their close associations with the German administration. As a result, efforts were made to uproot and concentrate them in a few main settlements, where they could be more easily protected with the help of their own self-defense forces. With this in mind, specific ethnic German platoons were also created within the indigenous police in General Commissariat Zhytomyr and designated Ethnic German Aux-

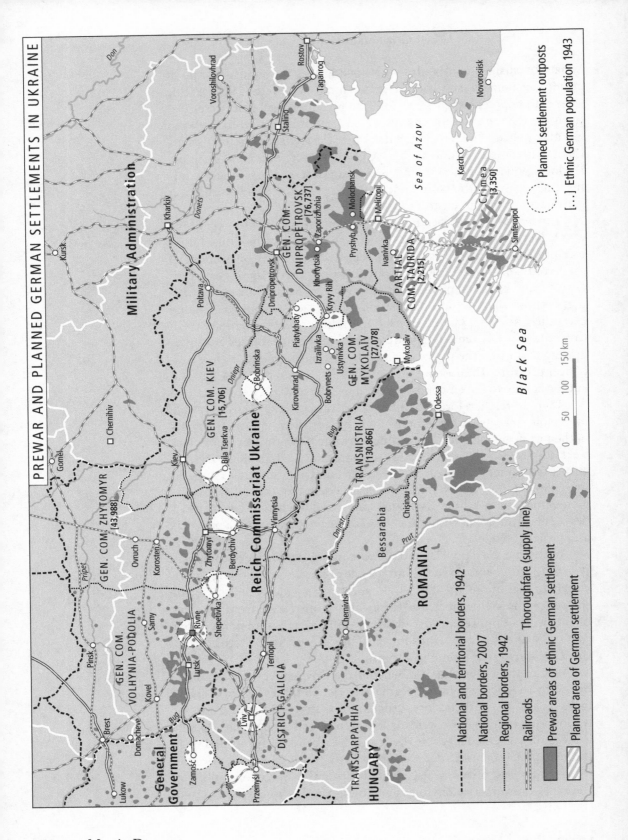

PREWAR AND PLANNED GERMAN SETTLEMENTS IN UKRAINE

iliary Police. As the Red Army advanced westward across Ukraine in 1943 and 1944, whole ethnic German communities were evacuated to the Reich in what were called "treks."

Ethnic Germans serving with the Gendarmerie and the local police were also evacuated together with their units.[102] Police personnel from southern Ukraine, including men from the Gendarmerie in General Commissariat Mykolaïv, can be found on the roster for Police Rifle Regiment 38, which was reorganized and re-outfitted during the retreat through Romania and Hungary in late 1944. The roster also includes a number of ethnic Germans from southern Ukraine.[103]

The Nazis' aim was to integrate the ethnic Germans gradually into a wider, strictly German national community (*Volksgemeinschaft*). In terms of police service, this can be seen in the efforts taken to prevent ethnic Germans from serving under Ukrainian command within the local police. This resulted in their rapid promotion to positions as senior NCOs and their employment as translators in the Gendarmerie. They were offered the long-term prospect of possibly receiving civil service status within the police, but that could only be granted once they had achieved full German citizenship.

The fusion of ethnic German interests with those of the Reich was only fully achieved during the closing phase of the war. The parents of ethnic Germans serving in the police, the Waffen-SS, and the Wehrmacht were registered as full German citizens on entering the Reich. Their sons also received citizenship as a result of a "Führer decree" granting citizenship to ethnic Germans serving in the German police and Waffen-SS.[104] Thus, only in retreat did ethnic Germans become fully integrated into the Reich—just in time to become full participants in the trauma of defeat.

The self-perception of ethnic Germans as "double victims" of history has generally overshadowed their role as instruments of Nazi policy. The case studies of a few individuals, such as Ernst Hering and Alfons Götzfrid, who were brought to justice in Germany in the late 1990s, are probably representative of many others who were punished in the Soviet Union or have escaped detection. These and other cases demonstrate that an influential number of ethnic Germans, serving as low-level perpetrators, came to perform key functions within the police structure of the RKU and to participate actively in the Holocaust at the regional and local level.

Notes

1. The precise date of the action is not clear from the Soviet witness statements. The main surviving eyewitness dated the shooting as May or June 1942; Australian Special Investigations Unit (SIU), Statement of Ivan Konstantinovich Zhilun, December 23, 1989. The general commissar for Mykolaïv reported that there were no longer any Jews or half-Jews in his commissariat as of April 1, 1942; see Dieter Pohl's chapter in this collection. The Jews of Bobrynets' County may have been caught up in the wholesale liquidation that took place in General Com-

missariat Mykolaïv in March, or they may have formed a group that managed to last another month or so after the region was declared free of Jews.

2. SIU (Security Service of Ukraine [SBU], Kirovohrad), Statement of Alexander A. Hübner (Gibner), March 20, 1947. This summary of events in Ustynivka was compiled mainly from statements in Soviet trials from the 1940s and 1950s. In spite of some discrepancies concerning dates and numbers, the statements appear to be reliable concerning the overall pattern of events. These accounts can also be compared with additional evidence collected by the SIU in the case of Heinrich Wagner and by the Dortmund Prosecutor's Office in the case of Ernst Hering.

3. SIU (SBU Kirovohrad), Statement of G.K.K., May 20, 1946, in own case.

4. SIU, Statement of Ivan K. Zhilun, December 23, 1989, and SIU (SBU Kirovohrad) G.K.K., May 20, 1946, in own case.

5. SIU (SBU Kirovohrad), statements of Alexander A. Gibner, March 20, 1947, and April 1, 1947, in own trial; F.F.S., March 1, 1958; and I.K.K., February 13, 1958, in Criminal Case File No. 4,419 (Mefody Marchyk).

6. Landgericht Köln (4. Grosse Strafkammer, 1. Jugendkammer), Urteil B. 104–28/97 in der Strafsache gegen Ernst Hering (Urteil Hering), December 19, 1997, pp. 43–49. Hering was under 21 at the time of the offense and therefore, according to German law, subject to trial before a juvenile court.

7. Urteil Hering, pp. 88f. The juvenile court's verdict is of particular interest as it also to some extent analyzes the family background and education of the accused as relevant factors in assessing the seriousness of the crime.

8. Police regulations issued in neighboring General Commissariat Zhytomyr in February 1942 indicate that policemen were permitted to resign with 14 days notice; see United States Holocaust Memorial Museum (USHMM), RG 53.002M (Belarusian National Archives Minsk [BNAM]), Reel 5, 658-1-1, p. 84, Kommando Befehl 6/42, February 18, 1942.

9. Landgericht Köln, Verdict 104-28/97, pp. 4–11.

10. Urteil Hering, pp. 4–11. Mefody Marchyk was tried and sentenced to death in Ukraine in 1958.

11. Adam Giesinger, *From Catherine to Khruschev: the Story of Russia's Germans* (Battleford, Sasketchewan: Marian Press, 1974), p. 308. See also similar comments by J. Otto Pohl, *Ethnic Cleansing in the USSR, 1937–1949* (Westport: Greenwood Press, 1999), p. 45.

12. Ingeborg Fleischhauer, *Das Dritte Reich und die Deutschen in der Sowjetunion* (Stuttgart: DVA, 1983), pp. 138–143.

13. Ibid., p. 163.

14. On the hitherto neglected aspect of German policing at the local level, see Martin C. Dean, "The German *Gendarmerie*, the Ukrainian *Schutzmannschaft* and the 'Second Wave' of Jewish Killings in Occupied Ukraine: German Policing at the Local Level in the Zhytomyr Region, 1941–44," *German History*, 14, no. 2 (1996), pp. 168–192.

15. Meir Buchsweiler, *Volksdeutsche in der Ukraine am Vorabend und Beginn des Zweiten Weltkrieges—ein Fall doppelter Loyalität?* (Gerlingen: Bleicher, 1984), p. 383.

16. Ibid., pp. 381ff.

17. On the role of the *Selbstschutz* in Transnistria, see Andrej Angrick, "Die Einsatzgruppe D: Struktur und Tätigkeiten einer mobilen Einheit der Sicherheitspolizei und des SD in der deutsch besetzten Sowjetunion," PhD diss., Technische Universität, Berlin, 1999, pp. 173–196. For a perspective based also on Romanian sources, R. Ioanid, *Holocaust in Romania: The Destruction of Jews and Gypsies under the Antonescu Regime, 1941–44* (Chicago: Dee, 2000), pp. 187–193.

18. The three main case studies here concern the Gendarmerie and *Schutzmannschaft* in the RKU precincts of Ustynivka, Khoiniki (now in the Gomel Oblast of Belarus) and Domachevo (now in the Brest Oblast of Belarus).

19. Richard H. Walth, *Strandgut der Weltgeschichte: Die Russlanddeutschen zwischen Stalin und Hitler* (Essen: Klartext-Verlag, 1994), p. 30.

20. Gosudarstvennyi Arkhiv Rossiiskoi Federatsii (GARF), 7021-148-183, Braune Mappe: Die Zivilverwaltung in den besetzten Ostgebieten. Teil II: Reichs-kommissariat Ukraine, 1941.

21. Fleischhauer, *Das Dritte Reich*, pp. 45f.

22. On the Makhno partisans' activities, see, for example, Orlando Figes, *A People's Tragedy: The Russian Revolution 1891–1924* (London: Cape, 1996), pp. 661–664.

23. GARF, 7021-148-183, Braune Mappe, Teil II. See also, for example, the village reports in Bundesarchiv Berlin (BA-B), R 6/620, 621, and 626.

24. J. Arch Getty, Gabor T. Rittersporn, and Viktor N. Zemskov, "Victims of the Soviet Penal System in the Pre-war Years: A First Approach on the Basis of Archival Evidence," *The American Historical Review*, 98, no. 4 (1993), p. 1,028, gives a figure of more than 18,000 ethnic Germans in GULAG camps in 1939.

25. J. Pohl, *Ethnic Cleansing*, pp. 39ff. The Presidium of the Supreme Soviet on August 28, 1941, issued a decree ordering the deportation of the Volga Germans behind the Urals. This gave further impetus to German plans to deport German Jews to the east as a form of reprisal. See A. Angrick, "Die Einsatzgruppe D," pp. 174ff. Valdis O. Lumans, *Himmler's Auxiliaries: The Volksdeutsche Mittelstelle and the German National Minorities of Europe, 1939–45* (Chapel Hill, London: University of North Carolina Press, 1993), p. 244, notes that the majority of ethnic Germans remaining in Ukraine consisted of women, children, and elderly people.

26. For an overview of the most important reports, see Buchsweiler, *Volksdeutsche in der Ukraine*, pp. 467–489; on the village reports prepared by Kommando Dr. Stumpp; see, for example, Eric J. Schmaltz and Samuel D. Sinner, "The Nazi Ethnographic Research of Georg Leibbrandt and Karl Stumpp in Ukraine, and Its North American Legacy," *Holocaust and Genocide Studies*, 14, no. 1 (2000), pp. 36–42.

27. Lumans, *Himmler's Auxiliaries*, p. 245. Lumans largely skates around the participation of ethnic Germans in war crimes and refers only to service in the *Selbstschutz* and the Waffen-SS.

28. Peter Klein, ed., *Die Einsatzgruppen in der besetzten Sowjetunion 1941/42: Die Tätigkeits- und Lageberichte des Chefs der Sicherheitspolizei und des SD* (Berlin: Edition Hentrich, 1997), pp. 214ff. and pp. 238ff., contains two reports on ethnic German communities. See also BA-B, R58/217-218, Ereignismeldungen UdSSR (EM) No. 86, No. 103, and No. 107.

29. Angrick, "Die Einsatzgruppe D," pp. 170ff.

30. Ibid., pp. 178f.

31. Buchsweiler, *Volksdeutsche in der Ukraine*, pp. 306–310, gives evidence that the initial response was not always overwhelming, as there was some concern that the Soviets might soon return.

32. Schmaltz and Sinner, "Nazi Ethnographic Research," p. 46. The ethnic German settlements in Ukraine included both Catholic and Protestant congregations. In particular, there were a number of Mennonites, Baptists, and Lutherans who had preserved their faith. The revival of religious life in these communities presented some difficulties for the German authorities. See also Angrick, "Die Einsatzgruppe D," pp. 181ff.; Fleischhauer, *Das Dritte Reich*, p. 164; Doris L. Bergen, "The Nazi Concept of 'Volksdeutsche' and the Exacerbation of Anti-Semitism in Eastern Europe," *Journal of Contemporary History*, 29, no. 4 (1994), pp. 569–582.

33. USHMM, RG 11.001M.13 (Records from the Former Special [Osobyi] State Archive, Moscow), Reel 92, 1275-3-661, Feldkommandantur 676, October 21, 1941: "Reimer ist ein aktiver energischer Mensch, dem es allerdings noch etwas an der nötigen Verwaltungserfahrung fehlt. Doch besitzt er praktischen Blick und Geschick, sodass er in seiner Arbeit auch teilweise recht gute Erfolge aufzuweisen hat." Schmaltz and Sinner, "The Nazi Ethnographic Research," p. 46, refer to a

meeting of Dr. Stumpp with the mayor of Zaporizhzhia; as he is described as a non-Mennonite, it was presumably Heinrich Wiebe from Zaporizhzhia. On March 24, 1942, the German authorities gathered the Jewish population of Zaporizhzhia together under the pretext of sending them to the town of Melitopol' for work. They then marched 3,700 people out of town to the Stalin State Farm, where they were shot; see A. F. Vysotsky et al., *Nazi Crimes in Ukraine, 1941–44* (Kiev: Naukova Dumka, 1987), pp. 142f. The role of the local ethnic German mayors is not mentioned in this report.

34. On the recruitment of ethnic Germans as translators for the Wehrmacht, see BA-B, R58/218, EM No. 107; on the efforts to recruit ethnic Germans as police translators, see RG 53.002M (BNAM), Reel 5, 658-1-1, p. 56, KdG Shitomir, Kommandobefehl 6/42, February 18, 1942.

35. BA-B, R6/307, pp. 121ff.

36. USHMM, RG 11.001M.13 (Osobyi), Reel 92, 1275-3-661, Feldkommandantur 676, September 8, 1941. On the recruitment of ethnic Germans as auxiliary police under an ethnic German mayor, see BA-B, R58/214, EM No. 26, and R58/217, EM No. 86.

37. On the dissolution of the *militsiia* and the creation of the *Schutzmannschaft* in General Commissariat Zhytomyr, see Zhytomyr Archive (ZhA), 1182-1-17, p. 132, Kommando Befehle, n.d. [December 1941]. Some sources attempt to translate *Schutzmann* and *Schutzmannschaft* literally. The word is merely an old-fashioned German word for police, which the Order Police apparently adopted to distinguish the indigenous police from the German police in its various manifestations (Gendarmerie, Security Police, etc.).

38. BA-B, R 19/464, pp. 139–143, Schnellbrief des RFSS, November 17, 1941. By 1940, the Order Police had called up 91,500 men born between 1901 and 1909 as police reservists. Subsequently, the call-up was extended to older age groups. See Christopher R. Browning, *Ordinary Men: Reserve Police Battalion 101 and the Final Solution in Poland* (New York: Harper Perennial, 1993), pp. 5f.

39. Martin Dean, *Collaboration in the Holocaust: Crimes of the Local Police in Belorussia and Ukraine, 1941–44* (London: Macmillan, 2000), p. 72.

40. BA-B, R 19/333, pp. 45f., RFSS, Betr.: Vorläufige Richtlinien für den Einsatz der Gendarmerie in den besetzten Ostgebieten, January 8, 1942.

41. For example, BA-B, R 94/7, Gendarmerie-Gebietsführer Brest-Litovsk an KdG Lutsk, October 6, 1942.

42. ZhA, 1182-1-15, List of *Schutzmannschaft* members for Ruzhyn and Vchoraishe posts in Ruzhyn County in summer 1942. An additional *Volksdeutsche Hilfspolizist* was assigned to the platoon in November 1942.

43. ZhA, 1182-1-17, p. 102, Gendarmerie-Hauptmannschaft Berditschew, October 21, 1943. This document implies that, while some ethnic Germans had been withdrawn from other platoons to form purely ethnic German units in some areas of German settlement, other ethnic Germans continued to serve with Ukrainian policemen. On this policy and the Hegewald settlement project, see Wendy Lower, "A New Ordering of Space and Race: Nazi Colonial Dreams in Zhytomyr, Ukraine (1941–44)," *German Studies Review*, 25, no. 2 (2002), pp. 227–254.

44. Bundesarchiv Dahlwitz-Hoppegarten (BA-DH), ZM 1462 Akte 5, Gend.-Gebietsführer Melitopol, August 21, 1942.

45. USHMM, RG 53.002M (BNAM), Reel 5, 658-1-3, p. 189, KdG Shitomir, Kommandobefehl 33/43, April 26, 1943. Of the 69 *Schutzmänner* listed (including non-NCOs), at least 25 were probably ethnic Germans; another list of *Schutzmänner* recommended for decorations in General Commissariat Zhytomyr contained only three probable *Volksdeutsche* out of 61 men listed; see USHMM, 1996.A.269 (ZhA), Reel 1, 1151-1-11, Kommando Befehl 52/43, August 1, 1943.

46. Pohl, *Ethnic Cleansing*, p. 44.

47. BA-B, R 19/266, Stärkenachweisung der Schutzmannschaft, July 1, 1942; BA-B, R 19/122, pp. 129–136, HSSPF Ukraine an RFSS, November 25, 1942.

48. In some areas, it was not possible to establish *Selbstschutz* units due to the shortage of able-bodied men, see ZhA, 1182-1-36, p. 121, Gend.-Gebiet Rushin, August 15, 1942.

49. Osobyi, 1323-2-255, pp. 22f., KdG Shitomir, September 23, 1942.

50. ZhA, 1182-1-17, p. 29; reference is made to the green uniforms in BA-DH, ZAI/5346 A.9, KdG Shitomir, Kommandobefehl 3/44, February 8, 1944.

51. USHMM, RG 53.002M (BNAM), Reel 5, 658-1-1, pp. 115f., KdG Shitomir, Gendarmerie-Hauptmannschaft Korosten, June 2, 1942.

52. Search File of G.R. in KGB Archive Brest, pp. 2f. and 15f. For Kirovohrad, see SIU (SSA Kirovohrad), Statement of Alexander A. Hübner [Gibner] of June 13, 1947, in own trial, and Staatsanwaltschaft Dortmund 45 Js 30/93, Statement of Ernst Hering, January 5, 1996.

53. USHMM, RG 53.002M (BNAM), Reel 5, 658-1-1, pp. 115f., KdG Shitomir, Gendarmerie Hauptmannschaft Korosten, June 2, 1942.

54. Nechama Tec, *In the Lion's Den: The Life of Oswald Rufeisen* (New York: Oxford University Press, 1990), pp. 106–111.

55. For example, ZhA, 1465-1-1, p. 9.

56. BA-B, R 58/217, EM No. 88, p. 8; USHMM, RG 11.001M.13 (Osobyi), Reel 92, 1275-3-665, OK I/253 in Kryvyi Rih, situation report of October 14, 1941.

57. USHMM, RG 11.001M.13 (Osobyi), Reel 92, 1275-2-663, OK I (V) 839 in Uman', situation report of August 30, 1941. The ethnic German concerned was accused of having belonged to the Communist Party and having maligned the Führer prior to the German invasion. He was removed from his post during the investigation. I am grateful to Wendy Lower for bringing this document to my attention.

58. On the disparity between the Zhytomyr and the Vinnytsia oblasts (both within the General Commissariat Zhytomyr) with regard to the timing of the Jewish killings, see Alexander I. Kruglov, *Unichtozhenie evreiskogo naseleniia Ukrainy v 1941–1944 gg.: khronika sobytii* (Mohyliv-Podol's'kyi: n.p., 1997), p. 96.

59. Zentrale Stelle Ludwigsburg (ZStL), II 204 AR-Z 128/67, Vol. I, pp. 139f., Soviet confrontation of witness A. F. Smoljanskij with accused Arthur Reglin, the police chief in Vchoraishe, December 30, 1951.

60. Dean, *Collaboration*, pp. 71, 96–99, and 165.

61. For evidence of the alleged participation of an ethnic German in actions against the Jews in the Iemel'chyne area of General Commissariat Zhytomyr in 1941, see ZStL, 204 AR 339/66. This file concerns the investigation conducted against Bernhard Blech, an ethnic German NCO in the Iemel'chyne police. For the participation of the chief of the Ukrainian police, Fritz Manthei, in the killing of Jews in Kovel', see Landgericht Oldenburg, 2 KS 1/64, cited in Shmuel Spector, *The Holocaust of Volhynian Jews, 1941–44* (Jerusalem: Yad Vashem, 1990), p. 179.

62. Giesinger, *From Catherine to Khruschev,* p. 301, notes that some 60,000 ethnic Germans left Soviet-occupied Volhynia following the announcement on November 24, 1939; for examples of ethnic Germans who left the Domachevo area, see U.S. National Archives and Records Administration (NARA), Einwanderungszentralstelle USSR, records for Boguslav Selent, who entered the Reich on January 30, 1940, and Romuald Ryll, who entered the Reich on February 1, 1940.

63. KGB Brest, Search File of G. G. Ryll. It appears the mill was confiscated by the Soviets.

64. KGB Brest, Search File of A. A. Savanyuk, and Criminal Case against I. E. Chikun, Arch. File No. 466, Vol. II, pp. 94–99.

65. KGB Brest, Search File of G. G. Ryll, Search File of A. A. Savanyuk, and Criminal Case No. 403, Arch. File 9057 (Mikhail D. Kozlovskii), pp. 26–30.

66. BA-B, R 94/7, Gendarmerie-Gebietsführer Brest-Litovsk, report of October 6, 1942.

67. BA-B, R 94/7, Gebietskommissar Brest-Litovsk, report of March 24, 1942.

68. UKGB Brest, Criminal Case No. 23552 against K-N.M.B. and M.E.N (1945); BA-B, R 94/7, Gebietskommissar Brest-Litovsk, report of February 24, 1942.

69. UKGB Brest, Criminal Case No. 23552 against K-N.M.B. and M.E.N (1945).

70. For various accounts of this atrocity, see Brest Oblast Archive, 514-1-195.

71. BA-B, R 94/7, Gebietskommissar Brest-Litowsk Lagebericht, October 9, 1942, mentions that a start had been made on furnishing the ethnic German kindergarten planned for Domachevo: "Der Kindergarten wird in dem früheren einheimischen Waisenhaus untergebracht in welchem bisher sowjetische Waisenkinder untergebracht waren, die inzwischen vom SD übernommen sind." On the fate of the Domachevo orphans, see Bernhard Chiari, *Alltag hinter der Front: Besatzung, Kollaboration und Widerstand in Weissrussland 1941–44* (Düsseldorf: Droste, 1998), pp. 195 and 204ff., and Christian Gerlach, *Kalkulierte Morde: Die deutsche Wirtschafts- und Vernichtungspolitik in Weissrussland 1941 bis 1944* (Hamburg: Hamburger Edition, 1999), p. 1,075.

72. BA-B, R 94/7, Contribution to the monthly report for the period October 1–31, 1942.

73. BA-B, R 94/8, Gebietskommissar Brest-Litowsk an den Generalkommissar, Lagebericht, December 23, 1942.

74. BA-B, R 94/8, Gendarmerie-Gebietsführer Brest-Litowsk, December 5, 1943.

75. BNAM, 3500-4-321, History of the Voroshilov partisan unit, p. 93; ethnic German workers in the area received twice the pay of other locals and equal rations with the Reich Germans, see BA, R 94/6, Brest Stadtkommissar, August 27, 1942.

76. BA-B, R 94/8, Gendarmerie-Gebietsführer Brest-Litowsk, February 3, 1944.

77. ZStL, 202 AR-Z 871/63, Vol. I, pp. 45–48, Interrogation of Albert Krüger (a.k.a. Alexander Ermolshik), April 6, 1964. I am grateful to Erich Haberer for assisting me with information regarding this complex.

78. Ibid.

79. Ibid.

80. ZStL, 204 AR-Z 871/63, Vol. III, pp. 768–772.

81. USHMM, RG 53.002M (BNAM), 658-1-3, p. 189, KdG Shitomir, Kommando Befehl Nr. 33/43, April 26, 1943.

82. USHMM, RG 53.002M (BNAM), 658-1-3, p. 27, Kriegstagebuch Gendarmerie Post Choiniki, February 18–22, 1943.

83. USHMM, RG 53.002M (BNAM), 658-1-3, p. 157, Gend. Post Choiniki, report of September 21, 1943.

84. *Justiz und NS-Verbrechen*, Vol. 19 (Amsterdam: Amsterdam University Press, 1978), p. 614 (pp. 560–566). For an example of an ethnic German who worked for the SD in Berdychiv, see Instytut Pamięci Narodowej (IPN), Warsaw, SWKt 193. See also Martin Dean, *Collaboration*, p. 61, which notes that a third option of transfer to a labor camp was subsequently introduced.

85. For background information relating to the case, see *Stuttgarter Zeitung*, April 28, 1999.

86. Staatsanwaltschaft Frankenthal, 9 JS 70/65, Vol. XIV, pp. 2,472–2,492, Statement of Alfons J.Götzfrid, September 26, 1973, and Vol. XIII, pp. 2,386–

2,390, Statement of A.J.G., September 22, 1971, Vol. XIV, p. 2,473, and Vol. XIII, p. 2,386; Landeskriminalamt (LKA) Stuttgart, Interview with A.J.G., May 8, 1996.

87. NARA, T-175, Roll 234, EM No. 150, p. 20, reports both the shooting of 17,645 Jews and an *Aktion* in Simferopol'. NARA, T-175, Roll 234, EM No. 170, p. 19, reports that almost 10,000 had been shot so far in Simferopol'.

88. StA Frankenthal, 9 JS 70/65, Vol. XIII, pp. 2,386–2,390, Statement of A.J.G., September 22, 1971, and Vol. I, p. 46, A.J.G., October 7, 1964.

89. A further translator, H., is named by witnesses; see ZStL, 208 AR 87/66, Vol. IV, p. 681, A.A.S., September 28, 1973; see also StA Frankenthal, 9 JS 70/65, Vol. I, p. 39, D.H., October 11, 1964.

90. Some members of the unit were captured in May 1942; see ZStL, 208 AR 87/66, Vol. IV, A.A.S., September 28, 1973, p. 677; D.N.N., September 25, 1973, p. 597; and G.P.W., October 1, 1973, p. 694.

91. StA Frankenthal, 9 JS 70/65, Vol. XIV, pp. 2,472–2,492, Statement of Alfons J. Götzfrid, September 26, 1973, and Vol. XIII, p. 2,387, Statement of A.J.G., September 22, 1971. On the development of the gas van and its use by Einsatzgruppe D from the end of 1941, see M. Beer, "Die Entwicklung der Gaswagen beim Mord an den Juden," *Vierteljahrshefte für Zeitgeschichte*, 35, no. 3 (1987), pp. 403–417.

92. A.J.G., September 26, 1973, p. 2,482; also A.J.G., September 22, 1971, p. 2,388.

93. A.J.G., September 26, 1973, p. 2,483, and September 22, 1971, p. 2,388. In his Soviet protocol of August 11, 1960, he states that the gas van "actions" in Stavropol' were carried out by Einsatzkommando 12.

94. A.J.G., September 26, 1973, p. 2,485, and September 22, 1971, p. 2,389; A.J.G., August 12, 1960; and Recommendation for Award KVK 2. Kl., Lemberg, August 12, 1943 (copy from LKA Stuttgart); ZStL, II 208 AR 87/66, Vol. V, p. 1,136. K. Weidauer, April 27, 1987, confirms that A.J.G. served with the Caucasian Company.

95. T. Sandkühler, *"Endlösung" in Galizien: Der Judenmord in Ostpolen und die Rettungsinitiativen von Berthold Beitz, 1941–44* (Bonn: Dietz, 1996), p. 268.

96. H. Grabitz and W. Scheffler, *Letzte Spuren* (Berlin: Edition Hentrich, 1988), pp. 328f.

97. LKA Stuttgart interview with Götzfrid, May 8, 1996.

98. During an interview, Götzfrid commented that in 1,000 years people would probably still dig him up to ask him questions.

99. For evidence of an ethnic German from Domachevo who joined the SD in Brest, see IPN, Warsaw, SWGd 71–77, Statement of Mikhail D. Kozlovskii, November 1, 1948.

100. On the privileged position of ethnic Germans within the RKU, see, for example, USHMM, 1996.A.269 (ZhA), Reel 2, 1151-1-21, p. 24, RKU an die Generalkommissare, April 7, 1942.

101. For an example of call-up papers for ethnic Germans in November 1943, from General Commissariat Zhytomyr, see USHMM, 1996.A.269 (ZA), Reel 1, 1151-1-6. See also Fleischhauer, *Das Dritte Reich*, p. 145.

102. See Dean, *Collaboration*, pp. 148f.

103. Wehrmachtauskunftstelle Berlin, Erkennungsmarkenverzeichnis (dog-tag list) Polizei-Schützenregiment 38, March 27, 1945; on the path of retreat taken by these units, see Dean, *Collaboration*, pp. 150f.

104. *Befehlsblatt des Chefs der Ordnungspolizei*, August 5, 1944.

VIII
Jewish Losses in Ukraine, 1941–1944

ALEXANDER KRUGLOV

A key component of the Nazis' plans for achieving global domination was an antisemitism that had as its strategic goal the universal, physical eradication of Jews around the world. This aim represented the most important and most consistent element of Nazi ideology and policy between 1933 and 1945. The tactical means to this end addressed several policy interests: first, in the realm of economic policy, confiscating Jewish property and exploiting Jewish labor so as to eliminate Jewish competition from domestic markets and enrich local economic interests; second, where domestic politics were concerned, consolidating and strengthening the Nazi regime and German nation at the expense of what was seen by Hitler and his followers as a subversive and corrupting element; third, in foreign policy, weakening and undermining the countries that were to become the victims of aggression by disseminating politically destabilizing and morally corrupting myths and lies about Jews; fourth, on the psychological front, inculcating Germans with feelings of racial superiority and hatred of others, particularly Slavs and Jews; and fifth, with regard to practical matters, improving means and methods of repressing and destroying local Jewish populations.

One of those territories where the Nazis attempted to implement these goals was Ukraine. There, as elsewhere in eastern Europe, the anti-Jewish genocide unfolded in a brazenly public and exceptionally brutal fashion. There, the Nazis did not feel themselves bound by any kind of conditions, as they did in the countries of western and central Europe. They acted with determination and ruthlessness, even killing highly qualified Jewish workers at a time when these were desperately needed.

In mid-1941, some 2.7 million Jews lived in the territory of what is today the independent state of Ukraine.[1] Taking the borders of Ukrainian Soviet Socialist Republic between June 1940 and June 1941, that is to say after Moscow seized eastern Galicia and western Volhynia from Poland and the northern half of Bukovina and Izmaïl territory from Romania, the Jewish population in Soviet Ukraine totaled over 2.47 million souls. In quantitative terms, the Jews of Ukraine were for this brief period the largest Jewish population in Europe and the second largest Jewish population in the world. Between 1941 and 1945, more than 1.6 million of them perished at the hands of the Nazis and their accomplices. Roughly 100,000 Jews survived the German occupation in hiding or in Nazi camps and ghettos. The rest, more than 900,000, escaped the Nazi genocide by fleeing with the Red Army into the Russian interior during the Soviet retreat in 1941.

Despite the scale of destruction and the high death toll among Ukraine's Jews, the Holocaust as it unfolded in that part of the Soviet Union has not attracted the level of scholarly attention typically given to Poland, where the extermination camps were located, or Germany, where the first steps that ultimately led to the Holocaust were taken in the mid-1930s and early 1940s. Indeed, most students and scholars of the Holocaust are unaware of the scale of killing that occurred in Ukraine.

This chapter, using the most recent documents to emerge from Ukrainian and Russian archives since the collapse of the Soviet Union in 1991, attempts to provide a quantitative survey of the total losses experienced by the Jews in Ukraine between June 22, 1941, and July 21, 1944, and does so by presenting these losses as they occurred in specific oblasts (Soviet regional-level administrative districts) and on a monthly basis. The documents cited here include contemporary German documents, witness statements, material gathered by Soviet investigators traveling in the rear of the Red Army, and survivor testimonies and memoirs.[2] This analysis also draws heavily from my own previous publications.[3]

Among the key Soviet sources frequently consulted are the records of the Extraordinary State Commission for Ascertaining and Investigating Crimes Committed by the German-Fascist Invaders and Their Accomplices, which was set up before war's end. Here, the commission's evidence is corroborated with contemporary German and Romanian documents; postwar criminal investigations and trial material, including indictments and verdicts, kept in Ukrainian and Russian security service archives, as well as similar materials compiled by West and East

German prosecutors and courts over the decades; and Jewish sources such as memoirs, diaries, and memorial books.

This statistical review covers the territory of today's Ukraine, including Transcarpathia, northern Bukovina (Chernivtsi Oblast), and the Crimea. However, the oblasts of Ukraine are discussed as they existed in early 1941, on the eve of the German invasion. This means that Kiev Oblast includes most of today's Cherkasy Oblast, and Mykolaïv contains most of present-day Kherson. Conversely, the Drohobych and Lviv oblasts and the Odessa and Izmaïl oblasts are treated individually.

Jewish Losses: 1941

The Nazis' war against the Jews is intertwined with the Third Reich's invasion of the Soviet Union, which began on June 22, 1941. That same day, in Sokal, the first large town encountered by the Wehrmacht on June 1941, German soldiers shot 11 Jews. During the days that followed, about 1,500 Jews in the oblasts of Lviv, Drohobych, and Volhynia were murdered.

The first "Jewish actions" in Ukraine were directed mainly against members of the Jewish intelligentsia as potential organizers of resistance. Jewish officials from the Communist Party of the Soviet Union and Jewish civil servants were also among the principal victims of the first massacres. In the western oblasts of Ukraine, thousands of Jews were killed in pogroms. Some of these pogroms were organized surreptitiously by the Germans, while others were spontaneous acts of anti-Jewish violence. In both cases, both factions of the Organization of Ukrainian Nationalists, the Melnykites and the Banderites, were often involved.

Thus in July, the death toll for Jews as a result of shootings and pogroms combined totaled 38,000–39,000 persons. The massacres during this period took place primarily in the western oblasts of Lviv (7,000 victims), Drohobych (1,600), Ternopil (9,000), Chernivtsi (9,000), Zhytomyr (3,000), Volhynia (2,500), Proskuriv (1,800, today Khmelnytsky), Odessa (1,000), Rivne (1,000) and Vinnytsia (800), and Stanyslaviv (several hundred, today Ivano-Frankivsk). On July 21, 1941, during a visit to Lviv, Himmler seems to have issued an unwritten order to his representative in Ukraine, Higher SS and Police Leader Russia South Friedrich Jeckeln, to kill all male Jews save for those who could be used for forced labor.[4] The following day, Himmler ordered the 1st SS Infantry Brigade to Lviv and subordinated it to Jeckeln's command, a clear signal that the HSSPF Russia South would need more manpower in the days to come.[5]

At first glance the death toll for Jews in Ukraine for the month of August—around 62,000 persons—would suggest that this order and the additional forces had resulted in the acceleration of mass murder that Himmler appears to have desired. This, however, did not come about so quickly. If one takes into consideration the Jews killed during the first three weeks of August, one arrives at a figure of 40,000 Jews, almost the same as in the month of July.

This "inactivity," from Himmler's point of view, led the Reichsführer-SS and chief of the German police to summon Jeckeln on August 12, 1941. During this meeting, Himmler probably issued a verbal order regarding the killing of Jewish women and children. Jeckeln shortly thereafter transmitted this order, also verbally, to his Order Police battalions and Einsatzgruppe C.

Thus, at the end of August, the mass murder of Jews took in Ukraine took on a new dimension, affecting all Jews without regard for gender or age. The watershed event came in the town of Kamianets-Podilsky. There, starting August 26, Jeckeln's Order Police formations murdered more than 22,000 Jews over the span of three days.[6] From this point on, no essential change would occur in the policy of mass murder against the Soviet Union's Jews. The number of oblasts and municipalities rendered "free of Jews" would grow until the Ukrainian lands were without any Jews save for those in hiding.

Taking all of August together, the Germans killed about 61,000–62,000 Jews in 15 oblasts. More than 31,000 Jews perished in Proskuriv Oblast, about 10,000 in Zhytomyr, over 3,500 in Rivne, 3,000 in Vinnytsia, 3,500 in Odessa, 3,000 in Volhynia, 3,000 in Kiev, and about 1,000 in the oblasts of Stanyslaviv and Mykolaïv. Additional massacres also occurred in Lviv, Drohobych, Kirovohrad, Chernivtsi, Dnipropetrovsk, and Ternopil oblasts.

By early September, the Order Police and Einsatzgruppe C were carrying out indiscriminate, near total liquidations of entire Jewish communities. Whereas male Jews had been the primary target in the first weeks of Operation Barbarossa, after mid-August 1941 elderly people, women, and children were gunned down by German police and SS forces and their local recruits. Not only did the scale of killing increase, but the speed with which the Nazis implemented the killing operations did as well. The SS and police forces, often with logistical and organizational support from the German armed forces, carried out killing operations involving tens of thousands of Jews in actions lasting but a few hours or days.

Again the figures provide the evidence for this brutal acceleration of the mass murder campaign. During September, the Germans and their accomplices killed about 136,000–137,000 Jews, mainly in the oblasts of Kiev (where 33,771 Jews were killed at Babi Yar on September 29–30), Zhytomyr (about 27,000, with 16,000 Jews perishing in Berdychiv and 4,000 in Zhytomyr), Vinnytsia (19,000 Jews, 15,000 of which were in the administrative center Vinnytsia, with another 1,500 in Haisyn), Mykolaïv (26,500, with over 8,000 in the town of Kherson and over 7,000 in Mykolaïv), Kirovohrad (5,200), Proskuriv (4,250).

Einsatzgruppe C and Einsatzgruppe D took the lead in organizing these killing operations, as is well documented and frequently described in Holocaust histories. However, the emphasis on studying the Sipo-SD commandos has come at the expense of underestimating Jeckeln's Order Police formations. These formations—Police Regiment South (Police Battalions 45, 303, and 314), Police Battalions 304 and 320, and the 1st SS Infantry Brigade—were crucial for carrying out the large-scale operations in cities and towns. No large massacre took place without their assistance, whether that support came in cordoning off killing sites or relieving their Sipo colleagues as shooters. Ultimately, the Order Police killed more Jews in Ukraine than the two Einsatzgruppen together. For example, Police Regiment South shot 4,414 Jews in Ostroh (Rivne Oblast) and Polonne (Khmelnytsky Oblast) on September 2, another 1,548 Jews in Ruzhyn (Zhytomyr Oblast) and Komsomolske (Vinnytsia Oblast) on September 10, and 1,255 (most likely in Koziatyn, Vinnytsia Oblast) on September 11.[7] Two of the regiment's battalions—45 and 303—were involved in the Babi Yar massacre in Kiev as well.

Both of Jeckeln's two reserve battalions were also very active in the mass murder of Ukraine's Jews. Advancing along the route that would ultimately become Thoroughfare IV (Durchgangstrasse IV), a major supply line for the Wehrmacht and a large forced labor project, Police Battalion 304 shot about 2,200 Jews in Vinnytsia on September 5; 486 Jews in Ladyzhyn (Vinnytsia Oblast) on September 13; 1,438 Jews in Haisyn (Vinnytsia Oblast) on September 16; and 4,200 Jews, including 600 Jewish prisoners of war, in Kirovohrad on September 30.[8] The other battalion at Jeckeln's disposal had carried out the aforementioned shooting at the Kamianets-Podilsky massacre, where no units from Einsatzgruppe C are known to have been involved.

Further north, on the Ukrainian side of the Pripet Marshes, and then later in the Dniepr Bend, the 1st SS Infantry Brigade was making its own contribution to the grim tally. Between September 10 and November 10 the brigade shot 5,397 persons (4,146 men, 1,033 women, 218 children) under the rubric of "actions according to the customs of war."[9] The brigade's maintenance platoon under SS 2nd Lieutenant Max Täubner shot 969 people: 319 Jews in Novohrad-Volynsky (Zhytomyr Oblast), 191 Jews in Sholokhove (Dnipropetrovsk Oblast), and 459 Jews in Oleksandriia (Kirovohrad Oblast).[10]

In October, Pol. Batl. 304 continued to comb the route of DG IV. The unit killed 305 Jews in Oleksandriia on October 4; 6,000 Jews (including about 600 prisoners of war) on October 8 in Uman (Kiev Oblast); and 47 Jews near Znamianka (Kirovohrad Oblast) on October 14.[11] Around October 20, when Zhytomyr Oblast and the Right-Bank parts of Kiev Oblast were transferred to civil rule, Einsatzkommando 5 (Ek 5) was broken up into detachments and sent back west to establish permanent offices of the Sipo-SD in the Reich Commissariat Ukraine. During the last ten days of October and the first week of November, these units went in search for communities that had been overlooked in September.

As a result of this methodical approach, about 118,000–119,000 Ukrainian Jews were killed in October. However, a full quarter of this total perished at the hands of Romanian troops in Odessa between October 16 and 25. This indicates that outside the Romanian zone of occupation, known as Transnistria, about 90,000 Ukrainian Jews died at the hands of the Germans in October. About 20,000 of these Jews, however, were shot in Stanyslaviv Oblast alone (including about 8,000 in the town of Stanyslaviv itself). Making allowance for the killing in the General Government, it appears that the killing in Dniepr Ukraine was beginning to let up somewhat. This appearance was probably rooted solely in demographics and timing.

By October, the German armed forces in the southern Soviet Union were fighting in Left Bank Ukraine, where many Jews had been able to escape, as many as two thirds in some towns, before the Germans crossed the Dniepr in late September 1941. Furthermore, the Ukrainian lands east of the Dniepr had historically been home to fewer Jews. Thus, the farther east Einsatzgruppen C and D and Police Regiment South advanced, the fewer Jews they found. They were by no means inactive, however. Large-scale actions took place throughout central and eastern Ukraine: 2,000 victims in Melitopol (Zaporizhzhia Oblast) on October 11, more than 11,000 victims in Dnipropetrovsk on October 14–15, 3,300 victims in Kryvy Rih (including about 800 prisoners of war) on October 15, over 8,000 in Mariupol (Stalino Oblast) on October 20–21, and about 3,000 in Kremenchuk (Poltava Oblast) on October 28, to name some of the larger killing operations.

In November, the overall rate of killing fell off further due to the reasons just mentioned. Nevertheless, Sk 4a was sweeping through the region northeast of Kiev, embracing an arc reaching from Chernobyl to Konotop via Chernihiv, and by mid-November, Special Commando 4b (Sk 4b) and Ek 6 were entering the heavily populated Stalino Oblast from the north and west respectively. At the same time, Ek 5's detachments were revisiting Jewish communities in Right Bank Ukraine. For example, 5,300 Jews were shot in Proskuriv on November 4 by a detachment of Ek 5 supported by mounted German police from the Reich and local Ukrainian policemen. The largest November massacre took place in the west, however, where some 15,000 Jews were murdered by Order Police troops (Police Battalions 315 and 320, the latter reinforced by a company of Pol. Batl. 33) in Rivne on November 6–7, so as to provide the civil administration with a work environment largely free of Jews. The total number of murdered Ukrainian Jews in November exceeded 65,000 persons.

In December, the total number of Jewish deaths in Ukraine rose to about 87,000 Jews. The Romanian camp of Bohdanivka in Transnistria accounted for the deaths of 34,000 Jews in the second half of the month. Deducting the Jewish deaths in Transnistria, some 48,000 Jews perished in German-occupied Ukraine. Almost a third of these murders took place in the Crimea, where more than 15,000 Jews were murdered in December.

In sum, more than 500,000 Ukrainian Jews were killed by the Ger-

Table 8.1. Jewish Losses in 1941

Oblast	June	July	August	September	October	November	December	Total
Military Administration				General Government as of August 1				
Drohobych	200	1,600	200	930	470	1,100	-	4,500
Lviv	800	7,000	100	70	30	4,000	-	12,000
Stanyslaviv	-	400	1,000	-	20,000	500	5,500	27,400
Ternopil	-	9,000	160	430	1,660	650	100	12,000
Sub-total	1,000	18,000	1,460	1,430	22,160	6,250	5,600	55,900
Military Administration				Reich Commissariat Ukraine (RKU), September 1				
Volhynia	500	2,500	3,000	500	600	-	-	7,100
Rivne	-	1,000	3,500	2,500	-	16,000	1,500	24,500
Proskuriv								
- indigenous	-	1,800	20,000	4,000	-	5,300	-	31,100
- Transcarpathian			11,000					11,000
Sub-total	500	5,300	37,500	7,000	600	21,300	1,500	73,700
Wehrmacht Administration					RKU, October 20			
Zhytomyr	-	3,000	10,000	27,000	5,500	3,000	-	48,500
Kiev	-	500	3,000	45,000	13,500	2,000	-	64,000
Vinnytsia								
- indigenous	-	850	3,000	19,000	2,800	6,570	2,800	35,020
- Bukovinian/Bessarabian					5,000	8,000	15,000	28,000
Sub-total	-	4,350	16,000	91,000	26,800	19,570	17,800	175,520
Wehrmacht Administration						RKU, November 15		
Kirovohrad	-	-	800	5,220	420	1,200	210	7,850
Mykolaïv	-	-	1,350	26,650	3,000	100	-	31,100
Sub-total	-	-	2,150	31,870	3,420	1,300	210	38,950

Oblast	June	July	August	September	October	November	December	Total
Wehrmacht Administration								
Dnipropetrovsk	–	–	200	300	16,500	2,000	5,000	24,000
Chernihiv	–	–	–	50	1,030	800	270	2,150
Poltava	–	–	–	500	5,000	3,500	–	9,000
Zaporizhzhia	–	–	–	–	3,000	250	150	3,400
Donetsk	–	–	–	–	8,000	500	1,000	9,500
Sumy	–	–	–	–	–	2,000	–	2,000
Kharkiv	–	–	–	–	–	500	1,500	2,000
Crimea	–	–	–	–	–	1,400	15,100	16,500
Voroshilovhrad (today Luhansk)	–	–	–	–	–	–	–	–
Sub-total	–	–	200	850	33,530	10,950	23,020	68,550
Romanian Occupation								
Chernivtsi (see also Vinnytsia & Odessa)	–	9,000	1,000	70	–	–	–	10,070
Odessa Indigenous	–	2,000	3,500	4,000	30,000	2,000	22,000	63,500
Bukovinian/Bessarabian	–	–	–	–	2,000	4,000	17,000	23,000
Sub-total	–	11,000	4,500	4,070	32,000	6,000	39,000	96,570
Hungarian Transcarpathia								
Transcarpathia (see Kamianets-Podilsky)	–	–	–	–	–	–	–	–
TOTAL	1,500	38,650	61,810	136,220	118,510	65,370	87,130	509,190

Note: In some cases, the dates in this table refer to the point when the greater part of an oblast passed from military to civilian rule.

mans, their allies, and their satraps in the second half of 1941. About 300,000 of the victims died at the hands of Police Regiment South, Police Battalions 304 and 320, and the 1st SS Infantry Brigade. Einsatzgruppe C shot more than 95,000 Jews, while Einsatzgruppe D killed at least 75,000. Some 100,000 Ukrainian Jews died as a result of killing operations and pogroms organized by Romanian forces.

The table below sums up the losses of Ukrainian Jews in the second half of 1941 in each oblast by month. It is broken down roughly along the lines of the differing occupation regimes and shows when the overwhelming share of a particular oblast was turned over to civil authorities (save for Dnipropetrovsk). It is imperfect, but it is accurate enough to show general trends under the different occupation regimes at given times. As can be seen here, the bulk of mass murders—particularly after the Kamianets-Podilsky massacre—took place as a rule before oblasts were transferred from military to civil administration, i.e., under the cover of military necessity, which merely underscores how the invasion of the Soviet Union and the mass murder of the Jews in 1941 were intertwined with one another.

Jewish Losses in 1942

By early 1942, the Germans had executed about a third of the Jewish population under its control in Ukraine. The larger communities in eastern Ukraine—Kiev, Mykolaïv, Chernihiv, Sumy, Poltava, Odessa, and Crimea—were the hardest hit. There still remained, however, more than 1.1 million Jews in Ukraine at the end of 1941, mostly in the western oblasts. Some 475,000 lived in Galicia, 170,000 in Volhynia, 175,000 in Khmelnytsky and Vinnytsia oblasts, and 100,000 in Transcarpathia. In addition, the Romanians had expelled to Transnistria over 25,000 Jews from the Romanian county of southern Bukovina, 9,000 from the Romanian county of Dorohoi, 20,000–25,000 from Bessarabia (largely present-day Moldova), and 50,000–55,000 Jews from northern Bukovina (Chernivtsi Oblast). The overwhelming majority of these Jews did not survive the next twelve months.

In the first half of the year, the Jews east of the Dniepr River and in the Crimea were systematically liquidated, along with most of the remaining Jews in the Kiev and Vinnytsia oblasts. In the second half of year, the Jews of the German civil administration's General Commissariat Volhynia-Podolia (which corresponded largely with the combined oblasts of Volhynia, Rivne, and Proskuriv) were killed. According to a report on anti-partisan operations dated December 29, 1942, Himmler informed Hitler that 363,211 Jews were killed in "Southern Russia" between September 1 and December 1, 1942 (31,246 in August; 165,282 in September; 95,735 in October; and 70,948 in November). Of these, as many as 300,000 Jews in the report came from within the borders of present-day Ukraine.[12] During 1942, the majority of Galician Jews, more than 300,000 people, were murdered. Almost a quarter of a mil-

Table 8.2. Jewish Losses in 1942

Oblast	Jews Killed
General Government	
Drohobych	60,000
Lviv	123,000
Stanyslaviv	90,000
Ternopil	65,000
Sub-total	**338,000**
RKU	
Volhynia	101,000
Rivne	70,000
North Vinnytsia	90,000
Proskuriv	75,000
Zhytomyr	4,000
Kiev	10,500
Kirovohrad	3,500
Mykolaïv	8,700
Sub-total	362,700
Wehrmacht Administration	
Chernihiv	1,500
Sumy	1,000
Poltava	2,500
Dnipropetrovsk	10,000
Zaporizhzhia	6,500
Kharkiv	10,500
Voroshilovhrad	2,000
Stalino	6,000
Crimea	8,000
Sub-total	48,000
Romanian Occupation	
Chernivtsi, Odessa & South Vinnytsia	25,000
Sub-total	**25,000**
TOTAL	773,700

lion were killed in the gas chambers of Bełżec (Poland). Altogether, Ukraine lost approximately 770,000 Jews in 1942.

Losses in 1943

By the beginning of 1943, the majority of Ukrainian Jews from the German and Romanian zones of occupation, about 1.3 million, had been killed. The remaining 350,000 Jews were concentrated in the oblasts of Drohobych, Lviv, Ternopil, and Stanyslaviv (Galicia) or scattered across

Table 8.3. Jewish Losses in 1943

Oblast	Jews Killed
General Government	
Lviv & Drohobych	80,500
Stanyslaviv	8,600
Ternopil	46,400
Sub-total	**135,500**
RKU	
Volhynia	1,500
North Vinnytsia	4,400
Zhytomyr	500
Kiev	100
Sub-total	**6,500**
Wehrmacht Administration	
Sumy	500
Sub-total	**500**
Romanian Occupation	
Chernivtsi, Odessa & South Vinnytsia	7,500
Sub-total	7,500
TOTAL	**150,000**

the oblasts of Vinnytsia, Chernivtsi, Odessa, and Volhynia in ghettos or camps.

Some 161,500 Jews were still registered in Galicia at the end of 1942, including several thousand in the districts of Lubaczów (Poland). These were for the most part held in 33 ghettos. In the 17 ghettos of Lviv Oblast, there were about 87,000 Jews, while in the 13 ghettos of Ternopil Oblast, about 40,000 Jews were still hanging on. The three ghettos of Stanyslaviv Oblast contained a mere 7,000 Jews.

Outside the ghettos, another 23,000–24,000 Jews worked in camps and work details. Some 3,000 Jews were spread out over five camps in Stanyslaviv Oblast (Stanyslaviv with about 450 Jews, Bolekhiv with 1,800 Jews, Vyshkiv with 400 Jews, Broshniv-Osada with 100 Jews, and Nebyliv with 250). In Ternopil Oblast, there were still more than 6,000 Jews in 14 camps, with another 3,000 on more than 20 manors. In Lviv Oblast, about 12,000 Jews were distributed over 16 camps, including 3,500 at the infamous Janowska Forced Labor Camp, 2,500 in Drohobych, and 1,500 in Boryslav.

In Vinnytsia Oblast, there remained about 74,000 Jews—almost all of whom were in the Romanian occupied part of the oblast. These in turn comprised 20,000 local Jews and over 50,000 Jewish deportees from Bessarabia and Bukovina. In the German part of Vinnytsia Oblast, some 3,500 Jews remained: 1,500 in the Khmilnyk ghetto and about 2,000 in labor camps along Thoroughfare IV (Lityn, Vinnytsia, Voronovytsia, Nemyriv, Raihorod, Haisyn, Krasnopilka, etc.).

The rest of the "legal" Jewish population in Ukraine was clustered in Chernivtsi Oblast, 15,000; in Odessa Oblast, 3,500–4,000 (with 2,500 in the Balta ghetto); in Volhynia Oblast, where some 1,500 Jews lived in a ghetto in Volodymyr-Volynsky; and in the southern Kiev Oblast with several hundred in labor camps.

By year's end, about 150,000 of these 350,000 Jews had also been murdered, mainly in Drohobych and Lviv (85,000), Ternopil (47,000), and Stanyslaviv (10,000) oblasts. About 10,000 of these Jews, mainly from the Lviv Oblast, were deported to Poland. More than 4,000 Jews were murdered in Vinnytsia Oblast as were the last 1,500 Jews in Volhynia Oblast and several hundred in the Odessa and Kiev oblasts.

Losses in first half 1944

By the beginning of 1944, the remaining 185,000–190,000 Jews who had managed to survive the war that long were located primarily in the Romanian occupied areas of Transnistria and Chernivtsi oblasts and in the Hungarian zone, Transcarpathia. In Transnistria and Chernivtsi, there were some 65,000–70,000 Jews, mainly deportees, and 15,000 Jews, respectively. In Transcarpathia, almost all 100,000 Jews of the oblast's prewar population were still alive.

Under direct German control, there were still some 4,000–5,000 Jews alive, mostly in Galicia: 1,500 in camps in Drohobych and Boryslav, several hundred in Lviv, several hundred in Tovste (Ternopil Oblast) and the surrounding area, and several dozen in Stanyslaviv. Of these, approximately 1,300 were murdered before the Germans were driven from northern Soviet Ukraine as it existed in 1941.

In March 1944, when the Germans occupied Hungary, the Jews of Transcarpathia also fell under German control. Over the next three months, more than 500,000 Jews from Hungary were deported to extermination camps in Poland. This figure included about 95,000 Transcarpathian Jews.

Conclusion: General Balance of Losses

Between 1941–1944, the Germans and their allies murdered some 1.6 million Jews in Ukraine. This figure includes over 65,000 Jewish refugees from Moldova and Hungary who fell victim to the SS and police forces that ravaged Ukraine. The allocation of victims by oblast breaks down as follows:

Table 8.4. Jews Who Perished as Part of Prewar Jewish Population

Oblast	1939 Jewish Population	Indigenous Jewish Victims	%
Less than One Third of Oblast's Jews Killed			
Kharkiv	136,746	12,500	9.1
Voroshilovhrad	19,949	2,000	10.0
Chernihiv	31,887	4,000	12.5
Sumy	16,363	3,000	18.3
Izmaïl	20,500	4,500	21.9
Zaporizhzhia	43,321	10,000	23.0
Poltava	46,928	11,000	23.4
Stalino	65,556	16,000	24.4
Dnipropetrovsk	129,439	35,000	27.0
Less than Two Thirds of Oblast's Jews Killed			
Odessa	250,000	100,000[1]	40.0
Crimea	65,452	27,000	41.3
Zhytomyr	125,007	55,000	43.9
Kirovohrad	26,419	12,000	45.4
Mykolaïv	66,402	33,000	49.6
Kiev	297,409	77,000	61.4
Chernivtsi	102,000	66,000[2]	64.7
More than Two Thirds of Oblast's Jews Killed			
Drohobych	120,000	87,000	72.5
Vinnytsia	141,825	115,000	81.1
Transcarpathia	123,000	100,000	81.3
Lviv	260,000	215,000	82.6
Rivne	112,000	95,000	84.8
Volhynia	123,000	109,000	88.6
Stanyslaviv	140,000	132,000	94.2
Proskuriv	121,335	115,000	94.7
Ternopil	136,000	132,000	97.0
Total	**2,720,538**	**1,568,000**	**57.6**

Notes

1. Around 8,000 Jews from the Odessa Oblast died in Mykolaïv Oblast.
2. Of this figure, 55,000 Jews perished in Transnistria. Around 45,000 Jews from Bukovina and Bessarabia perished in the former Vinnytsia Region of Transnistria, while some 25,000 Jews from Bukovina and Bessarabia perished in the Odessa Oblast.

Added to this figure are an estimated 50,000 Ukrainian Jews killed during hostilities, captivity, or in the northern Caucasus (where they had fled in 1941, and where the Germans caught up to them in 1942). Thus, the total number of Jews killed by the Germans can be estimated to be at least 1.6 million, around 60 percent of Ukraine's prewar Jewish population. Fifteen years after the war—after the return of refugees,

Table 8.5. Jewish Losses as Reflected in Comparison of the Ukrainian Population in 1939 and 1959 (using present-day oblasts)

Oblast	Prewar Jewish population	1959 Jewish population	Absolute decrease	Percentage vis-à-vis prewar population
Ternopil	136,000	1,600	134,400	1.2
Volhynia	123,000	1,500	121,500	1.2
Rivne	112,000	2,600	109,400	2.3
Ivano-Frankivsk (Stanyslaviv)	140,000	3,900	136,100	2.8
Lviv (incl. former Drohobych Oblast)	380,000	30,030	324,970	8.5
Transcarpathia	123,000	12,169	110,831	9.9
Khmelnytsky (Proskuriv)	121,335	19,050	102,285	15.7
Poltava	46,928	12,287	34,642	26.2
Zhytomyr	125,007	42,048	82,959	33.6
Vinnytsia	141,825	50,157	91,668	35.4
Kirovohrad	26,419	9,505	16,914	36.0
Kherson	28,000	10,437	17,563	37.3
Sumy	16,363	6,259	10,104	38.3
Chernihiv	31,887	12,562	19,325	39.4
Crimea	65,452	26,374	39,078	40.3
Chernivtsi	102,000	42,140	59,860	41.3
Odessa (incl. former Izmaïl Oblast)	270,500	121,377	150,623	44.6
Zaporizhzhia	43,321	20,811	22,510	48.0
Mykolaïv	38,402	20,276	18,125	52.8
Kiev	297,409	181,359[2]	116,050	61.0
Kharkiv	136,746	84,192	52,554	61.6
Dnipropetrovsk	129,439	73,256	56,183	56.6
Donetsk (Stalino)	65,556	42,501	23,055	64.8
Luhansk (Voroshilovhrad)	19,949	13,939	6,010	69.9
Totals	**2,720,538**	**840,329**	**1,865,709**	31.4

the de-Stalinization campaign, emigration, relocation to other Soviet republics, and a period of relative calm and normality—the damage inflicted on the Ukrainian Jewish population still left an enormous gap.

The greatest losses among the Jews (over 80 percent) took place in the western areas of Ukraine (Galicia, Volhynia, and Podolia). This occurred mainly for two reasons. First, German armies had seized these oblasts by mid-July, thus foiling almost any evacuation efforts that the

Soviet officials could have attempted (the city of Zhytomyr being an exception). Second, Galicia and Volhynia had been spared the ravages of Soviet rule between the wars. Local Ukrainians were therefore still more easily roused to primitive nationalism and more susceptible to outbursts of ethnic violence. Where Galicia is concerned, a more favorable German policy toward Galician Ukrainians played a key role in keeping non-Jewish losses relatively low. The higher number of Ukrainian deaths in Rivne and Volhynia oblasts vis-à-vis the four Galician oblasts is primarily the result of the various partisan wars that took place in the northwestern Ukrainian lands as well as the Ukrainian ethnic cleansing of Volhynia's Poles, which sometimes resulted in the killing of Jews hiding among Poles.

Jewish losses in eastern oblasts were less because the Germans started occupying these areas only in September 1941, over three months after the outbreak of the war. As a result, there had been more time to arrange evacuations. It seems that the further east the Germans advanced, the less regard they showed for human life in general. Where Jews were not to be found, the killing did not necessarily let up. Figures for civilian deaths in eastern Ukraine ranged into the six digits, but Jews often made up less than 20 percent of the victims.

Table 8.6, based on the records of the Soviet Union's official Extraordinary State Commission for Ascertaining and Investigating Crimes Committed by the German-Fascist Invaders and Their Accomplices, gives only some idea of civilian losses in Ukraine. Analysis of the Extraordinary State Commission records shows that the number of victims—Jewish and non-Jewish—is overstated for a number of oblasts (in particular Lviv, Poltava, Kiev, Zhytomyr, Donetsk, Odessa, and Kirovohrad as well as the Crimea), accounting for the discrepancy in the number of Jewish deaths given in Table 4 (1,568,000) and Table 6 (2,100,836). The figures, however, emphasize the German campaign against the Jews and shed some light on regional variations.

If the figures for non-Jewish victims and Jewish victims are overstated by the same percentage, this would not affect the overall ratio of non-Jewish deaths to Jewish deaths given in Table 6. The figures suggest that Jews made up around 60 percent of non–combat-related civilian deaths in Ukraine during the Second World War. Even if the number of non-Jewish victims were not overstated, Jewish non–combat-related civilian deaths would alone represent almost half of the overall total— and that from a segment of the population that accounted for less than 7 percent of Ukraine's inhabitants in mid-1940.

As the previous tables may suggest, the percentage of Jewish victims as a share of total non–combat-related deaths were highest in the geographic regions of Transcarpathia, northern Bukovina, Podolia, and Galicia (save for the Lviv Oblast). The oblasts with the lowest number of Jewish victims compared with overall civilian non-combat victims included several oblasts captured only in mid-September or later, by which point Soviet evacuation measures had become effective: Cherni-

Table 8.6. Jewish Non-Combat Related Deaths Compared to Those of the Overall Population in Ukraine

Oblast	Non-combat related civilian deaths	Jews	Share of Jews (%)
Ternopil	166,317	162,403	98
Stanyslaviv	215,035	212,103	98
Chernivtsi	15,707	15,308	97
Proskuriv	227,555	214,205	94
Vinnytsia	186,384	178,181	93
Transcarpathia	114,982	104,177	91
Drohobych	102,369	87,000	85
Kiev city	90,000	70,000	78
Mykolaïv	51,862	39,893	77
Izmaïl	5,194	4,000	77
Odessa	272,830	207,000	76
Volhynia	133,164	93,685	70
Rivne	198,008	130,074	65
Zhytomyr	117,840	75,764	64
Lviv	577,435	302,000	52
Dnipropetrovsk	70,660	35,792	51
Kharkiv	33,000[1]	15,000	45
Crimea	90,243	32,000	35
Zaporizhzhia	64,502	14,118	22
Poltava	112,850	25,000	22
Kiev[2]	179,268	37,000	21
Donetsk	126,342	25,133	20
Kirovohrad	66,745	12,000	18
Voroshilovhrad	12,614	2,000	16
Sumy	43,781	3,000	7
Chernihiv	127,778	4,000	3
Total	**3,402,465**	**2,100,836**	**61.7**

Notes

1. This figure reflects deaths by hunger.
2. Without the city of Kiev but including the contemporary Cherkasy Oblast.

hiv, Sumy, Poltava, Zaporizhzhia, Donetsk, and Voroshilovhrad. Furthermore, by late 1941 and early 1942, partisan groups had begun forming in parts of Kiev, Chernihiv, and Sumy oblasts, which in turn led to German retaliatory measures involving greater numbers of non-Jewish civilian deaths. It is also interesting to note that the ratio of Jewish to non-Jewish non-combat civilian deaths was lower in the "proletarian" oblasts of Donetsk, Zaporizhzhia, and Voroshilovhrad; there the German terror had been as political as it was racial. As the Jews had been largely evacuated, the Germans focused on other political enemies.

The overwhelming majority of Ukraine's Jews died near their homes on Ukrainian soil, while about 22 percent, some 345,000, were deported to Poland and gassed. Most of these were Galician Jews sent to Bełżec. More than 170,000 came from the Lviv and Drohobych oblasts (today unified into one oblast), more than 40,000 from Ternopil Oblast, and 41,000 from Stanyslaviv Oblast. The Jews of Transcarpathia met their end at Auschwitz. A small number of Jews from Ukraine were sent to Sobibór. The bulk of the remainder, 70 percent of Ukraine's Jews, were shot or worked to death, while about 5 percent, mainly in Transnistria, died of hunger and disease. Only in Galicia, Volhynia, Podolia, Transcarpathia, and in part of Right Bank Ukraine were Jews collected into ghettos. In central and eastern Ukraine, the Jews trapped behind German lines were exterminated almost immediately upon occupation of their hometowns by the Germans, or a few months later.

The greatest part of the killing took place in the 18 months from June 22, 1941 until December 31, 1942. In 1941, German and Romanian perpetrators killed on average 85,000 Jews per month, or more than 2,600 per day. In 1942, they murdered some 64,500 per month, or more than 2,000 per day. In 1943, they murdered over 12,000 per month, or 400 people per day. The duration of the process of extermination varied, of course, from each oblast to the next. In Galicia, the annihilation of the greatest part of Galician Jewry lasted two years (July 1941–July 1943); in Volhynia, the process took 1.5 years (July 1941–December 1942); and in Right Bank Ukraine, a little more than a year (August 1941–September 1942). In the rest of Ukraine, the greater part of the killing was done in roughly six months: in southern Ukraine from August 1941 to February 1942, and in Left Bank Ukraine from October 1941 to April 1942.

These figures should give the reader an idea of the scale of the killing that took place in the Shoah in Ukraine. They remain incomplete, but further research is unlikely to lead to significant fluctuation in the conclusions reached.

Notes

1. This figure was determined on the basis of the 1939 census of Ukrainian SSR, the results of which are reproduced in M. Altshuler, ed., *Distribution of the Jewish Population of the USSR 1939* (Jerusalem: The Hebrew University of Jerusa-

lem, Center for Research and Documentation of East-European Jewry, 1993); the 1931 Polish census given in *Statystyka Polski, II Powszechny Spis Ludności z 9 XII 1931 r. Seria C.*, Zeszyt 70, which was published in Warsaw in 1938; and materials related to the 1930 Romanian and Czechoslovak populations.

2. Many of these documents appear in A. I. Kruglov, *Sbornik dokumentov i materialov ob unichtozhenii natsistami evreev Ukrainy v 1941–1944 godakh* (Kiev: Institut iudaiki, 2002), and idem, *Evreiskii genotsid na Ukraine v period okkupatsii v nemetskoi dokumentalistike 1941–1944* (Kharkov-Ierusalim: Biblioteka gazety Bensiah 1995).

3. A. I. Kruglov, *Poteri evreev Ukrainy v 1941–1944 gg.* (Kharkiv: Tarbut Laam, 2005); idem, *The Losses Suffered by Ukrainian Jews in 1941–1944* (Kharkiv: Tarbut Laam, 2005); idem, *Khronika Kholokosta v Ukraine 1941–1944* (Dnipro-petrovsk: Tsentr "Tkuma" and Zaporizhzhia: Prem'er, 2004); idem, *Katastrofa ukrainskogo evreistva 1941–1944 gg.: entsiklopedicheskii spravochnik* (Kharkiv: Karavella, 2001); idem, *Entsiklopediia kholokosta: evreiskaia entsiklopediia Ukrainy* (Kiev: Evreiskii Sovet Ukrainy, 2000); idem, *Unichtozhenie evreiskogo naseleniia Ukrainy v 1941–1944 gg: khronika sobytii* (Mohyliv-Podil's'kyi, 1997).

4. By July 4, 1941, Jeckeln's command was based in Luts'k; U.S. National Archive and Records Administration (NARA), T 501, roll 5, frame 442. A week later, it moved to L'viv (NARA, T 501, roll 5, frame 459), where it remained until July 28, 1941, when it relocated to Shepetivka; Public Records Office, HW 16/6, Part 1: Summary of G.P.D. 275–323 for 3.7.-14.8.41, p. 5. It is quite probable that Jeckeln met with Himmler on July 21, 1941.

5. The Central Military Archive (Prague), Kommandostab RFSS, Order No. 20, July 22, 1941, and Peter Witte et al., eds., *Der Dienstkalender Heinrich Himmlers 1941/42* (Hamburg: Christians, 1999), p. 186, entry for July 21, 1941.

6. Klaus-Michael Mallmann, "Der qualitative Sprung im Vernichtungsprozess: Das Massaker von Kamenez-Podolsk Ende August 1941," *Jahrbuch für Antisemitismusforschung*, Vol. 10 (2001), pp. 239–264.

7. United States Holocaust Memorial Museum Archives, RG-48.004M (Military-Historical Institute, Prague), Reel 1 (Kommandostab des RFSS), HSSPF Russland Süd daily situation reports regarding activities and movements for September 1–30, 1941.

8. District Court Halle (German Democratic Republic), 1 Bs 26/78, 211–60–78, Judgment of October 26, 1978, in *DDR Justiz und NS Verbrechen*, Band 1 (Amsterdam: Amsterdam University Press, 2002), pp. 470–473. See also the diary of Otto Müller, a member of Pol. Batl. 304, for September–October 1941, Der Bundesbeauftragte für die Unterlagen des Staatssicherheitsdienstes der ehemaligen DDR, MfS-HA IX/11, ZUV 78, Bd. 6.

9. *"Unsere Ehre heißt Treue": Kriegstagebuch des Kommandostabes RF SS, Tätigkeitsberichte der 1. und 2. SS-Inf. Brigade, der 1. SS-Kav. Brigade und von Sonderkommandos der SS* (Frankfurt am Main, Wien, Zürich: Europa Verlag, 1965), p. 174.

10. See SS court verdict against Max Täubner from May 24, 1943, in Ernst Klee, Willi Dressen, Volker Riess, eds., *"Schöne Zeiten": Judenmord aus der Sicht der Täter und Gaffer* (Frankfurt am Main: Fischer, 1988), p. 184ff. See also, Y. R. Büchler, "'Unworthy Behavior': The Case of SS Officer Max Täubner," *Holocaust and Genocide Studies*, Vol. 17 (2003), No. 3, p. 409–429.

11. *DDR Justiz und NS Verbrechen*, Band 1, p. 474, and Müller diary, October 1941.

12. NO-511, Reichsführer SS, Betr.: Meldungen an den Fuehrer ueber Bandenbekaempfung, December 29, 1941. Scholars differ over how to break down the total number of murdered Jews mentioned in this document. Most, for example, believe that of the 363,211 victims, the 292,263 Jews killed before November 1 were almost exclusively from Reich Commissariat Ukraine. Subtracting from this fig-

ure an estimated 70,000 Jews from those Belarusian lands attached to the RKU leaves 222,263 Jews from within the borders of present-day Ukraine. The majority of the 70,948 Jews mentioned killed during November in Himmler's report are in turn thought to be from Białystok Region (*Bezirk Białystok*), a part of interwar Poland subordinated to East Prussia. The concentration of this region's Jews into larger ghettos for deportation to the death camps Treblinka and Auschwitz started on November 2, 1942, the very day after the Pinsk massacre in the RKU. HSSPF Ukraine Hans-Adolf Prützmann was simultaneously HSSPF for East Prussia and as such responsible for Białystok Region.

IX

Dina Pronicheva's Story of Surviving the Babi Yar Massacre: German, Jewish, Soviet, Russian, and Ukrainian Records

KAREL C. BERKHOFF

The largest single Nazi shooting of Jews in the Soviet Union occurred on September 29 and 30, 1941, on the western outskirts of Kiev in a large ravine known as Babi Yar. The occupying German army and SS and police forces began planning and implementing measures against the local Jews immediately after taking the capital of the Ukrainian Soviet Socialist Republic on September 19. They became all the more eager to rid the city of its Jewish citizens five days later, when mines laid by the retreating NKVD and Red Army exploded, igniting a fire that burned for over a week and demolished a full square kilometer (0.38 square miles or 247 acres) of the city center around the Khreshchatyk, Kiev's main street. To the German authorities, the explosions provided an acceptable rationale for the immediate eradication of the entire Jewish population.

On Sunday, September 28, the newly installed Ukrainian police posted 2,000 copies of an unsigned order in Russian, Ukrainian, and German to the Jews of Kiev and the surrounding area, instructing them to appear the next day before 8:00 AM at a certain intersection near the (Jewish and Orthodox) cemeteries and to bring along "documents, money, and valuables, and also warm clothing, underwear, etc." The largest of the texts on the trilingual poster, the Russian one, said that

"Yids" (*zhidy*) who disobeyed would be shot. Thousands of Jews, most of them expecting deportation, showed up at the intersection of Melnyk Street (today Melnykov Street) and Dehtiarivska Street, not far from where a freight train station was then located. Instead of being deported, however, they were marched to Babi Yar and shot by Sonderkommando 4a, a unit belonging to Einsatzgruppe C of the Security Police and Security Service. Reserve Police Battalion 45 and Police Battalion 303 of the regular German police assisted in the operation. Also present were Ukrainian auxiliary policemen. According to a contemporary report, the German forces on hand shot 33,771 Jews.[1]

After the war, the Communist Party of the Soviet Union (CPSU) prohibited serious study of Babi Yar—or the Holocaust in general. Preferring to emphasize that the Nazis also put to death tens of thousands of non-Jews at the ravine (or killed them elsewhere and dumped the bodies there), the CPSU refused to acknowledge that the first massacres at Babi Yar amounted to an unparalleled war crime, the attempt to kill every Jewish man, woman, child, and infant in the city at the time. Only on rare occasions did references to the Jewish background of the victims of the September 1941 massacre make it past the censor, primarily during the post-Stalin thaw under Nikita Khrushchev. Key examples were Yevgeny Yevtushenko's poem "Babi Yar" (1961), Dmitrii Shostakovich's Thirteenth Symphony (1962), and Anatolii Kuznetsov's novel *Babi Yar* (1966).

The political climate of 1970s, when the CPSU was producing an enormous amount of anti-Israeli propaganda with many antisemitic features, brought forth some of the worst distortions of Jewish suffering at Babi Yar. On March 12, 1970, *Pravda,* the Soviet Union's most important newspaper, went so far as to publish a statement signed by 51 Jews from Ukraine that included the following passage: "The tragedy of Babi Yar will forever remain the embodiment not only of the Hitlerites' cannibalism, but also of the indelible disgrace of their accomplices and followers: the Zionists."[2] Although the Soviet authorities did eventually place a large bronze sculpture at the site in 1976, in commemorating the "citizens of the city of Kiev and the prisoners of war" killed there between 1941 and 1943, the memorial made no mention of Jews.

In the West, awareness of the massacre remained limited, despite various trials of some of the murderers in West Germany and Western translations of Kuznetsov's novel. Some books and articles about the Holocaust referred to Babi Yar, but antagonistic Ukrainian-Jewish relations and spotty source material marred some of them. A 1981 article by Lucy S. Dawidowicz for *The New York Times Magazine* epitomized such cases: In discussing the spontaneous commemoration at Babi Yar of the twenty-fifth anniversary of the massacre in 1966, Dawidowicz, well known for her best-selling survey *The War Against the Jews,* said nothing about the courageous (and well-documented) condemnation of antisemitism that the Ukrainian writer Ivan Dziuba delivered during the ceremony. She also incorrectly cited a Security Police report as

The Germans were already planning the annihilation of Kiev's Jews when mines laid by the Soviets began exploding on September 24, 1941, five days after the city fell to the Wehrmacht. The explosions appear to have accelerated the massacre, which took place at the Babi Yar ravine on September 29–30. Ullstein.

evidence of the presence of Ukrainian police at Babi Yar.[3] Along with mistakes by other authors, Dawidowicz's error may have discouraged scholars within the Ukrainian diaspora—who were already on the defensive due to the 1958 bestseller *Exodus* by the Israeli novelist Leon Uris, which located the massacre "amidst the cheers of many approving Ukrainians"—from studying Babi Yar in detail.[4] This said, although the extant reports of the Security Police do not reveal it, postwar sources indicate that Ukrainian policemen were indeed involved in the Babi Yar massacre. Some of the few survivors have mentioned them,[5] and when a former member of Sonderkommando 4a testified in West Germany in 1959, he spoke of Ukrainians at the site who stripped and abused the Jews.[6]

In recent years, several scholarly analyses of Babi Yar have appeared. The collapse of the Soviet Union in 1991 expedited this, for not only did the study of the Holocaust finally become possible in Ukraine and other successor states, many Soviet archives opened up and provided new opportunities. In Germany, a fierce debate over the involvement of the Wehrmacht, the German armed forces, in the Holocaust produced several new studies of the Babi Yar massacre. Most of the latter contributions have drawn on German military records and postwar trial records. They have shed a great deal of light on the events preceding the massacre and the thinking of the Germans in Kiev at the time, and they make clear that, during one of several meetings in Kiev between September 25 and 27, 1941, top SS and police officials together with Wehrmacht officers made a collective decision to murder the city's Jews.[7]

This chapter moves the research beyond the perpetrator-focused documentation by exploring the testimonies of Dina Pronicheva, one of the handful of Jewish survivors of the Babi Yar massacre. Those familiar with the literature about Babi Yar will probably recognize her name, but even specialists generally have not known that Pronicheva went on record with her story not once or twice, but more than ten times. Her multiple accounts, which were given over decades, are in German, Russian, Ukrainian, and American repositories. Some have appeared in print in one form or another. What follows is a close reading that compares the 12 available narratives of the event and assesses their reliability.

As is to be expected, these narratives diverge in some ways. It is important to acknowledge these differences and to make an effort to explain them. Yet I believe a strong case can be made that the differences do not reduce the status of Pronicheva as a source. Careful scrutiny of her testimonies can establish with some authority various aspects and details about the Babi Yar massacre that are unavailable from Nazi records or indeed other postwar recollections. In general, this chapter demonstrates that the historiography of genocide and mass murder can be greatly enriched by careful comparison and analysis of survivors' recollections.

Dina Pronicheva's Multiple Testimonies

Dina Mironovna Pronicheva was born on January 7, 1911, in the northeastern Ukrainian town of Chernihiv, where her family lived until she was five years old. Like every Soviet citizen, she was registered under a specific nationality, and hers was that of her Jewish parents, the Russian-speaking glazier Miron Aleksandrovich Mstislavsky and his wife, Anna Efimovna Mstislavskaia. Dina received a secondary education and acquired a good knowledge of Ukrainian. In 1932 she married the Russian Viktor Aleksandrovich Pronichev. In the middle of 1941, she was 30, had a three-year-old daughter and a one-year-old son (both of whom were to survive the war in children's homes), and was working as an actress at the Puppet Theater in Kiev. Her two brothers served in the Red Army. On September 29, 1941, she went to Babi Yar with her parents and her younger sister, all of whom were murdered there. Dina Pronicheva, one of the tiny number of survivors of the massacre, is the only person known to have fallen into the ravine unwounded and feigned death. Assuming various non-Jewish identities and surmounting incredible obstacles, she survived the Nazi regime and after the war resumed her work at the Puppet Theater. Every year, she visited Babi

Yar, and she seems to have addressed a crowd there on the twenty-fifth anniversary of the massacre.[8] She died in Kiev on June 14, 1977.[9]

It is unfortunate that nobody seems to have interviewed Pronicheva with a tape recorder. But there are many written records of her testimony: 12 texts dating back to the 1940s, the 1960s, and the time thereafter. Their provenance varies greatly, and some were entirely unavailable before the dissolution of the Soviet Union. Four texts came about during Soviet and German judicial investigations and trial proceedings (1946, 1967–1968). Four others resulted from non-judicial interviews conducted by a Soviet journalist, Soviet Ukrainian historians, a Soviet Russian novelist, and a Jewish writer who later emigrated (1946, 1966–1970, 1983). Two texts are second-hand accounts by a Ukrainian émigré and another Jewish survivor (1963, 1994); one other is a letter by Pronicheva to a journalist (1967). Official censorship, self-censorship, and undue artistic or editorial license produced records that differ in substance and, especially, style. Most of the texts fail to meet the standards of contemporary oral history interviews.

The first record came about in connection with a Soviet military tribunal of one Austrian and 14 Germans held in Kiev in January 1946. The judges found all of the defendants, including Lieutenant General Paul Albert Scheer, the former commander of the regular German police in the Kiev region, "guilty of committing crimes stipulated by article 1 of the Decree of the Presidium of the Supreme Soviet of the USSR of April 19, 1943." That secret decree prescribed the hanging of all "German, Italian, Romanian, Hungarian, and Finnish fascist criminals" (as well as Soviet "spies and traitors") who had tortured or murdered civilians and Soviet prisoners of war.[10] Although three defendants were sentenced to 15 or 20 years of hard labor, the others did indeed soon hang from gallows on what is now Kiev's Independence Square. On January 12, 1946, less then a week before the start of the tribunal sessions, the Prosecutor's Office of the Kiev Military District questioned Pronicheva about Babi Yar. The result was a five-page report in Russian (hereafter, PR1) signed by her and the investigating major.

Fifty years later the document emerged from the central archives of the People's Commissariat for Internal Affairs (NKVD), a forerunner of the KGB, when Russia's Federal Security Service (FSB) donated a large set of photocopies dealing with Soviet trials of suspected war criminals to the United States Holocaust Memorial Museum.[11] Some years earlier, however, the German scholar Erhard Roy Wiehn was able to include a facsimile of an incomplete retyping of PR1 in a commemorative volume about Babi Yar.[12] In 2001, Ilia Levitas published an also incomplete version that he had edited for style.[13] The text used by Wiehn and Levitas was from Kiev, but the exact original location—the archives of the Security Service of Ukraine (SBU)—became formally known only in 2004, when PR1 appeared (*almost* in full) in a massive Ukrainian documentary collection about Babi Yar.[14]

On January 13, 1946, Soviet Ukraine's main Russian-language

newspaper, *Pravda Ukrainy,* published an article, "In Babi Yar," by "D. Pronicheva, Actress of the Central Republican Puppet Theater, Kiev" (PR2).[15] Written in the third person plural and the first person singular, it focuses on what she went through on September 29, 1941, and the following days. Over two decades later, in West Germany, Pronicheva was to state that on no occasion did she ever write down her testimony herself. But she had told it to a journalist once, she said. In view of the general slowness of the Soviet press, it is remarkable that *Pravda Ukrainy* published the interview, which was not identified as such, just one day after Pronicheva's visit to the Prosecutor's Office. The last paragraph differs significantly in tone from the rest of the text, suggesting the work of a journalist or editor: "Babi Yar has entered history as a symbol of death. The remains of the innocent, tortured people constitute a formidable indictment of the fascist henchmen. The blood of tens of thousands of hapless victims of Babi Yar cries out for a just retribution."

On the evening of January 24, 1946, Pronicheva took the stand at a session of the officially "open" tribunal. A Soviet camera crew captured her testimony, which appeared in part in a Soviet Ukrainian newsreel.[16] The official written record of this courtroom testimony (PR3) is in the FSB archives and hence beyond the reach of outside researchers, but one of the reports about the trial supplied to the Soviet media by the Soviet Ukrainian news agency RATAU quotes Pronicheva (PR3pub1). Here she is answering three questions from the prosecution ("Tell us, please, what do you know about Babi Yar?"; "Did the people know they would be taken to their execution?"; and "Were there many women, children, and elderly people?"). Thereafter, RATAU summarizes how she escaped, and it ends by saying that "it is impossible to convey in a few words the horrors that this courageous woman lived through."[17]

A 1995 book about the Kiev tribunal contains a longer version of Pronicheva's testimony on this occasion. Unfortunately its editor, Senior Legal Counsel Leonid Abramenko of Kiev, believed strongly in the "sufficiency of investigation before and during the trial." He perceived an "exceptional purposefulness and clarity" in the documentary record of the NKVD-supervised trial proceedings (22 FSB files) and was certain of the tribunal's fairness. Equally disturbing is his statement that in publishing the courtroom statements, he did so "selectively and also in a shortened and, we emphasize, adapted form (but while certainly retaining the contents of this or that testimony)."[18] Thus, Abramenko may have removed some questions from the prosecution as well as all of those from the defense. The testimony of Pronicheva in this book (PR3pub2) reads like a monologue.[19]

Three months after the tribunal, on April 24, 1946, a stenographer made a fourth and very detailed record of a testimony by Pronicheva, at her home in Kiev. The interview was conducted by the Commission on the History of the Patriotic War in Ukraine, a group of Soviet historians charged with researching the Great Patriotic War, as the Second World War was known in the Soviet Union. The result was twenty typed

Dina Pronicheva on the witness stand, January 24, 1946, at a Kiev war-crimes trial of fifteen members of the German police responsible for the occupied Kiev region. Her testimony was also recorded on film for use in a Soviet Ukrainian newsreel. USHMM, courtesy of Babi Yar Society.

pages, which Pronicheva signed and which are held at the Central State Archives of Civic Organizations of Ukraine (PR4).[20] A retyping with no signature is at another Kiev repository, the Central State Archives of the Higher Agencies of Power and Administration.[21]

There is no reliable publication of this important declassified document. In 1991, the Kiev-based authors Feliks Levitas and Mark Shimanovsky published it only partly (in a memorial book) and modified it in the process, replacing, for example, "Ukrainians" with ethnically indeterminate "policemen" (*politsai*), presumably for political reasons.[22] That same year Ukraine's leading history journal published the document in Ukrainian, but, in Soviet fashion, without informing the reader that this was a translation. This version is more a stylistic overhaul in another language; words and phrases have been removed without use of ellipses, added, or simply grossly mistranslated; the word "German," for instance, transforms into "fascist," "Hitlerite," or "occupier."[23]

In 1963, Kost Turkalo (1892–1979), a Ukrainian-American and a former member of the Central Rada, the Ukrainian government during the revolutionary period, published *Torture*, a memoir in Ukrainian of his life in the Soviet Union, including his conviction in 1930 to three years at a show trial for members of the fictitious Union for the Liberation of Ukraine. Very pleased by the arrival of the Germans in Kiev, Turkalo took charge of the technical department of the Ukrainian auxiliary city administration and later headed the administration of the city's Kurenivka District (which bordered on Babi Yar). He fled the city on September 19, 1943. Four pages in *Torture* contain the second-hand account of the ordeal of a young Jewish survivor of Babi Yar identified as "Dina" (PR5).[24] After the war, Turkalo adds, Dina passed on regards to him via his sister-in-law, who had remained in Kiev. On another occasion, Turkalo talked to a Ukrainian-American political scientist about how he helped Dina Pronicheva.[25] That he omitted her last name from his memoir is to his credit: Had the Soviet authorities found out about her ties to somebody they regarded a traitor, they might well have harassed her.

The sixth text based on Pronicheva's account has come to us from the aforementioned Anatolii Kuznetsov (1929–1979), born in Kiev of a Ukrainian mother and a Russian father.[26] This writer had already achieved fame within the Soviet Union when, using a diary he had kept under the Nazis, official documents, and his mother's memory, he wrote in Russian a "document in the form of a novel" about occupied Kiev and gave it the title *Babi Yar*. In view of the official taboo on mentioning the Jewish origins of Babi Yar's first victims, it was remarkable that a version of the manuscript then appeared in serialized form from August to November 1966 in *Iunost,* a Moscow monthly with a circulation of two million. One chapter, also called "Babi Yar," was entirely devoted to Pronicheva.[27] A slightly longer version of the novel—with no changes to the part about Pronicheva—appeared in Moscow as a book in 1967 in a print-run of 150,000.[28] There are three English translations of the Pronicheva chapter.[29]

As with almost all the other records, we do not know if Pronicheva had the opportunity to authorize this record. Kuznetsov asserted that it was her story "as I wrote it down myself from her own words, without adding anything of my own." Later, in exile, he was to add that he convinced her to tell her story of survival after "tremendous difficulty," for "she did not believe that it could ever be published or that it would serve any good purpose." She talked for several days, he says, and along the way suffered "a number of heart attacks." As will become evident below, this was not a candid description of the genesis of the text.

Readers in the Soviet Union and abroad received Kuznetsov's work warmly, but the CPSU soon decided that its publication had been a mistake and stepped up its surveillance of the author. During a visit to the United Kingdom in July 1969, Kuznetsov applied for and received political asylum. He denounced the Soviet regime as "fascist," left the CPSU, and, calling his former self "dishonest, conformist, cowardly," assumed the new name of A. Anatoli.[30] He also disowned the published versions of his books, citing editorial distortions. A microfilm of the *Babi Yar* manuscript, which he had smuggled out of the Soviet Union, served as the basis for a longer and definitive version that appeared in Germany in 1970, in the United States in 1986, and—at last—in Ukraine and Russia in 1991. Numbering 21 pages, the Pronicheva chapter in this publication (PR6) is longer than its Soviet incarnation, which lacked some passages such as a denunciation (although it did speak of western Ukrainian involvement).[31] The British journalist who helped Kuznetsov seek asylum has translated this uncensored version.[32]

Critics in Russia, Ukraine, and the West were less interested in the literary qualities of Kuznetsov's book than in its topic and the issue of authenticity.[33] Kuznetsov himself stated from the very beginning that *Babi Yar* contained "only the truth—AS IT REALLY HAPPENED."[34] Historians of wartime Kiev have found that the book contains errors, but Kuznetsov's description of that time and place remains on the whole remarkably accurate indeed.[35] For that reason, and because it is the most frequently cited record of Pronicheva's words, Kuznetsov's Pronicheva chapter would seem to merit serious attention—all the more so because the American writer D. M. Thomas received critical acclaim and commercial success in 1981 for a novel (*The White Hotel*) that reproduced passages from PR6 almost verbatim.[36] Yet, as I shall argue below, PR6 may be less a deposition (as claimed by Kuznetsov) than a combination of two testimonies. Therefore, its value as a historical document is uncertain.

Early in 1967, during their preparations for a trial of former members of Sonderkommando 4a, officials in the West German city of Darmstadt apparently asked the Prosecutor's Office in Kiev to question Pronicheva. The result of this deposition was a brief report in Russian, including the questions posed to her, dated February 9, 1967 (PR7). This text (or, more precisely, almost all of the text) became available in 2004, when a typed duplicate held at the SBU archives appeared in print in a documentary collection.[37] There also exists a German translation made in Germany (PR7ger), preserved at the Federal Archives branch in Ludwigsburg and at the Institute of Contemporary History in Munich.[38] Three of its seven German pages have been published.[39]

Perhaps confident after the outpouring of sympathy that resulted from Kuznetsov's book, Pronicheva wrote a letter to the Soviet journalist E. Litvin, identifying herself as probably the only person alive who "crawled out of Babi Yar in 1941 in the literal meaning of the word" (PR8).[40] It may have been that she wanted his help in getting another apartment. (She was still living at her prewar address, 41 Vorovsky Street, but moved out one year later.) Her motivations for writing are unclear, however, for the Moscow weekly *Literaturnaia gazeta* published only the part of Pronicheva's letter (PR8pub) that describes what happened to her relatives.[41] This seems to have been the last time any Soviet periodical mentioned her, but some more information, probably an excerpt of an interview or a letter, appeared early in 1968 in East Berlin in the organ of the Society for German-Soviet Friendship (PR9pub).[42] Here, Pronicheva is quoted describing events from 1942 only.

In the meantime, in October 1967, the case against ten former members of Sonderkommando 4a had finally gone to trial in Darmstadt. Over the course of 13 months, 175 people came to testify.[43] Witness 105, on the morning of April 29, 1968, was a survivor of the Babi Yar massacre who had traveled all the way from the Soviet Union: Pronicheva. She had made the journey to West Germany against her will, fearing that Nazis would attempt to kill her, but the reception she received allayed her fears.[44] The detailed Russian-language testimony that she gave in Darmstadt exists only as a 19-page record of the courtroom interpretation into German, which omits the questions posed to her (PR10). Like PR7ger, it is available in Ludwigsburg and Munich, but it has not been published.[45] Pronicheva did not recognize any of the defendants. In any case, she had not come to point at any of them, she said, nor did she wish to "avenge myself and do something bad to the German people. I know that it was not the German people as a whole but a group of people who imagined that they could conquer the whole world."

Interestingly, she mentioned near the end that she had testified at a Soviet tribunal in 1946 (which would refer to PR3), and that she had given the written record of that testimony to "a writer who used it in his book." She must have had Kuznetsov in mind. Thus, although the author of *Babi Yar* did not say so, for what became PR6 he had evidently used more than his own interview with Pronicheva. But that he could have employed PR3, as PR10 implies, seems unlikely. It is more likely that Pronicheva gave him PR4, the interview with Soviet historians, also because of remarkably similar sentences in PR4 and Kuznetsov's text.

In the 1970s and 1980s, any text based on Pronicheva's words could appear only abroad, as happened in 1983 in a Jewish memorial book published in Philadelphia. These are 13 pages in Russian entitled "Lively Greetings from Hell," which start as follows: "My name is Dina. Dina Mironovna Vasserman" (PR11).[46] The person who wrote these words was Shimon Kipnis, a Jewish writer and former Soviet citizen, who added that he talked with Pronicheva—for that name appears in his text as well—for two days, and that on the third day, before the end of her story, she fell ill, was taken to a hospital, and died there. Kipnis, like Kuznetsov before him, does not say when (or how) he recorded her words. There exist English and Yiddish translations of his text.[47]

The final known record, a second-hand account, came into being in an indirect fashion during the mid-1980s, when the Ukrainian journalist Iurii Petrashevych was studying the history of wartime Kiev. Among the people he interviewed for his planned book was G. Ia. Batasheva (*Ukr.* Batashova), another Jewish survivor of Babi Yar. Petrashevych's project never came to full fruition, but in 1994, the literary monthly *Kyïv* published Ukrainian versions of some of his interviews, including the one with Batasheva, who had met with Pronicheva after the war. Two pages here provide a Ukrainian translation of Batasheva's rendition of what she had heard from Pronicheva about the massacre (PR12).[48]

Thus, in spite of highly unfavorable circumstances, there exist numerous texts conveying the recollections of one of the very few people who survived Babi Yar. Let us now take a closer look, proceeding in order of the chronology of the events.

Babi Yar According to Pronicheva's Testimonies

Seven texts state that the Jews who assembled on September 29 thought they would be "taken somewhere" (PR1, 3pub2, 4–7, and 10). This was because the Jews had to bring valuables (PR1, 3pub2, 4, and 5) or because there was a train station nearby (PR3pub2, 6, and 10). PR6, the text in Kuznetsov's book, adds that Pronicheva's parents thought that they were bound for "Soviet territory." PR2, the 1946 interview in *Pravda Ukrainy,* quantifies the number of Jews who showed up as "tens of thousands." Both PR6 and PR10, the Darmstadt testimony, say that Pronicheva arrived at the designated site in the afternoon.

After reaching the intersection, the great mass of people walked on (obviously along Melnyk Street) and came upon a roadblock near the gate of the Jewish cemetery, which was on the right side of the street (PR1, 2, 3pub, 4, 6, and 10). The guarded checkpoint consisted of barbed wire and (Soviet) anti-tank obstacles, and there was a gap in it that anyone could walk through. According to PR1, the 1946 report from the Prosecutor's Office of the Kiev Military District, the guards were Germans wearing helmets and carrying rifles, and PR5, the section in Kost Turkalo's book, likewise speaks of "armed German soldiers." But other reports also mention non-Germans. PR7, the 1967 Prosecutor's Office report from Kiev, says that there were "also" *politseiskie*—which is probably the prosecutor's rendition of what Pronicheva (like others who survived the Nazis) would have called *politsai,* the colloquial Russian term for auxiliary, native policemen.

Three other texts go further and specify an ethnic background: PR4, the 1946 interview with Soviet historians, speaks of "Ukrainians," PR6 mentions "Ukrainian policemen in black uniforms with gray cuffs" (in addition to "Germans with numbers on their breast"), and PR10 refers to "two Germans and a Ukrainian" alongside "cuirassiers," or mounted soldiers with breast plates (which could refer to the oval gorgets worn by the Wehrmacht's field gendarmes).[49] Only Kuznetsov's text adds that "a very striking figure, a tall, energetic man in a Ukrainian embroidered shirt, with a long Cossack mustache, was giving instructions. . . . Everyone called him 'Mr. Shevchenko,' like the Ukrainian poet. Maybe that was his proper name, or maybe somebody had dubbed him that because of his mustache, but it sounded rather frightful, like 'Mr. Pushkin' or 'Mr. Dostoyevsky.'" Later, Pronicheva was to return to the entrance in an attempt to get out (which PR12, the interview with Batasheva, mentions as well). According to PR6, the man in charge there took one look at her Soviet identification card and called out in Ukrainian, "No, a Jew! Get back!" (*E, zhidivka! Nazad!*).[50]

Beyond the entrance Germans—and Germans only—robbed the

Jews of their coats, jewelry, and other valuables (PR1, 3pub2, 4, 6, 7, 10, and 11). PR2 uniquely mentions in this regard both "SS men" and (non-German) "policemen" (*politseiskie*). A German confiscated Pronicheva's fur coat (PR3pub2 and 6). PR6 says that "an enormous German came up to her and said: 'Come and sleep with me, and I'll let you out.' She looked at him as if he were out of his mind, and he went away." Only PR10 has something similar: A "German soldier," it says, told her with a smile, "If you want to stay alive, sleep with me, then you will be saved." The Jews were steered left, evidently down Kahatna Street (today Simi Khokhlovykh Street), which had a long fence on the left and the small Orthodox Bratske Cemetery on the right. The Jews then turned right into another street, evidently the wide Laherna Street (today Dorohozhytska Street), which separated the Bratske Cemetery from the large (and also Orthodox) Lukianivka Cemetery. Four texts mention a blind old man who asked for assistance in walking, which Pronicheva provided. She asked where everybody was being taken, and the man said something like, "Don't you know, my child, that we are going to pay our last debt to God?" (PR4, 6, and 10; PR2 has him say that they are "going to die").

Seven accounts state that the Jews then arrived at a horrible "corridor," or gauntlet, of Germans with rubber clubs, big sticks, and vicious dogs (PR1, 2, 3pub2, 4, 6, 7, and 10). Here the tendentiousness of the Kiev tribunal comes to light. PR3pub2 quotes Pronicheva as saying that these Germans wore "blue uniforms. I knew well that that was the German police." No other available text says this, and PR6 and PR10 actually refer to "soldiers." What Pronicheva said in Darmstadt in 1968 rings true: "At that time, I did not look carefully at what kind of uniforms these were. Later, I found out that the green uniforms belonged to the [German] policemen and that the soldiers had a gray uniform. I don't know the color of the uniforms there [at Babi Yar]" (PR10).[51] Therefore, it looks as if she may have given in to pretrial pressure from the Kiev tribunal prosecution to say certain things.

In any event, the seven accounts that mention the gauntlet state without exception that none of the Jews could avoid running it; all of them were beaten severely, and those who fell were attacked by the dogs. PR6 says that the blows drew blood, that those who inflicted them were laughing, and that the horrified victims trampled some of their own into the ground. PR7, Pronicheva's deposition for Darmstadt investigators, says simply that "many people" died in the gauntlet. PR10, Pronicheva's courtroom testimony in Darmstadt, states that "many fell down and were trampled into a thin mass."

Most versions of Pronicheva's testimony state or imply that the gauntlet led to a large "space cordoned off by troops, a sort of square overgrown with grass" (PR6), where policemen who were not German gave the Jews an equally terrifying reception (PR1, 2, 3pub2, 4, 6, 7, 10, and 12). In most texts, they are simply *politseiskie* (PR1, 3pub2, and 7), *politsai* (PR1, 2, and 4), or *politsaï* (PR12). But three documents speak of "Ukrainian policemen"—*ukrainskie politsai* (PR6), *ukrainische Polizisten* (PR10), and *politsai-ukraintsy* (PR11). "To judge by their accent," PR6 (Kuznetsov) adds, "they were not local people but from western Ukraine." No other version provides any information about accents, which is reason to be cautious about accepting this detail. The Darmstadt testimony, however, says the open space was "full of German soldiers and Ukrainian nationalists and Ukrainian policemen" (PR10).

It is appropriate to note here that new and newly found Ukrainian sources also name paramilitary and auxiliary police formations that were in Kiev at the time of the massacre: a squad of what was then simply called the "Ukrainian police" and the Bukovinian Battalion. Both were created or commanded by activists of the Melnyk faction of the Organization of Ukrainian Nationalists (OUN-M), a militant group dominated by western Ukrainians who saw themselves engaged in a struggle to free Ukraine from "Muscovite-Jewish gangs."[52] A document from the war years speaks of the arrival in the city of a squad of Ukrainian policemen on September 21 and of a full company two days later.[53] A recent book about the Bukovinian Battalion by veterans places members in Kiev from the time of the great fire, functioning as part of a "Ukrainian police": Having mentioned the encirclement of the Red Army near Kiev and the date of the German arrival in the city, the books says that "less than a week after these events, the Bukovinian Battalion, which had 700 to 800 members at that time, arrived in Kiev." Several newcomers took jobs in the city administration or went on to create police units in Vasylkiv, Bila Tserkva, and other places near Kiev, but others joined Kiev's "Ukrainian police": "With the remaining members of the Battalion, a military course was held. They participated in rescue efforts, helping the inhabitants of Kiev to extinguish the fires and to liquidate the consequences of the massive explosions." Likewise, in recently published memoirs the battalion's former commander, Petro Voinovsky (1913–1996), recalls that the unit arrived while "the Khreshchatyk was burning."[54] (This said, little noticed OUN émigré publications from the 1950s also report the battalion arriving in Kiev soon after the Germans.[55])

Every record of Pronicheva's testimony that describes the massacre itself states that the auxiliary policemen readied the Jews for their murder by stripping them. The non-German policemen, according to PR1,

> chased the fully undressed people one by one up a hill. The people reached the crest and there, through a cut in a wall of sand (*peschanaia stena*), neared the ravines. . . . Before my very eyes people went insane, they turned gray, all around there were heartrending cries and moans. All day long, there was machine-gun fire. I saw how Germans took children away from their mothers and threw them from the precipice into the ravine.

Here are present many elements that reappear in other reports: a sandy wall with a narrow passage cut through it (PR2, 3pub2, 4, 6, and 10); the sound of shots (PR2, 3pub2, 6, and 10); rapid whitening of hair within minutes or even seconds (PR2, 3pub2, 4, 6, 7, and 10); participation by Germans (PR2, 6, and 7) or "soldiers" (PR10); and babies who are ripped from their mothers and thrown into the ravine (PR4, 6, 7, and 10). PR1 does not, but other testimonies do also mention severe beatings. For instance, PR4 says that the policemen "abused them terribly, wherever and however they could—with their hands, feet, some of the policemen had brass knuckles. People walked to the execution covered in blood." (See also PR2, 3pub2, 7, and 10). PR6 uniquely speaks of commands in Russian, Ukrainian, and German to be quick, and of the policemen's "sadistic rage."[56]

Only two early testimonies mention that some victims were silent (PR2 and 3pub2). As for resistance, PR10 is the only testimony to use the word: "Of course nobody wanted to undress, the women in particular resisted. It was all so shameful and humiliating. If one stood there and tried to cover oneself with one's hands so as not to stand there entirely naked . . . there were beatings." This also is the one version where Pronicheva mentions the sight of her sister: "She was naked, lying on the ground. A policeman was beating her and kicked her in the face and in the head." Other differences between the various texts relate to the entry into the ravine. Whereas PR1 says that the victims were chased through the opening one by one and another speaks of a single line (3pub2), other records speak of groups, which was probably how it happened (PR4, 6, and 7).

Three texts say that immediately after Pronicheva escaped from the gauntlet but before anybody could undress her, she heard her mother call out something like, "My daughter, you don't look like one, save yourself!" (PR3pub2, 6, and 10). In a slight variation, another text says this was as Pronicheva was *entering* the gauntlet (PR4). The reports tend to repeat a single narrative about what Pronicheva then did. PR4 puts it as follows:

> I walked straight to a policeman and immediately asked him in Ukrainian where the commander was. He asked why do you need the commander. I answered that I was not a Jew but a Ukrainian. I accompanied my colleagues and ended up here by accident. He looked at me in a certain way and demanded my papers. I showed him the union member card and the labor booklet, which do not mention a nationality. He believed me for my last name is Russian, my patronymic also sounds a bit Russian, and he pointed to a hillock on which a small group of people were sitting. He says, "Sit down, wait until the evening. When we have shot all of the Yids, we will let you out (*Sadis, podozhdesh do vechera, kogda vsekh zhidov perestreliaem, vas vypustim*)."

The rendition of the man's words in Russian does not preclude the possibility that Pronicheva was thinking of a man who spoke Ukrainian, if only because she says he did speak that language in PR2 and PR6 (which here resembles PR4 a great deal; compare PR1, 7, and 12). PR10 again stands out, because here, for reasons unknown, Pronicheva claims to be Russian.

When it began to get dark, the group, by then about fifty (PR6 and 12), was still waiting. Seven texts state that a German in a position of authority came on the scene (PR1, 2, 3pub2, 4, 6, 7, 10, and 12), by most accounts in a car. With him was an interpreter (PR3pub2, 6, 7, and 10; PR6 calls that person a Russian). The German—possibly Friedrich Jeckeln, the higher SS and police leader for Russia South—demanded to know who the people sitting were. "It was explained to him that this was a group of Russians and Ukrainians, who must be let out" (PR3pub2). "'These are our people (*Tse nashi liudy*),' a policeman answered. 'They didn't know; they must be let out (*Ne znaly, treba ikh vypustyt*)'" (PR6). "[T]he policemen responded to his question that we had come here to accompany people. We had come to this place by accident and must be released" (PR7; PR10 is similar). But the German immediately ordered the execution of all of those waiting, for they had seen everything (PR1 and 7) and would talk (PR2, 3pub2, and 10); after that, no Jew would heed any summons (PR4, 6, and 10).

The group was not undressed (PR3pub2, 4, 6, and 12), "for it was already dark and the Germans were tired" (PR4). By eight accounts, Pronicheva was taken away and, along with the others, was chased through the ravine wall to a ledge inside (PR1, 2, 3pub2, 4, 6, 7, 10, and 12). The ledge was narrow and difficult to stand on (PR3pub2); it had been deliberately cut for the purpose of mass murder (PR6 and 12). Deep down she saw a sea of bodies and blood (PR2, 4, 10, and 12). PR6, in Kuznetsov's book, describes how the shooters had made themselves comfortable: "On the other side of the quarry, she could just make out the light machine-guns that had been set up there and a few German soldiers. They had lit a bonfire, and it looked like they were making coffee." Only PR12 has something similar: "a group of Germans sitting on overturned tree trunks." One German walked toward the gun and began shooting (PR6 and 12). It is possible that the greater detail in PR6 regarding the shooters—and earlier regarding the policemen's "sadistic rage"—stemmed from Kuznetsov's notion that he had some artistic license.

"When only one person was left before me [to be shot], I gathered all of my strength and jumped into the pit," Pronicheva said in Darmstadt (PR10). Other reports also say that she dropped down before being hit, landed on people covered in blood, and pretended to be dead (PR1, 2, 3pub2, 4, 6, 7, and 12). Only Batasheva's retelling (PR12) adds that Pronicheva then heard from above the clatter of "spoons and metal plates and dishes. They were having supper up there." At this point in Pronicheva's story, I shall omit some hair-raising details found in various texts.

Her ordeal was far from over. Germans came down into the ravine, walked across the pile of victims, and finished off survivors (PR1,

2, 3pub2, 4, 5, 6, 7, and 10), whom they sought out with flashlights (PR3pub2, 4, 6, and 12). Also down into this hellish place came non-German "policemen" (PR1, 2, 6, 7, and 10). PR6 mentions in this regard the policeman who had told Pronicheva to sit down on the hillock. The *Pravda Ukrainy* interview and the two testimonies related to the Darmstadt trial imply that not only Germans but also auxiliaries were doing the killing there: "Germans and policemen descended into the pit to kill off people who were still living" (PR2); "Here walked Germans and policemen who shot and finished off those still alive" (PR7); "Germans came down. They were two officers and two [non-German] policemen. With gun shots, they finished off those still alive" (PR10). Most accounts then say that one or two men approached Pronicheva, became suspicious because they saw no wound, and trampled her to verify that she was dead. She showed no sign of life (PR1, 2, 3pub2, 4, 6, 7, 10, 12). The texts variously describe this, often with great precision, but PR4 seems the most realistic in saying that the first to see her was "one of the policemen or Germans (I cannot remember)."

It should be noted that the texts produced by Turkalo and Kipnis provide a substantially different account. These versions do not mention a gauntlet, an open space, a wall of sand, or a long waiting period for Pronicheva. According to Turkalo in PR5:

> The [Jewish] cemetery was fenced off by a high stone wall. One side of that stone wall borders on a rather deep ravine called Babi Yar. In this wall was a gate. All of the Jews, having undressed down to their underwear and having taken off their shoes, had to walk along a path toward the gate. But somewhere behind the gate stood a machine-gun. Right after people walked through the gate they came under fire and fell into the ravine. Dina saw how her entire family came under fire and fell into the ravine. Fortunately, the bullets somehow missed Dina, and she was not wounded when she fell into the ravine.

PR11, Kipnis's version, does not even mention any kind of wall, of sand or stone: "All were taken to an open pit and shot by sub-machine-gunners. . . . I saw a young and completely naked woman breastfeeding her naked baby when a policeman ran toward her, grabbed the child from her breast, and hurled it into the pit. The mother rushed after the child. A fascist shot her, and she fell down dead." Pronicheva, as Kipnis tells it, showed her identity card to a "fat officer"; this passport said she was Russian. But, he goes on to record, "one policeman ran up to us and barked, 'Don't believe her, she's a Yid (*zhidovka*). We know her.'" The German told her to wait and then "took me to his superior, gave him my identity papers, and said, 'This woman says she is a Russian, but a policeman knows her as a Yid.' His superior took the papers, took a long look at them, and barked, 'Dina is not a Russian name. You're a Yid. Take her away!'" A policeman ordered her to undress. She dropped into the ravine "before any shots were fired." Unlike any of the other texts, PR5 and PR11 also state that people fell on top of Pronicheva.

Almost all of the reports tell us that Pronicheva and the others in the ravine were covered by a thin layer of earth or sand (PR1, 2, 3pub2, 4, 6, 7, 10, 11, and 12). PR2 says this started after somebody said, "Start shoveling! (*Davaite zasypat!*)." PR12 mentions Germans as shoveling, but PR4 has others in mind: "Some time later, I heard almost directly above my ear, 'Demidenko, get over here, start shoveling (*Demidenko, davai siuda, zasypai*).' Then I heard some kind of muffled thuds, then they came closer and closer, and I felt how sand poured down on me—they were covering the dead bodies." In this case, Kuznetsov's version (PR6) is very similar to PR4: "A few minutes later, she heard a voice calling from above: 'Demidenko! Start shoveling! (*Demidenko! Davai prikidai!*).' There was a clatter of spades and then muffled thuds of sand on bodies, closer and closer and eventually heaps of sand started coming down on Dina."

Somewhat later, Pronicheva snuck out of the mass grave and, while doing so, encountered a teenaged survivor who had done the same. Later, the boy was shot (PR1, 2, 3pub2, 4, 6, 7, 10, and 11). Three versions give his name as Motia, but Kipnis speaks of a Fima Shnaiderman (PR4, 6, 7, and 11). While hiding near the ravine, Pronicheva saw Germans rape and murder two young Jewish women and later shoot a woman and a young boy (PR4, 6, 7, and 10). The child's last words, given in PR4, 6, and 10, were "Grandma, I'm scared (*Babushka, ia boius*)." PR4 uniquely adds that "some kind of woman with a child came upon the scene, looked down, laughed, and chatted with the Germans who had shot [the two]."

It was already October 2 when Pronicheva approached a nearby cottage. By five accounts, the inhabitants looked evil and fetched a German, who came to arrest her almost at once (PR1, 4, 6, 7, 10). Three versions (PR1, 4, and 6) give the words of a boy at the house: "Look sir, *Jude* (*Os, pan, iuda*)." That all of the published Soviet versions—PR2, 3pub1, 3pub2, 8pub, and 9pub, and of course the Soviet edition of *Babi Yar*—lack this denunciation is not surprising. The German glanced at Pronicheva's profile (PR10) and took her to a nearby house, where some other Germans were having breakfast; later, she had to clean up there (PR1, 4, 6, 7, and 10; the last two texts do not mention a meal). After a while, all of the Germans left save for one who was left behind to guard her while she worked. He wanted her to live and urged her to flee through the window (PR6 and 10). Two Jewish girls were also brought in (PR1, 4, 6, 7, and 10). The Germans drove Pronicheva and other arrested Jews to a place with several garages (PR1, 3pub2, 4, 6, 7, and 10), but those turned out to be so jammed with people that the truck's German occupants were unable to squeeze them in (PR4, 6, 7, and 10). A woman fell out of one of the garages and was shot on the spot (PR6 and 7). Forced to continue on their way, the Germans drove on at high speed, but by six accounts, Pronicheva and a girl jumped off without the guards noticing (PR1, 2, 3pub2, 4, 6, 7, and 10; PR2 lacks the girl; PR10 calls the guards Ukrainian). The girl's name was Liuba Shamin, says PR1, but other texts speak only of Liuba (PR4, 6, and 7), who was a nurse (PR1, 4, 6, and 10).

At this point, the reports diverge to such a degree that overlap becomes rare. PR5 says that Pronicheva stayed briefly at the home of Turkalo and his wife, who knew her already and who together with Turkalo's sister-in-law gave her money for travel. PR7 does not add anything substantial after Pronicheva's leap from the car. Five texts say that Dina and Liuba spent the night with a relative of Pronicheva's and then went to Darnytsia on the eastern shores of the Dnieper river (PR1, 3pub2, 4, 6, and 10), and another text says the same while omitting the girl (PR2). But only two of these texts provide substantially more information than this. PR4 has nine pages with a detailed account of how, by working in theaters and fleeing many times, Pronicheva survived in Darnytsia, Kiev, Bila Tserkva, Rokytne, Ruzhyn, and Koziatyn. PR10 also talks about this period in some detail.

PR8pub, the letter in *Literaturnaia gazeta,* says little about the massacre itself ("My father, mother, and sister were shot in Babi Yar—I saw this") and continues with, "I ran from the ravine twice, I ran from the Gestapo twice, I ran from the Gendarmerie, and I ran after sitting in jail for 28 days and nights. I spent the night in ruined buildings, basements, in attics, in rubbish pits—hungry, half-dressed, sick, with severe injuries (not only to the heart) received from the blows of rifle butts, severe beatings."

PR9pub uniquely—and appropriately for a magazine devoted to German-Soviet friendship—says that a German helped Pronicheva in Darnytsia. By this account, one Hans Heinicke, who had a Jewish fiancée in Germany, gave her and her baby boy Vladimir food when she was under house arrest there. On February 22, 1942, Heinicke told her to flee, which she did the next day. (PR4 also describes a flight on that date.) PR11 lacks both the denunciation near the cottage and the leap from the car. It does say, however, and uniquely so, that Pronicheva became a housemaid for an elderly Kievan, and that a German by the name of Albert courted her. It concludes by saying that when her Jewish identity became known, this German quickly took her to an ethnic German in Bila Tserkva. That only Kipnis's version, produced near the end of Pronicheva's life, mentions a courtship by a German and a stay with an ethnic German does not disprove these events, for they are of a kind that most Soviet citizens would prefer to conceal.

PR4 and PR8pub discuss Pronicheva's family: Her husband Viktor saved their son Vladimir from being shot for being half-Jewish, but he himself was arrested and did not survive. Friends took the boy and his sister Lidiia to children's homes, where their mother found them in March 1944. Looking back, Pronicheva was amazed at her strength during the war. "Now I get upset by the smallest things and am moved to tears immediately." Fortunately, she had received many letters "from all corners of the Union, and they are all so tender, so touching, that

sometimes it seems that now I have the whole world as my friend"
(PR8pub).

Conclusion

In the line-up of *pronicheviana,* two texts stand out as odd. One is
PR5, Turkalo's account. Elsewhere in his book, there is also a strange,
obvious error: Turkalo has the first explosions and the outbreak of the
fire on the Khreshchatyk taking place *after* the massacre. And in describing events in Kiev in June 1941, he finds it necessary to state twice
that a building custodian who harassed him was Jewish.[57] If and when
Pronicheva spent time at his place after the massacre, did she dare tell
him everything she had experienced?[58] The other odd text is PR11,
which generally appears to render whatever Kipnis heard from Pronicheva in an inaccurate way. It should give us pause that only this text
gives her maiden name as Vasserman and her husband's first name as
Nikolai.

As noted, there is a specific problem with PR6. That text probably
contains information that Kuznetsov heard from Pronicheva, but his
failure to mention that she had also given him the record of a two decades' old statement, which perhaps explains the striking similarity
between various passages in PR4 and PR6, is reason to be cautious in
using this text.

The main finding is that most of the texts repeat details with considerable consistency. We found, for instance, that many texts say that
non-German policemen were present at the massacre, whereby many
call them Ukrainians, state or imply that one or more of those non-German auxiliaries spoke Ukrainian, or state that Pronicheva addressed
one of them in Ukrainian. (See, respectively, PR4, 6, and 10; PR3pub2
and 6; PR1 and 4.) We also heard of individual Germans who offered
to save Pronicheva.[59]

Of course, as historians, lawyers, and psychologists know, a person
may have consistent or vivid memories of an event, but this does not
suffice to prove that those memories are accurate.[60] Yet despite the risks,
historians of the Babi Yar massacre (as opposed to its legacy) should
use Pronicheva's and other testimonies much more extensively. There
is no methodological guideline other than an awareness of the need to
avoid the two extremes of utter skepticism and faith in everything recalled.[61] The fact remains that only very few sources come as close as
Pronicheva's testimonies do to the horrendous details of Kiev's Jewish
Holocaust.

In my opinion, researchers should take particularly seriously PR4,
the interview by Soviet historians, and PR10, the Darmstadt testimony. These Soviet and German records also happen to be the only ones
that mention Kiev's great fire on the eve of the massacre. PR4 is all the
more credible because a stenographer produced it and did so as early as

1946—in the Stalin period, but less then five years after the events and at a time when Pronicheva possibly felt safe, having just testified in the Soviet media and at a Soviet tribunal. PR4 does contain an obvious error when it quotes Pronicheva as saying that the city commandant had signed the poster summoning the Jews (he only ordered it printed[62])—but this does not invalidate the entire testimony.

The reader will also recall that PR4, PR10, and many other versions state that the hair of some victims at Babi Yar turned white (or gray) before Pronicheva's eyes. While such phenomena have been mentioned in many other times and places, rapid whitening of scalp hair in extreme situations is impossible.[63] Yet this is not the kind of error casting doubt on the veracity of a witness's statement. On the contrary, it should actually bring us closer to the person who made it: This kind of detail reminds us, even over a distance of several decades, that we are listening to somebody who experienced unspeakable horror, suffering, and trauma.

Acknowledgements

For their help in gathering elusive data and documents or their comments on earlier versions, I thank Nanci Adler (Center for Holocaust and Genocide Studies, Amsterdam), Marco Carynnyk (Toronto), Mary Ginzburg (Yad Vashem Archives), Tetiana Iemel'ianova (H. S. Pshenychnyi Central State Film, Photo-, and Phonographic Archives of Ukraine), Dmytro V. Malakov (Museum of the History of Kiev), Anatoly Podolsky (Ukrainian Center of Holocaust Studies, Kiev) Dieter Pohl (Institute for Contemporary History in Munich), Shmuel Spector (Yad Vashem), Jolande Withuis (Netherlands Institute for War Documentation), and the editors.

Notes

1. Facsimiles, contemporary photographs, and a succinct description of the massacre are in Hamburger Institut für Sozialforschung, *Verbrechen der Wehrmacht: Dimensionen des Vernichtungskrieges 1941–1944. Ausstellungskatalog* (Hamburg: Hamburger Edition, 2002), pp. 160–165. A reduced facsimile of the Russian-Ukrainian-German poster is in Erhard Roy Wiehn, comp., *Die Schoáh von Babij Jar: Das Massaker deutscher Sonderkommandos an der jüdischen Bevölkerung von Kiew 1941 fünfzig Jahre danach zum Gedenken* (Konstanz: Hartung-Gorre, 1991), p. 144. A facsimile of the relevant pages of the Security Police and Security Service report about the operation, "Ereignismeldung UdSSR Nr. 106" of October 7, 1941, is in John Mendelsohn, ed., *The Holocaust: Selected Documents*, Vol. 10: *The Einsatzgruppen or Murder Commandos* (New York and London: Garland Publishing, 1982), pp. 57–58 (with an English translation of the key passages on p. 50). The most informative study of pictorial evidence relating to the massacre is D. Malakov, "Kiev i Babii Iar na nemetskoi fotoplenke oseni 1941 goda," in Tat'iana Evstaf'eva and Vitalii Nakhmanovich, eds., *Babii Iar: Chelovek, vlast', istoriia. Kniga 1: Istoricheskaia topografiia. Khronologiia sobytii* (Kiev: Vneshtorgizdat Ukrainy, 2004), pp. 164–170. For a general survey of the relevant Russian- and Ukrainian-language sources (and historiography), see V. Nakhmanovich, "Istochniki i literatura: Problemy sistematizatsii i osobennosti izucheniia," in idem, pp. 21–65.

2. I. Iu. Barenboim et al., "Obuzdat' agressorov, presech' zlodeianiia sion-
istov," *Pravda,* March 12, 1970, p. 4, cited in a different translation in Jonathan
Frankel, "The Soviet Regime and Anti-Zionism: An Analysis," in Yaacov Ro'i and
Avi Beker, eds., *Jewish Culture and Identity in the Soviet Union* (New York and
London: New York University Press, 1991), p. 336.

3. Lucy S. Dawidowicz, "Babi Yar's Legacy," *The New York Times Magazine,*
September 27, 1981, pp. 48–50, 54, 59–60, 63, 65, and 67. Elsewhere, she wrote that
from June 1941 "the Ukrainians" were "Germany's most diligent collaborators."
Lucy S. Dawidowicz, *The Holocaust and the Historians* (Cambridge, MA, and Lon-
don: Harvard University Press, 1981), p. 80. The most comprehensive study of the
massacre's legacy is Richard Sheldon, "The Transformations of Babi Yar," in Terry
L. Thompson and Richard Sheldon, eds., *Soviet Society and Culture: Essays in Hon-
or of Vera S. Dunham* (Boulder and London: Westview Press, 1988), pp. 124–161.
See also Jeff Mankoff, "Babi Yar and the Struggle for Memory, 1944–2004," *Ab
Imperio,* no. 2 (2004), pp. 393–415.

4. Leon Uris, *Exodus* (New York: Bantam, 1958), p. 119; see also ibid., p. 80.
Critical comments about Dawidowicz's article are in Taras Hunczak, "Ukrainian-
Jewish Relations during the Soviet and Nazi Occupations," in Yury Boshyk, ed.,
Ukraine during World War II: History and Its Aftermath (Edmonton: Canadian In-
stitute of Ukrainian Studies, University of Alberta, 1986), pp. 56–57, note 63; and
in Yaroslav Bilinsky, "Methodological Problems and Philosophical Issues in the
Study of Jewish-Ukrainian Relations during the Second World War," in Howard
Aster and Peter J. Potichnyj, eds., *Ukrainian-Jewish Relations in Historical Perspec-
tive,* 2nd ed. (Edmonton: Canadian Institute of Ukrainian Studies, University of
Alberta, 1990), pp. 379–380 and 391, note 31. On the Ukrainian émigré community and war crimes, see John Paul Himka's article "War Criminality: A Blank Spot
in the Collective Memory of the Ukrainian Diaspora" in the e-journal *Spaces of
Identity,* at: http://www.yorku.ca/soi/_Vol_5_1/_HTML/Himka.html.

5. For example, Dina Pronicheva, G. Ia. Batasheva (see note 48), and Mariia
Grinburg, who is briefly interviewed in Sjifra Herschberg, "Er staat een standbeeld
bij Babi Jar," *De Volkskrant* (Amsterdam), October 5, 1991.

6. A translation of some of this testimony is in Ernst Klee et al., eds., *"Those
Were the Days": The Holocaust through the Eyes of the Perpetrators and Bystanders*
(London: H. Hamilton, 1991), p. 63.

7. The more comprehensive studies include Harmut Rüß, "Wer war verant-
wortlich für das Massaker von Babij Jar?" *Militärgeschichtliche Mitteilungen,* 57,
no. 2 (1998), pp. 483–508; M. V. Koval', "Tragediia Bab'ego Iara: istoriia i sovre-
mennost'," *Novaia i noveishaia istoriia,* no. 4 (July-August 1998), pp. 14–28; Klaus
Jochen Arnold, "Die Eroberung und Behandlung der Stadt Kiew durch die Wehrmacht im September 1941: Zur Radikalisierung der Besatzungspolitik," *Militärgeschichtliche Mitteilungen,* 58, no. 1 (1999), pp. 23–63; F. L. Levitas, "Babyn Iar
(1941–1943)," in S. Ia. Ielisavets'kyi, ed., *Katastrofa i opir ukraïns'koho ievreistva
(1941–1944): Narysy z istoriï Holokostu i Oporu v Ukraïni* (Kiev: Natsional'na akademiia nauk Ukraïny, Instytut politychnykh i etnonatsional'nykh doslidzhen',
1999), pp. 88–117; Wolfram Wette, *Die Wehrmacht: Feindbilder. Vernichtungskrieg.
Legenden* (Frankfurt am Main: S. Fischer, 2002), pp. 115–128; Karel Cornelis
Berkhoff, "Hitler's Clean Slate: Everyday Life in the Reichskommissariat Ukraine,
1941–1944" (PhD diss., University of Toronto, 1998), pp. 47–61, 404–405, 419,
423–428, 439–440, and 499; Karel C. Berkhoff, *Harvest of Despair: Life and Death
in Ukraine under Nazi Rule* (Cambridge, Mass.: The Belknap Press of Harvard
University Press, 2004), 29–33, 65–68, 75–78, and 302–303; V. Nakhmanovich,
"Rasstrely i zakhoroneniia v raione Bab'ego Iara vo vremia nemetskoi okkupatsii
g. Kieva 1941–1943 gg.: Problemy khronologii i topografii," in Evstaf'eva and Nakhmanovich, *Babii Iar,* pp. 84–163, esp. 94–128.

8. A. Anatoli (Kuznetsov), *Babi Yar: A Document in the Form of a Novel*, transl. David Floyd (New York: Farrar, Straus and Giroux, 1970), p. 475. According to this author, who was not there himself, "when they heard of the meeting, some cameramen from the Kiev news-film studios rushed down and filmed it, as a result of which there was a great row in the studio, the director was sacked and the film confiscated by the secret police." Confirmation of the confiscation is in Vladimir Khanin, ed., *Documents on Ukrainian Jewish Identity and Emigration 1944–1990* (London and Portland: Frank Cass, 2003), pp. 146–147.

9. The dates of her birth and death come from Dmytro V. Malakov, who received them from Pronicheva's son, Vladimir Viktorovich Pronichev.

10. Leonid Abramenko, ed., *Kyïvs'kyi protses: Dokumenty ta materialy* (Kiev: Lybid', 1995), pp. 201–203. See also Alexander Victor Prusin, "'Fascist Criminals to the Gallows!' The Holocaust and Soviet War Crimes Trials, December 1945–February 1946," *Holocaust and Genocide Studies*, 17, no. 1 (Spring 2003), pp. 1–30.

11. "Protokol doprosa svidetelia Pronichevoi Diny Mironovny. Gor. Kiev, 12 ianvaria 1946 g.," United States Holocaust Memorial Museum (USHMM) Archives, RG-06.025*02, box 41, No. 372. In the Central Archives of the Federal Security Service of the Russian Federation in Moscow, the document is among what the USHMM Archives describe as "records relating to war crime trials in the Soviet Union, 1939–1992," "N-18762, tom 17," fols. 257–261.

12. Wiehn, *Die Schoáh*, pp. 179–183. The retyping omits crucial information: the names Pronicheva and Kogan (the investigator), the place, the date, and the archival reference. A historian at the Academy of Sciences of Ukraine quotes from the same source in an article based on declassified testimonies. See Bogdan A. Martinenko, "Tragediia Bab'ego Iara: rassekrechennye dokumenty svidetel'stvuiut," in ibid., pp. 363–364.

13. "Dina Pronicheva," in Il'ia Levitas, comp., *Pamiat' Bab'ego Iara: Vospominaniia. Dokumenty* (Kiev: Evreiskii sovet Ukrainy, Fond "Pamiat' Bab'ego Iara," 2001), pp. 133–138. Contrary to a widespread belief in Ukraine, editing historical documents for style easily introduces distortion. Levitas changes, among other things, "skazal" into "kriknul" ("said" into "cried") and "tselyi den'" into "bezprestanno" ("all day" into "ceaselessly"). Whereas PR1 says that on their way to the point of assembly, "almost no one" among the Jews thought they might be massacred (*pochti nikto . . . ne predpolagal*), Pronicheva in Levitas's version is categorical: "they" did not think this (*ne predpolagali*).

14. "Iz protokola doprosa na Kievskom protsesse [*sic*; it was not an in-court testimony] v kachestve svidetelia spassheisia ot rasstrelov D. Pronichevoi," in Evstaf'eva and Nakhmanovich, *Babii Iar*, pp. 277–280, with reference to an "original" at Derzhavnyi arkhiv Sluzhby Bezpeky Ukraïny, fond 7, opys 8, sprava 1, arkushi 75–79. In this publication, ellipses replace the place (Kiev), the warning that Soviet Ukraine's Criminal Code penalizes false statements, Pronicheva's signature, and the name, title, and signature of the investigating major.

15. D. Pronicheva, "V Bab'em Iaru," *Pravda Ukrainy* (Kiev), January 13, 1946, p. 3. A retyping by a Kiev archivist is among the papers of the Jewish Anti-Fascist Committee at the State Archives of the Russian Federation in Moscow, fond 8114, opis' 1, delo 942, listy 11–15, and a photocopy of the retyping is at the Yad Vashem Archives, record group M.35, file 8.

16. *Kinozhurnal* "Radians'ka Ukraïna," No. 13–14, special two-part edition about the Kiev tribunal, 1946. It is available at the H. S. Pshenychnyi Central State Film, Photo-, and Phonographic Archives of Ukraine (Kiev), film collection, item 299. There may also exist more film footage of Pronicheva recorded on other occasions. On this, see also note 8 above.

17. RATAU, "Sudebnyi protsess po delu o zverstvakh nemetsko-fashistskikh zakhvatchikov na territorii Ukrainskoi SSR," *Pravda Ukrainy*, January 26, 1946, p. 3; RATAU, "Sudovyi protses u spravi pro zvirstva nimets'ko-fashysts'kykh za-

harbnykiv na terytoriï Ukraïns'koï RSR," *Radians'ka Ukraïna* (Kiev), January 26, 1946, p. 3. Words to the effect that the victims were Jews appear here only once, although according to PR3pub2, Pronicheva mentioned this several times.

18. Abramenko, *Kyïvs'kyi protses*, pp. 5 and 8.

19. Ibid., pp. 69–72.

20. "STENOGRAMMA besedy so svidetelem nemetskikh zlodeniaii po Bab'emu Iaru PRONICHEVOI Dinoi Mironovnoi," Kiev, April 24, 1946, at Tsentral'nyi derzhavnyi arkhiv hromads'kykh ob"iednan' Ukraïny (Kiev), fond 166, opys 3, sprava 245, arkushi 115–134. The stenographic report was prepared by Zh. B. Vil'kova, who also signed the document. A carbon copy on which were written the handwritten corrections that are also on PR4, and also new signatures by Pronicheva and Vil'kova, is at fond 166, opys 2, sprava 275, arkushi 1–20.

21. One may call the retyping PR4a. "Stenogramma vospominanii Pronichev-oi Diny Mironovny o zverskom unichtozhenii evreiskogo naseleniia v Bab'em iaru gor. Kieva," April 24, 1946, at Tsentral'nyi derzhavnyi arkhiv vyshchykh orhaniv vlady ta upravlinnia Ukraïny (Kiev), fond 4620, opys 3, sprava 281, arkushi 1–21. A photocopy of PR4a is at the Yad Vashem Archives, record group M.53, file 185.

22. Feliks Levitas and Mark Shimanovskii, *Babii iar: Stranitsy tragedii* (Kiev: Slid i Ko., 1991), pp. 23–32, lacks the first paragraph, the last sentence, and a sentence from the third folio. Whereas PR4a says, "U vkhoda stoiali nemtsy i ukraintsy, propuskavshie za zagrazhdenie. Tuda voiti mozhno bylo svobodno, a na vy-khod nikogo ne propuskali, krome podvodchikov," this publication (p. 23) renders this as, "U vkhoda stoiali nemtsy i politsai [*sic*], propuskavshie za zagrazhdenie. Tuda voiti mozhno bylo svobodno, a na vykhod nikogo ne propuskali, krome perevodchikov [*sic*]." A partial reprint of this unsatisfactory publication of PR4a is in Ol'ga Ungurian, "'Otets ob"iasnil, chto esli ia uvizhu mamu, nuzhno nazy-vat' ee 'tetia'—inache nas vsekh rasstreliaiut.' Vspominaiut deti Diny Mironovny Pronichevoi—geroini dokumental'noi knigi Anatoliia Kuznetsova 'Babii Iar'," *Fakty* (Kiev), September 7, 2001, p. 23.

23. "Babyn Iar (veresen' 1941-veresen' 1943 rr.)," *Ukraïns'kyi istorychnyi zhur-nal*, no. 9 (September 1991), pp. 80–85. For example, the two sentences quoted in the preceding note become, "Vkhid na kladovyshche [*sic*] rehuliuvaly fashysty [*sic*] i mistsevi politsaï [*sic*], ale nazad nikoho ne vypuskaly [*words omitted*]." Ibid., p. 81. The following sentences are neither replaced by ellipses nor translated: "Sna-chala menia obdalo vsiu krov'iu, po litsu stekala krov'. . . . Potom ia uslyshala ikotu predsmertnuiu, plach—eto vse iskhodilo ot nedobitykh trupov, ot umiraiu-shchikh." Equally striking is that "eto prisypali trupy" becomes "fashysts'ki neli-udy zamitaly slidy svoïkh zlodiian'." Levitas, "Babyn Iar (1941–1943)," pp. 104–106, provides part of PR4a in another Ukrainian translation, while misidentifying it as Pronicheva's Kiev tribunal testimony.

24. Inzh. K. T. Turkalo, *Tortury: (Avtobiohrafiia za bol'shevyts'kykh chasiv)* (New York: Nasha bat'kivshchyna, 1963), pp. 193–196.

25. The brief discussion of Pronicheva in Bilinsky, "Methodological Prob-lems," p. 380, refers to "the late K.T." In an e-mail message to me on August 8, 2001, Professor Yaroslav Bilinsky confirmed my conjecture that K.T. stood for Kost' Turkalo.

26. Kuznetsov had the same nationality as his father. He probably spoke Rus-sian with his friends, like most Kievans of his generation, even though he con-sidered Ukrainian his native language and had attended a Ukrainian-language school. Anatoli, *Babi Yar*, pp. 14 and 138.

27. The chapter about Pronicheva is in Anatolii Kuznetsov, "Babii Iar," *Iunost'*, 12, no. 8 (August 1966), pp. 22–23 and 26–28.

28. Anatolii Kuznetsov, *Babii iar: Roman-dokument* (Moscow: Moloda-ia gvardiia, 1967), relevant pages: 52–66, facsimile in Wiehn, *Die Schoáh*, pp. 199–213.

29. The first translation is "Babi Yar: Part One of A Documentary Novel," [transl. Jacob Guralsky and Mary Mackler] *The Current Digest of the Soviet Press*, XVIII, no. 39 (New York, October 19, 1966), pp. 15–19. The second translation is Anatoly Kuznetsov, *Babi Yar: A Documentary Novel*, transl. Jacob Guralsky (New York: The Dial Press, 1967), pp. 65–84; UK edition: (London: MacGibbon & Kee, 1967). The third English translation of the Pronicheva chapter, slightly condensed and with no mention of a translator, is in George St. George, *The Road to Babyi-Yar* (London: Neville Spearman, 1967), pp. 117–129. The German translation of the Soviet book is Anatoli Kusnezow, *Babi Jar: Ein dokumentarischer Roman*, transl. L. Robiné (Zurich: Diogenes Verlag, 1968). A Hebrew translation appeared in 1968.

30. Abraham Rothberg, *The Heirs of Stalin: Dissidence and the Soviet Regime, 1953–1970* (Ithaca and London: Cornell University Press, 1972), pp. 257–262. After the Bulgarian Communist regime murdered his friend and fellow-émigré Georgi Markov in late 1978, Kuznetsov developed heart problems; he died in June 1979 at the age of 49.

31. A. Anatolii (Kuznetsov), *Babii iar: Roman-dokument* (Frankfurt am Main: Possev, 1970, 2nd ed. 1973), relevant pages: 99–119; Anatolii Kuznetsov (A. Anatolii), *Babii iar: Roman-dokument* (New York: Possev-USA, 1986), relevant pages: 99–119; Anatolii Kuznetsov (A. Anatolii), *Babii iar: Roman-dokument* (Kiev: MIP "Oberig," 1991), relevant pages: 74–90; Anatolii Kuznetsov, *Babii Iar: Roman-dokument* (Moscow: Sovetskii pisatel'-Olimp, 1991), relevant pages: 68–83. The latest edition is Anatolii Kuznetsov, *Babii iar: Roman* (Moscow: Zakharov, 2001), relevant pages: 66–82. PR6 is also in Dr. Sh. Spektor [Shmuel Spector] and M. Kipnis, eds., *Babii Iar: K piatidesiatiletiiu tragedii 29, 30 sentiabria 1941 goda* (Jerusalem: Biblioteka-Aliia, 1991), pp. 45–66, and (except for the final paragraph) in I. A. Al'tman, ed., *Russkaia literatura o Kholokoste: Khrestomatiia dlia uchashchikhsia* (Moscow: Nauchno-prosvetitel'nyi tsentr "Kholokost," 1997), pp. 23–35.

32. Anatoli, *Babi Yar*, relevant pages: 99–120; UK edition: (London: Cape, 1970). My English quotations from PR6 are my adaptations of Floyd's translation. The German translation of the definitive version is A. Anatoli (Kusnezow), *Babij Jar: Roman*, transl. Alexander Kaempfe (Munich, Zurich, and Vienna: Axel Juncker Verlag, 1970), relevant pages: 94–114. A new Hebrew translation appeared in 1971.

33. Among the more thorough reviews are Zoya Vatnikova-Prizel, "*Babii Iar* A. Anatoliia (Kuznetsova)—novaia (sinkreticheskaia) forma memuarnoi literatury," *Russian Language Journal*, 31, no. 106 (East Lansing, 1976), pp. 143–152; and [Andreas Guski], "Babij Jar," in Wolfgang Kasack, ed., *Hauptwerke der russischen Literatur: Einzeldarstellungen und Interpretationen* (Munich: Kindler Verlag, 1997), pp. 560–561.

34. He also wrote: ". . . I take full responsibility, as a living witness, for the absolute TRUTH of everything I relate." Anatoli, *Babi Yar*, pp. 14 and 295.

35. Among the errors are Kuznetsov's assertion that the Nazis murdered 70,000 Jews at Babi Yar in September 1941; that the NKVD blew up the Dormition Cathedral of the Monastery of the Caves; and that the Ukrainian soccer team Start played its last game on August 9, 1942. Anatoli, *Babi Yar*, pp. 119, 195–202, and 294. Considerations of space prevent a discussion of these issues here. (On the soccer team, see Berkhoff, "Hitler's Clean Slate," pp. 298–299.) Kuznetsov is also inaccurate in a less substantial, but easily verifiable way: He says in the full version that he italicized all the passages that the Soviet version had removed or modified, but he actually does not italicize all of them. Recent editions of his book no longer contain any of these italics.

36. Therefore, the acknowledgment on the copyright page of a debt to *Babi Yar* seems insufficient. One of several reviews to discuss this matter is Alvin H.

Rosenfeld, "Perspectives on the Holocaust in Current Literature," *Simon Wiesen-thal Center Annual*, 1 (1984), pp. 205–216.

37. "Iz protokola doprosa v Prokurature v kachestve svidetelia spassheisia ot rasstrela v Bab'em Iaru D. Pronichevoi," in Evstaf'eva and Nakhmanovich, *Babii Iar*, pp. 283–291, with reference to Derzhavnyi arkhiv Sluzhby Bezpeky Ukraïny, fond 7, opys 8, sprava 1, arkushi 80–84. The final page (presumably arkush 85) was not published, as is evident from comparison with PR7ger. At issue on that page is the identity of the "military unit" that carried out the massacre; other witnesses known to Pronicheva; her lack of knowledge of the names of the German suspects Kallsen and Matner; the name of the interrogator (A. Potapenko); and Pronicheva's confirmation that the deposition is accurate. Also unpublished were data from arkush 80, such as the precise location and duration of the interrogation (the Public Prosecutor's Office, from 10:00 AM to 3:00 PM). The two mentions of "[. . .]" on page 289 are erroneous.

38. The translation, by Stanislaus Heimerl, is dated July 17, 1967. The record is filed in Germany at the Federal Archives-Ludwigsburg as 204 AR-Z 269/60 and at the Institute for Contemporary History in Munich as Gd 01.54/59. Dieter Pohl sent me a photocopy of the document from the latter location.

39. Peter Longerich with Dieter Pohl, ed., *Die Ermordung der europäischen Juden: Eine umfassende Dokumentation des Holocaust 1941–1945* (Munich and Zurich: Piper, 1989), pp. 124–127; reprint in Wiehn, *Die Schoáh*, pp. 175–177. An exhibition about the Holocaust at the German Historical Museum in Berlin (January–April 2002) included an audio recording of a reading of PR7ger, albeit in a stylistically improved version. In yet another indication of the widespread lack of clarity about Pronicheva, the caption stated that she made this testimony during "a war crimes trial in 1945."

40. Kuznetsov introduces his Pronicheva chapter (PR6) with the similar statement that Pronicheva was "the only eyewitness to come out of" the Babi Yar massacre. But he contradicts this at the end, where he summarizes a letter in which Pronicheva informs Kuznetsov that after the Soviet book edition of *Babi Yar* came out, a Kievan who did not give his name visited her apartment. The man told her that as a small boy he had also scrambled out of the mass grave. A Ukrainian family adopted him, and he had never told anyone about his escape. "To judge from the details he gave," Kuznetsov concludes, "his story was true." See Anatoli, *Babi Yar*, pp. 98 and 120.

41. "Pochta redaktora," *Literaturnaia gazeta*, no. 8, February 22, 1967, p. 13, partially translated in William Korey, *The Soviet Cage: Anti-Semitism in Russia* (New York: The Viking Press, 1973), p. 119. When exactly Pronicheva wrote the letter is unclear. The original may be in the *Literaturnaia gazeta* collection of the Russian State Archives of Literature and Art in Moscow.

42. Pjotr Krepki, "Auferstanden aus dem Grabe. Jüdische Künstlerin über-listete die Nazimörder," *Freie Welt*, no. 4 (1968). Dmytro V. Malakov gave me this article.

43. Korey, *The Soviet Cage*, p. 98; *Justiz und NS-Verbrechen: Sammlung deutscher Strafurteile wegen Nationalsozialistischer Tötungsverbrechen 1945–1999*, Bd. 31 (Amsterdam, Amsterdam University Press, 2004), pp. 7–275.

44. Personal communication to me from Dmytro V. Malakov (who personally heard from Pronicheva about her journey), January 22, 2002.

45. I am using a photocopy from the Institute of Contemporary History in Munich, Gd 01.54/78, folios 1758–1776 (original trial record pagination), supplied to me by Dieter Pohl. The original is at the Federal Archives-Ludwigsburg. The interpreter was Wera Kapkajew (born Mirman) of Frankfurt.

46. Shimon Kipnis, "Zhivoi privet iz ada," in Iosif [Joseph] Vinokurov, Shi-mon Kipnis, and Nora Levin, eds., *Kniga pamiati posviashchena zhertvam Bab'ego Iara* (Philadelphia: Publishing House of Peace, 1983), pp. 21–33. A reprint of the

first half is in Itskhak Arad, ed., *Unichtozhenie evreev SSSR v gody nemetskoi ok-kupatsii (1941–1944): Sbornik dokumentov i materialov* (Jerusalem: Yad Vashem, 1991), pp. 107–112.

47. Shimon Kipnis, "Greetings from hell . . . ," in Vinokurov et al., *Kniga pamiati*, English section, pp. 108–118; partly reprinted in "Greetings From Hell . . . by Dina Mironovna Pronicheva," in *Babi Yar 1941–1991: A Resource Book and Guide*, ed. and comp. The Staff of the Simon Wiesenthal Center (Los Angeles: Simon Wiesenthal Center, 1991), pp. 45–47. The translation is rather inexpert, stating for example that on September 29 the Jews "marched . . . three days in a row." A far better translation, by Zvi Gitelman, Leonid Livak, or John Squier, but of the first six Russian pages only, is "A Live Message of Greetings from Hell," in Zvi Gitelman, ed., *Bitter Legacy: Confronting the Holocaust in the USSR* (Bloomington and Indianapolis: Indiana University Press, 1997), pp. 275–278. The Yiddish translation is Shimen Kipnis, "A libendiker grus fun gehenem," in Vinokurov et al., *Kniga pamiati*, Yiddish section, pp. 19–28.

48. Iurii Petrashevych, "Tini Babynoho iaru: Novi fakty i svidchennia ochevydtsiv," *Kyïv*, no. 1 (January 1994), pp. 95–102, here 101–102. Batasheva's own account as reproduced here also mentions the presence of *politsaï* at the massacre, whereas the record of an official Soviet interview with her in 1980 apparently speaks only of "Hitlerites" and "fascists"; see Martinenko, "Tragediia Bab'ego Iara," pp. 365–366.

49. Folio 1762 of PR10 mentions "Panzerabwehrgeschütze," but the interpreter said later (see folio 1770) that her translation should have been "Panzerreiter," or cuirassiers. See also Gordon Williamson, *German Military Police Units 1939–1945*, Men-at-Arms Series, Nr. 211 (London: Osprey, 1989), pp. 9–10.

50. Here and below, for the sake of clarity I transliterate any words in PR6 that are in the Russian alphabet as if from Russian. With *zhidivka*, Kuznetsov evidently had in mind the Ukrainian word *zhydivka*, which usually translates as Jew, and not the derogatory Russian word *zhidovka*, or Yid.

51. The field uniforms of most Einsatzgruppe members were also gray. For the untrained eye, the differences in emblems and insignia would have been lost, particularly under such conditions.

52. John A. Armstrong, *Ukrainian Nationalism*, 3rd ed. (Englewood: Ukrainian Academic Press, 1990), pp. 12–16. The quotation is from *Surma: Chasopys Orhanizatsiï Ukraïns'kykh Natsionalistiv*, July 19, 1941, p. 2, a rare OUN-M publication held at the library of the University of Illinois at Urbana-Champaign. Ray Brandon provided me with a copy of this issue.

53. Levitas, "Babyn Iar (1941–1943)," p. 102, quotes an archival document stating that on September 21, 1941, Bohdan Konyk (the pseudonym of Bohdan Onufryk) arrived in Kiev from the Zhytomyr region with 18 policemen, who became the nucleus of the city's Ukrainian police. Two days later, Levitas's quotation of the document adds, "a Cossack company commanded by Ivan Kediumych [*sic*] arrived in Kiev to perform duties for the German military command." This was likely a reference to Ivan Kediulych, a Ukrainian from Transcarpathia with years of military training and experience in Czechoslovak and German service. Iaroslav Haivas, "V roky nadii i beznadii (Zustrichi i rozmovy z O. Ol'zhychem v rokakh 1939–1944)," *Kalendar-al'manakh Novoho Shliakhu 1977* (Toronto [n.d.]), p. 115, calls Kediulych the covert "plenipotentiary" of the OUN-M in Kiev's non-German police force in the period 1941–1943.

54. Andrii Duda and Volodymyr Staryk, *Bukovyns'kyi Kurin': V boiakh za ukraïns'ku derzhavnist', 1918, 1941, 1944* (Chernivtsi: Nakladom Tovarystva "Ukraïns'kyi Narodnyi Dim v Chernivtsiakh," 1995), pp. 84 and 86.; Petro Voinovs'kyi, *Moie naivyshche shchastia: Spomyny* (Kiev: Vydavnytstvo imeni Oleny Telihy, 1999), p. 254 (the last quotation).

55. One publication from 1955 says the battalion arrived in the city "shortly

after its liberation from the Bolsheviks," after which "the largest part joined the Ukrainian police." Vasyl' Shypyns'kyi, "Ukraïns'kyi natsionalizm na Bukovyni," in *Orhanizatsiia Ukraïns'kykh Natsionalistiv, 1929–1954: Zbirnyk stattei u 25-littia OUN* ([Paris]: Vydannia Pershoï Ukraïns'koï Drukarni u Frantsiï, 1955), p. 220. A man who volunteered in Lviv for police work recalled in 1957 that, under Voinovsky's command, he arrived in Kiev on November 9, 1941, as part of a group of 280 volunteers (all of whom like him were "thirsting for revenge.") At the police station in Korolenko Street, he met another group, of "about 350 volunteers; the sons of green Bukovina and Transcarpathia who also had volunteered for active struggle against the Muscovite occupiers. That group had advanced right behind the front line." Iu. Pasichnyk, "Ukraïns'ki 115 i 118 kureni v borot'bi z soviets'koiu dyversiieiu (Uryvky iz shchodennyka z 1941–1944 rr.)," *Visti Bratstva kol. Voiakiv 1 UD UNA*, VIII, 7–10 (78–81 [*sic*; = 81–84]) (November 1957), p. 9. Late in 1941, the members of the Bukovinian Battalion in Kiev were reorganized into Schutzmannschaft (auxiliary police) Battalion 115. During its service in Belarus the battalion was turned over to the Waffen-SS for the creation of the 30th Waffen-Grenadier Division of the SS and was transferred to Alsace. There the battalion's members in late 1944 deserted en masse to the French Forces of the Interior.

56. In translating the sentence in question, David Floyd mistakenly adds "by the Germans," evidently because he assumed that Kuznetsov was describing Germans, not Ukrainians. See Anatoli, *Babi Yar*, p. 106.

57. Turkalo, *Tortury*, pp. 180–181 and 197.

58. In oral communication, Turkalo also said Pronicheva told him that "she only saw individuals in grey-green overcoats, i.e., Germans." Bilinsky, "Methodological Problems and Philosophical Issues," p. 380.

59. PR6 uniquely mentions something else that was perhaps a rescue attempt: As Pronicheva was walking in the crowd toward the designated point of assembly, some German soldiers in Lviv Street (present-day Artem Street) called out to her, *Komm waschen!*—"Come do some cleaning here!"

60. Psychologists argue against any simple relationship between degree of emotion experienced during violent events and witnesses' memory of details about these events. See Willem A. Wagenaar and Jop Groeneweg, "The Memory of Concentration Camp Survivors," *Applied Cognitive Psychology*, 4, no. 2 (March-April 1990), pp. 77–87, and Sven-Ake Christianson and Birgitta Hübinette, "Hands Up! A Study of Witnesses' Emotional Reactions and Memories Associated with Bank Robberies," *Applied Cognitive Psychology*, 7, no. 5 (October 1993), pp. 365–379.

61. See Christopher R. Browning, "Survivor Testimonies from Starachowice: Writing the History of a Factory Slave Labor Camp," in his *Collected Memories: Holocaust History and Postwar Testimony* (Madison, Wisconsin: University of Wisconsin Press, 2003), pp. 37–44.

62. *Verbrechen der Wehrmacht*, pp. 160 and 162.

63. See Frederick Helm and Halina Milgrom, "Can Scalp Hair Suddenly Turn White? A Case of Canities Subita," *Archives of Dermatology*, 102 (July 1970), pp. 102–103. PR11 again has it differently: Looking into a mirror shortly after her escape, Pronicheva sees that her *own* hair has turned white.

X

White Spaces and Black Holes: Eastern Galicia's Past and Present

OMER BARTOV

The Borderland

Galician history began in Kievan Rus and, after a 750-year odyssey, this region is today once again part of a state ruled from Kiev. In between the destruction of Kievan Rus in 1241 and the constitution of independent Ukraine in 1991, Galicia changed hands numerous times. Becoming a part of the Polish crown lands in 1349, Galicia marked the borderland between the old Polish-Lithuanian Commonwealth and marauders and rival empires from the east and the south: the Tatars, the Cossacks, the Turkish Ottomans, and the Russians. In 1772, this territory was annexed by the Austrian Habsburg Empire and made officially into the province of Galicia. For the next 146 years, Galicia was an outpost of the Habsburg Empire on the border to the Russian Empire. Between the world wars, Galicia became part of reconstituted Poland and lay between the Polish heartland and Soviet Russia.

The land itself stretches from the outer edge of core Poland north of the regional capital Lviv (Lwów, Lemberg, Lvov) southward, to where the Prut flows into the former Austrian, later Romanian province of Bukovina on its way to Chernivtsi (Czernowitz, Cernăuți). It extends from the foothills of the Carpathian Mountains in the west, the far side of which once belonged to Hungary, to the Zbruch River in the east, by which point it has faded into Podolia, an erstwhile domain of the Russian tsar. As a consequence of its geographic location, Galicia was imbued with Polish and German-Austrian culture and exposed to influences from the wide plains, forests, and steppes of western Russia and Asia, vast territories in which Europe was but a rumor.

The peoples of Galicia also once constituted a rich mosaic of interdenominational and interethnic coexistence on the one hand and a volatile mixture of animosity, strife, and bloodshed on the other. Galicia was the birthplace or breeding ground of numerous intellectual, spiritual, and political movements. While Shabbateanism, Frankism, Hasidism, and Haskalah (enlightenment) flourished there among the Jews, the region's Roman Catholic Poles later produced a Romantic literature that glorified the rule of Poland's great noble houses over these lands. For Greek Catholic Ukrainians, Galicia was the homeland of Ukrainian literary and political nationalism, its towns and villages providing some of Ukraine's most distinguished political and cultural figures.[1] It was where the peasants were imagined as the carriers of an authentic Ruthenian or Ukrainian culture and tradition, and where the splendor and heroism of the Polish gentry, or *szlachta,* appeared to echo in the numerous castles built to ward off foreign enemies and rebellious serfs.[2] Interspersed among the larger ethnic groups were Germans, Lutheran and Catholic alike, farmers and bureaucrats, as well as groups such as the Hutsuls of the Carpathians.

For Jews, Galicia conjured up mixed images. To be called a *galitsyaner* was for long not much of a compliment for its Jewish inhabitants: It denoted folksy backwardness and at times also a petty mercantile mentality and moral shiftiness. The galitsyaner was someone who either spoke of leaving or had already left for better places (Vienna, Prague, Berlin, America—the *goldene medine*—where money grew on trees and a Jew could make a living). Increasingly, the galitsyaner came under the influence of Zionism and either dreamed of going to Eretz Israel or actually ended up in the Promised Land, only to discover that it had very little to offer save for more hopes and dreams.[3] Nonetheless, Galicia was also the land of great rabbis and religious colleges (*yeshivot*), of miraculous tales and vibrant community life, as depicted in the writing of Yosef Shmuel Agnon (1888–1970), who recreated his hometown of Buchach (Buczacz) as a microcosm of East European shtetl life, and given plastic expression in the paintings of Maurycy Gottlieb (1856–1879) of nearby Drohobych (Drohobycz).[4]

This Galicia, already strained by competing Polish and Ukrainian nationalisms between the world wars, was ultimately destroyed by successive occupations between 1939 and 1944. The Soviet occupation destroyed the region's social fabric and exploited antagonisms that had accumulated under Polish rule. By early 1940 the Soviets began deporting hundreds of thousands—Poles, Jews, and Ukrainians alike—to Siberia. Nazi Germany in the meantime had been allowed to resettle ethnic Germans from Soviet-occupied eastern Poland to Nazi-occupied western Poland. The German invasion of the Soviet Union in June 1941 signaled the start of the near total annihilation of the Jewish population in Galicia. And when the Germans were expelled, the Poles who remained in 1944 were in turn deported across the San and Bug rivers, leaving behind a society almost exclusively Ukrainian. Galicia is a land that has many claims to fame and infamy.

This corner of western Ukraine may be an ethnically homogenous land today, but it is a haunted land. Its ghosts freely roam the hills and valleys, clutter the unpaved streets, and congregate in cemeteries grazed by goats and in synagogues transformed into garbage dumps. And while the name Galicia no longer appears on modern maps and the names of its towns and cities, as well as its rulers and inhabitants, have changed many a time, it remains the site or object of prejudice, legend, and myth, of nostalgia and regret, of loss and oblivion.[5]

Contemporary Germans, for example, often speak in terms of a rustic idyll about the former ethnic German population of Galicia, expressing a nostalgia documented in numerous recent books that reflect disenchantment with the crowded modernity of the West, a nostalgia all the easier to elaborate as the passage of time transforms memory into fantasy.[6] But German scholars have also recently reconstructed the destruction of the Jewish population in these regions.[7] For Austrians, a vaguely romantic view of their long-vanished great empire coincides with vicarious memories of what used to be its most backward province. A young Austrian historian has recently shown that this familiarity with the land and its people also facilitated the involvement of Viennese policemen in mass murder during the Second World War.[8]

For contemporary Ukrainians, the western edge of their newly independent country—but for the briefest periods never a part of Russian-controlled Ukraine before 1939—is both an example of greater Western sophistication and a somewhat foreign and suspect territory. Its Ruthenian farmers till the black earth as their forefathers did, but as the changing names of its cities and towns indicate, urban culture blends an assertive Ukrainian nationalism, traces of a rich Polish and Jewish past, and the external trademarks of a spreading globalized modernity, even as many locals still refer to themselves as Galicians.[9] In all these respects, Galicia is a true borderland, the meeting-place of numerous cultures, religions, and ethnicities, which is at the same time located at their periphery, a site where identity is all the more vehemently asserted precisely because of its often tenuous and fluid nature.[10]

Today's inhabitants of eastern Galicia have little memory of its complex, rich, and tortuous past. This land is in the throes of creating a single national narrative of events, people, institutions, culture, and politics, an undertaking of massive simplification that not only distorts its past but threatens to impoverish its future. In a certain sense, this region exemplifies a larger trend that can be identified in much of the rest of Europe, despite claims to the contrary and notwithstanding differences in style and approach.

The pre-1939 world of Galicia is no more. But its past, and the denial of that past, is more visible than in many other parts of Europe, not least thanks to neglect, indifference, and forgetfulness. Western Europe has rapidly modernized, and has thereby covered the traces of destruction with concrete and rhetoric.[11] Eastern Galicia was left on the margin, a borderland territory between the West and the East, with little development and investment under Soviet rule, and a seething nationalism that kept up resistance to the "liberators" of this land well into the 1950s.[12]

Since the early 1990s, the Soviet distortion of the past has been replaced by, or combined with, the previously suppressed nationalist narrative. But in many parts of the land these cosmetic changes have had little effect on the general condition of ignorance and abandonment, dilapidation and oblivion. Here the Galician past is still bare, indifference still glaring, prejudices and denials and fierce loyalties still almost entirely bereft of the comforting West European glaze of sophistication. The inhabitants walk among the ruins and the ghosts, awakened to their presence only when asked by a stranger and forgetting them just as soon as he leaves.

Galicia is a region suspended in time, just for a little while longer, before it too will be swept with the tide of modernization and globalization, commemoration, and apology. Sooner or later, the people of western Ukraine's Galicia too will become aware of what they had lost and forgotten, but by then, they will have destroyed the last material traces of the past in their rush to catch up with the present and will have to recreate another past, one capable of more conveniently accommodating the spirit of tolerance and nostalgia that befits the modern temperament forged in the incinerators of difference and memory.

Travels in the Borderland

Lviv / Lwów / Lemberg

As western Ukraine's Galician territories begin to stir from decades of war, oppression, and economic decline, let us take a brief journey through this land of memory and oblivion, coexistence and erasure, dashed hopes and grand illusions.[13] We begin in Lviv, now located some 40 miles southeast of the Polish border (see map on p. 137). Once a mostly Polish and Jewish city and a thriving cultural, economic, and political center, it is now struggling to emerge from the decades of Soviet neglect and suppressed memories of mass murder, expulsion, and demographic upheaval. Boasting a population of 830,000 people, the city is the capital of Lviv Oblast and Galicia's main urban center.[14]

Two sites may remind us of this city's past diversity. The Armenian Cathedral, dating back as far as 1363, is a well preserved and moving edifice, testifying to the former presence of an important Armenian community, which eventually mostly assimilated into the local population.[15] The Armenians, along with the Karaites and Greeks, were the Jews' main competitors in commerce and business. Being members of a small Christian denomination and numbering far fewer people, the

Armenian community went into decline just as the Jewish population increased.[16] The Armenian Cathedral in Lviv is interesting not least because it served as the burial ground for some distinguished Polish intellectual and political figures of the nineteenth and twentieth centuries. This testifies both to the assimilation of the Armenians into the hegemonic culture of Lviv and to the strong Polish presence in a city, which defined itself as an inherent part of Poland despite the growing pressures from Ruthenian-Ukrainian nationalism and the predominance of Ukrainians in the countryside.[17]

The second site is the Golden Rose synagogue, of which almost nothing remains. A modest plaque carries the following inscription in Ukrainian, English, and Yiddish:

> Remnants of the old temple called "Di Goldene Royz." Built in 1580–1595 by the Nachmanowitch family in the memory of Rabbi Nachman's wife. The building designed by the Italian architect Pablo Romano, was destroyed by nazis [sic] and burnt in summer 1942.[18]

The site of the temple seems to be a popular nighttime hangout, as indicated by the empty beer bottles and other garbage strewn in the shallow pit next to the only remaining wall. The synagogue is located in the former Jewish quarter, next to the old city wall. One looks in vain for any explicit mention of the destruction of the Jewish community, let alone of the Ukrainian contribution to that destruction. Nowhere is it mentioned that somewhere between 7,000 and 10,000 Jews were murdered in the pogroms that followed on the heels of the German army's entry into the city on June 30, 1941.[19]

Walking the streets of this beautiful, old part of town, one still encounters the marks of mezuzahs on some of the doorways. Not far from the center is the oldest settlement of Jews, where the Great Synagogue of the Suburb (built in 1632) once stood. This formerly busy Jewish commercial district still displays Polish and Yiddish store signs under the peeling façades of handsome nineteenth-century buildings. Presumably, as the city modernizes, these last remaining traces of a vanished world will be erased. For now, very few people seem to notice them.

Until the Second World War, the extraordinary edifice of the Reform Synagogue (completed in 1845) stood nearby on Old Market. It is now commemorated with a rough stone, about three feet high, whose small plaque notes in Ukrainian and English the destruction of the temple by the Germans.[20] Since the city provides no indication about the site's location, it is difficult to find.[21] A couple of blocks away in St. Theodore Square still stands the former Hasidic Jakob (Yankl) Glazner Shul, built in 1842–1844, which has housed the Jewish Culture Society since 1991. Not far from there is a plaque in Yiddish and Ukrainian noting that the Yiddish writer Sholem Aleichem had lived in that house in 1906.[22]

From there, we proceed to the vast Jewish hospital built at the turn of the previous century in striking oriental style. While its tiled dome is decorated with Stars of David, no written indication is given of its history. Behind the hospital was the old Jewish cemetery, known to have had tombstones dating back to the mid-fourteenth century. Destroyed by the Nazis and paved over by the Soviets, it now serves as the town's main open market, where ragtag merchandise places Ukraine on the periphery of Europe and in another historical era.[23]

A couple of blocks farther down, we find the former Jewish gymnasium, a humanities-oriented secondary school, which now serves as Secondary School No. 52, without a single nod to its previous identity. A few minutes more on foot and we arrive at Lviv's only functioning Jewish house of prayer. Built in 1924 to echo the town's renaissance synagogues and overlooked by the oversized neo-gothic Church of St. Elizabeth, the Tsori Gilod Synagogue is a small, dilapidated, walled-in structure, a pale reminder of a once large and vibrant Jewish community, whose 160,000 members constituted approximately 45 percent of the city's total population on the eve of the Holocaust.[24]

The poverty of memory and the selective marginalization of the past are illustrated by what one of the city's brochures calls its "biggest and interesting collection" of Judaica at the Lviv Museum of the History of Religions in the baroque Dominican Roman Catholic church and monastery near the Jewish quarter. Visitors are assured that "this is the only museum in Ukraine, where you can see a permanent exposition of Judaism exhibiting approximately 100 original items."[25] In fact, the collection consists of a mélange of objects that fill a couple of glass cases and have all the dignity of loot collected at the local flea market. Indeed, the museum's Jewish "corner" looks more like a ghetto. The brochure informs us, however, that the "total number of [Jewish] articles rises to a thousand items in reserves of the museum," mostly "ritual articles," of which "the most valuable" is a "unique . . . collection of torahs of the fifteenth to nineteenth centuries in Ukraine (over 420 scrolls)." There is no access to these scrolls, and one must wonder about their condition in the basement of the church, and under what circumstances they might be allowed to see the light of day or be transferred to a safer resting place.

Since the fall of Communism, the destruction of the Jews of Lviv has received more attention. But it remains couched in euphemisms and distortions. In 1992, a Monument to the Lviv Ghetto Victims (1941–1943) was installed across from the railway bridge that had separated the German-imposed ghetto from the rest of the city.[26] This massive, quasi-abstract sculpture of an old Jew raising his arms to heaven in horror and supplication was financed by the Jewish community of Lviv without public assistance.[27] In front of the monument, under a steel menorah, is an inscription in Ukrainian that reads: "Remember and keep in your heart." A single memorial stone, lying flat on the ground, provides an English-language approximation of the events commemorated: "Through this 'road of death' in 1941–1943 were passing 136,800 Jewish victims martyred by the German Nazi-Fascist occupiers in Lvov Geto [sic]."[28]

A second monument was erected in 1993 next to the site of the former Janowska Forced Labor Camp just outside Lviv by camp survivor Alexander Schwarz.[29] Some 200,000 people, mainly Jews, were tortured and killed there. After the war, the camp was used by the Soviet secret police for its own prisoners and was later employed for training police dogs and breeding pigs. Thanks to Schwarz's pressure, this practice has recently ceased, but his efforts to create a commemorative complex on the site of the former camp—which includes the killing grounds and the mass graves—have failed due to resistance from the local authorities. The site of the camp itself is still sealed off with a fence and cannot be entered. As a result, Schwarz's memorial was erected outside the locked gate. This massive ten-ton granite boulder carries the following inscription in Ukrainian, Yiddish, and English: "Let the memory of all the Nazi genocide victims in Janowska forced labor camp remain forever: 1941–1943."[30] While the number 200,000 and a Star of David are inscribed on the boulder, the word "Jew" is nowhere to be seen.

On November 19, 2003—the sixtieth anniversary of the camp's liquidation—the International Holocaust Center, a non-governmental organization created by and named after Alexander Schwarz, installed a large plaque next to the boulder, which can be seen more easily from the road. The Ukrainian and English text reads:

> Passer-By, Stop! Bow Your Head! There is a spot of the former Janovska concentration camp in front of you! Here the ground is suffering! Here the Nazis tormented, taunted executed innocent people and sent them to the gas chambers. Let the innocently undone victims be remembered forever! Eternal damnation on the executers [sic].

This formulation further obfuscates the identity of the victims, never specifically identifying them as Jews nor providing any other symbolic indication of their identity. Perhaps it carries on the Soviet practice of never specifically mentioning Jewish victims; perhaps it reflects the fear of Lviv's small Jewish community of stirring more antisemitism by insisting on a clear statement of Jewish victimhood. Either way, this text allows the local population to view the victims of the camp as "belonging" to them rather than to a category of people whose history has been largely erased from public and collective memory and whose presence in the region has been almost entirely eliminated.[31]

Similarly, the modest memorial located in the New Jewish Cemetery is visible only to those who enter this vast and crowded terrain of the dead, adjacent to the Ianivsky Cemetery, on the road leading to the former camp. Inscribed in Yiddish and Ukrainian, the memorial again avoids any mention of Jewish victims. The Yiddish inscription reads: "In eternal memory of the martyrs who fell at the hands of the cruel Hitler-murderers." The Ukrainian is even briefer: "In memory of those who perished in the years of Hitlerite occupation in 1942–1943."

While most of the locals have no idea about the Janowska camp and its memorial, nor of other Jewish sites in Lviv and the surrounding towns, the city has been asserting its Ukrainian character, primarily by representing itself as the main victim of totalitarianism, prejudice, and violence. In this memory, there is no room for other victims, let alone for the victims of Ukrainians, and least of all, for the victims of Ukrainian nationalists, who can only be depicted as heroes and martyrs. Many of Lviv's streets have been renamed to emphasize the city's present-day Ukrainian character, and a variety of publicly funded monuments have been erected to celebrate its heroic Ukrainian sons.[32] Indeed, even though the monument to the victims of Soviet repression (unveiled in 1997) attempts to remind people that all nationalities were victimized by the Soviets, it seeks reconciliation by way of obfuscation and suppression of memory.

Built in front of the old prison, the memorial includes the figure of a tortured, crucified man within the frame of a cross that is lined with barbed wire, and surrounded by hundreds of names of NKVD (Soviet secret police) victims. The text on the monument reads:

> Between September 1939 and June 1941, within the prisons of Western Ukraine, 48,867 persons were killed. 1,238,256 were deported to Siberia. Within the prisons of Lviv Oblast, during six days in 1941, 3,348 Ukrainian, Polish, and Jewish prisoners were shot.

Quite apart from the inflated figures, the text fails to mention that, upon the Germans' arrival in Lviv, thousands of Jews were charged with the murder of Ukrainian patriots in Soviet prisons and subsequently brutalized and murdered by largely Ukrainian crowds. Precisely because it carries the three national symbols—the Ukrainian trident, the Polish eagle, and the Star of David—the monument liberates Ukrainian memory from the burden of invoking the crimes perpetrated by those freedom fighters now celebrated as national heroes.[33]

Lviv is the shop window of western Ukraine. Traveling deeper into Galicia, one discovers even starker examples of Ukrainian self-glorification alongside neglect, suppression, and even destruction of all signs of the land's multiethnic past and its violent end in mass murder and ethnic cleansing—which was accomplished with a high degree of Ukrainian complicity.[34] Let us then embark on a journey throughout the former province of Galicia.

Drohobych / Drohobycz / Drohobitsh (Drohobets)

The town of Drohobych is situated some 40 miles southwest of Lviv. Along with the painter Maurycy Gottlieb, Drohobych was also the birthplace of the Polish-Jewish artist and writer Bruno Schulz (1892–1942). The Ukrainian national poet Ivan Franko (1856–1919) and a co-founder of the Organization of Ukrainian Nationalists (OUN), Andrii Melnyk (1890–1964), were born in nearby villages. In 1939, Drohobych numbered some 10,000 Poles, 10,000 Ukrainians, and 15,000 Jews. The German occupation began with a pogrom by local Ukrainians and Poles, during which about 400 Jews were murdered. In the three years that followed, the vast majority of the Jews were either deported to the Bełżec death camp or killed in the town and its vicinity. Most of the Poles were deported over the border to Poland after the war.[35]

Those visiting Drohobych now would be hard put to discover any trace of its bloody past or the days in which it was described as "one and a half city: half-Ukrainian, half-Polish, and half-Jewish."[36] Coming to the handsome park at the center of town, we glimpse a large statue at the point where all the paths meet. The bronze figure represents Stepan Bandera (1909–1959), leader of a breakaway faction of the OUN (OUN-B), whose followers were deeply implicated in the genocide of the Jews and the ethnic cleansing of the Poles in eastern Galicia.[37]

Across from the park still stands the very same house next to which Bruno Schulz was shot by SS Staff Sergeant Karl Günther during a "wild" *Aktion* on November 19, 1942, as revenge for the killing of "his" Jew, the dentist Löw, by Schulz's protector, SS First Sergeant Felix Landau, for whom Schulz painted his last works.[38] In June 2004, my Ukrainian assistants and I were trying to locate the site of the shooting with a prewar photo from a book on Drohobych when an old man approached us.[39] "What are you looking for?" he asked. We showed him the photo. The man led us to the street corner, and then motioned to the park. "This is where the ghetto was," he remarked. "I still remember it. I was a teenager at the time." Bandera's statue could be seen gleaming between the trees, built, as it turns out, directly over the grounds of the ghetto, where the Germans had crammed the Jewish population of Drohobych before deporting it to the extermination camp of Bełżec or murdering it on the spot. But there is no indication anywhere that this was a site of suffering and despair by fellow citizens.

Drohobych recalled Schulz only decades after the war. A modest plaque on the house where he lived during the interwar period was apparently put up only after the discovery in 2001 of murals Schulz had painted in the room of Landau's son. "In this house," notes the plaque in Ukrainian, Polish, and Hebrew, "in the years 1910–1941, lived and worked the famous Jewish artist and great writer in the Polish language, Bruno Schulz." This brave attempt to encompass in a single sentence the multifaceted nature of life, identity, and letters in Galicia on the eve of the catastrophe remains largely hidden from public view: the Schulz house is not even marked on the city map. Nor can one find the "villa" in which Schulz painted the murals, whose removal from the wall and transportation to Israel by Yad Vashem was criticized by Ukrainians and Poles alike. Suddenly, everyone wanted to appropriate Schulz, who was shot like a stray dog on a nearby street and ignored for six decades.[40]

A young girl in Drohobych gazes up at a monument to Stepan Bandera. Bandera's faction of the Organization of Ukrainian Nationalists was responsible for the deaths of thousands of Jews during the pogroms in western Ukraine in 1941. Bandera's group, which by 1943 had become the driving force behind the Ukrainian Insurgent Army (UPA), also instigated a campaign of mass murder to expel local Poles from western Ukraine. Nonetheless, Bandera is today celebrated as a hero in western Ukraine. The Drohobych park, which bears Bandera's name, stands on the former site of the Drohobych ghetto. Courtesy of the author.

Not far from the Schulz house is the gymnasium, where Bruno studied between 1902 and 1910 and where he taught between 1924 and 1939. Farther on is an impressive structure, whose original Polish inscription, "Jewish Orphanage," has been erased from its façade, and the Star-of-David design of its windows has been altered.[41] We then reach Stryiska Street, which features as such in Schulz's writing.[42] Formerly known as Sholem Aleichem Street, it is currently named after Ivan Mazepa (1640–1709), the last ruler of the quasi-independent Cossack entity that briefly emerged in the seventeenth century.

A little alley off the main street has now been named after Bruno Schulz, but the street sign is obscured by a large colorful ad for a café-restaurant. From this spot, one could still see in June 2004 a handsome, though derelict, building that took up half a block farther down the street. A 1909 photograph of the building, which features a few ghostly figures in dark coats and hats, identifies it as the City Synagogue of Drohobych; a cheerier postcard dated 1910 features horse carriages and gentlemen with walking canes passing by the synagogue.[43] The Soviets transformed the building into the sports club Spartak. Since 2004, the structure has been beautifully renovated, and while it remains a sports club, the remnants of the Stars of David that were still visible two years earlier have now been removed.[44] Conversely, the vast Choral Synagogue still looms over the city as a dilapidated, empty shell on the verge of collapse, locked and sealed. Patches of paint still cling to the walls, while a few Hebrew words can still be seen over the main gate and on the interior arcs.[45]

The site of a great oil boom in the latter nineteenth century, and also known for its abundant salt mines, Drohobych proudly displays its beautiful sixteenth-century St. George wooden church, presents some wonderful old villas surrounded by lovingly tended gardens, and can generally be described as a tidy and elegant town gradually recovering from years of oblivion under Soviet rule in a semi-sealed security borderland region.[46] But it has almost completely erased its entire Jewish past.

Ivano-Frankivsk / Stanyslaviv / Stanisławów / Stanislev

Heading southeast of Drohobych, about 85 miles south of Lviv, we come to Stanyslaviv, renamed Ivano-Frankivsk for the poet Ivan Franko in 1962. Now the capital of Ivano-Frankivsk Oblast, the city boasts a population of over 204,000, making it the third largest city in the region. Founded in the mid-seventeenth century, by the end of the nineteenth century it included a Jewish population constituting about half of the total 30,000 inhabitants. This ratio declined in the next few decades, so that by 1931 Jews comprised just over a third of the total population of 72,000.[47]

As happened throughout the areas occupied by the Soviets in 1939, the Jewish community of Ivano-Frankivsk and its institutions were torn apart, political activists and industrialists were tried and deported, and most businesses were nationalized. In 1940, numerous Jewish refugees from German-occupied Poland were deported to Siberia, Kazakhstan, and other distant territories in the Soviet Union. When the Germans took over the city in late July 1941, the Jewish population numbered about 40,000, including refugees from central Poland, the Carpathians, and from nearby villages terrorized by local Ukrainians. An initial execution of several hundred members of the Jewish "intelligentsia" (professionals considered by the Germans to be potential leaders) was followed in October by the mass murder of about 10,000 Jews in a single day at the New Cemetery. Mass killing resumed in March 1942 until the city was declared "cleansed of Jews," or *judenrein*, in late February

1943. The few remaining labor camps were liquidated a few months later. When the city was liberated in July 1944, only about a hundred Jews were still alive; another 1,500 had survived in the Soviet Union and elsewhere.

Visitors to Ivano-Frankivsk will find it hard to believe that it had witnessed such massacres. The town boasts beautifully preserved churches and a tastefully renovated town center. The only surviving edifice from the once large and prosperous Jewish community is the Great Synagogue, although it has lost its four onion-domed steeples. The synagogue was handed back to the Jewish community in 1991 and is said to have 300 members.[48] It now shares the premises with a store and must therefore be entered through an unmarked backyard and a dark staircase, which leads to the back door of the still impressive but bare main space of the synagogue. When I visited the town in March 2003, only four middle-aged and elderly men were present at the service.

Recently, a memorial statue has been installed in front of the synagogue. Adorned with fresh wreaths in the blue and yellow of the Ukrainian flag and the black and red of the Ukrainian Insurgent Army, founded by others in late 1941 but taken over by Bandera's OUN in 1942, this quasi-abstract bronze figure of a man with hands tied behind his back carries a plaque commemorating 27 OUN members executed by the Germans at this site in November 1943.[49] The implications of remembering "their own" victims at the site of the Great Synagogue without mentioning—there or anywhere else in the town center—the mass murder of Ivano-Frankivsk's Jewish population may have been entirely missed by the city fathers. It can also be interpreted as another attempt to assert the predominance of Ukrainian memory and to ignore the historical reality of the town's Jewish population.[50]

The site of the notorious "bloody Sunday" massacre of October 1941 is not easy to find. In the local city map, it is confusingly marked with a cross.[51] The area is overgrown and neglected; many of the tombstones have been removed. A sign at the entrance, written only in Hebrew and English, announces that the "cemetery was restored with the help of Mr. Emanuel Schaefer from Israel" in memory of his parents and sisters who died in the Holocaust. The single official monument, clearly dating back to the Soviet era and inscribed only in Ukrainian, reads: "At this site in 1941–1944, the German-fascists executed over 100,000 Soviet citizens and prisoners of other lands." There is only one central post-Soviet monument to the Jewish community, apparently installed by private initiative. This modest pink stone carries a Star of David and inscriptions in Hebrew, English, and Ukrainian. But while the Hebrew and English texts read: "In memory of 120,000 Jews victims of the Holocaust 1941–1944," the Ukrainian text dispenses with any mention of Jews and reads instead: "In memory of 120,000 devoured in the Holocaust, 1941–1944." No other information is provided on what actually happened at this site or elsewhere in the city, let alone about the participation of locals in the massacre.

Situated at the foot of the Carpathians, the town of Kosiv is about 70 miles southeast of Ivano-Frankivsk, near the border to Bukovina. Walking down the main street, we soon come upon an elegant two-story nineteenth-century house facing the main town square. The plaques on either sides of the main door describe it as the National Art Museum, dedicated to "Hutsul Customs" and to "the Struggle for Liberation in Hutsul Lands."

The exhibit indoors has little to do with the Hutsul ethnic group that inhabits the region. Rather, what attracts the local teenagers and young couples, some with children and babies, to this cramped space is a nationalist display. The guide, an elderly, wiry, tough-looking man is holding forth. The room is dedicated to the freedom fighters of the region, the troops of the Ukrainian Insurgent Army (UPA). The walls are covered with the photographs of these young, handsome fighters, who kept up the hopeless struggle against the Soviet reoccupation of their lands in 1944. The youthful visitors seem inspired, and the old man, evidently a UPA veteran, lectures them about the sacrifice of these martyrs.

But the men in the photos are dressed in German army uniforms, armed with German weapons, and holding the leashes of fierce German dogs. For the moment, they seem quite happy in fulfilling their tasks, which, as we know, included going out on "Jew hunts" and assisting the Germans in local mass shootings. In one of the photos, the Lvy (lions) Company is posing by the banks of the Strypa River, which loops around the town of Buchach. The date is July 1944, and the men, armed to the teeth with German equipment, look eager for action. It is just 60 years prior to my visit.

Being Jewish—my mother's family left Buchach in 1935—I would not have fared well at the hands of the Lvy Company or of any other UPA unit. The little Kosiv exhibit does not divulge the darker aspects of the UPA's struggle for independence. The UPA saw itself engaged not only in a struggle for liberation from Polish rule, German occupation, and Soviet oppression; they also fought what they saw as Jewish exploitation and collaboration with Ukraine's enemies and oppressors. In this latter capacity, the UPA closely collaborated with the German occupiers and was consequently equipped and supported by them as an important tool in the mass murder of the Jews, even as it gradually turned against the Germans when it became clear that they had no intention of facilitating Ukrainian independence. But it is unlikely that the young visitors who crowded the room had any inkling of the crimes committed by this organization or of the predominant prewar presence of Jews in Kosiv, where the 2,400 Jewish inhabitants recorded in 1931 comprised half the total population. Indeed, not a single marker in town reminds the present inhabitants of the past. The museum guide surely knew what he and his comrades had been up to during the war. So did the elderly woman at the museum ticket booth; she could have been a girl during the war. As we leave, she asks us whether we know to whom this house once belonged. No, we answer, somewhat puzzled. This was the rabbi's house, she states, sounding almost relieved to be able finally to divulge this information.

I did not quite believe her. It seemed all too cynical to house an exhibition for a force that was possibly complicit in the murder of Kosiv's Jews in the home of their rabbi. I looked up Kosiv's memorial book and found there a hand-drawn map indicating the location of the rabbi's house—precisely where the museum is now situated.[52] Facing the rabbi's house in the main town square stands a new three-story city hall; its bright red roof tiles and pink façade clash with the dark green of the steep wooded hill in the background. In front of the building is a white sculpture of Mother Mary holding the infant Jesus. The Great Synagogue, once famous for its splendor, stood to the left of city hall, but there is no trace of it. To the right side is another steep, overgrown hill. A closer look reveals that it is dotted with hundreds of tombstones, most half covered with brush or sunken into the soil. This is the only surviving evidence of the city's Jewish past, gradually being swallowed into the earth while serving as pasture for local goats.

Goats were a main source of trade in nineteenth-century Kosiv, along with a successful tanning industry and the extraction of salt from springs in the area. Jews are known to have resided in Kosiv since the early seventeenth century and lived there under religious rule until the 1930s.[53] In the municipal elections of 1928, the three main ethnic groups agreed that the Jews would comprise half of the city council. Toward the end of the interwar period, the Zionists emerged as the strongest political faction in the town. Secular education, especially for girls, was on the rise, and the expansion of cultural activities, sports associations, youth groups, and political organizations indicated the rapid transformation of this strict religious community, which in the past had produced several important Hasidic figures.

In the fall of 1939, Kosiv was flooded with Jewish refugees from German-occupied Poland. Only a few young Jews managed to escape when the Soviets retreated in 1941. The town was initially occupied by the Hungarians who enacted a series of anti-Jewish measures. In September, Kosiv passed over to German control; acts of violence by the occupiers and the local Ukrainian population sharply increased. In mid-October 1941, about 2,200 Jews—more than half the community—were shot into two vast pits on a hill across the river, with active participation of the Ukrainian militia and members of the local population. In spring 1942, some 700 Jews were transferred to the ghetto in nearby Kolomyia, while the remaining community was also enclosed in a ghetto. That September, some 150 Jews were shot in town and another 600 were sent to Bełżec. The last survivors were sent to Kolomyia in November 1942. Kosiv was then declared *judenrein*. While some Jews were sheltered by gentile neighbors, many more were hunted down and murdered by the local population. There is nothing in contemporary Kosiv to remind locals or visitors of these events.

Buchach / Buczacz / Butschatsch (Bitshutsh)

Our path now takes us northeast to Buchach. We drive along the Strypa valley on a winding dirt road. My Ukrainian assistant notes that my great-grandfather—an estate manager for the noble Potocki family in nearby Zoloty Potik (Potok Złoty)—must have traveled on the same road at the turn of the previous century. It is a quiet and peaceful afternoon. The Strypa keeps flowing slowly to the Dniester, just as it did all those decades ago.[54]

Established in the fourteenth century, Buchach had a Jewish population at least since 1500. It was heavily damaged in the wars of the seventeenth century, but subsequently came to be known for its enormous synagogue (1728), its elegant town hall (1751), its churches, the Basilian monastery, the ruins of its renaissance fortress, and its remarkable location, perched on hills rising above the winding Strypa. On the eve of the First World War, Buchach numbered over 14,000 inhabitants, of whom over half were Jews, the rest being either Poles or Ukrainians. The city was devastated in the fighting, and its population was halved. It gradually recovered in the interwar period: It is estimated that there were some 10,000 Jews in the town at the outbreak of the Second World War.

The Germans occupied Buchach in early July 1941 and soon thereafter murdered several hundred "intellectuals" on the nearby Fedir Hill. In the first large-scale *Aktion* in October 1942, about 1,600 Jews were transported to Bełżec and 200 were shot on the spot by the Germans and their Ukrainian satraps. In November, another 2,500 were taken to Bełżec, and 250 were hunted down and shot. The ghetto, established in late 1942, also contained Jews from nearby towns. In February 1942, about 2,000 Jews were shot and buried in mass graves on Fedir Hill. The killings continued throughout the spring, costing the lives of 3,000 people. In June 1943, the remnants of the community were shot at the Jewish cemetery along with the inmates of the local forced labor camp. Remarkably, when the city was liberated in March 1944, about 800 Jews came out of hiding, but following a German counter-attack most of the survivors were murdered. By the time the Red Army returned in July, only 100 Jews remained. Not long thereafter, the region's Polish population was also deported west.

Nowadays, Buchach is ethnically homogeneous. How the town remembers the past parallels its ethnic and religious identity. A few individuals still remember the war, but there is no collective memory of the presence or the elimination of non-Ukrainians. Nor is there any official indication of the city's Jewish past. The Great Synagogue, still seen standing in a German aerial photograph from April 1944, is no more, and its unmarked site is in now an open market. One local resident, Oresta Synenka, whose father worked as the foreman of a building bri-

gade in Buchach between 1945 and 1950, reported in March 2006 that the synagogue had been heavily damaged in the fighting. "There was no sense in repairing the synagogue," she said, "so they demolished it. It was done by 1950."[55]

The study house (*beit hamidrash*) adjacent the synagogue was torn down only in 2001, despite the protests of Israeli tourists who photographed the demolition. The Jewish cemetery, on Bashty Hill overlooking the town, still contains some tombstones, including that of the Israeli writer Yosef Shmuel Agnon's father. The oldest gravestones date back to 1587.[56] No signs have been put up in town directing visitors to this site where thousands of Jews were shot. A memorial erected there after the war has vanished without a trace.

Similarly, the handsome gymnasium, built in the late nineteenth century, bears no commemorative plaque to the numerous Jewish and Polish students who ended up being deported by the Soviets or murdered by the Germans and their Ukrainian accomplices. Conversely, a plaque located inside the school commemorates the Ukrainian students arrested by the Soviet authorities.[57] Another plaque installed by the school gate indicates that it is now named after Volodymyr Hnatiuk, an important figure in the revival of Ukrainian culture, born in Buchach County in 1871.[58] Although the recently deceased "Nazi hunter" Simon Wiesenthal was born in Buchach and attended the gymnasium in the 1920s, no mention is made of him there.[59]

Walking up forested Fedir Hill, one would not be able to find the mass graves of the town's Jews or the lone memorial standing there without the help of a local guide. The memorial—a simple tombstone-sized edifice commemorating the victims of the first *Aktion*—merely carries the Ukrainian inscription: "Here rest 450 people slain by German executioners on August 27, 1941."[60] The victims' identity is not identified, although a Star of David is carved on the stone. For most of the Communist period, the stone lay broken on the forest floor. It was put up again only in the 1990s by retired official Roman Antoshkiv and the Jewish principal of the agricultural school on Fedir Hill.[61]

Conversely, the memorial to the town's UPA fighters—a large cross planted on a round mound of earth on top of Fedir Hill—can be seen from afar. The plaque below the cross is inscribed with the rhymed phrase: "Glorious heroes who have fallen [in the struggle] for freedom; holy knights, hear this in your graves: We swear here, by your grave, to preserve the freedom of Ukraine." This post-independence memorial constitutes the nationalist response to the Soviet-era monument, situated on the same hill. Featuring an oversized Red Army soldier and inscribed with the words "Eternal Memory to the Fallen Heroes" and the dates 1941–1945, this memorial is dedicated to the singular event of the Great Patriotic War and excludes, indeed refutes, the legitimacy of the Ukrainian struggle against the Soviets. But since 1991, a cross has been added to it.

The post-Soviet era has also seen the creation of a UPA museum in Buchach. Located in the former offices of the NKVD, the museum is directed by the same Oresta Synenka quoted above, who dedicates herself to preserving the memory of Ukraine's local freedom fighters and victims of the NKVD, one of whom was her husband, Ivan Synenky.[62] Finally, another monument has been erected in the yard of St. Nicholas Greek Catholic Church, on a hill overlooking the town center. In March 2003, this simple wooden cross commemorating the sixtieth anniversary of the Soviet-induced Ukrainian famine of 1933 was decorated with a bouquet of fresh flowers.

Only the humble museum in the main town square contains any reference to the former Jewish presence in Buchach. The few glass cases displaying books by and photographs of Agnon, mostly donated by visiting Israeli tourists, make a ghostly appearance in this space, for no context is provided for the presence of this yarmulke-wearing, Hebrew language author in what is otherwise now a purely Ukrainian town. Still, the belated discovery of this former resident's celebrity stimulated the municipality to rename the street on which he had lived. A marble plaque put up at 5 Agnon Street in 2003 to commemorate the author's residence—now a derelict tenement—was stolen soon thereafter and has been replaced by a wood frame sign, which reads: "In this house lived in 1888–1907 the writer, Nobel Prize laureate (1966) Shmuel Yosef Agnon (Chachkes), July 17, 1888–February 17, 1970." Written only in Ukrainian, the plaque fails to mention the author's Jewish identity or the language in which he wrote. Nor did the rediscovery of Agnon by his hometown prevent the demolition of the study house that features prominently in his voluminous writings on Buchach.[63]

Every other opportunity to commemorate Jewish life and death in Buchach has been missed. No plaque has been put up at the partially renovated local police station and jail, from which thousands were led to execution on Fedir Hill, or at the Christian cemetery, where the undertaker Manko Szwierszczak bravely hid several Jews for two years in a crypt and later under his house,[64] or at the train station, from which about 5,000 Jews were sent to Bełżec, or by the railroad tunnel, blown up by the Soviets and rebuilt under the Nazis by Jewish slave workers, most of whom perished, or at the site where the Jewish hospital stood, once the most modern in the region and the site of a ghastly murder by the Germans.

Nonetheless, in Buchach memory is experiencing a renaissance. The town is currently constructing a monument for Stepan Bandera on a hill across the Strypa, funded by public subscription among the good citizens of the town, despite its depressed economy. In January 2006, Buchach celebrated the ninety-seventh anniversary of Bandera's birth with solemn patriotic speeches and a performance by the women's choir.[65] This nationalist event took place in the building that had formerly housed the Polish gymnastics and cultural association Sokól (Falcon) and had provided space for Jewish and Ukrainian groups before the war. No reference is made these days to such interethnic cooperation in the past, and this elegant structure, built in 1905, is blandly called the District House of Culture.

Conversely, attempts to commemorate the fate of the Jews in Buchach cause consternation. In May 2005, a concrete base was built for a monument at the Jewish cemetery. One local resident complained that the foreign Jews who asked Mayor Overko to build the base never paid for the job, adding that the money they offered to erect a fence around the mass graves on Fedir Hill was insufficient and that people would steal the fence for the metal.[66] No fence was built, and the monument, which has now been completed in an isolated and unmarked spot over a mass grave behind the cemetery, is a shoddy piece of work that was already showing signs of dilapidation in spring 2007. Meanwhile, tombstones are being carted away to serve more immediate needs, and hens roam the area, picking the garbage that people dump in the cemetery.[67] Some, more future-oriented work is being carried out in Buchach. But while the prewar hotel of the Jewish Anderman family has finally been renovated, it now serves as a bank. Another recently opened hotel is not recommended to foreigners. Thus, just as contemporary Buchach has fewer facilities to accommodate tourists than it did 70 years ago, so, too, its citizens still balk at revealing the secrets of its past to the few visitors who pass through.

In March 1935, my maternal grandfather received a certificate of immigration to Palestine. My 11-year-old mother, her parents, and her two brothers landed at the port of Haifa in December that year. From a comfortable bourgeois existence, they were reduced to the status of blue-collar workers. My mother was the first in her family to gain a college degree. But the rest of the extended family, apart from one uncle who also left in 1935, disappeared without a trace. No one knows how they were murdered or where their bodies lie. I am the only member of my family ever to have returned to Buchach. By then, my mother had passed away. She had fond memories of her childhood there and took them to her grave without seeing the erasure of the postwar years.

Ternopil / Tarnopol / Ternopol

We head northeast to Ternopil on the Seret River, capital of Ternopil Oblast, located some 80 miles east of Lviv. With a population of 221,000 in 2004, this is the second largest city in Galicia.[68] It is an elegant town that proudly displays some elements of its past glory, most restored since the fall of Communism. Other reminders of the past have vanished.

Indeed, Ternopil seems especially anxious about revealing certain aspects of its history. The director of the archives, for instance, seemed rather worried that I might be seeking information on stolen Jewish property that could lead to demands for compensation—a worry echoed by a local cab driver—or that I would discover documents about Ukrainian collusion with the Nazis. The latter, in fact, were cited in the catalogue, but it took another three years to extricate them from the archive.[69]

It was consistent with this anxiety of past secrets being revealed that in March 2003 one of the city's main newspapers, *Ne Zdamos* (We Will Not Surrender), published a front-page article by its editor, Iaroslav Demydas, entitled "Jewish Pogrom."[70] Arguing that the long history of oppression and murder of the Ukrainians by the Jews had culminated in the corrupt and criminal administration of Leonid Kuchma's administration in Kiev—detested in western Ukraine and widely believed to be under Jewish influence—the article went on to "uncover" what it claimed to be the hidden truths of Ukraine's past.[71]

It is instructive to cite some of the statements made in this widely circulated Ternopil newspaper, in order to illustrate the extent to which obfuscation, lies, and ignorance still prevail in this region. Demydas notes that in the past, presumably under the Communists,

We were taught internationalism and a respectful attitude toward other peoples. In truth, we were encouraged to look at our own people with contempt. Those who fought for Ukraine were labeled "bandits." On the suffering of Ukrainians not a word was said, because in this falsified history it was Jews who suffered most. All other nations had to bow down to them, to be in their debt, to be afraid of them.

Perversely, in Demydas's view:

How was it possible not to be afraid of them when every high-ranking Soviet official either was a Jew himself or had a Jewish wife, and when they all had the ear of Stalin's Gestapo [the NKVD], which was swarming with Jews . . . ? By now, everyone understands that this Soviet regime was planned and established by Jewish magnates and that Jews held all the key positions.

Consequently, the Jews soon:

occupied executive positions in the people's commissariats, swam in blood at secret-police headquarters, and wielded axes, crowbars, bayonets, and pistols in the "slaughter yards" and "slaughter cells." They surrounded Ukraine with a cordon of commissars and set about butchering and pillaging. They snatched the last crust of bread from children and the last hope from their elders. Those who were still living were driven to graves and buried alive. All in the name of the "radiant future." Jews also . . . enriched themselves and lived in luxury by taking away from the Ukrainians their last family relics in exchange for a handful of groats or a couple of potatoes. They took away all the gold Ukrainians had, enriching themselves on blood and death.

This was not merely a matter of individual greed but of national essence and ideological drive:

For this is the Zionist profession: to act as parasites, to exploit, and to rob. These beasts in human form hurled seven million Ukrainians into their graves [an allusion to Stalin's state-directed famine of 1932–1933], and buried Ukraine's future. The Zionists wanted to rule the world and intended to make our abundant land into a bridgehead for their conquests . . . . Flowering orchards and cottages were turned into a desert, and weeds ravaged the once-fertile black earth. "A bit of bread!" a child would plead and then fall dead. Yes, Jewish commissars became infamous for their exceptional pitilessness and cruelty!

And after Ukraine was liberated from the Bolshevik-Jewish yoke, the Jews continued their dirty business under different slogans. Once more "they took away our economy from us; they trampled on our human rights and burdened us with a new yoke of injustice" in league with their "blood brothers," the Russian "Jew-oligarchs":

Jewish money bought up all the television channels, which are now, just as in the old [Soviet] times, lying about the guilt of the Ukrainians vis-à-vis the Jews. They're lying in an insolent and mean fashion! Contrary to historical evidence, they are making Ukrainians into the "greatest antisemites." They have robbed us to the bone and are now building a "civil society" in Ukraine. Build one for yourself in Israel! Even if you prostrate yourself before the oppressors, you won't find any pity, compassion, or understanding! There is only one conclusion: Nothing can compel the Jews to remove the brand of the "greatest antisemites in the world" from the Ukrainians. Even if we gave the Israelites all the riches of Ukraine, they would still leave us with this brand. Now if they could destroy every last Ukrainians, then there would certainly be no one left to be called an antisemite!

What is most striking about this article is the extraordinary mélange of resentment, hurt pride, and reversal of images, whereby the Jews are remembered as Ukraine's annihilators and Ukrainians are depicted as the Jews' innocent victims. That this is a view both of the past and of the present—informed by and in turn promoting a fantastic, indeed hallucinatory, powerful image of history—is a clear indication of the inevitable return of the repressed as compulsive obsession. The author's conclusion is simple:

> We have absolutely no doubt that it was precisely the Jewish oligarchs who perpetrated a spiritual and economic pogrom in Ukraine on orders from the Moscow special services that they served and are still serving . . . . Buttered bread is tastier, but is it worth the price of serving the Jewish oligarchs who have made Ukraine into a graveyard? Will the ordinary Ukrainian agree to put on the Jewish yoke and to take orders from Moscow's lackeys? Let us be friends with Jews on the ground of brotherly principles. The basis of fraternity must be truth and sincerity.

This extraordinary tirade is especially telling considering the violent destruction of the city's Jewish community.[72] Established in 1540 as a private town, Ternopil is known to have had a Jewish population since 1550. By 1880, Jews comprised half the total population of almost 26,000. The Jewish population stagnated in the next six decades so that on the eve of the Second World War there were less than 14,000 Jews in a city with a total population of about 36,000. Considered exceptional for the high measure of tolerance among its ethnic communities in the early twentieth century, Ternopil experienced growing tensions in the interwar period. The Soviet takeover in 1939 brought about the elimination of most Jewish educational and political institutions, expropriation of property, and deportations. Still, due to the presence of Jewish refugees from German-occupied Poland, there were some 17,000 Jews in Ternopil when the Germans entered the city on July 2, 1941.

The German conquest was followed by a week-long pogrom led by German and Ukrainian police. The discovery of prisoners murdered by the NKVD was used to incite the population against the Jews, and the jail again became a site of massive torture, humiliation, and butchery. It is reported that while at this point the Germans shot only men, Ukrainian pogromists also killed women and children, using crowbars, axes, and knives. About a hundred Jews were murdered in a synagogue, which was then set on fire. More massacres took place also in the surrounding villages; the violence was so intense that the German authorities eventually decided to bring it under control. Altogether during this first week of German occupation, some 5,000 Jews, mostly men, were murdered in Ternopil.

Shortly thereafter the Nazis murdered much of the town's Jewish intelligentsia and appointed a Jewish council. A ghetto was established in September and was surrounded by a fence in late 1941. People died there in large numbers due to hunger, cold, and epidemics; others were employed in forced labor camps in the area, using tombstones from the old Jewish cemetery for road construction. A series of mass killing operations between March and November 1942 cost the lives of 7,000–8,000 people, who were either shot in a nearby forest by German and Ukrainian policemen or deported to Bełżec. The remaining 8,000 Jews were murdered in two mass shooting operations in April and June, 1943, after which the city was declared *judenrein*. The 2,000–2,500 inmates of the Jewish labor camp (*Judenlager*, or *Julag*) were killed in July, and the few who escaped to the forests were mostly pursued and murdered by local Ukrainian peasants or denounced to the Germans, despite several known cases of Ukrainians and Poles sheltering Jews. Only a few hundred Jews survived the war, largely in exile in the Soviet Union. A memorial put up in Ternopil after the liberation was destroyed in the 1950s, along with two Jewish graveyards used to construct buildings and garages. Most of the 500 Jewish residents of postwar Ternopil—who mainly came from the east—have meanwhile left.

The only significant indication of the formerly massive Jewish presence in Ternopil is the New Cemetery, situated next to an unmarked road on a hill overlooking the town across the Seret River.[73] Containing several hundred tombstones dating back to 1903, about three quarters of which are standing in their original locations, the cemetery is now protected by a fence that was put up in 1991–1994 by initiative of Ukrainian and foreign Jewish groups. Along with the destroyed sixteenth-century cemetery, the city's extraordinary fortress synagogue, built in the seventeenth century, has also vanished, although its ruins were still standing at the end of the war. The local history museum contained a vehemently nationalist and anti-Soviet exhibition when I visited it in March 2003; it made no mention of former Jewish life—or death—in Ternopil. When asked about a glass cabinet displaying a few Jewish items rumored to have been there the previous year, a museum attendant responded that it had been a temporary exhibit.

The single reference to the Holocaust in Ternopil that I found is a Soviet-era plaque inscribed in Yiddish and Ukrainian by the main door of the medical faculty building. Even in this case, while the Yiddish speaks of "thousands of Tarnopol Jews" shot there in early July 1941, the Ukrainian version mentions only "hundreds." Conversely, there is no paucity of memorials and commemorative plaques dedicated to marking the persecution of Ukrainians by the Soviets and to glorifying local nationalist fighters. The gymnasium in central Ternopil, for example, bears a plaque commemorating UPA Major Marian "Iahoda," "Chernyk" Lukasevych, born in 1922 and a pupil at the school from 1930 to 1937, who was killed in September 1945, most probably by the Soviets.

To complete our tour, we head directly west to the town of Zhovkva, about 20 miles north of Lviv.[74] Built as a private fortress town in the late sixteenth century, the town boasts an impressive castle, several well-preserved churches, and a magnificent synagogue dating back to 1692, once considered one of the most beautiful in Europe due to its architecture and sumptuous interior. Uncharacteristically, a plaque is attached to the synagogue, noting that its interior was destroyed when the Germans tried to blow it up, and that following partial restoration in the mid-1950s the building was declared unusable. No mention is made of the community that once used this edifice or of its fate. In stark contrast to such beautifully renovated buildings as the Roman Catholic Saint Lawrence Collegiate Church, the synagogue's lamentable condition seems to suggest its approaching demise.[75]

Jews have resided in Zhovkva since the earliest days of the town's existence. By 1890, the nearly 4,000 Jewish inhabitants constituted just over half the total population. Following the First World War, the city stagnated and the Jewish population became impoverished. In 1931, there were some 4,400 Jews in Zhovkva, again about half the total population. Many of the Jewish refugees from German-occupied Poland who arrived in 1939 were deported by the occupying Soviet authorities. When the Germans marched in on June 28, 1941, the discovery of NKVD victims in the local prison led to a pogrom by local Ukrainians and Poles. According to one version, it was at that point that the Great Synagogue was set on fire.

The first deportation took place in March 1942, when about 700 sick and elderly people were sent to Bełżec. Throughout summer 1942, numerous trains traveled through Zhovkva carrying Jews from other towns in Galicia to extermination camps. Those who jumped out of the trains and tried to escape to the forest were hunted down by the Germans, the Ukrainian guards, and the local population. A second *Aktion* took place in Zhovkva in November: 2,000 Jews were concentrated in the yard of the castle, of whom about 300 were shot on the spot and the rest were deported to Bełżec. In March 1943, approximately 600 men were sent to the Janowska camp in Lviv, following which the ghetto was liquidated and whoever tried to escape was sought out by the local population. Most surviving Jews were executed in the nearby forest. The last labor camp in town was liquidated in July. Other Jews discovered in hiding were shot at the Jewish cemetery. Only some 70 Jews survived, pursued to the end by Bandera units active in and around Zhovkva.

One mass grave of Jews is located at the municipal cemetery in the center of town. The grave is neither marked nor protected. The main Jewish cemetery, still surrounded by a wall and containing unmarked mass graves, has been converted into an open-air market. The Germans had used the tombstones—some of which dated as early as 1610—for paving roads; other gravestones were incorporated into structures and used to repair the cemetery wall, probably already during Soviet rule. Yet another mass grave is located in the forest east of Zhovkva. It too is neither protected nor officially marked.[76] The day I visited Zhovkva, a Saturday afternoon in March 2003, the open market had just closed. The muddy field was strewn with garbage. A small "memorial tent" had been erected by the cemetery wall to commemorate former rabbis of the town. The rest of the field was taken up by half-buried vehicle tires marking out the path for commercial traffic and by several large sheds.

The memory of the atrocity will not go away. It resurfaces, distorted and hateful, as repressed memories will, with all the anger and resentment of unresolved guilt. This is not to say that Zhovkva displays total amnesia. Indeed, at the center of town a memorial has been placed to remind the population of one episode in the past. It reads:

> In the years 1939–1941, Zhovkva Castle housed the district section of the NKVD . . . . It deported hundreds of Ukrainian and Polish families and imprisoned hundreds of Zhovkva residents, accusing them of disloyalty to Soviet power. On June 23–28, 1941, before the German forces seized Zhovkva, tragic events occurred within the walls of the fortress. Sadistic NKVD men tortured and executed the prisoners without trial or judgment . . . The mutilated bodies of the innocent victims . . . rotting in the rooms and in several concealed pits in the area of the castle, were sorrowfully buried.

This lamentation of the bitter fate of Zhovkva's Christian population—both standing as a legacy of and symbolizing liberation from Communist subjugation—makes no mention of the Jews, let alone of the complicity of their gentile neighbors in their mass murder. But because of this repression of a past that still stares one in the face, the recent discovery of a new mass grave was greeted not as an opportunity to confront the past but as a trigger for renewed denial.

On September 29, 2002, Roman Woronowycz reported in the *Ukrainian Weekly* on the discovery three months earlier of the remains of 228 bodies in the basement of the Zhovkva Basilian Monastery. Only eleven bodies had bullet holes in the skull, while six had been struck on the head with sharp objects. No less than 87 bodies belonged to children, two of whom were unborn. The local Memorial Society in Lviv, which collaborated in the investigation, swiftly concluded that these were victims of a Soviet massacre. Mr. Hryniv, president of the Memorial Society and a former member of parliament, stated, "This was the work of the NKVD. We have evidence to show that this is undeniable." This evidence included postwar Soviet newspaper clippings and coins found next to the bodies. Hryniv noted that between 1946 and 1949 the NKVD used the Basilian Monastery as a garrison while it ferreted out UPA and OUN members, former Nazi satraps and "bourgeois nationalists." The bodies, Hryniv argued, belonged either to Ukrainians who had been deported by the Polish authorities after the war or to locals who had managed to evade deportation to Siberia.[77]

These speculations were completely rejected, however, by the Kiev journalist Danylo Kulyniak, the author of influential articles on Soviet mass killing sites discovered near Ivano-Frankivsk in 1990. For Kulyniak, the bodies found in Zhovkva had all the hallmarks of SS killings. As he wrote: "How come the bodies are not clothed, and why were there no gold teeth found?" The bodies also had no hair, and no clasps, jewelry, or buttons were discovered at the site. Kulyniak noted that while the Germans took everything they could from their victims, the Soviets were inclined to bury the bodies as they were and rarely stole gold teeth. He also stressed that Soviet perpetrators did not normally murder women and children, certainly not on such a large scale. Rather, they usually placed the children of families perceived as a threat to the Soviet state in special schools.

Kulyniak thus concluded that the remains belonged to the local Jews of Zhovkva. He hypothesized that they might have been killed in gas vans and then buried in the basement of the monastery, or they might have been buried there by the Soviet authorities who collected the remains of dead Jews, possibly victims of epidemics who were then robbed of their clothes and teeth and left behind by the Germans before they retreated. The Soviets, he wrote, were keenly aware of the local population's inability to distinguish between Nazi and Communist atrocities, which made the Soviets all the more eager to cover up the traces of German crimes as well as their own. Burying the bodies in the monastery might have also served the Communists as a symbolic act of desecration of a Ukrainian religious institution.

Hryniv would have none of it. For him, the mass grave was "the best evidence" that the Soviets waged "a war against the civilian population," namely the Ukrainians.[78] Clearly, Hryniv's theory is untenable and contradicts everything we know about Nazi and Soviet killing methods and the realities on the ground in Galicia. Why then his insistence on this idea? In part, this has to do with the desire to blame all evil deeds on the Soviets, an understandable urge after close to half a century of oppression, especially from the perspective of a Ukrainian from Galicia. But there is more in play here, which has to do not just with identifying the victims, but also with transforming them into perpetrators. To be sure, this is not mentioned explicitly by Hryniv. But a glance at some of the more extreme responses to the discovery of the mass grave at Zhovkva sheds a painful light on the long-term effects of repression. For while not a few Jewish survivors from these regions have maintained since the Holocaust that "the Ukrainians were worse than the Germans," the line of defense taken up by Ukrainian nationalists who identify with the UPA and OUN and with their antisemitic policies is that the "Soviets, led by the Jews, were worse than the Germans."[79]

Return

Ultimately, this is a story not only about exhuming bodies, but also about unearthing a past of destruction whose very objective was to bury the traces of its crimes and the identity of the murdered along with their bodies. But such crimes tend to resurface, both metaphorically and physically. They cannot remain hidden forever, and they cannot be confronted without a willingness to look back at all the hatred and atrocity and the beauty and creativity of a world that ended up being trampled by vast external forces even as it devoured its own inhabitants. Those who stare at that past with eyes wide shut can only conjure fictions, legends, nightmares, and phobias, however much they seek an identity that is pure and good and cleansed.

We cannot bring back the dead, but we can give them a decent burial. We cannot bring back a culturally rich, complex, and precarious multiethnic world, and we may not even want to do so, but we can recognize its failings and respect its accomplishments, not only for their own sake, but because we cannot understand ourselves and build a secure and confident identity without acknowledging where we come from and how we got to where we are today. We have just left behind us the bloodiest century in world history and seem to be heading right into one that could prove to be even bloodier. If we are to plunge into yet another ocean of blood, it behooves us to reflect on the causes and consequences of previous atrocities and to grasp the fact that the origins of collective violence invariably lie in repressing memory and misconstruing the past.

Notes

Author's note: This is a much abridged version of my book, *Erased: Vanishing Traces of Jewish Galicia in Present Day Ukraine* (Princeton: Princeton University Press, 2007).

1. Throughout this text, I use the current Ukrainian rendering of place names. At first mention, the Polish and Yiddish (with other Yiddish versions in parentheses) are provided, as is the Romanian where relevant. See also Timothy Snyder, *The Reconstruction of Nations: Poland, Ukraine, Lithuania, Belarus, 1569–1999* (New Haven, Conn.: Yale University Press, 2003); Andrei S. Markovits and Frank E. Sysyn, eds., *Nationbuilding and the Politics of Nationalism: Essays on Austrian Galicia* (Cambridge, Mass.: Harvard University Press, 1982); Christopher Hann and Paul Robert Magocsi, eds., *Galicia: A Multicultured Land* (Toronto: University of Toronto Press, 2005); Adam Zamoyski, *The Polish Way: A Thousand-Year History of the Poles and Their Culture* (New York: Hippocrene Books, 1994); Gershon David Hundert, *Jews in Poland-Lithuania in the Eighteenth Century: A Genealogy of Modernity* (Berkeley: University of California Press, 2004); Paul Robert Magocsi, *The Roots of Ukrainian Nationalism: Galicia as Ukraine's Piedmont* (Toronto: Toronto University Press, 2002).

2. John-Paul Himka, *Galician Villagers and the Ukrainian National Movement in the Nineteenth Century* (Houndmills and London: Macmillan, 1988); Keely Stauter-Halsted, *The Nation in the Village: The Genesis of Peasant National Identity in Austrian Poland, 1848–1948* (Ithaca and London: Cornell University Press,

2001). And see, e.g., the historical trilogy by Henryk Sienkiewicz (1846–1916): *With Fire and the Sword* (1884); *The Deluge* (1886), and *Pan Michael* (1887–1888).

3. Ezra Mendelsohn, *The Jews of East Central Europe between the World Wars* (Bloomington: Indiana University Press, 1983), pp. 19, 50f., 54f., 68–83; Yisrael Gutman et al., eds., *The Jews of Poland Between Two World Wars* (Hanover and London: University Press of New England, 1989), pp. 16–19, 24f., 114f., 123 (contributions by Ezra Mendelsohn, Gershon C. Bacon, and Antony Polonsky); Joshua Shanes, "National Regeneration in the Diaspora: Zionism, Politics and Jewish Identity in Late Habsburg Galicia, 1883–1907," PhD Diss., University of Wisconsin, Madison, 2002; Klaus Hödl: *Als Bettler in die Leopoldstadt: Galizische Juden auf dem Weg nach Wien* (Vienna: Böhlau, 1994). See also *The Galitzianer*, at: http://www.jewishgen.org/galicia/newsletter.html (accessed August 23, 2006).

4. Shmuel Yosef Agnon, *A Guest for the Night: A Novel*, Misha Louvis, trans. (Madison, WI: University of Wisconsin Press, 2004); Agnon, *The Whole City* (Jerusalem: Schocken, 1973, in Hebrew); Ezra Mendelsohn, *Painting a People: Maurycy Gottlieb and Jewish Art* (Hanover, NH: University Press of New England, 2002).

5. See, e.g., Joseph Roth, *The Wandering Jews*, Michael Hofmann, trans. (New York: W. W. Norton, 2001, orig. pub. 1926); Salcia Landmann, *Erinnerungen an Galizien* (Munich: Knaur, 1983); Guido Baselgia and Verena Dohrn, *Galizien* (Frankfurt am Main: Jüdischer Verlag, 1993); Stefan Simonek and Alois Woldan, eds., *Europa Erlesen: Galizien* (Klagenfurt: Wieser Verlag, 1998); Soma Morgenstern, *In einer anderen Zeit: Jugendjahre in Ostgalizien* (Berlin: Aufbau Taschenbuch Verlag, 1999).

6. See, e.g., Isabel Röskau-Rydel, ed., *Deutsche Geschichte im Osten Europas: Galizien* (Berlin: Siedler Verlag, 1999); Roswitha Schieb, *Reise nach Schlesien und Galizien: Eine Archäologie des Gefühls* (Berlin: Berlin Verlag, 2000); and n. 15, below. See also Valdis O. Lumans, "A Reassessment of *Volksdeutsche* and Jews in the Volhynia-Galicia-Narew Resettlement," and Doris L. Bergen, "The Volksdeutsche of Eastern Europe and the Collapse of the Nazi Empire, 1944–1945," both in Alan E. Steinwies and Daniel E. Rogers, eds., *The Impact of Nazism: New Perspectives on the Third Reich and Its Legacy* (Lincoln: University of Nebraska Press, 2003), pp. 81–100 and 101–128, respectively.

7. Dieter Pohl, *Nationalsozialistische Judenverfolgung in Ostgalizien 1941–1944: Organisation und Durchführung eines staatlichen Massenverbrechens* (Munich: Oldenbourg, 1996); Thomas Sandkühler, *"Endlösung" in Galizien: Der Judenmord in Ostpolen und die Rettungsinitiativen von Berthold Beitz, 1941–1944* (Bonn: Dietz, 1996).

8. Thomas Geldmacher, "Die Beteiligung österreichischer Schutzpolizisten an der Judenvernichtung in den galizischen Städten Drohobycz und Boryslaw, 1941 bis 1944" (MA thesis, Vienna University, 2001); Geldmacher, *"Wir als Wiener waren ja bei der Bevölkerung beliebt": Österreichische Schutzpolizisten und die Judenvernichtung in Ostgalizien 1941–1944* (Vienna: Mandelbaum Verlag, 2002).

9. "Forum: A City of Many Names: Lemberg/Lwów/L'viv/L'vov—Nationalizing in an Urban Context" (essays by Harald Binder, Anna Veronika Wendland, and Yaroslav Hrytsak), *Austrian History Yearbook* XXXIV (2003), pp. 57–109; John Czaplicka, ed., "L'viv: A City in the Crossroads of Culture," *Harvard Ukrainian Studies* Special Issue XXIV (¼) (2000).

10. On Galicia as the site of competing nationalisms, see Klaus Bachmann, *Ein Herd der Feindschaft gegen Rußland: Galizien als Krisenherd in den Beziehungen der Donaumonarchie mit Rußland (1907–1914)*, (Vienna: Verlag für Geschichte und Politik, 2001). See also papers linked to the research project led by Omer Bartov: "Borderlands: Ethnicity, Identity, and Violence in the Shatter-Zone of Empires Since 1848," Watson Institute for International Studies, Brown University, at: http://www.watsoninstitute.org/borderlands/ (accessed August 23, 2006). And see Peter Bugge, "'Shatter Zones': The Creation and Re-Creation of Europe's East,"

in Menno Spiering and Michael Wintle, eds., *Ideas of Europe since 1914: The Legacy of the First World War* (New York: Palgrave, 2002), pp. 47–69.

11. See, e.g., Karen E. Till, *The New Berlin: Memory, Politics, Place* (Minneapolis: University of Minnesota Press, 2005).

12. John A. Armstrong, *Ukrainian Nationalism*, 2nd ed. (Littleton, CO: Ukrainian Academic Press, 1980), pp. 290–321; Roger D. Petersen, *Resistance and Rebellion: Lessons from Eastern Europe* (New York: Cambridge University Press, 2001), pp. 209–230.

13. For other journeys into these regions, see, e.g., Alfred Döblin, *Journey to Poland*, Joachim Neugroschel, trans. (New York: Paragon House Publishers, 1991, orig. pub. 1925); Verena Dohrn, *Reise nach Galizien: Grenzlandschaften des alten Europa* (Berlin: Philo, 2000); Martin Pollack, *Galizien: Eine Reise durch die verschwundene Welt Ostgaliziens und der Bukowina* (Frankfurt am Main: Insel Verlag, 2001).

14. http://en.wikipedia.org/wiki/L%27viv (accessed August 23, 2006).

15. Another plaque dates the building back only to 1578, while one scholar dates it to 1635. See Yaroslav Hrytsak, "L'viv: A Multicultural History through the Centuries," in Czaplicka, *L'viv*, pp. 52. These dates seem to indicate reconstructions of the cathedral. Armenians lived in East Central Europe since the Byzantine era and in L'viv since the thirteenth century. The community reached its height in the seventeenth century and declined to merely 3,000 thoroughly Polonized members by the early nineteenth century. See Paul Robert Magocsi, *Historical Atlas of East Central Europe* (Seattle: University of Washington Press, 1993), 110; Paul Robert Magocsi, *A History of Ukraine* (Seattle: University of Washington Press, 1996), pp. 396. See also http://www.armeniapedia.org/index.php?title=L'viv (accessed August 23, 2006); http://www.travel.inL'viv.info/aguide/aguide5.php (accessed August 23, 2006).

16. Magocsi, *Historical Atlas*, pp. 107–110. Jews arrived in the region of L'viv already in the tenth century, mainly from Byzantium and Khazaria; the earliest Jewish tombstone found in the city dates back to 1348. But it was only after the creation of the Polish-Lithuanian Commonwealth in 1569—which brought vast areas of present-day Ukraine under Polish rule—along with increasing pressure on Jewish settlement and economic rights in western Poland and offers of opportunities farther east, that large numbers of Jews moved to these new territories. By the mid-eighteenth century close to half of Polish Jewry lived in Ukraine-Ruthenia. Some eighty percent of world Jewry today can trace their roots to the eighteenth-century Polish-Lithuanian Commonwealth. Danuta Dąbrowska et al., eds., *Pinkas Hakehillot: Encyclopedia of Jewish Communities: Poland*, Vol. II, *Eastern Galicia* (Jerusalem: Yad Vashem, 1980, in Hebrew), p. 1; M. J. Rosman, *The Lords' Jews: Magnate-Jewish Relations in the Polish-Lithuanian Commonwealth during the Eighteenth Century* (Cambridge, MA: Harvard Ukrainian Research Institute/Harvard Center of Jewish Studies, 1990), pp. 36–41; Hundert, *Jews in Poland-Lithuania*, pp. 3–20; Martin Gilbert, *The Routledge Atlas of Jewish History*, 6th ed. (New York: Routledge, 2003), pp. 32f., 46f., 56.

17. John Czaplicka, "Introduction: Lemberg, Leopolis, Lwów, Lvov: A City in the Crosscurrents of European Culture"; Hrytsak, "L'viv"; Alois Woldan, "The Imagery of L'viv in Ukrainian, Polish, and Austrian Literatures: From the Sixteenth Century to 1918," all in Czaplicka, *L'viv*, pp. 13–45, 47–73, and 75–93, respectively.

18. This is the English text of the plaque. The Yiddish text is much abbreviated. The Ukrainian text is also slightly abbreviated, leaving out the fact that the synagogue was built to commemorate the rabbi's wife.

19. Delphine Bechtel, "De Jedwabne à Zolotchiv: Pogromes locaux en Galicie, juin-juillet 1941," in Delphine Bechtel and Xavier Galmiche, eds., *Cultures d'Europe centrale 5: La destruction des confines* (Paris: CIRCE, 2005), pp. 69–92,

esp. 72. Among the numerous memoirs of the Holocaust in L'viv, see esp. David Kahane, *Lvov Ghetto Diary*, Jerzy Michalowicz, trans. (Amherst: University of Massachusetts Press, 1990); Kurt I. Lewin, *Przeżyłem: Saga świętego Jura spisana w roku 1946* (Warsaw: Zeszyty Literackie, 2006); Leon Weliczker Wells, *The Janowska Road* (New York: Macmillan, 1963); Eliyahu Yones, *Smoke in the Sand: The Jews of Lwów during the War 1939–1944* (Jerusalem: Yad Vashem, 2001, in Hebrew); Tadeusz Zaderecki, *When the Swastika Ruled in Lwów: The Destruction of the Jewish Community through the Eyes of a Polish Writer*, Zvi Arad, trans. (Jerusalem: Yad Vashem, 1982, in Hebrew). On Poles in World War II L'viv, see Grzegorz Hryciuk, *Polacy we Lwowie 1939–1944: Życie codzienne* (Warsaw: Książka i Wiedza, 2000). For the history of Jewish L'viv, see N. M. Gelber, ed., *Encyclopedia of the Jewish Diaspora: Poland Series*, Vol. IV: *Lwów* (Jerusalem: The Encyclopedia of the Jewish Diaspora, 1956); Dąbrowska, *Pinkas Hakehillot*, pp. 1–47.

20. Thanks to Delphine Bechtel and Sofia Grachova for directing me to this monument and to Artem Svyrydov for a photo.

21. See also Michael Stanislawski, *A Murder in Lemberg: The Assassination of Rabbi Abraham Kohn* (Princeton: Princeton University Press, 2007), and Albert Lichtblau and Michael John, "Jewries in Galicia and Bukovina, in Lemberg and Czernowitz: Two Divergent Examples of Jewish Communities in the Far East of the Austro-Hungarian Monarchy," in Sander L. Gilman and Milton Shain, eds., *Jewries at the Frontier: Accommodation, Identity, Conflict* (Urbana, IL: University of Illinois Press, 1999), pp. 29–66.

22. The sculptor Pesach (Peter) Palit, who designed the plaque, has meanwhile immigrated to Israel. Tiqva Nathan, *The Last Jews of Lwów (Lemberg)*, (Jerusalem: Reuven Mas, 1997, in Hebrew), p. 137.

23. On the dispute over the Jewish cemetery in L'viv, see: http://www.risu.org.ua/eng/news/article;4791/ (accessed August 23, 2006).

24. Yones, *Smoke in the Sand*, p. 257.

25. *Jewish Heritage of L'viv*, B. Mirkin, ed., A. Turkivskyy, trans. (L'viv: Centre of Europe, 2002). Vita Susak, director of the European Art Collection at the L'viv Art Gallery, gave me her last copy of this brochure and kindly showed me around the gallery in March 2003. The gallery displays some works of Jewish artists and depictions of shtetl life in Galicia, but provides no mention of Jewish fate. In an essay on this art, Ms. Susak curiously associated between the disappearance of such cultures as the "Phoenicians, Copts, Assyrians, and others," and the "vanished world" of Galician Jewry. Vita Susak, "Images of a Vanished World," in *Images of a Vanished World: The Jews of Eastern Galicia (From the mid-19th century to the first third of the 20th century)*, Exhibition International Holocaust Center, exhibition curators Halyna Hlembots'ka and Vita Susak, trans. Taras Kupriy, Jeffrey Wills and Cristina Teresa O'Keefe, eds. (L'viv: "Centre of Europe" Publishing House, 2003), 6–12. See also Vita Susak, "Les visages de la Galicie orientale dans les œuvres de ses peintres (fin XIXᵉ-début XXᵉ siècles)," and Delphine Bechtel, "'Galizien, Galicja, Galitsye, Halytchyna': Le mythe de la Galicie, de la disparition à la résurrection (virtuelle)," both in Delphine Bechtel and Xavier Galmiche, eds., *Culture d'Europe Centrale 4: Le Mythe des confins* (Paris: CIRCE, 2003), pp. 189–205 and 56–77, respectively.

26. The architect of the monument is Volodymyr Plykhivskyi. The sculptors, Luisa Sternstein and Yuriy Schmukler, have meanwhile immigrated to Israel. See *Jewish Heritage of L'viv*, p. 23; Nathan, *Last Jews*, p. 138.

27. See Harold Marcuse, "Six Day Trip to L'viv, 5–11 August, 1999," at: http://www.history.ucsb.edu/projects/holocaust/LvovTrip/lvivjrnl.998.htm (accessed August 23, 2006).

28. The differences in inscriptions written in several languages clearly indicate the real or anticipated sensibilities of potential readers as well as the agendas and historical understanding of those who formulated them.

29. "The story of Lvov citizen Alexander Schwarz, who survived Janovska camp," at: http://www.history.ucsb.edu/projects/holocaust/Resources/Janowska Survivor047.htm (accessed August 23, 2006), site managed by Harold Marcuse, taken from Gundula Werger, "Denk ich an Lemberg," *Die Welt*, July 19, 2004.

30. The Ukrainian and Yiddish versions are the same, save for replacing the word "Nazi" with "fascist," as was the convention in Soviet times.

31. See also http://www.holocaust.kiev.ua/eng/seminarse/lviv.htm (accessed August 23, 2006), the program of a conference that took place in L'viv in November 2003. B'nai Brith "Leopolis" supports 10–15 percent of western Ukraine's estimated 12,000–15,000 mostly elderly Jewish population. Schwarz's International Holocaust Center provides medical and food services for Jewish children and the elderly. Schwarz was awarded the Order of Merit by former German President Johannes Rau.

32. Yaroslav Hrytsak and Victor Susak, "Constructing a National City: The Case of L'viv," in John J. Czaplicka and Blair A. Ruble, eds., *Composing Urban History and the Constitution of Civic Identities* (Baltimore: The Johns Hopkins University Press, 2003), pp. 140–164.

33. Bechtel, "Zolotchiv," p. 85; Liliana Hentosh and Bohdan Tscherkes, "L'viv: In Search of Identity—Transformations of the City's Public Space," paper presented at: *Cities after the Fall: European Integration and Urban History Conference* (Minda de Gunzburg Center for European Studies, Harvard University, spring 2005). The sculptors of the monument are P. Shtaer and R. Ryvenskyi. Jews constituted 10 percent of the population in western Ukraine and western Belarus, but a third of the total number of deportees. Altogether from 1939 to 1941 between 309,000 and 327,000 people were deported from western Ukraine and western Belarus; between 110,000 and 130,000 people were arrested. Between a quarter and a third of those deported by the Soviets died; about 90–95 percent of the Jews under German occupation in these areas were murdered. Jan T. Gross, *Revolution from Abroad: The Soviet Conquest of Poland's Western Ukraine and Western Belorussia*, 2nd ed. (Princeton: Princeton University Press, 2002), xiv, 269f.; Stanisław Ciesielski et al., *Represje sowieckie wobec Polaków i obywateli polskich* (Warsaw: Ośrodek Karta, 2000), pp. 11–16. Up to 50,000 mostly Ukrainian prisoners were held by the Soviets in western Ukraine on the eve of the German invasion, of whom up to 30,000 were executed or died on forced marches during the Soviet retreat. Bogdan Musial, *"Konterrevolutionäre Elemente sind zu Erschießen": Die Brutalisierung des deutsch-sowjetischen Krieges im Sommer 1941* (Berlin: Propyläen Verlag, 2000), p. 137f.

34. John-Paul Himka, "Ukrainian Collaboration in the Extermination of the Jews During the Second World War: Sorting Out the Long-Term and Conjectural Factors," in Jonathan Frankel, ed., *The Fate of the European Jews, 1939–1945: Continuity or Contingency?* (New York: Oxford University Press, 1997), pp. 170–189; Aharon Weiss, "Jewish-Ukrainian Relations in Western Ukraine During the Holocaust," in Peter J. Potichnyj and Howard Aster, eds., *Ukrainian-Jewish Relations in Historical Perspective* (Edmonton: Canadian Institute of Ukrainian Studies/ University of Alberta, 1988), pp. 409–420; B. F. Sabrin, *Alliance for Murder: The Nazi-Ukrainian Nationalist Partnership in Genocide* (New York: Sarpedon, 1991); Martin Dean, *Collaboration in the Holocaust: Crimes of the Local Police in Belorussia and Ukraine, 1941–44* (New York: St. Martin's Press, 2000); and essays in this volume.

35. On the Jews of Drohobych, see N. M. Gelber, ed., *Memorial to the Jews of Drohobycz, Boryslaw, and Surroundings* (Tel Aviv: Association of Former Residents of Drohobycz, Boryslaw and Surroundings, 1959, in Hebrew and Yiddish); scanned copy at: http://yizkor.nypl.org/index.php?id=2312 (accessed August 23, 2006); partial translation at: http://www.jewishgen.org/Yizkor/Drohobycz/Drogobych.html (accessed August 23, 2006); Dąbrowska, *Pinkas Hakehillot,* 168–171. On the "Final

Solution" there, see Pohl, *Judenverfolgung*, pp. 70, 122, 143, 149, 190, 202, 224–227, 243, 250, 256; Sandkühler, *"Endlösung,"* pp. 303, 305–310, 312–318, 320, 323–29, 331–334, 336–339, 374–380, 398–399, 403. Further in Geldmacher, "Beteiligung"; and Geldmacher, *"Wiener."* Also see http://www.personal.ceu.hu/students/97/ Roman_Zakharii/drohobych.htm (accessed August 23, 2006); http://en.wikipedia .org/wiki/Drohobych (accessed August 23, 2006).

36. This saying is attributed to the Jewish-Polish writer Marian Hemar (1901–1972). See Leonid Goldberg, "Drogobych—One and a Half City," in *Jewish Ukraine* 7/26 (April 2002), at: http://jewukr.org/observer/jo07_26/p0203_e.html (accessed August 23, 2006). See also Jaroslaw Anders, "The Prisoner of Myth," *The New Republic Online*, Post date 11.14.02, Issue date: 11.25.05, at: http://www.tnr.com/doc .mhtml?i=20021125&s=anders112502&c=1 (accessed August 23, 2006); Denise V. Powers, "Fresco Fiasco," in *Forum: Żydzi-Polacy-Chrześcijanie*, at: http://www .znak.com.pl/forum/index-en.php?t=studia&id=67 (accessed August 23, 2006).

37. Wilfried Jilge, "The Politics of the Second World War in Post-Communist Ukraine (1986/1991–2004/2005)," *Jahrbücher für Geschichte Osteuropas* 54 (2006): pp. 50–81, esp. 55f. and n. 30; Ryszard Torzecki, "Die Rolle der Zusammenarbeit mit der deutschen Besatzungsmacht in der Ukraine für deren Okkupationspolitik," in Werner Röhr, ed., *Okkupation und Kollaboration (1938–1945), Beiträge zu Konzepten und Praxis der Kollaboration in der deutschen Okkupationspolitik* (Berlin: Hüthig, 1994), pp. 239–272; Karel Berkhoff and Marco Carynnyk, "The Organization of Ukrainian Nationalists and Its Attitude toward Germans and Jews: Iaroslav Stets'ko's 1941 Zhyttiepys," *Harvard Ukrainian Studies* XXIII (3/4) 1999: pp. 149–184; Dieter Pohl, "Ukrainische Hilfskräfte beim Mord an den Juden," in Gerhard Paul, ed., *Die Täter der Shoah: Fanatische Nationalsozialisten oder ganz normale Deutsche?* (Göttingen: Wallstein, 2002), pp. 205–234; Frank Golczewski, "Die Kollaboration in der Ukraine," in Christoph Dieckmann et al., eds., *Kooperation und Verbrechen: Formen der "Kollaboration" im östlichen Europa 1939–1945* (Göttingen: Wallstein, 2003), pp. 151–182.

38. Jerzy Ficowski, *Regions of the Great Heresy. Bruno Schulz: A Biographical Portrait*, Theodosia Robertson, trans. (New York: W. W. Norton, 2003), pp. 132–139. See also Pola Arbiser and Irene Frisch, *Give Me the Children* (Atlanta, GA: P. Arbiser, 2002); and Henryk Grynberg, *Drohobycz, Drohobycz and Other Stories: True Tales from the Holocaust and Life After*, Theodosia Robertson, ed., Alicia Nitecki, trans. (New York: Penguin Books, 2002). The German *Aktion* (pl. *Aktionen*) and its Polish equivalent *akcja* (pl. *akcje*), as well as the Yiddish and Hebrew derivations (*aktsya*, pl. *aktsye* or *aktsyot*), denote roundup and mass killing.

39. The book is Roman Pastukh, *Vulytsiamy Staroho Drohobycha* (Kamenyar: L'viv, 1991); the photo is in a batch of plates between pp. 64f.

40. Yad Vashem's agents had apparently struck a deal with the local Drohobych leaders behind the backs of the Ukrainian and Polish cultural authorities. On the controversy, see Ficowski, *Regions*, pp. 165–172; Powers, "Fresco Fiasco"; Ruth Franklin, "Searching for Bruno Schulz," *The New Yorker*, issue of December 16, posted December 9, 2002, at: http://www.newyorker.com/ critics/books/?021216crbo_books (accessed August 24, 2006); Anne Applebaum, "An Oddball Miles from Anywhere," *The Spectator*, March 15, 2003: http://www .anneapplebaum.com/other/2003/03_15_spec_oddball.html (accessed August 24, 2006); Amiran Barkat, "Yad Vashem Not Displaying Bruno Schulz Holocaust Art," *Haaretz*, July 4, 2005, at: http://www.isjm.org/news/040805har.htm (accessed August 24, 2006); Benjamin Paloff, "Who Owns Bruno Schulz? Poland Stumbles over Its Jewish Past," *Boston Review* (December 2004/January 2005), at: http://bostonreview.net/BR29.6/paloff.html (accessed August 24, 2006).

41. See prewar photo in Pastukh, *Vulytsiamy*, between pp. 64f.

42. See "The Street of Crocodiles," in *The Complete Fiction of Bruno Schulz*, Celina Wieniewska, trans. (Walker and Company: New York, 1989), 5.

43. Pastukh, *Vulytsiamy*, between pp. 64f.; and http://diaspora.org.il/chamber%20/pics/drohobyz.htm (accessed August 24, 2006); http://members.tripod .com/~mikerosenzweig/easteursyn.htm (accessed August 24, 2006).

44. See http://polishjews.org/synag/drohobycz2.htm (accessed August 24, 2006).

45. The synagogue is said to be presently under renovation. As can be glimpsed from pre-World War I photographs, restoring the exterior, let alone the opulent interior of this splendid edifice, will be an extraordinarily difficult task. See Pastukh, *Vulytsiamy*, between pp. 64f.

46. See, e.g., http://www.shtetlinks.jewishgen.org/Drohobycz/dz_histoil.htm (accessed August 24, 2006); Alison Fleig Frank, *Oil Empire: Visions of Prosperity in Austrian Galicia* (Cambridge, MA: Harvard University Press, 2005).

47. This account is based primarily on Dąbrowska, *Pinkas Hakehillot*, pp. 359–376; English translation at: http://www.jewishgen.org/yizkor/pinkas_poland/pol2_00359.html (accessed August 24, 2006). See also: http://en.wikipedia .org/wiki/Ivano-Frankivsk (accessed August 24, 2006), citing population figures from the 1931 Polish census: Poles: 120,214 (60.6%); Ukrainians: 49,032 (24.7%); Jews 26,996: (13.6%); Total: 196,242, presumably including Polish villages around the city and excluding those of Ukrainians and Jews. See also the full census record, at: http://www.halgal.com/1931popbylang.html (accessed August 24, 2006). The Polish administrative district of Stanisławów (excluding the city population) comprised on the eve of World War II 600,000 people, of whom 70 percent were Ukrainian, 20 percent Jews, and the remainder made up of smaller local ethnic groups. See Elisabeth Freundlich, *Die Ermordung einer Stadt namens Stanislau: NS-Vernichtungspolitik in Polen 1939–1945* (Vienna: Österreichischer Bundesverlag, 1986), p. 21.

48. For photos and information, see http://www.shtetlinks.jewishgen.org/ Stanislawow/syn.htm (accessed August 24, 2006).

49. For a photo of this execution with the wall of the synagogue clearly visible in the background, see Yury Boshyk, ed., *Ukraine during World War II: History and its Aftermath* (Edmonton: University of Alberta, 1986), in a batch of photos between pages 108–109. The tourist site "Discover Ukraine" notes that "The hearts of people are still aching when they recall the public execution of 27 patriots in the center of the city in November 17, 1943. In Stanyslaviv and its suburbs fascists killed more than 100 thousand peaceful people in total." The identity of these "peaceful people" is not given. See: http://tourism.pcukraine.org/info .php?site=Ivano-Frankivsk&oblast=Ivano-Frankivska&PHPSESSID=838b2e941 54ded958a77c2a936586a94 (accessed August 24, 2006).

50. The execution is also mentioned in the unpublished diary of Viktor Petrykevych, who lived in Ivano-Frankivs'k and Buchach during the German occupation. He notes that the executed were probably Banderivtsy. The so-called Banderivtsy (Banderowcy) units were loyal to OUN-B and UPA and became deeply complicit in the murder of Jews and Poles in Galicia and Volhynia. Thanks to Sofia Grachova for updating me on this memorial, supplying photos, and finding and translating sections from this extraordinary diary.

51. See more about the massacre in Pohl, *Judenverfolgung*, pp. 144–147; Sandkühler, *"Endlösung,"* pp. 150ff.; Freundlich, *Die Ermordung einer Stadt*, pp. 154– 164; Avraham Liebesman, *With the Jews of Stanislawow in the Holocaust*, Yosef Cohen, trans. (Tel Aviv: Ghetto Fighters' House, 1980, in Hebrew), pp. 22–31.

52. G. Kresel and L. Olitski, eds., *Yizkor Book of Kehilat Kosow (Kosow Huculski)* (Tel Aviv: Hamenora, 1964, in Hebrew and Yiddish), folded map after title page; available at http://yizkor.nypl.org/index.php?id=2312 (accessed August 24, 2006).

53. The following is based on Dąbrowska, *Pinkas Hakehillot*, pp. 481–486. See also Yehoshua Gertner and Danek Gertner, *The House is No Longer There: The De-*

struction of the Jews of Kosów and Żabie, Rinat Kahanov, trans. (Jerusalem: Yad Vashem, 2000, in Hebrew).

54. I am currently writing a history of Buchach. The bibliography is too vast to be covered here. For references see Omer Bartov, "Seeking the Roots of Modern Genocide: On the Macro- and Microhistory of Mass Murder," in Robert Gellately and Ben Kiernan, eds., *The Specter of Genocide: Mass Murder in Historical Perspective* (Cambridge: Cambridge University Press, 2003), pp. 75–96; Bartov, "Les relations interethniques à Buczacz (Galicie orientale) durant la Shoah selon les témoignages d'après guerre," in Bechtel and Galmiche, *La Destruction des confins,* pp. 47–67. See further in Dąbrowska, *Pinkas Hakehillot,* pp. 83–89; Yisrael Kohen, ed., *The Book of Buczacz* (Tel Aviv: Am Oved, 1956, in Hebrew), scanned copy at: http://yizkor.nypl.org/index.php?id=1854 (accessed August 24, 2006), English translation at: http://www.jewishgen.org/Yizkor/buchach/buchach.html (accessed August 24, 2006). Further information and sources at: http://www.shtetlinks.jewishgen.org/Suchostaw/sl_buczacz.htm (accessed August 24, 2006). For some memoirs, see Pesach Anderman, *The Strength of Life: Being Human* (Ramat Gan: Te'omim, 2004, in Hebrew); Mordechai Halpern, *A Family and a City: In Prosperity and in Ruin* (Tel Aviv: Traklin, 2003, in Hebrew); Etunia Bauer Katz, *Our Tomorrows Never Came* (New York: Fordham University Press, 2000); Mina Rosner, *I Am a Witness* (Winnipeg: Hyperion Press, 1990); Mali Karl, *Escape a la Vida* (Lima: Imprenta Charito E.I.R.L., 1989); Alicia Appleman-Jurman, *Alicia: My Story* (Toronto: Bantam Book, 1988). On three of the town's most famous sons, see Dan Laor, *S. Y. Agnon: A Biography* (Tel Aviv: Schocken, 1998, in Hebrew); Hella Pick, *Simon Wiesenthal: A Life in Search of Justice* (London: Weidenfeld & Nicolson, 1996); Samuel Kassow, "A Stone Under History's Wheel: The Story of Emanuel Ringelblum and the *Oneg Shabes* Archive," at: http://yiddishbookcenter.org/pdf/pt/43/PT43ringelblum.pdf (accessed August 24, 2006).

55. Interview of Oresta Synen'ka and her husband Ivan Synen'kyi conducted by Sofia Grachova and Andriy Pavlyashuk on March 2, 2006, in Buchach.

56. Michael Nosonovsky, *Hebrew Epitaphs and Inscriptions from Ukraine and Former Soviet Union* (Washington, D.C.: Printed from the PDF file provided by the author, 2006), p. 25. See also http://www.shtetlinks.jewishgen.org/Suchostaw/sl_buczacz.htm (accessed August 24, 2006).

57. This is according to Petro Pasichnyk (born in 1923), interviewed by Sofia Grachova and Andriy Pavlyashuk on March 3, 2006, in Buchach. I have not been able to enter the gymnasium to verify this information.

58. See: http://www.lvivbest.com/Sections+index-req-viewarticle-artid-140-page-1.html (accessed August 24, 2006).

59. Pick, *Simon Wiesenthal,* p. 42f.

60. Estimates of the number of people murdered in this so-called "registration *Aktion*" range between 350 and 700.

61. I interviewed Roman Antoshkiv in Buchach on June 21, 2004. Born in the 1930s, Antoshkiv remembers the deportation of the Jews from his village to nearby Buchach. His mother, he said, worked for the Jews and therefore could "distinguish between good and bad Jews." Antoshkiv has also donated money to erect the new Bandera monument (see below).

62. See n. 57, above. I am thankful to Sofia Grachova for photographing the memorials and the museum, translating the texts, and conducting the interviews. Oresta Synen'ka noted in her interview that on Fedir Hill the bones of the murdered Jews could still be seen, presumably because of the shallow graves. She commented: "I asked the mayor, as well as the principal of the college [presumably the agricultural school situated on the hill] many times: Take a few fellows from the college and make them scatter some earth over the grave. There are people lying about there, never mind who they were." Ivan Synen'kyi was born in Buchach in 1925 and served as a member of UPA, probably as of 1944, taking photographs of

Soviet agents, which would then be delivered to the UPA units in the forest. He was arrested on May 14, 1946, and spent ten years in Soviet camps. See also "The testimony of Ivan Iosypovych Synen'kyi," recorded for the *Poshuk Archive,* October 29, 2004.

63. Agnon's novel, *A Guest for the Night,* contains retrospectively tragic sections in which the author, who visited Buchach in 1930, looks out of the windows of the study house to Fedir Hill, where the community would be murdered ten years later, reminiscing about family picnics and lovers' rendezvous there before World War I. Agnon's posthumous book, *The Whole City,* is a vast collection of tales, legends, and historical accounts about Jewish life in Buchach, much of it centered around its many synagogues.

64. Mordecai Paldiel, *The Path of the Righteous: Gentile Rescuers of Jews during the Holocaust* (Hoboken, NJ: Ktav, 1992), 191ff.

65. See http://buchach.com.ua/?mhnews_id=206&mhnews_newsid=7310&mhnews_page=1 (accessed August 25, 2006). Among the speakers was the director of the Bandera Memorial Society, Oresta Synen'ka, mentioned above. The speeches are said to have been "beautiful and sincere . . . full of heartfelt feelings, reflections on the figure of Stepan Bandera in the history of our Fatherland and the region, and his enormous role in the formation of Ukrainian self-consciousness, national spirit, and the striving for freedom and liberty."

66. Interview with Mykola Kozak conducted in Buchach by Sofia Grachova on March 2, 2006.

67. For photos, see http://www.shtetlinks.jewishgen.org/Suchostav/Buchach/BuchCemIndex.html (accessed August 25, 2006).

68. http://en.wikipedia.org/wiki/Ternopil (accessed August 25, 2006).

69. For this I must thank my German research assistant, Dr. Frank Grelka. The documents in question are: State Archives of the Ternopil' Region, fond R-279, opys 1, sprava 1; fond R-274, opys 1, sprava 123; fond P-1, opys 1, sprava 608; fond P-69, opys 1, sprava 1–2, 8, 17, 19, 31, 35–37, 38–40, 47.

70. Yaroslav Demydas, "Zhydivs'kyi Pogrom," in *Ne Zdamos',* no. 3, March 2003, pp. 1, 7, also at: http://www.nezdamosia.te.ua/modules.php?name=News&file=article&sid=33 (April 8, 2003, accessed August 27, 2006). The word *zhydivs'kyi* is commonly used in western Ukraine but considered pejorative in other parts of Ukraine and in Russia (as the equivalent of "kike" or "yid"), where the standard term for Jews is *ievrei* or *evrei.* There is some debate over whether the Galician term *zhydy* carries an intentional pejorative meaning, reflecting traditional and persisting local antisemitic attitudes, or is a neutral designation related to the Polish *żydzi.* Some argue that Ukrainian Galicians view *ievrei* as pejorative because it connotes Soviet Jews and Russian/Soviet influence. Still, when restoring old Jewish street names in L'viv, it was decided to modify the original name of Starozhydivs'ka (Old Jewish) Street to Staroievreis'ka Street so as "to avoid offending Jewish people." See Hrytsak and Susak, "Constructing a National City," p. 156.

71. Leonid Kuchma was president of Ukraine in 1994–2005. His presidency ended with the Orange Revolution, which brought Viktor Iushchenko to power with massive support from western Ukraine. But Viktor Ianukovych, leader of the Party of Regions and prime minister of Ukraine in 2002–2004 under Kuchma, led his party to victory in the parliamentary elections of March 2006, receiving 32 percent of the vote, as opposed to Iushchenko's bloc, Our Ukraine, which received 14 percent. Consequently, in August 2006 Ianukovych was appointed prime minister by President Iushchenko.

72. The following is based on Dąbrowska, *Pinkas Hakehillot,* pp. 234–251, available in English at: http://www.jewishgen.org/Yizkor/pinkas_poland/pol2_00234.html (accessed August 25, 2006). See also P. Korngruen, ed., *Tarnopol* (Jerusalem & Tel Aviv: Encyclopedia of the Jewish Diaspora, 1955, in Hebrew); Pesach

Herzog, *In the Shadow of the Black Eagle: Memories of Tarnopol in 1939–1945* (Tel Aviv: Yaron Golan, 1996, in Hebrew).

73. The following is based on my own visit to the site in June 2004 as well as on "Jewish Cemeteries, Synagogues, and Mass Graves in Ukraine," United States Commission for the Preservation of America's Heritage Abroad, 2005, pp. 24, 50, 94, 119, at http://www.heritageabroad.gov/reports/doc/survey_ukraine_2005 .pdf (accessed August 25, 2006); and *International Association of Jewish Genealogical Societies—Cemetery Project,* US Commission Reports UA19010101 and UA19010102, at: http://www.jewishgen.org/cemetery/e-europe/ukra-t.html (accessed August 25, 2006).

74. For background see Dąbrowska, *Pinkas Hakehillot,* pp. 206–213; Nathan Michael Gelber and Y. Ben-Shem, *The Book of Żółkiew* (Jerusalem: The Diaspora Encyclopedia, 1969, in Hebrew); Sam Halpern, *Darkness and Hope* (New York: Shengold Books, 1997). See also Zhovkva: http://www.geocities.com/zhovkva/ zhovkva_e.html (accessed August 25, 2006); http://www.babylon.com/definition/ Zhovkva%20Synagogue/All (accessed August 25, 2006).

75. It has been reported that the synagogue will be restored as a regional Jewish museum, and that funds have been allocated to that purpose by the World Monuments Fund, a private New York–based historic preservation organization, and by the Ukrainian government. See "Jewish Cemeteries, Synagogues, and Mass Grave Sites in Ukraine," United States Commission for the Preservation of America's Heritage Abroad, 2005, at: http://www.heritageabroad.gov/reports/doc/ survey_ukraine_2005.pdf (accessed August 25, 2006), pp. 2, 21–22, 27, 62, 65–67, 76, 93, 136, 180. But on a visit to the town in spring 2007 I discovered that while the municipality had received and used funds for the restoration of historical sites, it did not deem the synagogue part of its historic heritage. A small amount of foreign money given specifically to restore the synagogue was employed to clean up its vast interior. Nothing has yet been done concerning the dilapidated external walls of the structure.

76. International Association of Jewish Genealogical Societies—Cemetery Project, at: http://www.jewishgen.org/cemetery/e-europe/ukra-z.html (accessed August 25, 2006).

77. Between 1945 and 1948, nearly 1.3 million Poles moved voluntarily or were forced from Volhynia and eastern Galicia to Poland (as Poland's borders were moved to the west). Conversely, close to 500,000 Ukrainians and Lemkos (a Carpathian ethnic group associated by the authorities with the Ukrainians) were moved from Poland to the newly incorporated western regions of Soviet Ukraine. Continuing UPA actions provoked the Polish Communist government to unleash Operation Vistula, in which 140,000 Ukrainians and Lemkos living in the Carpathian region were forcibly deported to the western and northern regions of Poland (recently annexed from defeated Germany). Many UPA members either escaped to the west or crossed over the border to keep up the fight in western Ukraine. See Magocsi, *History of Ukraine,* pp. 642, 649; Snyder, *Reconstruction of Nations,* pp. 187–201.

78. Roman Woronowycz, "Mass Grave at Zhovkva Monastery: The Mystery Continues," *The Ukrainian Weekly,* September 29, 2002, No. 39, Vol. LXX, at: http://www.ukrweekly.com/Archive/2002/390204.shtml (accessed August 25, 2006). Kulyniak was born in Zhovkva but moved to the Kherson region as a child. For an earlier report see Roman Woronowycz, "Soviet-Era Mass Grave Unearthed in Western Ukraine," *Ukrainian Weekly,* July 28, 2002, No. 30, Vol. LXX, at: http://www.ukrweekly.com/Archive/2002/300201.shtml (accessed August 25, 2006). The story received little coverage in the West. But see Peter Baker, "Soviet-Era Atrocity Unearthed in Ukraine: Remains of 225 Apparently Killed by Secret Police Are Found at Monastery," *Washington Post* (July 23, 2002): A1. Available at: http://www.artukraine.com/events/atrocity.htm (accessed August

25, 2006); http://www.theage.com.au/articles/2002/07/23/1027332376044.html (accessed August 25, 2006); "Mass Grave Found at Ukrainian Monastery," *BBC News* (Tuesday, 16 July, 2002): http://news.bbc.co.uk/1/hi/world/europe/2131954.stm (accessed August 25, 2006).

79. See, e.g., http://www.mail-archive.com/antinato@topica.com/msg06933.html (accessed August 25, 2006); http://litek.ws/k0nsl/detox/Carto-nine-reasons.html (accessed August 25, 2006). According to Shimon Redlich, "Metropolitan Andrei Sheptyts'kyi, Ukrainians and Jews During and After the Holocaust," *Holocaust and Genocide Studies* 5/1 (1990): pp. 39–51, while Sheptyts'kyi initially welcomed the Germans because they drove out the Soviets, he eventually concluded that they were worse than the Soviets.

Comparative Table of Ranks

U.S. Army	SS	Polizei und Gendarmerie	Wehrmacht
Private	SS-Mann	Unterwachtmeister	Soldat
Private First Class	Sturmmann	Rottwachtmeister	Obersoldat
Corporal	Rottenführer	Wachtmeister	Gefreiter
—	—	Oberwachtmeister	Obergefreiter
—	—	—	Stabsgefreiter
Sergeant	Unterscharführer	Revieroberwachtmeister / Zugwachtmeister	Unteroffizier
Staff Sergeant	Scharführer	Hauptwachtmeister	Unterfeldwebel
Technical Sergeant	Oberscharführer	Meister	Feldwebel
First Sergeant	Hauptscharführer	—	Oberfeldwebel
Master Sergeant	Sturmscharführer	—	Stabsoberfeldwebel
Second Lieutenant	Untersturmführer	Leutnant	Leutnant
First Lieutenant	Obersturmführer	Oberleutnant	Oberleutnant
Captain	Hauptsturmführer	Hauptmann	Hauptmann
Major	Sturmbannführer	Major	Major
Lieutenant Colonel	Obersturmbannführer	Oberstleutnant	Oberstleutnant
Colonel	Standartenführer	Oberst	Oberst
—	Oberführer	—	—
Brigadier General	Brigadeführer	Generalmajor	Generalmajor
Major General	Gruppenführer	Generalleutnant	Generalleutnant
Lieutenant General	Obergruppenführer	General der Polizei	General
General	Oberstgruppenführer	Generaloberst	Generaloberst
General of the Army	Reichsführer-SS and Chief of the German Police	Generalfeldmarschall	

Source: *The Holdings of the Berlin Document Center* (Berlin 1994), pp. 276-277.

Technical Design
and Computer Graphics:
PETER PALM,
Berlin

Research and Drafting:
RAY BRANDON,
Berlin

The following sources were used throughout in preparing maps for this volume:

Encyclopedia of Ukraine, Map and Gazetteer, Volodymyr Kubijovyc, ed. (Toronto: University of Toronto Press, 1984)
Ukraïna zahal'noheohrafichna karta (Kiev: Ministerstvo Ekolohiï ta Pryrodnykh Resursiv Ukraïny and Derzhavne Naukovo-Vyrobyche Pidpryiemstvo "Kartohrafiia," 2002)
Ukraïna, Karta avtomobil'nykh shliakhiv (Kiev: Holovne Upravlinnia Heodeziï, Kartohrafiï ta Kadastru pry Kabineti Ministriv Ukraïny, 1993)
Bundesarchiv-Militärarchiv, RW 41 (Wehrmacht Territorial Commanders)/ 1.
Der Generalbezirk . . . , Der Reichsminister für die besetzten Ostgebiete, Haupabteilung I, Raumplanung (Berlin: Reichsminister für die besetzten Ostgebiete, 1942). For Reich Commissariat Ukraine, booklets in this series are available for the general commissariats Volhynia-Podolia, Zhytomyr, Mykolaïv, Taurida, Kiev, Chernihiv, Kharkiv, Stalino, and Voronezh.
www.mapquest.com

Individual maps drew on the additional publications listed below:

Map 1.1

Klaus-Jürgen Thies, *Der Zweite Weltkrieg im Kartenbild,* Band 5: *Der Ostfeldzug 1941–1945.* Teil 1.1: *Der Ostfeldzug 1941—Heeresgruppe Mitte. 21.6 1941–6.12 1941,* map 80.
Das Deutsche Reich und der Zweite Weltkrieg, Band 4: *Der Angriff auf die Sowjetunion,* Beiheft, Ernst Boog et al. (Stuttgart: Deutsche Verlags-Anstalt, 1983), various maps.
Situation maps for Army Group South housed at the Bundesarchiv-Militärarchiv, Freiburg.
Note: The mass shootings carried out by Police Regiment South are not included on this map.

Map 1.2

Alexander Dallin, *German Rule in Russia, 1941–1945: A Study of Occupation Policies* (New York: St. Martin's Press, 1957), p. 94.
Das Deutsche Reich und der Zweite Weltkrieg, Band 4: *Der Angriff auf die Sowjetunion,* Ernst Boog et al. (Stuttgart: Deutsche Verlags-Anstalt, 1983), p. 420.

Maps 2.1 and 3.1

Statistisches Gemeindeverzeichnis des bisherigen polnischen Staates (Berlin: Selbst-verlag der Publikationsstelle, 1939).

Andrzej Żbikowski, "Local Anti-Jewish Pogroms in the Occupied Territories of Eastern Poland, June–July 1941," in Lucjan Dobroszycki and Jeffrey S. Gurock, eds., *The Holocaust in the Soviet Union: Studies and Sources on the Destruction of the Jews in the Nazi-Occupied Territories of the USSR, 1941–1945* (Armonk, NY: M. E. Sharpe, 1993).

Shmuel Spector, *Holocaust of Volhynian Jews, 1941–1944* (Jerusalem: Yad Vashem and Federation of Volhynian Jews, 1990).

Dieter Pohl, *Nationalsozialistische Judenverfolgung in Ostgalizien 1941–1944. Organisation und Durchführung eines staatlichen Massenverbrechens* (München: Oldenburg, 1996).

Krzysztof Popiński, "Ewakuacja więźień kresowych w czerwcu 1941 r. na pod-stawie dokumentacji "Memorial" i archiwum wschodniego," in *Zbrodnicza ewakuacja więźień i aresztów NKWD na kresach Wschodnich II Rzeczypo-spolitej w czerwcu-lipcu 1941 roku: materiały z sesji w 55. rocznice ewakuacji więźniów NKWD w głąb ZSRR, Łódź, 10 czerwca 1996 r.* (Warsaw: Instytut Pamięci Narodowej / Główna Komisja Badania Zbrodni Przeciwko Narodowi Polskiemu, 1997), pp. 75–77.

The contributions to this volume by Timothy Snyder, Frank Golczewski, and Omer Bartov.

Note: Not included on these maps are recorded pogroms in villages.

Map 4.1

Die Bevölkerungszählung in Rumänien 1941 (Wien: Publikationsstelle, 1943), map supplement.

Ekkehard Völkl, *Transnistrien und Odessa (1941–1944)* (Regensburg [i.e., Kall-münz]: Lassleben, 1996), p. 27.

Map 5.1

Bundesarchiv-Militärarchiv, RW 41 (Wehrmacht Territorial Commanders)/19K.
Bundesarchiv, R58 (Reich Security Main Office), Dienststellenverzeichnis des Re-ichssicherheitshauptamt.

Map 6.1

Der Generalbezirk Shytomyr (abgeschlossen am 15. März 1942) Entwurf! Der Re-ichsminister für die besetzten Ostgebiete, Haupabt. I, Raumplanung (Berlin: Reichsminister für die besetzten Ostgebiete, 1942).

Note: The locations of German settlements represent only the presence of sizeable German communities, not necessarily German majorities.

Map 7.1

Bruno Wasser, *Himmlers Raumplanung im Osten: Der Generalplan Ost in Polen 1940–1944* (Basel, Berlin: Birkhäuser, 1993), 302–303.

Hermann Kaienburg, *Die Wirtschaft der SS* (Berlin: Metropol-Verlag, 2003), p. 401.

Selected
Supplemental
Bibliography

Note: This bibliography is limited to recent works that were not referenced by the authors in this volume. For additional titles, readers are recommended to consult the footnotes in each chapter.

Abramson, Henry. "Nachrichten aus Lemberg: lokale Elemente in der antisemitischen Ikonographie der NS-Propaganda in ukrainischer Sprache." In Irmtrud Wojak and Susanne Meinl, eds., *Grenzenlose Vorurteile, Antisemitismus, Nationalismus und ethnische Konflikte in verschiedenen Kulturen.* Jahrbuch zur Geschichte und Wirkung des Holocaust 2002. Frankfurt am Main, et al.: Campus-Verlag, 2002: 249–268.

Anderson, Truman. "Germans, Ukrainians and Jews: Ethnic Politics in Heeresgebiet Süd, June 1941–December 1941." *War in History* 7 (2000) 3: 325–351.

Angrick, Andrej and Dieter Pohl. *Einsatzgruppen C and D in the Invasion of the Soviet Union Holocaust.* Holocaust Educational Trust Research Papers, vol. 1, no. 4. London: Holocaust Educational Trust, 2000.

Bernheim, Robert. "The Commissar Order and the Seventeenth German Army: From Genesis to Implementation, 30 March 1941–31 January 1942." M.A. thesis. McGill University, 2004.

———. "The Treatment of Ukrainian Jews by Forces of the Seventeenth German Army Command: 22 June 1941–31 July 1941." In Wolfgang Mieder and David Scrase, eds., *Reflections on the Holocaust: Festscrift for Raul Hilberg on His Seventy-Fifth Birthday.* Burlington, VT: The Center for Holocaust Studies at the University of Vermont, 2001: 21–38.

Brown, Kate. *A Biography of No Place from Ethnic Borderland to Soviet Heartland.* Cambridge, MA: Harvard University Press, 2004.

Bruder, Franziska. *"Den ukrainischen Staat erkämpfen oder sterben!" Die Organisation Ukrainischer Nationalisten (OUN) 1929–1948.* Berlin: Metropol, 2007.

———. "'Der Gerechtigkeit zu dienen': Die ukrainischen Nationalisten als Zeugen im Auschwitz-Prozess." In Irmtrud Wojak and Susanne Meinl, eds., *Im Labyrinth der Schuld: Täter, Opfer, Ankläger.* Jahrbuch zur Geschichte und Wirkung des Holocaust 2003. Frankfurt am Main, et al.: Campus-Verlag, 2003: 133–162.

———. "Kollaboration oder Widerstand?: die ukrainischen Nationalisten während des Zweiten Weltkrieges." *Zeitschrift für Geschichtswissenschaft* 54 (2006) 1: 20–44.

Carmelly, Felicia (Steigman). *Shattered! 50 years of Silence: History and Voices from the Tragedy in Romania and Transnistria.* Toronto: Felicia Carmelly, 1997.

Deletant, Dennis. *Hitler's Forgotten Ally. Ion Antonescu and His Regime, Romania 1940–44.* Houndmills, Basingstoke, Hampshire: Palgrave Macmillan, 2006.

Desbois, Father Patrick, and Edouard Husson. *The Mass Shooting of Jews in Ukraine 1941–1944: The Holocaust by Bullets.* Paris: Mémorial de la Shoah, 2007.

Dietsch, Johan. *Making Sense of Suffering: Holocaust and Holodomor in Ukrainian Historical Culture.* Lund: Dept. of History, Lund Univ., 2006.

Fishman, Lala and Steven Weingartner. *Lala's Story: A Memoir of the Holocaust.* Evanston, IL: Northwestern University Press, 1998.

Friedman, Henry. *I'm No Hero: Journeys of a Holocaust Survivor.* Seattle: University of Washington Press, 1999.

Gerlach, Christian and Götz Aly. *Das letzte Kapitel: Realpolitik, Ideologie und der Mord an den ungarischen Juden 1944–1945.* Stuttgart: Deutsche Verlags-Anstalt, 2002.

Gesin, Michael. *The Destruction of the Ukrainian Jewry during World War II.* Lewiston: Edwin Mellen Press, 2006.

Gotfryd, Anatol. *Der Himmel in den Pfützen: ein Leben zwischen Galizien und dem Kurfürstendamm.* Berlin: wjs Verlag, 2005.

Grelka, Frank. *Die ukrainische Nationalbewegung unter deutscher Besatzungsherrschaft 1918 und 1941/42.* Studien der Forschungsstelle Ostmitteleuropa an der Universität Dortmund 38. Wiesbaden: Harrassowitz, 2005.

Grynberg, Michał, ed. *Życie i zagłada Żydów polskich: 1939–1945, relacje świadków.* Warsaw: Oficyna Naukowa, 2003.

Heinen, F. A. *Gottlos, schamlos, gewissenlos. Zum Osteinsatz der Ordensburg-Mannschaften.* Düsseldorf: Gaasterland-Verlag, 2007.

Herbert, Ulrich, "Vergeltung, Zeitdruck, Sachzwang: die deutsche Wehrmacht in Frankreich und der Ukraine." *Mittelweg* 36 (2002) 6: 25–42.

Hofbauer, Ernst. *Verwehte Spuren: von Lemberg bis Czernowitz ein Trümmerfeld der Erinnerungen.* Vienna: Ibera-Verlag, 1999.

Hollander, Eugene. *From the Hell of the Holocaust.* Hoboken, NJ: KTAV Publishing House, 2000.

Hon, Maksym, ed. *Holokost na Rivnenshchyni (dokumenty ta materialy).* Ukraïns'ka biblioteka Holokostu. Zaporizhzhia: Prem'er, 2004.

Hunczak, Taras, and Dmytro Shtohryn, eds. *Ukraine: The Challenges of World War II.* Lanham, MD: University Press of America, 2003.

Katz, Menachem. *Na ścieŻkach nadziei.* Warsaw: Żydowski Instytut Historyczny, 2003.

Kulke, Christine. "Everyday life in L'viv under German occupation." Ph.D. diss. University of California Berkeley, forthcoming.

Langerbein, Helmut. *Hitler's Death Squads: The Logic of Mass Murder.* College Station: Texas A&M University Press, 2004.

Lapciuc, Israel. *Thou Shalt Not Forget.* Jersey City, NJ: Ktav Publ., 2004

Lerner, Sima. *Moi rok: vospominaniia.* Tel-Aviv: Izdatel'stvo Krugozor, 1998.

Liubchenko, Arkadij P. *Shchodennyk Arkadiia Liubchenka.* L'viv: Vydavnytstvo M. P. Kots', 1999.

Lower, Wendy. "Facilitating Genocide: Nazi Ghettoization Practices in Occupied Ukraine, 1941–1944." In Eric Sterling, ed., *Life in the Ghettos during the Holocaust.* Syracuse: Syracuse University Press, 2005: 120–144.

Melnyk, Oleksandr Ivanovych. "Behind the Frontlines: War, Genocide and Identity in the Kherson Region of Ukraine, 1941–1944." M.A. thesis. University of Alberta, 2004.

Mick, Christoph. "Ethnische Gewalt und Pogrome in Lemberg 1914–1941." *Osteuropa* 53 (2003) 12: 1,810–1,829.

———. "Kriegserfahrungen in einer multiethnischen Stadt: Lemberg 1914–1950." Habilitation. Tübingen University, 2003.

Pohl, Dieter. "Die Trawniki-Männer im Vernichtungslager Belzec 1941–1943." In *NS-Gewaltherrschaft: Beiträge zur historischen Forschung und juristischen Aufarbeitung.* Berlin: Edition Hentrich, 2005: 278–289.

———. "Hans Krüger-der 'König von Stanislau' Hans Krüger." In Klaus-Michael Mallmann and Gerhard Paul, eds., *Karriere der Gewalt. Nationalsozialistische Täterbiographien*. Darmstadt: Wissenschaftliche Buchgesellschaft, 2004: 134–144.

———. "Ukranische Hilfskräfte beim Mord an den Juden." In Gerhard Paul, ed., *Die Täter der Shoah. Fanatische Nationalsozialisten oder ganz normale Deutsche?* Göttingen: Wallstein-Verlag, 2002: 205–234.

Redlich, Shimon. *Together and Apart in Brzezany: Poles, Jews, and Ukrainians, 1919–1945*. Bloomington: Indiana University Press, 2002.

Rhodes, Richard. *Masters of Death: The SS-Einsatzgruppen and the Invention of the Holocaust*. New York: Alfred A. Knopf, 2002.

Richman, Sophia. *A Wolf in the Attic: The Legacy of a Hidden Child of the Holocaust*. New York: Haworth Press, 2002.

Rubenstein, Joshua, and Ilya Altman, eds. *The Unknown Black Book: The Holocaust in the German-Occupied Soviet Territories*. Bloomington: Indiana University Press, 2007.

Rubin, Arnon. *Against All Odds: Facing Holocaust: My Personal Recollections*. Tel-Aviv: Tel-Aviv University Press, 2005.

Sanders, Marian R. "Extraordinary crimes in Ukraine: An examination of evidence collection by the Extraordinary State Commission of the Union of Soviet Socialist Republics, 1942–1946," Ph.D. diss. Ohio University, 1995.

Steinhart, Eric Conrad. "Transnistria's Ethnic Germans and the Holocaust, 1941–1942." M.A. thesis. The University of North Carolina at Chapel Hill, 2006.

Sten, Ephraim F. *1111 Days in My Life Plus Four*. Takoma Park, MD: Dryad Press, 2006.

Stieglitz, Anita Lebowitz. *The Joy and the Sorrow: The Jews of Ungvar-Uzhorod and Vicinity, 1492–1944*. Denver, CO: Cyrano Publishing, 1997.

Tiaglyi, M. I., ed. *Kholokost v Krymu: dokumental'nye svidetel'stva o genotside evreev Kryma v period natsistkoi okkupatsii Ukrainy, 1941–1944*. Ukraïns'ka biblioteka Holokostu. Simferopol': Khesed Shimon, 2002.

Tyaglyy, Mikhail I. "The Role of Antisemitic Doctrine in German Propaganda in the Crimea, 1941–1944," *Holocaust and Genocide Studies* 18 (Winter 2004): 421–459.

Umanskij, Semen S. *Jüdisches Glück: Bericht aus der Ukraine 1933–1944*. Frankfurt am Main: Fischer-Taschenbuch-Verlag, 1998.

Völkl, Ekkehard. *Transnistrien und Odessa (1941–1944)*. Schriftenreihe des Osteuropainstituts Regensburg, Passau 14. Regensburg: Lassleben, 1996.

Wolfenhaut, Julius. *Nach Sibirien verbannt: als Jude von Czernowitz nach Stalinka 1941–1994*. Frankfurt am Main: Fischer, 2005.

Wolkowicz, Shlomo. *The Mouth of Hell*. Haverford, PA: Infinity Publishing, 2002.

Yones, Eliyahu. *Smoke in the Sand: The Jews of Lvov in the War Years 1939–1944*. Jerusalem, New York: Gefen, 2004.

Zabarko, Boris, ed. *Holocaust in the Ukraine*. The Library of Holocaust Testimonies. London: Vallentine Mitchell, 2005.

Żbikowski, Andrzej, ed. *Relacje z Kresów*. Archiwum Ringelbluma 3. Warsaw: Wydawnictwo ANTA, 2000.

———. *Rozwiązanie kwestii Żydowskiej w Dystrykcie Galicja*. Warsaw: Instytut Pamięci Narodowej, 2001.

Additional Bibliography for the Paperback Edition

Al'tman, Il'ia. *Opfer des Hasses: Der Holocaust in der UdSSR 1941–1945*. Gleichen: Muster-Schmidt, 2008.

Arad, Yitzhak. *The Holocaust in the Soviet Union*. Lincoln: University of Nebraska Press, 2009.

Berkhoff, Karel. "'Total Annihilation of the Jewish Population': The Holocaust in the Soviet Media, 1941–1945," *Kritika: Explorations in Russian and Eurasion History* 10 (2009) 1: 61–105.

Desbois, Father Patrick. *Holocaust by Bullets: A Priest's Journey to Uncover the Truth behind the Murder of 1.5 Million Jews*. New York: Palgrave Macmillan, 2008.

Hartmann, Christian. *Der deutsche Krieg im Osten: 1941–1944: Facetten einer Grenzüberschreitung*. München: Oldenbourg, 2009.

Himka, John-Paul. "Dostovirnist' svidchennia: reliatsiia Ruzi Vagner pro l'vivs'kyi pohrom vlitku 1941 r." *Holokost i suchasnist'* 2 (2008) 4: 43–80.

Hoffmann, Jens. *"Das kann man nicht erzählen: Aktion 1005." Wie die Nazis die Spuren ihrer Massenmorde in Osteuropa beseitigten*. Hamburg: KVV Konkret-Verlag, 2008.

Jilge, Wilfried. "Nationalukrainischer Befreiungskampf: Die Umwertung des Zweiten Weltkrieges in der Ukraine." *Osteuropa* 58 (2008) 6: 167–186.

Portnov, Andrij. "Pluralität der Erinnerung: Denkmäler und Geschichtspolitik in der Ukraine." *Osteuropa* 58 (2008) 6: 197–210.

RAY BRANDON (Editor) is a freelance editor, historian, translator, and researcher based in Berlin. A former editor at the *Frankfurter Allgemeine Zeitung, English Edition,* he has also lived and worked in Ukraine and Poland. He is translator of *The "Final Solution" in Riga: Exploitation and Annihilation, 1941–1944* by Andrej Angrick and Peter Klein.

WENDY LOWER (Editor) is research fellow and lecturer at Ludwig Maximilian University, Munich. Her publications include *Nazi Empire-Building and the Holocaust in Ukraine* (2005) and articles in *German Studies Review, Holocaust and Genocide Studies,* and the *Journal of Religion and Society.* Her latest work is *Escaping Oblivion: The Diary of Samuel Golfard and the Holocaust in Eastern Galicia* (forthcoming).

ANDREJ ANGRICK is a historian, consultant, and researcher with the Hamburg Foundation for the Promotion of Science and Culture. He was one of the co-editors of *Der Dienstkalender Heinrich Himmlers 1941/42* (1999) and, together with Klaus-Michael Mallmann, of *Die Gestapo nach 1945: Karrieren, Konflikte, Konstruktionen* (2009). He is co-author, with Peter Klein, of *The "Final Solution" in Riga: Exploitation and Annihilation, 1941–1944* (2009) and author of *Besatzungspolitik und Massenmord: Die Einsatzgruppe D in der südlichen Sowjetunion 1941–1943* (2003).

OMER BARTOV is the John P. Birkelund Distinguished Professor of European History at Brown University. His books include *Hitler's Army: Soldiers, Nazis, and War in the Third Reich* (1991), *Murder in Our Midst: The Holocaust, Industrial Killing, and Representation* (1996), *Mirrors of Destruction: War, Genocide, and Modern Identity* (2000), *Germany's War and the Holocaust: Disputed Histories* (2003), and *The "Jew" in Cinema: From* The Golem *to* Don't Touch My Holocaust (2005). His new book, *Erased: Vanishing Traces of Jewish Galicia in Present Day Ukraine,* was published in fall 2007.

KAREL C. BERKHOFF is associate professor, Center for Holocaust and Genocide Studies, an organization of the University of Amsterdam and the Royal Netherlands Academy of Arts and Sciences. His articles have appeared in *Jahrbücher für Geschichte Osteuropas, Holocaust and Genocide Studies, Kritika, the Slavonic and East European Review,* and *Harvard Ukrainian Studies.* His book *Harvest of Despair: Life and Death in Ukraine under Nazi Rule* (2004) was awarded the Wiener Library's Fraenkel Prize for Contemporary History, Category A.

MARTIN DEAN is an applied research scholar at the United States Holocaust Memorial Museum's Center for Advanced Holocaust Studies and author of *Collaboration in the Holocaust: Crimes of the Local Police in Belorussia and Ukraine, 1941–44* (2000). Before joining the Museum, he was senior historian for the Metropolitan Police War Crimes Unit in London. His most recent book is *Robbing the Jews: The Confiscation of Jewish Property in the Holocaust, 1933–1945* (2009).

DENNIS DELETANT is professor of Romanian studies at the School of Slavonic and East European Studies, University College, London, and at the University of Amsterdam and author of several books on modern Romanian history. His recent work on the Holocaust in Romania includes *Hitler's Forgotten Ally: Ion Antonescu and his Regime, Romania 1940–44* (2006).

FRANK GOLCZEWSKI, professor of East European history at the University of Hamburg, is author of *Deutsche und Ukrainer 1914–1939* (2010) and *Polnisch-jüdische Beziehungen: 1881–1922* (1981). He has written numerous articles on Ukraine, was editor of the collection *Die Geschichte der Ukraine* (1993), and is co-editor of the journal *Jahrbücher für Geschichte Osteuropas.*

ALEXANDER KRUGLOV of Kharkiv is the author and editor of numerous books and articles about the Holocaust in Ukraine. His most recent works, in Russian, include *The Encyclopedia of the Holocaust: A Jewish Encyclopedia of Ukraine* (2000), *The Catastrophe of Ukrainian Jewry, 1941–1944, An Encyclopedic Guide* (2001), *A Collection of Documents and Materials about the Nazi Destruction of the Jews of Ukraine in 1941–1944* (2002), *The Chronicle of the Holocaust in Ukraine* (2004), and *The Losses Suffered by Ukrainian Jews in 1941–1944* (2005, also available in English).

DIETER POHL is senior researcher at the Institute of Contemporary History in Munich and adjunct lecturer at Ludwig Maximilian University Munich. He has published widely on the Holocaust in Poland and Ukraine. His books include *Nationalsozialistische Judenverfolgung in Ostgalizien, 1941–1944* (1996); *Holocaust; Verfolgung und Massenmord in der NS-Zeit* (2000); and *Die Herrschaft der Wehrmacht: Deutsche Militärbesatzung und einheimische Bevölkerung in der Sowjetunion 1941–1944* (2007). He was also a co-editor of *Der Dienstkalender Heinrich Himmlers 1941/42* (1999).

TIMOTHY SNYDER is professor of history at Yale University. His publications include *Sketches from a Secret War: A Polish Artist's Mission to Liberate Soviet Ukraine* (2005) and *The Red Prince: The Secret Lives of a Habsburg Archduke* (2008). His 2003 book, *The Reconstruction of Nations: Poland, Lithuania, Ukraine, Belarus, 1569–1999*, earned him the American Historical Association's George Louis Beer Prize. His most recent book is *Bloodlands: Europe between Hitler and Stalin* (forthcoming), a history of German and Soviet mass atrocity.

Index

The letters "soft sign" and the "short i" in Ukrainian and Russian personal and place names were left out of the main text to facilitate reading for general readers. These letters are included in the index below as well as in the footnotes and bibliography.

Place names for locations that were in Poland or Romania prior to the Second World War are given in parentheses as are spellings that differ fundamentally from the more familiar transliterations from the Russian, e.g. Haisyn (Gaisin) or Mykolaïv (Nikolaev).

Romanian Intelligence Service, 172
Romanian Jews, 51, 156–181, 211, 251
Romanian Ministry of Finance, 175
Romanian Ministry of Internal Affairs, 161–162, 170, 172, 175–176
Romanian Security Police, 164
Roosevelt, Franklin D., 173–174
Roques, Karl von, 26–28, 34
Rosca, Augustin, 165–166
Rosenberg, Alfred, 2, 42, 47, 124–125, 175, 225–226, 228, 230–232, 234–235, 237, 242
Rostov on the Don, 193, 195, 198
Rokytne, 308
Rucker, Hans, 208
Rundstedt, Gerd von, 34
Russia, 23, 78, 117, 119–120, 122–123, 251, 318; Russian Revolution 24, 122; Russian Civil War 79, 115, 119, 251–252
Ruzhyn: town, 276, 308
Ruzhyn: County Commissariat, 234, 255, 257
Ryll, Gustav, 258

Sabrin, F. A., 145
Sachsenhausen, 134–135, 140
Safran, Alexander, 173
Sambir (Sambór), 145
Samhorodok, 13, 238
Sandkühler, Thomas, 7, 116, 192
Sanok, 127
Satanowski family, 100
Sauckel, Fritz, 201, 203
Săveni, 169–170
Schaefer, Emanuel, 329
Schechter, Simon, 145–146
Scheer, Paul Albert, 295
Schenk, Walter, 141
Scherer, Siegfried, 206
Schmidt, Hans, 228, *240*
Schnöller, Xaver, 204–205
Schulz, Erwin, 40
Schulz, Bruno, 325–327
Schwarzbart, Samuel, 122
Secret Field Police (*Geheime Feldpolizei*, GFP), 40, 47
Security Police (*Sicherheitspolizei*, Sipo), 10, 26, 28, 34, 38, 40, 43, 46, 47–49, 54–56, 59, 129, 132, 135, 144, 164, 191, 199, 205–206, 210, 214, 232, 234, 239, 249, 251, 261–262, 275–276, 292–293, 310. *See also* Reich Security Main Office
Security Service (*Sicherheitsdienst*, SD), 10, 26, 28, 34, 37–40, 43, 46–47, 49, 54, 56, 59, 129, 132, 135, 141, 144, 191, 199, 205–206, 210, 214, 228, 232, 237–240, 251, 259, 261, 275–276, 292. *See also* Reich Security Main Office
Security Service of Ukraine, 295, 299
Serbia, 39
Serebriia, 207
Sosenki, 43

Seventh-Day Adventists, 145
Scheffler, Wolfgang, 191
Shamin, Liuba, 307–308
Shepetivka, 28, 42
Sheptyts'kyi, Andrei, 144, 146
Sheptyts'kyi, Kliment, 144
Shimanovsky, Mark, 297
Shnaiderman, Fima, 307
Sholokhove, 276
Shostakovich, Dmitrii, 292
Shums'k (Szumsk), 85
Siberia, 89, 129, 252, 319, 325, 328, 341–342
Silver, Elsa, 145–146
Simferopol, 261–262
Sittig, Herbert, 230
Skoropads'kyi, Pavlo, 124
Slovakia, 6, 125, 129, 136, 234,
Snyder, Tim, 8, 14–15
Sobesiak, Józef, 100
Sobibór, 6, 140, 288
Sobieski, Jan, 78
Sofiïvka (Dnipropetrovs'k Oblast), 198
Sokal, 274
Sokół, 335
Sokyriany (Târgu Secureni), 164, 166
Sonderkommando (special commando), 26, 35; Sonderkommando 4a (Sk 4a), 26, 33–37, 39–40, 52, 277, 292–293, 299–300; Sonderkommando 4b (Sk 4b), 26, 37–38, 40, 52, 277; Sonderkommando 11b, 261; Sonderkommando 1005, 53–54, 58; Sonderkommando 1005-A, 54; Sonderkommando 1005-B, 54; Sonderkommando Plath, 38; Sonderkommando R, 48, 252
Sonthofen, 228
Soroca, 163
Soviet bloc, 116, 144
Spector, Shmuel, 3, 5
Sperber, Julius, 145
Speer, Albert, 193, 197–199, 213
SS and police base leaders (*SS- und Polizeistandortführer*), 50
SS and police leaders (SSPF) 10, 44, 49–50, 194, 196–198, 206, 214, 225, 239
SS Command Main Office (*SS Führungshauptamt*), 198
SS Economics and Administration Main Office (*SS Wirtschafts- und Verwaltungshauptamt*), 197
Stalin, Josef, 1–2, 14, 17
Stalindorf Precinct (*Rayon*), 38, 251
Stalingrad, 2, 38–39, 52, 178, 195, 209, 213
Stalino (today Donets'k), city, 38, 52, 192, 198
Stalino Oblast, 277, 281, 284–285
Stanyslaviv (Stanisławów, today Ivano-Frankivs'k), 12, 132, 328–330, 342
Stanyslaviv (Ivano-Frankivs'k) Oblast, 274–275, 277–278, 281–285, 287–288
Starokonstiantyniv, 50, 210
Stavropol, 262